JEWS IN THE GERMAN ECONOMY

Jews in the German Economy

The German-Jewish Economic Élite 1820–1935

W. E. MOSSE

CLARENDON PRESS · OXFORD
1987

Oxford University Press, Walton Street, Oxford OX2 6DP
Oxford New York Toronto
Delhi Bombay Calcutta Madras Karachi
Petaling Jaya Singapore Hong Kong Tokyo
Nairobi Dar es Salaam Cape Town
Melbourne Auckland
and associated companies in
Beirut Berlin Ibadan Nicosia

Oxford is a trade mark of Oxford University Press

Published in the United States
by Oxford University Press, New York

© W. E. Mosse, 1987

All rights reserved. No part of this publication may be reproduced,
stored in a retrieval system, or transmitted, in any form or by any means,
electronic, mechanical, photocopying, recording, or otherwise, without
the prior permission of Oxford University Press

British Library Cataloguing in Publication Data
Mosse, W.E.
Jews in the German economy: the German-
Jewish élite, 1820–1935.
1. Élite (Social sciences)—Germany—History
2. Jews—Germany—History
3. Germany—Economic conditions—19th century
4. Germany—Economic conditions—20th century
I. Title
330.943'08 HC285
ISBN 0-19-821967-9

Library of Congress Cataloging in Publication Data
Mosse, Werner Eugen.
Jews in the German economy.
Bibliography: p.
Includes index.
1. Jews—Germany—Economic conditions.
2. Germany—Ethnic relations.
3. Germany—Economic conditions
I. Title.
DS135.G33M63 1987   330.943'0089924   86-18080
ISBN 0-19-821967-9

Set by Hope Services, Abingdon
Printed in Great Britain
at the University Printing House, Oxford
by David Stanford
Printer to the University

Acknowledgements

A NUMBER of institutions and individuals, whose help is gratefully acknowledged, contributed to the completion of this study. The work was assisted by a generous grant from the Deutsche Forschungsgemeinschaft. A year spent at the Zentrum für interdisziplinäre Forschung in Bielefeld provided opportunities for research and writing. An early exploratory visit to academic institutions in the Bundesrepublik was financed by the Deutsche Akademische Austauschdienst. The Leo Baeck Institute in New York supported a visit to its library and archives.

The assistance of staff of the Bundesarchiv in Koblenz, the Deutsches Zentralarchiv in Merseburg and Potsdam and the Leo Baeck Institute in New York is gratefully acknowledged. Dr Friedrich-Carl Euler placed at my disposal besides the resources of his Institut zur Erforschung Historischer Führungsschichten in Bensheim Bergstr., his expertise on genealogical and biographical matters. Among archivists to whom I am indebted are Dr Sybil Milton (Leo Baeck Institute, New York), Dr Cecile Lowenthal-Hensel (Geheimes Staatsarchiv Preussischer Kulturbesitz, Berlin), Dr Klara van Eyll (Rheinisch-Westfälisches Wirtschaftsarchiv zu Köln), Dr Renate Köhne (Historisches Archiv der Friedr. Krupp GmbH, Essen), Dr Bodo Herzog, (Archiv der Gute-Hoffnungs Hütte, Oberhausen) and last, not least, Dr Carl-Friedrich Baumann (Thyssen AG, Duisburg).

Prof. Dr Jürgen Kocka (Bielefeld) was throughout a stimulating partner and critic. Helpful comments and suggestions were provided by Professors Richard H. Tilly (Münster) and Hartmut Kaelble (Berlin) and by Dr Heidrun Homburg (Bielefeld), each of whom read parts of the manuscript. My thanks for their help at different points are due to Henry Bondi (Princeton) and Dr Arnold Paucker (Leo Baeck Institute, London). Marjan Bhavsar (Norwich) did the typing from a sometimes difficult manuscript.

Contents

	List of Tables	viii
1	Introduction: the German-Jewish Economic Élite 1820–1935	1
2	Beginnings	34
3	An Élite of Notables	69
4	Entrepreneurial Activities	96
5	Anatomy of a Wealth Élite	172
6	The Corporate Élite	218
7	Corporate Structures	260
8	Weimar: Decline and Fall?	323
9	Conclusion	380
	Bibliography	406
	Index	411

List of Tables

1. Commercial Occupations of Jews and Gentiles	85
2. Geographical Distribution of Titleholders	86
3. Distribution by Branches of all Jewish Titleholders	89
4. Geographical Distribution of Jewish Titleholders	89
5. Evolution of the 'Sub-Élite'	91
6. Comparison of Jewish Family Wealth and Capital of Major Joint-Stock Companies	207
7. Relative Fertility of the Jewish and Gentile Wealth Élite	215
8. Relative Fertility of the Jewish and Gentile Sub-Élite	216
9. Relative Fertility of the Jewish Wealth Élite and Sub-Élite	216
10. Relative Fertility of the Gentile Wealth Élite and Sub-Élite	217

I
Introduction: The German–Jewish Economic Élite 1820–1935

I

ANY study of the German-Jewish economic élite raises a number of general or methodological problems. The first of these concerns the basic question as to who, in the particular context, is to be considered a Jew. It is, of course, in precisely this segment of the German–Jewish population that total assimilation, the abandonment first of Judaism and then of all remaining Jewish ties, became widespread (though not, perhaps, as widespread as is sometimes supposed). The question therefore arises how far men (and, to a lesser extent, women) of Jewish origin who had converted to Christianity and contracted Gentile marriages are nevertheless to be considered as Jews for the purpose of the present study.

In relation to the concept of an economic élite, to be examined presently, a definition of 'Jewishness' in terms of religious profession and observance alone would be extremely narrow. In general, the relationship between religious affiliation and economic role, discussed among others by Max Weber and Werner Sombart, is a complex one. Besides 'Puritan ethic', economic role is influenced to a significant extent also by wider social factors, among them membership of usually disadvantaged minority groups (in Weber's terminology 'pariah people'), general historical factors (often with a discriminatory legal base), participation in informal networks, and, in the opinion of some, also by 'racial' determinants. None of these are changed to any significant extent upon a member of the economic élite, hitherto part of the Jewish community, either changing his religious affiliation or marrying a Gentile. Important circumstances influencing economic opportunities and performance remain substantially the same, often over more than one generation. This is the reason why a narrowly religious definition of 'Jewishness' would, in the present context, be unsatisfactory.

Perhaps the most acceptable definition of 'Jewishness', whatever its imprecision, is that of membership of the Jewish 'ethnic group', as the term is understood in the United States. Ethnicity, in this sense, has its base in a common extraction reinforced by and expressed in endogamy and kinship networks, common customs and traditions, preservation of distinctive names, with religion as only one in a bundle of attributes. If such a 'pluralist' definition is adopted, membership of the ethnic group may be judged by the presence or absence of a number of different criteria. Not every member of an ethnic group, then, will necessarily possess every one of the group's common characteristics. At the periphery of any ethnic group, moreover, there will always be found marginal elements at different stages of shedding (or simply losing) their hereditary 'ethnicity' en route towards acquiring another. There will be others who, even though their ethnic characteristics have been diluted, still retain them in sufficient measure to be predominantly identified with the group of their origin. In fact it would be possible—more specifically in the case of ethnic minorities—to range their members by a combination of different criteria in something like a continuum (or possibly in concentric circles) with regard to the strength of their ethnicity.

While this would appear the most sophisticated and hence the least unsatisfactory model for defining membership of an ethnic group it is, of course, one difficult to apply in practice. Where, for the purposes of identifying group membership, is the line of division on the continuum to be drawn? Only an empirical answer is possible here. The borderline might reasonably be held to lie where the offspring of a mixed marriage in turn marries out of the original ethnic group. Thus a person with one non-Jewish parent who himself marries a Gentile may be considered to have abandoned the last vestiges of residual Jewish ethnicity. The 'half-Jew', on the other hand, might still be considered a peripheral or marginal Jew.[1]

In fact, in the majority of cases, ethnicity can be established without great difficulty. Unavoidably, there are marginal cases (that of Bernhard Dernburg, son of a baptized father and a non-Jewish mother, is typical), but such cases are relatively infrequent. Whether individuals in this position are included or not in any case barely affects the overall picture of the German–Jewish economic élite.

A second term requiring definition is that of 'economic élite'. Here,

[1] The rabbinical definition of a Jew as one born of a Jewish mother is, perhaps, less useful, at any rate in a patrilineal society.

any definition must obviously be based in the main on socio-economic criteria. Three of these suggest themselves as particularly relevant in the context of nineteenth- and twentieth-century Prussia/Germany.

The first, that of status, seems apposite more especially to the status-orientated Prusso-German society of the nineteenth century, with status determined essentially by standing within an estate or 'Stand'. In the age of early industrialization in particular, men active in commercial life were still thought of by authorities and public (possibly less so by themselves) as members of an 'honourable merchant estate'. Status within that estate was expressed through membership of and standing in the local merchant corporations (for Berlin in membership of the prestigious Korporation der Kaufmannschaft and more particularly of its college of aldermen—*Aelteste*). Later, this would be replaced by membership and office-holding in the less exclusive chambers of commerce (*Handelskammern*).

To the outside world, and distinct from standing within the local merchant corporation though quite closely related to it, status found confirmation, official recognition, and public visibility through conferment of the coveted titles of *Kommerzienrat* (KR) and *Geheimer Kommerzienrat* (GKR). At least until near the end of the nineteenth century, it was these titles which largely helped to determine standing (as well as credit rating) alike within the commercial community, with the authorities, and with the world at large. Quite rigorous selection procedures for the conferment of these titles were carefully elaborated by Prussian officialdom. In addition to matters like wealth and income (the official requirements were raised from time to time with the increase in Prusso-German prosperity), these took account of economic services to the state (exports, import substitution, innovation), public service (in a variety of elective offices, as advisers to the government, in religious communities, and so on), charitable activities, standing among peers (reported on conscientiously by a special commission), life-style, and, on a different plane, political allegiance. The criteria, then, for identifying respected, public-spirited, and innovative entrepreneurs (for a long time, only owners of family firms were considered eligible though, eventually, titles would be conferred also on outstanding employees) were both varied and comprehensive. Jews whose economic activities were seen as useful to the state (or the community) shared to the full in this bounty: evidence of discrimination (notwithstanding the occasional anti-semitic remark in the internal correspondence over recommendations) is small. Nor was discrimination on political grounds normally particularly severe: whilst conservatives were, marginally, preferred, liberals of all shades, if otherwise qualified, received their titles as well—though a few politically active ones might have their awards delayed. The Jewish share of commercial titles was in fact, if anything, a generous one.

Happily the investigations and recommendations preceding the conferment of titles on Jew and Gentile alike are recorded in some detail in the files left behind by a painstaking and conscientious bureaucracy. The authorities, in adjucating on recommendations and (somewhat less frequently) direct applications for the conferment of titles, carried out detailed investigations before reaching their decisions.

The group of notables honoured with the titles of KR and GKR, thus, was not an arbitrary one. The officials carefully selected recipients in accordance with increasingly well-defined criteria. Nearly everyone, moreover, operating at an appropriate level of commercial activity and prima facie eligible for the honour, would seek—a few eccentrics apart—to become a KR in order to obtain the resulting status and commercial advantage. The reservoir of title-holders, accordingly, included the great majority of eligible bankers, merchants, and entrepreneurs. Moreover, at any rate until the nineties (when the titles became increasingly purchasable through 'charitable' gifts), the authorities applied their criteria for selection with a degree of rigour and impartiality. In consequence, until the later eighties at least, possession of a title may be held to indicate membership of a genuine élite of commercial notables whether in metropolis, provincial city, or small town (with financial requirements for conferment carefully graded in accordance with the milieu). The total numbers of Jews or men of Jewish extraction on whom the title of *Kommerzienrat* was bestowed between 1819 (date of the first recorded conferment on a Jew) and 1901 (by which time the title had lost much of its earlier prestige) was approximately 250.[2] This, calculated against the roughly fixed number of annual conferments, may have amounted to something like 20 per cent of the total.

In fact the figure of around 200 Jewish KR embraces a structured élite, composed of three distinct strata. At the top are the men who

[2] In fact, I have identified 206 for the period but the figure has no claim to absolute accuracy. It is not always possible to identify men of Jewish origin, particularly among the more obscure provincial title-holders. I wish to acknowledge the invaluable assistance in the determination of ethnic origins of archivist Dr F. W. Euler of the Institut zur Erforschung Historischer Führungsschichten in Bensheim (Bergstr.).

became GKRs (entitled to be addressed to their no small delight as 'Geheimrat'). These, usually, were appointed at a relatively advanced age, normally after some ten years as KR. Such men, who may be considered leading figures in the economic life of the country, constituted roughly one quarter of the total number. The next stratum, which can be delimited only approximately, consisted of some 60 men who played a prominent but essentially local role in the economic and public life of leading commercial centres, like Berlin or Breslau. The remainder, rather less than a hundred, could be described as 'local worthies' and were drawn mainly from medium-sized towns in the eastern half of the monarchy.

With the entry of the German economy in the 1890s into a new phase of accelerated capitalist development and full industrialization (variously described as high capitalism, finance capitalism, or organized capitalism), the definition of the economic élite in terms of commercial titles apposite to the earlier age of notables becomes increasingly inappropriate. The old order of notables was now in process of being replaced by, on the one hand, a plutocratic society, on the other a managerial one. As the prestige of the commercial title declines along with the relative economic weight of the family firm, so that of 'naked' wealth on the one hand, of position on the boards and in the management of major joint-stock companies on the other, increases. New criteria, accordingly, become appropriate for defining membership of the economic élite.

Information regarding wealth and income of individuals is available from two separate sources. In the first place, in considering candidates for the title of KR, the authorities often, though not invariably, recorded their tax category, fortune, and income (as well as, on occasion, the turnover of their enterprises). More systematically Rudolf Martin, a retired economic expert from the Reich ministry of the interior, compiled information on German millionaires based on their triennial tax returns for the year 1908 (and, in some cases, 1911). Martin lists systematically all people with fortunes above one million marks. Those 'worth' at least five million, moreover, are honoured with short biographical entries listing family connections and sources of wealth. While Martin's work needs to be treated with some caution, for reasons to be discussed presently, it nevertheless provides invaluable information concerning the distribution of personal wealth (including, of course, Jewish wealth) in Germany in the immediate pre-war period.

Martin's data make possible the identification of a Jewish wealth élite while, at the same time, providing a convenient non-Jewish control group. An analysis of the Jewish wealth élite throws light on the distinctive distribution of Jewish economic activity. With the majority of individuals listed, it is clear whether their wealth is predominantly inherited or acquired. In any case, irrespective of whether the millionaire remained economically active or merely benefited from earlier economic activities, he would equally form part of the plutocratic élite. The lower limit for membership of the élite must, of necessity, be arbitrary, but Martin's break at the five million mark point appears a reasonable one. In terms of wealth, then, it is again possible to arrive at a fairly precise definition of the German (and equally the German–Jewish) economic élite. According to Martin's figures there existed in Prussia in 1908 747 millionaires with fortunes exceeding 5 million marks.[3] Of these at least 162 can be identified as of Jewish extraction. As in the case of the KRs, the Jewish component once again constitutes roughly one fifth of the total. The Jewish (like the Gentile) wealth élite, in fact, overlaps to some degree with the earlier élite of notables. Thus, among the 32 wealthiest Jewish millionaires, there are 9 KR and GKR, 6 men with (more highly valued) consular titles, and 1 *Wirklicher Geheimer Rat* (again a more prestigious title). Of 16 people without commercial titles, 8 were ennobled (among them several dowagers), leaving 8 untitled commoners. Within the group of Jewish multimillionaires, it is possible, by admittedly arbitrary criteria, to identify a central plutocratic core. There existed in Prussia, in 1908, a total of 29 families,[4] the combined fortunes of whose members exceeded 50 million marks. The 9 families in the total that were either Jewish or of Jewish extraction may be considered the top stratum of the Jewish wealth élite. It is equally plausible, if somewhat less informative, to define the top stratum of the Jewish wealth élite, again somewhat arbitrarily, as consisting of its 50 wealthiest individuals.

---

[3] The total number of millionaires in Prussia at the same time is given by Martin as being in excess of 8,300. (R. Martin, *Jahrbuch des Vermögens und Einkommens der Millionäre in Preussen* (Berlin, 1912), p. xiii.)

[4] It is, however, more instructive to consider the aggregate fortunes of families rather than those of individuals. While large family fortunes were as a rule derived from a single commercial source, they might however be held by anything from 1 individual (notably Silesian magnates: Hohenlohe, Tiele-Winckler, Ballestrem) to 10 (vom Rath) or even 13 (Haniel). Jewish family fortunes were shared by from 2 individuals (Speyer, Simon, Mosse) to 6 (Gans/Weinberg) and 7 (Rothschild/Goldschmidt-Rothschild).

However, by the turn of the century, as is well known, a growing differentiation was beginning to emerge between ownership and management. While some of the wealthiest millionaires had become *rentiers*, a growing number of influential 'captains of industry', *Direktoren* and *Generaldirektoren* as well as board chairmen, were men without large personal fortunes. While wealth and economic influence did often continue to go hand in hand, a further criterion needs to be applied to incorporate members of the economic élite like Albert Ballin or Emil Rathenau who, while extremely influential in economic affairs, did not in fact own great personal fortunes.

The economic élite of the twentieth century, in effect, consisted of a positional as well as a plutocratic component. With large joint-stock companies progressively replacing the entrepreneurial family firm, a new class of managers (including the influential 'barons of high finance' of the large joint-stock banks) assumes an increasing importance. This is a group capable of fairly precise delimitation both in the Wilhelmine era and in its aftermath in the Weimar Republic. It is represented above all by managing directors (*Generaldirektoren* or *Vorsitzende des Vorstandes*) and board chairmen (*Vorsitzende des Aufsichtsrats*) as well as by multiple board members (*Mitglieder des Aufsichtsrats*) of major public companies. (The hundred largest in terms of paid-up share capital have been listed for the years 1887, 1907, and 1927.) To these may be added the owners or senior partners of some large family firms (often nominally converted into joint-stock companies) which retained their importance into the age of finance or 'organized' capitalism. Together, these men constitute a positional or influence élite, which may in fact be seen as forming the core of the 'post-notable' economic élite as a whole. It could be described equally as a corporate élite. This corporate élite, in its turn, contained within itself elements of stratification. Walther Rathenau in 1912, in an oft-quoted statement, claimed that 300 men, each of whom knew every other, guided the economic fortunes of the European continent.[5] He did not indicate what proportion of these men were, in his view, of German nationality. However, if one attempted a rough estimate one might

---

[5] 'Dreihundert Männer', wrote Rathenau, 'von denen jeder jeden kennt, leiten die wirtschaftlichen Geschicke des Kontinents und suchen sich Nachfolger aus ihrer Umgebung.' The result was '... eine Oligarchie ... so geschlossen wie die des alten Venedig'. Walther Rathenau, 'Geschäftlicher Nachwuchs', in *Zur Kritik der Zeit*, 5th edn. (Berlin, 1912), p. 207. While Rathenau's striking statement is, perhaps, over-categorical, it points to the undoubted concentration of decision-making processes in developed capitalism and to the oligarchic character of the decision-making élite.

arrive at a figure in the vicinity of 125.[6] Of these, some forty to fifty would be of Jewish extraction. Among them it is possible to identify an inner core consisting of some fifteen to twenty men, among them Carl Fürstenberg, Albert Ballin, and the two Rathenaus, occupants of key positions in German economic life. The figures inevitably—like Rathenau's 300—contain subjective assessments and can only be rough approximations.[7] It is worth noting that this essentially 'Wilhelmine' group, though weakened by war, inflation (which, however, also favoured the rise of a number of new financial and industrial 'operators'), and generational change, survived into the brief and hectic days of the Weimar Republic.

Data on the management (*Vorstände*) and boards (*Aufsichtsräte*) of the major joint-stock companies can be found both in regularly published stock-exchange handbooks and in several compendia, both Jewish and general, of 'economic leaders' (*Wirtschaftsführer*) or of prominent people in general. Contrary to the conventional wisdom, moreover, propagated on occasion with apologetic intent, the role of Jews in the age of 'finance capital', of the development of electrical and chemical industries, of overseas trade and colonial enterprises, as well as of a domestic mass market for consumer goods, did not significantly diminish. Indeed, it might well be held that the 'Jewish' role was hardly less important in the managerial corporate élite of the joint-stock companies than it had been in the earlier entrepreneurial one. It was only with the gradual 'bureaucratization' of management in the Weimar Republic combined with the onset of the Depression (which *may* have hit types of enterprise with strong Jewish involvement somewhat harder than others—though the opposite also has been claimed), increased state intervention in economic affairs, and the rise of the last wave of 'Depression' anti-Semitism, that the Jewish role in German economic life gradually declined.

It is of course evident that the three élites, that of the notables (KR and GKR), that of the plutocrats (Martin's millionaires), and that of influence (primarily *Aufsichtsräte* and *Vorstände*), are not directly comparable. The first contains a significant proportion of men of purely local economic importance that is absent from the other two.

[6] This includes the most prominent members (board chairmen, multiple board members, and leading managing directors) of the 100 largest public companies (in terms of paid-up share capital) as well as senior partners in the most important private firms (in terms of their personal fortunes).

[7] There are, of course, no known criteria for determining relative economic importance.

Whilst the first two élites, those of the notables and the millionaires, represent largely—though not exclusively—the independent entrepreneurship of the owner, the last, under more advanced conditions of capitalist development, represents—even if not exclusively—the top stratum of salaried 'managers' with, perhaps, some capital invested in 'their' enterprise or others, but by no means the owners. Wealth and influence élites overlap to a degree, but there are those combining great wealth with an absence of significant managerial functions, like the later Rothschilds and Goldschmidt-Rothschilds, and others (Albert Ballin is a case in point) who enjoy great influence without significant wealth. There is also a core of families—with the Mendelssohns and Mendelssohn-Bartholdys perhaps the outstanding example—who pass naturally from the élite of notables into that of wealth while at the same time retaining to the end a position of prominence also in economic life (though, significantly, through a family firm and by recruiting able partners from outside the family circle). There are in fact elements of continuity as well as significant differences in the three overlapping élites. Structure and numerical strength, however, are roughly comparable. And, of major significance in the present context, the criteria, in each case, embrace the bulk of the German-Jewish *haute bourgeoisie* (excluding only a top stratum of successful professional men).

The German-Jewish economic élite thus defined by the criteria of status, wealth, and position can also be delimited in time. Disregarding (perhaps unjustifiably) the court Jews (*Hoffaktoren*) of the age of absolutism, studied by Schnee, the élite may be said to have originated in the multifarious commercial and financial transactions attending the revolutionary and Napoleonic wars and the subsequent age of early industrialization. It is during this period (roughly 1800–40) that a new entrepreneurial generation (not only in industry but also in commerce and banking) drawn from bourgeois or petty bourgeois strata of society gradually supersedes the last descendants of the court Jews[8] and of what Toury has described as privileged Jewish 'Adelsbürger'.[9] The

---

[8] The Jewish *Hoffaktoren* and their role are described in Heinrich Schnee's classic *Die Hochfinanz und der moderne Staat. Geschichte und System der Hoffaktoren an deutschen Fürstenhöfen im Zeitalter des Absolutismus*, 6 vols. (Berlin, 1953–67). See also Selma Stern, *The Court Jew. A Contribution to the History of the Period of Absolutism in Central Europe* (Philadelphia, 1950).

[9] The term coined by Jacob Toury to describe the highly privileged (by comparison not only with the bulk of their co-religionists but also with that of the non-Jewish population) court Jews and their families. Toury, 'Der Eintritt der Juden ins deutsche

economic activities of these new entrepreneurs as a group may be said to have reached their zenith in the course of the thirties and forties. Significantly, a decline (or withdrawal from commercial activity) often occurs already in the second generation. By mid-century, many (though not all) of the early entrepreneurial families (and with them their enterprises) have disappeared or lost their earlier importance.

The following generation, that of the fifties and sixties, can be seen as primarily that of the railway builders and financiers, from Abraham Oppenheim in Cologne through Bethel Henry Strousberg and Baron Maurice de Hirsch to Gerson von Bleichröder. This is the generation of the classic Jewish private banker, flourishing under the aegis and in the wake of the house of Rothschild. In the provinces, less conspicuously, Jews then enhanced their prominence also in the traditional produce trade and, through it, in the equally traditional business of war contracting, in connection with the wars of German unification. This is also the second phase (after an earlier one in Berlin) of the Jewish textile industry, more particularly in Silesia. Again, many families that achieve prominence during this period— though with exceptions—disappear from view in the following generation.

The period of the German empire sees the rise of a further generation of Jewish industrial entrepreneurs, conspicuously in machine building, armaments, Silesian heavy industry, as well as of a small but important trading élite (metals, coal, textiles, shipping, imports, exports, retail trade), and culminates in the emergence of a number of prominent bankers, financiers, and a sprinkling of major industrialists. The Wilhelmine era may be seen as the 'high noon' of the German-Jewish economic élite, outwardly expressed in the curious but significant phenomena of, on the one hand, the so-called 'Kaiserjuden', on the other a relatively large number of ennoblements. Typically—as with the Rathenaus, Fürstenbergs, or Mertons or with the long-lived Louis Hagen—this 'golden age' in fact covered not one single generation but something like a generation and a half.

Bürgertum' in Hans Liebeschütz and Arnold Paucker (eds.), *Das Judentum in der Deutschen Umwelt 1800–1850* (Tübingen, 1977), pp. 153 ff. Toury writes: 'In dem Prozess der jüdischen Verbürgerung kommt zunächst der Fürstengunst und der jüdischen Finanzkraft eine schwerwiegende Bedeutung zu. Denn diese beiden Faktoren begannen noch vor einer generellen Verbreitung der Aufklärung unter Juden und Nichtjuden wirksam zu sein. Selbst weniger "aufgeklärte" Herrscher oder gewisse geistliche Herren gewährten "ihren" Hofjuden und Finanzagenten weitgehende Vergünstigungen und räumten ihnen manchmal Positionen ein, die den Neid der Nichtjuden hervorrufen mussten' (ib., p. 153).

The final generation—many important figures of the imperial era died during the Great War or shortly afterwards—was in many cases one of epigones. This was the age of the great amalgamations (IG Farben, Vereinigte Stahlwerke, Schultheiss-Patzenhofer-Ostwerke, Darmstädter und Nationalbank, Deutsche Bank Disconto Gesellschaft, Hapag-Lloyd, and so on). It is the age of conglomerates (Stinnes) and of cartelization. Jews or men of Jewish extraction play a role in the 'organizing' phase—Louis Hagen, Maximilian Kempner, Jakob Goldschmidt, Paul Silverberg, Ludwig Katzenellenbogen—but are less prominent in the resulting organized bureaucracies. Their role in the large banking amalgamations is conspicuous, while some older private banking houses maintain or even regain their importance. More than is sometimes believed, the German-Jewish economic élite, though weakened by general economic and political trends, still continues to occupy a relatively prominent position in German economic life. Weakened further by the events of 1933, it may be said to have received its death-blow by about 1935.

It is thus possible to trace the fortunes of the German-Jewish economic élite, its adaptation to changing economic and political circumstances, over 4 to 4½ generations. The present study is concerned with the rise of the 'first generation' from about 1820 onwards and continues to the bitter end in 1935, a period of some hundred and twenty years of economic activity.

Next to location in time, that in space also is significant. For the nineteenth century, regarding the conferment of commercial titles, it is Prussian data that are most readily available in a systematized form. These in fact cover the major areas of early German industrialization, Berlin, Rhine-Ruhr, and Upper Silesia. Compared to these regions, developments in the rest of Germany were of relatively minor importance. From 1866 onwards, Prussian data also include the relatively advanced commercial areas around Hanover and the great financial and industrial centre of Frankfurt-on-Main. Martin's lists of millionaires on the eve of the Great War cover, in separate volumes, the greater part of Germany. Here also Prussia, and more particularly Berlin and its surroundings, emerge as the most important regions in both a general and a Jewish context. Data on the positional or influence élite, of course, relate to the whole of Germany. Overall, then, the German-Jewish economic élite, with the parameters sketched out, can be seen as a fairly distinctive and identifiable group. Its members, to a great extent, can be located within the economic and social context of time and place. Moreover, the basic sources normally provide, at least in theory, a Gentile control group, even if, for practical reasons, this cannot in every case be fully utilized. For what it is worth, moreover, much of the information concerning the German–Jewish economic élite is capable of quantification though the 'cliometric' approach, of course, has its well-established limitations.

II

The definition of terms and identification of the economic élite are, however, not in themselves sufficient. Doubt has been cast on the validity of singling out for study a 'Jewish' economic élite, of linking ethnicity and economic performance. Has 'Jewishness' a meaning in an economic context or is the association of the two terms a purely arbitrary one? This raises the question of how far, if at all, it is possible to detect, in the economic sphere, elements of Jewish specificity. Does ethnicity affect economic behaviour and, if so, in what respect? Answers to this and related questions can emerge only from an examination of the evidence and must, therefore, be reserved for the conclusion.

It may be useful none the less at this point to introduce a number of preliminary considerations. Among the hypotheses which can be tested in the light of the evidence is the perennial anti-Semitic charge of the alleged Jewish domination of major branches of German economic life. It is an assertion the validity of which can be tested (among others) in terms of the Jewish share in the German economic élite. Thus the proportion of men of Jewish origin among those given commercial titles during the nineteenth century can be determined with a fair degree of accuracy. So can the proportion of Jews (individuals as well as families) among millionaires on the eve of the World War, reflecting approximately one century of capitalist accumulation. Again it is possible to calculate the proportion of the largest enterprises in imperial Germany with men of Jewish extraction in prominent positions. Altogether, then, it is possible to determine, with reasonable accuracy, the proportion of Jews among economic 'leaders' during the evolution of the German economy from early industrialization to the fully fledged industrial age.

The 'Jewish' share in the German economic élite lies, for obvious reasons, well above that of Jews in the German population at large. Yet, how meaningful is this oft-repeated statement in the light of occupational and residential differences between Jew and Gentile? What, it may be asked, would be a proper basis of comparison, the 'norm' against which the Jewish share should be evaluated? It is self-evident that the proportion of Jews in the economic élite would exceed their share of the urban population as a whole with its large proletarian component (in which Jews were notoriously under-represented). What interpretation, therefore, is to be put on the fact that in 1914 Jews in Berlin, with 5 per cent of the population, raised over one third of the taxes?[10] Theoretically, perhaps the most apposite comparison would be between Jewish shares respectively of the urban middle class as a whole and the German economic élite. This would seem the only possible basis for assessing whether, and to what extent, the Jewish presence in the élite was, in fact, 'disproportionate'. Even then, it might be questioned how far the urban middle class as a whole and its Jewish component respectively, even were it possible to establish their numbers, could be considered comparable entities. In fact, there is no effective possibility of establishing a norm and then measuring the Jewish percentage against it. All that can be done is to quantify roughly the Jewish share in groups constituted on the basis of 'objective' criteria (commercial titles, millionaires) and to compare it with the Gentile one.

About the relative—or 'perceived'—prominence of men of Jewish extraction in leading positions in economic life, and of the importance of their collective presence, there can be no doubt. Jews, overall, though unevenly distributed over different branches of economic activity, were both relatively numerous and often conspicuous. It is accordingly tempting to speculate—though there is no way of reaching incontrovertible conclusions—on the reasons for their relative prominence. How far is such prominence attributable to the special motivations traditionally ascribed to members of religious and ethnic minority groups, struggling to secure economic compensations for social and political disadvantage? How far was it furthered by formal and informal networks characteristic more particularly of the social organization of minority groups suffering discrimination? Again, what part was played by specific elements of the Jewish religious and cultural tradition with its positive attitude towards economic activity in

---

[10] H. G. Zmarzlik, 'Antisemitismus im deutschem Kaiserreich 1871–1918', in Bernd Martin and Ernst Schulin (eds.) *Die Juden als Minderheit in der Geschichte* (Munich, 1981), p. 251.

contrast to a major strain in the Christian one which was negative?[11] How significant was a Jewish 'Puritan ethic'? What was the role of a century-old commercial tradition and of international connections, the combined product, of the Jews' minority situation and world-wide dispersion? How relevant is Sombart's well-known thesis about alleged Jewish ethnic (racial) characteristics, said to be conducive to successful capitalist activity: the dominance of will-power, egotism, and 'abstract mentality' ('das Vorwalten des Willens, des Eigennutzes und die Abstraktheit ihrer Geistesbeschaffenheit'[12])? Again in the specific German context, how significant was Germany's relative economic underdevelopment in providing opportunities for Jews in economic life not available to the same extent in economically more advanced countries? The relative weight of these and other related factors is, of course, impossible to determine. Only the comparative study of the economic fortunes of certain comparable minority groups and of Jewish economic élites in other countries could shed light on questions of this kind.

Nor is it easy to answer a further related question, though here the historian finds himself at any rate in the realm of quantifiable fact. As is well known, the Jewish distribution across different branches of economic activity—at the level of the economic élite as, indeed, below it—differed significantly from that to be found among non-Jews. This can be established concretely with the help of non-Jewish control groups more particularly in the case of the wealth élite. According to a certain conventional wisdom, Jews engaged predominantly in commerce and banking, Gentiles in manufacturing industry. Though not wholly false this is, demonstrably, an over-simplification. To the extent however that it is based on fact, it would seem to call for attempt at an explanation. Moreover, if one accepts the crude tripartite division of commerce, finance, and industry (in reality the three emerge as distinct activities only slowly and incompletely from earlier composite forms and are, indeed, never entirely separated), it is noticeable that,

---

[11] For a discussion of the relation of Judaism and capitalism see W. E. Mosse, 'Judaism, Jews and Capitalism. Weber, Sombart and Beyond', in *Year Book XXIV of the Leo Baeck Institute* (London, 1979), 3 ff. For Sombart's views on the 'materialism' of the Old Testament see W. Sombart, *Die Juden und das Wirtschaftsleben* (Leipzig, 1911), p. 255.

[12] W. Sombart, *Die deutsche Volkswirtschaft im neunzehnten Jahrhundert*, 4th edn. (Berlin, 1919), pp. 113 f. See also W. E. Mosse, 'Die Juden in Wirtschaft und Gesellschaft' in W. E. Mosse (ed.) *Juden im Wilhelminischen Deutschland 1890–1914* (Tübingen, 1976), especially pp. 108 ff.

within each of the subdivisions themselves, there were further Jewish peculiarities or 'anomalies'. Were there, one is in consequence led to ask, specific aspects of Jewish religiosity or tradition or, alternatively, of the Jewish economic or social situations which led to concentration on certain types of economic activity in preference to others? Can an underlying 'monocausal' explanation (or indeed bundle of causations) for occupational specificity be provided or has one to seek specific explanations for each separate area of concentration (or neglect)?

In short, the question arises—and in this lies one justification for isolating the study of Jews within the wider economic élite—as to whether elements of Jewish specificity exist within overall German economic activity. The evidence, in fact, strongly suggests the existence of such elements. There is, moreover, no shortage of attempts to explain both their nature and their causes. Thus one hypothesis asserts the general marginality of Jewish economic activity. Jews, it is claimed, engaged only in such forms of economic activity as were disdained by Gentiles. It was, predominantly, these activities which Jews entered in numbers and in which they were sometimes able to achieve striking successes. Jews, in this view, remained, at all times, outside the mainstream of German economic life. Their economic role was always marginal and they were therefore economically 'expendable' as 'proved' after their disappearance under Nazi rule. However successful in individual instances, they had in fact, collectively operated merely in the interstices of the wider German economy. Their opportunities and their choices alike had been determined by what Max Weber described as their 'pariah status'. This is a hypothesis that can, to a great extent, be tested against the facts.

A refinement of the 'marginality' theory, and one that raises somewhat different issues, is the assertion that alleged Jewish marginality steadily increased with the progress of industrialization and the growth of capitalist organization. Jews, it is conceded, may have fulfilled a significant entrepreneurial function in the age of early industrialization as financiers, risk-takers, and pioneers. However, with time, they steadily lost their innovative flexibility, contenting themselves with by then traditional commercial (mainly trading) activities, activities which were steadily losing their central place in German economic life. Moreover, Gentiles were steadily 'learning' from Jews and duplicating their techniques. Also while, at the beginning of industrialization, Jews may have found themselves in a favoured starting position, they inevitably lost their initial advantage.

This thesis, moreover, has a variant, involving at least a degree of 'objectivization'. Men of Jewish extraction, it is argued—with some support from statistical evidence—were to a much greater extent than non-Jews 'independents', committed to the autonomy of the family firm. They stuck to this congenial form of economic organization even when the family enterprise was being steadily superseded by the joint-stock company and, eventually, by the large private bureaucracies of organized or monopoly capitalism. (The extent to which different forms of economic organization continued to exist side by side is conveniently overlooked.) Men of Jewish origin, it is argued, were unfitted by temperament (and discouraged by corporate anti-Semitism) from making the transition from the family business to the larger corporate structures, in consequence of which their overall role in German economic life steadily declined. In the light of an examination of the German–Jewish economic élite over several generations and spanning the different phases of economic development, it is possible to test the validity of this hypothesis also.

Still another hypothesis which has found a degree of favour starts from the undeniably distinctive economic starting position of Jews in the early nineteenth century. This was ascribed, other causes apart, to the age-old familiarity of Jews with financial operations (in a still largely natural economy) and their consequent financial and commercial expertise and disproportionate command of mobile capital—to which might be added their determined pursuit of economic success following their recent escape from what were, in many cases, at best 'near-ghetto' conditions and their consequent willingness (again exceeding that of their Gentile competitors) to 'try their luck', to take risks, to work hard and single-mindedly, to experiment, and to invest. The result was a degree of economic success (though the model fails to explain fully why this should occur in some areas rather than others). Once economic success had been achieved in certain fields, the laws of persistence through the formation of dynasties would tend to perpetuate an existing pattern. So would the operation of informal economic networks. Gradually, the Jewish sector would tend to become ossified—and in a shape somewhat different from that of its Gentile counterpart. Rather quaintly, this theory is sometimes linked with another almost its opposite, to the effect that with the progress of capitalism there occurred, in fact, a growing convergence in Jewish and Gentile occupational patterns. The Jewish one, it is asserted (almost certainly with apologetic intent), had, by the time of the Weimar

Republic (that is by the last generation of the Jewish economic élite), become largely assimilated to the Gentile. Again it is a claim which can, to an extent, be tested against the evidence.

A somewhat different, 'structuralist' approach has also been used to explain if not the origins at any rate the persistence of distinctive Jewish economic patterns. In this view the peculiar Jewish occupational structure at the beginning of the age of industrialization would be perpetuated through an internal dynamic of dynasty formation, personal relations, kinship ties, socialization processes, and, in general, the operation of a variety of informal networks. At least until mid-century Jews tended to transact business mainly with fellow Jews, in part because Jewish ritual laws impeded, if they did not completely inhibit between Jew and Gentile the social intercourse almost inseparable from sustained business relations. Equally important, it is claimed, though this of course can be no more than an assumption, that relations of trust, so essential in commercial dealings, were more readily established among members of the same (disadvantaged) ethnic and religious minority group. Kinship ties also would tend to reinforce business relations among members of the same ethnic group. Where sons of Jewish élite members were sent to other houses for their apprenticeships (both at home and, more particularly, abroad) these, for a variety of reasons, would, as likely as not, be those of co-religionists (often relatives). Again, whether through kinship ties, greater confidence and sympathy, feelings of solidarity, or recommendations, there would be a marked tendency for Jews to employ fellow-Jews in positions of trust, as men having *prokura*, and eventually to raise them to a partnership. Close and harmonious business relationships reinforced by personal friendship, the friendship of families, and common leisure pursuits would, not infrequently, contain also an element of common 'Jewishness'. Thus cultural factors and social environment might help to explain first the emergence and later the persistence of something like a 'Jewish sector' within the German economy. Jewish economic specificity then would be based less on purely economic aspects, than on the operation of a number of social and cultural factors. The German–Jewish economic élite thus might be considered a social and cultural as much as a purely economic phenomenon.

Finally, the element of Jewish specificity in German economic affairs, the emergence of a successful Jewish business class, has been related also to Jewish minority status. The existence of a connection between membership of certain ethnic or religious minority groups and economic achievement is, of course, a commonplace. So far as Jewish economic success in Germany is more particularly concerned, this has been ascribed to a peculiar combination of political and social disrimination with economic opportunity. This combination was itself the product, largely, of the interested policies of rulers and governments who, while denying Jews many important chances, chose to grant them economic privileges, offering to the most enterprising opportunities for lucrative commercial employment. This situation, characteristic of the age of absolutism, had continued into the period of early industrialization when partly emancipated Jews—freed with regard to mobility and choice of a vocation (notably in Prussia since 1812)—still suffered from second-class (if any) civil status and exclusion from a wide range of 'public' functions. Discrimination had, inevitably, made Jews 'achievement orientated', more particularly in the economic sphere, one not only wide open to them but in which they were able to operate with official encouragement. Indeed it has frequently been stressed that one element in the Jewish situation favourable to the economic progress of individuals was that the state, in its search for economically active individuals (urgently needed for a variety of purposes at all times, but more especially during the Napoleonic crisis), had turned increasingly to its Jewish subjects (as also to those of Huguenot origin) on account of a marked shortage of entrepreneurial potential in the majority population. Members of the upper and middle classes of the majority would manifest, for a long time (if not, indeed, permanently), a marked disdain for 'low status' commercial pursuits. Those who did turn to commerce would often lack the tenacious and determined industry of members of the disadvantaged Jewish minority. There was indeed a particular challenge to the young Jew, often the modest Jewish family, to achieve upward social mobility through successful economic activity. In general, it could be held that in both psychological and environmental aspects the situation of the young Jew embarking upon a commercial career differed from that of his Gentile peers. In this respect also, the Jewish situation could be seen as distinctive.

A further question frequently raised—from different directions and with varied, often hostile intent—concerns the possible existence of a distinctive Jewish business ethic or style, of specific commercial methods employed by Jews (notably in advertising), of distinctively 'Jewish' business strategies. Did managerial or commercial decisions of firms vary with the ethnic composition of management? (In relation to this question comparisons like the obvious one between AEG and Siemens have been made; others, for instance between the Dresdner and the Deutsche Bank, founded almost simultaneously, or between Albert Ballin's Hapag and the Norddeutsche Lloyd, are possible.) This is, of course, an area where the historian must hesitate. Criteria of comparison are difficult to establish, the comparability of individual enterprises is doubtful. Even could these difficulties be overcome, it would not be easy to determine the relative weight of ethnic and other factors. Tempting though it may be to detect something like a 'Jewish style' in the economic activities of an Emil Rathenau, Oscar Tietz, or Albert Ballin, a Louis Hagen, Carl Fürstenberg, or Eugen Gutmann, the undertaking would of necessity be inconclusive and, perhaps, of questionable validity.

Nor is it profitable to speculate how the German economy might have fared in the absence of its Jewish component. About a degree of Jewish prominence in German economic development there can be no doubt. Neither is it to be doubted that Jews constituted a distinctive and identifiable element with the German 'body economic'. Whether the distinctiveness was due primarily to ethnic or environmental causes, to social or to psychological features, is a question that cannot readily be answered. Clearly many often interdependent factors were involved in producing and perpetuating the Jewish economic élite. In important respects, its members differed from their non-Jewish peers. While as a social group they were distinct, as an economic entity they possessed, at any rate, a number of distinctive characteristics. Their role in the German economy was, as will be seen, both significant and, in some respects, unique. They deserve study as a major factor in German economic development.

III

The German–Jewish economic élite as such has never been studied. The nearest approach to a description is Zielenziger's collection of twenty-one sketches of members of the élite ranging from the house of Rothschild to Jakob Goldschmidt.[13] It is a study which, of its kind, remains unsurpassed to this day. Several works devoted to the German economic élite in general cover also a number of its Jewish members.

[13] Kurt Zielenziger, *Juden in der deutschen Wirtschaft* (Berlin, 1930).

Thus Schnee's monumental study of court factors in the age of absolutism[14] covers a number of court Jews.[15] The period dealt with, however, precedes in the main that of the present study. Rachel and Wallich's study of entrepreneurs in Berlin in the age of early industrialization[16]—a work marred by its anti-Jewish bias—contains accounts of a number of Jewish entrepreneurs.[17] There are then few collective studies of members of the economic élite until the works of Pinner[18] and Achterberg[19] devoted to men prominent in the Wilhelmine age. Martin, in his year-books of millionaires, provides brief biographical sketches of those with fortunes exceeding five million marks.[20] In the *Reichshandbuch der deutschen Gesellschaft* published in 1930 there are brief accounts of Jews then prominent in economic life. More comprehensively, the *Neue Deutsche Biographie* currently being published contains descriptions of prominent members of the Jewish economic élite with helpful references to available monograph literature. Information relating more particularly to board membership of Jews under the Weimar Republic can be gleaned from a compendium published by Wenzel.[21] None of these works, however, are systematic studies of the German–Jewish economic élite. All are limited chronologically with an emphasis on either the eighteenth and early nineteenth centuries or the early twentieth. Several are confined to particular centres, notably Berlin. Some are works of a serious popular kind. What is presented is, in the main, thumbnail sketches, describing in more or less detail some of the more prominent individuals. Not one of the works mentioned, whatever their merit (sometimes considerable) in the provision of data, could, by any stretch of the imagination, be considered a systematic study of the German (or, as the case might be, German–Jewish) economic élite.

[14] Heinrich Schnee, op. cit., n. 8 above.
[15] See also Selma Stern, op. cit., n. 8 above.
[16] Hugo Rachel and Paul Wallich, *Berliner Grosskaufleute und Kapitalisten*, 3 vols. (Berlin, 1934–9).
[17] A number of Jewish entrepreneurs also figure in Hartmut Kaelble, *Berliner Unternehmer während der frühen Industrialisierung* (Berlin, 1972). Data on some members of the Jewish economic élite are to be found also in Stefi Jersch-Wenzel, *Jüdische Bürger und kommunale Selbstverwaltung in preussischen Städten 1808–1848* (Berlin, 1967).
[18] Felix Pinner, *Deutsche Wirtschaftsführer* (Charlottenburg, 1925). An earlier work of a somewhat similar nature is Dr E. Friedegg, *Millionen und Millionäre* (Berlin, 1914). Carl Fürstenberg described Pinner as 'einer der besten Kenner der neueren deutschen Wirtschaftsgeschichte'. Carl Fürstenberg, *Die Lebensgeschichte eines deutschen Bankiers* (Wiesbaden, 1961), p. 169.
[19] Erich Achterberg, *Berliner Hochfinanz. Kaiser, Fürsten, Millionäre um 1900* (Frankfurt-on-Main, 1965). [20] Rudolf Martin, op. cit., n. 3 above.
[21] Georg Wenzel, *Deutscher Wirtschaftsführer* (Hamburg, 1929).

Introduction

Beyond these collections, there exist a number of monographs devoted to prominent families, outstanding individuals, or, on occasion, enterprises. It may be worth listing briefly some of the more important. There exists, of course, a quite extensive literature on the Rothschilds.[22] There are publications devoted to the Mendelssohns.[23] Gerson Bleichröder has recently been the subject of an extensive biography by Fritz Stern[24] which, however, concentrates almost wholly on his relations with Bismarck, rather than his broader economic role. Albert Ballin[25] and the two Rathenaus have attracted historians and others. Yet while there is relatively little information on Emil Rathenau and the creation of the AEG,[26] the economic activities of Walther (almost certainly seriously overrated[27]) figure little in the extensive literature devoted mainly to other aspects of his life.[28] Besides such

[22] The standard work is Bertrand Gille, *Histoire de la maison Rothschild*, 2 vols. (Geneva, 1965 and 1967). See also Jean Bouvier, *Les Rothschild* (Paris, 1967) and Egon Conte Corti, *The Rise of the House of Rothschild* (London, 1928).

[23] There are two volumes of *Mendelssohn Studien*, published in Berlin in 1972 and 1975. The first contains an essay by Wilhelm Treue, 'Das Bankhaus Mendelssohn als Beispiel einer Privatbank im 19. und 20. Jahrhundert' *Mendelssohn Studien*, i (Berlin, 1972, 29 ff). A more fundamental source is several volumes of materials on the bank's activities down to the year 1875 assembled by Rudolf Loeb, one of the partners, as the basis for a planned history. These are preserved in the archives of the Leo Baeck Institute in New York. Felix Gilbert, *Bankiers, Künstler und Gelehrte* (Tübingen, 1975), a collection of nineteenth-century family correspondence with a long and informative introduction, deals primarily with social rather than with economic matters.

[24] Fritz Stern, *Gold and Iron* (New York, 1977).

[25] Besides the sources listed in Eduard Rosenbaum, 'Albert Ballin: A Note on the Style of his Economic and Political Activities' in *Year Book III of the Leo Baeck Institute* (London, 1958), 299, see now also Lamar Cecil, *Albert Ballin: Business and Politics in Imperial Germany 1888–1918* (Princeton, 1967).

[26] Probably the most useful source remains Felix Pinner, *Emil Rathenau und das elektrische Zeitalter* (Leipzig, 1918). The unpublished reminiscences of Felix Deutsch, 'Lebenserinnerungen' (copy in the archives of the Leo Baeck Institute in New York), contain valuable information especially on the early days of Deutsche Edison and AEG. Other works on Emil Rathenau are listed in Ernst Schulin, 'Die Rathenaus. Zwei Generationen jüdischen Anteils an der industriellen Entwicklung Deutschlands' in Werner E. Mosse (ed.), *Juden in Wilhelminischen Deutschland 1890–1914* (Tübingen, 1976), p. 120 n. 15.

[27] This is brought out by Hans Fürstenberg in his memoirs in a critical appreciation of Walther Rathenau, Hans Fürstenberg, *Erinnerungen: mein Weg als Bankier und Carl Fürstenbergs Altersjahre* (Düsseldorf and Vienna, 1968), pp. 97 ff. Hans Fürstenberg not only knew Rathenau well but, as a banker, was closely acquainted also with his activities in the economic sphere. Rathenau's relatively modest role in corporate industry outside the ambit of the AEG is confirmed by his board memberships. Cf. 'Liste der Aufsichtsräte in denen Rathenau zwischen 1907 und 1922 vertreten war' in Hartmut Pogge v. Strandmann (ed.), *Walther Rathenau Tagebuch 1907–1922* (Düsseldorf, 1967), pp. 287 f.

[28] It may be more than an accident that, in his extensive introduction to the correspondence between Maximilian Harden and Walther Rathenau, Hans Dieter

favourites of the biographers, other members of the élite have received their individual monographs, among them Wilhelm Merton,[29] Bernhard Dernburg,[30] Louis Hagen,[31] and Paul Silverberg.[32] Carl Fürstenberg provided his own near-autobiography,[33] whilst both Hermann and Paul Wallich left valuable autobiographical writings.[34] In a class by itself is Georg Tietz's monument to his father Oscar.[35] What is, on the whole, striking is the attention paid to unrepresentative and untypical figures like Bismarck's belated and anachronistic 'court Jew' Gerson Bleichröder or the Hamletic Walther Rathenau, a talented and many-sided cultural philosopher and aesthete, eaten up with political ambition. There are no biographies of more 'normal' and typical members of the élite, such as Eduard Arnhold,[36] James Simon, Isidor Loewe, or Max Warburg,[37] to name only a few of the more important. Among the scanty histories of Jewish firms, besides the account of the Tietz department stores already mentioned, that of the Warburg bank stands out.[38] There are descriptions of the Loewe concern[39] and of the Hirsch brass manufacture.[40] It is clear that, however valuable and

Hellige, while speaking of Rathenau as 'Wirtschaftsführer und Initiator grosser Fusionen' (p. 179), has disappointingly little to say about his actual economic activities. Hans Dieter Hellige (ed.), *Walther Rathenau Maximilian Harden Briefwechsel* (Munich and Heidelberg, 1983), pp. 176–8. Rathenau's diaries (op. cit.) would seem to confirm the relatively modest nature of his economic role, the full history of which remains, perhaps, to be written.

[29] Hans Achinger, *Wilhelm Merton in seiner Zeit* (Frankfurt-on-Main, 1965).
[30] W. Schiefel, *Bernhard Dernburg* (Zurich, n.d.).
[31] Hermann Kellenbenz, *Louis Hagen (1855–1932)* (Münster, 1974).
[32] Hermann Kellenbenz, *Paul Silverberg (1876–1959)* (Münster, 1967). For Louis Hagen and Paul Silverberg see now Werner E. Mosse, 'Zwei Präsidenten der Kölner Industrie- und Handelskammer: Louis Hagen und Paul Silverberg' in *Köln und das rheinische Judentum* (Cologne, 1984).
[33] Carl Fürstenberg, op. cit., n. 18 above. The memoirs, recorded by Hans Fürstenberg, were based on conversations with his father and approved by him.
[34] *Zwei Generationen im deutschen Bankwesen 1833–1914* (Frankfurt-on-Main, 1978).
[35] Georg Tietz, *Hermann Tietz Geschichte einer Familie und ihrer Warenhäuser* (Stuttgart, 1965).
[36] The nearest approach to a biographical study is Wilhelm Treue, 'Caesar Wollheim und Eduard Arnhold' in *Tradition*, 6 (Apr. and June 1961).
[37] It is to be hoped that the complete version of Max Warburg's reminiscences will, one day, belatedly see the light of day.
[38] E. Rosenbaum and A. J. Sherman, *Das Bankhaus M. M. Warburg & Co. 1798–1938* (Hamburg, 1976).
[39] Georg Tischert, *Aus der Entwicklung des Loewe-Konzerns* (Berlin, 1911).
[40] Siegmund Hirsch, *Revolution im Messing (1908–1929)* (Lammersdorf, 1967). There is also an unpublished family history by the same author, 'Die Kupferhirschs in Halberstadt 1780–1930', of which, thanks to Henry Bondi (Princeton), I possess a copy.

informative, such occasional works are not accounts of the German–Jewish economic élite.

In fact, the published sources on the Jewish economic élite in the nineteenth century (the élite of notables) are few, those on their successors in the imperial era if somewhat more plentiful remain fragmentary, unsystematic, and sometimes subjective. What is available is unevenly distributed and largely the product of chance. The present attempt at a systematic description and analysis of the élite is thus a pioneering venture with the inescapable weaknesses and deficiencies of such. It attempts, however, to fill a gap in the knowledge of German economic history. Nor does a (feasible) comparable study exist either of the German economic élite as a whole or of its Gentile sector alone—a major desideratum. A study on the Jewish economic élite in Anglo-Saxon countries, similarly, would yield valuable comparative data.

IV

The German–Jewish economic élite, as will be seen, played a prominent part in German economic development over the course of four generations from the age of early industrialization to the emergence of fully fledged industrial capitalism in the twentieth century. The economic role of Jews in Germany—though actual quantification is, of course, impossible—was greater than that in western industrialized countries like England, France, or Holland. It also exceeded almost certainly their role in the development of the American economy. Only in the Habsburg monarchy and its successor states may Jewish entrepreneurship have played a comparable role.

If one seeks to account for the special prominence of the Jewish economic élite in Germany, a number of reasons suggest themselves which, in their cumulative effect, help to explain not only the importance, but to some extent also the specific nature of the Jewish contribution. The causes, as one would expect, lie in both the German and Jewish situations. While some could be described as 'typical', others were highly specific. It is the latter, above all, which explain the distinctive nature of the Jewish function in German economic life.

At the very root of the Jewish economic role in Germany lie certain fundamental features of the German environment. The most important of these is the comparative 'underdevelopment', at least by western European standards, of German capitalist and entrepreneurial forces.

The reasons for this may be, in the first place, geographical: Germany's remoteness from the world's great seas, the Mediterranean, Atlantic, and Indian Oceans, with the consequent lack of overseas navigation, great trading companies, overseas settlements, the lucrative colonial trade (from spices to slaves), the banking, maritime insurance, and other financial institutions and devices associated with such trades. Even at the height of its influence, the scattered Hanseatic League hardly matched later counterparts like the Dutch or British East India Companies, the City of London, or the economic powerhouse devised by Colbert. Nor did fragmented Germany possess a political authority capable of providing single-minded backing for mercantilist ventures. Instead, the devastations of the Thirty Years War impoverished cities and impeded economic development. 'Development-minded' princes of the seventeenth and eighteenth centuries, in consequence, were forced to have recourse to foreigners, to Protestant refugees from Catholic persecution (whether in France, Salzburg, or elsewhere) or Jews, refugees from Catholic persecution in the Iberian Peninsula and seeking to fan out from their original places of refuge in Amsterdam, Altona, or Vienna. The virtual lack of an indigenous capitalist and entrepreneurial class was, in fact, the basic reason why German princes encouraged, by the grant of various privileges, the settlement in their territories of members of religious and ethnic minority groups. Thus, from the start, members of such groups filled gaps in the German economic system that were without close parallel in the countries of western Europe.

The weakness of the German commercial classes, largely due to 'natural causes', was reinforced by the low social status of their members. Except in some residual commercial enclaves such as Frankfurt-on-Main or Hamburg, the merchant estate in Germany ranked low in social esteem. It was socially separated, in a manner unequalled elsewhere, from the landowning and sword-bearing nobility and its bureaucratic extension. While France also had its *noblesse d'epée*, this was flanked by a *noblesse de robe* and, eventually, by an assertive *tiers état*. The indispensable tax-farmers also enjoyed a degree of social prestige. In Germany—this, of course, a generalization to which exceptions can be found—commercial pursuits (eventually, there was some exception made for 'patriotic' *manufacturers* like the Krupps) continued to occupy a low place in the social ranking order with the 'Koofmich', to the bitter end, a figure of fun and derision. Commerce (*Handel*) was a barely 'honest', let alone an 'honourable', occupation in a country which, to the end, remained essentially anticapitalist (as witness, among others, the widespread *völkisch* anticapitalism culminating in the quest for *Lebensraum*—core of the essentially anticapitalist economic ideology of the NS regime). It was an ideology (with Friedrich Nietzsche a fanatical and influential exponent) which kept members of the noble ruling classes away from commercial pursuits and left the field open to others content with low—or at any rate lower—status activities. It is no accident that the early industrialists of the Rhine and Ruhr were frequently men of 'foreign' extraction: Dutch, Belgian, French, Irish, or English and, moreover, in their majority Protestant. The low prestige of commercial avocations left, throughout, the economic sphere wide open for the 'outsider'.

There was, moreover, a curious interaction of cause and effect. While the low esteem enjoyed by commercial pursuits may in origin have been due to general social causes (going back to the age of *Landsknechte* and *Raubritter* as well as the social philosophy of the medieval Catholic Church) it was in its turn heavily reinforced by the fact that such pursuits, from an early period, had become, in fact, essentially the preserve of 'outsiders' in general and of the despised Jews in particular. So long as these conditions persisted, *Handel*, especially, remained a term with pejorative connotations as, indeed (the sources bear witness to the fact) did banking, the trade in money. The ridiculous distinction between 'raffendes' and 'schaffendes' *Kapital*—equated, idiotically, respectively with 'Jewish banking' and 'German industry'—was a late manifestation of the widespread attitude towards the economic activities of a despised minority. Owing to the prominence of members of minorities and, more particularly, Jews, capitalism, banking, trade (indeed any economic pursuit other than agriculture, *Handwerk*, and the armaments industry) could never, in Germany, gain the social esteem they enjoyed in more economically and socially advanced countries. The disesteem, moreover, was reinforced (though only partly on an anti-foreign or specifically anti-Jewish basis) by the rapid growth of various brands of socialism. Money, wealth, and the pursuits producing them (other than the apparently 'reputable' coal ownership of assorted magnates, assimilated to the 'noble' pursuit of agriculture) remained—partly as the domain of numerous 'aliens'—barely reputable to the end. Indeed, Gentiles entering commerical pursuits were assimilated to Jews in the minds of the apostles of anti-capitalist and anti-Semitic nationalism ('Jeder Christ treibt Judenschacher'). In Sombart's famous terminology a people of 'Helden', true Germans, looked down on alien 'Händler' (eventually however represented mainly by 'das perfide Albion'). So the incentive for young Gentiles to enter the despised field of commerce was relatively small. This may, moreover, in part account for the surprising (relative) absence of competition between Gentile and Jew in German economic life. On the whole, leading Gentile entrepreneurs appear not only to have been largely free from anti-Jewish prejudice, but even to have readily acknowledged Jewish achievement in this field. For such reasons, among others, there were near-empty spaces left in the German economy which it was open to Jews to fill.

Furthermore–another feature more typical perhaps of Germany than of many other countries—members of minority groups and Jews in particular were officially encouraged until a late date to fill such empty spaces. A related aspect, notably in the age of absolutism, was the multitude of principalities of all shapes and sizes in Germany. As is well known, the princes, their courts, and their military establishments were insatiable consumers of goods and services, in constant need of scarce resources whether for peace or war. There was thus a steady demand among princes for financiers to manage and indeed increase the revenues of their principalities and, above all, their (the princes') own. Management of coinage, tax-farming, the operation of salt and tobacco monopolies, military supplies, the provision of goods ranging from jewellery to horses or agricultural produce, and last, not least, credit were involved. And, in the relative absence of native capitalists, all this had traditionally been and remained the domain largely of Jews, the celebrated *Hofjuden* or *Hoffaktoren*, who had, inevitably, become also the court bankers of princes great and small. Compared to countries further west, the multitude of principalities in Germany thus created a unique and specific demand for Jewish financial and commerical services.

In particular, there was a demand for the services of Jews as war contractors and as the purveyors of a variety of goods (again largely for military purposes) on credit. The demand had reached unprecedented heights during the revolutionary and Napoleonic wars, when Jews had not only supplied and provisioned armies but had transmitted and distributed British subsidies, raised contributions for the French, financed military operations, transmitted French reparation payments, and provided loans for princes and estates financially exhausted by decades of war. Jews had become indispensable to the public finances of Germany and Europe. The multiplicity of principalities in Germany had produced a unique multiplication of demand. Moreover, the demand for Jewish financial and economic services was sustained not by princes alone but also by 'development-minded' bureaucracies. In Prussia among others, more particularly in the days of Chancellor Hardenberg, the importance of Jews for economic development had been recognized. It was a tradition which would persist to the days of Bismarck and Bernhard v. Bülow. However determined to discriminate systematically against at least professing Jews in the state service, the German authorities—some half-hearted measures (under pressure) to penalize stock-exchange transactions or department-stores apart— tended not only not to impede, but actively to encourage their economic activities. Here also the combination of the traditional weakness of the Gentile entrepreneurial class, the multiple demands of princes, and the stance of 'development-minded' bureaucrats combined to create a situation favourable to the unfolding of Jewish entrepreneurial skills.

Given these various factors in the main peculiar to the German situation, the external conditions for the development of an important Jewish economic élite could hardly have been more favourable. Sombart, indeed, was not far from the truth when proclaiming that if the Jew did not exist, he would have to be invented.[41]

But the Jew (luckily for the German economy) did not have to be invented. He was already to be found in Germany in numbers at the dawn of the age of early industrialization able and ready, for a variety of reasons, to take advantage of the economic opportunities offered by the peculiar German situation. A number of factors combined to enable German Jews to seize these opportunities. The first, a 'typical' one, was their minority status. The implications of this had already been spelt out in classic formulation by wise old Montesquieu in his *Lettres persanes*: 'On remarque que ceux qui vivent dans les religions tolérées se rendent ordinairement plus utiles à leur patrie que ceux qui vivent dans la religion dominante parce que, éloignés des honneurs ne pouvant se distinguer que par leur opulence et leurs richesses, ils sont portés à acquérir par leur travail et à embrasser des emplois de la société les plus pénibles.'[42] Sombart also (unlike Montesquieu with

---

[41] Sombart, op. cit., n. 11 above, p. 112.
[42] Charles Louis de Secondat, Baron de la Brède et de Montesquieu, *Lettres persanes*, (Paris, 1960), Letter LXXXV, p. 179.

specific reference to Jews) explains that mobile wealth—money—was the only possible equivalent available for the status denied them by the lawgiver's fiat.[43]

Minority status, moreover, normally involves for members of the minority group a sense of social solidarity, not a negligible economic asset. In the words of David Landes:

> I have had occasion to discuss elsewhere the success in trade and banking of such dispersed but cohesive religious and ethnic groups as the Jews, Calvinists, Greeks and Parsees. Their effectiveness rested on mutual confidence, especially precious before the days of institutionalized credit ratings and easy communication, on mutual support and on superior intelligence (in the military sense). Everywhere, they prospered out of proportion to their numbers; but their role was most important in those societies that were either incapable or scornful of trade—areas of backwardness or illiteracy for example, or countries in which business was looked upon as a degrading activity.[44]

If minority status in general—Max Weber would later speak of 'pariah people'—predisposed Jews towards exertions in the economic sphere, and thus towards filling the gaps left by gentile reluctance to engage in commerce, there were other more specific causes rooted in Jewish history to reinforce such general dispositions. In the first place, ever since their Babylonian exile, Jews had engaged in commercial pursuits, a fact reflected also in their ethic. Jewish scholars and teachers had gained their living by trade: the Talmud, in consequence (unlike traditional Christianity) had been positively disposed towards economic activity and the profit motive.[45] Unlike Christianity, Judaism tended to sanction capital and capitalism, a fact, moreover, recognized—from interested motives—also by the Christian authorities.[46] Judaism,

---

[43] The alleged Jewish 'idolatry' of money, Sombart considered, was the product of a number of causes. 'Vor allem ihre Zurücksetzung in rechtlicher Beziehung, ihre Ausschliessung von Ämtern und Würden der christlichen Gesellschaft. Da lernten sie denn im Gelde ein Mittel kennen, das ihnen zum grossen Teil ersetzte, was sie durch Machtspruch der Gesetzgebung entbehren mussten: Geltung und Ansehen. Und daraus ergab sich natürlich abermals eine gesteigerte Wertung dieses Stillers aller Schmerzen, dieses Heilers aller Wunden, dieses wundersamen Trösters in allen Leiden: das Geld.' Sombart, op. cit., n. 11 above, p. 115.

[44] David S. Landes, 'The Bleichröder Bank' *Year Book V of the Leo Baeck Institute*, (London, 1960), p. 203.

[45] See W. E. Mosse, 'Judaism, Jews and Capitalism', loc. cit., n. 11 above, 3 ff.

[46] Thus the Emperor Frederick II of Hohenstaufen in the Constitutions of Melfi (1231): 'Von der Verbindlichkeit dieses unseres Wuchergesetzes nehmen wir allein die Juden aus, die des unerlaubten Zinsnehmens, durch Gottes Gesetz verboten, nicht zu

as Siegmund Freud observed, was, unlike Christianity, a 'this-worldly' religion.[47] It was also a rationalistic one, imbued with the 'Protestant ethic' of labour and worldly (but divinely sanctioned) success. Sombart, after drawing a somewhat crude analogy between rationalism and capitalism, concluded that, since the Jewish religion had strong rationalistic features, there existed among Jews a natural affinity for equally rationalistic capitalism. Max Weber in turn considered that the rationality of the traditional Jewish way of life found expression also in a distinctive Jewish attitude to labour and hence economic activity in general. Kurt Zielenziger, historian of the German–Jewish economic élite, elaborates the point.[48]

Thus specific factors resulting from the nature of Jewish religiosity, the Jewish ethic, and the traditional Jewish way of life reinforced predispositions resulting from minority status in general. This was, in fact, a minority particularly well prepared by religion and history to take advantage of economic opportunities.

Yet even these causes taken together would not, by themselves, suffice to explain the emergence and success of the German–Jewish economic élite in the nineteenth century. Further factors arising on the one hand from the nature of the German environment, on the other from changes in that environment, concurred to promote the progress of Jews in nascent capitalist society. Prominent among these is the Jewish occupational distribution in the age of absolutism, determined on the one hand by a persistent 'feudal' society with its estates and guild privileges, on the other by the economic power and needs of princes. Jews, as is well known, were, in their overwhelming majority, permitted in traditional German society to engage only in occupations

zeihen sind da Sie—wie bekannt—nicht unter dem Gesetze der seligen Kirchenväter stehen.' Ernst Kantorowicz, *Kaiser Friedrich der Zweite* (Berlin, 1936), p. 245.

[47] 'Ich war überrascht zu finden, dass schon das erste, sozusagen embryonale Erlebnis des Volkes, der Einfluss des Mannes Moses und der Auszug aus Ägypten, die ganze weitere Entwicklung bis auf den heutigen Tag festgelegt hat—wie ein richtiges frühkindliches Trauma in der Geschichte des neurotischen Individuums. Voran steht hier die Diesseitigkeit der Lebensauffassung und die Überwindung des magischen Denkens, die Absage an die Mystik, beides auf Moses selbst zurückzuführen, und vielleicht... ein Stück weiter...' Siegmund Freud to N.N., 14 Dec. 1937, in Ernst and Lucie Freud (eds.), *Siegmund Freud Briefe 1873–1933* (Frankfurt-on-Main, 1968), pp. 454 f.

[48] 'Die strenge Rationalisierung ihrer Lebensführung, ihnen eingeimpft durch ihre Lehren, lässt ihnen als einziges Volk der Antike—darin stimmen wir Max Weber zu—den Beruf zur göttlichen Berufung, zum "Melocho" (Dienst) werden. Diese religiöse Bewertung der Arbeit führt die Juden zu rastlosem Vorwärtsstreben, das ihnen sittliche Aufgabe wird.' Zielenziger, op. cit., n. 13 above, p. 16.

disdained by Gentiles. This, in essence, confined them to petty, often ambulatory trade (mainly in second-hand goods but also, on occasion, in agricultural produce), petty pawnbroking, and money-lending. Jews (it might have corresponded to their inclinations and aptitudes in any case) were forced to become essentially a nation of petty traders. Lestschinsky claims that, at the beginning of the nineteenth century, practically the whole of German Jewry consisted of pedlars or small shopkeepers.[49] In Bavaria, for instance, in 1821 a statistical count showed 96 per cent of all Jewish families as being engaged in trade.[50] German Jews, moreover, had been petty traders already for generations. The fact was not without significance. Not only did petty trade involve the development of certain (not always 'desirable') aptitudes but also the accumulation, in many cases, of modest amounts of capital. It necessitated also a high degree of mobility (compared to peasant and even landowning groups and to urban artisans—other than during the period of apprenticeship), the development of networks of commercial relations among local (largely rural) populations, and, economically, a mediating role between town (typically the small residence or provincial town) and country. It also brought with it considerable experience, acquired from childhood, of quality and characteristics of a variety of materials and products. All these were aptitudes and relations germane to the emergence of the German–Jewish economic élite from the midst of the reservoir of petty traders.

No less significant was the demand of princes large and small (already referred to) for Jewish capitalists. Through it some Jews, sometimes over several generations, were able to acquire financial expertise, familiarity with economic problems, and some experience of management and organization. At the same time they were enabled (often very successfully) to build up close personal and sometimes social relations with (usually impecunious) rulers and nobles and to acquire, at any rate superficially, some of the manners and diplomatic skills of courtly or aristocratic society. They might also accumulate (in some cases not inconsiderable) wealth. A few also achieved a privileged social status akin to that of a secondary nobility which led Jacob Toury to apply to them the designation of 'Adelsbürger' (which, if not a contradiction in terms, would almost mean 'noble commoners'). At the beginning of the nineteenth century such 'Adelsbürger' may

---

[49] Jakob Lestschinsky, *Das wirtschaftliche Schicksal des deutschen Judentums, Aufstieg, Wandlung, Krise, Ausblick* (Berlin, 1932), p. 16.
[50] Ib., p. 22.

have constituted, according to Lestschinsky, something like 1–2 per cent of the total Jewish population.[51] Though numerically small this group constituted, of course, an important element in the emerging economic élite. The occupations forced on the Jews by surrounding society were thus a factor of importance in preparing some of them for subsequent economic success.

No less significant for Jewish economic progress was the change in the economic and legal environment which occurred in the first decades of the nineteenth century. It was a change which, in its cumulative effect, amounted to nothing less than the destruction, by government, of the traditional economic system. This itself was a result of a number of causes among which the widespread reception of Adam Smith's free-trade philosophy and the attack on privileged corporations (including economic) associated with the French Revolution deserve, perhaps, pride of place. The result was a steady erosion of (Christian) guild privileges and monopolies, a growing freedom of choice of occupation, and with it a larger element of geographical and social mobility.

Moreover, the gradual destruction of the economic *ancien régime* in Germany coincided (perhaps not accidentally) with the early stages in the emancipation of the Jews. Among the first freedoms to be granted were those in the economic sphere: freedom in the choice of occupation, enlarged (if by no means absolute) choice of residence, the right to acquire land. Though severe restrictions remained in some regions (notably in Bavaria with its notorious *Matrikelgesetz*) Jews in many parts of Germany, particularly in Prussia, may be said to have acquired what amounted to at any rate economic citizenship. This in turn would enable them to take advantage of the 'new economic order'.

Furthermore, the introduction of that order coincided (the causal relationship may be ambiguous) with what has become known as the 'age of early industrialization'. Partly perhaps as a result of Napoleon's 'Continental System' with its exclusion of British goods and colonial produce from Germany, partly in consequence of the need for manufacturers of different kinds created by decades of war, new industrial enterprises began to emerge in what would presently (more particularly with the beginnings of the 'railway age') become a self-generating process. Gradual urbanization, improvement in transporta-

---

[51] Ib., p. 16.

tion, and reductions (or outright abolition) of customs barriers would help to create growing markets. Even the relative economic stagnation reflecting a negative phase of the long secular waves (Kondratiev Cycle) which set in around 1819 could only slow down but not arrest the process. Early industrialization in fact created opportunities for successful entrepreneurship, both generally and, for reasons already made clear, for Jewish entrepreneurship in particular.

In taking advantage of the opportunities created by the coincidence of the three 'environmental factors' (the new economic system, economic emancipation, and early industrialization), moreover, Jews were assisted by two further features deriving largely from their own distinctive minority situation. In the first place, German Jews formed part of a scattered diaspora covering the whole of Europe as well as the North American continent. This meant, for many among them, considerable international contacts—including commercial ones, and particularly in more advanced countries—greatly in excess of those normally available to Gentile competitors. Such contacts, moreover, were considerably extended and reinforced in numbers, intensity, geographical and social distribution by wholesale emigration of Jews from Germany in the first half of the nineteenth century, mainly to English-speaking countries. Such contacts (and they existed also with centres like Paris, Vienna, and Amsterdam) constituted a major peculiarity—as well as a decisive commercial asset—of, among others, members of the German–Jewish economic élite.

Such international contacts, moreover, both reflected and reinforced a further characteristic of economically active Jews, a high degree of geographical mobility. Originally, perhaps, this may, on a local level, have been connected mainly with residence restrictions, expulsions, general insecurity, as well as the exigencies of particular forms of Jewish economic activity. However, Jewish dispersion, ethnic solidarity, social cohesion, and commercial institutions also had consistently favoured mobility over a wider area and, with it, the geographical extension of kinship ties. In turn, this had contributed to the internationalization of Jewish economic relations and, with it, to international mobility. As movements of capital, of goods, and of 'technology' came, more and more, to transcend local and national boundaries, the 'internationalism' of the Jewish community and, with it, the attendant geographical mobility, became an important economic asset. Jews more than Gentiles came to know—and, indeed to desire to know—what was going on elsewhere, an asset of no small value in economic transactions. Mobility, contacts across frontiers, and up-to-date economic intelligence thus helped to place members of the Jewish economic élite in particular in an advantageous competitive position.

Given all these circumstances, it causes no surprise that Jews came to participate vigorously in German economic development in the nineteenth century and that there emerged in Germany a relatively sizeable Jewish economic élite.

2

Beginnings

I

THE German–Jewish economic élite of the age of early industrialization (*c.*1800–*c.*1850)—it may have numbered some forty to fifty families—was, in at least one of its components, the descendant and heir of the court Jews (*Hoffaktoren* and *Hofagenten*) of the age of absolutism.[1] Not only were the Rothschilds, who in wealth and prestige for at least two generations overshadowed every other German–Jewish family, descended from a financial agent of the elector of Hesse-Kassel, the richest prince in Germany,[2] but a number of prominent banking families of the first half of the nineteenth century, among them the Seligmanns and Hirsches of Munich, the Kaullas in Stuttgart, Habers in Karlsruhe, Kaskels in Dresden, Oppenheims in Cologne, were equally the descendants of *Hoffaktoren*.[3]

The evolution of these and similar families shows certain common characteristics, which Heinrich Schnee has tried to combine into an 'ideal type'. The typical evolution of such families Schnee describes as being

> emergence from modest beginnings into the top stratum of Israelites in the service of German princes through salt—and tobacco monopolies, army contracts, industrial enterprises, founding of banks, the granting of loans to princes and governments on moderate terms. Ennoblement, the marriage of descendants into the old landed and imperial nobilities, notably the families of

---

[1] For the court Jews see, among others, Heinrich Schnee, *Die Hochfinanz und der moderne Staat. Geschichte und System der Hoffaktoren an deutschen Fürstenhöfen im Zeitalter des Absolutismus*, 6 vols. (Berlin, 1953–67), Selma Stern, *The Court Jew. A Contribution to the History of the Period of Absolutism in Central Europe* (Philadelphia, 1950), and Jacob Toury, 'Der Eintritt der Juden ins deutsche Bürgertum' in Hans Liebeschütz and Arnold Paucker (eds.), *Das Judentum in der deutschen Umwelt 1800–1850* (Tübingen, 1977), especially pp. 153 ff.

[2] Kurt Zielenziger, *Juden in der deutschen Wirtschaft* (Berlin, 1930), p. 34.

[3] Details on the genealogical links of several of these families are to be found in F. W. Euler, 'Bankherren und Grossbankleiter' in H. H. Hofman (ed.), *Bankherren und Bankiers* (Limburg and Lahn, 1978), pp. 85 ff.

counts ... finally separation from the family banking firm, acquisition of estates and castles, move into the countryside, absorption into the aristocracy, service to the monarchies as officials.[4]

However, while Schnee undoubtedly describes a typical evolution, there are in fact numerous exceptions and it is precisely these which are of economic significance. Thus the Rothschilds (Frankfurt branch) and Goldschmidt-Rothschilds after them continued their banking activities, if with diminishing vigour (particularly after the Prussian annexation of the free city in 1866). The Oppenheims, throughout the period, operated their banking business in Cologne. Schnee considers it the largest private bank in the Federal Republic of Germany today.[5] Other descendants of court Jews were prominently involved in the founding of joint-stock banks in which they retained a substantial interest. While the Oppenheims joined with others in founding the Bank für Handel und Industrie (Darmstädter Bank) (1853), the Kaskels (related by marriage to the Oppenheims) did the same in regard to the Dresdner Bank (1872). Seligmanns (Eichthal) and Hirsches joined with the Frankfurt Rothschilds in founding the Bayerische Hypotheken- und Wechselbank, again, according to Schnee, still the largest financial institute of its kind in the Federal Republic. Both Seligmanns (Eichthal) and Hirsches joined with other, mainly Jewish bankers in founding the Bayerische Vereinsbank,[6] while the Kaullas in Stuttgart were instrumental in creating the Württembergische Hofbank and descendants of other Hoffaktoren, the Pfeiffers, joined with still other Jewish bankers to start the Württembergische Vereinsbank. In short, descendants of court Jews played a prominent part in the creation of a number of joint-stock banks, begun and often continued in the original Residenzstädte.

[4] 'Aufstieg aus bescheidenen Anfängen in die israelitische Oberschicht im Dienste deutscher Fürsten durch Salz- und Tabakmonopole, Heereslieferungen, Industrie-Unternehmungen, Bankgründungen, Gewährung von Anleihen an Fürsten und Regierungen zu massvollen Bedingungen. Aufstieg in den Adel, Einheirat der Nachkommen in den alten Land- und Reichsadel, hier in die gräflichen Familien ... schliesslich Trennung vom ererbten Bankgeschäft, Ankauf von Gütern und Schlössern, Übersiedlung auf das Land, Aufgehen in der Aristokratie, Wirken als Beamten in den Monarchien.' (Schnee, op. cit., iv (Berlin, 1963), p. 237.)

[5] 'Das grösste deutsche Privatbankhaus Oppenheims in Köln mit führender Position in der deutschen Industrie ist zugleich das einzige in Deutschland bestehende Finanzinstitut, das nach dem Erlöschen des Hauses Rothschild in Frankfurt und Wien seinen Ursprung im Hoffaktoren des fürstlichen Absolutismus hat und Bedeutung und Rank in Wirtschaft und Gesellschaft behaupten konnte' (ib., p. 272).

[6] Details in ib., pp. 235 f. and Euler, loc. cit., p. 132.

Moreover, in the shadow of the Rothschilds and, not infrequently, as their clients, there emerged a network of lesser Jewish banking dynasties. These found their opportunities in towns like Frankfurt-on-Main, Hamburg, Mannheim, or Breslau which had no ruling princes (and hence no *Hoffaktoren* or court bankers), or Berlin, where the relatively effective bureaucracy of the Prussian monarchs had partly obviated the need for court Jews, while the military articulation of the monarchy had retarded the emergence of a commercial and financial patriciate. In centres such as these, starting at the end of the eighteenth century, had arisen some major Jewish banking dynasties, the core of Toury's 'Adelsbürger': the Speyers, Ellissens, Goldschmidts, Hahns, Erlangers, Sulzbachs, Sterns in Frankfurt, the Heines, Warburgs, Behrenses in Hamburg, the Mendelssohns and Mendelssohn-Bartholdys, Bleichröder-Schwabachs, Magnuses, Warschauers, Plauts in Berlin, the Ladenburgs in Mannheim, and the Heimanns in Breslau, to name only some of the more important. These, as distinct from the earlier court Jews, lent to governments rather than princes. They were the bankers of the age of railway construction. Some were involved in the formation of joint-stock banks like the Berliner Handels-Gesellschaft, while a few ventured, gingerly, into the field of early industrial investment. At the same time, with the development of communications, their operations became increasingly international in scope. Several, following in the footsteps of the Rothschilds, established their members in foreign financial centres, earlier in the century in Paris, later in London and New York. It is members of these banking dynasties who form a major component of the German–Jewish economic élite down to the foundation of the German empire in 1871 and, to some extent, beyond.

Between the original *Hoffaktoren* and their descendants and the newer banking dynasties of the 'railway age', there are elements of both continuity and discontinuity. One element of continuity is formed by the transitional Rothschilds, descended indeed from the late court Jews but engaging in the financial transactions of the 'railway age'. Again, several of the newer banking dynasties owed their rise from the ranks of the everyday Jewish money-changers and traders to Rothschild patronage, among them the Mendelssohns, Warburgs, Heines, Bleichröders, Behrenses and Ladenburgs. Rothschilds would either allow them a modest share in their business transactions or use them as agents in places where they themselves were unrepresented. They would also offer a safety net, credit in times of financial stringency.

Beginnings

What it meant, on the other hand, to fall foul of the house of Rothschild, was experienced by the Haber and Kusel banks in Karlsruhe which fell victim to the economic crisis of 1847–8 for lack of Rothschild support.

Major financial transactions, government loans, and railway flotations created links between the older Rothschilds and Oppenheims and the Mendelssohns, Magnuses, Warschauers, Plauts, and Bleichröders. A vast demand for money from governments and railway consortia brought together in the same transactions the descendants of court Jews and the newer private bankers. It was the older-style houses which were adapting themselves to the conditions of the railway age and taking advantage of the opportunities it afforded.

No less important than the elements of continuity, however, were the discontinuities. In the first place the two groups were—and perhaps more surprisingly remained—socially distinct. The descendants of court Jews, who usually converted to Christianity, either married among themselves[7] or saw at least their daughters marry into the non-Jewish nobility. The newer banking families more often retained their Judaism and intermarried with families of their own kind. Here also, members of converted families would often marry among themselves.[8] Intermarriage between members of the two groups was rare,[9] as was *connubium* between the later banking dynasties and the German nobility.

Moreover, with the exception of the Oppenheims in Cologne, the descendants of court Jews had, by the middle of the century, effectively disappeared from German economic life.[10] The sixties and seventies were the classic age of the Jewish private bankers from the newer 'bourgeois' dynasties.

---

[7] Among typical instances were the marriage in 1858 between Felix, *Freiherr* von Kaskel, of Dresden and Emma, daughter of Simon Oppenheim of Cologne, and the marriage ties between the von Hirsches of Gereuth and the Kaullas (Euler, loc. cit., p. 133).

[8] An instance of multiple marriage alliances among members of converted families here is that of the Warschauer, Oppenheim, and (von) Simson families, originally from Königsberg, and the Mendelssohns in Berlin.

[9] Among the few exceptions, in 1901 Lucie Lea Kaulla married Georges S. Warburg, son of the Hamburg banker Sigmund Warburg.

[10] While some, like the Habers and Kusels, had to put their banks into liquidation, others, like the Seligmann-Eichthals, the later Hirsches, and the later Rothschilds, effectively abandoned the family firms to become *rentiers*. Among the exceptions were the celebrated Baron Moritz von Hirsch, a railway entrepreneur in the Balkans, and Alfred von Kaulla, chairman of the board (1888–1900) of the Württembergische Vereinsbank, who, in close association with the Deutsche Bank, took a prominent part in railway construction in the Ottoman empire.

II

In the meantime, a new and distinctive group had joined the ranks of the German–Jewish economic élite, the entrepreneurs of the age of early industrialization. Due to the still limited scope of their operations, such entrepreneurs tended to form regional clusters, of which the most significant developed in and around Berlin between the Napoleonic wars and the wars of German unification. Typically, this entrepreneurial élite survived for only two generations, with the 'sons' tending to drop out of economic life by the second half of the sixties. While information on the modest early Jewish entrepreneurial activity in the rest of Germany is scarce and somewhat fragmentary,[11] that in Prussia and particularly in and around Berlin is relatively well documented.[12]

A glance at the more prominent Jewish entrepreneurial families of the period[13] reveals a number of peculiarities. First among these is their uneven distribution among different branches of industrial activity, their prominence in textile manufactures[14] and their almost complete absence from the metallurgical and machine-building industries. Again, Jewish entrepreneurs of the period usually started from a trading background, while their non-Jewish contemporaries more often did so from an artisan or peasant one.[15] The typical development of Jewish and of Gentile enterprises and entrepreneurial families is, accordingly, distinct.

Typically, the Jewish industrial enterprise originates either from the decision of a Jewish trader in a small provincial centre to branch out

[11] For some data see Toury, loc. cit., n. 1 above, pp. 203 ff.

[12] See H. Rachel and Paul Wallich, *Berliner Grosskaufleute und Kapitalisten*, iii (Berlin, 1967) and the papers on the nomination of *Kommerzienräte* in the Zentrales Staatsarchiv in Merseburg.

[13] Identified essentially through the conferment of the titles of *Kommerzienrat* and *Geheimer Kommerzienrat*.

[14] Thus in 1809, of the Jewish entrepreneurs in Berlin, 60 per cent were engaged in one branch or another of the textile industry. Toury, loc. cit., n. 1 above, p. 202.

[15] This view, forcefully but tendentiously propounded by Rachel and Wallich in their classic study of Berlin entrepreneurship in the age of early industrialization, especially pp. 188 f. (quoted in n. 53 below), has, however, been called in question. While it is recognized that few Jewish entrepreneurs had an artisan background, which, in any case, would have been difficult before the legislation of 1812 abolishing guilds, it is rightly stressed that numbers of non-Jewish entrepreneurs had a commercial one. Relative proportions are difficult to establish but, in addition to their own information on the Berlin machine-building industry, some evidence on the early Silesian textile industry as well as the cutlery industry of Solingen seems to lend at least some support to Rachel and Wallich's claim.

into manufacturing—often, though not invariably, using the raw materials of his trade—or from the investment decision of an established Jewish capitalist. The latter, as a rule, had multiplied a modest original capital by means of war contracts or loans to official bodies.[16] The enterprise, having been started in Berlin (or in the vicinity, with the entrepreneur himself having usually moved to the capital), is continued in the second generation, typically by two or three sons, more rarely sons-in-law or nephews of the founder. The changeover from first to second generation would occur, not infrequently, during the twenties and thirties. The enterprise would then grow under the management of the second generation in the thirties and forties with at least one member of the family receiving the accolade of being made a *Kommerzienrat*. With the death or retirement of the second generation, the firm, in the later fifties and sixties, would lose its commercial importance, to be liquidated with the onset of the depression in 1873. At the same time in the later sixties, a new and separate group of Jewish entrepreneurs would emerge, to continue into the imperial age.

A brief examination of some major Jewish entrepreneurial families of the 'first wave' will illustrate some of these features. It must begin with what was probably the major field of Jewish (and, probably, not only Jewish) entrepreneurial activity at this time, the textile industry.

The Meyers, for a time Berlin's most prominent silk manufacturers (they had originally established themselves in Brandenburg, where they also retained a manufacture), were in certain respects atypical, more particularly, because they had already been established in Berlin for several generations.[17] An ancestor had settled there as a silk merchant in 1714. His grandson, later in the century, had turned to manufacturing. In 1806, Jacob Abraham Meyer—already of the fourth generation—took over the management of the firm and its steep rise began. When, in 1841, his achievements were recognized by conferment of the title of *Kommerzienrat*, he employed in his two factories between 2,600 and 3,000 workers. Of the firm's capital of 800,000 thalers (almost 2½ million marks) he personally owned

---

[16] It would be instructive to examine in detail the contribution made by the revolutionary and Napoleonic wars, whether directly through war contracts or indirectly through associated financial operations, to Jewish capital formation and to the emergence and 'modernization' of the German–Jewish economic élite alike in banking, commerce, and industry.

[17] For the Meyer family see Stefi Jersch-Wenzel, *Jüdische Bürger und kommunale Selbstverwaltung in preussischen Städten 1808–1848* (Berlin, 1967), pp. 57 f.

300,000. Jacob Abraham was succeeded in the management of the firm by his nephew and senior partner Joel Wolff Meyer who had already in 1841 received the title of *Kommerzienrat* and, most unusually, that of *Geheimer Kommerzienrat* in the following year. Conferment of titles on two members of the same firm was unusual. The Meyers, in fact, enjoyed royal patronage.

Joel Wolff Meyer's younger brother Philip, who had married his cousin, a daughter of Jacob Abraham, had started his own silk manufacture in 1822. When, in 1843, he too received the title of *Kommerzienrat*—at the early age of 42—the police reported that his firm now 'competed with the greatest businesses in the land'.[18] For good measure, in the same year, Philip's partner and younger brother Julius Wolff Meyer also became a *Kommerzienrat*. Incredibly—and uniquely—within a short period of time, no fewer than four members of the same family had thus become *Kommerzienräte*. Moreover, all members of the family had remained faithful to Judaism. It was, however, not until 1856 that Philip Meyer was made a *Geheimer Kommerzienrat*, the delay betokening a decline in the economic importance of the firm. Indeed, from the mid-fifties, the much-titled Meyers fade from view.

Second only to the Meyers among Berlin's Jewish textile manufacturers came the Liebermanns, an old-established trading family (in calico goods) originating from Märkisch-Friedland and Sprottau.[19] Like the Meyers, the Liebermanns had turned to mechanical manufacture, this time calico printing, an industry which, after 1840, was experiencing boom conditions. Joseph Liebermann, celebrated for having introduced himself to Frederick-William IV as 'the Liebermann who had driven the English from the continent' (in calico printing) was made a *Kommerzienrat* in 1843 at the age of 60. His sons, who inherited the business, not only completed the transition from trading to manufacture but extended their activities also to machine building. Two of Joseph's sons in their turn became *Kommerzienräte*, Philip in 1860, Benjamin, the ablest, only in 1868 (after several refusals on account of his liberal political views). He was, however, granted the higher title four years later. One of his sisters married Moritz Rathenau, who, as a young man, had come to Berlin from the

[18] *Polizei Präsident* to *Ober-Präsident* of the Province of Brandenburg, 25 Oct. 1843, Z(entrales) S(taats)-A(rchiv) Merseburg, Rep. 120 A IV 5, vol. 3, fo. 17.
[19] For the Liebermanns see Rachel and Wallich, op. cit., n. 12 above, pp. 178 f. Information on the Liebermann family is, in general, inadequate.

Uckermark. Their son Emil would serve his engineering apprenticeship in his grandfather Joseph Liebermann's machine factory at the Wilhelmshütte near Sprottau.[20] Another of Joseph's grandsons was the painter Max Liebermann. However, though remaining socially distinguished, the Liebermanns, characteristically, had lost their economic importance by 1870.

Another prominent Jewish textile dynasty were the Reichenheims.[21] Leonor Reichenheim, born in Bernburg (Anhalt), after serving an apprenticeship in the family shop in Magdeburg, started jointly with his father a haberdasher's shop (*Manufakturwarenhandlung*) in Berlin.[22] In 1848, together with three of his brothers, he acquired from the Prussian state a textile mill (*Halbwollweberei*) at Wüstegiersdorf (Kreis Waldenburg) in central Silesia. Under the management, the mill expanded to become the core of the largest Jewish textile manufacture with a total of 2,400 employees. In 1856, Reichenheim's achievement was recognized when he was made a *Kommerzienrat*. In 1858, Leonor Reichenheim, unusually, branched out into politics, being elected a member of the Prussian *Landtag*. Louis Reichenheim, his son, who took over the management of the firm, in his turn became a *Kommerzienrat* in 1869, a *Geheimer Kommerzienrat* in 1874. In the 1890s, the Reichenheims sold out to another Jewish textile dynasty, the Kauffmanns of Breslau. In 1908, the fortune of Louis Reichenheim's only surviving brother, a doctor, was put at 12.12 million marks, that of his widow at 6.02 million. Though the Reichenheims ceased to be economically important, they continued to be socially prominent among Berlin Jews. They intermarried with a number of leading

---

[20] Cf. Zielenziger, op. cit., n. 2 above, p. 130.

[21] For the Reichenheims see Rudolf Martin, *Jahrbuch des Vermögens und Einkommens der Millionäre in Preussen* (Berlin, 1912), p. 306 and Ernest Hamburger, *Juden im öffentlichen Leben Deutschlands* (Tübingen, 1968), pp. 220 ff.

[22] For a different account see Jacob Toury, *Soziale und politische Geschichte der Juden in Deutschland 1847–1871* (Düsseldorf, 1977), pp. 98 f. 'Ähnlich hielten die Reichenheims ihrer Textilfirma generationenlang die Treue, nachdem sich die sechs Söhne eines Anhalter Kleinkinderlehrers und Schächters der Berliner Szene angepasst und das Unternehmen in Wüstegiersdorf organisiert hatten.' Toury's account is based on Ludwig Herz, *N. Reichenheim* (Berlin, 1936), mimeogr. in the Archives of the Leo Baeck Institute in New York. It is impossible to decide between his circumstantial account and the almost equally detailed one of Ernest Hamburger based on contributions to the *Allgemeine Zeitung des Judentums* in 1867 and 1868 (Hamburger, op. cit., p. 221 n.). Hamburger was familiar with the account of Ludwig Herz (ib.). If Herz is correct, the Reichenheim dynasty originated from another source of Jewish entrepreneurship, that of communal employees (teachers, cantors, occasionally rabbis) in small provincial communities.

Jewish entrepreneurs, bankers, and merchants, the Huldschinskys, Simons, von Klemperers, and (originally Gentile) von Leydens, through whom they were related also to the Oppenheims (of the still important banking house of Robert Warschauer and Co.).

Two other textile dynasties ranked in esteem only a little behind the Liebermanns and Reichenheims. The Weigerts, untypically, came from an artisan background.[23] Abraham Weigert, born in 1786 in Rosenberg (Upper Silesia), had, around 1800, been among the first Jews to become a weaver. Later, he had abandoned the declining trade of handloom weaving to try his hand in turn at potash manufacture, working as a publican (*Schankpächter*), vinegar manufacturing, distilling, and brewing.

Abraham Weigert's son Salomon had again been trained as a weaver. In 1839 he moved to Berlin where, with a partner, he started the mechanical weaving establishment of Marx and Weigert. His brother Hermann, following an apprenticeship as a weaver in the firm, replaced Marx as a partner. Hermann Weigert eventually took over the management of the Berlin mill. His brother Salomon, now a recognized expert in weaving technology, at the request of the Prussian government set up a mill at Schmiedeberg (Silesia) to provide employment for starving handloom weavers. He was made a *Kommerzienrat* in 1856. Hermann Weigert left the firm in 1869 to become a wealthy *rentier*. He now devoted himself to real-estate speculation, in which his success proved imperfect. The family business, in the seventies, went into a decline. A descendant, Max Weigert, was credited in 1908 with a fortune of 5.26 million marks.

The Kauffmanns, who in 1888 took over the spinning mills of the Reichenheims, began their commercial ascent when, in 1824, Meyer Kauffmann, born in Frankfurt-on-Oder, opened a drapery store (*Weisswarengeschäft*) in Schweidnitz in Silesia. Soon he began to operate a 'putting-out' system (linen and cotton materials) for cottage weavers in neighbouring villages. A few years later, he started a manufacture of his own. In 1839, the oldest son Salomon Kauffmann (1824–1900) entered the firm, followed in due course by three of his brothers. The business grew with substantial orders from Berlin, Stettin, Danzig, Königsberg, and Frankfurt-on-Main (met through

---

[23] For the Weigerts see Monika Richarz (ed.), *Jüdisches Leben in Deutschland: Selbstzeugnisse zur Sozialgeschichte 1780–1871* (Stuttgart, 1976), vol. i, pp. 317 ff. and Martin, op. cit., pp. 518 f.

manufacturing, the 'putting-out' system, and prison labour). In 1841, a branch office was opened in Breslau.

In 1851, the firm exhibited its products at the World Exhibition in London. During his stay in England, Salomon Kauffmann recognized the superiority of mechanical weaving over the handloom weaving still generally practised in Germany. The firm bought 200 English mechanical looms and, in 1852, opened its first mechanized mill at Tannhausen near Waldenburg. Subsequently, the Kaufmanns added four spinning mills (1859, 1863, 1875), the last, that of the Reichenheims, in 1888. Under the management of Salomon Kauffmann, the firm expanded. It received profitable military orders. The demand for cotton goods in the new German empire was such that even the dreaded annexation of Alsace with its developed textile industry produced no ill effects. The firm and its products became known far beyond the confines of Germany. For over forty years, Salomon Kauffmann was a member, eventually deputy chairman, of the Breslau chamber of commerce.

In 1905 Hans Schäfer, grandson of Meyer Kauffmann, a trained dyestuff chemist and textile engineer, entered the family business, now the Meyer Kauffmann Textilwerke AG. By this time the firm, run by several members of the family, had become a large enterprise, specializing in the production of coloured cotton prints for export to overseas markets. During the war, it received large military orders. Hans Schäfer, appointed managing director (*Generaldirektor*) in 1918, continued in that position until 1939. The Kauffmanns are an interesting example of adaptation to changing conditions from the original shop in Schweidnitz, through the 'putting-out' system, to mechanical manufacture and the formation of a group of textile mills producing largely for the export market. The firm remained a successful family business over three generations.

Perhaps even more successful than that of the Kauffmanns was the enterprise started by Samuel Fränkel (1801–81),[24] who in 1827 (three years after Meyer Kauffmann had opened his shop in Schweidnitz) had moved from the old, largely Jewish settlement of Zülz to neighbouring Neustadt (OS). He also began with a shop (*Schnittwarengeschäft*), then turned to the 'putting-out' system, to handloom—and, finally, to mixed handloom—and mechanical weaving principally of

[24] For Samuel Fränkel see Kurt Schwerin, 'Die Juden in Schlesien', *Bulletin des Leo Baeck Instituts*, 19, nos. 56–7 (Tel Aviv, 1980) pp. 43 f., and Wenzel, op. cit., n. 17 above, pp. 111 f. and 114.

damask and linen goods. Interestingly, Fränkel started his modest damask-weaving mill in 1847 in association with a non-Jewish weaving expert, Thill, who was responsible for important technical improvements. The business prospered and, in 1863, Samuel Fränkel's achievement was recognized by conferment of the title of *Kommissionsrat*.[25] Four sons, as well as a son-in-law, Joseph Pinkus, joined the firm. When the title of *Geh. Kommerzienrat* was conferred on Fränkel on the occasion of his wedding anniversary in 1872, the firm had come to employ 3,043 weavers (handloom and mechanical), 203 men in bleaching and finishing, 23 other tradesmen, and a clerical staff of 33. Its products—now mainly linen goods—were sought after not only in every major centre in Europe but also in New York and Tokyo, Cape Town and Melbourne.[26]

Josef Pinkus, Samuel Fränkel's son-in-law and effective successor, became a *Kommerzienrat* in 1881, *Geh. Kommerzienrat* in 1895, Fränkel's son Albert a *Kommerzienrat* in 1897. By this time the numbers employed by the firm had risen to over 5,000. Josef Pinkus played a prominent role in the textile industry for many years as deputy chairman of the central association of linen manufacturers (Zentralverein deutscher Leinenindustrieller) and executive member of the association of Silesian textile industrialists (Verband schlesischer Textilindustrieller) as well as being a member of the chamber of commerce in Oppeln. His son Max Pinkus (1857–1934) in due course also became a *Kommerzienrat* and chairman of the Oppeln chamber of commerce. By this time, however, the fortunes of the firm had passed their peak. By 1913, the number of its employees had fallen to 4,000 (working some 1,400 mechanical and 400 handlooms). The war provided orders neither for linen nor damask but, instead, meant a loss of export markets. The years following its conclusion saw a further decline in turnover. In 1934, the firm was converted into a joint-stock company. Three years later, Hans H. Pinkus, its last Jewish director, was forced to relinquish his position.

The Fränkel-Pinkuses, thus, were an entrepreneurial dynasty extending in all over four generations. Their enterprise appears to have reached its peak in the last quarter of the nineteenth century, its success based in no small degree on world-wide exports. It remained a pure family firm for an unusually long time. Unlike the Kauffmanns,

[25] It is not clear why Fränkel did not become a *Kommerzienrat*.
[26] Details of the firm's extensive commercial activities can be found in v. Hagemeister to *Graf* v. Itzenplitz, 18 Apr. 1872, in ZSAM Rep. 120 A IV 9 vol. 6 fos. 30 ff.

the Fränkels and Pinkuses had a strong Jewish commitment. The firm, since the days of Samuel Fränkel, who had sent his travellers to visit not only the whole of Germany but also Austria, Russia, Denmark, Switzerland, and Holland, while maintaining agents in Berlin, Hamburg, Paris, Constantinople, Riga, Naples, and Genoa, had developed a far-flung international sales organization. The authorities listed excellent connections ('die vorzüglichsten Verbindungen') with North America, France, Russia, Austria, Turkey, Italy, Switzerland, Holland, Belgium, Denmark, Sweden, and Norway, business with Latin America being conducted through a Hamburg exporting house. Curiously, the mechanization of production appears to have been late and incomplete.

A further Jewish entrepreneurial family in the textile industry but with an unusual development were the Goldschmidts.[27] Ruben Bendix Goldschmidt, a privileged Jewish merchant (*Generalprivilegierter*) in Berlin, had, with his brothers, conducted a calico trade and manufacture. Four of his sons, after their baptism Alexander, Eduard, Ferdinand, and Karl, had joined the ranks of Berlin's leading textile manufacturers. A daughter, Karoline Goldschmidt, married her cousin, the merchant Abraham Bendix Goldschmidt. In due course, the brothers Goldschmidt sold their calico manufacture and printing works to the more dynamic Liebermanns. So far, the story of the Goldschmidt resembles that of other Jewish entrepreneurial families in the Berlin textile industry like the Nauens, Loewes, or Reichenheims.

Albert Goldschmidt's son Karl Theodor Wilhelm Goldschmidt (1815–75), nephew of the four brothers,[28] entered the family firm,[29] where he gained an acquaintance with the practical aspects of textile chemistry (calico printing). After theoretical studies in chemistry (and baptism in 1834), Dr Theodor Goldschmidt served a practical apprenticeship in Prague, England, and France. In 1847–8 he founded, in the vicinity of the calico printing works, the Chemische Fabrik Th. Goldschmidt for the production of chemicals employed in dyeing and calico printing. It was an unusual transition from textile to

---

[27] For the Goldschmidts see *Th. Goldschmidt 1847–1937* (Essen, 1937) and W. Treue, 'Unternehmer und Finanziers, Chemiker und Ingenieure in der chemischen Industrie im 19. Jahrhundert' (off-print without details of publication), pp. 238 ff.

[28] On the data he provides he cannot, as Treue states, have been a cousin.

[29] Treue's account does not make clear whether this was the large manufacture of his cousins or a lesser one owned by an uncle on his father's side.

chemical manufacture. A significant element in the adaptation was Theodor Goldschmidt's academic training.

From modest beginnings, the firm developed, particularly under Theodor Goldschmidt's son Dr Karl Goldschmidt (1857–1926), who, according to Daniel Bernstein, took over the management in 1886,[30] and who later became a *Kommerzienrat*, and his brother Dr Hans Goldschmidt, like him a trained chemist. The firm, which had early transferred its major activities from textile to metallurgical chemistry (particularly de-tinning), moved to Essen in 1889,[31] after which it experienced a spectacular rise, based on valuable processes and patents. In 1911, the family business (*offene Handelsgesellschaft*) was converted into a joint-stock company with a capital of 15 million marks, a majority still held by members of the family. The management consisted of Dr Karl Goldschmidt, his brother Dr Hans Goldschmidt, and his son Dr Theodor Goldschmidt (1883–1965), who succeeded him as managing director. The firm never fully recovered from the effects of the Great War. While from 1911 to 1918 inclusive it had paid an annual dividend of 12 per cent on its capital, the dividend thereafter dropped to 5 per cent p.a.—being passed altogether in 1924 and again in 1931–4.

Apart from the transition from calico manufacture to chemicals, what is significant about the Goldschmidts (as about the Kunheims[32]) is, on the one hand, the early scientific training characteristic of much chemical entrepreneurship, on the other, so far as the Jewish aspect is concerned, the early baptism of the family. From the days of the Goldschmidt and Kunheim to those of Heinrich Caro, Franz Oppenheim, and Fritz Haber, the chemical industry was, quintessentially, for reasons on which one can only speculate, the industry of the baptized (late to include luminaries like the brothers Carl and Arthur von Weinberg and Fritz von Friedländer-Fuld). The fact that the Goldschmidt, like the Kunheim, owned and managed their businesses for three generations in the direct male line is probably fortuitous. The Goldschmidts are notable also as being among the small number of Jewish (or any other) entrepreneurs (Bethel Henry Strousberg, Albert Hahn, Ludwig Loewe, Benno Orenstein, Arthur Koppel, and the

---

[30] Daniel Bernstein, 'Wirtschaft: II. Handel und Industrie' in Siegmund Kaznelson (ed.), *Juden im deutschen Kulturbereich* (Berlin, 1962), p. 767. According to Treue, he entered the firm in 1888 (Treue, loc. cit., p. 239).

[31] According to Bernstein in 1890.

[32] The Kunheims in their turn had come into the chemical industry through the manufacture of alum, a chemical employed in textile printing.

Beginnings

Rathenaus among them), who moved their industrial interests—usually only in part—from Berlin to the western provinces of the Prussian monarchy; only Ludwig Loewe operated significantly to the south of the Main (Karlsruhe and Oberndorf/Neckar) as well as marginally the AEG at Rheinfelden.

If one considers the more important among the Jewish textile dynasties in Prussia in the age of early industrialization,[33] some significant features emerge. One aspect typical of a majority is the transition from trade to manufacture, whether in silken goods as with the Meyers, calico as with the Liebermanns, or retail trading as with the Reichenheims, Kauffmanns, or Fränkels. The exception is the Weigerts with a background of artisanship: two generations of weavers and an expert in weaving technology. Some turned directly from trade to manufacturing, in two cases (Reichenheim and Weigert) with active assistance from the Prussian state. The 'putting-out' system as an intermediate stage is mentioned more particularly for the Kauffmanns and the Fränkels.

Leading non-Jewish textile dynasties[34] in Silesia appear to differ somewhat in social origins from Jewish ones. Unlike the Jewish entrepreneurs, who often began as retail traders, the Gentiles either came from old-established merchant families in the wholesale trade, comparable to the 'silk-Meyers' in Berlin (like the Kramsta and Websky) or were the sons of peasants (Johann David Gruschwitz), handloom weavers (Christian Gottlob Dierig), or calico printers (Karl August Milde). Unlike their Jewish counterparts, Gentile newcomers either started as artisans or were artisans' sons (Dierig, Milde, Gruschwitz); among Jewish entrepreneurs, only the atypical Weigerts conform to this pattern. The intermediate stage of the 'putting-out' system is mentioned twice (Dierig and Milde). On the other hand, not one of the Gentile dynasties originated in retail trade. Thus, while the distinction is not absolute, there is clearly a difference in both the social origins and the early economic activity (they meet in the 'putting-out' system in a number of cases) of the Jewish and non-Jewish textile dynasties in Silesia. Whilst the 'silk-Meyers' enjoyed royal patronage, the Kauffmanns benefited from large military orders. The diversification of the Liebermanns into iron working and machine

---

[33] For a survey of Jewish entrepreneurial activity in the textile industry outside Prussia see Richarz, op. cit., n. 23 above, p. 37 and for more detailed accounts of some individual enterprises ib., pp. 268 ff.

[34] Details in Schwerin, loc. cit., n. 24 above, pp. 40 f.

building was unique. Perhaps characteristic aspects of Jewish entrepreneurial activity were the 'technology transfer' of Joseph Liebermann 'driving the English from the Continent' (in calico printing), Meyer Kauffmann's importation from England of 200 mechanical looms, his firm's later production of printed cotton goods primarily for overseas markets, and the Fränkel-Pinkuses' unusually developed international sales organization. Monika Richarz, on the basis of a wider sample, sums up factors promoting Jewish success in textile entrepreneurship:

> Zusammenfassend kann gesagt werden, dass verschiedene Faktoren gemeinsam den Erfolg der Juden in der Textilfabrikation bewirkten: die Entstehung der Textilfabriken aus jüdischen Handelsunternehmen, deren Kapital zu einem frühen Zeitpunkt in Produktionskapital umgewandelt wurde, ferner die frühzeitige Mechanisierung und der Erwerb von technischen Kenntnissen die Förderung durch die Regierungen und die häufige Übernahme der Vertriebsorganisation durch Familienmitglieder, wobei kaufmännische Erfahrungen und alte Handelsverbindungen genutzt werden konnten.[35]

This careful analysis suggests an innovative role together with certain features derived from the specific Jewish situation.

The Jewish dynasties described here characteristically originate, with the exception of the Meyers (silk production had played a major role already in the economic activities fostered by eighteenth-century rulers, including the kings of Prussia), in small provincial towns (Bernburg, Märkisch Friedland, Sprottau, Rosenberg, Schweidnitz, Zülz), mostly in Silesia, where the bulk of the manufactures were also located. Of the major firms started by Jewish textile entrepreneurs in Prussia during the period of early industrialization only two, those of the Kauffmanns and Fränkel-Pinkuses, survived the age of early industrialization. The rest declined and several owners retired to become wealthy *rentiers*. Interestingly, all the families remained, at any rate preponderantly, Jewish (there was, eventually, a Christian branch of the Meyers who were, in any case, atypical). The same is true of the following generation of prominent Jewish textile manufacturers in Prussia (now mainly in the linen industry), the Grünfelds, Dahlheims (belated cotton manufacturers), Hahns, Huldschinskys (shoddy), with the Rinkels a notable exception. It is interesting to speculate whether it was the textile industry or the Silesian connection (or yet other causes) which accounts for the persisting Jewish attachment. It may, indeed, be due to a combination of both factors: most Jewish families prominent

---

[35] Ib., p. 37.

not only in the textile but also in the textile-related 'making-up' industry as well as in wholesale trading in textiles remained Jewish as did—though with notable exceptions—members of the Jewish economic élite with their roots in Silesia.

Besides textiles, a favoured field of early Jewish entrepreneurial activity was brewing and distilling. This was an activity which could develop from trade in agricultural, less commonly colonial produce. A chemical component (especially the production of alum and, later, of synthetic dyestuffs) was often an offshoot of Jewish involvement in the textile industry.

Prominent among early entrepreneurs in this field were the brothers Berend,[36] Samuel Bacher and Levin (later Louis), sons of Bacher Beer from Tirschtiegel, until 1812 residents of Potsdam. Like numbers of other entrepreneurs, they had been successful war contractors, being engaged between 1806 and 1815 in supplying military hospitals beyond the Vistula. Already for the forced loans of 1812 and 1813 the Berends had been among the most highly assessed Berlin inhabitants. Following the war, the firm of Gebr. Berend, besides further loans to the Prussian government, was prominently involved in the emission of Saxon government bonds.

It was thus from the direction of finance that the brothers Berend entered industrial entrepreneurship when, in 1818, they set up a sugar-refinery in Berlin. In 1825–6, Samuel Berend, in association with another Jewish former war contractor, S. Heinrich Kunheim, began the manufacture of wood-vinegar (*Holzessig*). When Samuel Bacher died in 1828, the sugar-refinery was being run by his three sons and his brother Louis who, in 1830, became one of the early Jewish *Kommerzienräte*. In 1829, the Berends had sold their share in the chemical factory to their partner S. Heinrich Kunheim, in whose family the business would remain for generations until the days of the Weimar Republic.

After the death of Louis Berend in 1830, the management of the sugar-refinery fell to Bernhard Samuel Berend, his oldest nephew. Bernhard became a Berlin city councillor, a *Kommerzienrat* (1847), and a senior member of the Berlin merchant corporation (*Ältester der Kaufmannschaft*) (1855–61). He had by then abandoned sugar refining, as the production of sugar from imported cane was ceasing to be profitable in the face of competition from home-grown beet. The

[36] For an account of the brothers Berend see Rachel and Wallich, op. cit., n. 12 above, pp. 134 ff.

Berend refinery, therefore, was closed down in 1850. Bernhard Berend then set up (in partnership with three sons and with a brother as sleeping partner) a produce and commission business (*Produkten- und Kommissionsgeschäft*) which, however, languished. When he died in 1864, he left only a relatively modest fortune. The firm, though it lingered on until 1879, rapidly declined. For the Berends, industrial entrepreneurship had always been something of a sideline.

The same could be said of another Jewish entrepreneurial family, the Beers.[37] Like the Berends, the Beers were of provincial origin. Like them, they turned to sugar refining to augment an already substantial fortune derived in part from war contracting. The Beers, like the Berends, rose to prominence in the second generation, although, unlike them, partly through cultural achievements (in the persons of the composer Giacomo Meyerbeer and the poet Michael Beer, with Wilhelm Beer a gifted amateur astronomer). Like the Berends, they lost their economic importance after the second generation.

Jakob Herz Beer, born in Frankfurt-on-Oder in 1759, had moved to Berlin and there, in due course, married a daughter of Liepmann Meyer Wulff, presently the wealthiest man in Berlin, in whose general trading permit (*Generalprivileg*) he was thereupon included. Among others, Jakob Herz Beer secured contracts for supplying Prussian troops in Poland in 1794. Five years later, he acquired a sugar-refinery (*Zuckersiederei*). In 1805 the enterprise was still a modest one (employing twenty-five), the smallest of Berlin's four refineries. When it closed down in 1849, it ranked, in the quantity of production liable to excise duty, among the leading enterprises of its kind. Beer, in fact, was the founder of more than one substantial refinery not only in Prussia but also abroad, particularly in Italy. He is sometimes described as a banker. In fact, he had been drawn into financial operations through the forced loans of the Napoleonic period. In 1815, he had enjoyed the doubtful privilege of having the highest assessment in Berlin. As early as 1803, he had become president of the Berlin stock exchange (*Börsenvorsteher*). From 1823 until his death in 1825, he was a senior member (*Ältester*) of the Berlin merchant corporation.

On Jakob Beer's death, the management of the firm was taken over by his third son Wilhelm. Wilhelm, usually described as a banker, in his turned played a prominent part in the affairs of the Berlin merchant

[37] For the Beer family see ib., pp. 88 ff. and H. Kaelble, *Berliner Unternehmer während der frühen Industrialisierung* (Berlin, 1972), pp. 49 f.

corporation. He was a director of two railway companies, the Potsdam–Magdeburger and the Niederschlesische–Märkische. He was—unusually for a Jew—elevated to membership of the Prussian upper chamber. In 1849, Beer finally abandoned sugar refining as no longer profitable. The following year he died and with him the economic fortunes of the family. Of his two sons, one settled in Paris while the other lost what remained of his wealth in the crash of 1873.

Somewhat different from the entrepreneurial activities of the Berends and the Beers were those of the Herzes.[38] Salomon Herz, a grain merchant from Bernburg (Anhalt), moved to Berlin in 1823, the year in which he also opened an oil-press (*Ölmühle*) in Wittenberge. Vegetable oil (rape and beet) was then used for both fuel and human consumption (as a precursor of margarine, particularly in mining areas), as well as for some industrial purposes. The enterprise began modestly, employing some sixty to seventy labourers by the late thirties. Thirty years later, the numbers employed had risen to some 300. However, by this time, vegetable oils were beginning to fall from favour first as fuel and then also for domestic consumption. Wilhelm Herz, born in 1823, who had succeeded his father in 1865, reacted by opening in Berlin, in 1869, a factory for rubber products which, among others, developed *Faktis*, an important by-product of oil used for softening rubber. In 1869, Wilhelm Herz became a *Kommerzienrat*. He had achieved the difficult transition from first to second-wave entrepreneurship.

Wilhelm Herz also became director of a lignite mine. More important, involvement in the produce trade had brought with it contacts with the brewing industry. Herz was prominent among the founders of the Schultheiss Brauerei AG, being appointed chairman of its board. In 1878 he became *Geheimer Kommerzienrat*. Herz took a leading part in the affairs of the merchant corporation (*Korporation der Kaufmannschaft*) of Berlin, being elected vice-president in 1889 and president in 1895. Following the amalgamation, he became board chairman of the Schultheiss-Patzenhofer Brauerei AG, the largest brewing enterprise in Europe. When in 1902 a chamber of commerce was established in Berlin, Wilhelm Herz became its first president. In 1913, on the occasion of his ninetieth birthday, Herz, recognized as the 'Grand Old Man' of the Berlin merchant estate, was honoured by

---

[38] For Salomon Herz and his son Wilhelm see Zielenziger, op. cit., n. 2 above, pp. 88 ff., H. Kaelble, op. cit., pp. 49 f., Martin, op. cit., n. 21 above, pp. 81 f., and Bernstein, loc. cit., n. 31 above, p. 780.

the emperor with the title of *Wirklicher Geheimer Rat* (which carried the appellation of Excellency), the first merchant in Germany to be so honoured. Wilhelm Herz died in 1914. The oil mill, in which Herz's oldest son and a nephew had been associated, was sold only in 1929. The rubber factory—now producing, besides the softening material, tubes, tyres (including car tyres), and packaging materials—still operated in 1931.

The story of the Herzes is untypical. Though their entrepreneurial activities began in the age of early industrialization they extended, in the form of a family business, until the advent of Hitler. Wilhelm Herz, as already indicated, successfully accomplished the unusual transition from the first to the second wave of Jewish entrepreneurship, and from a modest oil-press in Wittenberge to chairmanship—among others—of the largest brewery concern in Europe, an enterprise of the period of fully fledged capitalism. The Herzes thus moved from the grain trade through the production of vegetable oils to that of rubber-softening materials and, finally, rubber products. Wilhelm Herz also became chairman of the board of the Deutsche Bank. His prestige—acquired more as a skilful diplomat and man of the world than through a forceful and domineering personality—had no exact parallel among either Jew or Gentile. His career, moreover, spanned the best part of two generations.

A further Jewish entrepreneurial family of an untypical kind were the Kunheims.[39] The Kunheims, like the Herzes, spanned the period from early entrepreneurship to the days of the Weimar Republic, operating a family business of some importance through four generations. Samuel Hirsch Kunheim from Ankuhn near Zerbst had acquired some capital as an army contractor and in 1825, as already indicated, had joined the brothers Berend in the manufacture of wood-vinegar acid (*Holzessigsäure*). In 1829, Kunheim bought out his partners.[40] Under his sole management, the firm became a substantial enterprise. In 1847, Samuel Kunheim handed over the reins to his son Louis, who directed the enterprise until 1878. In 1851 Louis, a trained chemist, bought from the Prussian state a disused alum factory near Freienwalde. When it failed to prosper he replaced it, after some years,

---

[39] For the Kunheims see Rachel and Wallich, op. cit., n. 12 above, p. 141, Zielenziger, op. cit., n. 2 above, p. 26, Martin, op. cit., n. 21 above, pp. 81 f. and Bernstein, loc. cit., n. 31 above, p. 780.

[40] Until then, Kunheim had been an employee of the Berend brothers with a generous annual salary of 1,000 thalers and a share of the profits.

with a brickworks. In 1870, he diversified further, by opening a lignite mine in the Niederlausitz.

Louis's son and partner Hugo Kunheim, like his father a trained chemist, was made a *Kommerzienrat* in 1868, a tribute not only to the relative importance of his firm but also to his own activities as adviser to the Prussian government on a variety of commercial and industrial matters. Hugo's son Dr Erich Kunheim, fourth owner in the direct male line and once again a trained chemist, joined the boards of several companies. He also became a *Kommerzienrat*. Married to the sole (adopted) daughter of the Jewish wholesale coal merchant Eduard Arnhold, he was credited in 1908 with a fortune of some 5 million marks. After his death in 1921, the family business was converted into a joint-stock company and, following several amalgamations, became the Kali-Chemie AG, ultimately a part of Rhenania-Ossag.

The story of the Kunheims, who early converted to Christianity, has some distinctive features. In the first place, this was a family business managed in the direct male line by four successive generations extending over the best part of a century (1829–1921). Among early Jewish industrial entrepreneurs of comparable significance only the Hirsches of Halberstadt, who (at the other extreme of the Kunheims) remained, in the main, religious and indeed observant Jews, showed a similar entrepreneurial longevity (combined, in later generations, with engineering training). The Kunheims, moreover, anticipate by at least one generation entrepreneurship based on a scientific training (instead of or in addition to a commercial one), a feature more characteristic of more recent entrepreneurs of the 'second wave'. The Kunheims exemplify the characteristic development from army contracting of the Napoleonic period to science-based manufacture of the age of developed capitalism and, with it, the possibility for specialized family businesses to survive into the age of 'organized capitalism' and large-scale joint-stock enterprise.

What may loosely be called the 'chemical' group of Jewish entrepreneurs of the age of early industrialization originated, like the textile entrepreneurs, mainly from small provincial localities. Their investment capital, in the majority of cases (Berend, Beer, Kunheim), derived in the main from military contracts, that of the Beers also from marriage with an heiress. The major products of their industrial activities—cane sugar, vegetable oil, alum—had lost much of their commercial importance by mid-century. The Berends and Beers, whose entrepreneurial interests had never been more than secondary, then entered into economic decline (following a typical generational pattern). The Herzes and Kunheims, on the other hand, adapted to new conditions by switching their activities in the one case to rubber products and involvement in brewing, in the other to lignite mining including chemical production. These developments, characteristically, took place in 1869 and 1870 respectively as part of the second wave of entrepreneurial activity. There is in the activities of these entrepreneurs little that is innovative. Sugar refining and oil milling were at the time common fields of entrepreneurship,[41] as was the production of alum. Wilhelm Herz's manufacture and use of *Faktis*, the rubber-softening agent derived from oil, may have been innovative, less so the production of rubber goods. Though Herz concerned himself actively with exporting,[42] and though his career in the Berlin merchant corporation, in corporate industry, and as a representative of the merchant estate was unique, he was not an innovator but shone, rather, as an organizer and a diplomat.[43] The distinction of the Kunheims, on the other hand, lay in the production of three generations of trained chemists. With the exception of the Kunheims, who converted to Christianity in 1839 early in the second generation, the early 'chemical' entrepreneurs (unlike the great majority of their successors) retained their Judaism with the Beers and, after them, the Herzes, joining the social and cultural élite of the Berlin Jewish community.

Prominent among early Jewish entrepreneurs in the metal industry were the well-documented Hirsches of Halberstadt.[44] In 1805 Aron Hirsch, the son of a rabbi, began in Halberstadt the sale of products of

[41] When, for example, the coal merchant Karl Haniel was thinking of diversifying his activities, he considered in turn sugar refining, porcelain manufacture, glass making, and steam-powered oil milling. (Hans-Joseph Joest, *Pionier im Ruhrrevier* (Stuttgart, 1982), p. 47.) David Seligmann (1814 Freiherr v. Eichthal), a Jewish banker in Karlsruhe, moved from investment in the production of dyestuffs to that of textiles and also beet-sugar. (Jacob Toury, *Jüdische Textilunternehmer in Baden-Württemberg 1863–1938* (Tübingen, 1984) pp. 20 ff.)

[42] After Wilhelm Herz had taken over the paternal business in 1865, he engaged more particularly in the export of large quanitites of oil to the USA. He was frequently called to England as an oil expert and acquired an international reputation as 'Ölherz'. Zielenziger, op. cit., n. 2 above, p. 95.

[43] 'Weniger Unternehmer grossen Stils, auch kein kühner Erneuerer, ist es sein organisatorisches Geschick, sein diplomatisches Talent, vor allem seine ausgesprochene gesellschaftliche Begabung, die ihn befähigen, Jahrzehntelang der erste Kaufmann der deutschen Metropole zu sein. Dieser Grandseigneur ist ein Exponent der Kaiserlichen Zeit . . .' (ib., p. 91).

[44] For the Hirsches see Siegmund Hirsch, 'Die Kupferhirschs in Halberstadt 1780–1930', typescript MS and the same, *Revolution im Messing* (Lammersdorf, 1967), and Zielenziger, op. cit., n. 2 above, pp. 199 ff.

the Harz metal forges. Five years later, he extended his activity to the manufacture of semi-finished products (in the first place lead shot). In 1820, he set up a small forge of his own. Three years later, he helped found a company to operate another forge, located at Ilsenburg, which presently became his sole property. Early products included, besides kitchenware, vats and tubs for Harz breweries. In 1837, on Aron Hirsch's oldest son Joseph being admitted to a partnership, the firm became Aron Hirsch & Sohn. Aron Hirsch died in 1842, leaving the business to be run by four of his sons.

A turning-point in the development of the firm was reached in 1863 with the acquisition from the Prussian state of the brassworks at Hegermühle near Eberswalde. Gustav, one of the brothers, took over the management while the others remained at Halberstadt. The oldest brother, Joseph, became a *Kommerzienrat* in 1869. Upon his death two years later he was succeeded as senior partner by his son Benjamin. The latter's major contribution consisted, characteristically, in the development of the firm's international connections—the transition from early to 'high capitalist' entrepreneurship. Benjamin Hirsch—the internationalism almost certainly a distinctive feature of Jewish commercial activity—became co-founder and only non-British member of the London metal exchange. In New York, he was prominently associated with a former senior employee in founding the firm of Vogelstein & Co., through which he established links with the major American copper and brass producers. Like his father before him, Benjamin acquired the title of *Kommerzienrat*.

In 1884 a second Aron Hirsch, son of the youngest of the four brothers, entered the firm. In 1899, he took over the management of the Eberswalde works and moved from Halberstadt to Berlin. By this time, a major product of the factory was parts for railway engines. In 1906, various manufacturing interests were amalgamated as Hirsch Kupfer und Messingwerke AG, a joint-stock company still however wholly controlled by members of the family. The war of 1914 brought vast orders for brass bases for infantry cartridges and artillery shells. With the profits, Aron's son Siegmund Hirsch organized the retooling of the works in Eberswalde, making them the most up to date of their kind. Under a long-term agreement, the AEG became a major customer for the Eberswalde works (to meet its requirements for brass products after it had abandoned its own production). However, the Depression put the Hirsch enterprises in jeopardy. While the parent (trading) company in Halberstadt, after a number of unsuccessful speculative ventures, was forced into amalgamation with another similar company, the manufacturing interests, shortly before 1933, passed into the hands of the AEG.

Another metal-based firm which successfully effected the transition from the age of early industrialization to that of 'organized capitalism' was that of Alexander Coppel in Solingen.[45] During the eighteen-twenties, Alexander Coppel had traded in bones, horn, and hooves (needed for handle-making in the cutlery trade). Somewhat later, he began to trade in cutlery and ironware, until he finally turned to the manufacture of pocket-knives and scissors. In 1851, his products gained a certificate of merit at the Great Exhibition in London. During the fifties, with some 160 workers, the firm was the third-largest manufacturer in Solingen. In the 1860s, Alexander Coppel turned to making arms, more particularly bayonets for use on the new breech-loading rifles.

When in 1869 Gustav Coppel joined his father (and his brothers Arnold and Carl) as a partner, he was already a prominent public figure in Solingen both in the Jewish community and in municipal affairs. He chaired the Jewish board of representatives from 1857 to 1859 and again from 1869 until 1885 He was a city councillor from 1867 until 1910, deputy mayor from 1892 until 1912. In 1881, Coppel was elected to the *Kreistag*. From 1867 until 1878, he belonged to the Solingen chamber of commerce, ending his career as its president (1877–8). In 1874, he became chairman of the federation of scissors manufacturers. From 1875 until 1910, he also chaired the model arbitration court for industrial disputes. Honoured with the title of *Geheimer Kommerzienrat*, Gustav Coppel became a freeman of Solingen in 1906. He died in 1914. Coppel's career recalls that of the better-known Wilhelm Herz. Both became prominent notables for their public as much as their commercial activities. Like Wilhelm Herz, Gustav Coppel sat on the boards of some joint-stock companies, notably the Hannover Continental Caoutchouc- und Gutta-Percha Compagnie (Conti), the connection of which with his own manufacturing interests is not readily apparent.

After Gustav Coppel, the most prominent member of the family was his youngest son Alexander. On his father's death, Alexander Coppel took over the management of the firm together with two of his brothers. The diversification of its manufacturing activities mainly into

---

[45] For details of the Coppel family see H. Rosenthal, 'Jews in the Solingen Steel Industry' in *Year Book XVII of the Leo Baeck Institute* (London, 1972), 205 ff.

the production of seamless steel tubing is documented by Coppel's chairmanship of the Verband für nahtlose Präzisionsrohre and his board membership of the union of bicycle-part manufacturers. Like his father before him, moreover, he occupied a seat on the board of what had become the Continental AG Hannover (Conti). Alexander Coppel sat on the Solingen municipal council from 1914 until 1929. When the firm was 'Aryanised' in 1936, it continued in business as Alexander Coppel, Stahlwaren- und Waffenfabrik GmbH Solingen. It had either continued producing military equipment or was re-entering a field which had helped to make its earlier fortunes. The Hirsches and the Coppels were the most important Jewish dynasties in the metal industry originating during the age of early industrialization. Both survived 'to the bitter end', thanks to a marked adaptability to new demands and diversification of products. Both were involved in the manufacture of small arms (as, in the second wave of entrepreneurship, would be the more famous Loewe brothers). Both the Hirsch and Coppel families were prolific, with the management of their family businesses continuing throughout in the direct male line. Both provided their native towns of Halberstadt and Solingen with a succession of respected notables.

More typical, perhaps, than metallurgy of early entrepreneurship was transportation, a field in which Jewish enterprise also played a part. Moses Henoch,[46] a protected Jew in Berlin, had been, like a majority of early Jewish entrepreneurs, a war contractor during the French revolutionary and Napoleoic wars, involved, at the same time, in parallel credit operations. After the return of peace he had set up, at first in association with a horse-dealer, Mortier, a licensed horse-drawn cab service. He had then graduated to horse-drawn buses and, in 1839, secured a licence to station three such vehicles outside the newly built Potsdamer Bahnhof, to meet incoming trains.

However, Moses Henoch's entrepreneurial activities had not been confined to horse transportation. In 1819, he had acquired a noble estate (*Rittergut*) on which, four years later, he had started a silk manufacture. In this, by 1836, he employed five to six hundred people. He had also opened an alum and lignite mine, which gave employment to a further fifty workers. In 1836, he had added the obligatory beet-sugar refinery. Utilizing the bathing facilities of his village, he

[46] For the Henochs see Rachel and Wallich, op. cit., n. 12 above, pp. 151 ff. and Kaelble, op. cit., n. 37 above, pp. 48 f.

succeeded in turning it into a popular spa. In 1836, Moses Henoch received the title of *Geheimer Kommissionsrat* (the rarely awarded higher grade of a commercial title ranking below that of a *Kommerzienrat*).[47]

In the development of his estate, Moses Henoch had been assisted by his son Hermann who, in 1837, had taken over the management of his father's cab service. Moving with the times, Hermann Henoch had soon transferred his attention from horse transportation to the rapidly developing 'iron horse'. In 1840, he became a director of both the Berlin–Anhaltische and the Berlin–Frankfurter Eisenbahngesellschaft. In the fifties, in addition, he came to play a prominent role in the development of insurance companies, a growing branch of economic activity. Hermann Henoch became a member of the Berlin city council (*Stadtverordneter*). In 1861, like his father, he was made *Geheimer Kommissionsrat*. With him, however, the family disappears from the economic scene.[48]

Somewhat different from that of the Henochs had been the development of another Jewish family at one time connected with horse-drawn transportation, the Güterbocks.[49] Levin Isaak Güterbock had started out as a successful cattle-dealer in Berlin. From 1806 onwards, in association with other members of his family, he had undertaken contracts to supply French garrisons with meat. At the same time, members of the family had made loans to the Estates of different Prussian provinces. Levin Isaak died in 1815. Three years later, a firm founded by his son Baer Levin, in company with a nephew, had acquired the licence to run the lucrative postal-coach service between Berlin and Potsdam. This, however, in 1825, passed into the hands of their partner Johann Gottfried Berr.

Baer Levin, meanwhile, had developed the firm of Güterbock Söhne into one of Berlin's leading carriage and banking businesses (*Speditions- und Bank Geschäft*). He died a well-to-do *rentier* in 1833, leaving behind eight sons and one daughter. In 1829, several of the sons founded the banking house of Moritz Güterbock & Co., which under the direction of Moritz Güterbock grew into a house of repute. In 1857, Güterbock became a *Kommerzienrat*. When, ten years later, he was granted the title of *Geheimer Kommerzienrat*, the authorities put

---

[47] Henoch had been recommended for the title of *Geheimer Kommerzienrat*. The reasons for appointment in the lesser grade are unclear.
[48] Moses Henoch's *Rittergut* had been sold in 1842.
[49] For the Güterbocks see Rachel and Wallich, op. cit., n. 12 above, pp. 143 ff.

his fortune at the substantial sum of 400,000 thalers.[50] Since 1846, Moritz Güterbock had been a director of the Anhalter Eisenbahn. He became a board member also of the Stettiner Eisenbahn. Güterbock had been baptized. A son—and later a grandson—became owners of estates (*Rittergutsbesitzer*) in Upper Silesia. The family bank, like other similar ones, faded from view in the seventies.

III

If one considers the group of the more prominent Jewish entrepreneurs of the age of early industrialization described here, certain features emerge. In the first place, there is among them and their successors so high a degree of individuality and diversity that, even in so small a sample, hardly a general characteristic is without exception. The development of individual entrepreneurs, their enterprises, and their dynasties reveals variations based on specific circumstances, accidents, and elements of seeming chance. Nevertheless, in seeking to characterize the 'ideal type' of the early German–Jewish entrepreneur, some generalizations would appear possible and justified by the evidence.

The first of these concerns the role of the revolutionary and Napoleonic wars in the accumulation of the original investment capital. Typically, the biography of the first-generation entrepreneur—with the exception however of those engaged in the textile industry—begins with involvement in economic transactions resulting from military operations or their consequences. Though such activities varied, ranging from war contracting through transfers of money to a variety of credit and loan transactions, there is, as a rule, no clear-cut distinction between these different forms of activity. Typically various kinds of operation are inextricably linked. Samuel Bacher and Levin Berend, Moses Henoch, Jakob Herz Beer, Levin Isaak Güterbock, Samuel Hirsch Kunheim, and, doubtless, others, had laid the foundations of their fortunes by undertaking to supply the armies of friend and foe during an age of revolutionary military upheaval. With the possible exception of Kunheim, they had lent money to credit-starved governments, rulers, and estates. With partial or full repayment, they then had sought investment opportunities. Typically they would, after the war, set up mixed enterprises combining banking, trading, and

[50] von Bernuth to von Itzenplitz, 24 Jan. 1867, ZSAM, Rep. 120 A IV 5, vol. 9, fo. 126.

industrial activities. Samuel Hirsch Kunheim, who appears to have concentrated single-mindedly on manufacturing, was exceptional in this respect. (Concentration on production was, of course, more typical of entrepreneurs in the textile industry which, however, itself contained a large commercial component.) An extreme expression of such early versatility is to be found in the activities of Moses and Hermann Henoch, who combined their original horse-transportation business with silk-manufacture, alum and lignite mining, beet-sugar refining, and (slightly later) railway management and the development of insurance companies. While others did not, perhaps, show such extreme 'diversification', the Berends also combined finance operations with sugar refining, chemical manufacture, and produce and commission trade, the Beers banking, sugar refining, and (somewhat later) railway management. In fact, men of this type could properly be described as 'men of affairs'. They formed one element among German–Jewish entrepreneurs of the age of early industrialization.

The textile manufacturers were a more heterogeneous group. Typically they or their ancestors had traded in certain types of goods before beginning to produce them. Thus the Meyers of Brandenburg and Berlin had traded in silken goods for several generations before turning to production, the Liebermanns, similarly, in cotton wares. (In the same way, Aron Hirsch the first had traded in the products of the Harz forges, the Caros in Breslau in those of the ironworks of Upper Silesia, Alexander Coppel in Solingen in bones, horn, and hooves, then cutlery, before turning to manufacturing.) The Reichenheims, Kauffmanns, and Fränkels started as retail traders. The Weigerts, untypically, beginning as handloom weavers, came out of the Silesian artisan tradition. Textile entrepreneurs, as a rule, confined their commercial activities to the production of textiles only (though the Liebermanns, exceptionally, diversified into extraction and machine building).

In general for both types of entrepreneur it would be true to say that manufacturing was an extension of trade, usually in the type of product later manufactured. Sometimes—the Hirsches in Halberstadt are a case in point—wholesale trade (also in money) continued to some extent by the side of manufacturing, but this was the exception rather than the rule. Where, as was common, several members of a family were business partners, there would normally be a degree of specialization, usually a division between technical and commercial functions.

Beginnings

Early Jewish entrepreneurship, it has been noted, was concentrated in certain branches of economic activity. Jews were prominent on the one hand in textile manufacturing, on the other in industries using raw materials in which they had previously traded (whether agricultural produce, colonial wares, or the products of extractive industry). They also involved themselves in transportation, whether by horse or rail. On the other hand, they were, as often noted, little represented in the extractive and metallurgical industries.

To understand the nature of early Jewish entrepreneurship it is necessary to examine the causes for its specific distribution, seemingly at variance with that of early entrepreneurship at large—though the difference cannot, of course, be quantified. The view has been put forward—and the evidence to a degree seems to support it—that, while Gentile entrepreneurship often, though by no means invariably, emerged from a craft tradition,[51] Jewish entrepreneurship was more

[51] The extent to which non-Jewish early entrepreneurship is of artisan or peasant origin is a matter of dispute. The early machine-building industry in Berlin, on which Rachel and Wallich base their conclusions, may be unrepresentative in this respect. Moreover, the authors probably exaggerated it in their tendentious dialectical (anti-Semitic) presentation. On the other hand, Kaelble, in his study of early Berlin entrepreneurs, overall seriously impairs the value of his conclusions by his failure to distinguish between those of Gentile and those of Jewish origin. Three relatively recent studies of early Saxon entrepreneurs stress their artisan origins. 'Die drei Autoren erkennen denn auch einen hohen Zustrom aus der Handwerkerschaft zur Unternehmergruppe und schliessen demzufolge auf eine hohe Mobilität der Unternehmer.' Hansjoachim Henning, 'Soziale Verflechtungen der Unternehmer in Westfalen 1860–1914' in *Zeitschrift für Unternehmensgeschichte*, 23, no. 1 (1978), 11 n. 24, which also offers some details. Evidence already quoted from the Solingen cutlery industry supports this view. Non-Jewish Silesian textile entrepreneurs, as has also been seen, may have been drawn in equal measure from artisans or peasants and old merchant families. Early entrepreneurs with a commercial background like the Haniel (of Huguenot origin), the Krops (better known as Krupp—of Dutch origin), or the Kramsta in Silesia—no doubt there were others—were the offspring of wealthy merchants of the eighteenth century (comparable to the Jewish court factors or the 'silk-Meyers' of Berlin and Brandenburg) and/or of foreign (mainly Huguenot) origin. Few came from the retail trade of petty dealers and shopkeepers, the nursery of early Jewish entrepreneurship. There is some evidence that retail trade may have formed the background of some *later* Gentile entrepreneurs. According to Henning's study of Westphalian entrepreneurs, of his sample of 27 between 1860 and 1889, 9 came from wholesale, 5 from retail trade, 4 from 'Gewerbe', only one from an artisan background. However, it is not stated what proportion of retail traders became actual independent entrepreneurs as distinct from entering what Henning calls 'high-management' ('hohes Management'—a category hardly known in the age of early industrialization). It is a pity Henning's study does not go back to the post-Napoleonic period. (See Henning, loc. cit., 5 ff.). What is, however, clear—and indeed predictable—is that artisans no longer become successful entrepreneurs in what may be called the 'middle period' of industrialization. Kaelble's findings in this respect ('Sozialer Aufstieg in Deutschland 1850–1914' in Konrad

likely to develop out of trading activities. Thus it has been noted that, even in the same branch of manufacture, there could be differences in the original starting-point:

The customary way to the top in Solingen was to start as an artisan outworker and eventually set up a factory of one's own . . . However, none of the Jewish manufacturers started in this way. Apart from the brothers Feist, who were originally tinware makers and therefore artisans, all started as traders in other types of goods and changed over to cutlery as the opportunity arose. It has been noted that even where Jews did become artisans, they tended to favour branches of production with a large commercial component.[52]

The difference is explained largely by the fact that, until 1812, Prussian Jews had been debarred from membership of craft guilds which enjoyed a monopoly of many trades. The difference is discussed by Rachel and Wallich in their classic study of early Berlin entrepreneurship, published under National Socialism and heavily anti-Semitic in tone (even though Paul Wallich was himself of Jewish origin). While the founders of the Berlin metallurgical industry, it is argued, came mainly from artisan stock and achieved success through 'iron' determination, inventiveness, and selfless devotion to their task—August Borsig and Werner Siemens are cited as outstanding examples—the Jewish 'huckstering spirit' achieved prominence in banking, in the cotton industry, and, above all, in the exploitative making-up business (*Konfektion*). It found no scope in the metallurgical industry where, for decades, no Jews were to be seen. Significantly, it is claimed, they made their entry into this branch only in the fifties with the introduction of the American sewing-machine.[53]

Jarausch (ed.), *Quantifizierung in der Geschichtswissenschaft* (Düsseldorf, 1976), p. 286), quoted by Henning (loc. cit., 11) are hardly surprising. Overall, the evidence does not seem to invalidate the view that men of artisan or peasant stock played a prominent part in Gentile entrepreneurship during the age of *early* industrialization.

[52] Richarz, op. cit., n. 23 above, p. 34.

[53] 'In den grossenteils aus dem Handwerkerstande hervorgegangenen Gründern der so mächtig emporgediehenen Berliner Matallindustrie offenbart sich eine eindrucksvolle Fülle von Begabung, Mut, Tatkraft und unermüdlicher Einsatzbereitschaft. Nur überlegenes Können, eiserner Fleiss und selbstloses Dienen am Werk hat sie so Grosses erreichen lassen. Jüdischer Händlergeist, der sonst in Berlin so stark hervortrat, so namentlich im Bankwesen, in der Baumwollbranche und der hier als besondere Eigenart entwickelten, arg ausbeuterischen Konfektion, hatte dort keinen Platz. So ist denn in der Metallindustrie Jahrzehnte hindurch kein Jude zu finden. Sie tauchen bezeichnenderweise erst auf mit der Einführung der amerikanischen Nähmaschine, also in engem Zusammenhang mit der verjudeten Bekleidungsindustrie. 1855–56 wurden hier die ersten Nähmaschinenfabriken von Beermann und Gutmann gegründet. Viel

Whilst the generalized opposition of the heroic Gentile Siegfrieds of the Berlin metal industry and the Jewish Fafners of the making-up trade is, of course, as presented by Rachel and Wallich, arrant mythologized nonsense, it is, nevertheless, based on some carefully researched data. Descriptions of non-Jewish and Jewish entrepreneurs in their study do indeed suggest some basic differences.

Typically—although there are of course exceptions—the Gentile entrepreneur in Berlin is indeed the son of an artisan or peasant. Typically also he is, like his Jewish counterpart, an immigrant.[54] The non-Jew would frequently complete a course of studies at the Royal Trade School (Kgl. Gewerbeinstitut), founded in 1821, followed by an industrial apprenticeship. Thus F. A. Egells who, in 1828, established the first private iron foundry in Berlin, had been an apprentice in the Royal Iron Foundry set up in 1804, for a long time Berlin's largest metallurgical undertaking. In the thirties, a new generation of apprentices would flock to Egells himself, amongst them the young August Borsig who, in 1837, opened his own workshop. Thereafter, newcomers would seek apprenticeships with the firms of either Egells or Borsig. The Gentile entrepreneur setting up on his own might then start a small workshop with capital partly saved, partly borrowed from family or friends, occasionally with a sleeping partner; the Jewish entrepreneur, more usually, would enter manufacturing with some capital already acquired through war contracting or retail trade, sometimes by buying an already existing small enterprise. In short, differences in the origins of 'typical' Jewish and Gentile entrepreneurship were marked. It seems possible also that whereas much Jewish entrepreneurship of the age of early industrialization dates from the Restoration, its non-Jewish counterpart developed more typically in *Vormärz* some ten to fifteen years later. It may also be that, whilst the non-Jew set up his workshop, after having served as an apprentice and journeyman, relatively young, the Jewish entrepreneur was more likely to turn to manufacturing at a more mature age.

später erst kamen die bekanntesten jüdischen Industriellen, Ludwig Löwe und Emil Rathenau, auf, nicht mit Erzeugnissen eigenen Geistes sondern wieder solchen amerikanischer Herkunft: Werkzeugmaschinen bzw. Glühlampen!' Rachel and Wallich, op. cit., n. 12 above, pp. 188 f.

[54] It would appear, from a limited sample, that Gentile entrepreneurs tended to be drawn from further afield. While the Jewish industrialists would move to Berlin mainly from small localities in Brandenburg, Anhalt, occasionally the eastern provinces, Posen and Silesia (the major migration of entrepreneurs from these provinces belongs to a later period), their Gentile counterparts might have come from Kassel, Münsterland, or Niedersachsen, from Breslau, Kiel, Naumburg, Magdeburg, Eschwege, or the Vogtland.

Why then, it may be asked, were so few Jews to be found in the metal and machine-building industries? Some of the causes seem clear. In the first place, at the time when some Jews entered manufacturing during the Napoleonic wars and in the following decade, a private metallurgical industry had hardly yet come into existence: the major enterprises in the field were royal arsenals and foundries in which Jews found little scope. By the time private entrepreneurs began to move into the field, Jews had already established their somewhat different entrepreneurial patterns. Moreover, Jews would now enter the field of engineering at a double disadvantage. In the first place, the manual skills required to start a workshop were more likely to be found in the sons of builders, bricklayers, carpenters, metal-workers, even peasants, than in those of shopkeepers and traders. Moreover, the entrepreneurs of the metallurgical industries soon came to constitute a fairly tight network, based on Egells and Borsig, into which it would not be 'natural' for young—let alone middle-aged—Jews to seek admission. (Emil Rathenau did indeed, if for a relatively brief period, work with Borsig—to the latter's satisfaction—but only after he had already served an apprenticeship in his grandfather's machine-building workshop near Sprottau and then, characteristically, gone abroad to complete his engineering education.) It may be significant that, in a later generation, when Jews did indeed take up machine building, dozens of Jewish engineers, many of whom would eventually set up their own, usually medium-sized and highly specialized firms, would serve their apprenticeships with 'Jewish' enterprises, Emil Rathenau's AEG, Ludwig Loewe, Benno Orenstein, or Arthur Koppel. Many would then be employed for a time (the equivalent of a period as journeyman) by the AEG before setting up their own workshops. Others would find permanent employment with AEG, Loewe, or Orenstein and Koppel. In short, by the last quarter of the century, there was available a network of Jewish engineering enterprises which, for good reason, had had no counterpart in the age of early industrialization. The link between the two ages is Emil Rathenau who, in his youth, had worked for Borsig and who, in his age, would become the hub of a Jewish engineering network.

What, then, positively determined the choices of Jewish entrepreneurs entering the manufacturing field? Here the evidence would seem to support the conventional view that, often, Jews entered manufacturing in areas using raw materials in which they had previously traded. Moreover, a fact less widely appreciated, this, in the age of early industrialization, in fact excluded only extractive industries[55] (to which they would gain access somewhat later, more particularly in Silesia) and engineering. Thus strong Jewish representation in the textile industry, quite apart from the fact that this was in any case the most important and probably fastest growing sector, can be explained also through their traditional involvement not only in the trade in rags and old clothes, but also in itinerant, retail, and even wholesale trade in textiles. Other industrial pursuits would emerge from trade in agricultural produce, in the products of extractive industries, or in overseas colonial products. Later, the coal trade also would lead to industrial activity.

Examination of early Jewish entrepreneurs refutes the view that they entered peripheral branches of industrial production at the 'interstices' of the economy. In fact, they are to be found in most branches of industrial activity, notably textiles and the nascent chemical industry, except for machine building and (somewhat later) the 'heavy industry' of the Ruhr (though not excluding the comparable, if less spectacular, 'heavy industry' of Upper Silesia). In fact, the widespread view of the concentration of Jewish entrepreneurship in certain areas requires at least some modification. As for their heavy involvement in the textile industry in particular, it would have to be shown that this did not simply reflect the fact that this was, in any case, the fastest-growing area of entrepreneurial activity in the age of early industrialization. To substantiate the theory of an atypical distribution of early Jewish entrepreneurs (other than in banking), it would also have to be demonstrated that there were, beyond those already mentioned, areas of entrepreneurial activity in which Jews were notably under-represented. In the absence of evidence to the contrary, it would seem reasonable to assume (quantitative analysis would seem impracticable) that, with a few exceptions, the areas of Jewish and Gentile entrepreneurial activity coincided. Jew and non-Jew alike took advantage (allowing for their rather different starting-points) of similar opportunities. In a number of cases successful Jewish entrepreneurs—like no doubt some of their Gentile counterparts—settled down to their definitive economic pursuits only after a number of false starts. That Gentile entrepreneurship tended to be more 'rectilinear', developing in a single craft tradition from apprenticeship onwards, is a supposition that cannot be verified. Early entrepreneurial activity in machine building alone

[55] One reason was the strong traditional engagement of the state in mining operations which, among others, militated against Jewish participation.

(mainly, though not exclusively, in Berlin) forms an inadequate basis for Rachel's and Wallich's generalizations. This is a proposition which will be examined once more with regard to the second wave of Jewish entrepreneurship.

A hypothesis partly confirmed by a study of the early Jewish entrepreneurial élite is that confining to two generations the 'normal' lifespan of entrepreneurial 'dynasties'. This, it would appear, resulted from a combination of technical, sociological, and biological factors. Thus certain processes or branches of industrial production—cane-sugar refining, silk manufacture, the production of vegetable oil, or horse transportation—became obsolescent with the result that once profitable enterprises had to change their activities or close down. On occasion, moreover, financial stringency or falling demand such as occurred, notably, in the seventies, would bring about the closure of marginal enterprises. Some businesses (the Herzes in changing from the production of vegetable oil to that of rubber or the Hirsches turning to the manufacture of railway-engine parts are cases in point) overcame technological obsolescence by switching to new products. Financial constraints could sometimes be overcome (typically, however, at a later period) by the conversion of a family business into a joint-stock company. The major sociological factor operating was the withdrawal from commercial activity of men preferring to live the life of a wealthy *rentier*. Some—Leonor Reichenheim and, later, Ludwig Loewe are cases in point, and at a different level, Wilhelm Herz or Gustav Coppel—chose eventually to devote the greater part of their time and energies to public affairs, whether national or communal. In the third generation (as with the Güterbocks) there was a noticeable tendency towards either 'feudalization', the purchase of *Rittergüter*, aristocratic marriages, and the adoption of a 'sub-feudal' life-style or towards academic or artistic pursuits. Lastly in biological terms, though this would become marked only in the imperial period, there is a striking tendency among leading members of the economic élite (or their wives) towards biological infertility, a tendency that has been ascribed to intensive urban commercial preoccupations.[56]

[56] For a discussion of 'economic man' as a lover, see Ernest K. Bramsted, *Aristocracy and the Middle-Classes in Germany* (Chicago and London, 1964), pp. 6 f. Bramsted quotes a suggestive, if over-dialectical observation by Sombart: 'A good householder, that is a good burgher, and a lover, of whatever rank, are irreconcilable antitheses. Either economic interests, in the broadest sense, or love-interests form the central point of all life's importance. One lives either to work or else to love. Work implies saving, love implies spending.' W. Sombart, *Der Bourgeois* (Munich, 1913), p. 263.

Whichever the factors involved and whatever their specific impact in particular cases, it is noticeable that perhaps a majority of early Jewish entrepreneurial families have disappeared—at any rate from any prominent position in economic life—by the sixties. Typically, such 'dynasties' extend over two generations only with the first raising the enterprise above those of their 'run of the mill' competitors, the second developing it to the highest level it is destined to reach—normally, rewarded with the accolade of a title. It must, however, be noted that there existed a goodly number of exceptions to this pattern: the Coppels, Kauffmanns, Fränkel-Pinkuses, Herzes, Hirsches, Kunheims, dynasties whose relative economic prominence outlasted the minimum of two generations. But these were still the minority. Among private banking dynasties, the Heines, Habers, Kusels, Güterbocks, Plauts, Warschauers and, finally, Rothschilds who lose their importance or disappear are, perhaps, more evenly balanced by the Mendelssohns, Oppenheims, Bleichröder-Schwabachs, Warburgs, Ladenburgs, Kaullas, and Behrenses who do not. Bankers, perhaps, were somewhat more adept at preserving and even increasing their capital than were industrialists.

IV

The German–Jewish élite then, in its beginnings in the age of early industrialization, was a composite body, made up of at least three major and distinct elements. Its core, arguably, consisted of the descendants of the last generation of court Jews, the Rothschilds, Kaullas, Hirsches, Seligmanns, Oppenheims. To these, due largely to the financial operations of the Napoleonic wars, to public loans, early railway construction, and last, not least, Rothschild patronage, were added private banking families of the first half of the century, the Heines, Behrenses, and Warburgs, Mendelssohns, Ladenburgs, Warschauers, Plauts, Erlangers, and Speyers. Lastly, there was the entrepreneurial group of the Meyers and Liebermanns, Beers, Reichenheims, and Herzes, some of whose members achieved a degree of social and cultural prominence. Between the three groups, there was some geographical distinction—even if divisions were by no means clear-cut. Thus, while the direct descendants of the later court factors tended to reside, naturally, largely in the major *Residenzstädte*, mainly in the south and west (Munich, Stuttgart, Karlsruhe, Mannheim,

Bamberg, and Würzburg),[57] the 'secondary' financial dynasties were to be found more often in the north and east (notably Hamburg, Berlin, and Breslau) but also in Frankfurt-on-Main, with Cologne occupying an intermediate positon. With the exception of Berlin, with a weakly developed commercial tradition, these were commercial centres dominated by influential patriciates. Jewish industrial entrepreneurship, though there were rudiments also in the south,[58] was concentrated largely in and around Berlin and in Silesia. Geography, in this way, reinforced the occupational[59] and social fragmentation of the German–Jewish economic élite (as, to some extent, did the political and religious fragmentation of Germany itself).

The German–Jewish economic élite, then, as it emerged in the first half of the nineteenth century, was essentially the product of economic opportunities provided by the revolutionary and Napoleonic wars and the subsequent beginnings of early industrialization. It benefited, in a variety of ways, both from the fiscal needs of governments and from state encouragement of economic development. Jewish entrepreneurship in the narrower sense, however, whether in the production of textile goods, sugar, vegetable oil, kitchen utensils, or cutlery, tended to look for its customers to an early consumer market. It also produced goods needed for industrial operations, alum and dyestuffs for textile manufacturers, vats for breweries, vegetable oil with industrial uses. There was an involvement in transportation from horse-drawn vehicles to railway finance and management.

The evidence suggests that, following vigorous beginnings, the economic activity of the German–Jewish economic élite tended to slow down towards mid-century. The number of new enterprises destined to achieve prominence diminished. The 'heroic age' of early industrialization (and with it of Jewish entrepreneurship) was over. The subsequent 'railway age', however, would offer new opportunities.

---

[57] They were to be found also in Dresden. The Rothschilds chose to stay in Frankfurt-on-Main rather than join their major princely client in Hanau or Kassel.

[58] For some details see Toury, op. cit., n. 22 above, pp. 20 ff. and Kurt Grunwald, *Türkenhirsch* (Jerusalem, 1966), pp. 1 ff.

[59] While, in the south, the Hirsches, Habers and Seligmanns financed early industrial development, northern capitalists, once banking had become separated from trade and industry, tended to abstain from industrial investment until the coming of the railways in mid-century.

3
An Élite of Notables

I

THE economic status élite in Prussia—as indeed in most of the rest of Germany—during the greater part of the nineteenth century consisted, besides the select few who could aspire to ennoblement, of men who achieved the coveted non-hereditary titles of *Kommerzienrat* and *Geheimer Kommerzienrat* (*Geheimrat*). In Prussia, conferment of these titles by the king on the recommendation of the minister of commerce[1] was the result of a quite rigorous selection procedure in which, with time, well-established criteria came to be applied. Down at any rate to the last quarter of the nineteenth century when, to some extent, the titles gradually became venal and fell into some disrepute, every successful merchant, banker, or entrepreneur (with infinitesimal exceptions) considered (or, indeed, thinking himself) to be of sufficient standing within the commercial community, would aspire to the honour of a title. The distinction, moreover, would confer more than mere status. A title for its owner could greatly enhance the standing of a business,[2] besides, more specifically, improving its credit rating.[3]

---

[1] The official designation was *Kgl. Staatsminister für Handel, Gewerbe und öffentliche Arbeiten*.

[2] Thus in 1859, the *Ober-Präsident* of Brandenburg, in explaining why a title was more valuable than a decoration, wrote that 'zumal in der kaufmännischen Welt durch den Raths-Character das Renommé der Firma besonders im Auslande, mehr gehoben wird als durch eine Medaille'. *Ob.-Präsident* of the Province of Brandenburg to *Handelsminister*, 4 Feb. 1859, ZSAM Rep. 120, A IV 5, vol. 6, fo. 168. Decades later, the minister of commerce, in deprecating the conferment of titles on two partners in the same firm, observed: 'Es möchte dies auch deshalb zu vermeiden sein, weil dadurch das Ansehen der Firma zum Nachtheil der Concurrenz-firmen in weitgehender Weise gehoben würde.' Brefeld to Wilhelm II, 2 Oct. 1897, ZSAM 2.1.1, no. 1590, fos. 70^{r-v}.

[3] Bismarck in 1888 commented, 'die Ertheilung des Titels eines Commerzienrates habe auf die Creditfähigkeit des Beliehenen einen gewissen Einfluss, und der Regierung fiele eine [illegible] Verantwortlichkeit zu; sie müsse deshalb bei Ertheilung des Titels von gewissen finanziellen Voraussetzungen ausgehen um keinen Irrthum beim Publicum zu erregen . . .'. Memorandum d. Friedrichsruh, 2 Sept. 1888, signature illegible, Zentrales Staatsarchiv in Potsdam (ZSAP), 07.01 Reichskanzlei 589, fo. 22. Years later, it was noted in the Prussian cabinet (*Staatsministerium*): 'Durch beide Titel

The reservoir for this economic status élite, in consequence, comprised the bulk of economically successful members of the Prussian business community (indeed the situation did not differ widely in the rest of the German states).

Recommendations for conferment of the title of *Kommerzienrat* addressed to the minister of commerce could originate from several different quarters. Most often, such recommendations came from partners or business associates. On occasion, they might also originate with a variety of public figures (royal princes recommending their private bankers), of suppliers, retired military men, and members of the nobility. Other recommendations would come from municipal corporations or dignitaries. Not infrequently, sons would submit the names of their venerable sires, usually in connection with some business jubilee, more rarely wives those of their husbands. A goodly number of nominations were clearly instigated by the hopeful beneficiaries themselves, a few of whom, to the indignation of the authorities, actually drew attention to their own merits.[4] Finally, for special conferments to mark royal visits to various provinces, recommendations would be submitted by the local authorities.

In the case of serious nominations, the minister of commerce would then invite a detailed report on the candidate, his reputation, standing, and political attitude,[5] from the *Ober-Präsident* of the province concerned, in the case of Berlin the *Polizeipräsident*. The report would normally include details on the nature and progress of the candidate's commercial activities. In addition, the minister would normally consult the directorate of the Prussian state bank (*Kgl. Preussisches Haupt-Bank-Directorium*) about the reputation of the individuals concerned

erhalte der damit Beliehene eine ganz andere Stellung und Kreditfähigkeit. Denn in diesen Titeln liege, da namentlich im Westen jeder wisse, dass die Verleihung nach einer Prüfung des Vermögens und Kredits nur dann erfolge, wenn ein Vermögen von mindestens 500.000 M. vorhanden sei geradezu eine staatliche Abstempelung der Kreditfähigkeit.' Sitting of the cabinet, Berlin, 19 Mar. 1909, Staatsarchiv Dahlem, Rep. 90, no. 2002.

[4] 'Wenn im Jahre 1858 Herr Flatau selber auf die Verleihung mit dem Kommerzienraths Titel bei den Staatsbehörden Anträge stellte, ein Schritt, der in gewöhnlicher Weise nicht gebilligt werden kann, so möchte derselbe seine Entschuldigung darin finden . . .' *Ober-Bürgermeister* Krausnick to *Ober-Präsident* von Flottwell (precise date not available), 1862, ZSAM Rep. 120 A IV 5, vol. 7, fo. 176.

[5] In 1885, for example, the minister called on the *Ober-Präsident* of Brandenburg 'unter Erörterung der persönlichen und gesellschaftlichen Verhältnisse der Genannten, sowie ihre politische Haltung sich gefälligst zu äussern'. *Minister für Handel etc.* to *Ober-Präsident*, Brandenburg, 27 Mar. 1885, ZSAM, Berlin, Rep. 120 A IV 5a, vol. 1, fo. 101.

An Élite of Notables

and their enterprises and their standing within the commercial community (*Handelsstand*). The more comprehensive report of the *Ober-Präsident* would usually include details about estimated wealth and income, tax-rating, business turnover, the number of employees, and other similar matters. There would also be information relating to specific criteria for conferment to be mentioned presently. Altogether, the data gathered by the authorities were nothing if not comprehensive.

Certain criteria—once recognized procedures for the conferment of commercial titles had been established (by the middle of the century)—were consistently (or almost) applied in decision-making and hence reflected also in the information provided. Thus in the first place, a successful candidate must still be active in commercial affairs: recommendations for *rentiers* who had retired after a successful business career, however meritorious, were usually rejected. Next the future *Kommerzienrat*, at any rate until 1886, must not only be owner or part-owner of his enterprise but must also take an active part in its management.[6]

A further criterion applied for the conferment of titles was the contribution of the individual concerned to the well-being of his locality (or, on occasion, to the national economy) by the development of new branches of industry, the provision of employment, import substitution. Contribution to exports and enhancement of Prussia's reputation abroad are sometimes stressed in the official reports. Purely economic attainments, on the other hand, were not by themselves considered sufficient. Great importance was attached also to the standing of a candidate among his peers, a matter regularly reported upon. Failure in this respect could prove fatal to the chances of a candidate.[7] In this regard, participation in public life, whether in

---

[6] 'Der Character als Kommerzienrath', von Itzenplitz informed the king in 1866 (in the spirit of the *Ständestaat*), 'ist nur für selbständige Handeltreibende bestimmt, denn nur diese können eine wirklich hervorragende Stellung im Handelsstande einnehmen.' v. Itzenplitz to the king, 14 Feb. 1866, ZSAM 2.2.1., no. 1581, fo. 4. From the eighties onwards, taking account of the evolution of economic organization, limited exceptions were made in favour of *Generaldirektoren* (managing directors of major joint-stock companies, mainly in the *Montanindustrie* of the Rhine and Ruhr). The first *Generaldirektor* recorded as receiving a title was Friedrich Knoblauch of the Magdeburger Feuerversicherungsgesellschaft: he became a GKR in 1879 and must have been made a KR some years before that date. (No data are available for the period 1872–9.) No *Direktor* or *Generaldirektor* is then recorded until 1886, when policy on appointing non-owners appears to have changed.

[7] 'Nach seinem Vermögen und seinem Character', ran a report of the sixties, 'verdient er diese Auszeichnung unbedingt, sonst nimmt er aber wohl kaum eine hervorragende Stellung unter seinen Stammesgenossen [*sic*] ein.' Another speaks of a

elective office, in commercial organizations, in municipal government, or in religious communities was held to be of major importance. So were charitable activities and benefactions, both private and public, and contributions to a great variety of 'good causes'.[8] Good labour relations also could be a recommendation. Not every candidate would score equally under all headings and a rough and ready law of compensations would appear to have prevailed. It was unlikely, however, for anyone to succeed who did not play some significant public role and could thus in some way be considered a 'notable'.[9]

Besides these different criteria, a minimum of personal wealth was considered an essential prerequisite for the conferment of a title.[10] In 1888, in connection with a candidate held to be somewhat doubtful in this respect, Bismarck observed that in earlier days, a fortune of at least 100,000 thalers (300,000 marks) had been looked for. Given the changed economic circumstances he felt that, in the absence of special factors, a minimum of at least 1 million marks would now be appropriate. In the case under consideration, a fortune of a mere

candidate who 'durch seine Fabriktätigkeit wie durch sein grosses, durch einige Betriebsamkeit erworbenes Vermögen zwar zu den angesehendsten Gewerbetreibenden Berlins gehört, im Handelsstande aber keine so hervorragende Stellung einnimmt, dass wir die für ihn in Anregung gebrachte Auszeichnung für angemessen erachten können'. Of yet another candidate it was reported: 'Seine Stellung im Handelsstande ist aber unseres Wissens nach keiner Richtung hin eine hervorragende . . .' (All in ZSAM, J. Rep. 120 ZU A IV 5). Clearly this was a hurdle some applicants failed to take.

[8] Typical of many is the commendation of a candidate as '. . . ein wahrhaft wohltätiger Mann . . . , welcher bei jeder sich darbietenden Gelegenheit mit vollen Händen gibt'. (von Bernuth to von Itzenplitz, 1 Oct. 1866, ZSAM, Rep. 120 ZU A IV 5.) Another candidate is described as 'stets zu Betheiligung an gemeinnützigen Unternehmungen bereit' (ZSAM, Rep. 120 ZU A IV 5).

[9] A negative report on an applicant listed the qualifications looked for: '. . . weder im Communal-Ämtern thätig gewesen, noch hat er dem öffentlichen Wohl auf dem Gebiete des Handels u. der Industrie besondere Dienste geleistet. Ebensowenig hat er sich in politischer Beziehung in conservativer Richtung hervorgethan [!] Es fehlt daher meines Erachtens an Veranlassung . . .'. von Jagow to von Itzenplitz, 14 Feb. 1865, ZSAM, Rep. 120 A IV 5, vol. 9, fo. 1. Interestingly, recommendations from *Regierungspräsidenten* in Münster appear, from around 1910 onwards, to have reduced emphasis on municipal office while continuing to stress membership of professional associations (*Interessenverbände*), chambers of commerce, and provincial diets (Henning, 'Soziale Verflechtungen der Unternehmer in Westfalen 1860–1914' in *Zeitschrift für Unternehmensgeschichte*, 23, no. 1 (1978), 17 n. 37). Clearly the concept of the 'notable' was undergoing a (somewhat belated) change.

[10] Thus the *Ober-Präsident* of the province of Westphalia informed the *Regierungspräsident* in Minden in an official circular of 25 February 1895 that the main prerequisite for appointment as KR was, besides some activity for the public good, 'Vorhandensein eines beträchtlichen, sicher fundierten und von der jeweiligen Geschäftslage unabhängigen Kapitalvermögens'. Quoted in Henning, loc. cit., 3 n. 9.

450,000 marks appeared somewhat meagre but, given the candidate's other qualifications, he was not indisposed to accede to the request.[11] When in 1909 the Prussian cabinet (*Kgl. Staatsministerium*) discussed raising the fees for newly appointed *Kommerzienräte*, the minister of finance observed that the minimum requirement in the wealthier provinces of the monarchy was, in fact, 500,000 marks.[12] The minister of commerce, in pleading for a lower registration fee than that proposed by his colleague, rejoined that the object in stipulating a minimum of wealth was to ensure that titles should not be disgraced by their bearers. A fortune of half a million in the provinces and of one million in Berlin would offer adequate security.[13] It is worth noting that, with all the attention paid to the fortunes of candidates, concern is expressed on occasion lest wealth become the sole criterion.[14]

[11] 'In früheren Zeiten habe man den Nachweis eines Vermögens von 100.000 th gefordert; nach den heutigen Verschiebungen möchte Seine Durchlaucht die als Unterlage erforderliche Summe, wenn nicht sonstige Gründe massgebend wären, wenigstens mit 1.000.000M. veranschlagen.
Im vorliegenden Falle schiene Seiner Durchlaucht das Vermögen von 450.000 demnach etwas gering; aniden sonstiger Eigenschaften des g. Wurmbach wäre er aber nicht abgeneigt, dem Gesuch zu entsprechen.' Memorandum d. Friedrichsruh, 2 Sept. 1888, signature illegible, ZSAP 07.01 Reichskanzlei 589, fo. 22.

[12] In the less developed eastern provinces, more modest fortunes had always been considered sufficient. In a report of 1898 the minister of commerce observed with regard to a candidate that his fortune of 186,000 M 'entspricht zwar nicht dem Vermögen, das als massgebende Voraussetzung für die Erwirkung des Characters als Kommerzienrath angenommen zu werden pflegt...', but it appeared adequate for the eastern provinces of the monarchy and, more particularly, Poznania (Brefeld to Wilhelm II, 21 June 1898, ZSAM 2.2.1, no. 1590, fos. 136^{r-v}.

[13] 'Die Prüfung des Vermögens finde wesentlich zu dem Zwecke statt, um Sicherheit zu haben, dass den Titeln durch ihre Inhaber keine Schande gemacht werde. In den Provinzen werde ein Vermögen von 1/2 Mill.M., in Berlin von 1 Mill.M., als ausreichende Sicherheit betrachtet.' Sitting of the cabinet, Berlin, 19 Mar. 1909, Staatsarchiv Dahlem, Rep. 90, no. 2002. These figures conflict with Henning's claim, based on a circular supposed to have been issued by the Prussian *Minister für Handel, Gewerk und öffentliche Angelegenheiten* of 8 October 1890 (of which, however, he could find no copy) to the effect that the requirement for the title of KR had been 'seit 1865 ein nicht betriebsgebundenes Vermögen von 750.000 M., seit 1893 von 1 Mill.M.—,..' (Henning, loc. cit., n. 9 above, p. 3). The figures seem too high, though they might, conceivably, have been the prerequisite for a GKR. Nor is it clear how a circular of 1890 could announce what the requirement had been since 1893 ('seit 1893').

[14] 'Unter diesen Umständen nehme ich Anstand, die Verleihung des Geheimen Commerzienraths Titels an den Simon Oppenheim zu befürworten, umso mehr als nach dem Dafürhalten des Ober-Präsidenten die durch Ernennung beider Brüder zu Geheimen Commerzienräthen dem Oppenheimischen Bankierhause gewährte exceptionelle Bevorzugung im Publicum wohl nur als eine dem—von besonderen Verdiensten nicht begleiteten—Reichthum zu Theil gewordene Berücksichtigung aufgefasst werden würde...', von der Heydt to the Prince Regent of Prussia, 16 Apr. 1859, ZSAM 2.2.1, no. 1580, fos. 209^v–210. A generation later (1900), on a non-Jewish candidate for the

A further matter taken into consideration was the political 'reliability' of the candidate. Whilst support of the government and its policies was no absolute *sine qua non*, it was, undoubtedly, a recommendation.[15] Conversely, active support of liberal (later left-liberal) parties, while not a total bar, was unquestionably a handicap[16] which had to be compensated by other qualifications. While opposition to government policy on questions thought to be of importance was considered an obstacle to the conferment of a title, only liberal activists ('agitatorisch tätig'), later active supporters of the *Fortschrittspartei*, were effectively debarred.[17] Not infrequently, people of an 'undesirable' political complexion got their titles only at the second attempt, after a possible delay of two to three years.[18]

The title of *Geheimer Kommerzienrat* was awarded, normally, by comparable criteria. It was conferred, with rare exceptions, on men who already possessed the lower honour,[19] normally after an interval of

title of a GKR, the *Regierungspräsident* of Minden would still write in an official report . . . 'die öffentliche Meinung würde es nicht verstehen, wenn einem Manne, dessen einziges Verdienst es ist, viel Geld zu verdienen und davon nur das Allernötigste auszugeben, solche Allerhöchsten Gnadenbeweise zuteil würden.' Quoted in Henning, loc. cit., n. 9 above, p. 14 n. 29.

[15] The political behaviour of candidates was reported on as a matter of course. In some reports, the candidate would be described as 'treuer Anhänger des Königs und der Regierung' or as a man 'welcher *stets* dem König und der Regierung ergeben war'. On numerous occasions 'streng conservativ' is the epithet applied to a candidate's conduct during the previous election.

[16] The crude comment of an *Ober-Präsident* of Brandenburg: 'Zur Gewährung einer Allerhöchsten Anerkennung an den g. Liebermann liegt keine Veranlassung vor, da er der Fortschrittspartei angehört' (Wintzingerode to von Itzenplitz, 15 Nov. 1865, ZSAM Rep. 120 A IV 5, vol. 9, fos. 45^{r-v}) is untypical and reflects the aftermath of the Prussian constitutional conflict. In general, the authorities were more sophisticated in their political assessments.

[17] Eventually in 1895 in order to remove uncertainties, the minister of commerce officially informed his colleagues 'dass Seine Majestät den Titel als Kommerzienrat auch an Angehörige der Fortschrittspartei, sofern dieselben nicht agitatorisch auftreten, zu verleihen pflegen'. Sitting of the cabinet, Berlin, 8 Oct. 1895, Staatsarchiv Dahlem, Rep. 90, no. 2002, fo. 20. It is worth noting that the minister did not introduce a new policy but merely restated existing practice.

[18] In 1903, for instance, in the case of an industrialist of considerable distinction, the minister of commerce felt impelled to ascertain the views of the *Reichskanzler* and Prussian prime minister. Bülow opposed the suggestion in view of the candidate's presidency of the *Handelsvertragsverein* which opposed the government's tariff policy. He added, however, that once the new trade treaties were 'safe and dry', the matter might be reconsidered. Wilhelm Herz, in due course, got his title.

[19] A memorandum of 1907 stated that, normally, only *Kommerzienräte* could be appointed to the higher grade. Exceptions could be made only 'in ganz vereinzelten, hervorragend geeigneten Fällen'. There had been only five such exceptions: Alexander Mendelssohn (1854), Adolf Hansemann (1868), Stadtrath Magnus (1879), Friedrich Alfred Krupp (1887), and, in somewhat different circumstances, Julius van der Zypen

An Élite of Notables

eight to ten years. In making the relatively rare award, the authorities were much concerned with the question of comparability in relation to other possible claimants.[20] Those eventually destined for the higher title seem, as a rule, to have received the lower one at an earlier age than the rest.[21] They either represented the more important enterprises or, more rarely, achieved unusual distinction at a relatively early age.

With the territorial growth and rapid economic expansion of Prussia in the sixties and seventies and the increasing number of requests and recommendations for titles, Bismarck decided to introduce a quota system. It was resolved that not more than twenty-five *Kommerzienräte* and five *Geheime Kommerzienräte* should be created each year.[22] On the basis of these quotas, the bureaucrats then devised a truly remarkable procedure, designed presumably to level out over the year the burden of the investigations. If sufficient worthwhile candidates were available, two recommendations a month for the title of *Kommerzienrat* would be submitted by the minister of commerce to the king during the first eleven months of the year. In the final month, however, there would be

---

(1898) (Richter to Loebell, 25 Apr. 1905, Reichskanzle: 589, ZSAP 07.01, fo. 256). The list is incomplete. Among those who received the title of *Geheimer Kommerzienrat* without having held the lower one was the silk manufacturer Jacob Abraham Meyer in 1841. *Polizeipräsident* Puttkammer to *Wirkl. Geh. Rat Präsident* Bassewitz, Berlin, 21 Oct. 1841, ZSAM, Rep. 120, A IV 5, vol. 2, fos. 156–60.

[20] In a case in 1857, when an advancement from *Kommerzienrat* to *Geh. Kommerzienrat* was proposed, the *Königlich-Preussische Haupt-Bank-Direktorium* reported that the appointment would cause 'ein gewisses Gefühl der Zurücksetzung bei zweien unserer hervorragendsten Börsen-Notabilitäten . . . welche dem Genannten in Bezug auf Verdienst und Stellung in keiner Weise nachstehen, wegen ihres gemeinnützigen Wirkens aber vielleicht noch nähere Anrechte auf eine derartige Auszeichnung haben dürften'. (KPHBD to v. Itzenplitz, 3 Dec. 1857, ZSAM, 2.2.1, no. 1590, fo. 139.) In general, the KPHBD almost invariably made it its special responsibility to report on how a conferment would be received by members of the commercial community.

[21] According to an official document (no date given) in the Staatsarchiv in Münster, qualified entrepreneurs until about 1890 received the title of KR aged between 55 and 60 years, thereafter around the age of 50 (Henning, loc. cit., n. 9 above, p. 3). A memorandum of 1905 explained: 'Wenn dem Hause Abel keine hervorragende kommerzielle Bedeutung beigelegt wird, so ist das wohl zutreffend. Dafür wird aber auch nur die Charakterverleihung zum einfachen Kommerzienrat für den 54-jährigen Geschäftsinhaber erbeten. Wenn es sich um Firmen von grosser Bedeutung handelt, so pflegt dieser Titel schon bei Erreichung des 40sten Lebensjahres verliehen zu werden und mit dem 50sten Jahre der als Geheimer Kommerzienrat nachzufolgen.' Memorandum enclosed in Möller to Loebell, 31 Mar. 1905, ZSAP ReichsKanzle: 589 07.01, fo. 127.

[22] The memorandum does not make clear whether this number included the appointments (normally 3 or 4) made each year in connection with royal attendance at manœuvres in different parts of the monarchy. The mode of procedure indicated does, however, suggest that such appointments were additional to the quota.

three submissions. In each of the first three quarters of the year, there would be one recommendation for appointment as *Geheimer Kommerzienrat*, two in the last quarter.[23] This procedure, it was claimed in 1888, had in practice already been followed for years[24] ('seit Jahren'). In 1897 under the pressure of applications, the quotas, it appears, were raised by one third.[25]

Bismarck's bureaucratic procedures, designed among others to save commercial honours from loss of esteem through 'inflation', failed however to prevent their gradual decay from another cause. With the importance known to be attached by the authorities (and, more particularly, the two queen-empresses) to contributions to a variety of charitable, religious, public, and, most frequently, patriotic causes—and their evident effect on the conferment of titles—the suspicion inevitably gained ground that such titles were being 'bought'. It had begun with isolated cases of patronage (*Feldmarschall* v. Gneisenau, the prince of Prussia (later Wilhelm I), Prince Karl v. Preussen, a little later *Herzog* von Ratibor and *Fürst* von Putbus) nor was Bismarck's patronage of his private banker Gerson Bleichröder or his timber merchants, the Behrends, wholly above suspicion. While some of the protégés thus put forward were probably well qualified for a title, with the recommendation merely initiating the process, others were of more questionable merit. Later, the correspondence contains occasional suggestions of candidates engaging in charitable activities merely to 'buy' a title.[26] *Freiherr* von Mirbach, chamberlain to the Empress Augusta (wife of Wilhelm I), became notorius for 'selling' titles to wealthy men in return for substantial contributions to the empress's church-building projects without regard to the religious persuasion of the 'donor'.[27] Even further, the press published documentation (from

[23] *Ministerium für Handel und Gewerbe* to Bismarck, 9 Nov. 1888, ZSAP, Reichskanzlei 589 07.01, fos. 27–8.

[24] The ratio had, however, been ignored in 1888 when the Emperor Friedrich III's 'accession honours' of 5 May had included 10 new *Kommerzienräte* and 6 *Geheime Kommerzienräte* (ib.).

[25] Sitting of the cabinet (extract), Berlin, 27 Dec. 1897, Staatsarchiv Dahlem, Rep. 90, A 2002, fo. 22.

[26] Thus it was said of one candidate: 'Goldberger gehört zu den in Berlin leider immer häufiger werdenden Personen, die sich bei allen Gelegenheiten vordrängen und deren mit Ostentation betriebenes Wohltun den unangenehmen Hintergrund der Sucht nach Auszeichnungen hat.' Berlepsch to Wilhelm II, 27 Sept. 1892, ZSAM 2.2.1, no. 1588, fo. 208.

[27] 'Um diese Zeit', writes Hermann Wallich, director of the Deutsche Bank, in his memoirs, '. . . erschien eines Tages ein Herr, Abgesandter aus dem Kabinett Ihrer Majestät von weiland Kaiserin Augusta. Der Herr, der kein empfehlendes Äusseres

An Élite of Notables

aggrieved parties) about a case where a self-appointed 'intermediary' had secured substantial sums by offering to use his connections to obtain a title. Already in 1893, the minister of commerce lamented that the title of *Kommerzienrat* had, 'in a manner of speaking', become venal.[28]

In any case, irrespective of creeping abuse, the title of *Kommerzienrat* was, by this time, beginning to lose its *raison d'être*. Originally designed as a mark of recognition for meritorious service in the *Kaufmannsstand*, it had, for a time, been confined by definition to independent owner-managers. Gradually, from 1886 onwards, reflecting economic change—indeed economic realities—some managing directors (*Direktoren* and *Generaldirektoren*) had also been made *Kommerzienräte* (without, however, significantly altering the general character of the distinction). By the late eighties and early nineties, however, economic life at large was undergoing a change. Only large joint-stock companies could, by this time, meet the capital requirements of large sections of industry (especially iron and coal—though, in this sector, family firms continued to coexist with joint-stock companies—electricity, machine building, and chemicals, besides, of course, the banking sector). The managing director to some extent replaced the private owner, though a good many of the latter continued to play a significant role in economic affairs. While, previously, influence and status had largely coincided in an élite of 'notables', the two were now beginning to diverge with the evolution of large-scale capitalist organization. Increasingly, those to whom the title of *Kommerzienrat* was still attractive had ceased to represent economic power or achievement at national level. More and more, commercial titles came to distinguish small-town dignitaries—even if many, in positions of real influence, also did not disdain them. On the other hand a goodly number, though still a minority, felt that a commercial title could add little to their status or influence. Men

hatte, er war einäugig, wollte mich allein sprechen. Mit der Eröffnung der Tagespost beschäftigt, bat ich ihn unwillig, im Beisein meiner Kollegen zu sprechen. Er eröffnete mir dann leise, es bestehe an hoher Stelle die Absicht, mir einen "Charakter" zu verleihen und zeigte dabei auf sein Portefeuille.' Hermann Wallich, *Aus meinem Leben* in *Zwei Generationen im deutschen Bankwesen* (Frankfurt-on-Main, 1978), p. 131.

[28] '... der Titel eines Kommerzienraths sei seit einiger Zeit gewissermassen käuflich geworden: Spenden für kirchliche u. a. Zwecke würden damit belohnt, und der Fhr. von Mirbach habe einen grossen Theil der von ihm patronisierten Sammlungen durch Verheissung solchen Titels zusammengebracht. Er, der Herr Minister, müsse sich gegen ein solches Verfahren, welches die Sache discreditiere, aufs Äusserste sträuben ...' Memorandum d. Berlin, 19 Apr. 1893, signed Goering, on behalf of Berlepsch, ZSAP Reichskanzlei: 589 07.01, fos. 50–1.

eligible, with the relevant aspirations, and who could afford to pay for the honour would, in the twentieth century, prefer ennoblement. In consequence of the Mirbach operation and one or two scandals, the title of *Kommerzienrat* in particular, fell into some disfavour.[29] Suitable candidates would now clamour instead for the title of a *Regierungsrat*—which, however, the higher bureaucracy reserved fairly rigorously for itself. On the other hand, when the AEG sought a distinction for its founder Emil Rathenau it applied for, and obtained, significantly, that of *Geh. Baurat*.[30] In fact, by the nineties, the classic age of the *Kommerzienräte* was over.

However, during the greater part of the nineteenth century, commercial titles had truly defined the Prussian economic status élite. By the operation of rigorous and painstaking selection processes Prussian officialdom had, in accordance with more or less established norms, chosen the people who could rightly be regarded as the pace setters (or the most distinguished members) of the economic community. They had, in the process, though that was hardly their prime purpose, gathered and preserved for posterity a mass of information about the evolution of Prussian economic life.

II

In the widespread scramble for titles men of Jewish origin had, from the start, participated to the full. Indeed, their natural thirst, as members of a despised and discriminated minority, for recognition,

[29] Hermann Wallich's retrospective comments are interesting in noting both that some people considered these titles 'ridiculous' and in his explanation why they persisted none the less: 'War es die Furcht, wiederholt für einen wohltätigen Zweck missbraucht zu werden, denn auf solchen Umwegen wurde gewohnheitsmässig der "Charakter" erworben, war es die Furcht, mich durch den Titel eines Kommerzienrats lächerlich zu machen, wie es unter meinen Intimen der Fall war, genug, ich antwortete dem armen Mann ziemlich unwirsch . . . Es war falsch, wie mir der Erfolg gezeigt hat. In einem Land wie dem unseren, wo so viel Wert auf Äusserlichkeiten und Rangunterschied gelegt wird, kann man nicht gut gegen die Stimmung ankämpfen und ist es jedenfalls fehlerhaft, eine Auszeichnung abzulehnen, wenn sie—namentlich in jungen Jahren—angeboten wird.' (Wallich, op. cit., n. 27 above, p. 131.)

[30] Already in the seventies, Werner Siemens had declined the title of KR. In 1877 he had, however, agreed to become a *Geh. Regierungsrat*. Entrepreneurs who saw themselves as primarily engineers or administrators, may well have disliked the association of the title with commerce throughout the second half of the nineteenth century, a misgiving which may have increased with time. The gradual growth of reservations about the title may have been connected with the increasing prestige of technology in the German empire documented in the rise of the *Technische Hochschulen*—the technological universities.

status, and prestige (previously satisfied largely in accordance with different, inner-Jewish criteria) made them avid for the title of *Kommerzienrat*. It was the seal of respectability in the world at large. Moreover, their developed commercial sense beyond doubt made them sensitive also to its economic advantages. The insistent pressure from Jewish bankers, merchants, and entrepreneurs for the conferment of titles developed in tandem with the commercial progress of members (or ex-members) of the Jewish community. In fact as early as 1836, a memorandum addressed to the king of Prussia from the ministry of finance commented critically on the tendency, said to be particularly prevalent among Jews, to record every meritorious proceeding in order to claim the reward. No encouragement, it was argued, should be given to this trend—in the interest of the 'moral education' of the Jews.[31] Some twenty years later, the same complaint was repeated, this time by the ministry of agriculture. Again it was remarked that Jewish candidates often applied on their own behalf, that they pushed their suits with persistence, and by a variety of means. The established stipulations about the necessary qualifications, therefore, should be rigorously enforced.[32] The president of police, in expressing reservations about simultaneous recommendations for two Jewish industrialists, struck a similar note.[33]

[31] '... bei den Juden insbesondere ist die Tendenz, sich über jede verdienstliche Handlung mit Dokumenten zu versehen und die Belonung dafür zur Befriedigung ihrer Eitelkeit selbst zu beantragen, so vorherrschend, dass es wohl zum besten ihrer moralischen Bildung zu gereichen scheint, ihm keinen Vorschub zu leisten.' Unsigned memorandum from ministry of finance to the king, Berlin, 25 Oct. 1836, ZSAM Rep. 120, A IV 5, vol. 1, fo. 177^v.

[32] 'Es hat sich in neuerer Zeit ein solcher Andrang der Gewerbetreibenden, insbesondere israelitischer Confession auf Gewährung öffentlicher Auszeichnungen bemerklich gemacht, dass es zunächst in den häufig vorkommenden Fällen wenn dergleichen Gesuche von den Beteiligten selbst vorgetragen und durch alle zugänglichen Mittel betrieben werden, zweckmässig sein dürfte, es mit den Angaben über die Verdienstlichkeit genau zu nehmen. Zu den sehr beharrlichen Bewerbern gehört auch der g. Flatau . . .' Vote of the cabinet for agricultural affairs, 27 May 1859, ZSAM Rep. 120, A IV 5, vol. 6, fos. 212^{r-v}.

[33] After listing several points in favour of the two applicants, *Freiherr* v. Zedlitz concluded: 'Gleichwohl befinde ich mich nicht in der Lage, die Anträge auf Verleihung des Commerzienraths—Titels für beide, Lehmann und Liebermann besonders zu befürworten. Es existieren hier noch christliche Kaufleute von mindestens gleichen Verdiensten um das öffentliche Wesen, denen bisher auch noch keine Auszeichnung zu Theil geworden ist, und wenn auch die Juden für gleichberechtigt anerkannt werden, so scheint es mir doch nicht unbedenklich sie, vielleicht nur weil sie weniger bescheiden sind, zu bevorzugen.' *Fr.* v. Zedlitz to *Ober-Präsident* of the Province of Brandenburg, Berlin, 4 Apr. 1859, copy in ZSAM Rep. 120, A IV 5, vol. 6, fos. 330^v–331. This in fact repeats a comment, only slightly less explicit, made by one of von Zedlitz's predecessors:

The authorities, in considering recommendations or applications for the title of *Kommerzienrat*, were, as a rule, well aware of the religious affiliation of the applicant. There are, however, curious inconsistencies. In the first place, though the religious profession of a candidate is often recorded, this is not invariably the case.[34] In particular, references to religion became less common during the eighties and nineties. It is difficult to escape the conclusion that, especially in the eighties, references to religion, where they do occur, were introduced with hostile intent. Further inconsistencies (which, however may be without significance though equally, they could reflect differences of attitude) occur with regard to the actual terms employed. These range from 'jüdischer Religion' and 'mosaischen Glaubens' to 'jüdischer Confession' and 'mosaischer Religion'. One reference only describes 'den jüdischen Kaufmann' N. N., while another sates that N. N. 'ist Jude'. That the higher authorities attached some importance to the religious aspect is documented by the fact that the reference to Jewish or Mosaic religion is frequently underlined in pencil. In the actual designations, no clear pattern is to be discerned, and it may be that their employment merely reflected personal idiosyncrasies. Christian associations are referred to more than once. Thus in two cases, bankers of Jewish origin are described as 'evangelischer Religion', in that of another, the writer feels impelled to add 'welcher übrigens der evangelischen Kirche angehört'. In yet other instances, reports state 'von Geburt jüdischer Religion, trat er im Jahre 1849 zum Christenthum über, lässt ... seine Kinder christlich erziehen', 'wogegen seine Söhne getauft sind', and 'seine Kinder hat er sämtlich christlich taufen lassen'. Though the reports in matters of religion are curiously unsystematic, it is difficult to escape the conclusion that, whereas references to conversion and to the Christian education of children are intended to strengthen an applicant's case (in extreme cases, men of Jewish origin are simply described as evangelical), those to Jewishness,

'... kann das Polizei-Präsidium dem Antrage auf Verleihung des Commerzienrathstitels an den älteren Philipp Meyer nichts Erhebliches entgegen stellen, bemerkt jedoch, dass sich wohl mancher gleich und mehr verdiente Mann unter dem hiesigen Handelsstande vorfinden möchte, welchen die Bescheidenheit von ähnlichen Anträgen zurückhält.' Puttkammer to *Ober-Präsident* of the Province of Brandenburg, Berlin, 25 Oct. 1843, copy in ZSAM Rep. 120, A IV 5, vol. 5, fos. 19^{r-v}.

[34] It is possible that, in some cases, well-intentioned officials omitted drawing attention to the religious affiliation of a candidate in order not to impair his chances of success. But in the matter of recording religious affiliations, officialdom was unsystematic whether for Jews or Christians.

An Élite of Notables

particularly from the later sixties onwards, may be introduced with the opposite intent. In some instances indeed, particularly in the eighties, the hostile intent is blatant.

Jewishness, moreover, came to acquire in the eyes of some high officials—largely erroneously, as will be seen elsewhere—a connotation of political liberalism, first after 1848 and, more particularly, during the constitutional conflict in Prussia. An attitude favourable to the policies of the government was sometimes, for Jews in particular, considered a strong recommendation.[35] The reverse could equally be the case.[36] The complicated considerations that might come into play are illustrated by the case of the brothers Gustav and Ferdinand Manheimer in Berlin. These (together with a third brother) were the joint owners of the largest Berlin 'makers-up' (*Confectionshaus*), giving employment to seven to eight thousand people. Whilst Gustav, the oldest, was the senior partner, Ferdinand, the younger, had had the major part in building up the firm. Unable to decide which of the brothers to honour, inspired by the laudable desire not to hurt the feelings of either, the minister of commerce, in 1897, forwarded to the king patents for the appointment of both. At the same time, while positively recommending both brothers, he drew the monarch's attention to the risk of anti-Semitic reactions to the conferment of titles on two partners in the same Jewish business.[37] Incidentally, and without stressing the point, the minister had routinely reported that

---

[35] '. . . Bei dieser guten politischen Gesinnung des Bendix, welche notorisch bei nicht vielen Juden angetroffen wird, glaube ich jetzt eine Auszeichnung desselben wohl befürworten . . . zu dürfen'. *Polizeipräsident* Bernuth to *Ober-Präsident* of the Province of Brandenburg, 20 May 1864, ZSAM Rep. 120, A IV 5, vol. 8, fo. 280.

[36] 'Zur Gewährung einer Allerhöchsten Anerkennung an den g. Liebermann liegt keine Veranlassung vor, da er der Fortschrittspartei angehört.' *Ober-Präsident* of the Province of Brandenburg to *Handelsminister* von Itzenplitz, 15 Nov. 1865, ZSAM Rep. 120, A IV 5, vol. 9, fos. 45^{r-v}.

[37] As already mentioned above, it was official policy not to confer titles on two partners in the same firm. Jewish 'making-up' firms, moreover, were an especial target of anti-Semitic attack. The minister, therefore, wrote as follows: 'Da es sich um eine jüdische Confectionsfirma handelt, so würde, wie ich befürchte, die gleichzeitige Auszeichnung zweier *Geschäftstheilhaber* in der unter dem Einfluss antisemitischer Kreise stehenden Presse einer abfälligen Beurtheilung, vielleicht sogar einer erregten Missbilligung unterzogen werden. Es scheint mir aber nicht rathsam zu sein, durch eine so ungewöhnliche Massregel wie die gleichzeitige Auszeichnung zweier Geschäftstheilhaber derselben Firma einer an sich unerwünschten Polemik Stoff zu geben. Es möchte dies auch deshalb zu vermeiden sein, weil dadurch das Ansehen der Firma zum Nachtheil der Concurrenzfirmen in weitgehender Weise gehoben werden würde.' Brefeld to Wilhelm II, Berlin, 2 Oct. 1897, ZSAM 2.2.1, no. 1590, fos. 70^{r-v}.

both brothers, though not militants, were of liberal political persuasion.[38] The emperor's reply may have surprised the minister. Whilst associating himself with Brefeld's misgivings, Wilhelm II, unlike the minister, stressed the political aspect.[39] In the circumstances, ran his Solomonic judgment, he would defer action until after the next elections. The minister might then resubmit his recommendations with a report on the brothers' political conduct.[40] Both Gustav and Ferdinand Manheimer became *Kommerzienräte* in 1899.

Reports on Jewish candidates also afford interesting glimpses of what might reflect equally Jewish stereotypes in the minds of officialdom, actual Jewish behaviour, or, indeed, a combination of both. One candidate, for example, was commended as being a stranger to the egotism characteristic of his co-religionists.[41] In another case it was noted that a candidate, although a Jew, employed in his office mainly Christian clerks.[42] Of yet another, it was reported that, though a Jew, he had always acted in a Christian spirit.[43] There was the curious comment on a further candidate that, though a Jew, he yet, as a businessman and owner of an estate, enjoyed a good social position.[44]

---

[38] Of Ferdinand, it was reported: 'Politisch ist er fortschrittlich gesinnt, ohne indessen bisher irgendwie agitatorisch hervorgetreten zu sein.' As for Gustav, Brefeld reported that 'dessen politische Stellung mit derjenigen seines Bruders im wesentlichen übereinstimmt', ib., fos. 68ᵛ–69.

[39] The chief of the civil cabinet informed the minister 'dass S.M. der Kaiser und König die Bedenken theilen, welche gegen eine gleichzeitige Verleihung der fraglichen Allerhöchsten Auszeichnung an zwei fortschrittlich gesinnte Geschäftstheilhaber einer jüdischen Firma bestehen, andererseits aber nicht erkennen, wie in der Verleihung des Titels an den jüngeren Bruder für den älteren eine kränkende Zurücksetzung liegen würde'. Chief of the civil cabinet to Brefeld, 16 Oct. 1897, ib., fos. 71ʳ⁻ᵛ.

[40] 'S.M. wolle unter diesem Umständen zur Zeit der gegebenen Anregung überhaupt keine Folge geben und zunächst abwarten, welche Haltung die genannten bei den nächsten Reichstags- und Landtags Wahlen einnehmen werden.' The minister might then resubmit his recommendation 'mit einer Äusserung in letzterer Beziehung' (ib.).

[41] '. . . zumal er dem sonst gewöhnlichen Eigennutz seiner Glaubensgenossen entfernt steht, dagegen nicht frei von Eitelkeit ist.' *Ober-Präsident* von Schlesien (v. Massow) to *Minister* von der Heydt, Berlin, 9 Jan. 1856, ZSAM Rep. 120, A IV 9, vol. 2, fo. 297ᵛ.

[42] 'Er beschäftigt, obwohl selbst Jude, in seinem Comtoir meist christliche Buchhalter.' *Polizeipräsident* to *Ober-Präsident* of the Province of Brandenburg, 30 Aug. 1883, ZSAM Rep. 120, A IV 5a, vol. 1, fo. 66.

[43] '. . . wenngleich Israelit, hat er doch überall im christlichen Sinne gewirkt, und wie ich vom Kreislandrathe vernommen habe, lässt er seine Kinder christlich erziehen.' *Regierungsrat* von Minutoli to *Regierungspräsident Graf* von Zedlitz und Trützschler, 3 July 1856, copy in ZSAM, Rep. 120, A IV 9, vol. 3, fo. 4ᵛ.

[44] N.N. '. . . ist Jude, nimmt aber als Geschäftsmann durch sein Vermögen und als Rittergutsbesitzer, eine gute sociale Stellung ein'. *Regierungspräsident* in Breslau to v. Itzenplitz, Breslau, 26 Apr. 1867, in ZSAM, Rep. 120, A IV 9, vol. 4, fo. 144ᵛ.

Of still another, it was said that precisely because he was a Jew and a traditional liberal, but in times of need a generous patriot, his appointment would be generally welcomed.[45] It is worth noting that comments of this kind occur only in the reports of local authorities and are not repeated in those of ministers to the king.

In general, the evidence seems to suggest, on the part of Prussian officialdom, peripheral prejudices against Jewish candidates but no systematic discrimination at any time. The merits of Jewish applicants are in general fairly, often indeed benevolently, assessed. Where merit, by the Prussian bureaucracy's accepted criteria, could be incontrovertibly established in a Jewish entrepreneur, he would receive the coveted title on equal terms with his Gentile peer. Discrimination against active left-liberals, not, of course, confined to Jews but among whom Jews figured quite prominently, was, except in the early sixties, episodic, unsystematic, and never persisted for any length of time,[46] in the face of commercial merit. Those who successfully passed the bureaucratic selection hurdle (particularly before about 1890), therefore, could be considered members of a genuine Jewish economic status élite.

III

Useful information can be gleaned from a representative sample of some 700 gazetted[47] *Kommerzienräte* (KR) (unless otherwise stated, the term includes *Geh. Kommerzienräte* (GKR)) appointed between 1819 and 1900.[48] The evidence is best presented in diagrammatic form.

Total KR and GKR: 713   GKR: 119   KR: 594
of whom Jewish: 110   21 (17.6%)   89 (14.8%)

Whereas 14.5 per cent (119 out of 603) of Gentile KR became GKR, the figure for Jews was 19.1 per cent (21 out of 110), probably

---

[45] Ibid.
[46] In a number of cases, political 'unreliability' meant a delay of usually two years after which a renewed application would, normally, succeed.
[47] Conferments of titles were published in the *Königlich Preussischer Staatsanzeiger*.
[48] Data are lacking for the periods 1853–60, April 1872–8 inclusive (the last a period with a distinctly above-average proportion of Jewish appointments), and the year 1882. The remainder of the sample is also slightly incomplete but such ommissions as occur are purely random ones. Possible understatement of the Jewish component due to the fact that ethnic origin of the more obscure appointees cannot always be determined is balanced by possible error in a few cases, where ethnicity has been deduced from the name only. Overall, the sample may cover some nine-tenths of all appointments.

betokening a somewhat higher proportion among the latter of important businesses or public figures.

To illustrate the movement over the course of the nineteenth century, this can be broken up into four periods (reflecting the nature of the evidence rather than economic or political factors): 1819–52; 1861–72; 1879–89 (without the year 1882); 1890–1901. Broken up into these divisions, the data present themselves as follows:

1819–52	*KR + GKR*	*GKR*	*KR*
Total:	150	18	132
Jewish:	15 (10%)	2 (11%)	13 (10%)
1861–72			
Total:	102	24	78
Jewish:	19 (18.6%)	4 (16%)	15 (19.2%)
1879–89			
Total:	165	35	130
Jewish:	33 (20%)	11 (31.4%)	22 (16.9%)
1890–1900			
Total:	296	42	254
Jewish:	43 (14.5%)	4 (9.5%)	39 (15.3%)

Several features deserve comment. One is the rise in the proportion of Jews appointed over the first three-quarters of the century, reaching a peak of one fifth of the total in the decade after 1879. Notable in that decade is the high percentage of Jewish GKR, reflecting the prominence of Jewish private bankers in Berlin during the period of German unification. The significant feature of the decade from 1890 is the 'inflation' of conferments in general due, as will be seen, largely to official recognition of economic development in the western provinces of the monarchy—in which Jews do not play a significant part. Overall, the Jewish proportion of appointments declines despite continued relative prominence in both Berlin and the eastern provinces of the monarchy.

Details of occupational distribution tend to confirm the conventional wisdom and strongly emphasize the different nature of the commercial occupations of non-Jew and Jew, as shown in Table 1.

What is significant in the Jewish distribution is the steady decline in the proportion of bankers accompanied by a rise in that of *Kaufleute* as well as of the small proportion of manufacturers (the figure of almost

An Élite of Notables

Table 1. Commercial Occupations of Jews and Gentiles

	Bankers		Merchants[a]		Manufacturers[b]	
	non-Jewish	Jewish[c]	non-Jewish	Jewish[c]	non-Jewish	Jewish[c]
1819–52	6	7 (58.3%)	60	3 (25%)	36	2 (16.6%)
1861–72	10	10 (47.6%)	27	9 (42.8%)	28	2 (9.5%)
1879–89	11	12 (41.3%)	37	13 (44.8%)	55	4 (13.7%)
1890–1900	16	13 (34.2%)	59	16 (42.1%)	137	9 (23%)
	43	42	183	41	256	17

[a] The term 'Kaufmann' covers a wide range of commercial activities, some with industrial connotations.
[b] These are variously described as 'Fabrikant', 'Fabrikunternehmer', 'Fabrikbesitzer', which designations clearly signify nuances. I have also included *Generaldirektoren*.
[c] Percentages of *Jewish* totals.

one quarter for the last decade is not negligible). The variations in the 'ethnic' distribution are, of course, striking. Whilst the *total* numbers of bankers are almost identical, Jewish merchants constitute 22.4 per cent of Gentile ones, 18.3 per cent of the merchant total, overall approximating the 'norm'. The latter fact, however, conceals great chronological differences. In the last decade, Jews constitute 21.3 per cent of all merchants, somewhat in excess of the 'norm'. The great difference is, of course, to be found in manufacturing. Here, there is no Jewish equivalent to the middle-range Gentile factory owners, notably in the western provinces who come to supply so large a part of the total of *Kommerzienräte*. The increase in the number of Gentile industrialists appointed is a striking phenomenon: the figure more than doubles in the last decade compared to the preceding one (as, indeed, does the Jewish figure if at an incomparably lower level). In general, while the number of bankers among *Kommerzienräte* remains almost static in absolute terms for Gentile and Jew alike and that of merchants increases steadily for both ethnic groups, the most striking phenomenon is the rise in the number of Gentile industrialists. The élite of economic notables in the period of its decline is undergoing a radical change of character. The owners of small to medium-sized factories which now flooded it (together, however, with the Haniels, Kirdorfs, Luegs, Poensgens, Krupps, Funkes, Goeckes, Guilleaumes, Klönnes, Schoellers, and others) could no longer be seen, like the old *Kommerzienräte*, as local dignitaries and luminaries of the merchant estate. Moreover, their importance was destined to decline precipitately in the era of the large joint-stock company and organized capitalism that was approaching fast. The age of the lesser provincial factory owner (including the Jewish one) would be of short duration.

The geographical distribution also confirms the view of significant differences between the two ethnic groups. For the present purpose, four regions may be considered, the eastern provinces (with the line drawn roughly at the river Elbe), Berlin and its immediate surroundings, central Germany and 'the west' (beginning very roughly on the river Weser). See Table 2.[49]

Table 2. Geographical Distribution of Titleholders

	Non-Jewish				Jewish					
	East	Berlin	Centre	West	East a	b	Berlin a	b	Centre	West
1819–1852	48	13	4	43	3 (5.8%) [21.4%]		9 (40.9%) [64.3%]		1	1
1851–1872	31	16	7	25	9 (22.5%) [43.0%]		9 (36%) [43%]		2	1
1879–1889	27	19	16	53	16 (37.2%) [48.5%]		15 (44.4%) [45.5%]		1	1
1890–1900	55	30	25	112	11 (16.6%) [29%]		22 (42.3%) [57.9%]		1	4
	161	78	52	233	39 (19.5%)		55 (41.3%)		5 (8.7%)	7 (2.9)

[a] Percentages of *total* for the area.
[b] Percentage of *Jewish* Kommerzienräte.

So far as the Jewish *Kommerzienräte* are concerned several features appear significant. The first is the exceptional position of Berlin with some 40 per cent of the total appointees of Jewish origin but with only just under 13 per cent of Gentile ones. At the level here considered, therefore, it could be said that something under half of economic activity in the capital was 'Jewish'. A further feature is the reduced proportion of Jewish *Kommerzienräte* in the eastern provinces, especially in the last decade, explained partly by the special factor of Magdeburg,[50] partly by the movement of eastern, especially Silesian members of the Jewish economic élite to Berlin. Notable also is the parallel shift among Jewish *Kommerzienräte* in the last two decades between the eastern provinces and Berlin. Jewish economic activity, at this level, is

---

[49] The north (Hamburg, Altona, Kiel, Emden) is excluded for the purpose of simplification. Citizens of Hanseatic towns did not, as a rule, accept Prussian titles (though there were a few exceptions—possibly residents who were not citizens).

[50] The picture would be altered somewhat if Magdeburg, which has been included with the eastern provinces, and which provided a surprisingly large number of KRs—not one a Jew—were, instead, to be considered as part of the centre, where it possibly belongs.

becoming (or has become) concentrated in the capital. In the notable overall shift of conferments to the west[51] and centre, Jews participate only marginally. In general, for members of the Jewish economic élite in Prussia, these shifts have a twofold implication: to the extent that significant economic activity moves from the east to the west, the centre, and non-Prussian parts of Germany, the Jewish economic role declines; to the extent, on the other hand, that economic decision-making comes to be concentrated in Berlin as, in fact, in the age of corporate structures it does to a marked extent, the Jewish role, overall, increases (though not necessarily that of members of the old élite of notables). As will be seen, the Jewish role more particularly of members of the economic élite based in Berlin in the age of 'organized capitalism' is a significant one. Berlin, if not the industrial, becomes increasingly (at the expense of centres like Frankfurt-on-Main, Cologne, or Hamburg) the financial heart of Germany.

IV

Thanks to the information assiduously gathered by Prussian officialdom, it is possible not only to quantify the Jewish economic élite but also to analyse its structure. For the purpose, it is helpful to divide the appointments into five periods (which, however, are arbitrary and unrelated to social or economic developments): pre-1848, 1848–70, 1871–9, 1880–9, and 1890–9.

As a second variable, the Jewish commercial notables of the nineteenth century can be divided into three separate strata. The first of these (I) comprises the *Geheime Kommerzienräte* (GKR), the core of the economic élite. Below this there existed a 'sub-élite (II) composed of men who either managed important businesses (which could be described loosely as 'enjoying a national reputation') or belonged to substantial commercial families—or both, without, however, being of standing to join the charmed circle of GKRs. These in turn shade into the 'rank and file' (III),[52] provincial worthies of purely local or regional

---

[51] According to records kept by the *Oberpräsidium* in Münster there lived in the province of Westphalia in the year 1885 only 24 KRs and 3 GKRs. By 1900, there were already 46 KRs and 5 GKRs. In 1910, the respective figures were 70 and 11. Henning, loc. cit., n. 9 above, p. 4.

[52] For members of this group, it is not always possible to determine ethnic origin with certainty, but errors are unlikely to be large.

importance (there are, of course, a few 'borderline-cases').[53] The numerical distribution between the three categories can be tabulated as follows:

	pre-1849	1849–1870	1871–1879	1880–1889	1890–1899
I	5	11	10	12	9
II	8	12	17	7	25[a]
III	5	12	27	15	20

[a] includes several men who later rose into category I.

Among the features worth noting, besides the overall numerical growth, are the steady proportionate decline, except in the final decade, of group II or, conversely, the rising proportion (not confined to Jewish appointees) of provincial 'rank and file'. Among the broader factors reflected here is undoubtedly a non-economic one, the desire of the Prussian government to reward Jewish notables in the eastern provinces of the monarchy for their 'Germanism' in opposition to Polish elements. As part of this policy the authorities sought to promote economic development in the eastern provinces which, to a great extent, meant encouraging Jewish enterprise. The striking increase in both absolute and percentage terms of category II in the last decade on the other hand is due on the one hand to the fact that the figure includes men who subsequently rose into group I, but may also reflect the growth of the 'sub-élite' as part of the economic expansion following the creation of the German empire. The sharp drop in the proportion of Jewish GKRs in the last decade, from 35 per cent in the previous one to 16.6 per cent—the comparable proportion for *all Geheime Kommerzienräte* is 12.3 per cent (figures for 1882 missing) and 14.9 per cent—would seem to indicate an 'abnormally' high proportion of Jewish GKRs in the earlier decade, probably reflecting the prominence of Jewish bankers and war contractors of the two preceding decades (the proportion of GKR's among Jewish appointees for the period 1871–9 had been 18.5).

[53] Henning's twofold classification of 'Grossunternehmer' including all GKR, KR, and the reservoir of KRs ('die Teilgruppe der Grossunternehmer, worunter die kommerzrätlichen und- ratsfähigen Unternehmer subsumiert wurden') on the one hand and remaining entrepreneurs on the other ('. . . die Teilgruppe der gewerblichen Unternehmer, worunter der Rest der Gruppe, die Kaufleute und Fabrikanten, gezählt wurde', Henning, loc. cit., n. 9 above, p. 3), ignores both the very special status of GKR and the fact that the title of KR could be conferred on relatively modest local notables (III). Moreover, how is one to identify the *papabile* ('kommerzienratsfähige Unternehmer')?

Before examining the groups separately, the totality of Jewish recipients of commercial titles may be considered. These are best broken down by firms rather than individuals (see Table 3).

Table 3. Distribution by Branches of all Jewish Titleholders:

	Banking	Trade	Industry
Vormärz:	8 (50%)	4 (25%)	4 (25%)
1848–1870:	20 (55%)	10 (28%)	6 (17%)
1871–1879:	15 (27%)	25 (46%)	15 (27%)
1880–1889:	14 (38%)	13 (35%)	10 (27%)
1890–1899:	18 (37%)	11 (23%)	19 (40%)

What is, perhaps, most striking in these figures is the percentage shift, after 1870, from trade to industry. As to those engaged in banking, while the figures show a steep percentage decline after 1870, this is followed by a recovery in the following decade, after which the proportion remains stationary at something over one third. As other evidence will show, the Jewish private banker played a significant role in economic life even in the age of fully fledged capitalist industry—more particularly before the massive amalgamations and take-overs of 1904.

Some information is to be gleaned also from a breakdown into capital and provinces (see Table 4).

Table 4. Geographical Distribution of Jewish Titleholders

	Berlin Banking	Trade	Industry	Provinces Banking	Trade	Industry
Vormärz:	5 (45%)	2 (18%)	4 (36%)	2 (50%)	2 (50%)	(—)
1848–1870:	10 (62%)	2 (12%)	4 (25%)	11 (55%)	7 (35%)	2 (10%)
1871–1879:	10 (33%)	12 (40%)	8 (27%)	6 (21%)	16 (55%)	7 (23%)
1880–1889:	7 (50%)	4 (28%)	3 (21%)	7 (29%)	10 (41%)	7 (29%)
1890–1899:	9 (41%)	5 (23%)	8 (36%)	9 (35%)	6 (23%)	11 (42%)
Totals:	41 (44%)	25 (27%)	27 (29%)	35 (34%)	41 (40%)	27 (26%)

The occupational distribution of Berlin Jewish *Kommerzienräte* and that of their peers in the provinces is thus roughly comparable. An exception is the higher proportion of bankers in the capital matched by one of merchants in the provinces, reflecting the relative prominence of local merchants among provincial appointees. The figure for industrialists in Berlin, especially in the final decade, is distorted by the fact that provincial manufacturers tended to take up residence in the capital. Certain fluctuations and trends in the different branches of activity have already been noted. Among the more striking is the increased proportion overall of provincial manufacturers.

V

It is now time to examine in more detail the separate strata and first the *Geheime Kommerzienräte*. The first GKRs were, predictably, leading private bankers: Nathan v. Rothschild (1834), August Heinrich Bendemann (1845), Wilhelm Beer (before 1845), Wilhelm Lehfeld (1853), Alexander Mendelssohn (1854), Abraham Oppenheim (1857 or 1858), Robert Warschauer (1863), Simon Oppenheim (1865), Gerson Bleichröder (1865), Moritz Güterbock (1867), Paul Mendelssohn-Bartholdy (1867), and Mortiz Plaut (1867). The only 'outsiders' were members of the Meyer silk-manufacturing clan, Jacob Abraham Meyer (1841), Joel Wolff Meyer (1842), and Philip Meyer (1856). Among the early GKRs, residents of Berlin predominate (the exceptions Nathan v. Rothschild in Frankfurt, the brothers Oppenheim in Cologne, and, somewhat surprisingly, Wilhelm Lehfeld in Glogau).

In the seventies, there is some diversification, with the arrival of manufacturers: Hugo Kunheim (chemical works) (1870), Benjamin Liebermann (cotton printing) (1872), Louis Reichenheim (textile manufacture) (1874), Wilhelm Herz (vegetable oil and rubber) (1878), and Meyer Magnus ('belated' silk manufacturer) (1879). It is to be noted that the manufacturers are drawn almost exclusively from the textile industry, reflecting the Jewish industrial pattern of the fifties and sixties. Industrialists, however, are still balanced by bankers: Heinrich Wolff (1873), Jacob Landau (1877), Julius Schwabach (1878), Franz Mendelssohn (1879), and Meyer Cohn (1879). The only 'outsider' is Bernhard Jaffé, president of the chamber of commerce and chairman of the municipal council in Posen (1877).

The eighties see a return of the bankers: Georg Fromberg (1880), Heinrich Heimann (1880), Hermann Eduard Veit (1883), Ernst Ladenburg (1883), Bernhard Seligmann (1885), Louis Ephraim Meyer (1886). These, in contradistinction to earlier banking notables, are the leading private bankers of provincial cities: Breslau (Fromberg and Heimann), Frankfurt-on-Main (Ladenburg), Koblenz (Seligmann),

Hanover (Meyer). The only representative of Berlin is Hermann Veit of the prominent banking house of Robert Warschauer. Interspersed with the bankers are a representative of the wholesale produce trade (Isidor Friedenthal, 1881), a leading producer of ladies' overcoats (Valentin Manheimer, 1885), a large-scale army contractor (Simon Cohn, 1887), a wholesale amber merchant (Moritz Becker, 1887), and a manufacturer of, incongruously, shoddy and seamless tubes (Albert Hahn, 1889). Significantly, these are mainly either provincials (Friedenthal in Breslau, Becker in Danzig) or newcomers to Berlin (Hahn from Gleiwitz, Cohn from Kreutzburg OS). An 'outsider' by the nature of his business is Hugo Pringsheim (1886), owner of a *Bank Commissionsgeschäft*. It is, overall, a group with strong provincial associations.

The GKRs of the nineties constitute a heterogeneous group. This includes a number of prominent Berlin bankers: Ludwig Max Goldberger (1893), Ernst Paul Mendelssohn-Bartholdy (1893), Edmund Helfft (1898), to which may be added Louis Gumpert from Brandenburg (1894). By their side figure a wholesale seed-merchant (Ernst Benary, Erfurt, 1892), a linen manufacturer (Joseph Pinkus, Neustadt OS, 1895), a wholesale textile merchant (Lewin Simon, Berlin, 1898) and, the first of a new breed, a leading machine builder and arms manufacturer (Isidor Loewe, Berlin, 1898). The majority of prominent Jewish industrialists, to the extent that they still hankered after titles, would realize their ambition only in the new century.

The evolution of the 'sub-élite' (II) across the different periods also deserves analysis. The relevant data has been tabulated in Table 5. In the 'Vormärz' group, 4 bankers (50 per cent) are matched by 3 men (37 per cent) engaged in trade and 1 manufacturer (12 per cent), predictably in the textile industry; 7 men (87 per cent) from Berlin face

Table 5. Evolution of the 'Sub-Élite

	Banking	Trade	Industry	Berlin	Provs.
Vormärz:	4 (50%)	3 (37%)	1 (12%)	7 (87%)	1 (12%)
1848–1870:	4 (33%)	3 (25%)	5 (42%)	6 (50%)	6 (50%)
1871–1879:	5 (29%)	8 (47%)	4 (23%)	12 (70%)	5 (30%)
1880–1889:	3 (43%)	1 (14%)	3 (43%)	3 (43%)	4 (57%)
1890–1899:	10 (40%)	3 (12%)	12 (48%)	14 (56%)	11 (44%)
Totals:	26 (38%)	18 (26%)	25 (36%)	42 (61%)	27 (39%)

1 (12 per cent) from the provinces (perhaps predictably, Breslau). The prominent commercial families represented are the Behrends, Liebermanns, and the first of the Silesian Friedländers.

In the next period (1849–70), there are striking changes of distribution. Four bankers (33 per cent) and 3 merchants (25 per cent) now confront 5 manufacturers (42 per cent) divided almost equally between engineering and textiles. Only 6 KRs (50 per cent) now come from Berlin, of the remainder, no fewer than 5 are natives of Silesia (Beuthen twice, Gleiwitz, Schmiedeberg, and Breslau—another, though resident in Berlin, is a Silesian textile magnate). Among the prominent families figure Benda, Borchardt, Gerson, Hirsch, Reichenheim, and further Silesian Friedländers. There is thus an almost complete shift from Berlin bankers and merchants to provincial (mainly Silesian) industrialists.

In the following phase (1871–9), the situation is almost reversed. Five bankers (29 per cent) are matched by 8 merchants (47 per cent) and only 4 industrialists (23 per cent). Equally the pendulum has swung back to Berlin with 12 residents (70 per cent) of that city as against 5 provincials (30 per cent) (2 bankers from Frankfurt-on-Main, 1 Breslau banker, and 2 representatives of the Silesian metal industry). The figures reflect the tendency, among others, for industrialists, irrespective of the location of their enterprises, to reside in the capital. The prominent names among the new KRs are Gerson, Reiss, Friedenthal, Caro, and Huldschinsky.

The group for the eighties (1880–9) is smaller than the previous ones. Of its members, 3 (43 per cent) are bankers, another 3 (43 per cent) manufacturers, 1 (14 per cent) is a merchant. Berlin with 3 representatives (43 per cent) and the provinces with 4 (57 per cent) are almost evenly balanced. Of 4 provincials 3 (75 per cent) are Silesians. The relative prominence of Silesian industrialists (both metal and textile) continues. Among the more important names are Kauffmann, Caro, and Kern.

Finally, the last decade (1890–9) sees a striking polarization between on the one hand 10 bankers (40 per cent) and on the other 12 manufacturers (48 per cent), with those engaged in trade reduced to 3 (12 per cent). Fourteen Berliners (56 per cent) outnumber 11 (44 per cent) provincials. Among the latter, the western provinces of the monarchy, perhaps predictably, now gain in prominence, providing 5 out of the 11 KRs (2 from Frankfurt-on-Main, one each from Solingen, Bedburg/Erft, and Metz).

What these figures show is a falling-off in the proportion of bankers between 1848 and 1880—an unexpected finding—and, consistently, of merchants (with the effects of the wars of German unification, however, contributing to an 'abnormal' increase in the decade 1871–9). So far as industrialists are concerned, what stands out is the relative decline in their numbers in the seventies. This may reflect the fact that Jewish industrial activity was passing through something of a trough in the fifties and sixties before the arrival of the second entrepreneurial wave. A relatively high proportion of provincial appointments distinguishes on the one hand the period 1848–70, on the other that of the eighties. There is no evidence of any consistent trend in the distribution between Berlin and the provinces. It may be that in so small a sample there is a large element of chance.

So far as group III, that of the local worthies, is concerned, a detailed analysis is neither possible nor necessary. In general this is a group dominated by provincial merchants (both wholesale and wholesale/retail) and industrialists of essentially local importance. There is also a minority of men engaged in economic pursuits in Berlin of merely local significance (including a number of court suppliers, *Hoflieferanten*), in whose selection patronage of one kind or another seems likely to have played a part. It is, of course, clear that members of this group did not form a reservoir for the recruitment of group II, both on account of significant social differences and because members of both groups in fact received the same title.

VI

Finally, it is possible to consider briefly the evolution of the group as a whole. In *Vormärz* (between 1829 and 1847 incl.) a total of 25 awards to men of Jewish origin is recorded. Twenty-three persons were involved (that is two individuals received two awards each). The number of enterprises, owners of which received awards was 20 (that is there were a few awards to more than one partner in the same firm). Of the firms, the nature of whose activities can be determined (16), 7 (44 per cent) were engaged in banking, 5 (31 per cent) in commerce, and 4 (25 per cent) in manufacturing. Eighteen (78 per cent) of the *Kommerzienräte* were inhabitants of Berlin.

Between 1849 and 1870 inclusive, a total of 46 awards were made, involving 40 individuals. Of enterprises whose activities can be clearly identified (in a few cases, the data are deficient, in some others, the enterprises were of mixed type, combining banking and commerce or commerce and industry), 20 (52 per cent) were banks—compared to 44 per cent in the previous period. This, in fact, was the golden age of the private Jewish banker. Ten firms (26 per cent) were involved in trade (as against 31 per cent previously). Finally, 8 firms (22 per cent) engaged in manufacturing, almost the same percentage as for the previous period. Overall, the only change to be observed is a slight move from commerce to banking (which may reflect some shift both in the occupational distribution of a somewhat wider German–Jewish economic élite and some modification of its function within the Prussian economy—as well as the evolution of the capitalist system in general). Of the awards 24 (52 per cent) went to people resident in Berlin (though some were recent immigrants from the provinces), a striking drop compared to the preceding 78 per cent. The change may reflect both increased economic activity in the eastern provinces (especially Silesia) and some change in official policy on the conferment of titles. Only 2 recipients were residents of the western provinces (bankers in Bonn and Cologne), another of newly acquired Hanover.

Between 1871 and 1879 inclusive, with some quickening of economic activity, a total of 69 awards was recorded, affecting 63 individuals. Of the firms involved among those capable of classification, 20 (34 per cent) were engaged in banking, a striking drop from the previous 52 per cent—reflecting, almost certainly, some decline in the importance of private banking in the face of the advancing joint-stock banks. On the other hand, the number of trading firms, 27 (47 per cent), showed a striking percentage increase over the previous 26 per cent. This reflected, on the one hand, the growing importance of wholesale trade in the German economy, on the other a government policy of conferring titles on merchants of regional importance in provincial centres. Finally, 11 manufacturing enterprises represented 19 per cent of the total, a slight drop compared to the previous period. The most striking feature overall is the increase in the share of merchants at the expense of bankers. Thirty-six awards (52 per cent) went to residents of Berlin, a stationary proportion. Among provincial KRs, there is some shift towards the western half of the monarchy. 'The west' now receives a total of 8 awards, still a small proportion of the total (two bankers in Frankfurt-on-Main, one in Hanover, a manufacturer in the province of Hanover, reflecting a conscious policy of rewarding or seeking friends in recently acquired territories, merchants in Kassel and Koblenz, a seed-grower in Erfurt, and, lastly, a manufacturer of leather goods in *Kreis* Kreuznach).

An Élite of Notables

From 1880 to 1889 inclusive 41 awards went to 40 men of Jewish extraction. Banking received 16 (38 per cent) as did commerce (38 per cent), while manufacturing, with 10 enterprises, claimed 24 per cent. The shift, compared to the previous decade, is from commerce to manufacturing, with the proportion of banking remaining almost stationary. Perhaps the most notable change is geographical with only 14 (33 per cent) of the titles now going to residents of Berlin as against the previous 52 per cent. Of the provincial awards, the majority went to residents of the eastern provinces with Silesia (12, not including some recent migrants to Berlin and Königsberg) being particularly favoured. Awards to the west of the monarchy are confined to 4 (one each in Frankfurt-on-Main, Cologne, Koblenz, and Hanover).

Lastly, between 1890 and 1899 inclusive, reflecting the increased number of nominations, there is a total of 52 appointments involving a similar number of individuals. Banking now obtains 18 (36 per cent), commerce 11 (22 per cent), and manufacturing 21 (42 per cent) awards, thus continuing the shift from trade to industry. The second wave of Jewish entrepreneurship, dating from the late sixties and early seventies, now begins to have an impact. Berlin provides 24 (46 per cent) of new KRs, reflecting a growing tendency for prominent Jewish (possibly more than Gentile) industrialists to reside in the capital irrespective of the location of their factories. As regards the provinces, there is some shift towards the west (3 Frankfurt-on-Main, one each from Burgsteinfurt Westf., Metz, Weilburg/Lahn, Solingen, Essen, and Bedburg/Erft).

Two overall conclusions about the Jewish status élite may perhaps be drawn from the data that have been discussed. The first is that the Jewish share of commercial titles amounts, on average, to some 15–18 per cent of total awards. The evidence relating to the conferment of these titles, moreover, suggests that this may be considered the approximate overall share of Jewish participation in Prussian economic life (and the proportions, outside Prussia, may not have been greatly different). In the second place, the evidence suggests that the general character of Jewish economic activity, in respect of distribution of both type and location, differed significantly from Gentile. A further point of interest is the attitude of the authorities towards economic activity in general and that of Jews in particular, and the role of the Prussian state in the creation of a commercial and industrial bourgeoisie. Some aspects, more particularly relating to distinctive features of Jewish economic activity, will be developed in the chapter that follows.

4
Entrepreneurial Activities

IN the economic pursuits of the Jewish KRs in the nineteenth century, it is possible to distinguish three phases. The first, that of early industrialization, extending roughly to mid-century, has already been examined. The second phase, broadly the age of railway construction covering the 'boom decades' of the fifties and sixties, is the classic age of the Jewish private banker and, to some extent, also of the Jewish military contractor of the wars of German unification. The final phase, coinciding broadly with the 'Great Depression' of the later seventies, eighties, and early nineties is marked on the one hand by the transition of Jewish private industry into the new corporate structure, on the other by a marked Jewish emergence in the rapidly expanding wholesale trade (coal, iron, non-ferrous metals, textiles, consumer goods). While the outlines of these developments reflect, of course, the general development of German industrial capitalism, it may be asked how far the details suggest the existence of specific Jewish features. It may also be considered how far the evidence supports the view of the Jewish entrepreneur as an innovator or, alternatively, as a 'marginal man' operating on the periphery of the economic mainstream. Finally, it may be asked how far the atypical distribution of Jewish entrepreneurship is modified during the period through the marked diversification of Jewish economic activity.

I

The earliest phase of Jewish entrepreneurial activity needs mention only in brief. The branches primarily represented were, as has been seen, textiles (mainly silk, calico, and cotton) and the production of consumer goods (mainly oil and sugar). There is also one substantial publisher (Carl Heyman in Berlin, originally Glogau). Among services gratefully acknowledged by the authorities are those to exports,[1]

[1] Thus, of the two Meyer silk manufactures, the senior (1841) was said to export its products to the whole of Europe and the United States, the junior (1847) to northern

military contracting, and the successful conduct of financial operations of provincial estates (the *General-Landstände*) of West-Preussen, Ost-Preussen, and Pommern—activities in which Jews in particular may have achieved prominence.

The scale of activity—no 'control figures' for Gentile enterprises are available—is indicated by figures giving the numbers employed. Thus L. B. Berend (1829) employed 70 families in his sugar refinery. Israel Moses Henoch (1836) gave employment to an estimated five to six hundred people on his industrial estate at Gleichen. There were 60–80 workers at the oil-presses of Salomon Herz (1837) in Wittenberge. On the other hand Joel Wolff Meyer (1839–40) employed 700 in his silk manufacture in Brandenburg, his uncle Jacob Abraham Meyer (1841) 1,200–1,500 in Berlin and a further 650 in Brandenburg. It was noted that he also provided employment for prisoners, some of whom joined his work-force after discharge. Gebrüder Meyer, the second of the Meyer silk firms, founded by Philip Meyer (1843), was reported as employing over 700. The calico printing firm of Ruben Goldschmidt, working largely for Joseph Liebermann (1843) employed 900–1,000. Finally, the publisher Carl Heymann (1845–6) had 250 employees. Jews were thus substantial employers of labour, more particularly in the textile manufactures of Berlin and nearby towns.

Four men of Jewish extraction may be taken as illustrating characteristic aspects of Jewish economic activity. The banker L. B. Berend (1829) was recommended for a title by Field Marshal Gneisenau.[2] Quartermaster-General (*Generalintendant*) v. Ribbentrop, whose opinion Gneisenau had sought, reported that Berend had not only been an exemplary army supplier during the wars of liberation (1813–15) but had also extended substantial credits to the Prussian army. Since the peace, his economic activities had gained him wide respect and the Prussian state considerable benefits through annual

and eastern Europe, but also to England. The more modest firm of Kiwi David Jacoby (1847) in Johannisburg in turn exported silk, woollen, and cotton textiles to Russia and Poland ('betreibt einen sehr ausgedehnten Handel mit seidenen, wollenen und baumwollenen Waaren nach Poland und Russland') (illegible to the king, Berlin, d. 15 Jan. 1847, ZSAM 2.2.1, no. 1579, fo. 102.).

[2] '. . . Ich selbst habe bei Gelegenheit einiger mit ihm verhandelter Geldgeschäfte seine Uneigennützickeit kennen gelernt und auch andere geben ein vortheilhaftes Zeugnis über ihn ab. Ein solches ist das hier beiliegende, dass ich über ihn von dem Generalintendanten v. Ribbentrop erfordert habe.' Gneisenau to ? *Handelsminister*, Berlin, 1 May 1829, ZSAM Rep. 120, A IV 5, vol. 1, fo. 111.

payments of excise duty from his sugar-refinery of more than 100,000 th. (300,000 marks).[3] In the case of the silk manufacturer Philip Meyer, the authorities commented on production, employment, and

[3] 'Der hiesige Banquier L. B. Berend ist mir in den Feldzügen 1813–14–15 von einer höchst vortheilhaften Seite bekannt geworden, ich habe mich daher auch späterhin häufig nach seinem Benehmen und seinen Schicksalen erkundiget [sic] um mich gelegentlich für eine Auszejchnung desselben durch Titelverleihung verwenden zu können.

In den Feldzügen zeichnete derselbe sich nicht nur durch pünktliche Erfüllung seiner Lieferungs-Verträge sondern auch dadurch aus, dass er stets bereit war, den Anträgen der Administration auf Geld-Vorschüsse Gehör zu geben, und dass er namentlich im Jahre 1815 dem General-Intendanten der Armee einen bedeutenden Credit eröffnete um die heimkehrenden Truppen in einen solchen Bekleidungs-Zustand zu versetzen, dass man an diesen durchaus keinen Mangel spüren konnte. Dadurch beförderte er, dass das Geld, welches die Französischen Autoritäten für die Loskaufung einer allgemeinen Requisition zahlen mussten zum vollständigen Retablissement des materiellen Theiles der Armee auf dem Grund einer Verabredung zwischen dem General-Intendanten und dem Minister der Finanzen nach Berlin geschickt werden konnte. Das auf des Berend Credit gezogene betrug ungefähr 200.000 th. und sollte zwei Monate nach Sicht der von dem General-Intendanten ausgestellten Wechsel durch den Finanz-Minister gezahlt werden, die Cassen waren aber damals erschöpft, der Berend musste auf Zahlung warten, und fügte sich auch ganz willig darin [sic].

Ausserdem habe ich in Erfahrung gebracht, dass der Berend eine Summe von mehr als 2000 th. zur Einkleidung freiwilliger Jäger, eine Summe von 600 th. zum Marsch eines Jäger Detachements nach Breslau, welches ohne diese Unterstützung nicht von hier fort konnte, hergegeben, für die Unterstützung der Blessierten bei Gr. Beeren u. vorzüglich bei Dennewitz rühmlichst gesorgt und überhaupt nicht kleine Opfer aus seinem Vermögen gebracht hat.

Nach hergestelltem Frieden legte derselbe in Gemeinschaft mit seinem nun mehr verstorbenen Bruder eine Zucker-Raffinerie an durch die über 70 Familien ernährt werden, und von welcher der Staat eine jährliche Accise von mehr als 100.000 th erhällt [sic]. Er geniesst in seinem ausgebreiteten Geschäfte die allgemeine Achtung der inländischen und ausländischen Kaufleute und erfreut sich der verdienten Achtung sämmtlicher [sic] corp. Behörden, sowie der Zuneigung und Liebe aller derer, die ihn kennen und dass er als anerkannter guter Patriot seinen so bedeutenden Credit zu Gunsten des Staats benutzen würde, wenn dieser in den Fall kommen sollte, davon Gebrauch zu machen, glaube ich mit Bestimmtheit behaupten zu dürfen.

Unter diesen Umständen, und wenn man berücksichtigt dass der Titel Geheim. Commerzien-Rath sehr vielen Personen zu Theil geworden ist, die ihm an Verdienst für den Staat bei weitem nachstehen und mit denen er nicht in eine gleiche Cathegorie [sic] gebracht werden kann, dürfte, nach meiner Ansicht, ihm der Titel: Geheimer Commerzien-Rath füglich zuzugestehen sein, und fühle ich mich um so mehr berufen, mich um diese Auszeichnung für ihn zu verwenden als seine Bescheidenheit ihm verbietet, diesfalsige Schritte zu thun, und ich es für rathsam halte, wohl erworbene Verdienste auch hinreichend zu belohnen und sich dadurch zugleich der künftigen Dienste eines Mannes zu versichern, der dem Staat in seinen verwickeltsten Lagen wahrhaft und ohne Interesse genützt hat.' Memorandum by *General-Intendant* von Ribbentrop, enclosed in Gneisenau to ?, 1 May 1829, ZSAM Rep. 120, A IV 5, vol. 1, fo. 112[r-v].

Entrepreneurial Activities

exports,[4] while the publisher Carl Heymann was commended for having built up a publishing house with a national reputation, especially in the field of jurisprudence.[5] Lastly, as a representative of the more modest type of KR one might select Kiwi David Jacoby of

[4] '... Im Jahre 1822 gründete er hier eine Seidenwaaren-Fabrik, deren Geschäfts Local sich am Cöllnischen Fischmarkt no. 4 befindet und jetzt so bedeutend ist, dass sie mit den grössten Fabriken des Inlandes wetteifert ... Der Umfang des Geschäfts ist so beduetend, dass gegenwärtig 507 Stühle, wovon sich 476 in Berlin und 31 in Bernau befinden, beschäftigt werden. An dem letzt genannten Orte haben die Gebrüder Meÿer im vorigen Jahre ein Grundstück zur Errichtung eines Fabrikgebäudes acquirirt, dessen Ausbau noch im Laufe dieses Jahres beendet sein und denselben zur Einrichtung einer bei weitem grösseren Anzahl von Stühlen Gelegenheit geben wird. Zur Zeit werden über 700 Arbeiter von ihnen beschäftigt. Die Handlung beschäftigt 14 Comtoristen und hat ein Betriebs Capital von 150 000 bis 200 000th.

Dem älteren Bruder Philipp Meÿer ist es, bei seinen gründlichen Kenntnissen in seinem Fache und durch seine mit grosser Umsicht ununterbrochen fortgesetzten Bemühungen gelungen seine Fabrik zu heben, dass sie den ausländischen Fabriken derselben Art nicht nur gleich steht, sondern sie in einzelnen Artikeln besonders in façonirten Seidenzeugen überflügelt. Der Geschäftsverkehr der Fabrik erstreckt sich ganz besonders auf Baiern [sic] und wird dafür ein Umsatz von 25.000th bis 30.000th gemacht ... Auch gehen die Fabrikate nach den anderen ZollvereinsStaaten, so wie nach Dänemark, Schweden, Russland, Polen, Gallizien [sic], Moldau und Wallachei, und stehen die Gebrüder Meÿer mit den geachtesten [sic] Handlungshäusern dieser Länder in Geschäftsverbindung, haben ausserdem neuerdings auch angefangen, ihre Waaren nach England zu versenden und hoffen, dass sie sich eines glücklichen Erfolges dieser Speculation werden erfreuen können.

Im October v. J. geruhten Seine Majestät der König aus der Fabrik der Gebrüder Meÿer einen Armstuhl mit façonirtem Seidenzeuge bezogen, anzunehmen, und die Fabrik ferner durch Ertheilung der goldenen Huldigungs-medaille zu begnadigen. Ebenso hatten sich die Gebrüder Meyer der allerhöchst belobenden Anerkennung der in ihrer Fabrik gefertigten Stoffe Seitens der Kaiserin von Russland und des Kaisers von Oesterreich Majestäten zu erfreuen, welche Allerhöchst Ihre Zufriedenheit mit den ihnen dedicirten Seidenzeugen durch sehr wertvolle Geschenke zu erkennen gaben...' *Polizeipräsident* von Puttkammer to *Ober-Präsident Ritter* von Meding, Berlin, 25 Oct. 1843, ZSAM Rep. 120, A IV 5, vol. 3, fos. 17–19.

[5] 'Der Buchhändler Carl Heÿmann, 52 Jahre alt, jüdischer Religion, aus Gr. Glogau gebürtig, ist der Sohn eines dort ansässigen sehr geachteten Mannes, der von seinen Renten lebt. Seine Schulbildung erhielt er auf dem katholischen Gymnasium in Gr. Glogau, von wo er in die Siegertsche Buchhandlung in die Lehre kam. Im Jahre 1813 trat er bei dem Jäger Detachement des 3ten Ostpreussischen Infanterie Reglements [sic] als Freiwilliger ein und wurde von Regiments-Kommandeur zweimal zum Offizier vorgeschlagen, von Sr. Majestät dem Könige aber nicht bestätigt. Ende des Jahres 1815, nachdem er seine Entlassung aus dem Militairdienste genommen hatte, übernahm Heÿmann in Gr. Glogau eine Verlags- und Sortiments-Buchhandlung, der er bis zum Jahre 1835 vorstand. Er übersiedelte sich demnächst nach Berlin und etablirte eine Verlags-Buchhandlung. Durch unermüdlichen Fleiss, Umsicht und strenge Rechtlichkeit gewann er sehr bald das Vertrauen der ausgezeichnetsten Literaten, vorzugsweise Preussischer Juristen, höherer Militairs, Architekten und Technologen, so dass er jetzt einer der bedeutendsten literarischen Producenten Deutschlands ist und aus keiner deutschen Verlagsbuchhandlung gehen so viele vaterländische Sachen hervor, als aus der seinigen. Er beschäftigt zur Zeit in seinem Comtoir 4 Commis und 2 Lehrlinge,

Johannisburg, a local small-town merchant, whose enterprise had yet acquired a more than local importance.[6] All four have in common the fact that their economic activities extend beyond the radius of the Prussian monarchy. War contracting, sugar distilling, silk manufacture, publishing, textile and grain trade in the eastern provinces with, on the one hand, exports to Poland and Russia, on the other the provision of grain for the authorities, are areas of economic activity that would clearly commend themselves to Jews and which, in the age of early industrialization, could not be considered marginal. While there is little evidence of technical innovation, the Meyers present an early instance of successful publicity (advertising) through the presentation of samples of their luxury products to a number of crowned heads.

II

The second phase of Jewish entrepreneurship, represented by men who became KRs during the third quarter of the century, reflects

ausserdem aber an Buchdruckern, Schriftsetzern, Schriftgiessern, Kupferstechern, Stereotypeuren, Zeichnern, Coloristen, Buchbindern, Colporteuren gegen 250 Personen.
... Hiernach weiss das Polizeipräsidium dem Wunsch des Herrn Ministers Mühler um Verleihung des Commerzionraths-Titels an den g. Heÿmann nicht nur nichts entgegenzustellen, es muss vielmehr diesen Antrag hiermit gehorsamst befürworten, da sich im vorliegenden Falle alle Momente vereinigten, die es nur wünschenswerth machen einem so geachteten Manne, welcher sich so vielseitig verdient gemacht hat, durch die beabsichtigte Titelverleihung eine öffentliche Anerkennung seitens des Staats zu Theil werden zu lassen.' von Puttkammer to von Meding, Berlin, 6 Feb. 1845, ZSAM Rep. 120, A IV 5, vol. 3, fos. 72–73^v. For further detail on Carl Heymann and the subsequent development of his publishing firm—which survives as an internationally known legal publishing house—see Kurt Schwerin, 'Die Juden in Schlesien' in *Bulletin des Leo Baeck Instituts*, 19, nos. 56–7 (Tel Aviv, 1980), 55.

[6] 'Der Kaufmann Kiwi David Jacoby zu Johannisburg, 45 Jahre alt, Vater von 9 Kindern und mosaischen Glaubens, betreibt einen sehr ausgedehnten Handel mit seidenen, wollenen und baumwollenen Waaren nach Polen und Russland. Ausserdem ist er auch Spediteur und macht als solcher sehr bedeutende Geschäfte da er sowohl das Vertrauen der Käufer als der Verkäufer besitzt. Durch seine Umsicht und Betriebsamkeit ist er ein sehr vermögender Mann geworden, was sich nicht allein in seiner grossartigen Lebensweise sondern auch an den mannigfachen Wohltaten offenbart, welche er so wohl seinen Angehörigen als einer Menge von Hülfsbedürftigen des In und Auslandes ohne Rücksicht auf ihr Glaubensbekenntnis zufliessen lässt. Namentlich hat er während des Notstandes Bedrängte in der mannichfachsten Weise unterstützt.
In den letztverflossenen Jahren hat er, in Folge der Uebernahme von Getreidelieferungen mit der Staatsverwaltung in näherer Verbindung gestanden, wobei er nicht nur seine Verbindlichkeiten auf das Pünktlichste erfüllt, sondern auch stets die grösste Bereitwilligkeit an den Tag gelegt hat, die Interessen der Verwaltung möglichst zu fördern . . .'? Wrisberg to the king, Berlin, 25 Jan. 1847, ZSAM 2.2.1, no. 1579, fo. 102^v.

essentially the age of railway construction. The representative Jewish personalities are in the first stage Abraham Oppenheim in Cologne, in the second Gerson Bleichröder (together with the bankers Robert Warschauer and Moritz Plaut) and the railway entrepreneurs Bethel Henry Strousberg (who however did not seek a commercial title) and Moritz von Hirsch. A second group of Jewish KRs consists of prominent army contractors of the wars of 1866 and 1870, Loebel Schottländer (who also did not seek a commercial title), Sigmund Aschrott, Simon Cohn, and Salomon Lachmann.

The largest single group of Jews whose public services were rewarded by the state were the leading private bankers. The bulk of these, predictably, resided in Berlin: Samuel Bleichröder (1855), his son Gerson (1861 and 1863), Sigismund Benda (1863), Moritz Plaut (1865), Moritz Güterbock (1867), Meyer Cohn, private banker to scions of the Prussian aristocracy (1871), and Julius Leopold Schwabach, Gerson Bleichröder's partner (1873). Other bankers of importance lived in Silesia: Ernst Heimann, Breslau (1852/3), Wilhelm Lehfeld, Glogau (1852), Leopold Kempner, Glogau (1860), and Otto Friedländer, Beuthen (1868). Those in other cities included Simon Oppenheim, Cologne (1859), and Louis Ephraim Meyer, Hanover (1871).

Apart from the bankers, textile manufacturers still figure prominently. Besides Philip Meyer (1865), they include Philip Liebermann (1859/60), in process of switching from the manufacture of silk thread to fashionable calico printing, the prominent calico manufacturers and printers Heinrich Joseph Loewe (1854), Benjamin Liebermann (1865), Adolph Liebermann (1870)—this, in Berlin textile manufacturing, could be considered 'the age of the Liebermanns' just as in private banking (equally with some exaggeration), it could be described as that of the Bleichröders. Besides them, there are the plush manufacturers Salomon Weigert in Schmiedeberg (1856) and Hermann Kauffmann in Thannhausen (1868), as well as the linen producer Samuel Fränkel in Neustadt OS (1869 and 1872). Towards the end of this phase the growing commercial importance of the leading fashion and dress store in Berlin, Gebr. Gerson, and of the leading German manufacturers of ladies' wear, Gebr. Manheimer, achieves recognition by the conferment of the title of KR on Benny Gerson (1871) and Valentin Manheimer (1873).

After the textile manufacturers, the largest group of Jewish KRs is that of wholesale merchants trading in products ranging from hops, wool, cotton, grain, and colonial products to wine, timber, coal, metals, seeds, lava and tuff. In the same category there are the war contractors supplying 'fodder' for man and beast. Other KRs engage in the production of consumer goods, ranging from oil, fresh milk, or mineral water (Karlsbad) to spoons, snuff, and paper products. There are jewellers supplying the wealthy and socially prominent. (The great age of the 'court supplier' (*Hoflieferant*), however, is deferred until the next phase under the German empire.)

Finally, there are some proto-industrialists; the financier brothers Oppenfeld (title refused 1854), co-founders of the Laura Hütte in Silesia (later taken over by Gerson Bleichröder), Moritz Friedländer (1854), and his son Dr Otto Friedländer (1868), both in Beuthen. These, characteristically, were bankers investing capital with indifferent success in Silesian mining operations. From a different direction came Philip Liebermann (1860) who, out of the textile industry, diversified (unusually) into mining and machine building. (It was at his Heinrichshütte near Sprottau that his celebrated grandson Emil Rathenau first learnt his trade.) The Hirsches of Halberstadt (Joseph Hirsch, 1869), long combining metal trading with manufacture, had recently (1863), as already mentioned, become owners of Messingwerk near Eberswalde, adapted to the manufacture of brass and copper parts (for locomotives among other things).

Within the general framework of these varied economic activities, certain contributions to the common good were singled out for notice by the authorities. As before, the provision of employment figured prominently. The orders of magnitude involved suggest what would, by later standards, be considered medium-sized enterprises employing hundreds rather than thousands (however it may be doubted whether many firms in Prussia—or *a fortiori* in the rest of Germany—at this time in fact employed more than 1,000 workers). The typical Jewish enterprise whose owner was made a KR may in fact have employed some five to eight hundred people:

Saling, Bonheim (1853)	spoons and silverware	150
Loewe, Heinr. Jos. (1854)	cotton (*Kattun*)	500
Friedländer, Moritz (1854)	mines and foundries	'several hundred'
Meÿer, Philip (1856)	silk	800
Weigert, Salomon (1856)	plush and carpets	*c.*600
Liebermann, Philip (1859/60)	cotton	700–800

Liebermann, Benj. (1865)	silk	400
Lehmann, D. J. (1859/60)	plush and woollen prod.	780
Gerson, Moritz (1868)	fashions	c.450
Hirsch, Jos. (1869)	brass and copper	500
Kauffmann, Hermann (1868)	cotton weaving	500
Herz, Wilhelm (1869)	vegetable oil	300
Dahlheim, Louis (1869)	cotton	1,000
Wolff, Moritz (1870)	cotton	400
Gerson, Benny (1871)	fashions	300
Bodenheimer, Gumpert (1871)	paper products	200
Fränkel, Samuel (1872)	linen (partly on 'putting-out' system)	3,300
Landau, Heinr. (1873)	tuff and lava	400
Manheimer, Valentin (1873)	ladies' coats (*Konfektion*)	1,000

Here the most distinctive contribution was the provision of work—with official backing—for near-destitute obsolescent Silesian handloom weavers.

The description of some characteristic businesses throws light on the evolution of Jewish manufacturing in this phase. Thus court supplier (*Hoflieferant*) Bonheim Saling (1853) at his foundry in Tassdorf near Berlin employed 100 workers and 50 hp. In his workshop in Berlin (*Schmelzerei*), he employed a further 50 people in the manufacture of silver and silver-alloy wares. His products found a market as far away as Australia.[7] Saling's was a skilled craft industry conducted on a relatively modest scale, but with some serial production (of spoons) and a considerable export market. A different type of commercial-industrial activity is described in the recommendation

---

[7] 'Der Kaufmann, Fabrikbesitzer und Hoflieferant Bonheim Saling . . . ist Besitzer des Hüttenwerkes Tassdorf bei Berlin, welches mit 50 Pferdekräften und 100 Menschen arbeitet. Dieses Hüttenwerk besteht in einer Giesserei, einem Walzwerke, einer Drahtzieherei und einer Löffelfabrikation. Es werden auf diesem Werke jährlich ca. 4000 Ctr Metalle verarbeitet, bestehend in Peru Silber, Bleche [*sic*] und Draht. Die Löffelhütte fertigt jährlich durchschnittlich 30 000 Dutzend Löffel an. Ausserdem hat Saling hier Monbijou Platz No. 3 eine Schmelzerei zu Tombai, Parasilber, Neusilber und echtem Silber. Er beschäftigt hier in und ausser dem Hause durchschnittlich über 50 Menschen . . . Ueber die gewerblichen Verdianste des g. Saling wird allgemein nur zu seinen Gunsten geurtheilt. Er belebt durch seine Thätigkeit den bereits angedeuteten Zweig der Industrie in einer Weise [illegible] seine Fabriken sich in voller Blüthe befinden und die Ausfuhr sich von Jahr zu Jahr mehrt, auch findet das von ihm erfundene Peru-Silber immer mehr Anklang und verspricht mit der Zeit einer der gesuchtesten Handelsartikel zu werden . . .' *Polizeipräsident* v. Hinckeldey to *Minister* v. d. Heydt, Berlin 14 Dec. 1853, ZSAM Rep. 120, A IV 5, vol. 4, fos. 215–16.

for Joseph Hirsch of Halberstadt (1869), commended more particularly for the manufacture of seamless tubes.[8] Here there is a substantial trading firm diversifying into large-scale factory production. In the textile industry also, mechanization was progressing as illustrated in connection with the conferment of a title on Moritz Wolff (1870). Wolff's factory is described as one of the most important in Germany.[9] Lastly, two enterprises with employees running into four figures show the top range of Jewish entrepreneurship towards the end of the period. One was the large linen manufacture built up by Samuel Fränkel (1872) in Neustadt OS, employing over 3,000 people.[10] This

[8] 'Der g. Hirsch, Mitinhaber der Firma Aron Hirsch & Sohn in Halberstadt, ursprünglich vermögenslos, begründete vor länger als 40 Jahren daselbst ein Handelsgeschäft mit Kupferwaaren, welches anfänglich nur in kleinem Umfange betrieben, durch die rastlose Thätigkeit und die unerschütterliche Solidität seines Gründers sich allmählich in einem Maasse erweiterte, dass es gegenwärtig zu den grossartigsten Metallgeschäften der Monarchie gehört und den Handel in dieser Branche nach allen Welttheilen vermittelt. Durch den g. Hirsch ist die Actien Kupferhammerbetriebsgessellschaft zu Ilsenburg ins Leben gerufen, die neben einem beträchtlichen Gewinn für die Actionäre, einer grossen Anzahl von Arbeitern die Existenz sichert. Er hat vor einigen Jahren das Messingwerk Hegermühle bei Neustadt-Eberswalde, welches bis dahin nicht prosperierte, vom Staate käuflich erworben und demselben durch seine Einsicht und Energie eine solche Ausdehnung verschafft, dass es jetzt mehr als 500 Personen lohnend beschäftigt. Er hat ferner in Halberstadt die Fabrikation von Kupfer- und Messingröhren ohne Naht eingeführt, die bei dem Betriebe der Dampfmaschinen wegen ihrer anerkannten Vorzüge sehr gesucht sind und bis dahin nur aus England und Frankreich bezogen werden konnten...' von Itzenplitz to the king, Berlin, 13 Jan. 1869, ZSAM 2.2.1, no. 1581, fos. 120^{r-v}.

[9] '... Moritz Wolff ... ist der älteste Chef des Handlungshauses *Nathan Wolff & Sohn*, welches in der Spandauerstrasse No. 17 sein Geschäftslokal und in Köpenick sein umfangreiches Fabrik-Etablissement hat. Der Betrieb des Letzteren, welches einen Flächenraum von 24 Morgen bedeckt, geschieht mittels dreier Dampfmaschinen zu welchen 7 Dampfkessel sowie 9 Walzen und Druckmaschinen gehören und erstreckt sich auf Fabrikation, sowie auf Bleichen, Drucken, Färben und Appretieren seidener wollener und hauptsächlich baumwollener Garne und Stoffe. Die Fabrik ist eine der bedeutendsten Deutschlands und wird ihrem Werthe nach auf 700 000th geschätzt. Durchschnittlich werden täglich 400 Arbeiter beschäftigt. Der jährliche Umsatz beträgt circa 200 000 Stück bedruckter Zeuge à 80 bis 85 Ellen Länge, so dass ein jährlicher Umsatz von etwa 3 Millionen Thaler erzielt wird. Der Absatz erstreckt sich nicht blos auf Europa, sondern ist auch auf Canada, Süd-Amerika und Japan ausgedehnt.' *Polizeipräsident* v. Wurmb to von Itzenplitz, spring 1870, ZSAM Rep. 120, A IV 5, vol. 11, fos. 193^{v}–194.

[10] 'Seit 25 Jahren besteht die vom Jubilar begründete Damast, Zwillich und Leinwandfabrik zu Neustdt O/S und hat während dieser Zeit einen Aufschwung erreicht dass sie Tausende von Arbeitern beschäftigt und ihre Waaren, ausser dem Absatze im Inlande, bis in das fernste Ausland versendet. Ein von mir eingesehener Ausweis thut dar, dass g. Fränkel gegenwärtig bei der Hand- und mechanischen Weberei 3043 Arbeiter, bei der Bleicherei und Appretur 205 Arbeiter, ferner 23 verschiedene Handwerker, in dem Comtoir 33 Commis, Buchhalter, Correspondenten

is a firm with extensive exports which appears, in large measure, to have accomplished the transition from manual work to mechanization. The second is the 'making-up' firm of the brothers Manheimer with Valentin (1873) the most active.[11] This represents a new branch of economic activity in Berlin and one in which the firm was destined for considerable expansion.

Among services to the economy stressed in the official reports, exporting is prominently figured (hops, Joseph Flatau (1853); silverware, Bonheim Saling (1853); silken goods, Philip Meyer (1856); silk thread, Philip Liebermann (1860); colonial produce, Theodor Jacob Flatau (1863); cloth, Joseph Behrend (1866); textiles, Hermann Kauffman (1868); linen goods, Samuel Fränkel (1869); coal, Emanuel Friedländer (1869); metal products, Joseph Hirsch (1869); textiles, Moritz Wolff (1870); ladies' coats, Valentin Manheimer (1873). While in some cases exports were on a world-wide scale, in others they were directed more

beschäftigt. Nächst dem befinden sich fast das ganze Jahr drei junge Leute auf der Reise, um die Kunden in Deutschland, Oesterreich, Russland, Dänemark, in der Schweiz und Holland zu besuchen, und in Berlin, Hamburg, Paris, Constantinopel, Riga, Neapel und Genua sind Agenten für den Verkauf angestellt. In Deutschland zählt jede irgend nennenswerthe Leinenhandlung, darunter auch einige in Elsass und Lothringen, zur Kundschaft der Fabrik, im Ausland und jenseits des Oceans besitzt letztere aber ebenfalls die vorzüglichsten Verbindungen, z.B. in Nordamerika, Frankreich, Russland, Oesterreich, in der Türkei, in Italien, in der Schweiz, in Holland, Belgien, Dänemark, Schweden und Norwegen, während die Bezüge für Mittel- und Südamerika durch Hamburger Exporteure besorgt werden.

Der Geschäftsgang ist in allen Stadien des colossalen Geschäfts ein musterhafter, wozu die vom g. Fränkel mit bemerkenswerther Umsicht gegebenen Intruktionen für die verschiedenen [?] wesentlich mitwirken. [There follows a description of social provisions, not relevant at this point.] Es liegt auf der Hand, dass die bedeutenden Beträge, welche durch die Fabrik in Circulation kommen, von wesentlichem Einfluss auf den Wohlstand der Stadt Neustadt und ihrer Umgebung sind. Dabei ist Commissionsrath [for some unknown reason Fränkel must have failed to meet the criteria for a *Kommerzienrat*, the more highly regarded distinction] Fränkel seinen Arbeitern gegenüber ein gütiger Fabrikherr und ein treuer Helfer . . .

Durch alle diese Kundgebungen tüchtiger Geschäftsverwaltung, industrieller Begabung und richtiger Behandlung seiner zahlreichen Arbeiter gilt Commissionsrath Fränkel in industrieller und finanzieller Beziehung als die hervorragendste Persönlichkeit an der oesterreichischen Landesgrenze . . . Seine Fabrikate sind bei allen Industrieausstellungen, zuletzt in Paris, premirt worden und er bereitet sich vor, die Wiener Welt-Ausstellung sehr reichlich zu beschicken . . .' *Regierungspräsident* von Hagemeister to von Itzenplitz, Oppeln, 18 Apr. 1872, ZSAM Rep. 120, A IV 9, vol. 6, fos. 30–31^v.

[11] '. . . Kaufmann Valentin Manheimer hierselbst . . . gilt für einen der grössten Industriellen und den eigentlichen Schöpfer des so bedeutend gewordenen Confectionsgeschäfts. Er bechäftigt über 1000 Arbeiter und sein Platz im Export Geschäft gehört zu den bedeutendsten. Unter den Manufacturisten Berlins nimmt er eine entschieden hervorragende Stellung ein . . .' von Itzenplitz to the king, Berlin, 11 July 1873, draft, ZSAM Rep. 120, A IV 5, vol. 13, fos. 151^{r-v}.

specifically towards eastern Europe. Imports figure more rarely: Moritz H. Güterbock (1857) bought grain for the Prussian government in Hungary, Theodor Jacob Flatau (1863) imported raw cotton from India, the USA, and England. There were cases of import substitution, Emanuel Friedländer replacing English coal with Silesian for the Berlin gasworks or Joseph Hirsch (1869) producing the seamless tubes hitherto imported from England and France. In general, the evidence suggests marked Jewish involvement in international trade as well as in manufactures with a substantial exporting potential.

Prominent Jewish bankers and merchants were commended for rendering to the authorities a variety of services. Abraham Oppenheim of Cologne, for instance, was able to serve the Prussian prime minister intriguingly in 'an important foreign matter'.[12] Moritz Plaut (1867 and 1868) supplied information on national and especially international commercial matters,[13] Heinrich Behrend in Danzig provided expert advice on international maritime law. Gerson Bleichröder (1863) assisted the Prussian government in its financial operations.[14] Philip Elkan (1873) not only supplied horses to the Prussian armies but, through his trade, was able to furnish valuable intelligence.[15] Salomon

[12] '. . . da für diese Auszeichnung in den, von Ersterem dem früheren Minister Präsidenten von Manteuffel in einer wichtigen auswärtigen Angelegenheit geleisteten Diensten ein besonderes Motiv vorlag.' von der Heydt to the king, 16 Apr. 1859, ZSAM 2.2.1, vol. 1580, fo. 204^v.

[13] 'Der Commerzienrath Moritz Plaut zeichnet sich durch Reichthum und Solidität, besonders aber durch ungewöhnliche geistige Begabung nicht minder aus. Er ist ebenfalls Mitglied des Centralausschusses der Preussischen Bank, unterstützt uns aber ausserdem, wie wir schon bei einer früheren Gelegenheit hervorgehoben haben, durch Auskünfte über hiesige und auswärtige Häuser, durch Rath und That bei unseren Silberbeziehungen, sowie durch die werthvollsten Mittheilungen über die Vorgänge an allen grossen Börsenplätzen fortlaufend und mit einer Uneigennützigkeit und Hingebung, welche nicht genug von uns anerkannt werden kann . . .' Kgl. Preussisches Hauptbank Directorium to von. Itzenplitz, 11 Feb. 1867, ZSAM REP. 120, A IV 5, vol. 8, fos. 139^v–140.

[14] '. . . Um dieselbe Zeit wurde auch die Preussische 4/2% Anleihe von 1859 nöthig. Gerson Bleichröder zeichnete eine grosse Summe und veranlasste hierzu auch andere grosse Häuser und Institute, so dass ein glückliches Resultat die Folge war. Ebenso hat derselbe der hiesigen Königlichen Münze Millionen Silbergeld geliefert, *Polizeipräsident* v. Bernuth to von Itzenplitz, Berlin, 14 Dec. 1863, ZSAM Rep. 120, A IV 5, vol. 8, fos. 172–3.

[15] '. . . Mit Hülfe seines erheblichen Vermögens ist es ihm möglich geworden, in den stattgehabten Kriegen, namentlich in dem Feldzuge 1870/1 der Militairverwaltung sehr nützliche Dienste zu leisten. In kurzer Zeit lieferte er eine bedeutende Zahl von Pferden in guter Qualität und trug dadurch zur Beschleunigung der Mobilmachung, namentlich der Kolonnen und der Formationen der Hauptquartiere wesentlich bei. Schon vorher hatte er in uneigennütziger und patriotischer Weise Nachrichten über die Pferde-

Lachmann rendered similar services in his capacity as a wholesale grain dealer.[16]

If one considers the Jewish industrial entrepreneurs of the 'second generation' as a whole, rewarded in the fifties, sixties and early seventies for their services, what appears significant is the continuing preponderance of men from the textile industry. They are based in Berlin and Silesia. If, as a control, one looks at an incomplete sample of Gentile KRs in the textile industry, what stands out besides the location of their manufactures (Görlitz, Züllichau, Salzwedel, Burg, Potsdam) is the fact that they are described mainly as cloth manufacturer (*Tuchfabrikant*), which seems to distinguish them from the 'Jewish' calico and linen manufacturers. The location of their manufactures is in small towns, usually on the periphery of the province of Brandenburg. Though the Gentile appointments considered here relate to the years 1836–52, while the Jewish ones occur mainly in the sixties, the differences are sufficiently marked to suggest at any rate the possibility that the Gentile cloth industry (no doubt producing mainly military uniforms) may have differed from the Jewish one devoted mainly to the production of consumer goods for domestic and foreign consumption.

For the sixties, comparisons are difficult as the authorities, in gazetting new KRs, all too often described them as 'Kaufmann' or 'Fabrikbesitzer' without further specification. It is, however, suggestive

Ankäufe der französischen Regierung beschafft und zu diesem Behufe Reisen auf eigene Kosten ausgeführt. Auch seit Beendigung des Krieges ist er fortgesetzt bemüht, der Regierung Burer Kaiserlichen und Königlichen Majestät nützliche und zuverlässige Mittheilungen über den Pferdebestand fremder Armeen und Pferde-Ankäufe für militairische Zwecke im Auslande zu machen . . .' von Roon to the king, Berlin, 11 July 1873, ZSAM 2.2.1, no. 1582, fo. 229. '. . . Die Verdienste des g. Elkan für das Militair und für die Orientierung über die einschlagenden Verhältnisse des Auslandes sind in der That sehr hoch zu schätzen und ist es von entschiedenem politischen Werth der bisherige Willfährigkeit des g. Elkan auch für die Zukunft möglichst zu sichern . . .' (ib., fo. 230).

[16] 'As the Prussian army and its allies entered Bohemia in 1866, the general staff did not know where the main force of the enemy was concentrated. One of the commanding generals, probably von Roon, told him about that difficult situation. Salomon Lachman answered him, he could find that out in a short time. He ordered his Berlin office by telegram, to wire buying orders of oats to all grain dealers located in the Bohemian border area with whom his company was in business relations, for immediate delivery. From the telegraphed answers he could easily pin down the battle line of the Austrian army. The army was where the oats were sold out. As a result, the Prussian army attacked and defeated the Austrians at Koeniggrätz . . .' From typewritten MS by Kurt Lachmann (Salomon Lachmann's grandson) d. Dachau, 15 Nov. 1970, original in possession of the Leo Baeck Institute in New York.

that Gentile KRs include the well-known cotton spinner Heinrich Gruschwitz in Neusalz (1865) (again, however, Jews were not prominent in the manufacture of thread—which, possibly, fed the cloth industry and hence the production of uniforms), a factory owner (*Fabrikbesitzer*), and a merchant and factory owner from Waldenburg and its region (1863 and 1869), where 'Jewish' enterprise was also active—both probably engaged in textile production. One Gentile silk manufacturer in Berlin had become a KR in 1847, a factory owner in Krefeld appointed in 1842 may have become a silk producer. Overall, though the evidence is fragmentary, it would appear that the overlap between the 'Jewish' and 'non-Jewish' sectors in the early textile industry was small.

Outside the textile field, the Jewish share in manufacturing was a modest one. Perhaps worth noting is Jewish participation in the early chemical industry (Kunheim, Goldschmidt, Paul Mendelssohn-Bartholdy in the AG für Anilinfabrikation in Treptow). In the commercial sector what is significant is the persistence, mainly against the background of the wholesale produce trade, of the traditional Jewish role as military suppliers and contractors (Schottländer, Cohn, Lachmann, Aschrott, Grünfeld, Elkan). This, in fact, is a field of activity in which Jews may have enjoyed a near-monopoly. The history of the contribution made by Jewish contractors to the unification of Germany (and here bankers like Gerson Bleichröder, Jacob Landau, or Ludwig Bamberger must be included) remains to be written. Arguably, in providing the tools such members of the Jewish economic élite were hardly inferior in importance even to the 'cannon king' Alfred Krupp himself.

III

In the banking sector, meanwhile, the major activity consisted in the financing of railway construction. The demand for investment capital in this field was huge, and it was met in no small degree by Jewish financiers. This was a sphere of activity frequently referred to in connection with the conferment on Jews of commercial titles. Such was the case with Ernst Heimann (1852/3), Moritz Ullmann (1856), Moritz Güterbock (1857), Gerson Bleichröder (1863), Paul Mendelssohn-Bartholdy (1867), Bernhard Jaffé (1868), Emanuel Friedländer (1869), Heinrich Fromberg (1869), Isidor Friedenthal

(1869 and 1871), and Moritz Wolff (1870). What is particularly striking is the number of provincial bankers prominent in regional railway financing: Heimann, Ullmann, Fromberg, and Friedenthal in Breslau, Jaffé in Posen, the brothers Oppenheim in Cologne, Moritz Cohn, native of Dessau (Thüringische Eisenbahn, Werra Bahn, Magdeburg–Halberstädter Bahn) and Seligmann Ladenburg in Mannheim. The role of the—mainly Jewish—private banker in mobilizing investment capital for early railway construction (extending from the mighty Rothschilds who, however, financed in the main construction outside Germany to the relatively modest provincial banking houses) awaits detailed elucidation. At the same time, Jewish railway entrepreneurs and managers ranged from men operating on an international scale like Bethel Henry Strousberg or Moritz von Hirsch (Baron Maurice de Hirsch) and, in a later generation, Alfred von Kaulla, to the more modest Pringsheims of Breslau engaged in railway management in Upper Silesia. A more detailed examination of Jewish involvement in railway construction and management (as well as in the production of railway parts and equipment) would, equally, require a separate study. For the moment, some illustrations of these activities must suffice.

Among earlier Jewish railway 'magnates', Abraham Oppenheim of Cologne perhaps takes pride of place.[17] Oppenheim, as a prominent banker, played a major part in the creation in 1835 of the company set up to construct the important line linking Cologne and Antwerp.[18] For the next forty-three years, he would devote himself indefatigably to the affairs of this Rhenish railway company,[19] first as provisional administrator, then, from 1837 to 1844, as, in effect, its managing director, finally as a vice-president. No less prominent was Oppenheim's part in the transactions producing the Cologne–Minden

[17] For some details see particularly 'Abraham Freiherr von Oppenheim (1804–1878)' in *Mitteilungsblatt der Industrie- und Handelskammer zu Köln*, 5, No. 19 (1 Oct. 1950), 297 ff. Cf. also Alfred Krüger, *Das Kölner Bankiergewerbe* (Essen, 1925), pp. 68 ff.
[18] '. . . So hatte sich Abraham Oppenheim in der Tat schon durch lange zuvor geführte Verhandlungen der Bereitschaft namhaftiger, zum Teil schon international bekannter Häuser zum Bau dieser ersten Bahn versichert. Seine "Comparenten-Liste" wies unter 27 befreundeten Firmen die Rothschildschen Häuser in Frankfurt, Paris und Neapel, die Häuser Mendelssohn in Berlin und Heine in Hamburg auf. Zusammen mit ihnen vertrat er rund ein Viertel der ursprünglich veranschlagten Bausumme' (loc. cit. n. 17 above, p. 298). The capital requirement had originally been estimated at 2 million thaler but this had soon risen to 3 million (ib.).
[19] It was described as the 'Iron Rhine' ('der eiserne Rhein von Köln nach Antwerpen'), loc. cit.

railway, key to the development of Westphalian industry,[20] as well as an essential link in the railway network of the Prussian monarchy. The role of the Oppenheim bank in the financing of this crucial line was, in fact, preponderant.[21]

Outside Germany, Oppenheim's financial involvement extended also to railway construction in France, the line from Paris to Versailles, the 'Ligne du Nord', and that linking Strasburg with Basle.[22] Abraham Oppenheim's contribution, through his activities as a railway financier, to the development of the Ruhr was immeasurable.[23] So, broadly, was his role in channelling international capital into the growing industries of the region.[24]

Another private bank involved in railway financing ws that of the Mendelssohns in Berlin. As Joseph Mendelssohn told a fellow banker in 1845, a firm that declined to participate endangered its position.[25]

[20] '... deren Linie über Duisburg und Dortmund mitten durch das Herzstück von Kohle und Stahl führen sollte' loc. cit.

[21] '... Bei der definitiven Gründung am 9 Oktober 1843 erreichten die notariellen Zeichnungen seines Hauses eine in dieser Form nie wieder erreichte Höhe von übe 8½ Millionen Talern—vergleichsweise das Doppelte von Schaaffhausen, das Vier- und Sechsfache anderer Häuser. Auch die für den weiteren Ausbau dieser Bahn benötigten Summen—in den Jahren 1847-1853 Obligationen in der Höhe von 9 Millionen Talern—sind von Abraham Oppenheim im Verein mit Deichmann, später mit Mevissen, übernommen worden' loc. cit. n. 17 above.

[22] Ib. For Oppenheim's prominent involvement in railway construction in the Habsburg Monarchy see ib., p. 299.

[23] '... und wenn man die Annalen auch nur oberflächlich durchblättert und bei den entscheidanden Gründungen der dreissiger und vierziger Jahre immer wieder dem gleichen Vorgang mit fast den gleichen Namen begegnet, so erkennt man bald dass die Bildung solcher finanziellen Kraftzentren eine der wesentlichen Bedingungen und Voraussetzungen für die industrielle Erschliessung des ganzen rheinisch-westfälischen Wirtschaftsraumes war' loc. cit.

[24] '... Die meist verwandtschaftlich durchsetzten Beziehungen zu einer Reihe der erlesensten Träger der europäischen Grossfinanz mit Sitz in Frankfurt a.M., Karlsruhe, Dresden, Berlin, Hamburg, Brüssel, Amsterdam, Paris, Wien und Prag, die seit den 30er Jahren ausgebaut wurden, haben die Beteiligung des Bankhauses nicht nur an zahlreichen deutschen Finanzgeschäften ausserhalb Rheinland-Westfalens sondern auch an grossen ausländischen Finanzgeschäften im Gefolge gehabt. Sal. Oppenheim jun. & Co. spielten ferner im 2. Jahrhundertdrittel die vorzügliche Mittlerrole bei der Hinzuziehung belgisch-französischen Kapitals für die Finanzierung werdender industrieller und sonstiger Grossunternehmer der deutschen Westmark.

Besonders hervorzuheben ist in diesem Zusammenhang das bereits sehr zeitig entwickelte Freundschaftsverhältnis zur Spitze der europäischen Grossfinanz, dem Hause Rothschild, dass sich häufig und in verschiedenster Richtung auswirkte, obwohl es auf die Dauer nicht immer einen einheitlichen Zug aufwies . . .' (Krüger, op. cit., n. 17 above, p. 68). The Oppenheims eventually began to engage in financial enterprises designed to break Rothschild near-monopolies.

[25] '... aber in Rücksicht auf Eisenbahnactien gleichen sich Paris, London u. Berlin wie ein Ei dem Andren. Diese Actien verschlingen alles Geld, alle Speculation und alles

Among the flotations in which the Mendelssohns had earlier had a stake had been that of the Berlin–Stettiner Eisenbahn in 1836. Shares to a nominal value of more than ¾ million thalers had been subscribed with Jewish private bankers prominent among the subscribers. Friedrich Gottlieb v. Halle (80,000 th.) was followed by F. Mart Magnus (75,000 th.) and by the brothers Joseph and Alexander Mendelssohn (50,000 th.) Thirty thousand th. each were subscribed by Jacobson & Riess, M. Oppenheims Söhne, and the presumably Gentile banker Carl W. I. Schultze, 26,000 th. by E. F. Meyer, 25,000 each by Meyer & Co. and the Gentile house of Anhalt & Wagener. Subscriptions for 20,000 each came from S. A. Liebert & Co. in Berlin and from the firm of Jacquier & Securius.[26] While no useful purpose would be served by working out percentages, names on the list of subscriptions clearly indicate a preponderance of Jews.

When, a generation later (in 1866), the grand duchy of Baden raised a 4½ per cent loan of 5 million Prussian thalers to finance railway construction,[27] 4 million were allotted for distribution by the Direction der Disconto-Gesellschaft in Berlin, the rest for distribution by the Jewish banking house of W. H. Ladenburg & Söhne in Mannheim. Those underwriting the issue included, besides the Königl. Seehandlungs Societät (the Prussian State Bank), the Berliner-Handels-Gesellschaft, S. Bleichröder, F. Mart. Magnus, Mendelssohn & Co., Gebr. Schickler, and Robert Warschauer & Co.—the élite of the Berlin banking establishment. The actual allocation of shares, presumably reflecting approximately the financial strength of the different houses, reads as follows:

	Thalers
Direction d. Disconto-Ges.	1,650,000
Kgl. Seehandlungs Societät	800,000
W. H. Ladenburg & Söhne	650,000
S. Bleichröder	500,000

Interesse der Börse. Wer da nicht mitspielt, der ist auf die Seite geschoben—wir sind darin ganz neutral wir haben in einig [sic] Eisenbahnen etwas angelegt u. das liegt ruhig. Indessen ist bey uns poco a poco das Spiel auch nach den Provinzen gelangt u. wir haben [illegible], ja täglich recht hübsche Aufträge darin, die wir wohl unserer vollkommenen Neutralität in diesen Actien verdanken. Ich wünsche von Herzen dass es Ihnen auch so gehen möge.' Joseph Mendelssohn to Leo, Berlin, 18 Feb. 1845. Mendelssohn MSS in the archives of the Leo Baeck Institute, New York.

[26] List of share subscriptions to the Berlin–Stettiner = Eisenbahn, ib.
[27] '... zur Weiterführung der Staatseisenbahnbauten' (ib.).

	Thalers
Mendelssohn & Co.	400,000
Gebr. Schickler	250,000
Berliner Handels-Gesellschaft	250,000
Robert Warschauer & Co.	250,000
F. Mart. Magnus	250,000

In fact, 'Jewish' private banks absorbed shares to the value of 2,050,000 thalers, more than half the total. Jewish capital, moreover, was involved also in the Berliner Handels-Gesellschaft.

A not dissimilar picture emerges from a loan with the nominal value of 24 million thalers in 4½ obligations, floated on behalf of the Prussian government (not for railway construction) in 1868. This time, shares in the operation were allocated in the following proportions:[28]

Die General Direction d. Seehandlungs Societät	8/24
Directorium d. Kgl. Pr. Hauptbank	
Direction d. Disconto-Ges.	4/24
M. A. v. Rothschild & Söhne	3/24
S. Bleichröder	3/24
Mendelssohn & Co.	1/24
F. Mart. Magnus	1/24
Gebr. Schickler	1/24
Robert Warschauer & Co.	1/24
B. Handels-Ges.	1/24
Sal. Oppenheim jun. & Co. (if desirous of participating)	1/24

The share allocated to Jewish private bankers (excluding the BHG) amounts to 10/24 of the total, exceeding that of the Prussian state and, by a large margin, those of the Disconto-Gesellschaft and of Gentile private banks. Finally, the picture of the place of Jewish private banking in the 'railway age' may be completed by an examination of the composition of the consortium which, in 1870, offered the General Direction der Seehandlungssozietät to place Prussian five-year Treasury Bonds (*Schatzanweizungen*) to the value of either 34 or 51 million thalers. If the smaller amount were to be decided upon, this was to be apportioned as follows:

---

[28] Ib.

Entrepreneurial Activities

	Mill. th.	Quota
Direction d. Disconto-Ges.	7.2	72/340
S. Bleichröder	5	50/340
B. Handels-Ges.	2	20/340
Norddeutsche Bank	1.6	16/340
Robert Warschauer & Co.	1.5	15/340
H. C. Plaut	1.5	"
F. Mart. Magnus	1.5	"
Mendelssohn & Co.	1.5	"
Sal. Oppenheim jun. & Co.	1.5	"
Pr. Central Boden Credit AG	1	10/340
Gebr. Schickler	1	"

The proposed share of the Jewish private banks in this time totals 125/240 again exceeding that allotted to the Disconto-Gesellschaft. It is worth noting, moreover, that, this time, the (declining) house of Rothschild is unrepresented. Of the 51 million thalers nominal *Schatzanweisungen* (5 per cent) of the North German Confederation eventually issued, while the *Seehandlung* took up bonds to the value of some 11 million thalers and the *Disconto-Gesellschaft* almost 10½, the combined share of the Jewish private bankers amounted to 18 million.[29]

To return to railway financing in particular, Mendelssohn & Co., during the so-called 'Gründerjahre', joined with an engineer called Plessner in floating a railway construction company which secured concessions for a number of branch lines mainly in central Germany.[30] The firm had to go into liquidation early in 1875. Unedifying lawsuits followed. Mendelssohn & Co., like, no doubt, other private banking houses, resolved henceforth to avoid altogether any form of industrial financing and to decline, for its partners, all seats on company boards (*Aufsichtsräte*).[31]

---

[29] Loc. cit., n. 25 above.

[30] 'Von allen Transaktionen, die Mendelssohn & Co. jemals tätigten, sind die mit der "Bau-Gesellschaft für Eisenbahn-Unternehmungen, Commerz Gesellschaft auf Aktien F. Plessner" [established on 20 March 1870], die unerquicklichsten und verlustreichsten gewesen. Die Bauten folgender Eisenbahnlinien: Altenburg–Zeitz; Angermünde–Schwedt; Kohlfurt–Falkenberg; Chemnitz–Komotau; Gera–Plauen; Oels–Gnesen; Erfurt–Hof u.a., bei denen M. & Co. (führend), Börsen-Handels-Verein, A Borsig, Meyer Cohn, Helfft Gebrüder, J. L. Eltzbacher & Co.; v. Erlanger & Söhne [Meyer Cohn, Helfft, Eltzbacher, and Erlanger were Jewish banking houses] sowie viele andere bedeutende Banken beteiligt waren (durch Kautionen, Darlehnsverträge, Emissionen) konnten einen Konkurs nicht aufhalten.' Ib.

[31] 'Nach dieser aufregenden Krisis der sog. "Gründerjahre" fassten M. & Co. den

A similar disaster, as is well known, overtook the more grandiose enterprises of Bethel Henry Strousberg, together with the more internationally active Maurice de Hirsch, the leading railway entrepreneur of the sixties.[32] Strousberg, significant, above all, as a pioneer of vertical integration, was a man before his time, 'one of the swallows who announced the coming summer of large-scale business'.[33] Not only did Strousberg, as a direct entrepreneur, increase Germany's railway network by some 1,700 km., largely in East Prussia, Lower Silesia, and Saxony,[34] but he also created a remarkable, if short-lived, industrial empire based on a degree of vertical integration,[35] the first of its kind in Germany. When, towards the end of the Franco-Prussian war, Strousberg consolidated his various enterprises as the Allgemeine Eisenbahnbaugesellschaft, the capital of the new company reached the then gigantic sum of 18 million thalers (54 million marks).[36]

Entschluss, sich Industriegeschäften fernzuhalten u. sich auch nicht durch einen Teilhaber als Aufsichtsrat wählen zu lassen. Hieran hielt die Firma fest.' Ib.

[32] For details of the activities of Strousberg see Kurt Zielenziger, *Juden in der deutschen Wirtschaft* (Berlin, 1930), pp. 75 ff. and Fritz Redlich, 'Two Nineteenth-century Financiers and Autobiographers' in *Economy and History*, vol. 10 (Lund, 1967), 104 ff. For Hirsch see Kurt Grunwald, *Türkenhirsch: A Study of Baron Maurice de Hirsch, Entrepreneur and Philanthropist* (Jerusalem, 1966).

[33] Redlich, op. cit., p. 108.

[34] 'Im Jahre 1863 erhält Strousberg die Konzession für den Bau der Ostpreussischen Südbahn zwischen Königsberg und Lyck, ein Jahr später den für die Berlin–Görlitzer Bahn. 1865 baute er die Rechte Oderuferbahn, 1867 die Märkisch-Posener Bahn, 1868 die Bahn zwischen Halle–Sorau–Guben, und im selben Jahr auch noch die Strecke Hannover–Altenbeken . . .' Zielenziger, op. cit., p. 82.

[35] 'Während der sechziger Jahre ist Strousberg nicht nur der grösste Bauunternehmer geworden, er hat inzwischen auch Fabriken der verschiedensten Art erworben und einen Vertikalkonzern, vielleicht den ersten seiner Art, aufgebaut. Denn mit dem Ankauf der Eggestorfschen Maschinenfabrik in Hannover, der Neustädter Hütte bei Hannover, der Einrichtung des Hochofenwerks bei Ostfresen, der Angliederung der Dortmunder Hütte, aus der er unter Umwandlung in die Dortmunder Union das erste gemischte Eisen- und Stahlwerk errichtete, und auf der er wieder als erster das Bessemerverfahren in Deutschland einführt, mit dem Erwerb der Zeche Glückauf und anderer Kohlengruben im Rheinland sowie im Waldenburger Revier und einer Zahl von Eisengruben im Siegerland hatte Strousberg sich für die Herstellung des Eisenbahnmaterials unabhängig machen wollen. Daneben hatte er bereits in Böhmen, und zwar in Zborow, ein riesiges Unternehmen gegründet, zu dem Wälder, Eisen- und Kohlenbergwerke gehörten, und in das er bereits Millionen hineingesteckt hatte. Der Eisenbahnbau führt ihn aber auch zur Lebensmittelversorgung. Schon frühzeitig gründete er in Geestemünde eine Fischereigesellschaft und erbaute als erster in Berlin den Viehmarkt und die Markthallen, um, wie er selbst schreibt, "dem Berliner Publikum gutes Fleisch, frische See- und andere Fische und die Hauptnahrungsmittel zu den billigsten Preisen zu liefern" . . . . einer der grössten Grundbesitzer . . . . Der Journalist von einst schafft sich in der "Post" ein eigenes Organ' (ib., pp. 85 f).

[36] Ib., p. 86.

Strousberg has been criticized for his hostility to banks and bankers,[37] for his 'technical ignorance',[38] his lack of innovation whether in the fields of railway technology or business finance.[39] With a heavy dose of hindsight, he is blamed for his failure to create an adequate financial base for his industrial activities.[40] If Strousberg was not yet an Emil Rathenau, whose genius, to a degree, lay precisely in these fields, he was yet a significant precursor. His lasting memorials which survived his personal failure (and, indeed, failings) were 1,700 km. of railway track and the Dortmunder Union, destined for an important, if not a brilliant, industrial future.

With the failures of Plessner (the Mendelssohn protégé) and Strousberg the golden age of private railway financing, in which Jews had played so prominent a part, came to a close. The major railway lines, moreover, would presently be nationalized. This, however, did not end Jewish activity in the field. In the next phase, Jewish enterprises would be involved in producing materials for railway construction as well as rolling stock and accessories—already pioneered by the Hirsch foundries with their manufacture of locomotive parts.

The financial transactions of the fifties and sixties overall show a striking participation of private banking houses owned by families of Jewish extraction (though, with few exceptions, no longer of the Jewish faith). With the slightly doubtful exception of Gebr. Schickler, there are few Gentile houses to compare with the Mendelssohn & Co., S. Bleichröder, F. Mart. Magnus, Robert Warschauer, and H. C. Plaut in Berlin, with M. A. von Rothschild & Söhne in Frankfurt, W. H. Ladenburg & Söhne in Mannheim, or with Sal. Oppenheim jun. & Co. in Cologne. It was firms like these which, during this period, were active in placing government issues, both German and foreign, and, above all, in financing railway construction. Why did Berlin (Gebr. Schickler apart) have no comparable Gentile banks capable of participating in these activities? Why, at the same time, were the most prominent among Hamburg bankers the Heines, Behrenses and Warburgs? Why did the Oppenheims become the leading bankers in Cologne, the Kaskels in Dresden, the Ladenburgs and Hohenemsers in Mannheim, the Heimanns in Breslau? Why did the Rothschilds, Erlangers, Speyers, Wertheimers, Goldschmidts play a leading part in

[37] Redlich, op. cit., n. 32 above, pp. 106 f. [38] Ib., p. 106.
[39] 'No innovator in technical matters . . . Nor was he an innovator in his own field, corporate finance' (ib., p. 105).
[40] 'He did not create a sound financial basis for his empire, nor did he coordinate it successfully' (ib,.). He has been described as 'essentially a brilliant speculator' (ib).

Frankfurt, the Kaullas in Stuttgart, the Hirsches, Seligmanns, Kaullas, and Wassermanns in Munich? Not all were old-established houses though several went back to at least the late eighteenth century. Among recent (or relative) newcomers were the Bleichröders, Warschauers, Plauts, Moritz Cohn (from Dessau), and the Heimanns (Breslau). Many of these banking families—the Bleichröders are a case in point—were in fact Rothschild protégés who owed their rise largely to the patronage of the 'Mighty Five'. To some extent, thus, the prominence of Jewish private bankers in the fifties and sixties was a by-product of the Rothschilds' earlier pre-eminence.

Even then, however, does the influence of the Rothschilds really explain the almost complete lack of comparable Gentile bankers? To their great scarcity, the numbers and even more the nature of Gentile KRs drawn from the banking world between 1861 and 1881 bear witness. A sample of 17 of these is possibly incomplete but it is a random one. While the leading Berlin bankers of Jewish extraction were rising to become GKRs, only one Gentile banker from Berlin is recorded (1866) as being made even a KR. There is, moreover no other record of the obscure Christoph Nicolaus Engelhard. Of the remaining 16, 3 came from Frankfurt. (1 in 1871, 2 in 1879), 3 from Halle (1881, 1888, and 1889), and two from Cologne (1871 and 1881). The remainder hailed from Elberfeld, Frankfurt-on-Oder, St Johann bei Saarbrücken, Dortmund, Trier, Flensburg, Nordhausen, and Naumburg. Altogether, only 3 of the 17 bore well-known names (Gustav-Adolf Neufville, Frankfurt, 1871, Wilhelm von Born, Dortmund, 1879, and Adolf Deichmann, Cologne, 1885), the rest, like the three bankers in Halle (Streckner, Bethcke, and Lehmann), were obscure local worthies. Even the single GKR among the number, Johann Philipp Petsch-Goll (GKR 1885), did not belong to a well-known banking family. (It is, of course, likely that a number of Frankfurt bankers disdained Prussian titles.) The great majority of the group consisted of obscure local bankers, testifying to an almost complete absence in Prussia at least of Gentile banking houses comparable in importance to the Jewish ones.

The question has still to be answered why this should be so. Had there, earlier, been Gentile private banks that had succumbed to Jewish competition? It appears that, in 1860, there may have existed in Berlin a total of 106 Jewish as against 51 Gentile banks.[41] A survey for

---

[41] Jacob Toury, *Soziale und politische Geschichte der Juden in Deutschland 1847–1871* (Düsseldorf, 1977), pp. 85 f.

the year 1871 suggests that of 580 firms some 40 per cent were Gentile, 23 per cent purely Jewish, and 37 per cent 'mixed'.[42] Why then did so few of the Gentile houses achieve any real eminence? The Jewish houses which were able to rise to the front rank probably enjoyed some major competitive advantages. It is clear that 'Rothschild power' helped the favoured, found predominantly in the Jewish group. Again, once Rothschild patronage had helped a firm to draw ahead of its competitors, its relative advantage might well increase with higher credit rating and greater amounts of available capital. A KR or GKR among the partners would further significantly enhance its standing. Again, numbers of Jewish bankers, whether through business or family connections, enjoyed privileged access to an international information network in which co-religionists were prominent and which might not be at the disposal of Gentile competitors. Whether Jewish banks, in a period of economic boom, realized greater speculative gains than their more cautious non-Jewish counterparts must be a matter for speculation.

It is worth noting that, of the prominent Jewish private banks in Berlin in the mid-nineteenth century, only that of the Mendelssohns retained its standing in the twentieth century, followed, at a distance, by the house of Bleichröder. The rest either declined into insignificance or were absorbed, by 1904, by the large joint-stock banks. On the other hand, a fact sometimes overlooked, some provincial private banks, notably those of the Oppenheims in Cologne, the Warburgs and Behrenses in Hamburg, and the Hirschlands in Essen, flourished, as did newcomers like Gebr. Arnhold in Dresden. Some of the latter, prominent among them the Hardys, actually established themselves in Berlin. While the role of the Jewish private banker had, perhaps, reached its peak during the fifties, sixties, and early seventies, and while many of the houses then prominent later declined, the importance of the Jewish private bank was far from over (especially if a hybrid variety, Carl Fürstenberg's BHG, is taken into account).

Given the general importance of Jewish private banks in the period under consideration, their prominence in railway financing was an almost automatic consequence. They disposed both of credit and of investment capital which railway construction demanded in vast amounts. This was, indeed, the great economic operation of the age (other than its armies and wars which, however, took second place).

[42] Ib.

There were, as the varied experiences of Abraham Oppenheim, of Bethel Henry Strousberg, of Moritz von Hirsch, and of the Mendelssohns showed, vast fortunes to be made but equally great risks to be incurred. It was also shown that simple investment and flotations were safer than entrepreneurship involving actual construction. But, whatever their ultimate fortunes, unless the state chose actively to involve itself in railway building, members of the Jewish economic élite would, of necessity, have to play a leading role. Their prominence in railway construction alone makes complete nonsense of the theory of their alleged marginality. Jewish finance and even entrepreneurship were filling a gaping gap, a near-vacuum resulting from the relative weakness of Gentile private banking and, indeed, even of pioneering enterprise in actual railway building.

IV

Between 1873 and the end of the century, in the main the age of the 'Great Depression', the major spheres of Jewish economic activity persist, albeit with a measure of diversification. While men from the textile industry continue to figure prominently among KRs, while several branches of wholesale trade are strongly represented, and while the number of men engaged in manufacturing increases, there is some decline in the proportion of private bankers. While the scale of industrial activities rewarded shows a notable increase, the bankers now honoured are, in the main, either residual small-town notables or second-generation partners—still esteemed among their peers—of slowly declining houses.

Among textile manufacturers made KRs also, there are still to be found bearers of the great names of the previous generation, Louis Reichenheim (1875), Moritz Wolff (1875), Louis Dahlheim (1877), Joseph Pinkus, the son-in-law of Samuel Fränkel in Neustadt OS (1881 and 1895), and his brother-in-law Albert Fränkel (1897), also Julius Kauffmann (Thannhausen) (1884) and Valentin Manheimer (1885 and 1897).

Such old-established family names are joined by those of newcomers, evidence of continued involvement of Jews in textile entrepreneurship. Albert Hahn (1887 and 1889), with Salomon Huldschinsky at one time Germany's largest exporter of rags to England (for the manufacture of shoddy), had later been instrumental in transplanting this branch of manufacture to Upper Silesia.[43] The amply documented story of the linen manufacturers F. V. Grünfeld in Landeshut shows so many characteristic features that it deserves more detailed consideration.[44] Valentin Grünfeld (1837–97) was the fifth son of a poor (Jewish) communal official in the small Upper Silesian locality of Leschnitz. Following apprenticeships in a variety of textile firms (mainly Jewish and including half a year with the renowned S. Fränkel in Neustadt), Grünfeld, in 1862, set up a minute shop for textile goods ('ein kleines Schnittwarengeschäft').[45] With the shop went manufacture, on the most modest scale, of coarse packing materials.[46] In 1864,

[43] '... Die Initiative zu allen vor der Firma Hahn & Huldschinsky geschaffenen Werken hat zunächst unstreitig wohl Hahn gegeben, während das Verdienst der praktischen Ausführung und Ausnutzung dem g. Huldschinsky zugesprocehn werden muss. Keiner von ihnen hatte ursprünglich ein technisches Studium mit ins Geschäft gebracht, oder eine Idee von der Fabrikation der Kunstwolle gehabt. Beide handelten bis zum Jahre 1852 nur mit Lumpen nach England, natürlich in grossartigsten Umfange. Erst durch Hahn's persönliche Anwesenheit in England und durch die gewährten genaueren Einblicke in die Fabrikation daselbst kam ihm der Gedanke, die bisher von ihm nach England ausgeführten Rohprodukte selber im Inlande zu verarbeiten. Ob der g. Huldschinsky ohne Hahn's festes Einwirken eine Kunstwollen-Fabrik hier eingerichtet hätte, ist sehr zweifelhaft... und soll es jedesmal harte Kämpfe zwischen den beiden Socien gekostet haben, wenn Hahn von England zurückgekehrt wieder eine neue Maschine oder eine grössere Veränderung resp. Verbesserung in der Fabrik einführen wollte...' v. Madai to Dr Achenbach, Berlin, 18 Aug. 1877, ZSAM Rep. 120, A IV 5 vol. 18, fos. 198^v–199.' ... alleiniger Besitzer [since 1873] einer Kunstwollfabrik und einer Spinnerei... Die Erzeugnisse der Fabrik erfreuen sich einer allseitigen Anerkennung und sind auf den Ausstellungen zu London, Paris, Moskau und Wien prämirt worden. Die Fabrik beschäftigt gegenwärtig 200 Arbeiter beiderlich Geschlechtes... Die Fabrik nimmt neben der des Commerzienraths Schöller in Düren den ersten Rang unter den Kunstwollfabriken Deutschlands ein: sie hat wesentlich dazu beigetragen, einen neuen Industriezweig in Deutschland einzuführen und versorgt mit ihren Erzeugnissen nicht nur Deutschland und Oesterreich, sondern auch Holland, England, Russland, Schweden, Dänemark und Italien. Der jährliche Umsatz beziffert sich auf rund eine Million Mark.' Achenbach to the king, Berlin, 8 Oct. 1877, ZSAM, 2.2.1, no. 1581, fos. 41^{r-v} '... Ist Chef und Haupttheilhaber der hier unter seinem Namen bestehenden sehr bedeutenden Kunstwollfabrik Spinnerei und Weberei... Die Firma welche auf ihren Niederlassungen etwa 300 Männer und ebensoviel Frauen beschäftigt hat das Verdienst, mit ihrer Kunstwollfabrikation einen neuen Industriezweig in Deutschland eingeführt zu haben, versendet ihre Erzeugnisse nach fast allen Ländern Europas und geniesst überall den besten Ruf...' Boetticher to the king, Berlin, 13 Oct. 1889, ZSAM 2.2.1, vol. 1587, fos. 192^{r-v}

[44] For the following see, besides Boetticher to the king, n. 43 above, also Heinrich Grünfeld, *Falk Valentin Grünfeld und sein Werk* (Berlin, 1934), privately printed; Fritz F. Grünfeld, *Das Leinenhaus Grünfeld: Erinnerungen und Dokumente*, ed. Stefi Jersch-Wenzel (Berlin, 1967), and Schwerin, loc. cit., n. 5 above, p. 46.

[45] Schwerin, loc. cit., n. 5 above, p. 46: '... als Grünfeld, 25 Jahre alt, in einem winzigen halbdunklen Laden an einer Marktecke 1862 ein eigenes Sortimentmanufakturwarengeschäft aufmachte.'

[46] 'Eine Herstellung wurde nur in kleinstem Umfang mit "Liebauer Taft"

Grünfeld was able to move into a larger building, thanks mainly to the dowry of 2,000 thalers of his wife Johanna Schück, whose father owned a fashion magazine in Oppeln.[47] From this moment onwards, Valentin Grünfeld, after his humble beginnings, would never look back.

Grünfeld's outstanding business acumen, more particularly as a salesman, soon found a number of significant outlets. In the first place, so characteristic of much Jewish entrepreneurship, Grünfeld, thanks to the Austro-Prussian war of 1866, received substantial military orders.[48] One consequence of these orders was the establishment of a department for men's wear and another for ready-made women's clothing. The necessary materials were produced largely by the 'putting-out' system in neighbouring villages.

It was, however, in the field of salesmanship that Grünfeld showed the greatest enterprise. His youngest brother-in-law gave up his own business to visit on his behalf the industrial centres of Saxony and Lusatia to sell working clothes. So did two other representatives who sold also high quality sewing-machines for which Grünfeld had wisely secured an agency.

However, thanks to his outstanding ability as a salesman, Grünfeld had acquired also a very different clientele. In fact, he had soon become the favourite supplier of textile goods to members of Silesia's landed gentry.[49] It was on the recommendation of some of his aristocratic patrons that Grünfeld in 1873 received the gracious permission of the Emperor Wilhelm I to present him, for a

aufgenommen, starkem Rohleinen aus Abfallgarn, das an Lieferanten und Grossisten als Packleinen verkauft wurde.'

[47] The significance of the sum can be measured by the fact that Grünfeld's original inventory (furnishings and stock) had been valued at 278 thalers, his cash reserve at 63 thalers.

[48] '1866, im Kriege mit Österreich, kam die Armee des Kronprinzen Friedrich . . . über Landeshut. Ein Zahlmeister eines durchziehenden Reiterregiments bestellte im Ladengeschäft für 6.000 thaler Futtersäcke. Der junge Geschäftsmann und seine Frau hatten Bedenken wegen der knappen Frist, lieferten dann aber noch drei Stunden vor deren Ablauf, was der Zahlmeister nie vergass. Es folgten jetzt und im deutsch-französischen Krieg weitere Aufträge, so auf die Lieferung von Drellmannschafts- und Lazarettanzügen.'

[49] 'Wie schon angedeutet, hatten die Eltern es schon sehr früh verstanden, gerade das Vertrauen der besten Gutsbesitzer- und Adelskreise nicht nur geschäftlich, sondern persönlich, fast gesellschaftlich zu erwerben . . . dass die strenge Zuverlässigkeit die Grundlage dieses freundschaftlichen Vertrauens war, das sich zeitweise in der Förderung geschäftlicher Interessen günstig auswirkte.' Heinrich Grünfeld, op. cit., n. 44 above, p. 30.

forthcoming visit to St Petersburg, with a warm quilted jacket filled with Silesian wool (*Waldwolle*). Through the intermediary of the same circles, notably court marshal Perponcher and lady-in-waiting Countess Udo Stolberg, the firm, twice yearly, now received extensive orders for linen for the imperial household. In 1875, Falk Valentin Grünfeld received the coveted title of *Hoflieferant*.

Parallel with the move into the 'upper end' of the market went changes in production, a shift from the coarser types of wear to the manufacture of high quality goods. When in 1887 Grünfeld was 'honoured' with the somewhat inferior title of a *Kommissionsrat*,[50] the authorities noted that, in addition to seventy to eighty people employed directly, the firm (described as 'Schnitt-Modewaaren-Garderoben') provided a livelihood on the 'putting-out' system for several hundred others engaged in weaving, in embroidery, and in needlework. What was noted in particular was the production of high-quality damask goods to the firm's own designs and the fact that these had won prizes at several exhibitions.[51]

So far, the development of the business, though unusual in some respects, had shown strong traditional features. These, however, were being increasingly combined with very 'modern' techniques, not least among them advertising, the stimulation of demand.[52] From the mid-seventies, moreover, Grünfeld had begun to operate a mail-order business.[53] The goods advertised in the firm's catalogues became increasingly diversified.[54]

[50] As in some other cases, it is not clear why he was not made a *Kommerzienrat*.
[51] '. . . Der Schwerpunkt des Geschäfts liegt in dem Absatz von Leinen- und Damastartikeln, welche letztere Grünfeld nach eigenen Mustern anfertigen lässt. Seinen hervorragenden Leistungen auf diesem Gebiete hat er auch das ihm mittelst Allerhöchster Ordre vom 23 Juni 1875 [?] Prädicat eines Königlichen Hoflieferanten zu verdanken. Auf verschiedenen Ausstellungen gewerblicher Erzeugnisse sind [?] rühmliche Auszeichnungen zu Theil geworden . . .' Boetticher to the king, Berlin, 5 Dec. 1887, ZSAM 2.2.1, no. 1587, fos. 63^{r-v}
[52] '. . . die ständige Fühlungsnahme mit den damals führenden Modezeitungen, "Bazar", "Modenwelt", "Victoria", "Illustrierte Frauenzeitung" usw., die teils seine Neuheiten ihren Lesern vorführten, teils Anregungen gaben für die Neuaufnahme von Artikeln.' Heinrich Grünfeld, op. cit., n. 44 above, p. 31. 'Mit der Zeit wurde den Provinzzeitungen, zuerst nur in Schlesien, ab und zu auch eine Beilage mitgegeben. In späteren Jahren brachten über 350 mittlere und kleinere Provinzialzeitungen etwa alle 14 Tage ein wechselndes kleines Inserat im Anschluss an den redaktionellen Text und mussten dafür auch zwei oder drei Reklamenotizen aufnehmen. Zugleich gehörte Grünfeld neben Mey u. Edlich und Rudolph Herzog zu den ersten, die ganzseitige Anzeigen in den gelesensten Familienzeitschriften wie Gartenlaube, Daheim, Leipziger Illustrierte Zeitung usw. aufgaben.'
[53] 'An Lehrer und Gemeindebeamte hatte sich Grünfeld um Anschriften kaufkräftiger

Among the reasons for the growing success of the firm, Grünfeld's older son Heinrich gave pride of place to the still relatively novel principle of fixed prices (which, however, by this time was beginning to spread among progressive retailers) and, following this, the practice of offering only quality goods (also spreading at this time)—both the reverse of the anti-Semitic stereotype of the Jewish 'huckster' peddling his shoddy wares. To these must be added Grünfeld's genius as an advertiser (sometimes considered a widespread Jewish talent) as seen among others in the provision of gratis refreshment for customers.[55]

To these (typical perhaps of the more traditional aspects of the Jewish family firm) must be added the active participation of Grünfeld's wife Johanna, described as 'Silesia's most efficient mechant's wife' ('Schlesiens tüchtigste Kaufmannsfrau').[56] In fact F. V. Grünfeld, notwithstanding rapid growth and the adoption of many modern, indeed avant-garde business practices, remained a closely knit family firm (*Offene Handelsgesellschaft*) to the bitter end. The capital remained in the business. In this as in other respects the Grünfelds recall the Tietzes, owners of the great department stores, a family to which they were one day to be united by marriage. Falk Valentin Grünfeld was assisted by his sons Ludwig (1864–1929) and Heinrich

Familien aus ihrem Umkreis gewandt; als Gegenlohn versprach er Barlohn oder Entgegenkommen bei Einkäufen. An diese Anschriften gingen einmal im Jahr Warenangebote in Form vierseitiger Zeitungsbeilagen, bald auch eines kleinen Büchleins.'

[54] Until 1878 the goods offered comprised only 'leinene, halbleinene, baumwollene Schneidezeuge, weiss oder farbig, Tischzeuge, Hand- und Wischtücher, aber noch keine genähten Sachen'. The only novelties were, in the list of 1875, universal hammocks (for the use mainly of invalids) and, in 1878, specially fitting bibs ('abgepasste Kinderservietten zum Umhängen), which proved a roaring success, to such an extent that Grünfeld had to involve three major textile works in their production. Thousands of dozens were exported to Africa and Australia. In 1882 came the first offer of bathing costumes in red or blue calico, in 1883 men's shirts, collars, and cuffs. In 1885–6 there was an offer of complete trousseaus, valued from 340 to 3,590 marks.

[55] '... 1869, leistete er sich einen neuen Umbau für 5.500 thaler. In ihm wurde der Laden verlängert, grosse Schaufenster eingebrochen, in den Eingang auf ein Marmortischchen eine Riesenbowle gestellt, die im Sommer den einströmenden Landkunden Himbeerwasser, im Winter heissen Punsch spendete.' This, indeed, remained a hallmark of the firm. In 1930 the British efficiency expert Herbert Casson, in one of its Berlin stores, could still admire the successor of the original bowl, 'unsere Limonadenquelle, wo jedem, ohne zu fragen, ob er etwas gekauft hat oder nicht, etwas gegeben wird—*ohne Firmenaufdruck!*' Fritz Grünfeld, op. cit., n. 44 above, p. 84.

[56] The son of Heinrich Grünfeld recalls that, until 1879, his parents probably took a midday meal together with their 'living-in' staff in different shifts. Least of all was a family meal possible on Sundays or feast-days, the busiest in the shop. Nor yet could they take joint holidays.

(1865–1938) who, in due course, took over the management of the business.

In 1889, ushering in a new phase in the firm's development, a store was opened in Berlin. In 1900, though the old base in Landeshut was retained, Berlin becme the main seat of what was now named Landeshuter Leinen- und Gebildeweberei F. V. Grünfeld. The 'modern' phase—a feature shared with a number of Jewish (and no doubt other) firms—owed much to the adoption of Anglo-Saxon, especially American, 'know-how':

> Erfahrungsaustausch mit der englischen und amerikanischen Geschäftswelt war bei uns zu einer Art Tradition geworden, seit der Firmengründer bei der Rückkehr von seiner ersten Amerikareise im Jahre 1891 . . . begeistert wiederkam . . . Danach hat—angefangen mit Ludwig Grünfelds Studienreise im Jahre 1892 und Heinrich Grünfelds im Jahre 1893 (zur Weltausstellung in Chicago)—jeder von uns ein oder mehrere Male die Vereinigten Staaten von Amerika besucht, weil aus keinem anderen Lande so viele Anregungen für neue Gedanken aus dem Gebiet der Organisation und Werbung zu gewinnen waren. Jeder brachte von solcher Reise—mit intensiven Betriebsbesichtigungen —Anregungen mit, die—mutatis mutandis—auf die Verhältnisse unseres Betriebes übertragen werden konnten.[57]

Indeed, like Georg Tietz a little later, Falk Valentin Grünfeld regretted the impossibility of settling in the USA, which he considered the ideal venue for his entrepreneurial activity.[58] It may be that, in the end, the Grünfelds had in some respects, outstripped their teachers. At any rate, in 1930, after visiting the Grünfeld stores in Berlin, a British business consultant noted no fewer than twelve features (including a conveyor system for transporting goods—a *'Warenpaternoster'*—and the famous lemonade fountain) which he had never met before. He promised—little did he know!—that in a report for his journal he would describe F. V. Grünfeld as the specialist store ('das Spezialgeschäft') of the forties.[59]

A significant feature of the Grünfeld enterprise in Berlin is recorded

[57] Ib., p. 84.
[58] On his return from his first visit to the United States in 1891, F. V. Grünfeld in his enthusiasm told his wife meeting him in Hamburg: 'Wenn wir uns hier nicht mit Grund und Boden festgelegt hätten, würde ich bestimmt dafür sein, sofort mit Kind und Kegel überzusiedeln; das ist das richtige Land für meinen privaten Unternehmergeist' (ib.).
[59] He told Heinrich Grünfeld: 'Nun habe ich schon zwölf Dinge bei Ihnen gesehen, die ich bisher in noch keinem Geschäft der Welt sah. Ich werde darüber in meiner Zeitschrift einen Bericht bringen und Ihr Geschäft das Spezialgeschäft von 1940 nennen' (ib.).

by a member of the third generation. The original store had been located in the centre of Berlin. In 1928 a new, ultra-modern one was opened in the west end. Fears were expressed that the original store would now be eclipsed by the new one. In fact, the more traditional shop and the new functioned happily side by side, each with its own distinctive clientele and a sales-staff to some extent adapted to its character. While the ultra-modern store acquired an almost magnetic attraction for the world of fashion and the arts as well as foreign visitors,[60] the more traditional branch continued to serve both provincial customers and the 'old distinguished clientele' (die 'vornehme alte Kundschaft').[61] As in the Grünfeld business in general, the ultra-modern and the more traditional could exist harmoniously side by side. Whether the Grünfelds were in fact running—no doubt quite unconsciously—one store for a predominantly Jewish (or at any rate mixed), another for an overwhelmingly Gentile clientele must remain a matter for speculation. When, in the days of Weimar, politicians, among them Franz von Papen, Konstantin von Neurath and Hjalmar Schacht,[62] visited the traditional store in the Leipziger Strasse, they usually asked to see Heinrich Grünfeld. He had become a recognized public figure, a *Wirtschaftsführer*. Having succeeded in organizing the fragmented German retail trade as the Hauptgemeinschaft des deutschen Einzelhandels, he had become its principal representative and spokesman. He had become also vice-president of the Berlin chamber of commerce and industry, and member of a number of official bodies. His leading role in his trade association in particular

[60] 'Sehr bald bildete sich sogar in unserem eigenen Verkaufspersonal ein anderer "Typ" für den Westen heraus als für die Altstadt—entsprechend der Kundschaft. Die gesamte Prominenz von Film, Theater, Musik, die gesamte Kunst- und Modewelt und die Besucher der Reichshauptstadt aus dem Auslande fühlten sich geradezu magnetisch zu dem "Grünfeld am Kurfürstendamm" hingezogen, was die übrige Käuferschaft—und die Angestellten—dieses Verkaufshauses sichtlich beeindruckte.' Fritz Grünfeld, op. cit., n. 44 above, p. 98.

[61] 'Andererseits bevorzugte die "Kundschaft aus der Provinz" der Mittelstand, Offiziere und Beamte die Atmosphäre des Hergebrachten im Hauptgeschäft, zu dessen Kunden auch eine andere Gruppe Prominenter zählte: wie früher die kaiserliche Familie, der Hof, der Adel, Gutsbesitzer, Diplomaten und Minister zu den Stammkunden der Leipziger Strasse zählten so folgten . . . die führenden Kreise der Weimarer Republik dem Beispiel ihrer Vorgänger. Die beiden Präsidenten der Republik, sowohl Ebert wie Hindenburg mit ihren Familien waren hier regelmässige Käufer, und nach wie vor tätigte "man" seine Einkäufe vom Hausbedarf und Geschenk bis zur Brautaussteuer bei Grünfeld in der Leipziger Strasse' (ib., pp. 98 f).

[62] 'Schachts berühmte hohe Kragen bedingten in unserer Herrenwäsche-Abteilung stets eine Sonderanfertigung' (ib. p. 99).

was typical of the organizing activities of several members of the Jewish economic élite.

If the story of F. V. Grünfeld has been told in some detail, it is in part for its value in illustrating a number of features characteristic of Jewish economic activity. In this connection, it might be noted that distinctively 'Jewish' business strategies or techniques are most likely to occur in branches of economic activity where Jews achieved particular prominence. In Germany, modern retailing in the shape of department and large specialist stores is one such branch—there were no Gentile Tietzes, Wertheims, or Grünfelds (just as there are in Great Britain no Gentile Marks and Spencer, among whose precursors the German–Jewish stores might be numbered). At the same time the preponderance of Jews among the owners of German department stores was unique[63] and requires explanation in terms of German conditions also.

Among the features contributing to the success of F. V. Grünfeld, a leading place must belong to salesmanship of the highest order by means of the most modern sales technique (advertising, various forms of publicity, service to customers) combined—an essential feature—with quality of the goods sold. Another element was organization, advanced methods of stock-control, and technological innovation like the conveyor system admired by the British consultant. A major aspect was constant contact with the most advanced practices in the USA (and, to a lesser extent, England). For Germany, the methods adopted by retailers like the Tietzes or the Grünfelds were not just innovative but downright revolutionary. They entered a field where Gentile competition was minimal. Were they innovators merely in the German context or on a wider scale? This is a question to be answered convincingly only on the basis of specialist investigations not to be attempted here. While one might feel inclined to stress the transfer of advanced techniques observed abroad (in Paris as much as in New York or London) Casson's comments on Grünfeld's new store on the Kurfürstendamm might lead one to hesitate.[64]

---

[63] It has often been pointed out that, of the great Paris department stores, the pioneers of the genre, only a minority were Jewish-owned. On the other hand, several New York and most Berlin (indeed German) stores were. Perhaps the greatest department store, Woolworth, is, of course, non-Jewish.

[64] Heinrich Grünfeld considered that, in important respects, his father was ahead of his time. '. . . Nachlesen dieser ersten Preislisten aus den Jahren 1877 bis 1880 bietet namentlich mir . . . immer wieder Beweise der wahrhaft genialen, und dabei von praktischer Menschenkenntnis getragenen, geschäftlichen Befähigung und Grosszügigkeit

A second significant aspect of the Grünfeld success story 'from rags to riches' lies, besides an opportune small dowry, in the presence among the Grünfelds to a marked degree of the 'Puritan' minority virtues of hard work irrespective of hours (as in coping with the first military order in 1866), reliability, the invaluable commercial and social contribution of a wife, and a strongly developed family sense with the resulting preservation of business capital (family members owned relatively little private wealth). It is not possible here to distinguish between features characteristic of members of certain minorities in general and more specific ethnic attributes.

One feature that may be a joint product of the two characteristics discussed is a happy blend in Grünfeld business strategies between traditional and innovative elements: ethnic, and immigrant pioneering attitudes. It seems significant that Falk Valentin Grünfeld, towards the end of a strikingly successful career, told his wife, on returning from his first visit to the USA, that he would prefer to live there as this was a country in harmony with his private entrepreneurial ethos. Somewhat later Georg Tietz, equally, after some months in the USA, could be induced to return to Germany only by strong paternal pressure. For Grünfeld, at any rate, the reasons for the preference were economic as much as social. The question is raised about a possible affinity of some Jewish entrepreneurs for an American business ethic they did not find in Germany. How far, one might ask, were their economic strategies and successes the product of an American-style business philosophy? There may indeed have existed something like a 'Jewish' entrepreneurial style, embodied in men like F. V. Grünfeld or Oscar Tietz with affinities with American approaches (through which, of course, a number of Jews in the American economy also prospered).

Nor was Grünfeld the only 'new style' textile entrepreneur among the KRs of this period. Several newcomers and their businesses acquired reputations in no way inferior to that of F. V. Grünfeld. Among the distinguishing features shared with Grünfeld was that textile production was increasingly combined with either trade or with 'making-up', *Konfektion*. The trading element was assuming increasing

unseres Vaters. Immer wieder stösst man . . . auf Sätze die, der Zeitauffassung weit voraus, heute noch oder wieder Geltung haben könnten. So die Begründung für die Preissenkungen in den Jahren 1878/79, für die strenge Durchführung des Grundsatzes "Nur gegen Vorausbezahlung oder Nachnahme" und die ständige Fühlungnahme mit den damals führenden Modezeitungen . . .' Heinrich Grünfeld, op. cit., n. 44 above, p. 31. *Mutatis mutandis*, Georg Tietz would express similar views about his father Oscar Tietz.

importance. Prominent among the Jewish families rivalling the Grünfelds in importance were the Gersons (1871, 1873, 1875). When Moritz Gerson became a KR (1868), the firm was already the largest fashion house in Berlin.[65] When three years later his brother Benny received the same accolade, the house was described as 'world-famous'.[66] when a third brother, Jacob (Julius), was so honoured—a unique occurrence—he owed this more particularly to the patronage of the queen-empress.[67] Then, following a period of decline, the fortunes of the house of Gerson once more revived under the management of Philipp Freudenberg (1899).[68]

Of greater importance among the newcomers than the fashion

[65] 'Moritz Gerson... ist einer der Chefs der hiesigen Handlung Hermann Gerson... Dieselbe gehört der Corporation der Kaufmannschaft an und darf als das grösste Etablissement ihrer Art in hiesiger Residenz bezeichnet werden. In den weiten, elegant ausgestatteten Räumen sind an Buchhaltern, Commis, Lehrlingen, Directricen, Verkäuferinnen, Hausdienern immer mindestens 200 Personen thätig, wenigstens 100 Arbeiterinnen werden im Hause beschäftigt, um schleunige Bestellungen auszuführen und erhalten ausser dem Hause durchschnittlich noch 150 Familien Arbeit und Verdienst. Der jährliche Umsatz beträgt circa 3 Millionen... Das gesammte Vermögen der Handlung resp. der Theilhaber beträgt mehrere Millionen. Wenn das Geschäft sich durch Reellität und solide Führung auszeichnet und dadurch nach und nach eine so bedeutende Ausdehnung gewonnen hat, so ist andererseits auch der Ruf der Wohlthätigkeit, welche stets und bereitwillig ausgeübt wird, für die Handlung Gerson ein allgemein verbreiteter geworden...' v. Wurmb to *Ober-Präsident* v. Jagow, Berlin, 2 June 1868, ZSAM Rep. 120, A IV 5, vol. 10, fos. 61–2.

[66] 'Der g. Gerson ... gründete im Jahre 1836 gemeinschaftlich mit seinem inzwischen verstorbenen Bruder Hermann Gerson das unter der Firma "Hermann Gerson" hier bestehende weltbekannte Confections-Geschäft, welches, abgesehen von den dort beschäftigten zahlreichen Arbeitern ein Geschäftspersonal von nahezu 300 Köpfen zählt. Zu dem Aufblühen dieses Geschäfts ... hat der g. Benny Gerson durch seine Thätigkeit wesentlich beigetragen ...' v. Itzenplitz to the king, Berlin, 27 June 1871, ZSAM 2.2.1, no. 1582, fos. 39[r-v]

[67] 'Ihre Majestät die Kaiserin und Königin haben mir zu erkennen gegeben, dass sich der g. Gerson nach einer vierzigjährigen Thätigkeit auch die Allerhöchste Zufriedenheit in so hohem Masse erworben habe, dass es den Wünschen Ihrer Majestät entsprechen würde, wenn derselbe gleich seinen Brüdern zum Commerzienrath ernannt werden könnte...' Achenbach to the king, 1875, ZSAM 2.2.1, no. 1583, fo. 81.

[68] 'Der Kaufmann Philipp Freudenberg ... steht als Senior-Chef an der Spitze des hier unter der Firma "Hermann Gerson" schon lange bestehenden grossen Handelshauses ... eine offene Handels-Gesellschaft, die seit dem ersten Januar v. J. unter Beitritt von stillen Gesellschaftern mit einem Betriebskapital von 5 Millionen Mark fortgeführt wird. Das Geschäft, welches sich hauptsächlich mit dem Vertriebe von Modewaaren befasst, ohne im Wesentlichen selbst zu fabriciren, gehört zu den grössten und bekanntesten seiner Art nicht nur in Berlin, sondern in ganz Deutschland und findet für einzelne seiner Artikel auch Abnehmer im Auslande. Freudenberg hat vor längerer Zeit das damals im Niedergange begriffene Geschäft als Hauptinhaber übernommen und es seitdem durch intelligente und rastlose Thätigkeit wieder zu einem Hause ersten Ranges emporgehoben...' Thiele to the king, Berlin, 30 Mar. 1899, ZSAM 2.2.1, no. 1590, fos. 207[r-v]

house of Hermann Gerson was the leading textile wholesale firm of Gebr. Simon.[69] When Isaak Simon was recommended for the title (1877) the police president of Berlin (who actually preferred the claims of the younger brother Lewin) launched into a veritable panegyric of the firm.[70] When Lewin finally joined his brother (1888) the assessment, if more sober, was no less appreciative.[71] Admiration

[69] The banker Carl Fürstenberg, who was briefly employed by Gebr. Simon, describes the business as follows in his memoirs: 'Als Louis [Lewin] Simon sich dann im Jahre 1852 mit seinem Bruder Isaak selbständig machte, brachte er die eigene Firma verhältnismässig schnell an die Spitze seiner Branche. Das Unternehmen spezialisierte sich auf den Handel mit Baumwollgeweben und insbesondere Kattunen. Gepflegt wurde in erster Reihe das sogenannte "Ausrüstungsgeschäft", das Appretieren, Färben und Mustern der Rohwaren. Diesen Zweigen sind Gebrüder Simon auch in der Folge treu geblieben. Der Deutsch–Französische Krieg sollte der Firma einen weiteren gewaltigen Aufschwung bringen, wie dann später der Weltkrieg mit seinen Nachwirkungen sie letzten Endes zugrundegerichtet hat.' Carl Fürstenberg, *Die Lebensgeschichte eines deutschen Bankiers*. Recorded by Hans Fürstenberg (Wiesbaden, 1961), p. 22.

[70] 'Der Kaufmann Isaak Simon ... und der Kaufmann Lewin Simon ... betreiben seit dem Jahre 1852 unter der der hiesigen Corporation angehörigen Firma "Gebrüder Simon" ... eine Leinen- und Baumwollenfabrik, verbunden mit einer en gros Handlung in sehr bedeutendem Umfange ...
Wenn sich das Geschäft anfänglich nach seiner Gründung in den bescheidensten Grenzen bewegte, so ist es namentlich des jüngeren Bruders Lewin Simon Verdienst, dass es in kurzer Zeit rasch emporblühte und jetzt zu den ersten Deutschlands in der betreffenden Branch gezählt werden darf, da es einen jährlichen Umsatz von 24 Millionen Mark erzielt. Nach dem Urtheile Sachverständiger war es speciell Lewin Simon, welcher verstanden hat, durch colossale Ankäufe von Baumwolle, durch einen grossartigen, [one feels the, possibly reluctant, admiration of the Prussian official for the dynamic of developing capitalism] von Jahr zu Jahr wachsenden Umsatz, die englische Industrie immer mehr und mehr von den deutschen Märkten zu verdrängen und der deutschen Industrie in seiner Branche den Sieg zu verschaffen [a second cause for official admiration]. Die grossen Fabriken für halbwollene Stoffe in Sachsen, dem Rheinlande und in Westphalen, die Spinnereien und Webereien in Baiern, und Württemberg, geben ein beredtes Zeugnis dafür ab und verdanken gewisser Maassen der Genialität und der rastlos eifrigen Arbeit des Lewin Simon der die Seele des Simon'schen Geschäftes ist ihre jetztige Grösse, ja es wird behauptet das in gewissem Sinne tausende von Arbeitern ihre Subsistenz der Firma "Gebrüder Simon" zu verdanken haben. Denn während andere Branchen in dem verflossenen traurigen Jahre feiern mussten, haben die "Gebrüder Simon" im Interesse der darniederliegenden Industrie in der ganzen Zeit fast ohne Nutzen gearbeitet nach wie vor aber durch billige Preise, welche den Abnehmern gestellt wurden, einen sehr bedeutenden Umsatz erzielt und auf diese Weise auch anderen Fabriken grosse Aufträge ertheilen können, welche wiederum zurückwirkend es diesen möglich machten, ihren Arbeitern dauernd Beschäftigung und Brod zu geben ...' von Madai to *Ober-Präsident* von Jagow, Berlin, 21 Sept. 1877, ZSAM Rep. 120, A IV 5, vol. 19, fos. 31ᵛ–33.

[71] 'Der Kaufmann Lewin Simon hierselbst ... hat sich durch rastlose Thätigkeit und Energie eine hochgeachtete Stellung in den hiesigen kaufmännischen Kreisen erworben. Er ist Mitinhaber einer hier unter der Firma Gebrüder Simon zu hoher Blüthe gelangten Baumwollwaarenfabrik und Leinen- und Manufacturwaarenhandlung en gros, welche zu den ersten Deutschlands gehört und die englische Industrie mehr

breaks through again when, aged 70, Lewin Simon became a GKR.[72] Finally among the newcomers there was Hermann Rinkel (1899), a Silesian textile manufacturer in the traditional mould, though with a completely mechanized mill of more than local importance.[73] These last conferments, interestingly, mark the end of Jewish prominence in the German textile industry. In fact, the geographical centre of gravity of the industry was shifting away from Berlin and Silesia, where Jewish enterprise had been prominent, to Saxony and, more particularly, Rhineland–Westphalia, where it was not. Some of the older Jewish family firms, indeed, continued to operate, but their importance diminished. A similar fate befell textile enterprises developed by Jewish entrepreneurship in southern Germany.[74] In the new joint-stock companies of the western provinces (and partly Silesia), Jews played little part. The reasons for the geographical shift

und mehr vom deutschen Markte verdrängt hat. Sein Vermögen wird auf 5 Millionen Mark, das seiner Firma auf mindestens 8 bis 10 Millionen Mark geschätzt. Er macht von diesem Vermögen durch grosse Opferwilligkeit für gemeinnützige und für wissenschaftliche Zwecke den besten Gebrauch . . .' Boetticher to the king, Berlin, 15 Dec. 1887, ZSAM 2.2.1, no. 1587, fos. 69^{r-v}

[72] 'Der im 70. Lebensjahre stehende Kommerzienrath Lewin Simon hierselbst ist ältester Leiter und Mitinhaber der von ihm vor 45 Jahren begründeten, durch seine rastlose Thätigkeit und Energie [a certain repetitiveness becomes evident] aus kleinen Anfängen zu hoher Blüthe gelangten hiesigen Firma Gebrüder Simon, die hauptsächlich die Herstellung von Baumwollenwaaren betreibt und im Elsass, sowie in Süddeutschland und Schlesien, eine grosse Anzahl von Etablissements beschäftigt, in denen viele Tausende dauernde Arbeit finden. Die Firma gehört zu den bedeutendsten ihrer Art in Deutschland und geniesst fast Weltruf. Es ist ihr gelungen, die englische Waare, die hier früher ausschliesslich bezogen wurde, zu Gunsten der heimischen Erzeugnisse mehr und mehr vom deutschen Markte zu verdrängen. Simon . . . ist zur Ergänzungssteuer mit einem Vermögen von über 13 Millionen Mark herangezogen . . .' Brefeld to the king, Berlin, 4 Apr. 1898, ZSAM 2.2.1, no. 1590, fos. 117^{r-v}

[73] 'Der Fabrikbesitzer Hermann Rinkel zu Berlin . . . ist alleiniger Inhaber der Firma I. Rinkel zu Landeshut in Schlesien.Diese besitzt in Nieder-Leppersdorf, Kreis Landeshut, eine mechanische Weberei mit 700 Stühlen, Appretur-Anstalt und Näherei [i.e. a vertically integrated enterprise of a type different from the Jewish-owned manufactures of the mid-century] für Tapisserie-Zwecke und beschäftigt in diesen Anlagen dauernd 900 Personen, für deren Wohl bestens gesorgt wird. Ausser dem in Landeshut befindlichen Hauptgeschäft werden Zweiggeschäfte in Berlin, Wien und Trautenau unterhalten . . . Als Förderer gemeinnütziger Bestrebungen hat er sich in letzter Zeit um die Stadt Landeshut und deren Umkreis sehr verdient gemacht, insbesondere ist seinem zielbewussten Vorgehen und seiner Opferwilligkeit das Zustandekommen der Ziederthalbahn Landeshut-Schöneberg-Albendorf zu danken, deren Betriebseröffnung zum 1. Oktober d. J. bevorsteht . . .' Thiele to the king, Berlin, 5 Sept. 1899, ZSAM 2.2.1, no. 1590, fos. 257^{r-v}

[74] For a summary description of Jewish entrepreneurship in the textile industry in Germany with some details on such activity outside Prussia see Jacob Toury, op. cit., n. 41 above, pp. 89 ff.

in German textile production and the consequent diminution of the Jewish role lie outside the scope of the present study. However, the reduced role of Jews in textile manufacture was accompanied by an increased wholesale trade, based largely in Berlin, in textile materials, clothing, and fashions.

Besides those engaged in the textile trade, there appear among the new KRs several industrialists engaged in the metallurgical industry. Prominent among these are the Caros (1875, 1894, 1897, and 1899), descended from generations of rabbis, and the allied Kerns (1855), the brothers Ludwig and Isidor Loewe (1889 and 1898), the Hahns (1877, 1889), and the Huldschinskys (1876). All except the brothers Loewe were associated primarily with Silesia, as were the coal wholesalers Fritz Friedländer (1897) and Eduard Arnhold (1900). The enterprises represented by these men were large family firms which, with growing capital requirements, were destined, normally by fusions, to become absorbed into large joint-stock companies. All the firms, except for Ludwig Loewe, arose from wholesale trading. With their extension into industrial activities and their eventual absorption into corporate structures, they represent the second wave of Jewish industrial entrepreneurship.

An enterprise in this group worth examining in some detail is that of the Caros, iron industrialists in Upper Silesia.[75] Its history is of interest as an instance of Jewish entrepreneurship in 'heavy industry' on a substantial scale. How far there were features in the evolution of the firm reflecting a distinctive—possibly 'Jewish'—management style is a matter to be considered.

The iron wholesale business of M. I. Caro & Sohn in Breslau had been founded by Moritz Caro in 1807. His son Robert (1819–75) had acquired in 1848 a water-mill and a small iron-foundry for the production of semi-finished products at Laband near Gleiwitz.[76] Robert Caro had entrusted its technical management to his brother-in-law Alois Kern, the commercial direction to Alois's brother Heinrich. Two characteristic features of the evolution of the firm are the branching out of a trading house into small-scale production (the same development occurs, among others, with Aron Hirsch & Sohn in

---

[75] For the following see Konrad Fuchs, 'Zur Rolle des schlesischen Judentums bei der wirtschaftlichen Entwicklung Oberschlesiens' in *Zeitschrift für Ostforschung*, 28 (1979), no. 2, 270 ff, Schwerin, loc. cit., n. 5 above, pp. 37 f. and Alfons Perlick, *Oberschlesische Berg- und Hüttenleute* (Kitzingen, 1953), pp. 79 ff.

[76] Fuchs, loc. cit., p. 279.

Halberstadt) and the Jewish family management of the Caros and the Kerns. Characteristic also is the division between technical and commercial management among the Kern brothers under the overall financial and commercial direction of Robert Caro. In fact, it was the Kern brothers who saw the modest enterprise through the crisis years 1857–65 and even succeeded in effecting a modest expansion.

In 1865 Heinrich Kern, looking for greater scope for his managerial talents, set up a wire manufacture, Heinrich Kern & Co., in competition with the nearby works of the Gentile Wilhelm Hegenscheidt. Robert Caro became a partner in the enterprise, Kern having persuaded him that the wire manufacture would become a major customer of his ironworks. Presently, Kern's manufacture overtook that of Hegenscheidt at least in quantity of output if not in its quality. The latter, however, was achieved when, in 1881, Victor Zuckerkandl, a retired Austro-Hungarian army officer of Jewish extraction, took over the management of the works.[77] A ruinous price war between Kern and Hegenscheidt ensued. It was in connection with this that Georg and Oscar, sons of Robert Caro and third generation in the firm of M. I. Caro & Sohn, acquired a new ironworks, the Moritzhütte. A degree of vertical integration was achieved with a coke oven, rented by the Caros in 1878, to supply the Moritzhütte which, in turn, provided the semi-finished materials for Kern's wire manufacture. It was in fact independence from outside suppliers which enabled Kern to compete effectively in the price war with Hegenscheidt.

In 1886–7 Kern and Hegenscheidt decided to amalgamate their enterprises. While the units producing semi-finished products (together with iron ore deposits and limestone quarries) were joined as the Oberschlesische Eisenindustrie AG für Eisenhüttenbetrieb und Bergbau (with an initial share capital of 8 million marks), the two wireworks in turn became the Oberschlesische Drahtindustrie AG (with a foundation capital of 4.8 million marks). Rivalry between the two companies led in turn to their amalgamation with effect from 1 January 1889 as Oberschlesische Eisenindustrie AG für Eisenhütten und Bergbau (Obereisen), presently to become a pillar of Silesian heavy industry. From its creation in 1889, Obereisen, under Oscar Caro's management (1889–1904), developed rapidly.[78] When Caro became a KR in 1894,

---

[77] For Viktor Zuckerkandl, see Dr Ernest Koenigsfeld, 'Viktor Zuckerkandl—ein oberschlesischer Wirtschaftsführer' in *Gleiwitzer-Beuthener-Tarnowitzer Heimatblatt*, 21 (Jan. 1971), no. 1, 20 ff.
[78] For some detail see Fuchs, loc. cit, p. 281.

he was in charge of an enterprise employing some 8,000 workers.[79] Yet, interestingly, when he was made a GKR five years later, it was his role in the parent house of M. I. Caro & Sohn, by then domiciled in Berlin, which the authorities chose to emphasize (perhaps due to the fact that commercial titles traditionally recognized ownership rather than management).[80] Obereisen's share capital in 1907 stood at 25.2 million marks. In 1904, Oscar Caro's place as managing director had been taken by Victor Zuckerkandl, who was to guide the firm through the difficult years of war and inflation. The financial transactions involved in the original fusions had been conducted by Carl Fürstenberg, who remained the firm's financial adviser.[81] While Oscar Caro joined the board of the BHG, Carl Fürstenberg in exchange became deputy chairman of the board of Obereisen.

Several aspects of this evolution are worth noting, more particularly the transformation of a family firm into a corporate enterprise, the rapid integration, both horizontal and vertical, the strong Jewish involvement not only in the provision of capital (the Caros, father and sons) and corporate financing (Carl Fürstenberg) but also in management (Heinrich Kern, Viktor Zuckerkandl, Oscar Caro), but, equally, a relatively rare instance of the successful fusion of 'Jewish' and 'non-Jewish' firms. (Caro and Hegenscheidt).

No less characteristic than that of Obereisen had been the development of the parent house, the iron wholesale firm of M. I. Caro

[79] 'Der Generaldirektor der Oberschlesischen Eisen-Industrie Aktien-Gesellschaft für Bergbau und Hüttenbetrieb, Oscar Caro in Gleiwitz, steht dem genannten Unternehmen als erster Leiter vor. Vermöge seiner Bildung, Erfahrung und rastlosen Thätigkeit ist es ihm gelungen, dieses bedeutende Aktienunternehmen zu hoher Blüthe zu bringen, so dass es eins der hervorragendsten der Provinz geworden ist. Es werden darin gegen 8000 Arbeiter beschäftigt, für die in ausgiebiger Weise durch Wohlfahrtseinrichtungen aller Art gesorgt ist. Wesentliches Verdienst hat sich Caro um die Bildung des deutschen Walzwerkverbandes erworben, in dessen Vorstand er seit Bestehen des Verbandes die Interessen der oberschlesischen Gruppe als Delegierter vertritt. Auch als Beirath für die russisch–deutschen Zollverhandlungen ist er thätig gewesen. Caro ist ein sehr reicher Mann, der sich durch private Wohlthätigkeit auszeichnet und in allen Kreisen Oberschlesiens das grösste Ansehen geniesst...' Berlepsch to the king, Berlin, 10. Mar. 1894, ZSAM Rep. 89 H vol. 7, fos. 16[r–v]

[80] 'Er betreibt seit einer Reihe von Jahren gemeinsam mit seinem Bruder in Berlin ein, in Deutschland zu den grössten zählendes Eisengrossgeschäft, welches einen Jahresumsatz von etwa 8 Millionen Mark erzielt, ist Vorsitzender des Aufsichtsraths der Oberschlesischen Eisenindustrie, und Aufsichtsrathsmitglied anderer Aktiengesellschaften. Im Handelsstande geniesst er hohes Ansehen, gilt als eine Stütze der oberschlesischen Eisenindustrie und besitzt ein Vermögen von vielen Millionen, von dem er zu Wohlthätigkeitszwecken fortgesetzt guten Gebrauch macht...' Thiele to the king, Berlin, 6 Apr. 1899, ZSAM 2.2.1, no. 1590, fos. 13[r–v]

[81] Cf. Fürstenberg, op. cit., pp. 191 f.

& Sohn managed since 1875 by Georg Caro, Oscar's older brother. Around 1890 the firm had moved the bulk of its activities from Breslau to Berlin. By the time Georg Caro became a KR in 1897 it could be described as it among the most important of its kind in Germany[82] with, in 1899, an annual turnover of some 8 million marks.[83] In 1906, Georg Caro was ennobled, a tribute to his position in German economic life.[84] Three years later, M. I. Caro & Sohn was amalgamated with the Deutsche Eisenhandels AG, founded in 1906 by Berlin's leading iron wholesaler GKR Louis Ravené (the Ravenés, sometimes erroneously described as of Jewish origin, were, in fact, of Huguenot descent). The amalgamation (including also some other firms) made the new Deutsche Eisenhandels AG the largest iron merchants in Germany. Its original share capital of 8.5 million marks had by 1913 been increased to 23 million. Georg Caro became its deputy chairman, his brother Oscar a board member.

Moreover, though the original Caro interests had by then been absorbed into larger corporate units, a 'fourth generation' also would be prominent in German economic life. Robert (b. 1885), the son of Oscar Caro, became not only board chairman of the Linkesche Waggonfabrik (later Linke-Hoffmann-Werke) in Breslau but also partner in the important Hamburg merchandizing house of Coutinho & Co., which then assumed the title of Coutinho, Caro & Co.

More significant, however, than the role of Robert Caro was that of Leo Lustig (1860–1932). Lustig, whose commercial talents had early been spotted by Georg and Oscar Caro, had, as their employee, been charged with creating a corporate organization of traders in Upper Silesian iron products. In 1887, Lustig had set up the *Schlesischer Händlerkonzern*, an association of all major firms in eastern and central Germany trading in the products of Upper Silesian rolling mills. For

---

[82] '... Dr jur. Georg Caro in Berlin, Mitinhaber und alleiniger Vertreter der Firma M. I. Caro & Sohn, betreibt hier ... in Gemeinschaft mit seinen Brüdern ein Eisengrossgeschäft, das zu den grössten derartigen Geschäften Deutschlands gehört und mit seiner Zweigniederlassung in Breslau als eine Stütze der oberschlesischen Eisenindustrie gilt. Caro geniesst demzufolge und als Besitzer eines Vermögens von mehreren Millionen Mark hervorragendes Ansehen im Handelsstande. Von seinen reichen Mitteln macht er ausgedehnten Gebrauch zu Wohlthätigkeitszwecken ... Caro ist in Berlin als Handelsrichter thätig ...' Brefeld to the king, Berlin, 18 May 1897, ZSAM 2.2.1, no. 1590, fos. 30^{r-v}

[83] ZSAM 2.2.1, no. 1590, fos. 13^{r-v}

[84] Though the title had been acquired partly by a vast 'gift' for charitable purposes and its award facilitated by conversion to Christianity and an absence of male heirs, it remained, none the less, a tribute to his economic standing.

years, it fell to Lustig to guide the fortunes of the association. His achievement in reconciling various conflicting interests earned him not only the title of KR but also a partnership in M. I. Caro & Sohn. When, moreover, in 1910 Lustig succeeded in bringing the Ravené AG into his association he had become the unchallenged leader of the iron wholesale trade in Germany. Shortly thereafter, he was appointed managing director of the Deutsche Eisenhandels AG, a position he would occupy until 1930 (when he became board chairman). During this later stage of his career, Lustig's major achievement lay in the organization of corporate interest groups, typical of advanced capitalist development. He became the founder of the association of German wholesale merchants (Reichsverband des Deutschen Gross- und Überseehandels) and, for many years, its vice-president. He also chaired the association of German ironwholesalers (Vereinigung der Eisenhändler Deutschlands) and represented it in the International Chamber of Commerce. He also helped to develop the Eastern Europe Institute of Breslau University and was rewarded with an honorary doctorate.

The development of the 'Caro group' has been described in some detail on account of a number of interesting features. It shows the evolution, over four generations, from Moritz Caro's modest iron trade to Leo Lustig's role in organizing German wholesale trade. It illustrates the progress of a family business through stages of corporate organization to activities in economic interest groups. There is a characteristic interaction of trading and manufacturing activities, with the former, seemingly, retaining pride of place. What is also worthy of note is the relatively modest role played by bank-capital.

Are there aspects of the 'Caro story' that may have an ethnic base? In this context, a striking feature is the existence of a Jewish core (Caro, Kern, Zuckerkandl, Lustig) based partly on kinship ties, partly on 'elective affinities'. There are also close commercial ties with enterprises with strong Jewish connections: BHG, Bismarckhütte, since 1895 the Caro's supplier of special steels, the Huldschinsky and Friedländer enterprises. What is notable also is the prominence of Jews in management, the brothers Kern, Oscar Caro, and Victor Zuckerkandl on the industrial side, Leo Lustig on the commercial. However, if the Caro businesses had marked 'Jewish' associations, there was, on the other hand, the equally notable and seemingly harmonious association with the Gentile Hegenscheidts and Ravenés.

Was there, in the direction of the Caro enterprises, anything that could be considered as a distinctively 'Jewish' style of business strategy? Unlike family-dominated firms like Krupp, Thyssen, Klöckner, or Siemens (a form comparatively rare among major Jewish industrial firms in the age of full industrialization and developed capitalism—the metal-manufacturing Hirsches were the exception), Obereisen was not owned by members of the Caro family, though they were, of course, major shareholders. The Caros remained, indeed, owners of the parent firm of M. I. Caro & Sohn which, however, had itself become integrated in a larger unit. On the other hand, the Caro 'style' differed radically from that of the large joint-stock companies (Harpen, Gelsenkirchen, Mannesmann, in its later phases also Gutehoffnungs-Hütte) dominated by powerful managing directors and influenced, to some extent, by their banking connections. Except as the representatives of banking interests, Jews, as a rule, played no part in these large joint-stock enterprises though, exceptionally, there could be powerful Jewish managing directors like Albert Ballin or Alfred Berliner of the Schuckert-Werke in Nuremberg (later Siemens & Schuckert). Large Jewish firms, on the whole, tended instead to develop the 'intermediate' form of organization typified by the Caros. It was to this model that the AEG, Ludwig Loewe, the Friedländer concern, the Mertons' Frankfurter Metallgesellschaft, and the AG für Anilinfabrikation (Agfa) in a greater or lesser measure approximated. Such firms, except for Ludwig Loewe, did not bear the name of a family (the small parent firm might still do so, as was the case with Caro and Friedländer, in fact Ludwig Loewe also was the name of a relatively small parent firm). Nor were they owned by members of a family, while there were yet strong family associations. The form of organization thus was intermediate between the family-controlled enterprise and the anonymous joint-stock company (essentially 'Gentile' forms). It is a form comparatively rare among 'Gentile' enterprises (significantly, perhaps, an approximation can be found in the position of the Haniel family—not by accident of French origin and traders before they became industrialists—in the Gutehoffnungs-Hütte). By and large, Gentile family firms did not enter capitalist corporate structures in this particular manner. 'Jewish' ones did so readily.

Another characteristic feature is the activity of Leo Lustig (sponsored by the Caro brothers) of creating and directing important professional associations (recalling comparable activities of, among others, Oscar Tietz, Heinrich Grünfeld, Emil Guggenheimer, Siegmund Hirsch, Georg Solmssen, and Paul Silverberg). Jews, in fact, though they had of course no monopoly of 'business diplomacy', may yet have possessed special skills for reconciling divergent interests and mitigating, on occasion, the effects of cut-throat competition. The transatlantic shipping-pools negotiated by Albert Ballin would later be an outstanding example. Whether men of Jewish origin were particularly gifted for or disproportionately prominent in this aspect of 'organized capitalism' it is impossible to determine with certainty. What is certain is that the case of Leo Lustig was far from being unique.

Different aspects of Jewish industrial activity are illustrated by the careers of Salomon Huldschinsky and Albert Hahn. Following their introduction into Germany of the manufacture of shoddy (studied by Hahn in England), they then proceeded to copy a further British speciality, seamless steel tubes. The combination of Hahn's initiative with Huldschinsky's skills as a manager resulted in the establishment of an ironworks in Gleiwitz[85] which, in 1876, employed some four to five hundred workers.[86] Local officialdom paid tribute to its importance for the province of Silesia.[87] Following the dissolution of the partnership in 1873, Huldschinsky had remained the sole owner, while Hahn had set up a new factory in Düsseldorf specializing in the

[85] 'In gleicher Weise trat aber auch die geistige Superiorität Hahn's bei der Begründung des Gleiwitzer Werkes hervor. Die vaterländische Industrie kannte noch keine Röhrenwalzwerke, dieser Artikel kam ausschliesslich aus England. Von dort ist auch dem Hahn die Idee zu dem Unternehmen gekommen. Er bemerkte mit richtigem Scharfblick die ungeheuere Wichtigkeit dieses Handelsartikels, wie zugleich den Vortheil welchen die Fabrikation desselben den schlesischen Eisenhütten bringen musste. Wenn sich der g. Huldschinsky auch hier wieder anfänglich sträubte, auf die Errichtung des Gleiwitzer Werkes einzugehehn, so fügte er sich doch endlich, wie immer, der Hahn'schen Energie und als sich die lohnenden Früchte des Unternehmens erst zeigten und das Werk einen wahrhaft colossalen Ertrag erzielte: im Jahre 1872 900,000M:, da ward auch Huldschinsky der beste und unermüdlichste Leiter dieses Werkes, welches er später, bei der Auflösung der Société, gänzlich für sich übernommen hat.' von Madai to Dr Achenbach, Berlin, 18 Aug. 1877, ZSAM Rep. 120, A IV 5, vol. 19, fos. 199[r-v]

[86] 'Der g. Huldschinsky ist Besitzer einer grossen Stabeisenfabrik und eines Röhrenwalzwerkes zu Gleiwitz, beschäftigt dort unter specieller Leitung seines Neffen und Schwiegersohnes 400 bis 500 Arbeiter und hat hier im eigenen Hause ... Comtoir und Lager. Im hiesigen Comtoir sind zwei Buchhalter, vier Correspondenten, drei Commis, ein Hausdiener und ein Kutscher beschäftigt ...' von Madai to von Jagow, Berlin, 17 Jan. 1876, ZSAM Rep. 120 A IV 5, vol. 16, fo. 110.

[87] 'Salomon Huldschinsky ist Mitbegründer der im Jahre 1868 zu Gleiwitz unter der Firma Hahn und Huldschinsky errichteten Röhrenwalzwerkes, welches seit dem Jahre 1873 unter der Firma S. Huldschinsky & Söhne, Berlin und Gleiwitz betrieben, das erste grössere derartige Etablissement in Schlesien, und welches nicht allein für den Oberschlesischen Industriebezirk, sondern auch für die Provinz überhaupt von grösster Bedeutung ist ...' Ober-Präsident of the province to Silesia to Dr Achenbach, Breslau, 3 Apr. 1877, ZSAM Rep. 120, A IV 9, vol. 18, fos. 144[r-v]

production of heating pipes.[88] After Huldschinsky's death in 1877, the management of the firm passed jointly to his son and a nephew. There followed the characteristic integration into the corporate system already seen in the case of the Caros. In 1894, the firm became Huldschinsky's Hüttenwerke AG, with Huldschinsky's son Oscar as board chairman. A period of rapid expansion and diversification followed. The capital, a modest 3 million marks in 1894, had, by 1898, been raised to 20 million. Following a series of fusions the Huldschinsky interests, in 1905, became the core of a major joint-stock company, Oberschlesische Eisenbahnbedarfs AG. As manufacturers of steel tubes the firm—known on the stock-exchange as Oberbedarf—became noted for the production of boiler-tubes for the imperial navy and merchant marine.[89] Characteristically, the original contribution of Hahn and Huldschinsky had been the transfer to Germany of British technology. Such transfers, first from Britain and later above all from the USA, were a common feature of Jewish industrial entrepreneurship, almost certainly a by-product of general mobility and international connections. The other feature worth noting is, once again, the integration of a family business into a larger corporate structure.

Technology transfer and arms production played a part also in the much more important industrial activities of the brothers Ludwig and Isidor Loewe. Their factories were significant on the one hand for the early adoption of new production methods, on the other for the introduction of precision machinery. Ludwig Loewe in fact was the pioneer, in Germany, of advanced methods of mass production copied from the USA. Within a generation Ludwig Loewe & Co., from a modest family firm, had grown into the parent company of a major industrial concern. Ludwig's brother Isidor Loewe, the second managing director, had become a prominent industrial magnate. It is, more

---

[88] 'Ein fernerer Beweis für den grossen Unternehmungsgeist des g. Hahn ist die Thatsache, dass er sofort nach der Trennung der Societät im Jahre 1873, in Düsseldorf ein neues Röhrenwalzwerk erbaute, welches dem Gleiwitzer Werke bereits ebenbürtig zur Seite steht und durch eine neue Specialität, Heizröhren sogar das englische Fabrikat verdrängt und den Export nach England ermöglicht hat. Huldschinsky dagegen hat sich auf die Erhaltung und Fortführung des alten solidem Gleiwitzer Werkes beschränkt und dasselbe auch auf seiner früheren Höhe erhalten, ein Verdienst, welches mit Rücksicht auf den inzwischen eingetretenen Niedergang der Eisen-Industrie jedenfalls nicht zu verkennen ist...' von Madai to Dr Achenbach, Berlin, 18 Aug. 1877, ZSAM Rep. 120, 1 IV 5, vol. 19, fos. 200^{r-v}

[89] Details in E. von Zalewski, 'Kurze Chronik', *Gleiwitzer-Beuthener-Tarnowitzer Heimatblatt* (1967).

particularly, the early history of the group that is of interest in the present context, showing the Loewe brothers as industrial pioneers and pace-setters of the age of full industrialization and developing *Hochkapitalismus*.[90]

Late in 1869, at the start of the 'second wave' of Jewish entrepreneurial activity, Ludwig Loewe, son of a poor cantor in Thuringia[91] (Heiligenstadt auf dem Eichsfeld), received authorization to start in Berlin a company for the manufacture of sewing-machines. Early in 1870 his firm, Ludwig Loewe & Co, Kommandit-Gesellschaft auf Aktien für Fabrikation von Nähmaschinen, was entered on the Berlin commercial register with a nominal share capital of 1 million thalers of which a quarter (750,000 marks) was paid up. The bulk of the capital was provided by a 'Jewish' private banking house (Born u. Busse), one of the two prepared to provide risk capital for hopeful industrial entrepeneurs.[92] (The other was Jacob Landau, the early financiers of Emil Rathenau.) Typical of the second wave of entrepreneurship, Ludwig Loewe & Co., from the start, was a form of joint-stock company. Also, unlike earlier Jewish ventures, it was, from the beginning, a pure manufacturing company. Loewe's object was serial production (not necessarily confined to sewing-machines), by means of American precision machinery. In 1870, accompanied by a specialist engineer, he visited the USA to study American production methods. He applied his experience on his return when he set up an American-style factory. The delivery of American machinery proving from the start both slow and unreliable, the factory at once began to produce its own machine tools copying American designs, an interesting and extreme case of technology transfer by a Jewish entrepreneur.

Loewe's manufacture of sewing-machines, however, remained

[90] For details on the Loewe concern see Georg Tischert, *Aus der Entwicklung des Loewe-Konzerns* (Berlin, 1911) and Zielenziger, op. cit., n. 32 above, pp. 99 ff. and Otto Jeidels, *Das Verhältnis der deutschen Grossbanken zur Industrie*, 2nd edn. (Munich and Leipzig, 1913), especially pp. 243 ff.

[91] Characteristically, the eldest of the brothers, Sigmund emigrated to England, where he became an intimate friend of Sir Ernest Cassel and, in due course, chief executive of Vickers at a time when, besides its other industrial activities, the firm was engaged in the mass production of the Maxim gun. (Gerald Oliven, *The Ludwig Loewe Group, its Personalities and Interconnections from the Early Foundations until its Forced Dismantlement under the Nazis*, unpublished MS in the archives of the Leo Baeck Institute (New York).

[92] This is, of course, the time of the so-called *Gründerjahre*. Largely under the influence of anti-Semitic propaganda, a great deal more attention has normally been paid to the enterprises which failed than to those which succeeded.

modest in scale due largely to American competition.[93] It would be discontinued finally in 1879. Almost at once, however, the firm turned to production of a very different kind. When, in the Franco-Prussian war of 1870, the French chassepot rifle had proved its unquestioned superiority, the Prussian government resolved to equip its army with an equally effective infantry weapon, the Mauser rifle Mod. 71. Since the royal ordnance factories lacked the equipment needed for mass production, it had turned to private industry. The only factory in Germany equipped to combine precision work and serial production was found to be that of Ludwig Loewe. By 1875, the bulk of the firm's output consisted of rifle parts, more particularly sights and extractors, small and complex items requiring extreme precision. Loewe began to manufacture these on a large scale,[94] later adding also artillery components. For a time production of weapon parts became the firm's main activity.[95]

The enterprise developed rapidly. In 1878 Isidor Loewe, Ludwig's younger brother, became a full partner (*persönlich haftender Gesellschafter*). In 1886, on Ludwig's death, Isidor Loewe became the senior partner. The following year, the share capital of the firm was increased by 1¼ million marks to finance large-scale production of rifles for the Turkish and German governments. At the same time, Loewe acquired shares to a nominal value of 2 million marks in the renowned small-arms factory of Mauser in Oberndorf am Neckar. In 1889, the capital of Ludwig Loewe & Co. was raised by a further 1¼ million marks. At the same time, together with explosives manufacturers in Hamburg and Cologne, Loewe acquired the Deutsche Metallpatronenfabrik von Lorenz in Karlsruhe. In 1890, with the active participation of Loewe, the explosives manufacturers amalgamated to form the Vereinigte Köln-Rottweiler Pulverfabriken.

When in 1889 Isidor Loewe was proposed for the title of KR[96] it was refused. The true reason was almost certainly his Jewishness (combined with the left-liberal sympathies of the Loewe brothers), publicized by a vicious anti-Semitic campaign. When in 1890, in

---

[93] Production of sewing-machines: 1873: 8,421; 1875: 5,570; 1876: 2,355; 1877: 1,147. Tischert, op. cit., p. 18.

[94] Production of rifle sights: 1873: 70,199; 1874: 309,813; 1875: 373,659. In 1875, Loewe also produced 305,345 extractors (ib.).

[95] In 1875, whilst the value of the production of machines and machine tools was 634,000 marks, that of weapon and munition parts had risen to 3¼ million (ib.).

[96] 'Isidor Löwe ... seit dem Tode seines Bruders Ludwig Löwe (1886) alleiniger kaufmännischer und technischer Leiter der von ihm mitgegründeten Kommanditgesell-

schaft auf Aktien "Ludwig Löwe & Comp.". Diese Gesellschaft findet sich im Besitz der oben erwähnten Fabrik so wie einer zweiten in Oberndorf in Württemberg, betriebt mit beträchtlichem Betriebskapital und etwa 2 700 Arbeitern ausser Waffen- und Munitionsfabrikation auch Werkzeug-Maschinenbau nach amerikanischem System sowie Dampfmaschinen und Röhrenkesselbau und ist unter Leitung des verstorbenen Ludwig Löwe zu hoher Blüthe gelangt. Soweit die Firma nicht durch Aufträge der preussischen und deutschen Regierungen in Anspruch genommen wird, hat sie Lieferungen nach Russland, Oesterreich, Italien, China und der Türkei auszuführen...' Boetticher to the king, Berlin, 1 Aug. 1898, ZSAM 2.2.1, no. 1587, fo. 179^{r-v} The petition for the award of the title submitted on Isidor Loewe's behalf described the activities of the firm until that time in detail: 'Die Firma Loewe & Co. ist seit dem Jahre 1872 von dem Königlichen Kriegs-Ministerium in sehr umfangreichem Maasse zu den Arbeiten der Neubewaffnung der Armee herangezogen worden und hat seitdem wiederholt Gelegenheit gehabt, dem Königlichen Kriegs-Ministerium wesentliche Dienste zu leisten dadurch, dass sie mit Aufwendung grosser Energie und Geldmittel die amerikanische Präcisionstechnik nach Deutschland verpflanzt und dadurch das Königliche Kriegs-Ministerium in den Stand gesetzt hat, die grossen Verbesserungen, welche im letzten Jahrzehnt auf dem Gebiete der Militärtechnik gemacht worden sind, schnell und zuverlässig und ohne Preisgabe des Geheimnisses für die eigene Bewaffnung nutzbar zu machen.

So hat die Firma gerade dieser Tage wiederum für das Königliche Kriegs-Ministerium eine Arbeit beendet, an deren schleunigster und intelligenter Durchführung das Königliche Kriegs-Ministerium ein grosses Interesse hatte. Dadurch, dass die Firma ihre Leistungsfähigkeit auf das äusserste [sic] anspannte, ist es ihr gelungen, diese Arbeit in der erstaunlich kurzen Frist von circa 1½ Jahren zu bewältigen. Hätte, wie das früher geschehen musste, die amerikanische Industrie mit dieser Arbeit betraut werden müssen, dann würde die Ausführung 3 bis 4 Jahre gedauert und mindestens 1½ Millionen Mark mehr gekostet haben, überdies aber wäre das Königliche Kriegs-Ministerium gezwungen gewesen, seine geheimsten Intentionen dem Auslande Preis zu geben.

Die Haupt-Leistungen der Firma Loewe seit dem Jahre 1874 sind die folgenden:
(1) Während 1874–1877: Lieferung von ca 1 Million Visieren und Schlosstheilen für das Infanterie und Jäger-Gewehr M/71.
(2) Im Jahre 1875: Lieferung von ca. 1 Million Granatzündern–eines neuen Systems für das Königliche Feuerwerks-Laboratorium
(3) Vom Jahre 1872 bis in die heutige Zeit Lieferung der Neuausstattung resp. Ergänzung der Fabrikations-Einrichtungen der Königlichen militärischen Fabriken und unausgesetzte Vervollkommnung dieser Einrichtungen. [There follows a list of not only Prussian but also Bavarian and Saxon armaments factories.]
(4) In den Zeiten, in welchen das Königlich Preussische Kriegs-Ministerium die Dienste der Firma nicht in Anspruch nahm, war diese auch für befreundete, auswärtige Regierungen, speziell Oesterreich, Russland, China etc. beschäftigt und hat für ihre Leistungen überall uneingeschränkte Anerkennung gefunden.
(5) Nebenher waren die Leistungen der Firma Loewe von der Königlichen Staats-Regierung auch für friedliche Zwecke vielfach in Anspruch genommen; ...

Auch in der Privat-Industrie, welche auf Betreiben der Firma Loewe die amerikanische Fabrikations-Methode vielfach und überall mit glänzendem Erfolge eingeführt hat, stehen die Leistungen der Firma in ausgezeichnetem Rufe und es wird allseitig anerkannt, dass dieselben der deutschen Industrie zu hoher Ehre gereichen.

Die Fabrik beschäftigt durchschittlich
ca. 500 Arbeiter im Maschinenbau und
7–800 Arbeiter in der Massen-Fabrikation (ausschliesslich Waffentheile und Munition)

consequence, Isidor Loewe separated the armaments—from the machine-tool division, the firm was employing some 5,000 workers. In 1891, it raised a loan of 7½ million marks. The following year, in conjunction with Thomson Houston Electric Co. of Boston, it branched out into the electricity industry by subscribing one third of the capital of the new Union Elektricitäts-Gesellschaft. When, in 1893, Ludwig Loewe became a fully fledged joint-stock company quoted on the stock exchange, it received the capitalist accolade of acquiring its own financial consortium (Direction der Disconto-Gesellschaft, Dresdner Bank, S. Bleichröder) to finance, more particularly, its expensive electrotechnical venture. In 1894 the consortium founded, with a share capital of 15 million marks issued at 136 per cent, a new company, Gesellschaft für elektrische Unternehmungen (Gesfürel) to finance electrotechnical enterprises and secure orders. Actual construction work would be carried out by the Union Elektricitäts-Gesellschaft under the technical supervision of Ludwig Loewe. Isidor Loewe, with the help of bank capital, was taking steps to build up a sophisticated concern.

In 1896, Isidor Loewe transferred his weapons division to the Deutsche Metallpatronenfabrik now renamed Deutsche Waffen- und Munitionsfabriken (Karlsruhe). Loewe received shares in the new company to a nominal value of 6 million marks, as well as a small cash payment. He and his associates obtained positions on the board of the new company which, moreover, undertook to buy its precision machinery exclusively from Ludwig Loewe. 6 million marks were invested in modernizing the factories of the parent company.

In 1898, Ludwig Loewe & Co. sold its electrical division to Union Elektricitäts-Gesellschaft which, at the same time, increased its share capital by 15 million marks. Shares of a nominal value of 4½ million marks remained in the Loewe portfolio. In the same year, the Schaaffhausensche Bankverein in Cologne, the bank *par excellence* of German 'heavy industry', joined the Loewe consortium. Loewe further diversified his interests by entering (with indifferent success) the field of heavy machine construction, by founding the Deutsche Niles-Werkzeugmaschinenfabrik and the Ascherslebener Maschinenfabrik.

---

ferner nahezu 1000 Arbeitsmaschinen, einen Park, der selbst die grossartigsten amerikanischen derartigen Etablissements weit übertrifft' (ib. fos. 183–86).

When, in 1898, Isidor Loewe was again proposed for the title of *Kommerzienrat*, he was the head of a major industrial concern. Those who had opposed his previous application were forced to recognize his changed position.[97] The Loewe brothers had, in fact, created one of the early German *Grosskonzerne*. Its subsequent history belongs to a later period.

Certain aspects of the early history of the Loewe concern are worth noting. Somewhat unusually, as already pointed out, Ludwig Loewe went straight into manufacturing. The parent company remained in manufacturing to the end (though the increasingly important Gesfürel became largely a service and finance company). A second feature was the importance, especially in the beginning, of advanced American technology. In fact, Ludwig Loewe was a major industrial innovator—at least so far as the German economy was concerned. His industrial activities controvert the view of Jewish entrepreneurship as being confined to peripheral areas or to the 'interstices' of the German economy. At the same time, of course, Ludwig Loewe (unlike Emil Rathenau) was not a trained engineer or inventor but had to rely, for technical expertise, on the services of others. In this sense he does perhaps conform to the anti-Semitic stereotype of the alleged lack of originality in Jewish entrepreneurship. A further feature of the Loewe's

---

[97] '... Nach den übereinstimmenden Berichten des hiesigen Polizei-Präsidenten und des Präsidenten des Reichsbank-Direktoriums, die über den Antrag, den sie befürworten, zunächst von mir vertraulich befragt worden sind, haben sich die früher dargelegten persönlichen und geschäftlichen Verhältnisse des Loewe, sowie die Stellung der genannten Gesellschaft inzwischen wesentlich geändert. Loewe . . . hat durch seine Umsicht und Thatkraft das von ihm geleitete industrielle Unternehmen, das sich die Waffen- und Munitionsfabrikation, sowie den Werkzeug-Maschinenbau zur Aufgabe gestellt und in neuester Zeit auch mit dem Bau von elektrischen Maschinen und Apparaten begonnen hat, zu einem der bedeutendsten und umfangreichsten Deutschlands auszugestalten und zu erheben verstanden. Die Firma, deren Ruf namentlich auf dem Gebiete der Waffentechnik über Europa verbreitet ist, beschäftigt in ihren Fabriken zahlreiche Arbeiter und erfreut sich sehr guter finanzieller Erfolge. Nach Mittheilung des Kriegsministers sind die Loeweschen Fabrik, sowie auch diejenigen Fabriken, bei denen er hervorragend betheiligt ist, ihren Verpflichtungen der Militärverwaltung gegenüber stets nachgekommen und haben die sehr bedeutenden Lieferungen von Waffen, Munition und sonstigem Kriegsmaterial zur Zufriedenheit ausgeführt. Loewe, der aus Anlass von Lieferungen für das Ausland mehrfach durch Verleihung fremdländischer Orden ausgezeichnet worden ist, geniesst wegen seiner Tüchtigkeit und der von ihm erreichten Erfolge in der Geschäftswelt hohes Ansehen und Vertrauen, das durch seine Wahl zum Mitgliede des Ältesten-Kollegiums der Berliner Kaufmannschaft Ausdruck gefunden hat. Ausserdem gehört er dem Aufsichtsrath mehrerer grosser und angesehener Aktien-Gesellschaften an . . .' Brefeld to the king, Berlin, 4 Feb. 1898, ZSAM 2.2.1, no. 1590, fos. 100–1.

strategies is adaptability. When American precision machinery proved difficult to obtain, they built their own. When it proved unprofitable to manufacture sewing-machines, they turned to weapon parts. They were ready to diversify by branching out into the rising electrical industry, construction, and servicing and into machine building. A distinctive feature of Isidor Loewe's commercial policies is the readiness to sell off divisions of his firm in return for a stake in large specialized undertakings and guaranteed orders for the parent company. It is arguable whether the Loewe 'empire' was in fact an early conglomerate or could still be considered an integrated concern. Isidor Loewe's share transactions were distinctive (and very different from Emil Rathenau's financial management of the AEG). It is, of course, a matter of pure speculation whether one chooses to detect ethnic characteristics in Isidor Loewe's remarkable agility in his share dealings and participations. Finally, the Loewe concern illustrates the evolution of a relatively modest engineering firm started by a man without means of his own, with 'risk capital' provided by private Jewish bankers, into a large corporate organization financed by a consortium of major banks (composed of both joint-stock and private banks, both 'Gentile' and 'Jewish'). Again, the Loewe family, while retaining a role to the very end, blends into a corporate structure in a way characteristic of Jewish entrepreneurs. A comparison (stressing both similarities and differences) with the 'management style' of the Rathenaus at the AEG, however interesting, lies beyond the scope of the present study.

If, for the brothers Loewe, arms manufacture was only a part (though an important one) of their varied economic activities, other Jewish entrepreneurs made their contributions—and fortunes—as their predecessors had done before them, through military contracts in the three wars of German unification. Indeed, the place in Jewish entrepreneurship of war contracts—possibly of contracts with public authority in general—is a subject which would repay detailed investigation. In particular, it would be interesting to know (though quantification may be difficult, if not impossible) whether and to what degree Jewish involvement in meeting the needs of the authorities was indicative of overall economic activity in Prussia–Germany, how far, as is almost certainly the case, there was an element of Jewish specificity—a continuation of the services rendered to rulers by court Jews of the age of absolutism.

Prominent among suppliers of the Prusso-German armies in

1870–1 were the grain dealers Salomon Lachmann of Berlin[98] and Simon Cohn of Kreuzburg in Upper Silesia. The authorities, both military and civil, paid eloquent tribute to their services.[99] Not only did both become KRs in 1872 but they were also made GKRs, Salomon Lachmann in 1880,[100] Simon Cohn, who by then had moved to Berlin,

---

[98] 'Salomon Lachmann . . . who came to Berlin in the mid-thirties of the 19th century as an apprentice in the office of a wholesale grain merchant, had become a big grain merchant in companionship with his brother Louis in the fifties.

When the Prussian army went to war against Denmark in 1864, Salomon Lachmann was entrusted with the supply of food to the fighting forces. He fulfilled the same function in the Prussian wars against Austria in 1866 and against France in 1870–1. In that function, he was always attached to the headquarters of the army . . . (Kurt Lachmann, loc. cit., n. 16 above).

[99] '. . . Als im Laufe des Krieges die Preise aller Bedürfnisse in Frankreich unverhältnismässig gesteigert waren, bemühte sich die Armee-Verwaltung vergeblich, auf dem Lieferungswege ein Herabgehen derselben herbeizuführen. Selbst in Elsass-Lothringen behaupteten sie sich trotz der Nähe von Deutschland auf jener ausserordentlichen Höhe. Als einziges Mittel blieb der Verwaltung nur der Selbstankauf durch tüchtige Kaufleute und zwar in der Art übrig, dass die bedeutendsten Lieferanten, welche den Markt beherrschten, von demselben entfernt wurden. Zu den letzteren gehörte auch der g. Lachmann. Er wurde aufgefordert, den Ankauf für die Verwaltung zu übernehmen und that dies gegen Bewilligung der sehr mässiger Provision von ½%. Es wurde durch diese Operation eine Verminderung der Preise von 30 bis 50% zu Wege gebracht, und, nach der Angabe des Armee-Intendanten Engelhard eine Ersparniss von mindestens 6 Millionen Thalern für den Staat herbeigeführt. Der Kriegs-Minister und der General-Lieutenant von Stosch haben sich deshalb lebhaft für eine Allerhöchste Auszeichnung des g. Lachmann verwendet . . .' Itzenplitz to the king, Berlin, 15 Jan. 1872, ZSAM 2.2.1, no. 1582, fos. 163[r–v]

'. . . Zu den Lieferanten, welche in dieser Weise mit der Armee-Verwaltung in Geschäftsverkehr traten und sich ihr besonders nützlich erwiesen, gehört auch der Kaufmann Simon Cohn zu Creutzburg. Der Kriegsminister, der General von Manteuffel und der General-Lieutenant von Stosch haben sich deshalb lebhaft für die Gewährung der gleichen Auszeichnung an den g. Cohn verwendet, welche dem Kaufmann Lachmann zu Theil geworden ist.

'Der g. Cohn hat sich durch die Lieferungen während des Krieges mit Oesterreich und des letzten Krieges ein sehr beträchtliches Vermögen erworben . . . und hat sich hierbei als in hohem Grade uneigennützig und zuverlässig erwiesen. Ganz besonders sind diese rühmlichen Eigenschaften aber in seinem Verhältnisse zu den Militairbehörden hervorgetreten, welche ihm nicht blos das Zeugniss eines äusserst thätigen und gewandten: sondern auch eines streng rechtlichen Geschäftsmannes geben. Für gemeinnützige Zwecke macht er von seinem Reichthum in liberaler Weise Gebrauch . . .' v. Itzenplitz to the king, Berlin, 21 Feb. 1872, ZSAM 2.2.1, no. 1582, fos. 181–2.

[100] '. . . Lachmann betreibt ein Bank- und Wechselgeschäft in ziemlich bedeutendem Umfange. Sein ursprünglich schon beträchtliches Vermögen hat sich durch glückliche Geschäfte und grosse Lieferungen welche er in den Jahren 1864, 1866 und 1870/71 für die Armee übernommen hat, im Laufe der Zeit so vermehrt, dass dasselbe gegenwärtig auf etwa 15 Millionen Mark geschätzt wird . . .

Durch seine Solidität, sowie durch seinen Charakter und Reichthum nimmt der g. Lachmann eine hervorragende Stellung im Handelsstande ein und erfreut sich auch in den übrigen bürgerlichen Kreisen allgemeiner Achtung. In Folge des Vertrauens seiner

in 1887.[101] Another important contractor, however, also hailing from Silesia, remained untitled, as did his son, almost certainly by choice.[102] Somewhat unusually, also, this was a family which, even with great wealth, continued to reside in Breslau. The Schottländers, remarkably, were a family whose members, while preserving the Jewish faith, also became Silesian magnates.[103]

Israel Ben David Schottländer,[104] the ancestor, had settled in 1803 in the small town of Münsterberg in Silesia where, in 1812, he had acquired Prussian citizenship. Schottländer was an optician, trading in spectacles and other optical wares which he sold not only locally but also at markets and fairs. He died in 1827. His son Johann Leib (Loebel), born in 1809, married in 1824 into a trading family. By 1835, he had become a prosperous trader and farmer, the owner of several estates around Münsterberg. His oldest son Julius, born in 1835, had moved to Breslau to run a mill. When Loebel followed him around

Mitbürger und Glaubens-Genossen zu manchen Ehrenämtern berufen, entwickelt er fortdauernd eine gemeinnützige Thätigkeit . . .' Hofmann to the king, Berlin, 27 Mar. 1880, ZSAM 2.2.1, NO. 1583, fos. 26[r–v]

[101] 'Der . . . Kaufmann Simon Cohn . . . siedelte im Jahre 1872 von seinem damaligen Wohnorte Kreuzburg O/Schl. nach Berlin über und betreibt hier ein nicht unbedeutendes kaufmännisches Geschäft, welches sich namentlich mit der Ausführung belangreicher Lieferungen für die Armee-Verwaltung sowie für die provinzialständischen Anstalten der Provinzen Pommern, Brandenburg und Westpreussen befasst. Zur bessere Abwickelung dieser Lieferungs-Geschäfte, welche sich auf 1 Million Mark jährlich beziffern, werden in Mainz und Metz, sowie in Landsberg a/W, Straussberg, Lübben, Prenzlau, Uckermünde, Neu-Stettin, Konitz ziemlich bedeutende Agenturen unterhalten.

Cohn ist Mitglied der Corporation der Berliner Kaufmannschaft und lebt in sehr günstigen Vermögens-Verhältnissen; er besitzt u.a. drei Rittergüter . . . Wegen seines ehrenhaften Charakters erfreut er sich allgemeiner Achtung. Bei jeder sich darbietenden Gelegenheit bethätigt er, ohne damit zu prunken, eine seltene Opferwilligkeit zur Förderung wohlthätiger und gemeinnütziger Zwecke . . .' Boetticher to the king, Berlin, 9 July 1887, ZSAM 2.2.1, no. 1587, fos. 39[r–v]

[102] For detailed information about three generations of Schottländers, Loibel, Julius, and Dr Paul, see Lisbeth Ledermann, 'Familie David Schottländer', typescript MS in the archives of the Leo Baeck Institute in New York; the same, Schottländersche Familienstiftung, ibid. and Rudolf Martin, *Jahrbuch des Vermögens und Einkommens der Millionäre in Preussen* (Berlin, 1912), pp. 108 ff.

[103] When Julius Schottländer died in Breslau in 1911, he was said to have left a fortune of 50 million marks. 'Er lehnte alle Orden und Auszeichnungen ab. Als ihm aber von höchster Stelle für seinen zehntausend Morgen grossen Gutsbesitz das Majorat [erblich] angeboten wurde, wurde er der erste und einzige jüdische Majoratsherr in Deutschland.' Ledermann, 'Familienstiftung', op. cit., fo. 10. Julius Schottländer was, according to Martin, in 1908 the second wealthiest person—after Prince Pless—resident in the country in *Regierungsbezirk Breslau* and ranked twenty-second among Prussian millionaires. Martin, op.. cit., p. 109.

[104] Named after a suburb of Danzig, from where the family originated.

1860, the estates near Münsterberg were left in the care of two younger sons. Loebel presently branched out into new fields of activity. He started a cement factory in Oppeln, bought real estate in Breslau, owned brickworks, and acquired interests in Oder navigation. In 1864, he built himself a town house.

The first 'quantum jump' in the fortunes of the Schottländers came with the wars of German unification. Their landed estates, combined with their farming skills, enabled them to become major suppliers of the Prussian and Prusso-German armies.[105] In 1872, Loebel Schottländer added a further source of revenue by renting the world-famous mineral waters of Karlsbad in Bohemia.[106] Loebel Schottländer died in 1880, a wealthy man.

Under his son Julius, the patriarchal Jewish family business somewhat changed its character. Following the example of Moses Henoch in Gleissen—but on a larger scale and in a new capitalist spirit—Julius Schottländer, on the basis of his agricultural interests, became an entrepreneur and developer (of the city of Breslau). He was already the owner of mills (for both oil and grain), of landed estates, and brickworks, as well as of a coal-mine. Now he turned to real estate development. His landed estates in fact were in part located at the very gates of Breslau and a whole quarter of the city came to be built

[105] 'Im Familienarchiv wurden Schriftstücke aufbewahrt, in denen von dem Befehlshaber einer preussischen Armee bescheinigt wird, wie vorzüglich in den Feldzügen 1864 und 1866 gegen Oesterreich die Verpflegung der Armee durch Loebel Schottländer für den Durchzug durch Schlesien war. Loebel und seine Söhne waren durch ihre Güter und ihre Mühlen in der Lage, den grössten Anforderungen gerecht zu werden. Sie lieferten Vieh, Getreide und durch die eigenen Brennereien auf ihren Gütern auch Schnaps für die Verpflegung. Bei Ausbruch des deutsch-französischen Krieges 1870, übergab die Heeresleitung wiederum vertrauensvoll derselben Familie einen Teil der Verpflegung. Als Haupt der Familie leitete Loebel die Geschäfte, zwei Söhne und zwei Schwiegersöhne waren mit dem Heer im Felde, und Vertrauensleute sorgten für Verpflegungsnachschübe. Als erfahrene Landwirte garantierten sie die besten Lieferungen. Aus wohlhabenden Männern wurden reiche Leute.' Lederman, 'Familie David Schottländer', loc. cit., p. 5.

[106] 'Als jährlicher Kurgast in Karlsbad interessierte es Loebel, wie die Pachtung der dortigen Mineralwasser von der Stadt Karlsbad, die von der Familie Mattoni-Gieshübel, gepachtet wurde, vor sich ging. Als er im Sommer 1872 wieder zur Kur in Karlsbad war, wurde wieder, wie alle 15 Jahre, die Pachtung neu ausgeschrieben. Die Pachtsumme musste geheim geschätzt werden.

Halb im Spass gab Loebel sein Angebot ab und schlug mit seiner richtigen Schätzung die alten Pächter aus dem Felde. Bis 1938 die Nazis in die Tschechoslowakei einrückten, blieb die Pachtung 66 Jahre ununterbrochen im Familienbesitz... Bis zu dem 1894 erfolgten Tode von Henriette Schottländer [Loebel's widow] besass sie die enorm hohen Revenuen von Karlsbad allein und verteilte am Familientag grosse Summen an ihre Enkelkinder' (ib., pp. 7 f.).

principally on his land. He was also a house owner in Breslau on his death in 1911, the possessor of thirty-five properties. Julius Schottländer provided milk for hitherto poorly supplied quarters of the city by building a dairy on one of his streets. On land to the south of the town, he also built a sugar-refinery. The total value of the real estate in town and country owned by Julius Schottländer (partly in conjunction with his oldest son) was estimated at 26 million marks.[107]

The cement manufacture in Oppeln that had belonged to Loebel Schottländer was taken over, at a valuation of some 2½ million marks, by the Oberschlesische Portland-Cementfabrik founded in 1888, of which Julius Schottländer was board chairman. His son Dr Paul Schottländer also sat on the board. Julius Schottländer was chairman also of the Schlesische Immobilien AG in Breslau, founded in 1871. When he died in 1911 he left, according to the family, a fortune of some 50 million marks.[108]

Comparable to Loebel and Julius Schottländer—a wealthy war contractor and real-estate developer—this time in Kassel, was the banker Sigmund Aschrott. Here, however, contrasts are more important than similarities. Where the Schottländers were modest and retiring, Aschrott was pushing, ostentatious, and given to self-advertisement. He duly attained his title of KR, though not at the first attempt. Again, while the probity of the Schottländers was above suspicion, Aschrott's activities as a war supplier drew on him judicial proceedings in which, however, he was acquitted. Whereas the Schottländers remained in Breslau, Aschrott moved to Berlin. Also, while the Schottländer transactions retained their agricultural base, Aschrott's activities came to be concentrated in the field of banking.

Sigmund Aschrott[109] was born in 1826, the son of a wine-grower of Hochheim (Main). Since 1821, the father had also owned a linen business in Kassel, to which city he migrated in 1838. Sigmund Aschrott, after an apprenticeship in the food trade in Frankfurt-on-Main, returned to Kassel in 1844 to enter the paternal business. This

---

[107] Martin, op. cit., p. 11.
[108] Ledermann, loc. cit., n. 105 above, p. 10. Martin is of the opinion that Julius Schottländer's taxable fortune in 1908 did not exceed 38 million marks (Martin, op. cit., p. 109). The two figures are almost certainly based on different calculations—Martin's on tax returns.
[109] For details on Aschrott see Anon. 'Aufzeichnungen über den Geheimen Kommerzienrat Sigmund Aschrott (1826–1915) und dessen Bedeutung für die wirtschaftliche und städtebauliche Entwicklung von Kassel', typewritten MS, and Paul Arnsberg, *Die jüdischen Gemeinden in Hessen* (Frankfurt, 1971), pp. 373 and 423.

he helped to develop greatly—characteristically through the 'putting-out' system and by means of credit transactions with the neighbouring peasantry.[110] From this traditional base, Aschrott, again typically, moved into textile manufacture. He acquired several derelict or ailing textile mills and was involved in starting others. He revealed a gift for choosing able employees, several of whom, in due course, became independent entrepreneurs themselves. In fact Aschrott came to be regarded as the father of the Kassel textile industry. He left the field (with justification) particularly with belated mechanization in the late eighties and early nineties, to men he had trained (several of whom later became KRs): the majority Jews. Aschrott's mills had produced primarily sailcloth and the material which, throughout the Anglo-Saxon world, became known as 'hessian'.

In the sixties, Aschrott had branched out into property developing, an activity which, for decades, would form his main occupation.[111] Through complicated real-estate and building transactions he became the creator, in accordance with a unified plan, of the western sections of the city of Kassel. When, in 1900, the authorities came to assess the value of this part of Aschrott's activities, they concluded that, despite much criticism levelled against them, their public utility was undeniable, that there was indeed a certain grandeur in his conceptions.[112] The

[110] '. . . er stellte das väterliche Unternehmen derart um, dass er in zunehmendem Masse Handweber . . . mit Rohstoffen (Garnen) belieferte und ihnen die Erzeugnisse abkaufte, um sie dann in den Handel zu bringen.' 'Aufzeichnungen', op. cit., p. 1. A hostile article in 1911 in an anti-Semitic paper (quoting another, in the *Deutsche Montagszeitung*) described in detail the nature of Aschrott's dealings: 'Er borgte . . . den Weserbauern Geld, er verkaufte ihnen Manufakturwaren, Klee- und Oelsaat, kurz alles, was der Bauer braucht . . . Auf der andern Seite konnte der Weserbauer bei Aschrott alles das los werden, was Haus und Hof hergab; selbst das handgesponnene Leinen, die sogenannten "Packen" . . .' *Deutsches Wochenblatt*, 24 June 1911.

[111] 'Auf seinen vielen Reisen im In- und Ausland hatte er seit langem die Entwicklung grösserer Städte beobachtet. Das hatte in ihm die Idee wachgerufen, dass auch Kassel dank seiner unvergleichlich schönen Lage mit der herrlichen Wilhelmshöhe, entwicklungsfähig sei.' ('Aufzeichnungen', op. cit., p. 12).

[112] '. . . Die gesammten hierdurch [a variety of benefactions] der spekulativen Verwerthung entzogenen Geländeflächen entsprechen somit 25% des überhaupt in den Bebauungsplan einbezogenen und 33 ⅓% des zur käuflichen Verwerthung gelangenden eignen Terrains von Aschrott. Dieselben lassen erkennen, dass er in dieser Beziehung mit Opfern nicht gegeizt hat.

Die Frage, ob Aschrott diese ganze unzweifelhaft mit einem Zuge ins Grosse angelegte und mit ausserordentlichem Geschick betriebene Operation vorzugsweise aus dem Gesichtspunkt einer idealen, seiner Heimathsstadt gewidmeten Thätigkeit eingeleitet hat, wie er selbst es behauptet, ist schwer zu beantworten. Ich glaube, dass Motive dieser Art mitgewirkt haben, dass sie aber weder vorwiegend noch ausschlaggebend gewesen sind. Die Aussicht auf Geschäftsgewinn war wohl das veranlassende Motiv.

assessment of Aschrott's performance does credit also to the minister in its fairness towards an unpopular and less than prepossessing Jewish candidate.

The greatest increase in Aschrott's fortune, however, had come from his activities as a war contractor in 1870–1. Here also, though Aschrott's honesty had been impugned, the minister felt inclined, after receiving detailed reports from two general officers as well as from a retired senior official, to give Aschrott the benefit of the doubt and to stress the great usefulness of his services to the Prussian armies.[113]

From the start, Aschrott had been connected also with a modest family banking business in Berlin. There, anti-Semites alleged, he had engaged in a number of highly speculative transactions.[114] Around 1900, Aschrott moved his domicile permanently to Berlin. His fortune (popularly believed to be in the range of 40 to 50 million marks) was assessed by Martin in 1912 more realistically at 20 million. While enjoying among members of the business community a reputation as a somewhat unscrupulous 'operator' and successful real-estate speculator, he was, none the less, valued by the Prussian minister of commerce.[115]

Hierbei wirkte aber die ehrliche Absicht mit, seiner Heimathsstadt dadurch zu nützen und sich in ihr und darüber hinaus nicht nur einen Namen zu machen, sondern diesen damit aus der Beschattung herauszuheben in welche ihn die mit den 1870 übernommenen Kriegslieferungen in Verbindung stehenden Verhältnisse gebracht haben . . .' Brefeld to the king, Feb./Mar. 1900 (exact date not available), ZSAM 2.2.1, no. 1591, fos. 12^{r-v}

[113] Über letztere [Aschrott's war contracts] ein volles eigenes Urtheil zu gewinnen, ist mir nicht möglich gewesen, da ich die Einsicht in die hierüber Aufschluss gebenden Akten nicht erlangt habe. In hohen militärischen Kreisen hier in Cassel ist man indessen der Ansicht, dass diese Vorgänge gegenüber der ausserordentlichen Leistungsfähigkeit und den dem Allerhöchsten Dienst zu gute gekommenen Vortheilen um so weniger geeignet seien, Aschrott mit dauernder moralischer Belastung erscheinen zu lassen, als das seiner Zeit eingeleitete Strafverfahren zur Freisprechung geführt habe und auch sonst manche Umstände bei jenen zu seinen Gunsten sprächen' (ib. fos. 12^v–13).

[114] 'In Berlin war er schon damals Stammgast. Jeder, der auf dem Grundstücksmarkt oder sonstwie spekulativ tätig war, "hing" mit ihm. Wenn irgendwo ein Terrain oder eine Fabrik zwangsweise versteigert wurde, so konnte man annehmen, dass unter den Reflektanten Aschrott aus Cassel sich befand. Er hatte ausserordentlich geschickte Zuträger, meistens Leute, die einst bessere Tage gekannt hatten . . .' *Deutsches Wochenblatt*, 24 June 1911.

[115] '. . . Allerdings steht Aschrott in dem Ruf, seinen Vortheil mit grosser Energie zu verfolgen. In kaufmännischen Kreisen ist man ihm wenig geneigt. In diesen sieht man in ihm vorwiegend den allerdings glücklichen aber ziemlich skrupellosen Geschäftsmann und Grundstückspekulanten und will demgegenüber das Verdienstliche seiner Thätigkeit nicht anerkennen . . .

Ich vermag diesen Einwendungen kein ausschlaggebendes Gewicht beizumessen und glaube dass der Banquier Aschrott nicht unwürdig für die Verleihung des Titels als Commerzienrath ist, sondern dass im Gegentheil die sehr wichtigen Dienste, welche er

In 1907, Aschrott 'bought' the title of GKR by repeatedly placing large sums for 'charitable purposes' at the disposal of the ever-greedy Empress Auguste Viktoria.[116]

Aschrott, in fact, combined uniquely in his career a number of economic activities in which Jews were prominent, ranging from produce trade and the 'putting-out' system accompanied by credit transactions, through textile manufacture and banking to real-estate dealings and development to war contracting. In many respects, thus, Aschrott conforms to the negative stereotype of the Jewish 'man of affairs', one, moreover, who made his early career, significantly, in Hesse with its widespread popular anti-Semitism. In fact, Aschrott's combination of activities and characteristics may have had few counterparts among Gentile entrepreneurs. This, however, was also the very antithesis of 'royal merchants' of Jewish extraction like Eduard Arnhold or James Simon (or the Mendelssohns). Even among war contractors, men like the Schottländers or Simon Cohn of Kreuzburg were above reproach. However, it may be more than an accident that the grain dealer Salomon Lachmann, another great war contractor, subsequently lost a substantial portion of his vast fortune in real-estate speculations in Berlin (as would his descendant, Hans Lachmann-Mosse, after him). Real-estate transactions could indeed produce large fortunes like those of the Schottländers or the Haberland family in Berlin but could equally cost the daughter of the banker baron Moritz Cohn several million marks on account of her late father's 'negligence' in supervising a real-estate company for which he was responsible. The speculative aspect of some Jewish entrepreneurship is conspicuous in Jewish involvement in real-estate development.

A very different category of Jewish merchants were the great Silesian coal wholesalers Emanuel Friedländer and Caesar Wollheim and, in the next generation, their successors Fritz von Friedländer-Fuld and Eduard Arnhold. The firms of Emanuel Friedländer & Co. and Caesar Wollheim became the leading exporters of coal from Upper Silesia, whose interests, however, would, in time, come to extend to related fields like the gas industry or coal-based chemistry. Their

---

sowohl der äusseren Entwicklung der Residenz Cassel wie den allgemeinen Wohlfahrtsinteressen in derselben geleistet hat, den erbetenen Allerhöchsten Gnadenerweis gerechtfertigt erscheinen lassen . . .' Brefeld to the king, Feb./Mar. 1900 (loc. cit., n. 112 above).

[116] Arnsberg, op. cit., n. 109 above, p. 374.

activities help to confute the claim of the alleged marginality of Jewish entrepreneurship.

The Jewish pioneer in this area was Emanuel Friedländer in Gleiwitz. When, in 1866, he received the title of KR, the authorities noted that, during the fifteen years preceding, he had successfully expanded the sales of Silesian coal. Rather curiously, in view of later developments, they also recorded his services to the local economy through the provision, on his estate, of facilities for the large-scale preparation of flax.[117] Emanuel Friedländer, however, would have remained a local Jewish celebrity without wider importance—indeed, when he died in 1880, he bequeathed to his son Fritz a family business faced with serious financial problems. It was Fritz who would make Emanuel Friedländer and Co. the nucleus of an important industrial concern.[118] A major factor in Fritz Friedländer's early rise was his success in negotiating agreements with several Silesian magnates (notably Count Hans Ulrich Schaffgotsch von Koppitz) for the sale by his firm of the entire output of their mines. A second achievement was his close relationship with Carl Fürstenberg, the rising star of the Berliner Handels-Gessellschaft, specialist in large-scale industrial financing.

In the late eighties, Fritz Friedländer moved from Gleiwitz to Berlin, determined, Fürstenberg later noted, to take that city by storm.[119] In 1890, the foundations of a future industrial empire were laid by the founding (in conjunction with Fürstenberg's BHG) of the Oberschlesische Kokswerke und Chemische Fabriken AG (Oberkoks) in Gleiwitz. Share capital of 4.5 million marks was raised and 1.5 million marks of obligations were placed through the good offices of the BHG. Oberkoks pioneered in Upper Silesia new technical processes for the distillation of gases released in coke production. It

---

[117] '... Seit fünfzehn Jahren an diesem Orte etabliert, ist es ihm durch angestrengte persönliche Thätigkeit und nicht ohne zeitweise bedeutende Opfer gelungen, den Kohlenhandel Oberschlesiens in Gang und zu dessen jetziger Blühte gebracht zu haben. Durch Errichtung einer grossen Flachsbereitungs-Anstalt auf seinem Gute Gross-Peterwitz, Kreis Ratibor, hat er dem Flachsbau in diesem Theile Oberschlesiens einen neuen erwünschten Aufschwung gegeben. In jeder Frage, welche die gewerklichen und kommerziellen Verhältnisse Obserschlesiens berührt, können die Behörden auf seinen Rath und seine Mitwirkung zählen...' v. Itzenplitz to the king, Mar. 1866 (exact date not available), ZSAM 2.2.1, no. 1581, fos. 2ᵛ-3.

[118] For Fritz Friedländer see Carl Fürstenberg, op. cit., n. 69 above, *passim*, and references in Schwerin, loc. cit., n. 5 above, p. 37 n. 123.

[119] '... wollte Friedländer die Reichshauptstadt im Sturme erobern', Fürstenberg, op. cit., n. 69 above, p. 255.

also exploited chemical by-products of coke manufacture as well as undertaking the construction for customers of coking and distillation ovens.

In 1896, in close association with the Caros' Obereisen, Oberkoks raised its share capital to 12 million marks. At the same time Fritz Friedländer, a director since 1890, sold the greater part of his shareholding[120] and became board chairman of the enlarged company. He then acquired a mine at Moravska-Ostrava in Bohemia and options on other coal deposits. He also joined the board of Fürstenberg's BHG. When he became a KR in 1897, he already ranked among the leading German industrialists.[121] Aged only 38, he had made the paternal trading firm the nucleus of an industrial grouping. His taxable wealth already exceeded 24 million marks, while his annual income reached an almost unrivalled two million marks.[122] In due course Fritz v. Friedländer-Fuld would become the wealthiest man in Berlin. The Friedländers, thus, belonged to the Jewish entrepreneurial families which successfully accomplished the transition from family firm to industrial concern, like the Loewe brothers in close association with 'Jewish' banking capital.

Not wholly dissimilar from that of the Friedländers, yet with significant differences, was the evolution of another Silesian enterprise. In 1840 Caesar Wollheim,[123] son of a Jewish merchant in Breslau,[124] was admitted to the Corporation der Berliner Kaufmannschaft. He

---

[120] According to Fürstenberg, in consequence of a shrewd assessment of the longer-term price trends of coal by-products and in order to occupy an intermediate position between the two interest groups (ib., p. 262).

[121] 'Der Kaufmann Fritz Friedländer hierselbst . . . ist Mitinhaber der von ihm im Wesentlichen allein geleiteten, in Gleiwitz mit einer Zweigniederlassung in Berlin bestehenden Firma Emanuel Friedländer und Comp., die in der Kohlenindustrie eine der ersten Stellen einnimmt. Friedländer gehört zu den hervorragendsten Grossindustriellen Deutschlands, hat sich auf industriellem Gebiete vielfach verdient gemacht [Friedländer's multiple activities were clearly too complicated for the minister either to know, to understand, or to wish to present to the sovereign] und steht wegen seiner Intelligenz und Gewandtheit sowohl im Handelsstande, wie auch in anderen Kreisen in hohem Ansehen . . . Auf seinen bedeutenden und umfangreichen Kohlenbergwerken beschäftigt er ungefähr viertausend Arbeiter, für die er auf das Beste sorgt . . .' Brefeld to the king, Berlin, 14 July 1897, ZSAM 2.2.1, no. 1590, fos. 52a[r-v].

[122] Ib., fo. 52a[v].

[123] For Caesar Wollheim see Wilhelm Treue, 'Caesar Wollheim und Eduard Arnhold', *Tradition*, 6 (April 1961), 65 ff.

[124] The *Jüdisches Gemeindeblatt für Oberschlesien*, reporting a lecture by Kurt Schwerin, claims—in opposition to Treue—that Caesar Wollheim had been born Leiser Wollheim in the province of Posen. *Jüdisches Gemeindeblatt für Oberschlesien*, no. 9 (13 May 1937), p. 2.

had begun—in a manner characteristic of many Jewish merchants 'on the make'—by trading in a variety of products, but specializing increasingly, until the late fifties, in textiles.[125] Already in 1856 however, recognizing the potential importance of Silesian coal for the growing city of Berlin, he had begun trading wholesale in the 'black gold'. For a time, he was associated with Emanuel Friedländer in Gleiwitz,[126] who had in fact pioneered the introduction of Silesian coal to the Berlin market: indeed, Wollheim started his activities in the coal business as Friedländer's agent. Soon, however, the two firms had separated, though continuing a friendly co-operation.

During the sixties, with the demand for coal, especially in Berlin, increasing at a rapid rate,[127] Silesian coal was progressively replacing British imports. Caesar Wollheim, while himself helping to promote them, profited from both developments. A close association with state-owned Silesian coal mines in particular enabled him to extend his business—especially as supplier to a number of gasworks. Among Wollheim's customers were gasworks in Spandau and Potsdam, from 1865 the municipal gasworks in Berlin, as well as major manufacturers like the machine builders Schwartzkopf and Borsig, the chemical factories of Kunheim & Co. and Siemens & Halske. Later, he also supplied railway companies. In fact, during the sixties, Caesar Wollheim developed into a large international trading firm with suppliers ranging from Scotland to Westphalia and customers extending to Austria and Poland. Wollheim, at the same time, began to indulge in large-scale stock-exchange speculations.[128] He became a KR, though the actual documentation is lost.

As a board member of the Dessauer Wollgarnspinnerei, Wollheim regularly visited Dessau. During one of these visits, a mutual acquaintance introduced him to the family of a Jewish ophthalmologist, Dr Adolph Arnhold. Wollheim was so impressed with the ability of

---

[125] 'Er war ein betriebsamer Mann, der zunächst mit mancherlei Waren handelte: mit Getreide und Textilien, mit Eisen und Schrott—kurz, ein Kaufmann, der jedes Geschäft wahrnahm an dem es etwas zu verdienen gab ... Allmählich spezialisierte er sich auf die "Manufakturwarenbranche": viele Geschäftsbriefe noch aus den Jahren 1858–1860 betrafen kleine und mittlere Geschäfte mit Leinen- und Baumwollwaren.' (Treue, loc. cit., p. 66).
[126] Treue, mistakenly, has Beuthen.
[127] Figures in Treue, loc. cit., pp. 68 f.
[128] 'So war zum Beispiel Cäsar Wollheim nicht nur ein Kaufmann grössten Stils, der sein Kohlenhandelsunternehmen zu einem Betriebe von nationaler Bedeutung entwickelte, sondern er bewies auch mehr als einmal in umfangreichen Effektengeschäften eine glückliche Hand ...' Fürstenberg, op. cit., n. 69 above, pp. 314 f.

Arnhold's young son Eduard that he invited the parents to apprentice the boy to his firm. In 1863, Eduard Arnhold duly entered the office of Caesar Wollheim.

Arnhold,[129] treated almost as an adopted son,[130] rapidly gained his chief's confidence. In 1875, aged only 26, he was given a partnership; in 1882, on Wollheim's death, he took over the management (though Wollheim's widow and, for a time, one of his sons-in-law retained an interest in the firm). Under Eduard Arnhold's direction, the business expanded rapidly in several directions. In the first place, agreements were concluded with a number of Silesian mine-owners under which Caesar Wollheim undertook to sell their entire output.[131] Prominent again were the mines owned by the Prussian state. For years, Caesar Wollheim had found customers in the growing gas industry. In order to expand the market, the firm, with some others, now formed a company for the construction and management of gasworks, particularly in smaller communities which lacked the resources to build their own. Eventually, in this way, the company helped to construct more than a hundred gasworks, mainly in the eastern provinces of the monarchy, which, naturally, bought their coal from Wollheim. (This creation of demand finds parallels in the proceedings of, among others, Emil Rathenau, Isidor Loewe, and Fritz Friedländer.) Close involvement in the gas industry in turn led to participation in machine construction, notably through the founding of the Berlin-Anhaltische Maschinenbau AG (Bamag) in Dessau (1872). Eduard Arnhold, a board member since 1881, became its chairman in 1900. Caesar Wollheim, moreover, had always been interested in navigation, more particularly on the river Oder. This branch of the firm's activity, based on its own shipyard and shipping line in Breslau, was considerably developed. Eduard Arnhold, moreover, became a leading expert on rail transportation and all tariff matters. Another of his activities was the creation of an extensive sales organization to extend the market for Silesian coal. When, in 1890, the Silesian coal producers combined to form the Oberschlesische Kohlenkonvention, the two firms of Emanuel Friedländer and Caesar Wollheim between them took over the sale of 59 per cent of its total

---

[129] For Eduard Arnhold see, besides Treue, loc. cit., n. 123 above, especially Johanna Arnhold, *Eduard Arnhold: Ein Gedenkbuch* (Berlin, 1928), private printing; also Zielenziger, op. cit., n. 32 above, pp. 155 f.

[130] Wollheim had no sons of his own.

[131] For details of the mines involved in such agreements see Treue, loc. cit., n. 123 above, pp. 77 f.

production, Wollheim alone a quota of 36 per cent in 1903.[132] When Arnhold became a KR in 1891, the recommendation dwelt on his services both to the state-owned coal-mines and to the expansion of Silesian coal sales in general.[133] When, ten years later, he was made a GKR, he was numbered among the ablest and most successful German wholesale merchants.[134]

A number of conclusions can be drawn from the careers of Fritz Friedländer and Eduard Arnhold, two of the most prominent industrial 'magnates' of Wilhelmine Germany. Both were based primarily on the wholesale trade in Silesian coal. Both Friedländer and Arnhold, in seeking to extend the market for their products, diversified their interests to include coke and coal chemistry, gas, machine building and transportation. Both thus came to supplement original trading interests with related industrial ones. In both cases, a modest family firm was integrated into a more substantial corporate structure. Both enterprises developed, characteristically, in association with predominantly Jewish banking institutions, respectively Carl Fürstenberg's BHG (later, however, replaced by the Deutsche Bank) and Eugen Gutmann's Dresdner Bank. There are characteristic generational patterns. While in the Friedländer firm there was a 'normal' transition from father to son, that from Caesar Wollheim to

[132] Treue, loc. cit., n. 123 above, p. 81.

[133] '... Mitinhaber und seit etwa 12 Jahren alleiniger Leiter der hiesigen grossen Firma Cäsar Wollheim, welche mehr als 30 Jahre hindurch als Hauptabnehmer der Kohlen der Königin Luisegrube und stets tadelloser Geschäftsführung sich um die staatliche Bergwerksverwaltung namentlich in Zeiten schwierigen Absatzes wohl verdient gemacht hat. Ihrer Vermittelung ist es zu danken, dass die oberschlesische Kohle sowohl in den städtischen Gasanstalten Berlins, als auch in den Provinzen Pommern, Ost-und Westpreussen, sowie in Dresden, Leipzig, Hamburg und Bukarest Absatz findet...' Brefeld to the king, Berlin, 27 Apr. 1891, ZSAM 2.2.1, no. 1588, fos. 80^{r-v}.

[134] 'Arnhold ist Mitinhaber und Leiter des in Berlin unter der Firma Caesar Wollheim bestehenden alten und sehr bedeutenden Steinkohlen-Grossgeschäfts. Er zählt zu den gewandtesten und fähigsten Gross-Kaufleuten und erfreut sich wegen seiner hervorragenden Eigenschaften hohen Ansehens im Handelsstande. Die Firma, welche in Breslau eine eigene Werft und Rhederei zur Verfrachtung der Kohlen und in Zabrze eine Steinkohlenbrikettfabrik besitzt, hat seit 41 Jahren den Absatz der Produkte der oberschlesischen Steinkohlen-Industrie vermittelt und sich als Hauptabnehmer der staatlichen Steinkohlenbergwerke Oberschlesiens um deren Entwicklung verdient gemacht... Er ist Mitglied des Aeltestenkollegiums der Berliner Kaufmannschaft, des Landeseisenbahnrats und mehrerer Bezirkseisenbahnräthe und bekleidet noch viele andere Ehrenämter, ist auch Aufsichtsrathsmitglied vieler industrieller Unternehmungen ... Sein Vermögen beträgt über 10 Millionen Mark, sein Jahreseinkommen über 1½ Millionen Mark...' Brefeld to the king, (exact date not available), 1901, ZSAM 2.2.1, no. 1591, fo. 244.

Eduard Arnhold was a case (these were relatively rare, at all events without some kinship ties) of the deliberate selection, training, and 'adoption' of a youthful Jewish successor. Moreover Arnhold, the doctor's son from Dessau, came from a non-commercial background. In both cases, there is a high degree of adaptation to changing circumstances, from the coal trade to ancillary industries and from the family firm to corporate positions. Both Fritz Friedländer and Eduard Arnhold were provincials who moved to Berlin to pursue their successful careers. When one considers these careers by the side of that of the Caro brothers (and, perhaps, less strikingly, those of Salomon Huldschinsky and Albert Hahn), a distinctive type of Silesian Jewish industrialist (outside the textile industry) appears to emerge. There is a strong family likeness in the careers of leading Jewish Silesian-based industrialists.

One other Jewish family firm that successfully achieved the transition from modest trading activities (in this case principally in imported dyestuffs) to science-based manufacture in the age of large corporations was that of Leopold Cassella & Co. In Frankfurt-on-Main. Founded in 1828 by Leopold Cassella, the business first passed by marriage to the Gans family, finally to achieve its widest international reputation, in association with Farbwerke Hoechst, under the Weinberg brothers (whose mother belonged to the Gans family). Leopold Cassella would achieve its most significant expansion during the nineties through the production of new diamin and sulphur dyes. When, in 1895, Leo Gans became the senior partner (the firm was an *Offene Handelsgesellschaft* owned by members of the Gans and Weinberg families), the firm employed some 1,000 workers.[135] Its final adaptation to the structures of developed capitalism belongs to a later phase.

Besides economic activities the national importance of which was acknowledged by conferment of the title of KR, there were others of purely regional or local significance, which still attracted attention. An example of such local enterprise is the development by GKR Moritz Becker of the East Prussian amber industry. The enterprise, which

---

[135] 'Der Fabrikbesitzer Dr. phil. Leo Ludwig Gans in Frankfurt a.M. ist Mitinhaber und Leiter der von ihm begründeten und jetzt unter der Firma Leopold Cassella & Comp. betriebenen sehr bedeutenden chemischen Fabrik in Fechenheim, die gegen 1000 Arbeiter beschäftigt, für deren Wohlfahrt in hervorragender Weise gesorgt ist . . . Er ist als Kaufmann sehr angesehen, besitzt ein bedeutendes Vermögen . . .' *Frhr.* v. Berlepsch to the king, Berlin, 29 Sept. 1895, ZSAM 2.2.1, no. 1589, fo. 104.

eventually came to employ some 2,000 workers, had become, by the late eighties, East Prussia's largest industrial undertaking.[136]

In examining Jewish entrepreneurial activity in the last quarter of the nineteenth century as it presents itself in the conferment of commercial titles, a number of features emerge. In the first place, the conventional 'Sombart' view of the Jewish entrepreneur as, at least in origin, primarily a trader is, in general, confirmed. Jews achieved recognition as wholesale merchants in textiles (Gebr. Simon), coal (Emanuel Friedländer and Caesar Wollheim), metals (Aron Hirsch, Ralph Merton, Robert and Georg Caro), dyestuffs (Leopold Cassella), agricultural produce (Salomon Lachmann and Simon Cohn), horses (Philip Elkan), and rags (Albert Hahn and Salomon Huldschinsky). It is trading in agricultural products which led to their prominence among army contractors in the German wars of unification (Loebel Schottländer, Sigmund Aschrott, Lachmann, Cohn, Elkan). While a few remained primarily wholesale merchants (the Simons, Eduard Arnhold), the majority of this generation diversified into various forms of production with, however, the boundaries between commercial and industrial activities remaining fluid (this is notably the case with the Caros, the Hirschs of Halberstadt and Messingwerk, the Friedländer concern and the Metallgesellschaft in Frankfurt). Reversion into banking and high finance or property development (Sigmund Aschrott, Salomon Lachmann) is exceptional. Several of the enterprises set up at this time were transitional in character between the pure family trading firms and the mixed commercial-industrial enterprise developed with the aid of some banking or public finance. The Loewe brothers, on the other hand, could be seen as pioneers of a new type of enterprise in which industrial production was financed directly with the aid of banking capital (with the original risk capital being provided not by large joint-stock banks but by small Jewish banking houses). With the Loewes (as with Emil Rathenau's AEG) the emphasis was on production (as is the case with Heinrich Kern, Oscar Caro, Salomon

---

[136] 'Der Geheime Kommerzienrath *Moritz Becker* (1830–1901) war der Gründer der modernen deutschen Bernstein-Gewinnung und-Verwertung. Er schuf den ersten Grossbetrieb auf diesem Gebiet und stellte erstmals den Dampfbagger und die moderne Tauchausrüstung und-technik in den Dienst dieses Gewerbes. Ende der achtziger Jahre stellten seine Bernsteingewinnungs- und -verarbeitungsbetriebe das grösste ostpreussische Industrieunternehmen mit ca. zweitausend Arbeitern dar. Später wurde diese von ihm aufgebaute Organisation vom preussischen Staat übernommen.' Daniel Bernstein, 'Wirtschaft' in Siegmund Kaznelson (ed.), *Juden im deutschen Kulturbereich* (Berlin, 1962), pp. 785 f.

Huldschinsky, Albert Hahn, and Gustav Hirsch, but with some of these in the role of industrial managers within essentially commercial dynasties).

The leading Jewish enterprises of the period were, predictably, transitional also in another respect. Starting usually in the sixties as pure family businesses on a modest scale, they expanded in the eighties and nineties, typically under second-generation management. With this expansion, generally in the decade 1885–95, they were converted into joint-stock companies (not infrequently as part of an early process of amalgamation, rationalization, or consolidation). Less commonly, they became *offene Handelsgesellschaften*, usually with a strong element of family ownership (normally by more than one member) and family management, with 'the family' usually providing the board chairman. Here again the Loewe firm, beginning from a different starting-point, was a stage ahead of the rest. Under the direction of Isidor Loewe, the original firm became the nucleus of a corporate structure combining its production of machine tools with the functions of a holding company. The original Loewe firm developed into a diversified industrial concern with, as its major element of integration, besides financial links, the obligation of associated enterprises to buy their equipment from the parent firm. In a similar manner, another of the new industrialists, Fritz Friedländer created, on the basis of participation by the family business of Emanuel Friedländer and with the help of bank capital (Carl Fürstenberg's Berliner Handels-Gesellschaft), a network of associated and partly owned companies (not subsidiaries) based eventually on his own coal production (in the Rybnik area of Upper Silesia). Loewe and Friedländer, among others, illustrate the early and middle stages in the development of a concern with partial vertical integration. Analogous developments can be seen in the corporate evolution of the Caro enterprises. The development of these firms and the assumption by members of the owning families of managerial as well as commercial functions confounds the thesis of the allegedly reduced role of Jews in economic life with the relative decline of the privately owned family firm. Jewish owners, in fact, often adapted to corporate development as readily as, if not indeed more readily than, others. How far Jewish entrepreneurs in this were following a general trend in German industry, how far they were pioneering it, it is impossible to say.

Another distinctive feature concerns the extent to which Jewish commercial activity at this time—in contrast with the preceding and following 'Berlin periods'—is concentrated in Silesia, both in textiles and heavy industry. Breslau, Landeshut, Beuthen, and Gleiwitz are the centres around which much of Jewish entrepreneurship (and a good deal of its financing) revolves. The reasons are manifold: trading links with the east and south-east (particularly Poland and Austria, to a lesser extent Bohemia and, more remotely, Russia and the Balkans—indeed it might be asked if historical connections with the Habsburg monarchy did not play a part); the presence of raw materials ranging from coal and iron to flax; the particular concern of the Prussian state for the economic development of the region; the presence of established Jewish communities with links with co-religionists in Lodz, Warsaw, and Vienna; the availability of 'merchant capital', in part the product of the export trade to east and south; possibly an element of 'self-sustaining' growth once Jewish entrepreneurship had reached a certain level. Again, it was railway construction and improvements in navigation—particularly on the river Oder—which facilitated dealings with the rest of the monarchy. The extension of the economic network of Silesia to include fast-growing Berlin must have played a major part. Characteristically, the Caros, whilst moving their flourishing trading activities to Berlin, retained their manufacturing base in Upper Silesia. Emanuel Friedländer & Co. in Gleiwitz at first employed Caesar Wollheim as their agent in Berlin and, for a time, the firms of Friedländer and Wollheim co-operated. Later, while Eduard Arnhold in Berlin developed Caesar Wollheim's Silesian business, Fritz Friedländer moved to Berlin, without abandoning his mining and industrial interests in Silesia. Hahn and Huldschinsky combined the original shoddy manufacture in Berlin with the production of seamless tubes in Gleiwitz. In fact, the general tendency for Silesian entrepreneurs (including the Grünfelds of Landeshut) to move to Berlin (sometimes, one family member would move to the capital, while another stayed behind) helped to extend the geographic and commercial range of Silesian Jewish entrepreneurship.

In other eastern provinces of the monarchy, only some of the 'Silesian' conditions prevailed (there was a lack of raw materials), often in an attenuated form. Jewish entrepreneurship, while by no means lacking, operated on a more modest scale. Berlin, on the other hand, the stage of earlier Jewish activity, may, after 1848, have entered a phase of relative economic stagnation (exept in a few specialist branches like the production of clothing (*Konfektion*) or some aspects of wholesale trade), not to be fully overcome until the imperial age. In the western provinces of the monarchy, Jewish communities tended to be smaller, with indigenous economic initiative supplemented rather by entrepreneurs and capitalists from France and Belgium (indeed it may be doubted whether Jewish entrepreneurial activity would have flourished in Silesia, had that province bordered on France and Belgium rather than Poland and the Habsburg monarchy). Germany outside Prussia will be considered in a different context. So far as the Prussian monarchy was concerned, the Jewish entrepreneurial role in Silesia in the period under discussion—its 'golden age'—was unique. The 'Silesian phase' of Jewish entrepreneurial activity would end roughly with the end of the century. In this respect, as in others, Ludwig Loewe & Co., with their interests spreading westwards from Berlin to Karlsruhe, Oberndorf/Neckar, and Cologne, pointed the way, as indeed did Albert Hahn, in extending his tube production to Düsseldorf and, perhaps, Eduard Arnhold in co-founding the Bamag in Dessau.

V

In considering KRs of Jewish extraction appointed between 1874 and 1901, a number of features may be noted. The first is their distribution over different branches of economic activity. Consistently, throughout, the textile industry in all its aspects (wool, linen, cotton, chintz, spinning, weaving, knitting, 'making-up') figures prominently. Altogether, 22 KRs and GKRs were drawn from some branch of the textile industry. Unlike the earlier concentration in Berlin, it is now the provinces which predominate in manufacture (14 recipients out of 22). Berlin, on the other hand, becomes the centre of Jewish entrepreneurship in the clothing industry as well as in retailing. Among the provinces, Silesia with 10 titles (with Landeshut, Leobschütz, and Neustadt OS prominent locations) takes pride of place.

Textile manufacturing provided substantial employment for local populations (lack of precision in some figures is due mainly to the 'putting-out' system or cottage industries):

1875	Louis Reichenheim (resident in Berlin)	Thannhausen	'thousands'
1875	Heymann Pariser	Luckenwalde	500–600 (and domestic workers).
1877	Albert Hahn	Berlin	200
1877	Louis Dahlheim	Berlin	1,200

1878	Benjamin Holländer	Leobschütz	'thousands'
1879	Moritz Teichmann	„	1,600
1881	Joseph Pinkus	Neustadt OS	over 5,000
1884	David Aaron Levin	Berlin	150 + 1,500–2,000
1884	Julius Kauffmann	Thannhausen	1,740
1885	Valentin Manheimer	Berlin	3,000–4,000
1887	Falk Valentin Grünfeld	Landeshut	70–80+ 'several hundred'
1895	Joseph Pinkus	Neustadt OS	6,000
1897, 1899	Valentin Manheimer	Berlin	7,000–8,000
1897	Albert Fränkel	Neustadt OS	5,000
1900	Hermann Rinkel	Landeshut	900

The second significant group among the KRs are those connected with mining and metallurgy. This is a smaller group also associated mainly with Silesia:

1875	Robert Caro	1889	Albert Hahn (GKR)
1876	Salomon Huldschinsky	1894	Oscar Caro
1877	Albert Hahn	1897	Georg Caro
1885	Heinrich Kern	1897	Gustav Coppel
1889	Isidor Loewe	1897	Fritz Friedländer

These too were substantial employers of labour:

Robert Caro	1875	500–600
Sal. Huldschinsky	1876	4,500 (probably includes textile works in Berlin)
Heinrich Kern	1885	Over 2,000
Oskar Caro	1894	c.8,000
Fritz Friedländer	1897	c.4,000

Representatives of the chemical industry begin to figure in the later nineties. Besides the old-established Kuhnheims (Hugo Kuhnheim, 1894) these include Leo Ludwig Gans (1895), Fritz Friedländer (1897), and Nazary Kantorowicz (1900). While the Gans business of Leopold Cassella employed some 1,000 workers (1895), Kantorowicz's firm of Milch in Posen gave employment to 350 (1900).

Two other branches of industry represented among the KRs can be noted. One was the paper and packaging industry:

1886	Moritz Behrend	Varzin (not without the patronage of the local 'lord of the manor' Otto v. Bismarck)
1888	Martin Schlesinger	Berlin
1889	Hermann Süssmann	Ratibor

However, these were modest enterprises, with Schlesinger, owner of a luxury paper and lithographic business, for instance, employing in 1888 some 250 workmen.

Others honoured with the title of a KR engaged in curing tobacco and in the manufacture of cigars:

1883	Emanuel Münzer	Oppeln
1892	Adolph Rotmann	Burgsteinfurt (Westph.)
1895	Bernhard Loeser	(Berlin, but manufacturing mainly in Elbing)
1897	Louis Grosskopf	Königsberg Pr.

These were medium-sized employers, with Emanuel Münzer (1883) employing 460, Louis Grosskopf (1897) 400–500, and the most important, Hermann Loeser (1895), 1,800. A few other manufacturers operated in a variety of specialized fields, usually on a modest scale.

A second branch of economic activity pursued by KRs—on occasion diversified to include also industrial entrepreneurship or participations —was wholesale trade. In this area, a threefold division prevailed. At the top, there are the 'royal merchants', the large wholesale traders operating on a national and, indeed, as a rule an international scale, among them coal wholesalers Eduard Arnhold and Fritz Friedländer, the textile merchants Gebr. Simon, metal traders like the Hirsches in Halberstadt, Robert and Georg Caro, and, last but not least, Wilhelm Merton of the Metallgesellschaft in Frankfurt-on-Main. Men such as these indeed constituted something like a Jewish merchant patriciate, whose members were distinguished by wide cultural, social, and general public interests.

Below these 'merchant-princes' came the sometimes extremely wealthy war contractors, the Schottländers, Cohns, Lachmanns, and Aschrotts who, from local bases in rural areas, laid the foundations for nationally important wholesaling operations. At perhaps a roughly comparable economic level (though normally somewhat less wealthy) there are the major retailers mainly of articles of clothing and fashions, located principally in Berlin, among them the Gerson family and its successors, the Manheimers (in whose activities however, 'making-up', that is manufacture, played the major part) and the Grünfelds. The great department store owners, with the Tietzes and Wertheims in the lead, though their businesses did originate in this period, achieved prominence and recognition only later. The same is true of the publishing families of the Mosses and Ullsteins. Such later entrepreneurs, moreover, would not, as a rule, seek commercial titles. Not infrequently, being 'oppositional' in their attitudes, they would disdain 'distinctions' conferred by the imperial authorities.

The 'lowest' stratum of commercial KRs consisted of comfortably off wholesalers of purely regional importance, usually in the eastern provinces of the monarchy (and, typically, resident not in Silesia but in Posen and, to a lesser extent, West and East Prussia), trading in timber, building materials, colonial produce, sugar, wine, grain, spirits, seeds, textiles, or agricultural machinery. On occasion, they would combine such produce trade with credit and banking operations. Sometimes their commercial activities would extend beyond the eastern confines of the monarchy. Occasionally, the authorities refer specifically to the beneficial effects for local economic development of the activities of such notables—as, indeed, they do also for industrial entrepreneurs operating at a similar level. The recognition of economic activities such as these would seem to reflect the relative economic underdevelopment of the eastern provinces (with the exception of Silesia) as well as the desire of the Prussian authorities to secure Jewish goodwill for the perennial struggle against the Poles.

The third branch of economic activity represented among the KRs is, of course, the old-established one of banking. Here also, a certain stratification is to be observed. At the top, there are the old-established wealthy banking families led by the Mendelssohns and Mendelssohn-Bartholdys, the Schwabachs (as heirs to the Bleichröder), and the Oppenheims (of the still prestigious firm of Robert Warschauer). Below these figure the owners or senior partners of solid and respected private banking houses, represented in Berlin by GKR Heinrich Wolff, by Abraham and Ernst Joachim Meyer, and by Berthold Simon of Gebr. Veit.

Below such solid and respected pillars of the banking establishment there operated a number of venturesome 'buccaneers', adventurers, and (sometimes successful) speculators. Pride of place in this group belongs to members of the Landau family, sons of Jacob Landau of Breslau who was believed to have started his not undistinguished career as a somewhat shady horse-dealer. Others included Max Ludwig Goldberger (adviser to Caprivi on international tariff policy, a man of affairs whose commercial activities had started with a lucrative trade in metal chains alleged to offer protection against or even to cure rheumatism), Wilhelm Kopetzky, a leading member of the Berlin stock exchange, and the Kassel 'developer' Sigmund Aschrott.

A further group of KRs was drawn from successful bankers in

growing provincial cities, typified by, among others, Heinrich Heimann in Breslau, Jacques Reiss in Frankfurt-on-Main, Ludwig Landsberg (Breslau), Bernhard Seligmann (Koblenz), Louis Ephraim Meyer (Hanover), Albert Warburg (Altona), and Georg Fromberg (Breslau, later Berlin). Such men received recognition for their part in stimulating local economic activity (and in nursing local industry through recurrent economic crises).

In conferring titles on these men, the authorities repeatedly commented on various services rendered either to the economic life of the country or, indeed, to themselves. During the seventies, services mentioned include assistance to young merchants (Louis Joachimsthal, Berlin, 1876),[137] confidential advice to the Reichsbank directorate (Louis Gumpert, Brandenburg, 1876), services in the setting up of loan banks (*Darlehnkassen*) (the same), and financial services to German diplomats abroad (Meyer Cohn, Berlin, 1878). In the eighties, there is mention of financial services to the imperial navy (Hermann Wallich, Berlin, 1885), help to landowners in financial difficulties (Gustav Friedmann, Breslau, 1886), services to the beet-sugar industry (Samuel Auerbach, Posen, 1886), assistance to local industries (Louis Ephraim Meyer, Hanover, 1886), services to the state-owned coal-mines in Silesia (Eduard Arnhold, Berlin, 1891). In the nineties, among services referred to figure expert advice during Russo-German trade negotiations (Oscar Caro, Gleiwitz, 1894), similar advice in the stock-exchange inquiry (Wilhelm Kopetzky, Berlin, 1895), assistance to local landowners (Hugo Kempner, Glogau, 1895), and the supply of information useful to the foreign ministry (Julius Schwabach, 1897).

There is repeated mention of import substitution normally at the expense of British goods (Albert Hahn, Berlin, 1877, Lewin Simon, Berlin, 1877, Valentin Manheimer, Berlin, 1897), while references to

[137] 'Am 27 d. Mts. 50 Jahre lang der Corporation der Berliner Kaufmannschaft angehörend, hat Joachimsthal sich stets bestrebt diesen Stand zu heben und gerade in der Branche, welche er vertrat, junge strebsame Kaufleute zu unterstützen, wo er nur konnte. Es giebt [*sic*] hier in Berlin eine Menge Colonialwaaren Handlungen, deren Inhaber mittellos zu Joachimsthal kamen und seine Unterstützung durch Gewährung von Credit erbaten. Keiner dieser Leute, wenn sie sonst fleissig und redlich waren, hat unerhört das Joachimsthal'sche Haus verlassen und bezeugt das Blühen und Wohlergehen der meisten dieser Firmen den Segen, den der heutige Jubilar solcher Weise in dem Aufblühen dieser Geschäfte dem Gemeinwesen durch diese seine Handlungsweise bereitet hat . . .' von Madai (*Polizeipräsident*, Berlin) to von Jagow (*Ober-Präsident* of the Province of Brandenburg), Berlin, 7 July 1876, ZSAM Rep. 120 A IV 5, vol. 17, fo. 60ᵛ, copy.

successful exporting activities are too numerous to mention. These were exports, above all, of textiles, but also of items like iron, agricultural machinery, precision machinery, sugar, cardboard, paper, and seeds. Among the markets for such exports figure most European countries with Russia, Bohemia, Scandinavia, and Italy prominent. There is reference to exports to Turkey, Japan, China, the USA, and Australia.

While, in general, much of the economic activity of the Jewish notables still bears the characteristics of the entrepreneurial capitalism of the early family firm, there are, among members of the last 'generation' of KRs examined here, first indications of adaptation to the forms of corporate capitalism. Thus the brothers Loewe, in their enterprises, combine new methods of mass production with forms of organization and finance characteristic of developed capitalism. Among early firms geared to supplying industries of developed capitalism with raw materials or semi-finished products, sometimes from overseas, are enterprises like those built up by, among others, Wilhelm Merton, Fritz Friedländer, Eduard Arnhold, and Lewin Simon. While Rudolf Mosse pioneered systematic advertising (that is the artificial stimulation of demand), soon to be a feature of a developed economy, Oscar Tietz (following, to some extent, foreign models) was developing another, the large department store. Eduard Arnhold, similarly, was helping to build up a gas industry to consume Silesian coal.

Of the companies founded by Jewish entrepreneurs during the *Gründerjahre* some survived the crash of 1873 to become substantial enterprises. Among their number were Strousberg's Dortmunder Union and the Königs- und Laura Hütte, in the financing of which both Gerson Bleichröder and Jacob Landau had played a part. Anton Emil Wolff (partner of GKR Heinrich Wolff, 1876) was co-founder of the Aktienbrauerei Friedrichshöhe vorm. Patzenhofer, destined to become part of Schultheiss-Patzenhofer, Europe's largest brewery. From the mid-nineties onwards, the number of board members of joint-stock companies among the KRs increased, with the brothers Caro in the lead. There is an early cartel, the Deutscher Walzwerksverband, in the setting-up of which *Generaldirektor* Oscar Caro (1894) played a prominent part. Thus the end of the age of the notables (and of early capitalism) saw some Jewish entrepreneurs ready to move into positions of prominence in the growing corporate structure of developed capitalist commercial organization.

The Jewish economic élite of notables in the nineteenth century, as represented by Jewish KRs in Prussia, thus reflects a variety of types of economic activity, making generalization hazardous. If Jewish entrepreneurial activity has some distinguishing features, these are, perhaps, to be sought less in outright innovation or invention than in a special aptitude for economic 'mediation' in the forms of the export of German goods, of 'secondary innovation', technology transfer through the introduction into Germany of processes and methods observed abroad, and in new techniques for the creation (or stimulation) of demand. Nor were such contributions (as rabid anti-Semites either claimed or implied) less valuable to the German economy than those of a small handful of inventors like Werner von Siemens, the brothers Mannesmann, or Rudolf Diesel. The Prussian authorities, the evidence suggests, appreciated the advantages to German economic life of the contribution made by Jewish enterprise. They had special reason also to recognize the financial services rendered to governments, railway development, industry, and private individuals by Jewish bankers. In these spheres, the Jewish contribution to German economic development at all levels and in most regions was, indeed, outstanding.

VI

The German–Jewish entrepreneurship examined may be viewed in the light of the model of Jewish economic behaviour devised by the economist Simon Kuznets.[138] Minorities, Kuznets observes, invariably show a narrower occupational base than the population at large, a claim confirmed by the occupational distribution of the German–Jewish economic élite, more particularly in the first half of the nineteenth century. Jews, unlike Gentiles, are virtually unrepresented in the extractive, metallurgical, and engineering industries (as they are, of course, in agriculture).

Jewish entrepreneurship at this stage, according to Kuznets, tends to be concentrated in branches of industry that are relatively new and expanding more rapidly than the economy in general. The reason for this is that such branches are less occupied than others and yield a

---

[138] Simon Kuznets, 'Economic Structure and Life of the Jews' in Louis Finkelstein (ed.), *The Jews: Their History, Culture and Religion* (London, 1961) ii. 1597 ff. The Kuznets analysis is here used as elaborated by Professor Yehuda Don of Bar-Ilan University, Ramat-Gan.

higher rate of return on capital than more traditional pursuits. They may also be the reflection of an 'economic heritage', a pre-existing traditional Jewish skill structure. In the present instance, such new 'growth industries' attracting Jewish entrepreneurship would appear to be sugar distilling, some branches of the textile industry (notably cotton and calico printing, later wholesale clothing manufacture and fashions), and mechanical transportation: railway financing, construction, management, and the production of railway materials. Whether these branches of entrepreneurship preferred by Jews did indeed offer a higher rate of return on capital than 'heavy industry', which Jews rarely entered, is a question that cannot be considered here. It appears, in any case, doubtful whether the 'Gentile' branches were originally more 'occupied' (assuming it were possible to measure density of occupation or 'absorptive capacity') than the ones in which Jews achieved some prominence. In any case, Jewish entrepreneurship was equally present in 'traditional' branches of economic life: silk or woollen manufacture, the production of traditional consumer goods, or horse transportation. Again, Jews continued to be conspicuous in 'traditional' occupations like trade in agricultural produce, the basis of large-scale war contracting. Whether private banking, in which Jews achieved prominence, is considered a 'traditional' or an 'innovative' occupation must remain a matter of opinion. While loans to governments and public authorities (now in the guise of underwriting government stock issues) had a long tradition behind them, the mobilization of investment capital, notably for capital-intensive railway construction (and, more particularly, in the form of share flotations and stock-exchange operations pioneered by the Rothschilds), may be considered 'innovative'. Certainly the traditional Jewish skill structure, orientated on the one hand towards financial transactions, on the other towards the production and sale of consumer goods, helped to determine the character and distribution of early Jewish entrepreneurship. It may, however, be questioned to what extend traditional Jewish skills influenced the investment of capital and energy in activities like sugar distilling, calico printing, production of dyestuffs or horse transportation. On the whole, Jewish entrepreneurs of the first half of the century tended to invest 'unemployed' capital (derived largely from war contracts and associated credit transactions) in branches of economic activity that seemed to offer substantial returns. If, overall, there was some conformity to the Kuznets model, that conformity was far from absolute.

Kuznets (whose main illustrative material is taken on the one hand from the Jewries of Russia and Poland, on the other from Jewish immigrants into the USA and Palestine-Israel) discusses Jewish adjustment to industrial society and adaptation to the occupational patterns of the Gentile majority. The smaller, proportionately, the Jewish minority, the closer its approximation to the occupational pattern of the majority. The degree of 'normalization' would depend also on the attitude towards Jewish economic activity of the host societies, both governments and populations. Again, there might be obstacles to adaptation in the shape of minority economic heritage, language differences, and distinctive cultural customs and traditions.

In Prussia (and, indeed, the rest of Germany), all such factors, on the whole, tended to favour Jewish economic diversification and, with it, approximation to the general economic pattern. Compared to the Jewries of central and eastern Europe or the USA, German Jewry constituted a relatively small (if often concentrated) minority. Official attitudes towards Jewish economic activity were almost uniformly benevolent. The Gentile commercial community (though there were some exceptions) came to be well disposed towards mutually beneficial commercial relations with Jews. The bulk of the urban Gentile public meanwhile was more than ready to profit from the 'good value' offered by Jewish retailers and the quality of many Jewish-produced consumer goods. They may have responded positively to Jewish sales techniques, advertising, assiduity, and readiness to be of service. Finally relations, economic and personal (with localized exceptions), with rural populations also were, on the whole, positive and mutually advantageous. In short, the 'general climate' consistently favoured Jewish entrepreneurship (if hardly social integration or a significant public role).

Moreover, as is well known, German Jewry was favoured in its economic activities by rapid and successful acculturation. By mid-century, the use of a separate language (Yiddish) had largely disappeared. So had traditional observances impeding Jewish integration: observance of the sabbath and of the ritual laws which had, to some extent, promoted the maintenance of a distinct Jewish economic network. At the same time, some economically favourable aspects of the Jewish social tradition survived: the closely knit Jewish family and elements of the solidarity often found among members of underprivileged minorities. These latter features, however, while conducive to economic advancement, would at best be neutral in terms of assimilation of occupational distributions.

In such a climate, according to Kuznets, Jews would be able to progress economically relatively faster than corresponding Gentiles. They could get wealthy more rapidly. They could acquire a significant, in some cases a dominant share in some branches of economic activity. Jewish and Gentile wealth on the eve of the Great War, the fruit largely of differential economic activity, will be considered in the following chapter. To some extent here the picture bears out the analysis offered by Kuznets.

It is in these conditions that an economically upwardly mobile group enters fully industrialized capitalist society with its preponderance of large production units, huge demand for investment, and large corporate structures. According to Kuznets this phase, which in Germany may be dated from the last quarter of the nineteenth century, is marked by a rapid growth particularly of the 'tertiary sector', more particularly commerce (wholesale trade, banking, and finance rather than 'service industries'). This is a rapidly growing sector, employing an ever-growing proportion of labour. Jews and Gentiles alike move from handicrafts and manufacturing to commerce, the former mainly from industrial occupations, the latter from agriculture.

Kuznets assigns several reasons for what he considers the Jewish move from industry to commerce. Commercial activity (which includes banking, insurance, import-export trade, property development, and so on) is more lucrative than industrial pursuits and also confers a higher social status. Jewish craftsmen and artisans (like their Gentile counterparts) were losing ground in competition with the mass production of factories. Again, there was the example of others already successful in large-scale commercial activity. Economic modernization, Kuznets appears to argue, pushes Jews (like Gentiles) into commercial activities.

While the shift to commercial activities might not be unfavourable to Jewish entrepreneurship, the coming of full industrialization and developed capitalist structures is, according to Kuznets. The reason is to be found in certain traditional Jewish attitudes and preferences in both industry and commerce. The preference of Jewish producers, Kuznets considers, is for the production of consumer goods to be sold in the open market-place direct to the individual consumer. Production takes place mainly in small units employing simple technologies and with low capital requirements. Typical industries of this kind are the manufacture of clothing, paper, jewellery, leather goods, and furs, or printing and food processing. Jewish entrepreneurs, on the other hand, are not typically involved in large-scale, capital-intensive industries: mining, metallurgy, engineering, or large-scale mechanized textile manufacture.

Jewish trading activities, on the other hand, are, according to Kuznets, based typically on small capital, rapid turnover, and the employment of individual skills and dexterity. Jews prefer areas of open competition least subject to discrimination. They gravitate towards trades in which Jews are already employed. They prefer independent economic activity to even senior employment in large companies. Indeed, aversion to all dealings with large bodies (whether public or private) and the attempt to minimize all contacts with them (as a precaution against possible discrimination) are a distinguishing feature of Jewish economic strategies.

Such Jewish attitudes, Kuznets argues, stand in sharp contrast to economic modernization. In fact, modern industry with its advanced technology, capital-intensiveness, mass production, and wholesale orders from large bodies (whether governments or private corporations), progressively makes Jewish entrepreneurship uncompetitive and obsolescent. Jews, with traditional adaptability, turn to the professions, hospitable to many Jewish traditional attitudes. They also turn to economic activities related to the professions: accountancy, company law, salesmanship. The basic nature of Jewish economic preferences, an open market-place and the avoidance of dealings with the authorities, has remained unchanged.

On the face of it, this part of Kuznet's model (based largely on petty Jewish entrepreneurial activity in eastern and central Europe, the USA, or Israel) seems barely applicable to the German–Jewish economic élite of the Industrial Revolution and the age of full industrialization. It may, however, draw attention to the emergence, from the sixties onwards, of two separate sectors of German–Jewish entrepreneurship, one traditional, the other modern. While the former is indeed in fairly rapid decline—some substantial Jewish enterprises, notably private banking houses, disappear from the seventies onwards—the second operates with conspicuous success within the new capitalist and large industrial structures. There is also, as has been shown, rather more successful adaptation to the new conditions by both individual Jewish entrepreneurs and their firms than the Kuznets model allows for. In any case, almost by definition, the bulk of the Jewish economic élite of the new age belongs to the 'modern' sector. Jews (with Strousberg, the Loewe brothers, and a number of Silesian industrialists as pioneers) enter the field of large-scale capitalist industry. They do so in branches of industry (to which the electrical and chemical industries will presently be added) in which Jews, until this time, had hardly played a part. Jews also came to play a prominent role in the large joint-stock banks, major instruments of economic modernization. They are conspicuous in the international capital and commodity markets of the new age and in its vital export trade. These were developments conforming to Kuznets's thesis of Jewish economic diversification and approximation to the general occupational distribution under a liberal economic regime (at any rate internally). Jews important in economic life would, in the face of growing opposition from powerful interests, seek also to defend (relative) freedom of trade in the international sphere. In respect of freedom of trade, there were elements of continuity in Jewish entrepreneurial attitudes throughout. On this point, there was agreement also between the traditional and modernizing sectors of the 'Jewish' economy'. Both, as will be seen, would be represented in the German as in the German–Jewish wealth élite.

5
Anatomy of a Wealth Élite

I

THE fortunes acquired by Jews prominent in economic life in the nineteenth century (like their annual incomes) naturally showed considerable variations. As has been seen, the minimum qualification required by the authorities for the conferment of a commercial title varied with time and place. It was a matter for investigation by the authorities. Yet, though wealth and annual income of candidates were normally recorded, this was not always the case. The records none the less provide a representative sample of fortunes (and incomes) of many of the KRs to be. While the recorded wealth usually represents estimates, the income figures (and corresponding tax groups) are based on actual returns. Until the early seventies such figures are recorded in thalers and must be multiplied three fold to obtain the mark equivalent. The figures, besides recording the approximate wealth of individuals, also reveal broad trends in the size of fortunes as well as the branches of economic activity which helped to produce them.

Three instances illustrate the fortunes of *Vormärz*:

			Thalers
1837	Salomon Herz	vegetable oil producer	100,000–150,000
1838–9	Ludwig Lessing	banker	400,000–500,000
1841	Jac. Abraham Meÿer	silk manufacturer	c.300,000

For the fifties, sixties, and early seventies, information is more plentiful:

1853	Alexander Mendelssohn	banker	2,000,000
1854	Moritz Borchardt jun.	banker	800,000
1854	Moritz Friedländer	banker and industrialist	200,000
1865	Emanuel Friedländer	coal wholesaler	120,000–150,000
1867	Moritz H. Güterbock	banker	400,000
1868	Hermann Kauffman	textile manufacturer	200,000
1869	Wilhelm Herz	vegetable oil producer	700,000
1869	Louis Dahlheim	textile manufacturer	200,000
1870	Adolf Liebermann	textile manufacturer	300,000
1870	Valentin Manheimer	manufacturer of ladies' wear	800,000
1870	Moritz Wolff	textile manufacturer	300,000

			Thalers
1871	Salomon Lachmann	grain merchant and war contractor	4,000,000
1872	Heinrich Wolff	banker	300,000
1872	Wilhelm Herz	vegetable oil and rubber (softening) producer	1,000,000

Some features are worth noting. Among them is the increase in the fortunes of the two Herzes from just over 100,000 thalers in 1837 to 700,000 in 1869 and 1,000,000 in 1872. Notable also is the wealth of Alexander Mendelssohn which, however, represents no more than part of the capital of his bank. Significant is further the size of the fortune accumulated by Salomon Lachmann, one of an entirely new order of magnitude. Other war contractors, the Schottländer, Aschrott, Simon Cohn, also acquired considerable wealth during the German wars of unification. War contracting clearly, as in the age of Napoleon, remained a factor in the growth of the German-Jewish capitalist class. Below such outstanding fortunes, those of successful bankers range between one and two million marks. Among manufacturers, apart from the Herzes, the Manheimer brothers are the first to own several million marks.

For the seventies, relatively full figures of annual incomes become available, based on tax returns. Some of the top incomes are worth noting (figures in thalers converted into marks; the incomes are arranged in descending order);

		Tax class	marks	
Jacob Landau	1876	34	360,000–420,000	banker
Meyer Cohn	1879	30	168,000–204,000	banker
Louis Reichenheim	1875	28	120,000–144,000	textile manufacturer
Isaak and Lewin Simon	1877	28	120,000–144,000	textile wholesalers
Max Ludwig Goldberger	1879	26	96,000–108,000	banker
Robert Caro	1875	–	80,000–100,000	iron wholesaler

These are followed by, in tax class 25, Abraham Meyer (banker, Berlin, 1876) and Emanuel Lohnstein (banker, commission merchant, and textile manufacturer in Lodz; Berlin, 1879) and, in tax class 24, Salomon Huldschinsky (industrialist, Gleiwitz and Berlin, 1876), Albert Hahn (industrialist, Berlin and Düsseldorf, 1877), and Heinrich Wolff (banker, Berlin, 1876). Thus, though the largest incomes were in the main those of bankers, leading wholesalers (Robert Caro, the Simon brothers) and industrialists (Reichenheim, Hahn, Huldschinsky) also figured.

In the last quarter of the century, fortunes and incomes, predictably, increase dramatically. The largest fortune of the eighties, and by a wide margin, is still that of Salomon Lachmann, credited in 1880 with assets of some 15 million marks. Lewin Simon's fortune, recorded in 1887 as 3 million marks, had, by 1898, increased to an astonishing 13 million. It is in fact in the nineties that a renewed upward turn of the secular wave combined with the spectacular growth of the German economy in particular to produce a striking growth in individual fortunes. By 1897, Fritz Friedländer, with an estate exceeding 24 million marks, had taken the lead in the wealth table, followed by Lewin Simon with 13 million. Next in wealth were the brothers Ferdinand and Gustav Manheimer, credited in 1897 with fortunes of 5 million each. Significantly, the lead has passed from private bankers to merchant-industrialists (Fritz Friedländer and Georg Caro, 'worth several million' in 1897 and both destined for baptism and ennoblement), a wholesale merchant (Lewin Simon), and clothing manufacturers (*Konfektion*) Valentin and Gustav Manheimer. Significantly Isidor Loewe—manager and financier rather than owner (prefiguring men like Emil Rathenau or Albert Ballin)—is credited with a 'mere' 3 million (1898). The wealthiest banker of the period for whom data are available is Georg Fromberg (*c.*4 million in 1897), whose bank had moved to Berlin from Breslau, followed by Edmund Helfft, scion of an old and respected Berlin banking family (*c*2 million in 1898) (of course there were far wealthier Jewish bankers, notably the Bleichröders, Schwabachs, and Mendelssohn-Bartholdys).

Incomes, naturally, were related to the size of fortunes. Thus in the eighties the largest income was declared by Salomon Lachmann (class 35, 420,000–480,000), followed by two Berlin bankers, both placed in 1889 in the thirty-third class (300,000–360,000), Hugo Oppenheim and Max Goldberger. It is worth noting, however, that the latter's income had been halved by 1892, the result of unfortunate speculations. Next came two further army contractors, Gustav Friedmann of Breslau (240,000 in 1896) and Simon Cohn (120,000 in 1887), followed in their turn by the highly paid director of the Deutsche Bank, Hermann Wallich (class 26, 96,000–108,000 in 1885).

Incomes, like fortunes, rise spectacularly with the commercial upturn of the nineties. Fritz Friedländer, predictably, heads the list

Anatomy of a Wealth Élite

with the princely annual income of some 2 million marks in 1897, followed by Lewin Simon with c.930,000 in 1898. As against this affluence, Ferdinand Manheimer in 1897 earned 300,000 marks, Georg Fromberg 230,000. Isidor Loewe declared an income of 'only' 160,000 (1898) as did Edmund Helfitt (also 1898). The remaining incomes, by comparison, were relatively modest.

Collectively the wealthiest group among new Jewish KRs, then, were the army contractors, while the wealthiest individuals were wholesalers and industrialists, Friedländer, the Simons, and the Manheimers. Bankers, Oppenheim, Fromberg, Goldberger, and Helfft, occupy a more modest position. These figures (disregarding the earlier wealth of the Rothschilds, Mendelssohns, Bleichröders) reflect in fact the partial eclipse of the Jewish private banker, now overtaken in the Jewish wealth league both by the largest wholesale merchants and by corporate industrialists and men of affairs.

II

A full picture of the developed Jewish wealth élite in the age of high capitalism emerges from the tax declarations for 1908 and 1911, which serve as the basis for Martin's well-known studies. Rudolf Martin based his year-book of Prussian millionaires[1] on a Prussian official publication, *Mitteilungen aus der Verwaltung der direkten Steuern im preussischen Staate. Statistik der preussischen Einkommensteuer-Veranlagung für die Steuerjahre 1908–1910. Im Auftrag des Herrn Finanzministers bearbeitet vom königlichen preussischen statistischen Landesamt* (Berlin, 1908) and the corresponding publication for the tax years 1911–13.[2] However, though detailed geographically, the figures contained in these statistics were anonymous, that is no names were supplied.[3] Martin, a retired official of the ministry of the interior, set

---

[1] R. Martin, *Jahrbuch des Vermögens und Einkommens der Millionäre in Preussen* (Berlin, 1912, 2nd rev. edn., Berlin, 1913). Unless otherwise stated, the earlier edition has been used.

[2] In the introduction to his work, Martin writes as follows: 'Eine Statistik des Einkommens besteht seit dem Jahre 1892 und des Vermögens seit dem Jahre 1895 für das Königreich Preussen und hat sich ohne Zweifel ständig vervollkommnet. In dieser Statistik schlummert im Verborgenen eine gewaltige Kulturarbeit, die sich aus der Selbstdeklaration und der fleissigen Tätigkeit der Veranlagungs- und Schätzungskommission zusammensetzt. Ich habe es mir zum Ziel gesetzt, das tote Zahlengerippe der amtlichen Statistik zum Leben zu erwecken . . .' (ib., p. vi).

[3] '. . . die Zahlen stehen fest. Sie sind durch die amtliche Statistik gegeben und zwar im grossen ganzen für jede Stadt, von Ausnahmen bei kleineren Städten abgesehen, und für jeden ländlichen Regierungsbezirk' (ib., p. x).

himself the task on the basis of his officially acquired knowledge of German economic life,[4] to marry figures to names.[5] While freely admitting to the possibility of some errors,[6] Martin claims, reasonably, that these were least likely to occur in respect of the largest fortunes.[7] Moreover, he was able to correct such errors as came or were brought to his notice by those concerned.[8] On 10 March 1911, the police searched Martin's flat as well as the offices of his publisher, took away his notes, his manuscript, and some galley proofs and subsequently started proceedings against him. However, on 25 May 1911, he was informed that the prosecution had been dropped and the confiscated materials were returned.[9] In a curious way, the government, by this decision, gave some kind of official imprimatur to the data collected by Martin. In October 1911, Martin authorized publication, and the first edition of his work appeared in 1912.

In all, Martin lists wealth and incomes of some 8,300 Prussian millionaires, with special attention given to the 747 with fortunes exceeding 5 million marks. For the bulk of the latter Martin, in the second part of his study, provides biographical notes, with some details on family and source of wealth. While the coverage varies, the data are, on the whole, reliable. Nor would it have been entirely safe for either author or publisher to have printed seriously inaccurate information.

In 1913, Martin published the invaluable second edition of his work on Prussian millionaires based, this time, on the tax returns for 1911.[10]

[4] 'Ich würde niemals daran gedacht haben, dieses schwierige Werk in Angriff zu nehmen, wenn ich nicht durch 8 Jahre von 1897 bis 1905 als Referent im Reichsamt des Innern bei Produktionserhebungen des Wirtschaftlichen Ausschusses zur Vorbereitung des Zolltarifs und der Handelsverträge mir die Fähigkeit angeeignet hätte, schnell und sicher die Grössenverhältnisse von zehntausend gewerblichen Betrieben im Deutschen Reiche zu beurteilen, und wenn ich nicht in ganz ungewöhnlichem Masse in dieser Stellung Gelegenheit gehabt hätte, die besitzenden Klassen im Deutschen Reiche persönlich kennen zu lernen' (ib., p. 15).
[5] 'Meine Arbeit besteht darin, dass ich zu der Zahl die Namen setzte' (ib., p. x).
[6] 'Obgleich das Jahrbuch zum ersten Male erscheint, dürfte die Zahl der Fehler nicht grösser sein, als sie mit einem so ausgedehnten Unternehmen notwendig verbunden ist' (Martin, op. cit., n. 1 above, p. xiii).
[7] 'Die obersten Sprossen des Zahlengerippes der amtlichen Vermögens- und Einkommensteur-Statistik in jeder einzelnen Stadt und in jedem einzelnden ländlichen Regierungsbezirk sind also am leichtesten mit den richtigen Personen zu besetzen' (ib., p. x).
[8] 'Ich habe mich bemüht, die zu meiner Kenntnis gelangten Fehler in den beiden Nachträgen zum ersten und zweiten Teil richtig zu stellen ...' (ib., p. xiii).
[9] Ib., pp. xiv f.
[10] Rudolf Martin, *Jahrbuch des Vermögens und Einkommens der Millionäre in Preussen* 2nd edn (Berlin, 1913), 2vols.

This not only has the advantage of breaking down information by provinces, but also takes into account information and corrections elicited by the original publication from some of the people concerned.[11] Moreover, the new edition throws light also on the growth of individual fortunes between the tax declarations of 1908 and 1911.[12] Besides his work on Prussian millionaires, Martin also published comparable studies for the non-Prussian states and regions of Germany with the regrettable exception of Baden, the Palatinate, the Saar, and Alsace-Lorraine.[13] Even allowing for some possible errors, Martin thus presents a unique picture of the total German wealth élite on the eve of the war of 1914 at, arguably, the culminating point in its history.

Although Martin's compilation is both unique and informative, its use must, of course, be subject to a double caution. In the first place, while the figures are official, the attribution of specific fortunes to particular individuals depends, essentially, on Martin's judgment alone—even if serious errors, for reasons explained by the author, are unlikely. The second reservation concerns the figures themselves which, clearly, are at best approximations. Not only would the true value of factories or estates be difficult to assess (not to speak of 'goodwill' and so on) but these, and especially annual income, would be subject to variations from year to year. Also, there are the vagaries of death, inheritance, or marriage settlements. While the declarations themselves, agreed by the authorities, might be presumed to be approximately 'correct', they can represent only the state of affairs about the time of the declaration, some time in 1908 or 1911. Clearly, therefore, what Martin provides are approximations, orders of magnitude, a rough 'ranking order'. However, his data are fully adequate to establish in what forms of activity great fortunes were made, by whom, and, to some extent, their duration. For present purposes Martin's data reveal the structure (or anatomy) of the

[11] As Martin explains in the introduction to the 1913 edition of his work on Prussian millionaires: 'Das neue Werk ist in allen seinen Teilen von Grund aus eine neue Arbeit und beruht in erheblichem Umfange auf der Selbstdeklaration der preussischen Millionäre, die dem Verfasser eine Fülle wertvoller Berichtigungen und Ergänzungen eingesandt haben. Es ist kaum anzunehmen, dass sich in dem kommenden Jahrbuch der Millionäre in Preussen noch irgendeine Person befindet, die nicht wirklich Millionär ist, und dass irgendein erheblicher Irrtum in der Höhe des Vermögens oder Einkommens sich ereignet hat' (ib., p. 2).
[12] According to the official statistics the total number of millionaires in Prussia rose from 8,335 in 1908 to 9,341 in 1911 (ib.).
[13] Publication of the relevant volume was overtaken by the war in 1914.

German–Jewish wealth élite. Moreover, they provide an invaluable Gentile control group. They also contribute to an assessment of the place occupied by Jews in the German economy as a whole.

III

The Jewish wealth élite as it emerges from Martin's compilations reflects, of course, only to a limited extent the actual economic importance of individuals or their enterprises in the year 1908 (or 1911). Rather, it tends to represent economic achievements of an earlier age, magnified on the one hand by successful marriage strategies, on the other by the investment opportunities provided by the great economic upturn since the mid-nineties. The wealth recorded by Martin thus may, in fact, to some extent be the product of economic activity since the later sixties.

As a result, there is some overlap between the élite of notables, the *Kommerzienräte*, and that the millionaires of developed capitalism. At the same time, Martin's wealth élite also includes varieties of 'new wealth' not contained in the earlier group as well as the fortunes of those who either would not or could not become *Kommerzienräte*. The wealth élite, in fact, is the more comprehensive of the two. It also differs from that of the notables, among others, by including women (either dowagers or heiresses). Indeed, in some respects it is more informative to consider the wealth of families (hence, usually, the capital of enterprises) rather than the 'accidental' private fortunes of individuals.

The Jewish wealth élite, therefore, is perhaps best approached, in the first instance, by an examination of Jewish families with aggregate fortunes in excess of 50 million marks.

	Million marks	
Rothschild and Goldschmidt-Rothschild	310 (7)	(number of individuals
Speyer and Beit von Speyer	121 (2)	sharing the fortune
Mendelssohn and Mendelssohn-Bartholdy	101 (5)	in brackets)
Gans/Weinberg	71 (6)	
Bleichröder/Schwabach	70 (3)	
Freiherrn v. Oppenheim	68 (4)	
Schottländer	61 (5)	
Simon	53 (2)	
Mosse	51 (2)	

Anatomy of a Wealth Élite 179

The salient features of this list are clear. The leading group in the Jewish wealth élite consists of private banking dynasties with the Rothschilds and their successors, the Goldschmidt-Rothschilds,[14] symbolically and justly at the head. Of the nine wealthiest Jewish families, five (Rothschild, Speyer,[15] Mendelssohn,[16] Bleichröder,

[14] Willy von Rothschild, the last male member of the Frankfurt branch, died on 25 January 1901. His daughter Minna had married Maximilian Benedikt Goldschmidt. The Goldschmidts had, since the seventeenth century, been importers and merchants, originally of textile goods, in Frankfurt-on-Main. In 1827, Hayum Benedikt Goldschmidt had started trading in Russian and Polish products, particularly raw hides and leather, wholesale and retail. Minna Goldschmidt née Rothschild died on 1 May 1903. On 6 September 1903 *Generalkonsul* Maximiliam Goldschmidt was raised to the Prussian nobility as *Freiherr* 'von Goldschmidt-Rothschild'. (It is interesting to compare his elevation—comparable also for its symbolic value—with the almost simultaneous one of Gustav (Krupp) von Bohlen und Halbach.) Maximilian von Goldschmidt-Rothschild became the richest Jew (he actually retained his Jewish faith) in Germany. 'Freiherr Maximilian von Goldschmidt-Rothschild hat frühzeitig mit den alten steifleinenen Traditionen des Rothschild'schen Hauses gebrochen und sich modernen Geschäften zugewandt. Insonderheit hat er in Verbindung mit Wernher, Beit & Co. sich mit grossem Erfolge in südafrikanischen Goldshares betätigt. Auch ist Freiherr von Goldschmidt von Haus aus recht vermögend.—Einschliesslich des Vermögens seiner Ehefrau hat er im Jahre 1902 ein Vermögen von 139 Millionen Mark versteuert.' Martin, op. cit., ii. 22 ff. By 1908, the fortune had fallen to 107 million, possibly due to a dowry and some gifts. The evolution of the Goldschmidt-Rothschilds—one of Maximilian's sons married the daughter and sole heiress of Fritz von Friedländer-Fuld—forms an illustration of one form of adaptation of traditional Jewish businesses to the conditions of developed capitalism.

[15] The Speyers had once been wealthier than the Rothschilds. In 1799, while Meyer Amschel Rothschild declared a fortune of 60,000 fl., three Speyers (records of Speyers prominent among Frankfurt Jews go back as far as 1644) declared theirs at 604,000 fl. Joseph Lazarus Speyer (1783–1840) had married Jette Ellissen, heiress to yet another banking fortune. Their three sons adopted the name of Speyer-Ellissen. In 1836, the banking house of Lazard Speyer-Ellissen was founded in Frankfurt. It was destined to become not only the largest private bank in the city but part of an international banking group.

Gumperz—later Eduard Joseph—Speyer-Ellissen, son of Joseph Lazarus, had three sons. While Georg (died 1902) directed the parent house in Frankfurt, two brothers emigrated as young men, James Speyer, who conducted his business mainly in New York, but also in Frankfurt and Paris, and Edgar (in 1906 Sir Edgar), who operated mainly in the City of London (but also in Berlin). Their sister Lucie married, in 1892, the banker Eduard Beit, offspring of a wealthy Hamburg family.

Dr Ferdinand Beit, Eduard Beit's father, was the son of a cloth merchant, who had later added wholesale trade in dye-stuffs and chemicals. The son, Ferdinand, a trained chemist, had expanded the business to include both manufacture (especialy of saltpetre) and wholesale trade and adopted for the parental firm the name of Chemie und Farbenfabriken Fa. Beit & Co. He had married Johanna Ladenburg of the Mannheim branch of the wealthy banking family. His brother, who had moved to London, became the 'diamond king' Alfred Beit.

When Eduard Beit married Hanna Lucie Speyer in 1892, three great fortunes had thus become linked. In 1896, Eduard Beit became a partner in the house of Lazard Speyer-Ellissen. In 1901, KR Eduard Beit—by then a Protestant—was raised to the

See p. 179 for n. 15 cont. and n. 16

Oppenheim) are those of bankers linked directly or indirectly (through the Rothschilds) to the court Jews of the age of absolutism.

It is the four remaining families which introduce a new element. The Gans/Weinberg of Frankfurt-on-Main, owners of Leopold Cassella & Co., are the only industrialists in the group. The rest are engaged in commercial rather than industrial pursuits. The Schottländers, almost alone among the major Jewish contractors of the wars of unification, had preserved and, indeed, enlarged their fortune (another who did so was Sigmund Aschrott). The Simons, as has been seen, dominated a major branch of German wholesale trade. These fortunes were, by 1908, well established in the second or even third generation with members of the families concerned still active in economic life. An unusual feature of the third generation of Schottländers is that members of the family continued to reside, in relative obscurity, near Breslau. Newcomers in the first generation were the brothers Rudolf and Emil Mosse with fortunes derived from the first major advertising agency established in Germany, enhanced by successful publishing activities connected originally with advertising interests.[17] The Mosse family, like the Schottländers, though possibly

Prussian nobility as Beit von Speyer (1860–1933). For most of the foregoing information see Fredrich Wilhelm Euler, 'Bankherren und Grossbankleiter nach Herkunft und Heiratskreis', in Hans Hubert Hofmann (ed.), *Bankherren und Bankiers* (Limburg an der Lahn, 1978), pp. 122 f. Martin credits Eduard Beit von Speyer with a fortune of 76 million marks and with an annual income for the years 1909 and 1910 in excess of 2 million marks. Martin, op. cit., n. 10 above, ii. 40).

[16] Like some other banking fortunes (more than non-banking ones), that of the Mendelssohns was in part the product of successful marriage strategies. When Ernst von Mendelssohn-Bartholdy, wealthiest member of the family (Martin, for 1908, credits him with a fortune of 43 million marks), after being given a partnership in the bank in 1874, married the following year his cousin Marie Warschauer, heiress of the banker Robert Warschauer, the Warschauers were probably still the richer of the two families. Martin, op. cit., n. 10 above, ii. 90.

[17] 'Rudolf Mosse ... eröffnete im Jahre 1867 in Berlin ein Annoncenbureau, dem bald zahlreiche Zweigniederlassungen in allen grösseren Städten Deutschlands und in den Hauptstädten des Auslandes folgten. Im Jahre 1872 begründete er das Berliner Tageblatt von dem im Jahre 1889 die Berliner Volkszeitung abgezweigt wurde. Im Mai 1884 nahm Rudolf Mosse seinen jüngeren Bruder Emil Mosse als Teilhaber der Firma Rudolf Mosse auf ... Bis vor wenigen Jahren bestand die Haupteinnahme Rudolf Mosses in dem Reingewinn seiner grossen Annoncen-Expedition, welche den Reingewinn aus dem Berliner Tageblatt weit überragte. In den letzten Jahren dürfte sich durch da enorme Steigen der Abonnentenzahl des Berliner Tageblatts, der Berliner Morgenzeitung und der Berliner Volkszeitung ... dies Verhältnis etwas geändert haben ... Das von den beiden Inhabern der Firma Rud. Mosse zusammen versteuerte Vermögen betrug also rund 51 Mill. Mark. Da dieses Vermögen in der Hauptsache von den beiden Inhabern selbst geschäftlich verdient worden ist, wird kein Sachverständiger ein höheres Gesamtvermögen erwarten.' Martin, op. cit., n. 10 above, ii. 102 ff.

for different reasons, never joined the élite of notables. Being left-liberals and oppositional in their political views, they kept their distance from the Hohenzollern dynasty. It is worth noting, and not accidental, that the fortunes of the great banking dynasties are (except for that of the Gans/Weinberg) larger than those of the 'newcomers' whose wealth was derived from non-banking activities.

If, instead of the wealth of families, one looks at Jewish individuals with private fortunes exceeding 30 million marks, members of the same families predominate:

	Million marks
Freiherr Max von Goldschmidt-Rothschild	107
Freifrau Mathilde von Rothschild (widow)	76
KR Eduard Beit von Speyer	76
Frau Franziska widow of banker Georg Speyer	45
Ernst von Mendelssohn-Bartholdy *Wirkl. Geh. Rat*	43
Fritz von Friedländer-Fuld	40
Rudolf Mosse	40
Julius Schottländer	38
Freiherr Albert von Goldschmidt-Rothschild	38
Freiherr Rudolf von Goldschmidt-Rothschild	37
GKR Eduard Arnhold	35.5
Hans von Bleichröder (banker)	30.8
James Simon	30.2

In fact, the only change compared to the wealthiest Jewish families is the addition of the coal wholesalers and industrialists Fritz Friedländer and Eduard Arnhold.

Even if the list is extended to a band of owners of between 20 and 30 million marks, the changes are still relative few:

	Million marks
Oscar Huldschinsky	25
Freiherr Albert von Oppenheim	24–5
Freiherr Eduard von Oppenheim	24–5
Freiin Lucy von Goldschmidt-Rothschild	23–4
Dr James von Bleichröder	23.6

	Million marks
GKR Dr Eduard Simon	23.2
Robert von Mendelssohn	21.38
GKR Leopold Koppel	21.26
Freiherr Erich von Goldschmidt-Rothschild	20–1
GKR Sigmund Aschrott	20

Several points emerge. In the first place, these are still the old names with only one 'newcomer', Leopold Koppel. A second point which stands out, as it does in the previous group, is the frequency of ennoblement among members of the Jewish wealth élite, characteristic of the early twentieth century. Another aspect worth noting is the fact that the newcomers to the wealth élite do not include a single banker. Industrialists, however, are still confined to the Gans/Weinbergs, Fritz Friedländer, and Oscar Huldschinsky. The new entrants into the 'plutocracy' are, instead, drawn in the main from commerce. Of particular interest is the career of Leopold Koppel, a banker who, from modest provincial beginnings, by shrewd financing operations in two rising industries succeeded in amassing a large fortune.[18] His was an outstanding example of the Jewish private banker adapting his activities to the opportunities of the new corporate age. Koppel also illustrates, though success stories like his were uncommon, the entry into the wealth élite of obscure provincials in the course of a single

[18] The commercial career of Leopold Koppel was a curious one. 'Koppel begann als Handlungsgehilfe in dem früheren Bankhause Hrch. Roksch Nachfolger in Dresden, dessen Inhaber der Geh. Kommerzienrat Victor Hahn war, begründete dann selbst ein kleines Bankgeschäft in Dresden, siedelte aber nach einiger Zeit nach Berlin über, wo es ihm gelang das Gasglühlichtgeschäft und das Zentralhotel in die Hand zu bekommen' (ib., p. 185). 'Es dürfte wenige Personen in Berlin geben, die in den letzten 20 Jahren so viel Geld verdient haben wie Leop. Koppel. Seine Interessen lassen sich aus seinen Aufsichtsratsstellen ersehen. Er ist Vorsitzender des Aufsichtsrats der Deutschen Gasglühlicht A.G. in Berlin, der "Panzer" A.G. für Geldschrank-Tresorbau und Eisenindustrie, stellv. Vorsitzender des A.R. der Hotel-Betriebs A.G. in Berlin, Mitglied des A.R. der Arthur Koppel A.G. und der Monoline Maschinenfabrik A.G. in Berlin', (ib., p. 184). The Deutsche Gasglühlicht A.G. had been founded in 1892 with a capital of only 1.3 million marks. In 1911, however, the stock exchange valued its nominal share capital of 13.2 million marks at some 97 million. Hardly less successful had been Koppel's second venture, the Hotel-Betriebs-Gesellschaft. Founded in 1897 with a nominal capital of 2 million marks, increased to 9.8 million by 1911, it was then valued by the stock exchange at some 22 million marks (ib., pp. 184 f). 'Es ist nicht zu verwundern, dass das führende Bankhaus dieser beiden grossen Gesellschaften Millionen über Millionen verdient hat, und dass der alleinige Inhaber dieses Bankhauses sein Vermögen um vielleicht 20 Millionen vermehrt hat' (ib., p. 185).

generation. In this respect Koppel's story resembles that of the more significant Eugen Gutmann (coincidentally also from a modest private banking house) and foreshadows that of Jakob Goldschmidt, except that Gutmann and Goldschmidt achieved their positions of eminence through the corporate banking system rather than private banking.

Predictably, the dilution of the old wealth élite through men of a 'new formation' is somewhat more evident in the fortunes between 10 and 20 million marks. This, the level of 'lesser' members of the wealthiest families, lay within the reach of the most successful among the men operating within the new corporate structures. Though the numbers involved are somewhat greater, it is desirable to include them within the purview of the present study:

	Million marks
Paul von Schwabach	18.7
Carl von Weinberg	18–19
Arthur von Weinberg	18–19
Leopold Sonnemann	17–18
Franz von Mendelssohn	17–18
GKR Leo Gans	16–17
KR Dr Georg Heimann	15–16
GKR Dr Georg von Caro	15.04
GKR Isidor Loewe	14.32
James Hardy	14.02
Dr Wilhelm Merton	14–15
Fritz Gans	13–14
Berthold Israel	13.02
Adolf Gans	13–14
Carl Fürstenberg	12.64
Adolf Salomonsohn	12.60
Eugen Gutmann	12.22
Moritz H. Reichenheim	12.12
GKR Ludwig Max Goldberger	12.04
Max Baer	12–13
Max Steinthal	12–13
Geh. Reg.-R. Richard von Asser-Kaufmann	12–13
Paul Schottländer	12–13
GKR Wilhelm Kopetzky	11.96

	Million marks
KR Philip Freudenberg	11–12
Otto von Mendelssohn Bartholdy	11–12
GKR Otto Braunfels	11–12
KR Ernst Ladenburg	11–12
August Ladenburg	11–12
KR Louis Hagen	11–12
GKR Wilhelm Herz	11
Emil Mosse	10.9

At this level of wealth, the German–Jewish wealth élite is clearly a composite body, composed of heterogeneous elements. Out of 33 names only 3 (Paul von Schwabach, senior partner in the Bleichröder bank, Franz von Mendelssohn, and his distant cousin Otto von Mendelssohn Bartholdy, a *rentier* connected until 1904 with the old-established banking house of Robert Warschauer and also with the AG für Anilinfabrikation zu Treptow (Agfa), represent established banking families in Berlin. They are joined by an interesting newcomer, one of the handful of private bankers to establish a house of the first order in the age of the universal joint-stock banks, James Hardy.[19] Other representatives of established financial interests and pillars of the commercial-financial establishment of Berlin were GKR Ludwig Max Goldberger,[20] Geh GKR Wilhelm Kopetzky,[21] and

---

[19] 'Zu denjenigen Bankhäusern, die nach dem Kriege von 1870/71 zu aussergewöhnlicher Bedeutung gelangt sind, gehörte das Berliner Bankhaus Hardy & Co. Seine Entstehung geht auf James Hardy zurück. Er hat das Bankunternehmen von 1881–1889 als offene Handelsgesellschaft geführt, und es dann in eine G.m.b.H. umgewandelt. Hardy war ein ausgezeichneter Kenner des internationalen Bankgeschäftes. Er hatte besonders gute Beziehungen zu russischen und englischen Finanzkreisen. [James Hardy belonged to an Anglo-Jewish family called Nathan.] Die Verbindung mit dem Londoner Geldmarkt wurde noch verstärkt durch das von seinem Bruder gegründete City-Bankhaus Hardy, Nathan & Sons. Den Auslandsbeziehungen des Berliner Hauses kam auch die Gründung eines anderen Bruders zugute, der in Hamburg die ebenfalls schnell bekannt gwordene Firma Hardy & Hinrichsen aufbaute. Durch diese Querverbindungen haben die drei Hardys den Warenhandel und vornehmlich den deutschen Export finanziell sehr fördern können' Daniel Bernstein, 'Wirtschaft' in Siegmund Kaznelson (ed.), *Juden im deutschen Kulturbereich* (Berlin, 1962), p. 727.

[20] 'Geh. Kommerzienrat *Ludwig Max Goldberger* (1848–1913), der Schöpfer der Berliner Gewerbeausstellung von 1896, baute die väterliche Firma J. T. Goldberger zu einem Bank-Kommissionsgeschäft grossen Stils aus ... Er gehörte u.a. zu den Mitbegründern der Dresdner Bank und der Internationalen Bank in Berlin, die auch die Firma J. T. Goldberger übernahm. Seiner finanziellen Geschicklichkeit gelang es, die

GKR Wilhelm Herz, the dean (doyen) of the Berlin merchant community. Equally old-established interests originating from an earlier age were represented by members of a number of old provincial banking houses, notably Dr Georg Heimann (Breslau), *Generalkonsul* Max Baer (partner in Erlanger & Söhne, Frankfurt-on-Main),[22]

schweizerischen und italienischen Staats- und Eisenbahntransaktionen, die bisher ein unbestrittenes Monopol Frankreichs gewesen waren, grösstenteils nach Deutschland zu ziehen. Als im Jahre 1891 die Internationale Bank in den Interessenkreis der Berliner Handels-Gesellschaft überging, verzichtete Goldberger auf jede weitere geschäftliche Tätigkeit und legte gleichzeitig seine Aufsichtsratsmandate nieder. Von diesem Zeitpunkt an gehörte sein Wirken der Allgemeinheit. Er stand nun zehn Jahre an der Spitze des Vereins Berliner Kaufleute und Industrieller und war gleichzeitig Vorsitzender des Zentralausschusses Berliner kaufmännischer, gewerblicher und industrieller Vereine. Goldberger hatte einen wesentlichen Anteil an der Errichtung der Handelskammer zu Berlin. Ihm ist auch die Neugestaltung des kaufmännischen und gewerblichen Fortbildungsschulwesens zu verdanken. Er arbeitete ferner führend in dem von der Reichsregierung eingesetzten Wirtschaftlichen Ausschuss zur Vorbereitung und Begutachtung handelspolitischer Massnahmen. An der Gründung der Zentralstelle für Vorbereitung von Handelsverträgen, des Mitteleuropäischen Wirtschaftsvereins und des Kaiserlichen Automobilklubs war er ebenfalls beteiligt ...' (Bernstein, op. cit., pp. 794 f.). Goldberger was unique as an organizer of interest groups, specialist adviser to the government, and publicist (in 1902, following an extended mission to the United States on behalf of the German government, he published a book under a title destined to gain immortality: *Das Land der unbegrenzten Möglichkeiten*).

Goldberger, born in Tarnowitz in 1848, had married in 1877 Klara Simon, daughter of GKR Louis (Lewin) Simon, partner in the wholesale textile firm. Goldberger's father had already been a millionaire several times over, mainly through the production of anti-rheumatism metal chains (according to Martin a common panacea in the nineteenth century) (Martin, op. cit., n. 10 above, pp. 307 ff).

[21] 'Der Geh. Kommerzienrat *Wilhelm Kopetzky* (1847–1924) führte die Berliner Börse durch gute und schlechte Zeiten ... Kopetzkys erstes öffentliches Auftreten geht bis in das Jahr 1875 zurück. Damals wurde er Direktor der Deutschen Union-Bank und gleichzeitig Mitglied der Korporation der Kaufmannschaft. Im Jahre 1896 wurde er zum Ältesten der Kaufmannschaft von Berlin gewählt und trat dann bei der 1902 erfolgten Gründung der Handelskammer in diese ein. 1914 wurde er zu ihrem ersten Vizepräsidenten bestellt ... Gleichzeitig hat Kopetzky mit grossem Geschick ... die Einrichtungen der Berliner Börse ausgebaut. Er wurde 1889 Mitglied des früheren Börsen-Kommissariats und später Mitglied des Börsenvorstandes. Nachdem er zum stellvertretenden Vorsitzenden der Wertpapierbörse und im Jahre 1905 zum ersten Stellvertreter des Gesamtbörsenvorstandes gewählt worden war, trat er 1918 als erster Vorsitzender an die Spitze des Gesamtbörsenvorstandes sowie der Wertpapierbörse ... Seine Lebensarbeit galt vornehmlich der Berliner Wirtschaft, der er auch viele Jahre als Vorsitzender des Aufsichtsrates der Schultheiss-Brauerei gedient hat ...' (Bernstein, op. cit., pp. 731 f.). For a time, Kopetzky was a board member of the Deutsche Bank. He also sat on the board of the Grosse Berliner Strassenbahn Gesellschaft and belonged to the Verwaltungsrat of the Schweizerischer Bankverein in Basle.

[22] Baer is one of the many examples of the adaptation of private bankers to the structures of the corporate age. When, in 1904, his firm was absorbed by the Dresdner

GKR Otto Braunfels (senior partner in Jacob S. H. Stern in Frankfurt-on-Main),[23] KR Ernst Ladenburg and his brother August Ladenburg (joint owners of E. Ladenburg in Frankfurt-on-Main).[24] All the private bankers from Frankfurt show characteristic links (as do the Hardys) with other private banks directed by members of the same family both inside Germany and, more importantly, in London or New York, with joint-stock banks, and with some substantial industrial or commercial enterprises. It was a combination of these features which enabled bankers from private family firms to play a significant role even in the age of corporation capitalism.

In contrast to the 'traditional' sector of German–Jewish private banking going back, directly or indirectly, to the Jewish financiers of the age of absolutism were Jews prominent in the direction of the large joint-stock banks: Adolf Salomonsohn (founder of a dynasty prominent in the Direction der Disconto-Gesellschaft), Eugen Gutmann (founder and managing director of the Dresdner Bank), Max Steinthal (prominent in the direction of the Deutsche Bank and the Mannessmannröhren-Werke), and, occupying an intermediate position between the directors of large joint-stock banks and partners in the old private banking houses (with one of which he had served his apprenticeship), the great financier Carl Fürstenberg of the Berliner Handels-Gesellschaft. With these might be listed some others not included by Martin in this particular wealth range: Jacob Riesser and Bernhard Dernburg of the Bank für Handel und Industrie, Eugen Landau of the National Bank für Deutschland, and Hermann Wallich (Deutsche Bank). Since men such as these were important more for their positions than their wealth, they will be considered in connection with

---

Bank, he joined the board of that bank. He also became chairman of the board of a major private banking house in Berlin G. Schlesinger, Trier & Co. In fact, Baer sat on the boards of 24 companies, including Elektrizitäts AG vorm. W. Lahmeyer & Co. in Frankfurt-on-Main of which he was deputy chairman, as well as Felten & Guilleaume-Lahmeyer Werke (Martin, op. cit., n. 10 above, ii. 311 f.).

[23] Like Baer, Braunfels was a private banker who successfully entered the corporate sphere. His 12 board memberships included the Deutsche Bank and the Berg- und Metallbank (part of the Merton concern). He was actively associated also with German financial interests in China. Ib., p. 345.

[24] The bank house E. Ladenburg in Frankfurt maintained close connections with the 'related' firm of Ladenburg Thalmann & Co. in New York. It was also associated with the Süddeutsche Disconto-Gesellschaft AG in Mannheim, successor of the original parent house of W. H. Ladenburg und Söhne. A sister of Ernst and August Ladenburg was married to Wilhelm Merton. August Ladenburg occupied a seat on the board of the Berg- und Metallbank, the financial arm of the Merton concern (ib., pp. 347 f.).

the 'corporate élite', as will their Cologne counterpart Louis Hagen, the 'king of the board members' (*König der Aufsichtsräte*).

Among industrialists, the owners of the chemical firm of Leopold Cassella in and near Frankfurt-on-Main (Carl von Weinberg, Arthur von Weinberg, GKR Leo Gans, Fritz and Adolf Gans) represent the most considerable agglomeration of industrial wealth, an aggregate of almost 80 million marks. Theirs was an enterprise which, largely thanks to the brothers Weinberg and, indeed, their father Bernhard, who had married into the Gans family, had successfully accomplished the transition—over four generations—from a modest Jewish trading house of a traditional kind to a major science-based industrial enterprise of the era of high capitalism.[25]

[25] For Carl and Arthur von Weinberg see Carl von Weinberg, *Jubiläumsschrift* (Sept. 1931), Bernstein, op. cit., n. 19 above, pp. 777 FF., MARTIN, OP. CIT., N. 10 above, ii. 209 ff., and Zielenziger, *Juden in der deutschen Wirtschaft* (Berlin, 1930), p. 26. At the time of the Continental System, David Loeb Cassel (Leopold Cassella) of Friedberg had opened a sugar-refinery in Frankfurt-on-Main. It had collapsed with the end of the System. Cassell, with the aid of Dutch connections, had then started an import business which in time began to specialize in the importation of dyestuffs. The business passed to Ludwig Aron Gans, husband of Cassell's niece Rosette. In 1858, Gans's daughter Pauline married Bernhard Weinberg who became a partner in the firm and indeed its moving spirit. Under Bernhard Weinberg's direction the business changed from wholesale importing to industrial manufacture of dyestuffs. Of Bernhard Weinberg's sons, Arthur became a world-famous chemist, Carl an outstanding commercial organizer. In particular, Carl set up an efficient sales organization, largely abroad. Carl Weinberg (like Felix Deutsch of the AEG) attached particular importance to personal contacts between manufacturers and consumers to enable the former to keep in touch with the rapidly changing requirements of their customers. The technical 'break through' of Leopold Cassella & Co came between 1892 and 1897 with the development of the firm's new diamin and sulphur dyes. The firm had, for some time, been closely associated with AG Farbwerke vorm. Meister, Lucius & Brüning (later Farbwerke Höchst), who supplied a number of Cassella's new materials. In 1904, Cassella became a joint-stock company with a nominal share capital of 20 million marks. It also issued obligations nominally valued at 10 million marks. The brothers Weinberg were made joint managing directors (with their less able Gans cousins continuing as partners and board members).

'Der durchschnittliche Reingewinn der offenen Handelsgesellschaft Leopold Cassella & Co. betrug in den letzten Jahren vor der Begründung der G.m.b.H. im Jahre 1904 30 bis 35% des investierten Kapitals. Die G.m.b.H. Cassella & Co. verteilte in den Jahren 1905 bis 1907 je 30%. Später ist die Dividende nicht mehr veröffentlicht worden. Die Höchster Farbwerke besitzen jetzt 6 875 000 M. Cassella-Anteile. Cassella & Co. besitzt für 800 000 M. Aktien der Firma Kalle & Co. Zwecks Herbeiführung der Interessengemeinschaft erhöhten die Höchster Farbwerke ihr Aktienkapital um 5.5 Millionen, welche an die Firma Cassella & Co. begeben wurden. Dafür erhielten die Höchster Farbwerke den gleichen Betrag Anteile der Firma Cassella. Das Stammkapital der Firma Leopold Cassella & Co. wurde im Jahre 1908 um 5 Millionen erhöht und beträgt jetzt 25 Millionen. Schon bei Begründung der G.m.b.H. im Jahre 1904 wurde für das eingebrachte Fabrikunternehmen ein Wert vom 26 500 000 M festgesetzt' (Martin, op. cit., n. 10 above, ii. 210 f).

Comparable to the evolution of Leopold Cassella & Co. from modest traditional beginnings to an important technological capitalist enterprise was that of Wilhelm Merton's Frankfurter Metallgesellschaft.[26] The transformation of the old metal traders P. A. Cohen into a major concern by three Jewish families linked by ties of kinship under the leadership of an innovating industrial entrepreneur is among the outstanding examples of the transformation of an old family business going back to court Jews of the age of absolutism into a commercial enterprise that has survived the vagaries of time.[27]

[26] For Wilhelm Merton and the Frankfurter Metallgesellschaft see H. Achinger *Wilhelm Merton in seiner Zeit* (Frankfurt, 1965), Dr Franz Lerner (ed.), *Das tätige Frankfurt* (Frankfurt, 1955), pp. 371 ff.; Martin op. cit., n. 10 above, ii. 267 f., and Bernstein, op. cit., n. 19 above, pp. 836 ff.

[27] Philip Abraham Cohen (1790–1856) belonged to an established family of courtbankers (*Kammeragenten*) in Hanover. Having married into the old-established Jewish merchant and banking family of Wertheimer, he set up business in Frankfurt-on-Main. His firm, registered formally only in 1850, was described as 'Handlung in Metallwaren, Wechsel, Kommission und Spedition', a typical mixed produce-trading, discount, commission, and transport enterprise. In fact, the early prosperity of the firm was due principally to its monopoly of the sale of minerals mined in the kingdom of Hanover and the duchy of Braunschweig.

Philip Abraham Cohen had only two daughters. The elder, Sarah Amalie, had been married in 1837 to Raphael Moses, later Merton, the son of the London merchant Abraham Lyons and his wife Abigail Moses. A successful merchant in London and Paris, Raphael had, as a young man, visited Hanover and Frankfurt in 1837, before settling permanently in the latter city in 1854. In 1855, he had changed his name to Ralph Merton. Under his direction, the firm of P. A. Cohen flourished. In 1881, it became the Frankfurter Metallgesellschaft. Ralph Merton died two years later.

Of the sons of Ralph Merton and Sarah Cohen (they had nine children) two became bankers in the City of London (R. Merton & Sons, the old family firm Henry R. Merton & Co. Ltd., and Merton Metallurgical Co. Ltd.). Another, Sir Thomas Merton, became a director of Vickers (as had a brother of Ludwig and Isidor Loewe). Another, William, later known as Wilhelm Merton, married to Emma Ladenburg (daughter of the banker GKR Emil Ladenburg in Frankfurt), took over the management of the Metallgesellschaft. Members of two allied and related Jewish families, Philip Ellinger from Mainz and KR Zacharias Hochschild, became partners in the firm and joined in its management.

The speciality of the Metallgesellschaft was participation in mining ventures overseas. In 1897, Wilhelm Merton founded the Metallurgische Gesellschaft (with a nominal share capital of 9 million marks), to engage in the sale of mining expertise (what would now probably be described as 'consulting engineers'), especially overseas, with the original Metallgesellschaft becoming primarily a wholesale trading firm.

In 1906, Merton took the lead in founding the Berg- und Metallbank AG, its share capital of nominally 40 million marks being subscribed, among others, by Fürstenberg's Berliner Handels-Gesellschaft, by the Direction der Disconto-Gesellschaft (partner of the Ladenburgs), and by a number of private Frankfurt banks including E. Ladenburg, Lazard Speyer-Ellissen, and Jacob S. H. Stern. The major function of the bank was to finance participations by the group in large mining and refining ventures. The concern developed into an early 'multinational' through the acquisition by the Metallbank of shares in Henry R. Merton & Co. Ltd. in London with a nominal value of £118,750 and

One significant feature of the Jewish wealth élite is the prominent place occupied in it by members of the Jewish community in Frankfurt.[28] By the side of the representatives of traditional banking wealth, the Rothschilds, Speyers, Goldschmidt-Rothschilds, figure the only slightly less conspicuous Sterns, Erlangers, Hahns, and Ladenburgs.[29] In commerce and industry, on the other hand, there are the Ganses, Weinbergs, and Mertons. Finally, the list of Frankfurt millionaires contains a representative figure who, in his own sphere, had a major impact on commercial life: Leopold Sonnemann, whose Frankfurter Zeitung significantly enhanced the role of Frankfurt as a major centre of economic life.[30]

The only other names of significance to be found among men credited by Martin with fortunes of between 10 and 20 million marks are those of Berthold Israel, owner of a department store for linen and

a book value, in 1911, of 3,391,500 marks. There were lesser holdings in Merton Metallurgical Co. Ltd. in London, the American Metal Co., and the Metallurgical Co. of America.

[28] The role of Jews in establishing the privately financed university of Frankfurt in 1912 is eloquent testimony to their economic position. Contributions were distributed as follows:

Jewish	Million marks	Gentile	Million marks
Wilhelm Merton	2.3	Lucius, von Meister, vom Rath	0.7
Leo Gans	1	Metzler, Grunelius, Passavant	0.6
Rothschild and Goldschmidt-R.	1	Mumm von Schwarzenstein	0.5
Theod. Stern	0.7		
Arthur v. Weinberg	0.6		
E. Beit von Speyer	0.25		
Adolf Gans	0.25		
W. Sulzbach	0.25		
Moritz Oppenheim	0.25		
Total:	6.6		1.8

Achinger, op. cit., n. 26 above, p. 218. The 14 substantial gifts from Jews to the university, mainly for the endowment of chairs or institutes, included benefactions from Carl Meyer von Rothschild, Dr Wilhelm Merton, Georg and Franziska Speyer, Charles Hallgarten, Theodor Stern, Otto and Ida Braunfels, Arthur von Weinberg, Jacob H. Schiff, Mathilde, *Freifrau* von Rothschild, and *Freiherr* von Goldschmidt-Rothschild (Bernstein, op. cit., n. 19 above, p. 860).

[29] For the Ladenburgs see Rudolf Haas, *Die Entwicklung des Bankwesens im deutschen Oberrheingebiet* (Mannheim, 1970), pp. 67 ff.

[30] In 1853, on the death of his father, Leopold Sonnemann had taken over the latter's textile mill (later a trading firm) in Höchberg near Würzburg. In 1855 he had become a banker, the following year co-founder of the Frankfurter Handelszeitung, mouthpiece of south-west German liberalism. In 1867, Sonnemann became sole owner and publisher of the Frankfurter Zeitung. He died in Frankfurt in 1909.

cotton goods, dowries, and furniture and of KR Philip Freudenberg, successor to the Gerson brothers in the management of the great fashion store of Hermann Gerson, both in Berlin.

Below the owners of fortunes in the range of 10 to 20 million may be said to begin, in a manner of speaking, the *Mittelstand* ('middle estate') of Prussian millionaires. It includes, in Martin's compilation, a number of unexpected names. Among these is that of Oscar Tietz, credited with a fortune of 'only' 9 million marks.[31] Like the Tietz family, their

[31] For the Tietz department stores see Georg Tietz, *Hermann Tietz: Geschichte einer Familie und ihrer Warenhäuser* (Stuttgart, 1965), Zielenziger, op. cit., n. 25 above, pp. 206 ff., and Bernstein, op. cit., n. 19 above, pp. 789 f. 'Unter der Leitung von Hermann und Leonhard Tietz, die später getrennt arbeiteten, sind zwei der grössten Warenhauskonzerne Deutschlands entstanden. Während sich Leonhard Tietz, ausgehend von seiner Gründung in Köln, die später in eine Aktiengesellschaft umgewandelt wurde, vornehmlich auf Süd- und Westdeutschland beschränkte, hat Hermann Tietz seine Haupttätigkeit nach Berlin verlegt ... Hermann Tietz, nach dem die Weltfirma ihren Namen trägt, rief gemeinsam mit seinem Neffen Oscar Tietz im Jahre 1882 das Stammhaus ins Leben. Es führte die Firma "Garn.-, Knopf-, Poamentier-, Weiss- und Wollwarengeschäft en gros und en detail Hermann Tietz". Der erste Tageserlös betrug 34.50 mark. Fünfzig Jahre später, im Jahre 1932, wurden jährlich mehrere hundert Millionen Mark umgesetzt ... Die aus Amerika importierten Ideen liessen Oscar Tietz mit grösster Beharrlichkeit den Plan verfolgen, auch in Deutschland durch niedrige Preise, durch grosse Auswahl und durch billigen Verkauf (auf Grund entsprechend billigen Einkaufs, möglichst unmittelbar beim Fabrikanten) eine preissenkende Wirkung für den Verbraucher zu erzielen. Da sich eine solche Geschäftspolitik in Gera allein nicht durchführen liess, veranlasste Oscar Tietz auch andere Mitglieder der Familie, ihren Bedarf zusammenzulegen und ihre Bestellungen gemeinsam zu machen. Aus diesen Erwägungen entstand im Jahre 1896 in Gera das erste Warenhaus Hermann Tietz, das bald stark erweitert werden musste ... Inzwischen war auch von Oscar Tietz in München ein Warenhaus errichtet worden, dass sich ebenfalls günstig entwickelte. Man musste auch hier bald an einen Neubau denken, und so entstand in der Hauptstadt Bayerns der erste grosse Warenhauspalast der Firma Hermann Tietz, mit Zweiggeschäften in Karlsruhe, Strassburg i.E. und in Stuttgart. Jetzt war der Weg nach Berlin für die Firma Hermann Tietz frei, und in der Reichshauptstadt wurden nacheinander die drei imposanten Warenhäuser ... errichtet. Im Jahre 1897 wurde auch in Hamburg eine Niederlassung der Firma eröffnet' (Bernstein, op. cit., n. 19 above, pp. 789 ff.). The major development of Hermann Tietz into a vast concern which, at the death of Oscar Tietz in 1923, embraced forty associated companies, seven wholly owned textile mills, and several clothing manufactures, belongs to a later period.

At the same time and parallel with that of his brother, Leonhard Tietz also had expanded his enterprise. 'Das Unternehmen ist jetzt nicht nur an Umfang, sondern auch durch die Verschiedenheit der Waren die es feilbietet, so gross geworden, dass man am 17 März 1905 seine Umwandlung in die *Leonhard Tietz Aktiengesellschaft* mit einem Kapital von 10 Millionen Mark beschliesst. Die Aktien befinden sich zunächst im Besitz der Familie ... Schon zwei Jahre später wird das Aktienkapital auf 12,5 Millionen erhöht. Im Jahre 1909 werden die Aktien als erstes deutsches Warenhauspapier an der Berliner Börse eingeführt.

... Als Leonhard Tietz am 15 November 1914 stirbt, hinterlässt auch er einen Konzern von grösster Ausdehnung ... In den verschiedensten Gegenden Deutschland,

Anatomy of a Wealth Élite

main competitors in Berlin, the Wertheims[32] range below the 10 million mark, due however mainly to the fact that the family fortune was shared among 4 brothers (7–8 million marks apiece).[33] In fact, the Wertheim department store in Berlin and those of Hermann and Leonhard Tietz occupy between them a dominant position (and one giving rise to much resentment among shopkeepers unable to compete with their efficiency and economies of scale) in the German retail trade.

The founder-directors of another major enterprise are unaccountably missing from Martin's compilation, Benno Orenstein and Arthur Koppel.[34] The two men had founded, in 1876, a firm with the object of introducing into Germany narrow-gauge tipper-railways for agricultural and industrial uses, which had already proved their worth elsewhere. Lacking the capital to start production on their own, they

---

aber auch in Paris, hatte man eigene Einkaufshäuser eingerichtet, in der Südeifel war man mit der Begründung einer Strumpffabrik zur Eigenfabrikation übrgegangen...' (Zielenziger, op. cit., n. 25 above, pp. 217 ff.).

As in the case of Hermann Tietz, the subsequent development of the Leonhard Tietz group belongs to a later period.

[32] For details of the Wertheim department store (*Kaufhaus*) see Zielenziger, op. cit., n. 25 above, pp. 213 f and Martin, op. cit., n. 10 above, p. 435. In 1885, four brothers Wertheim had moved from Stralsund to Berlin and set up a specialist clothing and fashion shop (*Manufaktur und Modewaren*). In 1894, this had become a modest department store. Two years later, they began constructing the large store than was to make them famous. Starting as a family firm (*offene Handelsgesellschaft*), Wertheim presently became a joint-stock company under family control. The nominal capital, originally a mere 100,000 marks, was raised in 1909 to just over 5 million. At the same time, a real-estate company was founded with a nominal capital of 4,200,000 marks. There were also a Wertheim bank with a nominal capital of 1,200,000 and several subsidiary companies. In 1909, one of the brothers, Wolf, withdrew from the partnership and was, as his share, paid some 6 million marks with which he established several new companies.

[33] Another fortune concealed by the fact that it was shared by several individuals is that of the publishing family of Ullstein. Divided almost equally between the widow of the founder, Leopold Ullstein, and his five sons—with each share 4–5 million marks—it may, in fact, altogether have amounted to some 27 million marks. Leopold Ullstein (1826–99), a paper merchant from Fürth, had founded a publishing house in Berlin in 1877. 'Das Haus Ullstein, das von Leopold Ullstein gegründet worden war und nach dessen Tode im Jahre 1899 von seinen Söhnen geleitet wurde, kaufte eher Blätter als dass es neue gründete; es begann 1877 mit der *Berliner Zeitung*, der ältesten Berlins, und kulminierte in dem Erwerb der *Vossischen Zeitung* im Jahre 1914. Das Unternehmen lancierte auch die *Berliner Morgenpost*, die die höchste Auflage in der Hauptstadt aufwies, sowie die *B.Z. am Mittag* und die äusserst populäre *Berliner Illustrirte Zeitung*...' Peter Pulzer in Werner E. Mosse (ed.), *Juden im Wilhelminischen Deutschland* (Tübingen, 1976), p. 218.

[34] For details, particularly of Benno Orenstein, see Zielenziger, op. cit., n. 25 above, pp. 166 ff.

had begun by purchasing and assembling rails, sleepers, and other equipment. From an early period, they had persuaded suppliers to work to their own specifications. In 1886, due to differences of temperament, there had been an amicable separation between the two partners, with each starting his own company with a limited co-operation between them.

In 1893–4 the original firm, now directed by Orenstein alone, had turned to the manufacture in Berlin and near Dortmund of wagons and points for narrow-gauge railways. In a suburb of Berlin, Orenstein then added the construction of locomotives. Production (on lines pioneered by the Loewe brothers) was based on the use of assembly lines to turn out standardized products—an innovation in the field of narrow-gauge railways. Further diversification followed with the construction of branch lines for standard railways, the manufacture of tramways, and the sale of specialist wagons and machinery. In 1897, under the auspices of the Dresdner Bank, the original firm of Orenstein und Koppel was transformed into a joint-stock company, AG für Feld- und Kleinbahnbedarf, with a nominal share capital of 4 million marks. The capital was doubled in 1898 and raised to 11 million in 1905.

The sister firm of Arthur Koppel and Co., meanwhile, had specialized in construction work, particularly overseas. In 1905, it became a joint-stock company in its turn with a nominal share capital of 9 million marks. At the same time, the two firms entered into a formal partnership (*Interessengemeinschaft*). Following Arthur Koppel's death in 1908, they amalgamated as Orenstein und Koppel Arthur Koppel AG, with a nominal capital in 1909 of 26 million marks. In 1911, this was raised to 36 million. By 1912, the firm had become a world-wide undertaking with some 15,000 workers and employees. In 1913, it produced its five thousandth locomotive.

Neither Benno Orenstein nor Arthur Koppel's heirs, however, despite the importance of the firm, figure prominently in Martin's list of millionaires. In this they are typical of a group of men whose fortunes, notwithstanding their economic importance, remained below the ten million mark: among them, the leading men of the AEG, Emil Rathenau (7.68 million), Felix Deutsch (4.87 million), and Paul Mamroth (4.32 million). In a similar position were leading directors of the Deutsche Bank: Hermann Wallich (9–10 million marks),[35] Paul Mankiewitz (9.38 million), and Oscar Wassermann

---

[35] Surprisingly, when Martin compiled a list of millionaires in the province of

(5.12 million). So would have been Albert Ballin who, however, as a citizen of Hamburg, does not figure among Prussian millionaires. Economic power—the influential directors of great companies, especially in the field of heavy industry bear witness to the fact—no longer involved, necessarily, membership of the higher strata of the wealth élite.

IV

Perhaps the most striking feature of the Prussian Jewish wealth élite as a whole, as it emerges from Martin's data, is the persistence of fortunes, mainly derived from banking, dating from the beginning of the nineteenth century. Though some of the great early fortunes (like those of the Habers, Kusels, Heines or Reutlingers) have disappeared, the top stratum of the Jewish wealth élite, in large part, can nevertheless trace its descent back to the later court Jews of the age of absolutism. The place occupied by Frankfurt bankers is conspicuous already at this level. Below these representatives of traditional wealth lies a stratum of men who, in the main, owed their economic success to various forms of wholesale trade. This, including the major contractors of the wars of unification, originates mainly in the seventies and eighties. The commercial wealth élite is located largely in Berlin. Only two representatives of Silesian industrial interests, resident in Berlin, Fritz Friedländer and Oscar Huldschinsky (more marginally, Eduard Arnhold), have acquired fortunes at this level. No other industrialist has done so. Only two of the commercial millionaires could be considered 'self-made men': Rudolf Mosse, son of a poor medical practitioner in a remote provincial township, and Leopold Koppel, who rose to prominence from modest beginnings in Dresden. Eduard Arnhold, son of another provincial medical man, had 'inherited' Caesar Wollheim's already substantial business; Sigmund Aschrott came from a relatively modest commercial background in Kassel; Fritz Friedländer had inherited a firm which, though close to bankruptcy, was old established. He belonged, moreover, to a prominent and respected commercial family. At this

Brandenburg (which included Charlottenburg, Wilmersdorf, and Grunewald) based on the tax declarations for 1911, the list was headed by Wallich (31 million marks) ahead of Wilhelm von Siemens (26–7 million), Franz von Mendelssohn (25 million), and Oscar Tietz (24 million). Rudolf Martin, *Jahrbuch . . . der Millionäre in der Provinz Brandenburg* (Berlin, 1913), p. 1. The discrepancy in the two figures for Hermann Wallich, though based on different tax declarations (1908 and 1911), is difficult to explain.

level, there occurs some 'circulation of élites': while names like Caro, Lachmann, or Warschauer that have earlier figured among the very wealthy disappeared, newcomers like Aschrott, Mosse, or Koppel have joined the charmed circle of great wealth (if not of social esteem).

The next lower stratum, besides representatives of traditional wealth (Wilhelm Herz, Moritz Reichenheim, Franz von Mendelssohn, Otto von Mendelssohn Bartholdy, Ernst and August Ladenburg in Frankfurt, Georg Heimann in Breslau) or of 'stagnating' wealth of the second generation (Georg von Caro, the Ganses in Frankfurt, Paul von Schwabach) also contained men responsible for building up enterprises and increasing fortunes in the second generation: Carl and Arthur von Weinberg, Isidor Loewe (following his brother Ludwig), Wilhelm Merton. Besides these figure newcomers, 'self-made' men like Leopold Sonnemann, Carl Fürstenberg, Eugen Gutmann, Max Steinthal, and, last but not least, Louis Hagen. Equally, Ludwig Max Goldberger and Wilhelm Kopetzky represent little but their talents; as does, at any rate, in economic terms, Adolf[36] Salomonsohn, born in Inowrazlav in the province of Posen, descendant of two generations of rabbis. The largest group of newcomers to this stratum of the wealth élite is the directors of the large joint-stock banks: Gutmann, Salomonsohn, Steinthal, in a slightly different position Carl Fürstenberg.

One feature of the élite is the sons-in-law (sometimes themselves sons of wealthy families): Maximilian Goldschmidt (-Rothschild), Eduart Beit (von Speyer),[37] or their offspring: those of Bernhard Weinberg and Pauline Gans or of Rafael Moses (Ralph Merton) and Sarah Amalie Cohen. While Richard von Asser-Kaufmann owed his position in the wealth élite to marriage into the Cologne banking family of Eltzbacher, the Sterns of Frankfurt are represented by Otto Braunfels, the Erlangers by Max Baer, the Gersons of Berlin by Philip Freudenberg. The business of the still wealthy Hans von Bleichröder is effectively run by his second cousin Paul von Schwabach. However, the 'golden age' of the sons-in-law was yet to come: a surprising number of the very wealthy had single or adopted (no doubt in some cases natural) daughters.[38]

---

[36] Though 'Adolph' in most of the literature, the name is printed 'Adolf' in the memorial which his son Georg Solmssen devoted to his parent.

[37] Himself offspring of the marriage between Dr Ferdinand Beit of Hamburg and the banking heiress Emma Ladenburg from Mannheim.

[38] This is, of course, by no means a 'Jewish' phenomenon: thus Arthur Gwinner and Carl A. Martius owed part of their economic success to marriage into wealthy Jewish banking families, whilst Gustav Bohlen and Carl H. Ziese, among others, married Gentile industrial heiresses.

The Prussian Jewish wealth élite at this stage reveals—curiously, in descending order of wealth—traditional elements, representatives of 'modernizing' family firms, and members of a new joint-stock 'corporate élite'. Moreover, these distinctions can be observed not only in banking and industry but also, if more doubtfully, in commerce (with the 'modern' sector represented by a successful corporate financier like Leopold Koppel, by influential managing directors like Albert Ballin of the Hapag, and by owners of 'modern' family businesses like the brothers Tietz). Characteristic of the period is the co-existence (successful in economic terms) of representatives of three distinctive phases of economic activity and capital accumulation. Arguably, in some respects, it is a hybrid form of economic organization like Carl Fürstenberg's Berliner Handels-Gesellschaft or the curious corporate activities of a private banker like Louis Hagen that are the most characteristic and significant. The position of men such as these marked the declining importance (except for some traditional industrial connections—such as those of the Bleichröder-Schwabach or of the Oppenheim in Cologne and a now limited role as shareholders) of members of the old wealth élite. Both family and individual wealth had lost much of their significance in the age of 'high capitalism' and corporate finance. Increasingly, the place of the Jewish man of affairs, also, would now depend on his position in the corporate structure.

V

Martin's list of millionaires based on the tax declarations for 1908 and on which the foregoing analysis is based is of course confined to Prussia, that is to people filing their tax returns in that kingdom. Data are available also for taxpayers outside Prussia, mainly, though not exclusively, from separate publications by Martin. They are based, more often, on tax returns for the year 1911.

In fact, outside Prussia, there were relatively few people of Jewish origin whose fortunes exceeded or, indeed, reached 10 million marks. In Bavaria, for instance, Martin noted six:

	Million marks
Oscar Tietz	25
Dr Max Embden	25

	Million marks
Professor Karl *Freiherr* v. Kaskel	14
Geh. Hofrat Prof. Alfred Pringsheim	13
Kgl. Univ. Prof. Dr Leo Graetz	10
Emil *Freiherr* v. Hirsch	10[39]

The list reflects, among others, the comparatively slow development of economic life in Bavaria (possibly also the relatively modest role of Jews in that development). Oscar Tietz, whilst he may still have filed his tax returns in Munich, had in fact moved to Berlin in 1900. He figures, with a fortune of 24 million, in Martin's list for the province of Brandenburg, based on the declarations for 1911.[40] Dr Max Embden is described as partner in the firm of M. I. Embden Söhne and the department store A. Jandorf in Berlin. Karl *Freiherr* von Kaskel is a late member of the wealthy Jewish banking family in Dresden, Alfred Pringsheim of a prosperous Jewish family in Breslau, several of whose members later moved to Berlin. Three of the Jewish millionaires in Munich are academics, Pringsheim, Kaskel (described as a Saxon professor), and Leo Graetz, inventor of the Graetz lamp. Emil *Freiherr* von Hirsch, co-founder of the Bayerische Vereinsbank, married to Mathilde Ladenburg of the Mannheim branch of that family and brother of the more famous Maurice de Hirsch ('Türkenhirsch'), had indeed been prominent in the economic life of the Bavarian capital. He is described as 'land and brewery owner' (*Land und Brauereibesitzer*). The only prominent entrepreneur of the six, however, is Oscar Tietz, whose department store had indeed passed in Munich through a crucial stage in its development. Only Hirsch (the origins of the Embdens and Graetz are not known) could be considered a 'Bavarian'.

In Württemberg[41] only one millionaire of Jewish extraction was credited with a fortune of 10 million marks, *Geh. Hofrat* Dr Eduard von Pfeiffer.[42] Pfeiffer had played a prominent role in the economic life

[39] R. Martin, *Jahrbuch des Vermögens und Einkommens der Millionäre in Bayern* (Berlin, 1914).

[40] R. Martin, *Jahrbuch des Vermögens und Einkommens der Millionäre in Preussen* 2nd edn., (Berlin, 1913), vol. 1; *Brandenburg*, p. 1.

[41] For Württemberg see R. Martin, *Jahrbuch des Vermögens und Einkommens der Millionäre in Württemberg* (Berlin, 1914); for some additional information cf. Maria Zelzer, *Weg und Schicksal der Stuttgarter Juden* (Stuttgart, 1964), especially pp. 58 ff. and 72 ff.

[42] Even this fortune was attributable significantly to Pfeiffer's marriage to Julie Benary née Kaim, widow of Louis Benary in Paris. Intermarriage between members of wealthy families clearly lies at the root of some of the largest Jewish (as indeed, Gentile) fortunes.

Anatomy of a Wealth Élite

of Württemberg as board chairman of both the Württembergische Vereinsbank and of the Württembergische Metallwarenfabrik (as well as board member of the Württembergische Bankanstalt). Of more than local economic significance was the second in the list of Jewish millionaires, Alfred von Kaulla (son of Dr med. Hermann Kaulla in Strassburg and Clarisse Pfeiffer). Kaulla, with a fortune of nine million marks, from his economic base as board member of the Württembergische Vereinsbank, had joined the boards also of important industrial enterprises of the region, notably the Badische Anilin- und Sodafabrik, the Daimler-Motorengesellschaft in Untertürckheim (of which he was board-chairman), and Gebr. Mauser KG in Oberndorf (Neckar). It was through the latter connection that he had helped to secure for the Deutsche Bank an Anatolian railway concession, the beginning of the Baghdad railway. In consequence, Kaulla joined not only the board of the Deutsche Bank but also that of the Anatolian railway company in whose affairs he took a leading part. The third-ranking among Jewish millionaires in Stuttgart was another Kaulla, offspring of a different branch of the old family of Württemberg court Jews, Professor Dr jur. Rudolf Kaulla. Having married into the wealthy banking family of Stern in Frankfurt, he also was credited with a fortune of 9 million marks. His mother Jeanette Kaulla, née Goldschmidt of Frankfurt, had been left, on her husband's death in 1906, with a fortune which, in 1914, amounted to a further 4 million marks. The joint estates of mother and son thus reached a total of 13 million marks. Next, with assets of 7 million marks, figures a Kaulla connection, Gabriel Georg Warburg, son of Siegmund Warburg of Hamburg, married to Lucie Eva Kaulla in Stuttgart. Warburg is described as a landowner (*Rittergutsbesitzer*). Probably no less wealthy than Alfred von Kaulla and Rudolf Kaulla was GKR Kilian von Steiner, founder of the Württembergische Vereinsbank and closely associated with the Deutsche Bank since its beginnings under Georg von Siemens. When Steiner died in 1903, he left his widow 5 million marks, but there is no record of the fortune of his son who, as a Christian and a landowner, chose to adopt the name of Adolf Wohlgemut. The third wealthiest Jew in Stuttgart in terms of annual income (0.7 million marks) and credited with a fortune of some 7 million was an industrialist, Max Levi (known as 'Salamander Levi'), a partner in the firm of J. Sigle and Co., a shoe factory in Kornwestheim (Salamanderwerke, founded in 1890). While the Jewish wealth élite of Württemberg thus could compare in neither size nor wealth with comparable groups in Berlin or Frankfurt-on-Main, it gains significance through its close and continual associations with the major industrial enterprises of the region[43] and through its marital links with Jewish banking families not only within the region but also outside it. It should, however, be noted that the place of Jews in the Württemberg wealth élite which included, besides numerous aristocratic landowners, also a number of wealthy industrialists, was a relatively modest one. Eduard von Pfeiffer, Alfred von Kaulla, and Rudolf Kaulla rank respectively, twenty-first, twenty-second, and twenty-third on Martin's list. Alfred von Kaulla, at any rate, belongs to the corporate or influence rather than the wealth élite. In addition to the board memberships already listed, he was also board chairman of the Württembergische Notenbank and of the Württembergische Bankanstalt vorm. Pflaum & Co.

No detailed information is available about millionaires in Baden and Hessen (Martin did not produce volumes for Baden, Hesse, Alsace-Lorraine, the states of Thuringia, and eight other lesser principalities). There were, however, at least two Jewish families in these regions whose wealth must have equalled, if it did not exceed, that of the Stuttgart bankers. The first of these was the Ladenburgs in Mannheim,[44] descendants, like the Kaullas, of earlier *Hoffaktoren*. Carl Ladenburg (1827–1909) had, on his father's death in 1873, taken over the direction of the family banking business of W. H. Ladenburg & Söhne, founded by his grandfather. He had at the same time succeeded his father as board chairman of the Badische Anilin- und Sodafabrik, with which both bank and family had been closely associated ever since its foundation. Similarly, the Ladenburgs had taken an active part in the founding and early financing (eventually in conjunction with others) of the Zellstoff-Fabrik Waldhof. Since 1868, W. H. Ladenburg & Söhne had worked in close association with the Disconto-Gesellschaft in Berlin. In 1905, with the strong participation of Disconto, W. H. Ladenburg & Söhne had been converted into the

---

[43] Zelzer, referring to an earlier period, describes the role of Jewish private bankers in this sphere. 'Alexander Pflaum, der nachmalige geadelte Kommerzienrat, beherrschte lange Zeit hindurch gemeinsam mit Kilian Steiner aus Laupheim, nachmals auch geadelt und Geh. Kommerzienrat, weitgehend das Württembergische Bankwesen und die gesamte Württembergische Volkswirtschaft. Die Mehrzahl der industriellen Gründungen der siebziger und achtziger Jahre sind auf diese beiden Männer zurückzuführen. Mehr in der Stille wirkte der Geh. Hofrat Dr. Eduard von Pfeiffer, der spätere Ehrenbürger.' Zelzer, op. cit., p. 58.

[44] For the Ladenburgs see Rudolf Haas, *Die Entwicklung des Bankwesens im deutschen Oberrheingebiet* (Mannheim, 1970), pp. 67 ff.

Süddeutsche Disconto-Gesellschaft AG with a nominal share capital of 20 million marks, raised in 1911 to 50 million. There were three Ladenburgs among the directors of the new bank. On its board, chaired by Carl Ladenburg, sat also two members of the Frankfurt branch of the family which had subscribed a part of the original share capital. Another family of Jewish origin in the region that acquired wealth and economic importance were the Schotts (originally Schottländer). Paul Schott (1843–97), son of a chemist and apothecary, and himself trained as a chemist, became managing director of the Portland-Cementwerke Heidelberg-Mannheim in Heidelberg which, with a nominal share capital of 15 million marks and 2,500 employees, ranked in 1907 among Germany's hundred largest industrial enterprises (in terms of nominal share capital).[45]

Characteristic of the Jewish wealth élite of southern Germany is the fact that, although once again composed primarily of bankers, it is closely associated with the development of major local industries. Not without significance also are associations from an early date with major joint-stock banks in Berlin, of W. H. Ladenburg & Söhne with the Disconto-Gesellschaft and of the Württembergische Vereinsbank with the Deutsche Bank. Sooner or later, the rapidly increasing demand for large amounts of capital came to exceed the resources of old-established regional banks (whether private or corporate).

Somewhat different is the history of the wealthiest Jewish family outside Prussia, the Kaskels in Dresden. These also, like the Kaullas or Ladenburgs, derived from *Hoffaktoren* and would remain court bankers to the Saxon royal family.[46] Intermarriage in successive generations, with the Fränkels in Warsaw and the Oppenheims in Cologne, had led to the accumulation of a very large fortune. This, in turn, had contributed substantially to the founding of the *Dresdner Bank* in 1872,[47] though the Kaskels themselves took little part in its

[45] Norbert Horn and Jürgen Kocka (eds.), *Law and the Formation of the Big Enterprises in the 19th and early 20th Centuries* (Göttingen, 1979), p. 107.
[46] Kaskels had achieved prominence in the economic life of Saxony in the later eighteenth century. Michael Kaskel (1775–1845) had been a noted 'Heeres- und Münzlieferant'. In 1838 his son Carl had become president of the Sächsische Bank, the official state bank, in which capacity in 1866 he had organized the finances of both the Saxon and Austrian campaigns. In 1831, he had married Victoire von Fränkel from a wealthy Jewish banking family in Warsaw. In 1867 he received a patent of Austrian nobility, in 1869 the title of *Freiherr*.
[47] In 1872 Carl, *Freiherr* von Kaskel, in association with his son Felix (who, in 1858 had married Emma, the daughter of Simon Oppenheim of Cologne) and the banker Eugen Gutmann, played the major part in founding the Dresdner Bank. Besides

management. However, the early prosperity of the bank helped greatly to swell the family's wealth. Emma *Freifrau* von Kaskel (née Oppenheim) was credited by Martin with a fortune of 21 million marks.[48] Since this amount included only one-third of the estate of her late husband, *Freiherr* Felix von Kaskel (who had died in 1894), as well as her own considerable assets, the total Kaskel wealth must have been formidable.

Less wealthy than the Kaskel, though still with an aggregate fortune of 11.5 million marks (divided, however, unevenly among five members of the family) were the Arnholds of Dresden, owners of the banking firm Gebr. Arnhold.[49] The firm, founded by Max and Georg Arnhold, brothers of GKR Eduard Arnhold in Berlin, was of considerable local importance, largely through its involvement in the financial affairs of the brewery and china industries.

Hamburg also contained some wealthy families of Jewish extraction. Far and away the wealthiest were the Behrenses,[50] erstwhile clients of the Rothschilds. Founded in 1796 as a trading house (*Manufaktur-*

providing the stock of its capital—'Man kann sagen, dass die neue Aktienbank aus dem K.schen Familienunternehmen hervorgegangen ist'—the Kaskels through their family ties with the Fränkels and Oppenheims and their close business associations with the Rothschilds in Frankfurt and the Magnuses and Bleichröders in Berlin, were able to draw all these houses into the founding consortium. Felix, *Freiherr* von Kaskel, became chairman of the board of the Dresdner Bank, his father (until his death in 1874) a board member. The Kaskels, at the same time, remained the private bankers of the king of Saxony as well as of many families of the Saxon aristocracy. *Neue Deutsche Biographie*, xi. 318). The story of the Kaskels has an interesting feature. Whereas, in other instances—the Württembergische Vereinsbank in Stuttgart or the Süddeutsche Disconto-Gesellschaft are cases in point—Jewish family banks, transformed into local joint-stock banks, were eventually absorbed into large universal banks, in the case of the Kaskels the family business (though not under their management) may be said to have been transformed (and in a relatively short period of time) into an actual universal bank.

[48] Emma, the widowed *Freifrau* von Kaskel, was the largest taxpayer in Saxony. (Rudolf Martin, *Jahrbuch des Vermögens und Einkommens der Millionäre im Königreich Sachsen* (Berlin, 1912), p. 207.) Martin's data are somewhat speculative: 'Das Vermögen des Freiherrn Felix von Kaskel dürfte nach dem Tode seines Vaters im Jahre 1874 bereits 7 000 000 M betragen haben. Freifrau von Kaskel geb. Freiin von Oppenheim dürfte nach dem Tode ihres Vaters im Jahre 1880 und ihrer Mutter im Jahre 1885 zusammen mindestens 6 000 000 M geerbt haben. Dieses grosse, auf das beste verwaltete Barvermögen des Freiherrn und der Freifrau von Kaskel hat den glänzenden wirtschaftlichen Aufschwung der letzten 40 Jahre mitgemacht und dürfte an der rüstigen Vorwärtsbewegung der Dresdner Bank und der ihr nahestehenden industriellen Gesellschaften in besonderem Masse teilgenommen haben' (ib.).

[49] Adolf Diamant, *Chronik der Juden in Dresden* (Darmstadt, 1973), p. 258

[50] For the Behrenses see Dr Paul Friedeberger (ed.), *Industrielle Vertreter deutscher Arbeit in Wort und Bild* (Berlin, n.d.) and R. Martin, *Jahrbuch des Vermögens und Einkommens der Millionäre in den drei Hansastädten* (Berlin, 1912).

warengeschäft) which as early as 1830 had set up an office in England, the Behrens firm had become a bank in 1850. Eduard Ludwig Behrens, of the third generation, had joined the ranks of the most respected Hamburg bankers whose advice had frequently been sought on a variety of banking questions. Under his direction, moreover, the bank had acquired a world-wide reputation. When E. L. Behrens died in 1895, he left the house to two sons, Eduard Ludwig and Theodor, together with a partner, Eduard Constantin Hamburg. Subsequently, one member of the following generation also became a partner. When Rudolf Martin compiled his statistics, he described the firm as probably the largest private bank in Hamburg. There were then four partners, the senior of whom, *Generalkonsul* Eduard L. Behrens, the fifth wealthiest man in Hamburg, was credited with a fortune of 31 million marks. His brother Theodor, the twelfth wealthiest, owned some 26 million marks. Eduard Constantin Hamburg owned 11 million marks, Georg, the son of Eduard Ludwig, a lesser amount. Between them, the four partners thus possessed about 70 million marks.

Compared to the Behrenses, the Warburgs were, at least in terms of wealth, a relatively modest family. Although established in 1798, M. M. Warburg & Co. had, for decades, operated in the shadow of the Rothschilds, inferior in importance to both the wealthy Salomon Heine and their bitter rivals, the Behrenses. The modern importance of the bank dates essentially from the year 1895 when the Warburgs concluded a double matrimonial alliance with the families of partners in the New York banking house of Kuhn, Loeb & Co.[51] The extremely close business associations which resulted enabled the Warburg bank to maintain its independence at a time when other, similar houses had

---

[51] Felix Warburg, one of the five sons of Moritz M. Warburg, married Frieda Schiff, the daughter of Jacob H. Schiff, senior partner in Kuhn Loeb & Co. His brother Paul married Nina Loeb, the daughter of Salomon Loeb, a founder of the firm. He left Hamburg in 1902 to become a partner in Kuhn Loeb & Co. Close personal and financial ties between Paul Warburg and his older brother Max M. Warburg (1867–1946) persisted. 'Trotz ihrer geographischen Trennung nahm die enge Zusammenarbeit zwischen den beiden Brüdern ihren Fortgang: Paul blieb Teilhaber von M. M. Warburg & Co. und verbrachte jedes Jahr mehrere Monate in Europa; die Beziehung zu Kuhn, Loeb & Co. intensivierte und entwickelte sich zu einer Verbindung, die für den Hamburger Familienzweig allergrösste Bedeutung erlangte.' E. Rosenbaum and A. J. Sherman, *Das Bankhaus M. M. Warburg & Co. 1798–1938* (Hamburg, 1976), p. 125. Felix Warburg also remained a partner in M. M. Warburg & Co. until forced to abandon the connection when the United States entered the war in 1917 (ib., p. 148).

to accept absorption into large joint-stock banks.[52] In 1905, in fact, the firm, then led by Max M. Warburg, received the accolade of being formally admitted to the prestigious state loan consortium.[53]

The fact that the estate of Moutz Warburg had had to be divided among his five sons, together with the relatively modest marriage of Max, the second oldest,[54] meant that the Warburgs (credited by Martin with fortunes of 5 million each for each of the three brothers remaining in Germany) hardly qualify for inclusion in the wealth élite. The wealth of the German brothers bears no comparison with that, for instance, of the Behrens partners. The Warburgs, and more particularly Max M. Warbug, in effect belong to the influence more than the wealth élite.

VI

Martin's compilation, based on the tax returns for 1908, provides a convenient Gentile control group. In the first place, this makes it possible to establish, roughly, the Jewish share. Of the 29 families with aggregate fortunes of 50 or more million marks, 9 (31 per cent) were Jewish or of Jewish origin. Their place in the general ranking order—with, in brackets, the number of individuals among whom the fortune is shared—is the following:

	Million marks		Million marks
Haniel	394 (13)	Krupp	250 (3)
Rothschild, incl.	310 (7)	Hohenlohe	151 (1)
Goldschmidt-R.		Speyer	121 (2)
Henckell	252 (7)	Waldthausen	103 (9)

[52] 'Die Kapitalsummen, die nunmehre erforderlich waren, um das Wachstum der Grossindustrie zu finanzieren, begannen die Mittel auch der grössten Banken zu übersteigen. Die Folge war eine zunehmende Tendenz, sich auszudehnen oder sich innerhalb des Bankensektors zusammenzuschliessen, wobei zahlreiche Privatbanken durch Fusion in den grossen Bankaktiengesellschaften aufgingen. M. M. Warburg & Co., befanden sich dank ihrer eingefahrenen internationalen Verbindungen und aufgrund ihrer frisch geschlossenen Familienbande mit New York und anderen wichtigen Finanzplätzen in ausreichend fundierter Lage, um an dem jüngsten Aufschwung der deutschen Wirtschaft teilzunehmen ...' (ib., p. 120).

[53] 'Den endgültigen "Ritterschlag" erhielt die Bank 1905, als sie "en nom" zu dem prestige- und gewinnträchtigen Reichsanleihenkonsortium zugelassen wurde, dem engsten Kreise von etwa 50 Repräsentanten der deutschen Hochfinanz' (ib.).

[54] He had married, in 1899, Alice Magnus, from a family distantly related to the Altona branch of Warburgs.

Anatomy of a Wealth Élite

	Million marks		Million marks
Mendelssohn incl. Mendelssohn-B.	101 (5)	von Rath Mumm von Schwarzenstein	67 (10) 63 (7)
Schaffgotsch	100 (2)		
Pless	93 (2)	Schottländer	61 (5)
Thyssen	79 (3)	Ballestrem	56 (1)
Stumm	78 (4)	Dippe	55 (4)
Tiele-Winckler	74 (1)	Henschel	54 (2)
Arenberg	74 (2)	Simon	52 (2)
Gans/Weinberg	71 (6)	Schichau/Ziese	53 (2)
Bleichröder/Schwabach	70 (3)	Mosse	51 (2)
Guilleaume	69 (5)	Borsig	51 (3)
Oppenheim	68 (4)	Metzler	50 (4)

Clearly, there are differences between the Jewish and Gentile 'sectors' with regard to the kind of economic activity on which capital accumulation was based. The major source of Gentile wealth in Prussia is coal: whether in the case of the Haniels (whose interests, however, from an early moment, also included rolling mills and machine building), Waldthausen and Arenberg in the Ruhr, Stumm in the Saar, or that of Silesian magnates, the Henckells (under Guido Henckell von Donnersmark in successful combination with other industrial pursuits), Hohenlohes, Schaffgotsches, Plesses, Tiele-Wincklers, and, at a distance, Ballestrems. Obviously, and for obvious reasons, there was no Jewish counterpart (though, if in a different and perhaps characteristic way, the fortunes of Fritz Friedländer and Eduard Arnhold also derive from coal). Coal ownership, among Gentiles, is followed by iron and steel (Krupp and Thyssen), by metallurgy and machine building (Guilleaume, Henschel, Schichau/ Ziese, and Borsig). These also are groups which, for obvious reasons, have no 'Jewish' counterparts. Branches comparable to those prominent in the Jewish 'sector' are weakly represented among Gentiles, confined as they are to the vom Raths, the largest German sugar producers (resident in Cologne but with large interests in Silesia) and the Dippes, plant breeders and seed-merchants from Quedlinburg (comparable to the, originally Jewish, Benarys in Erfurt). Two Gentile Frankfurt banking houses figure in the list—somewhat fortuitously, in consequence of wealthy marriages—the Mumm and the Metzler.[55]

[55] '... Die Metzler und die Grunelius gehören zu den reichsten Bankierfamilien in Frankfurt a.M. Durch das Zusammentreffen beider Vermögen in der Person von Carl von Metzler wurde ein Vermögen von besonderer Grösse geschaffen, sodass Bankier

Very different in character is the Jewish 'sector' of the 'upper' Prussian wealth élite, headed by the traditional banking dynasties, the Rothschilds, Speyers, Mendelssohns, Bleichröder/Schwabachs, and Oppenheims. These have no Gentile counterpart. The Gans/Weinbergs, on the other hand, could be compared to the vom Raths. There are, however, no Gentile representatives of commercial interests comparable to the Schottländers (why did not comparable Gentile landowners join the war contracting?), the Simons, or the Mosses (though one misses, in Martin's list, the name of August Scherl). In short, the area of overlap (or comparability) in the economic origins of the largest fortunes in Prussia is negligible. The sectors of the economy in which the largest non-Jewish and Jewish fortunes were made were, by and large, distinct.

If one turns from families (and, thus, enterprises) to individuals it is useful, once more, in the first place, to establish the Jewish proportion. Of the 25 richest individuals in Prussia listed by Martin, no fewer than 11 (44 per cent) were of Jewish origin. Of the 200 wealthiest millionaires, 55 (27.5 per cent) were of Jewish origin. Lastly, of the 800 wealthiest men and women, 190 (23.7 per cent) were Jewish. The Jewish proportion thus declined in descending order of wealth, but even among the wealthiest 800 it still amounted to almost one quarter. It is a figure which gains support from the fact that it resembles that for the Jewish share in the élite of notables of the *Kommerzienräte* and *Geheime Kommerzienräte* as well as, indeed, that of the corporate élite to be considered later. To anticipate one of the overall findings of the present study, the Jewish share in German commercial activity at the level under consideration here, may be quantified as lying somewhere in the neighbourhood of twenty per cent.

It is instructive, once more, to compare, on this larger scale, the origins of Jewish and Gentile fortunes. For this purpose, a rough classification (there are, of course, marginal cases) into five categories may be adopted: (I) extractive industry (primarily the mining of 'black gold', coal); (II) manufacturing industry; (III) wholesale trade; (IV) banking and finance; and (V) agriculture and forestry. If one confines

Carl von Metzler unmittelbar hinter den Rothschilds und Speyers an der Spitze der grossen Vermögen in Frankfurt a.M. steht' (Martin, op. cit., n. 10 above, ii. 222 f.). Albert Mumm von Schwarzenstein in his turn, senior partner in a banking firm founded in 1805, owed his great wealth to some extent to his marriage. 'Da Albert in eine sehr vermögende Industriefamilie geheiratet hat, so konzentriert sich in seiner Person ein Vermögen von ungewöhnlichem Umfange' (ib., p. 237).

Anatomy of a Wealth Élite

oneself to the fortunes of the 25 wealthiest individuals in Prussia, 14 Gentile, 11 Jewish, the distribution appears as follows:

	I	II	III	IV	V
Gentiles:	9 (64%)	5 (36%)	–	–	–
Jews:	–	–	4 (36%)	7 (64%)	–

The difference (and this computation includes individuals not figured in the previous 'family list') could hardly be more marked.

When it comes to the 200 richest millionaires—a category of 'other' (VI) has to be added—the differences, though somewhat less clear cut, remain striking:

	I	II	III	IV	V	VI
Gentiles:	31 (21%)	47 (32%)	12 (8%)	26 (18%)	19 (13%)	10 (7%)
Jews:	–	8 (14%)	14 (25%)	33 (60%)	–	–

At this level, then, some diversification occurs in the Gentile group compared to the previous one-sided preponderance of coal magnates. In the Jewish group, similarly, there is a degree of diversification from wholesale trade into manufacturing industry.

When considering the following 200 millionaires in descending order of wealth, the picture is roughly as follows:

	I	II	III	IV	V	VI
Gentiles:	14 (9%)	55 (34%)	14 (9%)	32 (20%)	33 (20%)	12 (8%)
Jews:	–	10 (25%)	6 (15%)	23 (57%)	–	1 (3%)

The Gentile 'sector', at this level, shows a high degree of stability compared to the previous sample. In the Jewish group, there is some decline in the fortunes derived from trade and some increase in those from manufactures. Overall, the lower one descends in the Jewish wealth scale, the larger becomes to proportion of fortunes derived from manufacture, the smaller than from trade.

Among the following two hundred, the respective proportions are as follows:

	I	II	III	IV	V	VI
Gentiles:	12 (8%)	42 (29%)	16 (11%)	12 (8%)	43 (30%)	21 (14%)
Jews:	–	13 (25%)	9 (16%)	27 (50%)	–	5 (9%)

At this level, the percentages for industry and trade in the two groups begin to approximate. However, while Jewish wealth is derived to a much greater extent from banking and finance, a substantial proportion of Gentile fortunes stems from landownership and agriculture.

For the final 200 millionaires to be considered here, the data are as follows:

	I	II	III	IV	V	VI
Gentiles:	12 (7%)	48 (30%)	8 (5%)	26 (16%)	38 (24%)	27 (17%)
Jews:	–	8 (20%)	9 (22%)	13 (32%)	–	11 (27%)

This shows a further continuation of the trend that, the smaller the fortunes, the smaller the share of Jewish wealth derived from banking and financial activities. The falling trend in the proportion of fortunes derived from trade is here reversed. The discrepancy in the proportions of wholesale trade and banking in the two groups, 19 per cent (Gentile) and 66 per cent (Jewish), in the previous sample, is now reduced to 21 per cent and 54 per cent respectively. The steady increase in the percentage of wealth derived from land in the Gentile sample is reversed.

If the total of 800 Prussian millionaires is considered (omitting, this time, people difficult to classify or not fitting into the categories employed here) the final result is the following:

	I	II	III	IV	V
Gentiles:	69 (13%)	192 (35%)	50 (9%)	96 (18%)	133 (25%)
Jews:	–	39 (22%)	38 (22%)	96 (55%)	–

The difference is underlined. While no 'Jewish' fortunes are made from extractive industries or agriculture, in short from the land (marginal entrepreneurs like Fritz Friedländer or the Schottländers are probably best classified as wholesale merchants in spite of their respective interests in coal-mining and agriculture), these sources account for 38 per cent of Gentile fortunes. On the other hand, while Jewish wealth derived from wholesale trade and banking amounts to 77 per cent of the total, the 'Gentile' proportion is 27 per cent. Clearly, Jewish and Gentile fortunes were drawn, typically, from different sources and from different forms of economic activity. While both Jews and Gentiles had the technical opportunity of making their fortunes in most branches of economic activity, they did so in very different proportions. Whether the variables were the numbers of Jews and Gentiles respectively in the different branches of economic activity or the respective degrees of economic success in these branches (or both), and the reasons for such differences cannot be examined here.

The amount of capital controlled by the Prussian wealth élite on the eve of the First World War is substantial, as can be seen by comparing it to the nominal share capital of the largest joint-stock companies. The comparison is of particular interest with regard to the Jewish fortunes as, unlike those of their Gentile counterparts, they tended to be 'mobile' rather than in the form of landed property or coal deposits and royalties, making them perhaps more readily comparable with the nominal share capital of companies which, however, would also represent immobile assets.

Table 6. Comparison of Jewish Family Wealth and Capital of Major Joint-Stock Companies

Wealth of Jewish families 1908	Mill. marks	Nominal share capital 1907	Mill. marks
Rothschild & Goldschmidt-R.	310	Deutsche Bank	200
Speyer & Beit von Speyer	121	Friedr. Krupp AG	180
Mendelssohn & Mendelssohn-B.	101	Dresdner Bank	180
Bleichröder/Schwabach	70	Disconto-Gesellschaft	170
Oppenheim (Cologne)	68	Bank f. Handel u. Industr.	154
		AEG	100[56]

It should, of course, be noted that the stock-exchange value of the large joint-stock companies could far exceed their nominal share capital, but the figures nevertheless suggest that the largest private banking fortunes were substantial even when measured against the share capital of the major joint-stock banks. Thus the private fortune of the Rothschilds exceeded the share capital of the Deutsche Bank, while that of the Mendelssohns equalled that of the AEG. When it comes to economic influence, on the other hand, particularly through industrial financing, the importance of the joint-stock banks and their managing directorates greatly exceeded that of the private firms. So far as Jews in economic life also were concerned, the wealthy, though not without influence, had to yield pride of place to the corporate influence élite of the age of high capitalism.

[56] The AEG had, however, major daughter companies.

VII

Martin's data show a very uneven geographical distribution of the Jewish wealth élite. There was, in fact, a heavy concentration, both in actual numbers and in proportion of the total wealth élite, in two centres, Berlin and Frankfurt-on-Main. In Berlin, the ranking order of the twenty wealthiest men according to their tax returns for 1911 is the following:

	Fortune (Million marks)	Income (Million marks)
1. Wilhelm II	140	22
2. Fritz v. Friedländer-Fuld	46	3.35
3. *Verlagsbuchhändler* Rudolf Mosse	45	3.2
4. GKR Sigmund Aschrott	41	1.5
5. *Rentier* Richard Haniel	41	2.7
6. GKR Eduard Arnhold	40	2.8
7. James Simon	35	2.4
8. *Wirkl. Geh. Rat* Dr jur. Willi v. Dirksen	30	2
9. Hans v. Bleichröder	29	2
10. *Geh. Justizrat* Eduard Uhles	27	2
11. GKR Louis Ravené	27	2.2
12. Oscar Huldschinsky	27	1.8
13. *Generalkonsul* Robert v. Mendelssohn	25.2	2
14. GKR Dr jur. Eduard Simon	25	1.7
15. GKR Leopold Koppel	21	1.6
16. KR Julius Bötzow	21	1.3
17. Rudolph Hertzog	20	1.1
18. *Generalkonsul* Dr phil. Paul v. Schwabach	20	1
19. Banker James Hardy	19	1
20. *Rentier* G. W. Gerson	18.5	0.8
21. Arnold v. Siemens	18.5	1.2

Thus, of the twenty wealthiest Berliners, no fewer than twelve were of Jewish extraction, with the last place shared between a Jew and a Gentile. Certain particulars are worth noting. Among Jewish names, though they include besides an insigificant Bleichröder, a Mendelssohn, James Hardy, and Paul von Schwabach, the bankers now yield pride of place to the merchants (Friedländer-Fuld, Mosse, Aschrott, Arnhold, the two Simons, Koppel, and Gerson). Oscar Huldschinsky is the lone ex-industrialist, though the activities of Friedländer and, to a lesser extent, Arnhold, have an industrial aspect. With the exception of Bleichröder, Gerson, and, possibly, Huldschinsky and Aschrott, Jewish millionaires remain active in economic life. The highest ratio of gross income to fortune among 'Jewish' millionaires is achieved, perhaps predictably, by Robert von Mendelssohn (almost 8 per cent) followed by Leopold Koppel (7.6 per cent), Friedländer, Mosse, Arnhold, and Simon (c.7 per cent each).

The Gentile group, by contrast, is a curious one. Wilhelm II apart, it contains two beneficiaries of the Haniel fortune (Richard Haniel and *Geh. Justizrat* Ules, married to Clara, widowed Haniel, née Haniel) and Willi von Dirksen, with a fortune derived from inherited estates in Silesia and marriage into the Cologne banking family of Schnitzler. It is only after these 'exotica' that the more authentic 'Berliners', the iron wholesaler Ravené, the brewer Boetzow, department store owner Hertzog, and industrialist Arnold von Siemens, appear.

The wealth élite of Berlin extends into that of the province of Brandenburg which, until 1920, included 'satellite localities' favoured by Jews, like Charlottenburg, Wilmersdorf, and Grunewald. Here, according to the tax returns for 1911, seven people declared fortunes of 18 million marks or over:

	Fortune (Million marks)	Income (Million marks)
1. Hermann Wallich, *rentier*	31	1.8
2. *Geh. Regierungsrat* Wilhelm v. Siemens	26–7	1.3
3. Franz von Mendelssohn	25	2.6
4. Oscar Tietz	24	2.0
5. *Freifrau Reg.-Assessor* Tilo v. Wilmowski	20	0.8
6. *Fürst* zu Solms-Baruth	20	0.8
7. Ernst v. Borsig	18	1.4

Of the seven wealthiest Brandenburgers, therefore, three (Wallich, Mendelssohn, and Tietz) were of Jewish extraction, a joint-stock banker, a traditional family banker, and the owner of a large department store. The large fortune of Hermann Wallich is somewhat inexplicable. His income was no more than 6 per cent of capital. Franz von Mendelssohn, senior partner in a flourishing private banking house, on the other hand, achieved an income exceeding 10 per cent of his wealth. Oscar Tietz, in his turn, obtained a relatively good return of more than 8 per cent.

The Gentile group, again, is a somewhat curious one, including, as it does, besides the old established industrialists Siemens and Borsig, *Freifrau* von Wilmowski (née Barbara Krupp) and a territorial magnate, Solms-Baruth. Striking (though not, perhaps, surprisingly) is the low return obtained by, on the one hand, the Krupp heiress (4 per cent), on the other the landowning magnate (also 4 per cent). While Siemens secures only a modest 5 per cent. Ernst von Borsig attains an above average 7.7 per cent. (It must be noted, however, that income could vary from year to year.) One feature of the wealth élite of Berlin and Brandenburg in 1911 is the strikingly small number of indigenous entrepreneurs and industrialists in the Gentile group, confined as they are to members of the Siemens family, Borsig, and the brewer Bötzow. The rest, with the exception of Hertzog, are a somewhat fortuitous collection.

For the second great centre of Jewish wealth, the province of Hesse-Nassau (including the city of Frankfurt and the town of Kassel), the data presented by Martin for the year 1911 are as follows:

	Fortune (Million mark)	Income (Million mark)
1. *Freiherr* Max v. Goldschmidt-Rothschild	163	3.86
2. *Freifrau* Mathilde v. Rothschild (widow)	92	3.45
3. KR Eduard Beit v. Speyer	88	2.905
4. GKR Carl Henschel (factory owner)	54	3.815
5. Frau Lucie Fleischer (née Cokerill)	47	2.845
6. *Freiherr* Albert v. Goldschmidt-Rothschild	40	1.8
7. *Freiherr* Rudolf v. Goldschmidt-Rothschild	39	1.8
8. *Freiherr* Ferdinand v. Krauskopf	30	2.25
9. Dr Herbert v. Meister (landowner)	25–6	1.83
10. *Freiin* Lucy von Goldschmidt-Rothschild	25–6	1.1
11. Alexander Friedrich Landgraf von Hessen	25–6	1.6
12. *Freiherr* Erich von Goldschmidt-Rothschild	25–6	under age
13. *Generalkonsul* Carl v. Weinberg	25–6	2.2
14. Dr phil. Arthur v. Weinberg	25–6	2.2

	Fortune (Million mark)	Income (Million mark)
15. GKR Leo Gans	22–3	1.7
16. Banker Carl v. Metzler	17–18	0.75
17. Banker Albert Mumm von Schwarzenstein	17–18	0.9
18. Fritz Gans (factory owner)	17–18	1.3
19. Adolf Gans (merchant)	17–18	1.3
20. Widow of GKR Henschel	16–17	0.91

Thus, of the twenty leading tax payers of Hesse-Nassau, twelve were of Jewish origin. What stands out, of course, is the wealth of the Rothschilds and Goldschmidt-Rothschilds with an aggregate fortune of 384 million marks. These are followed by members of the Gans/Weinberg families of Leopold Cassella & Co. 'worth' 108 million marks. The fortune of Eduard Beit von Speyer reaches 88 million marks. What is striking is the very different returns on capital. While the Weinbergs, with their flourishing enterprise, achieve 8.8 per cent (Leo, the senior Gans, obtains 8 per cent, other members of the family 7.6 per cent), the Goldschmidt-Rothschilds, no longer significant in economic life, secure returns ranging from 2.4 per cent (Maximilian) to 4.5 per cent (Albert and Rudolf). Eduard von Speyer's income also reaches no more than 3.3 per cent of his fortune.

The Gentile group consists essentially of manufacturers, Henschel in Kassel and von Meister of Farbwerke Höchst, and the wealthiest among Gentile bankers, Metzler and Mumm. The 'exotic' element is provided by the *Landgraf* of Hesse and by Lucie Fleischer (née Cokerill, heiress to an industrial fortune acquired mainly in Liège and Aachen). The distribution of return on capital resembles that of the Jewish millionaires. Here also, the highest returns are obtained from industry (Henschel and Meister) while those on traditional banking fortunes are low (Metzler 4.4 per cent, Mumm 5.3 per cent). The *Landgraf* of Hesse and Lucie Fleischer occupy an intermediate position (with 6.4 and 6 per cent respectively).

While men and women of Jewish origin thus occupy a conspicuous place in the highest stratum of the wealth élite in Berlin/Brandenburg and Hesse-Nassau (Frankfurt), their position in other parts of Germany is, predictably, modest. Thus in the *Rheinprovinz*, the three highest placed Jews in terms of wealth, all members of the Oppenheim family, occupy respectively places 32, 42 and 43 in the wealth table, followed by Louis Hagen at 51. While Hagen, predictably, achieves a high income ratio, 8.6 per cent (of which, however, a significant proportion must have consisted of *Aufsichtsrat* fees), the Oppenheims' ratio is 6.6 per cent, probably a reflection, compared to the Frankfurt bankers, of a more active residual involvement in the industrial financing of the joint-stock age. In Westphalia, amidst relatively smaller fortunes in general, the Jewish share is negligible. The wealthiest Jew, KR Emil Paderstein, a banker in Paderborn, credited with a fortune of 5–6 million marks and an income of 0.36 million marks (between 6 and 7 per cent), figures twenty-ninth on the list of millionaires.

Another region where Jews do not figure prominently among the very wealthy is the kingdom of Saxony. Here Emma, *Freifrau* von Kaskel, with her fortune of 21 million marks, is indeed the second wealthiest person in the kingdom (after Friedrich-August, king of Saxony, with 25 million), but the next Jew, GKR Sieskind Sieskind of the old-established banking house of H. C. Plaut in Leipzig, with a fortune of 7.3 million marks and an income of 0.45 (6.1 per cent), ranks only thirty-sixth. It is, perhaps, significant that *Freifrau* v. Kaskel only achieves a return of 6.6 per cent on her capital.

More surprising, perhaps, than their relative paucity in Rhineland-Westphalia or Saxony is the relative lack of people of Jewish origin among 'top' millionaires in the eastern provinces of the Prussian monarchy. Thus in Silesia, the first person of Jewish origin in the table and wealthiest man in Breslau, KR Dr jur. Georg Heimann, owner of the old-established banking firm of E. Heimann, ranks only twelfth after a succession of territorial magnates. His fortune of 24 million with an income of 1 million (something of the order of 4 per cent) must, moreover, be due in part to his marriage into the old-established Gentile trading family of Molinari. Dr Paul Schottländer, the next Jew, ranks twenty-ninth.[57] In the province of Posen, the most prominent Jew, the iron merchant GKR Michael Herz with a fortune

[57] The wealthiest millionaire in Silesia and since 1905 in Prussia, Prince Guido Henckel von Donnersmarck, returned a fortune of 254 million marks and an income of 13.145 million (*c.*5.2 per cent). The prince attributed his striking economic success largely to the acumen of his third wife, a Jewess, née Therese Lachmann. After her death, the prince recorded his gratitude: 'Sie war ein kaufmännisches Genie; ihren Ratschlägen allein verdanke ich meinen Reichtum' (Bernstein, op. cit., n. 19 above, p. 906). For the incredible career of the legendary and repulsive Païva—she died in 1884—see ibid., pp. 905 f.

of 5–6 million marks and an income of 0.2 (*c*.4 per cent) ranked sixteenth amid a mass of ethnically Polish landowners. Again, in the province of Pomerania (effectively, for this purpose, the commercial port and shipbuilding centre of Stettin), GKR Rudolf Abel, a prominent banker (whose ethnic origin, however, cannot be established with alsolute certainty), is followed in tenth place by *Konsul* Wilhelm Kunstmann, a Jewish shipowner,[58] whose fortune of 5–6 million marks produced an income of 0.36 million (*c*.7 per cent). The fourteenth place belonged to *Generalkonsul* KR Georg Manasse, partner in a wholesale business, with a fortune of 4–5 million marks and an income of 0.32 million. Nor did Jews figure prominently in the wealth élite of Hamburg, even though two Behrens brothers with fortunes respectively of 31 and 26 million marks occupied places 5 and 10. Their incomes reached the high proportion of 9 and 9.9 per cent respectively.[59] In the province of Hanover, finally, a man of Jewish origin, GKR *Generalkonsul* Bernhard Caspar, board chairman of the Continental Caoutchuc und Gutta-Percha-Compagnie AG, figured third on the list of millionaires with a fortune of 9–10 million and an income of 0.63 (6–7 per cent).

Overall, then, Jews in the top stratum of the German wealth élite (as indeed at the next level of wealth) were unevenly distributed geographically. Though much of the wealth was, not surprisingly, acquired in banking (more particularly in centres like Frankfurt-on-Main and Hamburg), a good deal of the newer wealth derived from commerce, with a sprinkling of large fortunes derived from industry. In general this may be held to reflect the overall pattern of Jewish economic activity at the highest level in the final decades of the nineteenth century.

VIII

If one looks at the Jewish wealth élite as a whole, a number of features (most of them predictable) stand out. One is the high proportion of bankers. Although some merchants figure in the top stratum, few industrialists were able to amass comparable fortunes. A second fact—again self-evident—is that large accumulations of capital tended

---

[58] For the Kunstmann shipping line see Zielenziger, op. cit., n. 25 above, pp. 192 ff.
[59] In general, return on capital in Hamburg may have been high. Three Warburg brothers, for instance, achieved returns of 8 per cent. Two Emdens had incomes equalling 8.5 per cent of their fortunes. Albert Ballin, with the inclusion of salary and fees, achieved a return of 10 per cent on a fortune of 5 million marks.

to occur above all where several large fortunes were combined. Thus some of the wealthiest men, Eduard Beit von Speyer (Beit-Ladenburg-Speyer-Ellissen) or Felix *Freiherr* von Kaskel (Kaskel-Fränkel-Oppenheim) owed their massive fortunes to the fortunate combination of a wealthy mother and a wealthy wife. More common were the cases where men from already wealthy families in turn married wealthy wives. It is a curious fact (though possibly again predictable) that this form of capital accumulation was practised primarily among bankers. It was less common among merchants or industrialists, though not unknown, as shown by the case of the entrepreneur Dr Ferdinand Beit of Hamburg who married a Ladenburg from Mannheim or, still more strikingly, by Maximilian Goldschmidt from Frankfurt, who secured the hand of a Rothschild heiress. In general, however, more likely than not, merchants and industrialists would contract modest marriages (with Fritz Friedländer, who married into the wealthy Amsterdam banking family of Fuld, a possible exception).

In general, the wealth obtained from banking was largely traditional or, at least, contained a large traditional element of steady accumulation over several generations. There were, among the bankers listed here, no true 'self-made men'. James Hardy, perhaps, comes nearest to the description, together, possibly, with Leopold Koppel or 'men of affairs' from small banking houses like Wilhelm Kopetzky or Ludwig Max Goldberger. As against this, the wealth derived from wholesale trade or industry was more likely to be of recent origin (reflecting economic opportunities of the eighties, and, particularly, the nineties).

It is hard to escape the impression that wealth from banking, once it had reached significant proportions, showed a relative stability (to which marriage strategies in many cases contributed). On the other hand, the fortunes made from wholesale trade or industry appear comparatively precarious. For this, there may be a number of reasons. In the first place, almost by definition, non-bankers were less likely than bankers to be conscious of the imperative need (or urge) to preserve and increase their capital. Moreover, the impression may, to some extent, rest on an optical illusion: the great banking fortunes which did survive to the eve of the First World War had, in fact, passed through the hands of one or more extra generations. Lastly, there is the curious fact—to be discussed presently—that the self-made (or nearly) men who had worked their way to the top, tended to lack male offspring (exceptions like the Mertons, Ullsteins, or Wertheims notwithstanding). Banking dynasties, the Speyers, Mendelssohns,

Oppenheims, Ladenburgs, Bleichröders, Warburgs, Kaullas, on the other hand, tended to produce the requisite male offspring for generations, and readily to 'adopt' talent, whether through marriage or partnership, where the natural succession failed. Prominent merchants or industrialists, on the other hand, often failed to establish dynasties, possibly, among other reasons, because entrepreneurial skills were perhaps more difficult to transmit than the 'naked' ability to handle money.[60]

The relative infertility of members of the highest stratum of the Jewish wealth elite, compared both to the equivalent Gentile group and to the succeeding Jewish stratum is too striking to be the result of pure chance (see Table 7).

Table 7. Relative Fertility of the Jewish and Gentile Wealth Élite

| | Owners of fortunes of 15 million marks and over ||
	Jewish	Gentile
Total number	31	82
Information available	30	64
Precise data available	26	59
Total no. offspring	63 av. 2.4	201 av. 3.4
sons	21 av. 0.8	113 av. 1.9
daughters	42 av. 1.6	88 av. 1.5
No male offspring	13 (50%)	10 (17%)
One child only	6 (23%)	6 (11%)
4+ children	8 (31%)	29 (50%)

The differences, particularly with regard to the production of male offspring, are striking. While the relative infertility of the Jewish group compared to the Gentile may be explained in terms of social differences (with the Gentile sample including many territorial magnates and members of the nobility) and of Sombart's thesis about the relative infertility of the marriages of men engaged in 'money-making' (and unhampered by religious considerations), the notable gender difference in the offspring is inexplicable except by hypotheses alike fanciful and incapable of proof.

[60] These are, of course, general statements, none without exceptions. The German branch of the Rothschilds eventually became extinct, though perpetuated as the Goldschmidt-Rothschilds with full preservation of capital. On the other hand, there were non-banking dynasties like the Cassella/Gans/Weinbergs, the 'Kupfer-Hirschs' of Halberstadt, or the Philip Cohen/Merton/Hochschild/Ellingers, but these may be exceptions which prove the rule.

An oddly different picture emerges from an examination of the lower wealth stratum (see Table 8).

Table 8. Relative Fertility of the Jewish and Gentile Sub-Élite

	Fortunes of 5–15 million marks	
	Jewish	Gentile
Total no.	66	268
Information available	40	229
Precise data available	26	212
Total no. of offspring	79 av. 3	680 av. 3.2
sons	51 av. 2	354 av. 1.67
daughters	28 av. 1	316 av. 1.5
No male offspring	4 (c.15%)	64 (30%)
One child only	2 (8%)	14 (6.6%)
4+ children	8 (c.30%)	83 (39%)

Compared to the previous sample, several features emerge. In general, the striking differences between the Jewish and the Gentile group have disappeared. More, the gender balance in the offspring of the two groups has been reversed. The proportion of those lacking male offspring is now higher among Gentiles than among Jews.

It is intructive, finally, to compare the two Jewish groups (see Table 9).

Table 9. Relative Fertility of the Jewish Wealth Élite and Sub-Élite

	Fortunes of 15+ million	5–15 million
Total no.	32	66
Information available	26	40
Precise data available	20	26
Total no. of offspring	48 av. 2.4	79 av. 3
sons	15 av. 0.75	51 av. 2
daughters	33 av. 1.65	28 av. 1
No male offspring	11 (55%)	4 (c.15%)
One child only	6 (30%)	2 (8%)
4+ children	6 (30%)	8 (c.30%)

The most striking features are the differences in the proportions of sons, of those lacking male offspring, and those with a single child only. There is clear evidence, in the wealthier group of a relatively high degree of infertility combined with an 'abnormal' gender distribution.

Finally, to complete the analysis, it is interesting to compare the two Gentile groups (see Table 10).

Table 10. Relative Fertility of the Gentile Wealth Élite and Sub-Élite

	Fortunes of 15+ million	5–15 million
Total no.	82	268
Information available	64	229
Precise data available	59	212
Total no. offspring	201 av. 3.4	680 av. 3.2
sons	113 av. 1.9	354 av. 1.67
daughters	88 av. 1.5	316 av. 1.5
No male heirs	10 (17%)	64 (30%)
One child only	6 (11%)	14 (6.6%)
4+ children	29 (50%)	83 (39%)

The figures show a much higher degree of correspondence for the two groups than in the Jewish sample. The 'lower' economic stratum contains a higher proportion of men without male heirs, a lower one of people with four or more children. Those in the wealthier groups produce relatively more sons.

What overall appears to emerge from these data is the existence of a degree of correlation between Jewishness, scale of wealth, and fertility (as well as gender distribution of offspring). The only conclusion to be drawn from this fact is perhaps the lesser likelihood of the largest Jewish fortunes remaining in the same family over several generations as against the greater possibility of Gentile ones being fragmented through division among a larger number of siblings. Overall, the proposition might tentatively be advanced that demographic factors marginally favoured the preservation of Jewish fortunes as against non-Jewish. The same may be true of marriage strategies—to be discussed elsewhere—more particularly in the case of Jewish banking families. Altogether, while the Jewish wealth élite was, of course, unstable like any other, there may have been present some factors tending to promote a relative comparative stability. Certainly among the millionaires examined by Martin there existed, thanks to the strikingly favourable economic conditions from the mid-nineties onwards (notwithstanding a short sharp recession) a tendency for many (perhaps most) large fortunes to grow, sometimes rapidly. It was difficult for the wealthy, before 1914, and more particularly for wealthy bankers, not to become wealthier still.

6
The Corporate Élite

IF the wealth élite was largely past-orientated, traditional, and of declining economic importance, the corporate élite, by contrast, was new (composed, almost entirely, of 'self-made men'), important in determining economic strategies (primarily of enterprises or branches of economic activity, their influence on public policy is a different matter), and devoid of (very great) wealth. Members, typically, managed the capital of others rather than their own or directed enterprises that did not belong to them. While the wealth élite was essentially 'dynamic', with many of the greatest fortunes the result of successful marriage strategies, the corporate élite was based on financial and managerial skills less likely than economic assets to prove transferable. To some extent, co-option (or adoption) replaces heredity as the structuring principle even if a tendency towards dynasty formation (more often than not unsuccessful) persists. There was, in the corporate élite, less room for the feeble heir, less pressure on (less suitable) sons to succeed fathers. In short, the corporate élite, seen as a group, constitutes a major step towards what might be described as capitalist 'meritocracy' with merit measured increasingly in terms of economic performance.

The rise of the new élite reflects, of course, well-known changes in economic organization, with the family firm yielding pride of place to the large joint-stock enterprise. The need for ever-increasing amounts of capital by stages replaces 'private' financing by private banking firms with massive stock-exchange flotations. Capital, at the same time, is concentrated largely, if as yet by no means exclusively, in the large deposit banks with branches all over the country. The size of industrial units also increases with the processes of fusion, integration, and diversification. Commercial and financial transactions are conducted between units of unprecedented size and complexity.

The adaptation of men of Jewish origin to the corporate age of high (organized) capitalism is a striking phenomenon. So is the large element of discontinuity between the traditional Jewish economic élites of status and wealth and the new influence or power élite. It reveals the adaptability of the matrix (or substratum) of Jews engaged in economic activities at lower or intermediate level in providing talent to operate in the new conditions. And not of the economically active alone. As with earlier Jewish élites (and, indeed, with Gentile ones too), men originating in the professions make their contribution to the formation of the new corporate élite. Contrary to what is sometimes asserted, the role of Jews in corporate economic activity in Germany was scarcely, if at all, inferior to the part they had played in the days of earlier industrialization, of private banking houses, and of individual entrepreneurship.

It is against this general background that the role of the Jewish corporate élite in the Wilhelmine period, the classic age of the German joint-stock company, must be seen. That élite was, in fact, a composite one. It was, in part, positional, consisting of chairmen (*Vorsitzende*), of *Vorstände* or *Direktionen* (often with the title of *Generaldirektor*), and of chairmen and deputy chairmen of boards or *Aufsichtsräte*. Overlapping with the latter group though not identical with it were a number of leading 'pluralists' on the boards of major companies. These included, in the main, a relativey small number of leading joint-stock bankers.

If, moreover, the distribution of members of the Jewish corporate élite among the major enterprises is examined, a picture emerges of a number of companies with significant Jewish representation in the top positions, which constitute something of a network with certain common features and common interests. The contours emerge on the one hand of a relatively small number of Jewish bankers associated with a number of major companies and, on the other, of some major firms linked by interlocking board membership through a small number of influential individuals.

I

As a first step towards studying the Jewish corporate élite it is necessary to examine the place of Jews in the direction of the large joint-stock banks. Contrary to a still widespread belief (encouraged, perhaps, with apologetic intent) to the effect that, with the relative decline in the importance of the private banking houses (which also has been overstated), the role of Jews in German banking declined, men of Jewish extraction were, in fact, prominent also in the managements of the joint-stock universal banks. In the Disconto-

Gesellschaft,[1] for example, founded in 1851, the most prominent partners (*Geschäftsinhaber*) and directors were the two Hansemanns, David (1851–64) and Adolph (1853–1903),[2] descended from Protestant clergy. However, there had existed, side by side with them, a dynasty descended from a line of rabbis, the Salomonsohns from Inowrazlaw (Posen).[3] The founder of that dynasty, Adolf Salomonsohn,[4] had become *Syndikus* of the bank in 1864, *Geschäftsinhaber* (partner) in 1869. As a leading member of the directorate, he had represented the bank above all in its stock exchange and credit transactions. He had played a prominent part in its operations connected with railway finance, in overseas enterprises, and in developing industrial connections. In 1888 he had withdrawn from the management of the bank but would remain a member of its *Aufsichtsrat* until his death in 1919.

When, in 1888, Adolph Salomonsohn had retired as *Geschäftsinhaber* of the bank, his nephew Arthur had entered its service to become, in 1895, *Geschäftsinhaber* in his turn. As such, he had played a prominent part in developing its association with major industrial enterprises (heavy industry, shipbuilding and navigation, the potash industry). In 1912, Arthur Salomonsohn assumed the chairmanship of the *Geschäftsinhaber*, the premier position in the bank. This he would occupy until its fusion with the Deutsche Bank in 1929. He then became board chairman of the new bank, a position he occupied until his death in 1930.[5]

In 1911 Georg Salomonsohn, son of Adolf and cousin of Arthur, who, since his conversion to Christianity in 1900, had adopted the name of Solmssen, had become in his turn *Geschäftsinhaber* of the bank. Solmssen also occupied important directorships notably in the petroleum industry and in telecommunications and played a prominent role in the eventual absorption by Disconto of the Schaaffhausensche

---

[1] Full title: Direction der Disconto-Gesellschaft.

[2] For a list of *Geschäftsinhaber* of the Disconto-Gesellschaft see Ernst W. Schmidt, *Männer der Deutschen Bank und der Disconto-Gesellschaft* (Düsseldorf, 1957), p. 21.

[3] For the Salomonsohn see Zielenziger, *Juden in der deutschen Wirtschaft* (Berlin, 1930), pp. 112 ff. and Bernstein, 'Wirtschaft' in Kaznelson (ed.), *Juden im deutschen Kulturbereich* (Berlin, 1962), pp. 737 ff.

[4] For Adolf Salomonsohn see Georg Solmssen, *Gedenkblatt für Adolf und Sara Salomonsohn zum 19 März 1931*, privately printed (Berlin, 1931).

[5] 'Wenn man von dem sporadischen Wirken David Hansemanns in den ersten Jahren der Disconto absieht, hatte diese Grossbank in den rund 75 Jahren ihres Bestehens nur drei Seniorchefs gehabt: Adolph von Hansemann, Alexander Schoeller und Arthur Salomonsohn. Diese drei Männer haben die Bank geprägt ...' Fritz Seidenzahl, *Hundert Jahre Deutsche Bank* (Frankfurt, 1970), p. 311.

Bankverein. On the death of Jakob Riesser in 1932, Georg Solmssen was elected president of the central organization of German bankers (Centralverband des deutschen Bank- und Bankiergewerbes), a position which, however, he had to reliquish the following year. In 1933, he replaced Oscar Wassermann as speaker of the directorate of the Deutsche Bank, another position he was unable to retain for long. He remained, however, a board member until 1937. The Salomonsohns had thus accompanied the Disconto-Gesellschaft through three generations almost from its beginnings, through the period of its greatest expansion to the 'bitter end' of its fusion with the Deutsche Bank and beyond. Solmssen remained a member of the *Vorstand* of the Deutsche Bank-Disconto-Gesellschaft until 1934, of its board until 1936. The dynasty of the Salomonsohn-Solmssen, besides being an interesting example of dynasty formation in a large joint-stock bank, also shows how the 'secondary dynasty' of the Salomonsohns eventually replaced that of the Hansemanns as the leading one in the bank. (While there were, of course, in the management of the Disconto-Gesellschaft prominent Gentile directors, there was no 'dynasty', after the decline of the Hansemanns, comparable to that of the Salomonsohn-Solmssens.) Besides the Salomonsohns, the Disconto-Gesellschaft had other less prominent Jewish *Geschäftsinhaber*. Of the twenty-two men who held that position between 1851 and 1929, five were of Jewish extraction, a sixth a half-Jew.

If the Disconto-Gesellschaft had a Jewish 'secondary dynasty' which after 1912 moved into the 'driver's seat' so, in its own way, did its great rival and ultimate partner, the Deutsche Bank.[6] While the leading men in the first decades of that bank's history were Georg von Siemens, Rudolf von Koch, and Arthur von Gwinner (married to a daughter of Georg Speyer of Frankfurt-on-Main), several Jewish directors, in a curious order of apostolic succession, played a prominent and, ultimately, a leading part in its affairs.

Among those prominent in the founding of the Deutsche Bank had been Ludwig Bamberger, the liberal politician, descended from a Jewish banking family in Mainz and trained as a banker by his uncles the Bischoffsheims in Paris. In Paris, Bamberger had met Hermann Wallich,[7] whose services for the new bank he secured. Wallich, as member of the *Vorstand* from its setting up in 1870 until 1893,

---

[6] For the history of the Deutsche Bank, see Seidenzahl, op. cit.
[7] For the memoirs of Hermann Wallich see H. Wallich, *Aus meinem Leben* in *Zwei Generationen im deutschen Bankwesen 1833–1914* (Frankfurt-on-Main, 1978).

rendered signal service to the bank, more particularly in developing its overseas activities.[8] After 1893, Wallich, by then a wealthy man, became an influential member of the *Aufsichtsrat*.[9]

If Bamberger 'begat' Wallich, Wallich in his turn 'begat' Steinthal.[10] On the occasion of a journey to the island of Sylt, Wallich had, by chance, made the acquaintance of and been impressed by the younger man. In 1873, at Wallich's suggestion, Max Steinthal joined the *Vorstand* of the bank, a position he retained until 1906.[11] While, at first, Steinthal had been concerned mainly with stock-exchange transactions,[12] the scope of his activities presently widened. From 1890 onwards he took an active part in floating industrial issues. Then, at the request of Georg v. Siemens, he assumed responsibility for the reorganization of the ailing Mannesmannröhren-Werke in which the bank had a major stake. As chairman of the Mannesmann board (from 1896), Steinthal had helped to turn the loss-making enterprise into a successful industrial giant.[13] He remained chairman of the *Aufsichtsrat* until 1936,

[8] 'Für die Bank war es ein Segen', writes Seidenzahl, 'dass Wallich engagiert wurde. Ihn herangeholt zu haben, ist das unbestreitbare Verdienst von Ludwig Bamberger. Hermann Wallich war zunächst der einzige, der das Bankfach erlernt und es in dieser Branche zu verantwortlicher Stellung gebracht hatte.' Seidenzahl, op. cit., pp. 29 f.

[9] Another Jewish banker prominent in the early days of the Deutsche Bank was Dr Kilian Steiner of the Württembergische Vereinsbank in Stuttgart, already referred to. Not only was his bank a substantial contributor to the foundation capital of the Deutsche Bank, but he soon became the confidential adviser of Georg von Siemens. He is described as 'der vertraute Gesprächspartner des leitenden Mannes der Deutschen Bank' (ib., p. 19). Steiner helped the Deutsche Bank, during the crisis of 1873, to acquire two substantial Berlin banks in financial difficulties. As a member of the *Aufsichtsrat* of the bank, Steiner, in 1888, was instrumental in initiating its interest in the Anatolian railway project, brought to his notice by his colleague in the Vereinsbank, Alfred von Kaulla (ib., pp. 41 f. and 65 f.).

[10] For Max Steinthal see Max Fuchs, *Max Steinthal* (Berlin, 1930), Bernstein, loc. cit., n. 3 above, pp. 739 f., R. Martin, *Jahrbuch ... der Millionäre in der Provinz Brandenburg* (Berlin, 1913), pp. 128 f., Hartmut Pogge von Strandmann, Unternehmenspolitik und Unternehmensführung (Düsseldorf and Vienna, 1978), *passim*, and Seidenzahl, op. cit., n. 5 above, *passim*.

[11] Fuchs, op. cit., p. 6.

[12] As Hermann Wallich wrote in his memoirs: 'Das einzige Fach in dem ich nicht glänzte, war das Börsenfach, und es blieb Herrn Steinthal und den von ihm herangebildeten Kräften vorbehalten, auch auf diesem Gebiet unsere Bank zu einer massgebenden Stellung zu bringen.' Hermann Wallich, *Aus meinem Leben* (Berlin, 1929, private printing), p. 160.

[13] 'Steinthals Ausdauer und Klugheit war es zu danken, dass die Mannesmannwerke zu einem grossen erfolgreichen Unternehmen aufsteigen konnten. Bereits 1896 wurde Steinthal zum Aufsichtsratsvorsitzenden ernannt. Trotz des Dritten Reiches stand er bis 1936 auf diesem Platz und gehörte dem Kollegium noch zwei weitere Jahre als reguläres Mitglied an. Unentbehrlich selbst im Zeitwandel.' Seidenzahl, op. cit., n. 5 above, p. 190. It was largely attributable to Steinthal that by 1930 Mannesmann had become the

a member of the board for a further two years. In 1905, after leaving the *Vorstand* of the Deutsche Bank, Steinthal had become a member of its board, its deputy chairman in 1914. After the fusion of the Deutsche Bank with the Disconto-Gesellschaft in 1929, he would share the position of chairman of the new *Aufsichtsrat* with Arthur Salomonsohn of the Disconto-Gesellschaft.

Steinthal, as a young man in Berlin, had served part of his apprenticeship in the bank of A. Paderstein in company with another aspiring young banker, Paul Mankiewitz.[14] The links then established were sufficient to ensure for Mankiewitz the degree of protection needed for a successful career in the Deutsche Bank. Thanks to Steinthal, he was promoted from early subaltern employment to the stock-exchange division, the traditional starting-point for a career in joint-stock banking. This proved, in fact, a field suited to Mankiewitz's talents and one which enabled him to build up a reputation as the 'King of the Stock Exchange'. Mankiewitz joined the *Vorstand* in 1898. In 1919, in succession to Gwinner, he was chosen speaker (*Sprecher*) of the bank, its most prestigious position. He left the *Vorstand* in 1923. Pinner, less than enthusiastically, describes him as a man lacking outstanding ability but with a certain *élan* and financial flair.[15]

Mankiewitz, in his turn, as head of the stock exchange division, had helped to develop the talents and promote the career of Oscar Wassermann,[16] offspring of an old Jewish banking family in Bamberg. After working in the Berlin office of the family firm, Wassermann in 1912 had joined the directorate of the Deutsche Bank. Starting as Mankiewitz's assistant in the stock-exchange division, he had soon extended his interests to other branches of the bank's activities. He succeeded Mankiewitz first as *Börsendirektor*, then (in 1923) as *Sprecher*. In this position, he would play a major part in the fusion in 1929 of the Deutsche Bank and Disconto-Gesellschaft. He would continue to occupy a leading position in the directorate of the new

---

ninth largest German joint-stock company with a share capital of just over 185 million marks and some 30,000 employees (Fuchs, op. cit., p. 21). See also Pogge, op. cit., *passim*.

[14] For Mankiewitz see Felix Pinner, *Deutsche Wirtschaftsführer* (Charlottenburg, 1925), pp. 207 ff.

[15] 'Er war ein Individualist und Impressionist' (ib., p. 211). '... ein ganz seltener Rechner ... blitzschnelle Zahlenkombinatorik ... ein Mann der Tradition ... die Linie des sogenannten gesunden Menschenverstandes' (ib., pp.209 f.). A man of this type could adapt only with difficulty to a war economy and to an inflation economy not at all.

[16] For Wassermann, see Pinner, op. cit., pp. 222 f.

bank, which he helped to steer through the financial turmoil of 1931.[17] In 1933 he was forced to resign his position and he died the following year.

Oscar Wassermann's career is an interesting example of the adaptation of old-established Jewish banking families to the age of the joint-stock banks, 'einer der Fälle, in denen ein Bankier aus altem Hause vorzog, seinen Weg als Bankdirektor zu machen'.[18] It was, indeed, a remarkable development which had led from the small-town Swabian shopkeeper Amschel Elkan Wassermann (1773–1833) through the *Kgl. bayerischen Hofbankier* Emil Wasserman (1842–84) to the latter's son Oscar, speaker of the Deutsche Bank. A decisive step had, of course, been the opening of a branch office of the family bank in Berlin which had made possible the career of both Max von and Oscar Wassermann.

Besides the members of this 'apostolic chain', two further Jewish directors of the Deutsche Bank deserve mention. Elkan Heinemann,[19] whose wife was a relative of Hermann Wallich, made a rapid career in the service of the bank. Having joined it in 1885 at the bottom of the ladder, he became a deputy director in 1902, a full director 4 years later. He remained in this position until 1923, when he resigned from the bank.[20] Heinemann's speciality was to nurse, with almost scientific care and precision,[21] a number of overseas ventures, especially the Deutsche-Überseeische Elektrizitätsgesellschaft, founded in 1898. He continued on the board of that company after in 1920 it had become Chade,[22] and after he had left the service of the Deutsche Bank.

---

[17] Pinner describes Wassermann as 'nicht nur ein sehr kluger, manchmal vielleicht etwas zur Überklugheit neigender Bankier, sondern auch ein auf vielen Lebens- und Wissensgebieten gebildeter Geist, dessen dialektische Überlegenheit ihn im kollegialen Fachgremium der Deutschen Bank trotz seines verhältnismässig jungen Dienstalters, an die führende, zugleich repräsentative Stelle brachte'. Pinner, op. cit., p. 223.

[18] Seidenzahl, op. cit., n. 5 above, p. 271.

[19] For Elkan Heinemann see 'Elkan Heinemann' MS note by Fritz Seidenzahl in the archives of the Leo Baeck Institute in New York. This forms the basis of a publication in *Historisches Archiv* in 1965.

[20] Seidenzahl suggests that Heinemann was 'squeezed out' by the progress of Wassermann and Stauss. Seidenzahl, op. cit., n. 5 above, p. 6.

[21] 'Nach Erscheinung und Veranlagung mehr Gelehrter als Kaufmann', it was Heinemann's speciality 'gewisse grosse Finanzierungs- und Beteiligungsgeschäfte, namentlich auf elektrotechnischem und überseeischem Gebiet mit einer nahezu wissenschaftlichen Präzision und Gründlichkeit zu entwickeln'. Pinner, op. cit., n. 14 above, p. 223.

[22] Compania Hispano Americana de Electricidad, Madrid. For details of the formation of Chade see Seidenzahl, op. cit., n. 5 above, pp. 254 ff.

Finally among men trained by Mankiewitz in the stock market division should be mentioned Selmar Fehr, who had joined the bank in 1899 as a specialist dealer in mining shares (*Kuxenhändler*). In 1916, he became a deputy director, from 1923 to 1926 he would be a director and member of the *Vorstand*. Men of Jewish extraction thus occupied positions of prominence in the bank's directorate. From the time of its foundation, they provided about one third of the members of its *Vorstand*, several in influential positions. Again, as in the case of the Disconto-Gesellschaft, the relative prominence of Jews tended to increase with time (following the 'Siemens–Koch–Gwinner era').

If both the Disconto-Gesellschaft and the Deutsche Bank thus had 'mixed' directorates, another of the great joint-stock banks, the Dresdner, could be described as predominantly Jewish. The bank was, in essence, the creation of one man, Eugen Gutmann.[23] From its foundation in 1872 until his retirement in 1920, Gutmann stood unchallenged at its head and, during that time, succeeded in turning it from a modest provincial institute into a bank of world renown.[24]

Eugen Gutmann had been a 'rank and file' banker in Dresden in the second generation when, aged 32, he persuaded the owners of the old-established banking house Michael Kaskel to transform their firm into a joint-stock bank.[25] In 1881, over the resistance of some shareholders, a branch office was opened in Berlin: its turnover, in its first year, already exceeded that of the parent house in Dresden. In 1884, the central direction of the bank was transferred to Berlin and Eugen Gutmann also moved to the capital. The steep ascent of the Dresdner Bank began.[26]

---

[23] 'Derjenige Direktor der Dresdner Bank, der sie von den ersten Anfangsstadien, nämlich 9,6 Millionen Mark Aktienkapital im Jahre 1873, zu ihrer jetzigen Grösse, nämlich 200 Millionen Mark Aktienkapital gebracht hat, ist Eugen Gutmann, Geheimer Kommerzienrat und Konsul' (Martin, op. cit., n. 10 above, ii. 305). While Fürstenberg described him as 'der eigentliche Kopf des Unternehmens' (Fürstenberg, *Die lebensgeschichte eines deutschen Bankiers* (Wiesbaden, 1961), p. 213), Pinner in turn sees Gutmann as 'Gründer und Schöpfer' of the bank (Pinner, op. cit., n. 14 above, p. 225).
[24] For Eugen Gutmann see Kurt Hunscha, *Aus der Geschichte der Dresdner Bank 1872–1969* (Frankfurt-on-Main, 1969), Martin, op. cit., n. 10 above, pp. 305 f., Pinner, op. cit., n. 14 above, p. 225, Fürstenberg, op. cit., pp. 213 ff. and Bernstein, loc. cit., n. 3 above, pp. 743 f.
[25] Of the original capital, ⅜ was subscribed by the Kaskels, Gutmann, and a few private individuals, the rest by a consortium of joint-stock banks mainly of the second order (Hunscha, op. cit., p. 23).
[26] 'Von diesem Tag an datierte der Aufschwung der Dresdner Bank, die Eugen Gutmann allmählich zu einer Weltbank ersten Ranges gemacht hat' (Bernstein, loc. cit., n. 3 above, p. 744).

The rapid progress of the bank—as early as 1887 it became a member of the prestigious state loan syndicate (Reichsanleihekonsortium)—is attributable on the one hand to the systematic establishment of branch offices (this parallels Georg von Siemens's policy at the Deutsche Bank), on the other to Gutmann's exceptional talent for stock-exchange operations. With the capital accumulated thanks to these two activities, the bank was able to engage in successful industrial financing and flotations. A first landmark was reached when, in 1893, it took the lead in placing a 4 per cent loan of 24 million marks for the house of Krupp.[27] Then, after weathering a serious crisis in 1901, it resumed its expansion. By 1925 its turnover (*Bilanzsumme*) stood second only (if at some distance) to that of the Deutsche Bank.[28] The success of the Dresdner Bank as well as its distinctive character, Fürstenberg, in a critical appreciation, attributed to the unique personality and aptitudes of the founder: a blend of painstaking and systematic effort in creating a network of branches with a 'buccanneering spirit'[29] in carrying out—often successfully—stock-exchange and financial coups.[30] Eugen Gutmann, like other prominent directors of joint-stock banks, occupied seats on the boards of numerous industrial companies. Before 1914, he held some 34 such posts, being chairman of 7 and deputy chairman of another 4 boards.

If Eugen Gutmann dominated the Dresdner Bank until his retirement in 1920, he also gathered around him a number of capable colleagues, frequently of Jewish extraction. Thus the affairs of the bank in Dresden (where its legal seat remained until 1950) were managed by Gustav von Klemperer, a member of the *Vorstand* from

[27] Hunscha, op. cit., p. 25.   [28] Seidenzahl, op. cit., n. 5 above, p. 316.

[29] Pinner, somewhat colourfully, speaks of Gutmann as 'eine Vollblutnatur, ein Draufgänger, eine Persönlichkeit voll Konstruktion und Ideen', though sometimes carried away by his enthusiasm (Pinner, op. cit., n. 14 above, p. 225).

[30] 'Es ist für mich immer sehr interessant gewesen', writes Fürstenberg, 'festzustellen, wie die führende Persönlichkeit, die eine grosse Bank geschaffen hat, deren ganzem Betrieb einen unverwischbaren persönlichen Stempel aufdrückt. Die Dresdner Bank Eugen Gutmanns unterschied sich in grundlegender Hinsicht von der Deutschen Bank Georg von Siemens' und von der Disconto-Gesellschaft Hansemanns. Auf der einen Seite sollte es Gutmann gelingen, systematische Mitarbeiter zu finden, die in ruhiger Arbeit das Filialwesen gerade dieser Bank zu besonderer Stärke entwickelt haben. Auf der anderen Seite war Gutmann nicht ein Mann des Details, sondern besass einen bemerkenswerten Blick für grosse Gewinnmöglichkeiten und einen ausgesprochenen Börsenverstand ... Wenn ich hier andeute, dass Eugen Gutmann wirtschaftliche Vorgänge unter dem Gesichtspunkt der Hausse oder der Baisse anzusehen pflegte, so will ich den Verdiensten dieses grossen deutschen Bankiers damit nicht etwa Abbruch tun. Das vortreffliche Werk, das er hinterlassen hat, zeugt für das hohe Mass seiner Tüchtigkeit.' Fürstenberg, op. cit., n. 23 above, pp. 213 f.

1891 until 1913, when he became deputy chairman of the *Aufsichtsrat*. In the *Vorstand*, his place was then taken by his son Victor von Klemperer. More surprisingly, Gutmann acquired as a member of his directorate Julius Stern, himself the leading figure in the Nationalbank für Deutschland. Nor did Gutmann overlook members of his own family. For a period of ten years, the board included Johann Jacob Schuster, his son-in-law, a former banker from Basle. Gutmann's son Herbert, a socialite whose talents as a banker were appraised critically,[31] also formed part of the management. Gutmann's right hand, however, was Henry Nathan,[32] who had joined the Berlin branch of the bank in 1895, had been made a deputy director in 1898 and a member of the *Vorstand* in 1903. Nathan had assumed responsibility for the bank's major financial operations, both foreign and domestic, its budgetary dispositions, and its larger credit transactions. In 1920, on Gutmann's retirement, he would take over the overall direction of the bank as *primus inter pares* among its directors.[33] Of Nathan it was said that, although an excellent banker, he lacked the charisma and dynamism of his predecessor.[34] By his side worked Wilhelm Kleeman who had been taken over with the co-operative bank (*Genossenschaftsbank*) Soergel, Parrisius and Co. Kleeman had joined the *Direktorium* of the Bank as a deputy in 1907. He was to be a full member of its *Vorstand* from 1916 until 1932. Yet another member of some distinction was Samuel Ritscher, specialist in major financial transactions outside Germany. A member of the *Vorstand* from 1919 until 1923, he then joined an official financial institution. He would return to the *Vorstand* as representative of the government on the bank's reorganization after its collapse in 1931.

The Dresdner Bank, one of Germany's largest, could thus be described as a 'Jewish' enterprise. Its *Direktorium*, in 1907, besides Eugen Gutmann, consisted of *Geh.-Ober-Finanzrat* Waldemar Müller

---

[31] He is described as a man 'der bei seinen geschäftlichen Transaktionen oft keine glückliche Hand hatte' (Bernstein, loc. cit., n. 3 above, p. 744).

[32] For Henry Nathan see Pinner, op. cit., n. 14 above, p. 225 and Bernstein, loc. cit., n. 3 above, p. 744.

[33] He is described by Pinner as 'heute unbestritten der geistige Mittelpunkt der Dresdner Bank' (Pinner, op. cit., n. 14 above, p. 225).

[34] '... eine kühle, ruhige, sehr gemessene und zurückhaltende Natur, aber ein Bankier mit sachlichen Weit- und Tiefblick, mit Einfühlungsfähigkeit und klugem Verständnis für die Verschlungenheit des modernen Wirtschafts und Bankprozesses, der dem Zentrum der Probleme vielleicht näher kommt als die meisten übrigen Bankdirektoren.' He only lacked 'Instinkt ... Schwung ... Temperament um ein wirklich grosser Bankdirektor zu sein' (ib.).

(the one prominent Gentile and link with the imperial authorities), Henry Nathan, Johann Jacob Schuster, GKR *General Konsul* G. Klemperer (Dresden), Louis von Steiger (Frankfurt) (where in 1904, the Dresdner Bank had absorbed the old-established Jewish bank of Erlanger & Söhne), *Reichsbank-Direktor a. D.* A. Dalchow (a second Gentile retired official chosen for his official contacts), Felix Jüdell, and Julius Stern.

Another of the big banks in which men of Jewish extraction came to play a prominent role was the Berliner Handels-Gesellschaft.[35] This bank, founded in 1856 on the model of the Disconto-Gesellschaft (with the participation of leading Berlin private banks Mendelssohn & Co., S. Bleichröder, Robert Warschauer and Co., Gebr. Schickler (non-Jewish)) was intended as an institute to provide credit for industry and commerce. During the seventies, the bank had lost much of its former prestige and had suffered some heavy losses. By the early eighties, it was ripe for reorganization.

The attention of interested bankers had then been drawn by an economic journalist to a youthful employee of S. Bleichröder named Carl Fürstenberg,[36] who in 1883 had agreed to assume responsibility, together with two associates. The operation had proved a brilliant success. In 1902, Fürstenberg had become the senior partner (*Seniorgeschäftsinhaber*), a position he was to fill with distinction until 1930. Under Fürstenberg's direction, the BHG became the bank *par excellence* of Germany industry.

The BHG, which had no branches, catered for a twofold clientele. On the one hand, it became the banking connection of provincial banks eager to maintain their independence in the face of the expansionist tendencies of the great deposit banks. Such banks secured access to the Berlin capital market through Fürstenberg, who was ready to satisfy their capital needs without any threat to their independence. The second group of customers consisted of industrial enterprises in need of expert financial management and advice without the danger of bank control. Fürstenberg was known never to

[35] For the history of the BHG see Carl Fürstenberg, op. cit., n. 23 above, and Rolf E. Lüke, *Die Berliner Handelsgesellschaft in einem Jahrhundert deutsche Wirtschaft 1856–1956* (Berlin, 1956). See also Hans Fürstenberg, *Erinnerungen* (Düsseldorf and Vienna, 1968).

[36] For Carl Fürstenberg see, besides Fürstenberg, op. cit., n. 23 above, Zielenziger, op. cit., n. 3 above, pp. 147 ff., Pinner, op. cit., n. 14 above, pp. 201 ff., Hans Fürstenberg, op. cit., and, for a critical assessment, Paul Wallich, *Lehr- und Wanderjahre eines Bankiers* in *Zwei Generationen im deutschen Bankwesen* (Frankfurt, 1978), pp. 363 ff. *passim.*

subordinate the interests of his industrial clients to those of his own bank. Indeed it was a certain disinterestedness based on the deliberate renunciation of every form of 'expansionism' or exercise of control which accounts in large measure for Fürstenberg's great popularity as the banker of large industrial enterprises (as indeed also of provincial banks).[37] Carl Fürstenberg inspired trust.

For many years, Fürstenberg occupied more board seats than any other German banker. At the end of 1929 (he had then reached the age of 79) he would still sit on fifty boards.[38] Moreover, unlike some of his peers, Fürstenberg took a serious view of his duties as a board member. With the aid of thorough examination of a company's affairs he sought to form a soundly based judgement of the needs of its financial management. Among the many enterprises for which Fürstenberg was thus a trusted financial adviser were the AEG, where

[37] Pinner, op. cit., n. 14 above, pp. 201 f. *Die Rote Fahne* in 1920 noted with evident distaste: '... Fürstenberg wollte die Taler und Groschen des mittleren und kleinen Kapitalismus nicht, sein Institut will eine Bank des Grosskapitals sein. Es ist ihm tatsächlich gelungen, die Berliner Handelsgesellschaft als Trust des Industriegrosskapitals zu erhalten. Die Berliner Handelsgesellschaft wurde das Finanzierungsinstitut Emil Rathenaus und ist noch heute die Bank der A.E.G. Sie machte mit und förderte die ganze ungesunde Expansion der Allgemeinen Elektrizitäts-Gesellschaft ...' *Die Rote Fahne*, no. 172 (2 Sept. 1920).

A more sympathetic appreciation of Fürstenberg and the BHG was that of Georg Tischert in the *Deutsche Bergwerkszeitung* in 1929:
'... Wer wissen will, was Carl Fürstenberg für das deutsche Finanz- und Wirtschaftsleben gewesen ist, der muss einen Geschäftsbericht der Berliner Handelsgesellschaft etwa aus dem Jahre 1907 und 1913 zur Hand nehmen. Was für Namen hat dieser Mann um sich zu scharen verstanden: Emil Rathenau, Oskar Caro, Fritz von Friedländer-Fuld, Fritz Lob von den Hohenlohewerken, Müller von Consolidation, Müser von Harpen, Oechelhäuser von Dessau Gas, Oswald von Rombach, Pintsch, Brückmann von Schwartzkopf, Kestranek, Lindner von Hibernia, Segall von den Rütgerswerken, Man überfliege auch die Finanzgeschäfte dieser Jahre ... Die Berliner Handelsgesellschaft war eine grosse Emissions- und Börsenbank. Sie war führend in den Börsenbewegungen vor dem Kriege. Rombach, Rheinstahl, Bochumer Verein, Hohenlohewerke, Harpen, Hibernia, Stahlwerke Richard Lindenberg, Körting waren die Domäne der Berliner Handelsgesellschaft. Erinnert sei nur noch an Caro-Hegenscheidt und Bismarckhütte, auch an die Grundstücksinteressen, an den Konzern Lenz, an die kolonialen Unternehmungen wie Diamanten-Regie, ferner an die Süddeutschen Baumwollspinnereien. Die AEG ist ohne Carl Fürstenberg nicht zu denken. Zu dem gewaltigen Aufschwunge der deutschen Elektroindustrie ... an der imponierenden Entwicklung der Montan-Industrie sowohl des Westens wie auch Oberschlesiens hat Carl Fürstenberg in einzig dastehender Weise beigetragen. Er hat auch die deutsch-österreichischen Montanbeziehungen aufgebaut ...' Georg Tischert, *Deutsche Bergwerkszeitung*, no. 35 10 Feb. 1929).

[38] Zielenziger, op.cit., n. 3 above, 152. Fürstenberg was almost unique among *Aufsichtsräte* in that he handed over his *Aufsichtsrat* fees (*Tantiemen*) to his firm and insisted that his associates do likewise.

a close personal friendship linked him with Emil Rathenau, and the Harpener Bergbau AG, where he helped the young Director-General Robert Müser to build up the largest coal-producing enterprise in the Ruhr. In general, Fürstenberg's contribution to the tempestuous development of German industry from the mid-nineties onwards was inestimable.[39]

Within his bank, Fürstenberg was an autocrat. Of the many able men (mostly of Jewish extraction) who became his partners (*Geschäftinhaber*) in the BGH, many left after a few years. One, Paul Wallich, the son of Hermann Wallich of the Deutsche Bank, described his discouraging experiences at the BHG.[40] Walther Rathenau also, who became a *Geschäftsinhaber* in 1903, returned to the AEG five years later. Walter Merton, son of Wilhelm Merton of the Metallgesellschaft in Frankfurt, was another *Geschäftinhaber* for some years before 1914. On the other hand, Hermann Rosenberg[41] (*Geschäftsinhaber* 1883–1902) had long been Fürstenberg's close assistant. Three prominent *Geschäftsinhaber* in Fürstenberg's declining years would be Otto Jeidels (1918–38),[42] Siegfried Bieber (1919–33), and Fürstenberg's son Hans who, however, lacked his father's talents (1919–36), all men of Jewish extraction. Fürstenberg's BHG, like Gutmann's Dresdner Bank, could—so far at least as its management was concerned—be described as a 'Jewish bank'.

Jewish bankers played a hardly less prominent part in the banking institutions which would, eventually, constitute the Darmstädter und Nationalbank (Danat). The Bank für Handel und Industrie, better known as the Darmstädter Bank, had been founded in 1853 with Abraham Oppenheim as vice-president of its *Verwaltungsrat*.[43] Compared to its major rivals the BHI, under mediocre management, had

---

[39] 'Unter Fürstenberg's Leitung wird die Handelsgesellschaft das Kreditinstitut der deutschen Industrie. Ihre Entwicklung wäre undenkbar ohne das Eingreifen und ohne die Initiative Fürstenbergs ... Hier liegt die Bedeutung Carl Fürstenbergs. Dieser jüdische Bankier ist es in vielen Fällen gewesen, der zahlreichen Unternehmungen erst die Wege zu ihrem Emporsteigen geebnet hat. In der Handelsgesellschaft sammeln sich die Aktienpakete der grössten Werke des Kohlenbergbaus, der Eisenindustrie und vieler anderer Wirtschaftszweige an. Fürstenberg hätte de Möglichkeit gehabt, sich zu ihrem Beherrscher aufzuschwingen, hätte schon vor dem Kriege Truste aufbauen können. Er kennt diesen Ehrgeiz nicht.' Zielenziger, op. cit., n. 3 above, pp. 150 f.

[40] Paul Wallich, loc. cit., n. 36 above, pp. 363 ff. *passim*.

[41] For Hermann Rosenberg see Fürstenberg, op. cit., n. 23 above, *passim*.

[42] Described by Bernstein as belonging to 'den meisterhaften Finanzdiplomaten Deutschlands' (Bernstein, loc. cit., n. 3 above, p. 737).

[43] Together with the Gentile Gustav Mevissen, Oppenheim had played a prominent part not only in obtaining the concession for the bank but also in raising its initial capital.

developed slowly.[44] Then, in 1888, Jakob Riesser, for eight years a practising lawyer, had joined the *Vorstand* and, under his guidance, it had entered a dynamic phase.[45] Between 1893 and 1902, it had developed two specialities, the financing of secondary railway companies (especially in southern Germany) and the reorganization (*Sanierung*) of banks in difficulties (combined, in some cases, with a 'take-over'). In 1905, Riesser left the bank to take up a professorship at the University of Berlin and to work as a publicist.

It was through the reorganization of broken-down banks that Riesser had first met Bernhard Dernburg,[46] the banker son of a journalist, who was rapidly acquiring an enviable reputation as a successful 'company doctor'.[47] In 1901, Dernburg joined the *Vorstand* of the Darmstädter Bank, where he distinguished himself in company restructuring, notably that of Hugo Stinnes's Deutsch-Luxemburgische Bergwerks- & Hütten-Aktien-Gesellschaft. He also increased the bank's involvement in the industrial issue market. In 1906, however, Dernburg left the bank to become state secretary in the Colonial Office (*Staatssekretär im Reichskolonialamt*).

Like other joint-stock banks at this time, the Darmstädter Bank during the Riesser-Dernburg era had absorbed several private banks with Jewish connections. Thus, in 1902, it had taken over the Breslauer Disconto Bank and with it Siegmund Bodenheimer, who was to play a prominent part in its later management. With the take-over of the once prestigious house of Robert Warschauer & Co. two years later, its directorate was joined by Georg von Simson[48] and Paul Bernhard.

---

[44] 'Neben diesen Banken behauptete die Bank für Handel und Industrie ihren altangesehenen Platz, obgleich man von einer grossen Aktivität bei diesem Institut kaum mehr sprechen konnte.' Fürstenberg, op. cit., n. 23 above, p. 214.

[45] 'Aus diesem Kreise ragte der Rechtsanwalt Dr. Riesser hervor, der später auch auf wissenschaftlichem und politischem Gebiet Bemerkenswertes geleistet hat und Vorsitzender des Verwaltungsrats der mit der Nationalbank für Deutschland fusionierten Bank geworden ist,' (ib., p. 215). Riesser has been described as 'Einer der grössten Führer des deutschen Bankgewerbes und des deutschen Kaufmannsstandes überhaupt' (Bernstein, loc. cit., n. 3 above, p. 794).

[46] For Dernburg see W. Schiefel, *Bernhard Dernburg* (Zürich, n.d.), Fürstenberg, op. cit., n. 23 above, pp. 429 ff. and Bernstein, loc. cit., n. 3 above, p. 747. Although a baptized half-Jew, Dernburg was regarded by friend and foe alike as a 'Jewish banker'.

[47] In banking circles, Bernhard Dernburg became known as the 'Sanitätsrat'. Fürstenberg, op. cit., n. 23 above, p. 430.

[48] Simson, though of Jewish origin, was, like Dernburg, baptized already in the third generation. Whether by accident or design, the Darmstädter Bank appears, to some extent, as the bank of baptized Jews or half-Jews.

In 1925 the Darmstädter Bank, once more steadily falling back behind its rivals, would join forces with the Nationalbank to form the Darmstädter und Nationalbank (Danat). The Nationalbank für Deutschland,[49] dominant partner in the Nationalbank, could be described as Jewish. Its origins went back to 1881. In 1907, with a share capital of 80 million marks, its most prominent directors were Richard Witting (originally Witkowski, a former mayor of Posen and brother of the journalist Maximilian Harden) and the banker Julius Stern.[50] Stern, described by Carl Fürstenberg as a 'talented banker',[51] had been close to the bank since its foundation and had helped to raise it to the rank of a 'big bank' (Grossbank). Besides Witting and Stern, the directorate had contained several Jewish bankers of lesser calibre. The brightest star in the firmament of the new Danat bank, however, and the man who would, for some years, make it one of the country's leading joint-stock banks, was Jakob Goldschmidt,[52] whose career, falling into the period of the Weimar Republic, will be considered later.

One further bank, though not quite ranking with the great join-stock banks in Berlin, should be mentioned in the present context, the Schaaffhausensche Bankverein in Cologne. This was an old-established regional bank, closely connected with major industrial enterprises on the Rhine and Ruhr.[53] In spite of opening an office in Berlin in 1891 (and though one of its leading men, Karl Klönne, had become a prominent director of the Deutsche Bank), Schaaffhausen had remained a regional banking institute. At a time of widespread amalgamations on the German banking scene, Schaaffhausen in 1903, through the intermediary of the Cologne banker Louis Hagen, entered into a close association with the fast-growing Dresdner Bank which became effective in 1904. The new arrangements brought into

---

[49] For the Nationalbank für Deutschland, product of the amalgamation of two Jewish private banks, see (somewhat inadequately) Dr Max Lewy, *Die Nationalbank für Deutschland zu Berlin 1881–1909* (Berlin, 1911).

[50] For Julius Stern see Bernstein, loc. cit., n. 3 above, p. 748.

[51] 'ein begabter Bankier', Fürstenberg, op. cit., n. 23 above, p. 215.

[52] For Jakob Goldschmidt, see Bernstein, loc. cit., n. 3 above, pp. 745 ff., Pinner, op. cit., n. 14 above, p. 226, and Zielenziger, op. cit., n. 3 above, pp. 264 ff. Pinner describes Goldschmidt as 'ein echtes Finanztalent mit ausgesprochenem Bankiersinstinkt und sehr anschlägigem Kopf'. Pinner, op. cit., p. 226. He also refers to Goldschmidt's rise 'vom kleinen Bankangestellten zum mächtigsten Grossbankdirektor'. Zielenziger, op. cit., p. 265.

[53] For the history of the A. Schaaffhausensche Bankverein see Jacob Riesser, *Die deutschen Grossbanken und ihre Konzentration* (Jena, 1912), pp. 408 ff.

prominence *Geh. Regierungsrat* Siegfried Samuel who, having served an apprenticeship with S. Bleichröder, had become a director of Schaaffhausen in 1900. Associated closely with several enterprises of the Ruhr, Samuel became the bank's chief representative on the boards of companies with which it was prominently associated.

Schaaffhausen's association with the Dresdner Bank—concluded for a period of thirty years—did not last. Following disagreements, it was terminated with effect from 1 January 1909. However, Schaaffhausen was still looking for a partner among the great joint-stock banks. In 1914, it entered into a new association, this time with the Disconto-Gesellschaft. It was a partnership destined to last. The Disconto-Gesellschaft sent to Cologne one of its leading men, Georg Solmssen, to supervise and direct the reorganization of Schaaffhausen. Solmssen stayed in Cologne from 1914 until 1921.[54] Schaaffhausen, though remaining nominally autonomous, ceased in this time to rank among the major joint-stock banks.[55]

The financial world of Cologne contained, however, a celebrity, a man who, from modest beginnings, was able, thanks largely to extraordinary skills in corporate manipulation (in which he, to a certain extent, anticipates Jakob Goldschmidt of the Danat bank), to acquire a leading place in the German corporate banking élite. Louis Heyman Levy, better known as Louis Hagen (1855–1932),[56] was the son of a relatively modest private banker in Cologne (who, however, had increased his capital by marriage (1852) to Johanna, daughter of Alexander Coppel, the well-to-do Jewish metal manufacturer in Solingen). After an apprenticeship in the banking firm of Jacob Landau, he had on his father's death (1873) entered the paternal bank

---

[54] See Zielenziger, op. cit., n. 3 above, p. 124.

[55] The Commerz und Disconto—later Commerz- und Privatbank—is included among the big joint-stock banks neither by Fürstenberg nor by Riesser who, perhaps unjustly, allows it no more than a footnote in one of his appendices (Riesser, op. cit., p. 722 n. 2). Certainly figures for turnover, creditors, and debtors for the twenties show it lagging well behind the big deposit banks. However, between 1926 and 1929 it was gaining rapidly on its nearest rival, the Disconto-Gesellschaft (Seidenzahl, op. cit., n. 5 above, p. 316). The only man of some prominence among directors of Jewish extraction was Curt Sobernheim, who had joined the *Vorstand* in 1911 and whose main responsibility was the development of links with both German and foreign merchants and industrialists. Pinner describes him as a 'gewandte Vermittlernatur' (Pinner, op. cit., n. 14 above, p. 227).

[56] For Louis Hagen see H. Kellenbenz, *Rheinisch-westfälische Wirtschaftsbiographien*, 10 (Münster, 1974), and W. E. Mosse, 'Zwei Präsidenten der Kölner Industrie- und Handelskammer: Louis Hagen und Paul Silverberg' in *Köln und das rheinische Judentum* (Cologne 1984), pp. 308 ff.

of A. Levy. In 1886—his ability to secure well-situated private clients had gained him entry into Cologne society—he married Emma Hagen, daughter of a (Gentile) metal merchant. At the same time, he became a convert to Catholicism. In 1893, he adopted his wife's name, under which he would become famous.

Through his acquaintance with the founder of the Rheinisch-Westfälische Pulverfabriken, Hagen became associated with the explosives industry and in 1890 co-founder of and major shareholder in the leading enterprise in this field, the Köln-Rottweiler Pulverfabriken. This was the start of a career in corporate industry, in the course of which Hagen became its leading 'marriage broker'. Among the fusions which he helped to negotiate (each profitable to himself and each providing a seat on one or more boards), perhaps the most conspicuous were those associating Schaaffhausen first with the Dresdner Bank and subsequently with the Disconto-Gesellschaft, and the linkages between Felten Guilleaume-Carlswerk in Cologne-Mülheim and the AEG and between the Hörder Bergwerks- und Hütten AG and Phoenix AG für Bergbau und Hüttenbetrieb. On the eve of the war of 1914 Hagen carried out, in association with Simon, *Freiherr* von Oppenheim, the transformation of the Scherl publishing empire into the Deutscher Verlagsverein in Düsseldorf. Finally, in 1922, Louis Hagen, after many years of co-operation, would become a partner in Sal. Oppenheim jun. & Co. As such, he would represent their joint interests on the boards of no fewer than sixty-three companies. Hagen, by his 'brokering' talents, had become a prominent member of the corporate banking élite as an outsider, that is, one operating outside the structures of the great joint-stock banks.

Another such outsider, by a curious coincidence Hagen's brother-in-law, was the lawyer *Geh. Justizrat* Maximilian Kempner (1854–1927).[57] Kempner's major corporate achievement was the formation of the Potash Syndicate (1909–10) whose chairman he would remain for many years. He would also be prominently associated with other industrial enterprises, among them AG für chemische Produkte vorm. Scheidemandel (chemical products from bones), and Chamotte-Didier (fireproof ceramics). With Kempner, who lived in Berlin, must be named another lawyer (academic as much as practical), Julius Flechtheim, who had moved from Berlin to Cologne in 1901.[58] Flechtheim became managing director of the Vereinigte Köln-

---

[57] For Kempner see Bernstein, loc. cit., n. 3 above, p. 781.
[58] For Julius Flechtheim see ibid., pp. 653 f.

Rottweiler Pulverfabriken in Berlin and subsequently joined the directorate of IG Farben. Of the many boards of which he was a member, the most notable were those of the AEG, the Deutsche Bank and the Gelsenkirchener Bergwerks-AG. Flechtheim, who was often called on for 'expert opinions' on economic matters, thus became, like Hagen and Kempner, a prominent member of the corporate élite. His career, like that, to a lesser extent, of Maximilian Kempner, reveals a curious mixture of legal (both practising and academic), managerial (particularly in the case of Flechtheim), corporate, and financial talents. The two could be described as 'universal capitalists' without, however, themselves either possessing or acquiring conspicuous wealth.

If one looks at the 'banking sector' of the corporate élite as a whole, a number of facts emerge. In the first place, perhaps unexpectedly, this is a completely new group. Its reservoir, with insignificant exceptions, is not to be found among the traditional Jewish banking families of Berlin. Indeed, with few exceptions (among them Eugen Gutmann, in the second generation from a small banking house in Dresden, Louis Hagen, from a similar house in Cologne, and Oscar Wassermann, from a junior branch of an old-established banking dynasty in Bamberg), members of the joint-stock élite are not drawn from Jewish private banking (though a few members would enter joint-stock banking in less than prominent positions through the amalgamations of 1904). Instead, the group was recruited from intellectuals (Adolf Salomonsohn, Jacob Riesser, Bernhard Dernburg), from relatively prosperous Jewish merchants in the middle range (Carl Fürstenberg, Max Steinthal), from modest business (Hermann Wallich), or though this was exceptional, from the Jewish petty bourgeoisie (Jakob Goldschmidt). Still others emerged from modest beginnings about which no details are available (Paul Mankiewitz, Maximilian Kempner). Almost without exception, these were self-made men, more particularly in the economic sphere, though those from an intellectual background at least came from families of some distinction.

Besides having this distinctive background, members of the corporate élite in the 'banking sector', almost without exception were provincials drawn from places as far apart as Bamberg, Darmstadt, Bonn, Cologne, Hanover, Dresden, Inowrazlaw and Kempen in the province of Posen, and Danzig. Only Max Steinthal was a 'Berliner born and bred' as were the later Salomonsohn-Solmssens. Perhaps significantly, not one of the major Jewish directors of joint-stock banks was a native of Frankfurt, possibly because Prussia was so detested that the adventurous would seek their fortunes in London or New York rather than in the Prussian capital.

It is also possible to distinguish, among the joint-stock banking élite, three separate generations. The first of these is that of the pioneers of the early banks: Adolf Salomonsohn, Jacob Riesser, Hermann Wallich, Kilian (von) Steiner, and Bernhard Dernburg. These are followed by the great figures of the 'classical' age, towering among them Eugen Gutmann, Carl Fürstenberg, Arthur Salomonsohn, and Louis Hagen, and including men like Max Steinthal, Paul Mankiewitz, and Maximilian Kempner. Lastly, there is the third generation of 'heirs', prominent among them Oscar Wassermann, Georg Solmssen, and Henry Nathan, and including, as an 'outsider', the buccaneer Jakob Goldschmidt.

Members of this group, heterogeneous in many respects and not rooted in the traditional Jewish economic élite (few acquired large fortunes, few came from old-established families, and many, though not all, chose to dispense with titles), shared certain common features. The majority, however influential, managed the capital of others rather than their own. Indeed Maximilian Kempner and Louis Hagen were forerunners, with the later Jakob Goldschmidt as a high priest, of the next phase of capitalist development, the formation of large industrial combines by the successful manipulation of share capital. Again these, as already indicated, were self-made men, though with a tendency to dynasty formation, successful in the case of the Salomonsohn-Solmssen (somewhat less so in those of the Walliches, Gutmanns, and Fürstenbergs to whom, from a different segment of the corporate élite, might be added the Loewes and Rathenaus). Attempts at 'dynasty formation' were resisted by corporate structures and usually frustrated by the almost invariably inferior commercial talents (or outside interests, often of an intellectual nature) of the heirs.

II

A separate segment of the corporate élite consisted of industrialists and merchants. This can itself be subdivided. Its senior stratum was composed of men who had successfully integrated family firms into larger corporate structures, prominent among them Isidor Loewe, Fritz Friedländer, and Eduard Arnhold. Such men, through board membership of large joint-stock companies, had become part of the corporate economic sector. Others, Wilhelm Merton and Benno Orenstein come to mind, had achieved a similar result mainly through corporate representation on the boards of their own companies. These men and their enterprises represent the transitional stage between the private family firm and the corporate structure of interlocking joint-stock companies. While, from a managerial point of view, such enterprises still bore a resemblance to private firms, their capital structure (indeed the need for much larger capital resources than their owners could normally muster) ensured their firm integration into the corporate business sector.

A second component of the corporate industrial élite consisted of the managing directors (*Generaldirektoren*) of major companies, of whom Albert Ballin (1857–1918) of the Hamburg-Amerikanische Paketfahrt-Aktien-Gesellschaft (Hapag) may be taken as the prototype.[59] Of humble origin in the Jewish petty bourgeoisie—his father, owner of a small shipping agency, had died when Ballin was 17—Albert Ballin, by outstanding ability and drive, achieved a position where he could justly be described as 'the uncrowned king of Hamburg' and 'the greatest Hamburger' (no pun intended).[60] Ballin's early career had been linked to the paternal shipping agency which he had joined at 17 and of which he had become partner and sole director four years later. While extending the agency, modernizing its methods, and linking it to some British shipping lines, he did not long remain content with these activities. His ambition was to develop his own shipping fleet.

In fact, Ballin found employment first with the Norddeutsche Lloyd in Bremen (where he organized the steerage transportation of emigrants), then with the Carr Line in Hamburg. When, in 1886, the Union Line of which Carr had become a partner, joined the Hapag, the latter, then a stagnating shipping line of no great importance, acquired the man who was to give it (and the port of Hamburg) world renown. It was a symbolically fitting start to the career of a leading member of the corporate élite.

Upon joining the Hapag in 1886, Ballin was placed in charge of the passenger department. Two years later, on joining the *Vorstand*, he

---

[59] Among the massive literature on Albert Ballin, the following might be mentioned as useful appreciations of the man and his work: Zielenziger, op. cit., n. 3 above, pp. 175 ff., Pinner, op. cit., n. 14 above, pp. 133 ff. and Lamar Cecil, *Albert Ballin* (Princeton, 1967).

[60] Pinner, op. cit., n. 14 above, pp. 133 f.

gave up his partnership in the family agency. In 1900, Ballin became *Generaldirektor* of the Hapag, a post he would occupy until his death in 1918.

Ballin's achievement, from his entry into the Hapag until 1914, is reflected in the figures showing the growth of the company.[61] Between 1886 and 1914, its share capital rose from 15 to 180 million marks, the quotation of its shares from 74 to 134. Its loans increased from 6 to 73 million marks, its reserves from 3 to 43 million. While the annual profit in the year of Ballin's joining had amounted to 2 million marks, it had, by 1913, risen to 40 million. Last but not least, the tonnage of the Hapag's fleet had grown from 65,000 to 1,500,000 tons.

Ballin's prestige, in his latter years, was unrivalled, resting on organizational and technical achievement in creating the world's largest shipping line (with technical innovations like new combined passenger and cargo vessels and the largest and most luxurious ships afloat) and on his international reputation (gained largely through outstanding skill in international 'shipping diplomacy', the negotiation of a succession of pool agreements, and the well-known favour extended to him by the Emperor Wilhelm II (proud of the world-wide impact of 'his' major shipping line). It was a striking career, if not an uncontroversial one,[62] for a lower middle-class Jew, one moreover though married to a Gentile, who, refused to abandon the religion of his fathers.[63]

Other managing directors of Jewish origin, though not attaining to Ballin's eminence, helped to build up substantial industrial enterprises. A number of these were to be found in the chemical industry. Thus *Konsul* Sally Segall (1867–1925), following years in the tropics, setting up branch organizations for Orenstein & Koppel, on his return to Germany became managing director of the Rütgers-Werke in Charlottenburg, producers, above all of impregnating fluids. In 1907, with a share capital of 12 million marks, Rütgers ranked among the

[61] E. Friedegg, *Millionen und Millionäre* (Berlin, 1914), p. 383.
[62] Ballin became, for anti-Semitic circles, a symbol of the new capitalist forces that were destroying their traditional way of life. 'Many of these workers [non-socialist artisans and handicraftsmen] looked to the crown for protection and redress, and they were therefore alarmed when they noted the influence which Ballin seemed to enjoy at court. "It has come to the point," one critic [the antisemitic Reichstag deputy Böckler] lamented, "that our highest echelons are Ballinized (*verballinisiert*), that foreigners from Palestine and America enjoy entrée even at the uppermost steps of the throne, while the simple, hardworking German people, our craftsmen, small businessmen, our peasantry — ... their path has been made difficult." [sic].' Cecil, op. cit., p. 132.
[63] Ballin's adopted daughter also was a Gentile.

hundred largest firms.[64] At Segall's suggestion, the Rütgers-Werke were amalgamated with the Deutsche Petroleum AG in Berlin which, in 1907, had a nominal share capital of 20 million marks. Segall, thereupon, became chairman of its board. *Generaldirektor* M. Salomon, in turn, was founder of the AG für chemische Produkte vorm. Scheidemandel in Berlin already referred to which, in 1927 (though not in 1907), figured among the hundred largest firms, with a nominal share capital of 25 million marks.

The lawyer Julius Flechtheim, a close associate of Louis Hagen, became, as already indicated, managing director of the Vereinigte Köln-Rottweiler Pulverfabriken in Berlin, which figured among the hundred largest industrial companies in 1887 and again in 1907 with a nominal share capital respectively of 5.76 and 16.5 milliion marks.

Another Jewish member of the managerial élite was Dr Alfred Berliner (1861–1943).[65] A physicist, born in Breslau, Berliner had entered the service of Siemens & Halske as an engineer (*Projektierungsingenieur*) in 1888. After three years in charge of the firm's Chicago office, he returned to Berlin to its communications division (*Verkehrsabteilung*). He became its director in 1900 and, the following year, entered the directorate (*Vorstand*) of Siemens & Halske. In 1903, he moved to the recently formed Siemens & Schuckertwerke as their managing director while retaining his directorship of Siemens & Halske AG. He thus came to occupy a key position in the Siemens concern.[66] Berliner's ambition, expansionism, and drive brought him into rivalry and indeed conflict with Wilhelm von Siemens, board chairman of the parent company. Although supported by the Deutsche Bank, the chief financier of the Siemens concern, Berliner in the end lost the battle. In 1912, he was replaced by Carl Friedrich von

---

[64] Details of the hundred largest industrial companies in Germany in 1887, 1907, and 1927 in Jürgen Kocka and Hannes Siegrist, 'Die hundert grössten deutschen Industrieunternehmen im späten 19. und frühen 20. Jahrhundert' in Norbert Horn/Jürgen Kocka, *Recht und Entwicklung der Grossunternehmen im 19. und frühen 20. Jahrhundert* (Göttingen, 1979) pp. 55ff. and Hannes Siegrist, 'Deutsche Grossunternehmen vom späten 19. Jahrhundert bis zur Weimarer Republik' in *Geschichte und Gesellschaft* 6. Jahrgang 1980/Heft 1.
[65] For Alfred Berliner see J. Kocka, *Unternehmensverwaltung und Angestelltenschaft* (Stuttgart, 1969) pp. 391, 438f. and 454ff.
[66] Kocka observes that Berliner combined technical and commercial talents to an exceptional degree. (Kocka, *op. cit.* p. 391 n.34). He became Siemens & Schuckert's 'most powerful director' (mächtigster Geschäftsführer). (*ibid.* p. 391). He was influential also in the parent concern as a member of both its directorate and finance committee (*ibid.* pp. 438f.).

Siemens, the following year, given the 'consolation prize' of board membership of Siemens & Halske. The large shareholder of the erstwhile family firm had triumphed over the talented and ambitious manager without capital.[67]

More fortunate than Berliner was his contemporary Dr Emil Guggenheimer (1860–1925), director of the Ver. Maschinenfabrik Augsburg-Nürnberg, a joint-stock company since 1898 which, in 1907, figured among the hundred largest enterprises with a nominal share capital of 12.34 million marks.[68] Also engaged in engineering was the AG für Feld- und Kleinbahnbedarf (Orenstein & Koppel), managed by Benno Orenstein (1851–1926). Its nominal share capital in 1907, 11 million marks, placed it in the top hundred. Benno Orenstein was, in fact, an 'intermediate' figure, as, though without significant capital of his own, he was not only the managing director but also co-founder of the enterprise. (In this, his position resembles that of the more famous Emil Rathenau to be considered later.)

Another member of the Jewish 'directorial' élite was Walter Sobernheim (born in 1869), stepson of the banker Jacob Landau, who, in 1903, had become a director of the Aktienbrauerei Gesellschaft Friedrichshöhe vorm. Patzenhofer in Berlin, and four years later its managing director. In 1920, Sobernheim would help to bring about the fusion of Patzenhofer with the Schultheiss Brauerei in Berlin which made Schultheiss-Patzenhofer the largest brewery company in Europe. Since Walter Sobernheim's major corporate activities belong to the period after the First World War, they will be considered later.

A very different type of Jewish company director was Heinrich Caro (1834–1910), an eminent dyestuff chemist who in 1868 had joined BASF as director of scientific research. In 1883 he had become a member of its directorate. Another Jewish chemist who played a significant part in corporate management, *Geheimrat* Dr phil., Dr-Ing.

---

[67] 'Im Sturz Berliners und Sieg Siemens' erwies sich dass in diesem Unternehmen weiterbestehende Übergewicht des kontrollierenden und disponierenden Grossaktionärs und 'Erben', der sich nicht auf seinen Aufsichtsratssitz beschränkte, sondern sich *quasi* als Generaldirektor in den Vorstand hineinschob, über den brillianten, anerkannten, aus eigener Kraft aufgestiegenen und als Vorstandsvorsitzender nach der höchsten Macht im Unternehmen—nach der des Generaldirektors—greifenden Direktor ohne Kapitalbesitz, einen Typ der generall in den nächsten Jahrzehnten an Einfluss gewinnen sollte.' (*ibid.* p. 456).

[68] 'Ein vielseitiger Kaufmann und Gelehrter war der Geheime Justizrat Dr. Emil Guggenheimer . . . Er war nicht nur Vorstand der grössten Bayerischen Maschinenfabrik Augsburg-Nürnberg, der er zu grosser Blüte verholfen hat, sondern auch einer der Führer des Reichsverbandes der Deutschen Industrie . . .' Kaznelson, *op. cit.* p. 769.

h.c. Franz Oppenhim,[69] whose mother Margarete was a daughter of the banker Alexander Mendelssohn, had entered, in 1880, the AG für Anilinfabrikation (Agfa)[70] in Treptow, of which his brother-in-law Dr Paul Mendelssohn-Bartholdy was managing director. (The Mendelssohns had participated in the founding of Agfa.) A trained chemist, Oppenheim had first entered the business 'temporarily' in 1880 as a 'stand-in' for his seriously ill brother-in-law (who died shortly afterwards of a heart attack). Six years later, Oppenheim had joined the directorate. In 1899, on the resignation of C. A. (von) Martius, Franz Oppenheim had become its leading personality, a position he would retain until the Agfa became part of IG Farben in 1925. It was Oppenheim who directed the Agfa, lagging somewhat behind the 'big three' in dyestuff manufacture, into the promising new field of photography,[71] and, additionally into that of synthetic fibres (*Kunstseide*). In 1899, when Oppenheim took over the management, the firm employed 50 chemists, 90 office, and 1,500 manual workers. Its nominal share capital amounted to 5 million marks. When it joined IG Farben in 1925, it had 1,370 chemists, engineers, and commercial employees while the number of manual workers stood at 9.200. The nominal share capital had risen to 58 million gold marks.[72]

A yet further company with a man of Jewish origin prominent in its management during the crucial phase of its growth was the clumsily named Continental-Caoutchouc- und Gutta-Percha Compagnie AG (generally known as Conti) in Hanover.[73] GKR Dr.-Ing. h.c. Siegmund Seligmann (1853–1925)[74] had entered the firm in 1876,

[69] For Franz Oppenheim see manuscript history of the Agfa in the Bayer archive, Leverkusen pp. 36ff. I have to thank the *Bayer AG* in Leverkusen and their chief archivist Dr. Göb for permission to consult materials in their archives.

[70] The *A.G. für Anilinfabrikation* does not figure in the list of the hundred largest industrial enterprises for 1907. It reached that status only with an issue of shares to the nominal value of 5 million *mark* in that year which brought its total nominal share capital up to 14 million *mark*. For the capital issues of *Agfa* see *Acten der AG für Anilin-Fabrikation* zu Berlin Abt. 1 12 Bd 2 in the Bayer archive in Leverkusen.

[71] 'Er hat photographische Industrie bei uns geschaffen, ohne dass er ein Photograph war, und ebenso anderes überragend wichtige, ohne das sachliche Specialkönnen, das unsere Zeit für die Voraussetzung des besonderen Erfolges und seiner Anerkennung ansieht.' Firtz Haber, 'Franz Oppenheim zum Gedächtnis am Jahrestag seines Todes' in *Zeitschrift für angewandte Chemie* (1930), 43. [72] Ib., p. 143.

[73] While Conti did not rank among the hundred largest companies in terms of nominal share capital in 1907, it did so in 1927.

[74] For some details on Siegmund Seligmann see, besides Bernstein, loc. cit., n. 3 above, p. 781, E. G. Lowenthal, 'Siegmund Seligmann, Industrieller in Hannover' in *Allgemeine jüdische Wochenzeitung* (Düsseldorf, 24 Sept. 1971), and the same, 'Fakten mit und ohne Kommentar, Zur Firmengeschichte von Continental', ibid. (2 June 1972).

originally as an accountant. Three years later, he had joined the board of directors. Seligmann, a 'self-made' man, was closely associated with the rise of Conti. On joining its management, he had found a business employing 250 workers. When he died in 1925, the total number of those employed was 15,000. The main activitity of Conti was, as it well known, the manufacture of car-tyres.

To the managerial élite of Jewish extraction also belonged Victor Zuckerkandl (already referred to), an Austrian regular officer who moved to Gleiwitz to become the first managing director of the Oberschlesische Eisenindustrie AG.[75] Zuckerkandl (1851–1927), after abandoning the military service for reasons of health, in 1881 had joined the wire factory, formerly Heinrich Kern & Co., in Gleiwitz, then managed by Oscar Caro. When, in 1887 it was merged into the Oberschlesische Eisenindustrie AG für Bergbau und Hüttenbetrieb, Zuckerkandl was appointed first commercial director of the new company. In 1904, he became its managing director. The nominal share capital of Obereisen, in 1907 was 28 million marks, while its employees numbered 9,500.[76] Less eminent than Zuckerkandl were managers of Jewish origin connected with other Silesian-based enterprises; among them Adolf Nothmann and later Hans Bie, managing directors of Friedländer's Oberschlesische Kokswerke und Chemische Fabriken AG in Berlin, and KR Emil Marx[77] (almost certainly of Jewish origin) (1858–1907), managing director of the Bismarckhütte, part of the Kattowitzer AG für Eisenhüttenbetrieb.

The most important managerial enterprise directed by men of Jewish origin, however, was beyond a doubt the Allgemeine Elektrizitäts-Gesellschaft, the AEG. Three men—two of them natives of Breslau—guided the mammoth concern from its modest beginnings in 1883 until the eve of the Great Depression of 1929: Emil Rathenau (1838–1915),[78] Felix Deutsch (1858–1928),[79] and Paul Mamroth

---

[75] For Viktor Zuckerkandl see Ernst Koenigsfeld, 'Viktor Zuckerkandl' in *Gleiwitzer-Beuthener-Tarnowitzer Heimatblatt*, 21, no. 1 (Jan. 1971) 19 ff. and Alfons Perlick, *Oberschlesische Berg und Hüttenleute* (Kitzingen/1953), pp. 191 f.

[76] 'Ein gründlicher Kennis der Bedürfnisse und Aufnahmefähigkeit der für die oberschlesische Industrie erreichbaren und zu behauptenden Märkte und ein energischer Organisator, hat er wesentlich dazu beigetragen, die Werke der genannten Gesellschaft den Fortschritten der Technik gemäss auszubauen und ihrer Produktion immer weitere Absatzgebiete zu erschliessen' (from an obituary notice, quoted in Perlick, op. cit., p. 192). Zuckerkandl also became known as the initiator of a private retirement pensions scheme for his employees and workers.

[77] For Emil Marx, a 'self-made man', see Perlick, op. cit., pp. 188 f.

[78] For Emil Rathenau see Felix Pinner, *Emil Rathenau und das elektrische Zeitalter*

(1859–?). (Mamroth left the directorate of the AEG in 1927 and died after 1930.[80])

Emil Rathenau, unlike other members of the Jewish managerial élite (perhaps nearest to him are Wilhelm Merton and Franz Oppenheim, though, in both cases, there are important differences), was the descendant of two established commercial families. However, the modest fortune assembled by Rathenau's paternal grandfather had since dwindled as a result of unsuccessful business ventures. Emil Rathenau's parents, in consequence, had had little capital to leave to their son. Emil Rathenau, in fact, was a rare case of the offspring of two declining entrepreneurial families of the age of early industrialization rising to prominence in the corporate élite of the age of full industrialization.

Following a good secondary education, Emil Rathenau had been apprentice in a machine-building establishment owned by his maternal grandfather. For a period of four years, he had worked 'at the bench'. Then a modest inheritance had helped him finance engineering studies at *Technische Hochschulen* in Hanover and Zurich. Following this (again in the best tradition of the Gentile artisan of an earlier generation), he had joined the establishment of August Borsig in Berlin. However, though valued by his employer, Rathenau felt that the work offered little scope and soon left on friendly terms. He then began a number of slightly belated 'Wanderjahre', working mainly in British factories.

In 1865, in associated with another aspring entrepreneur of Jewish origin, Rathenau bought a small engineering works. Marriage into a 'middle-range' Jewish banking family made possible the construction of a larger and more modern factory. During the '*Gründerjahre*' of hectic flotations, the firm, with the assistance of a Berlin bank, was converted into a joint-stock company. Rathenau—wisely as it turned out—took the payment for transferring his assets to the new company in cash rather than, as was more usual, in shares. In the financial crisis of 1873 the bank which had floated the company went into liquidation. The factory, with which Rathenau had severed all connections,

(Leipzig, 1918) and the same, *Deutsche Wirtschaftsführer* (Charlottenburg, 1925), pp. 11 ff. See also Zielenziger, op. cit., n. 3 above, pp. 125 ff. and Jürgen Kocka, 'Siemens und der aufhaltsame Aufstieg der AEG' in *Tradition*, 3–4 (1972).

[79] For Felix Deutsch see Pinner, *Deutsche Wirtschaftsführer*, op. cit., pp. 259 ff.

[80] For Paul Mamroth, who has received less attention than Emil Rathenau or Felix Deutsch, see Pinner, *Emil Rathenau*, op. cit., pp.397 f. and Bernstein, loc. cit., n. 3 above, pp. 774 f.

eventually passed to Ludwig Loewe & Co. and became part of the Deutsche Waffen- und Munitions Fabriken. Rathenau, with a relatively modest fortune of ¾ million marks, from 1875 until 1883 lived the life of a comfortably-off, underemployed, and unsatisfied *rentier*.

Some features of Rathenau's 'first career' are worth nothing. That career, in a curious way, reproduced as late as the fifties and sixties, at least outwardly, those of earlier Gentile engineers with an artisan background. Yet there are significant differences and there is little doubt that these could be attributed mainly to the 'Jewish factor'. Rathenau, unlike his Gentile counterparts, came from a moderately prosperous bourgeois background. Unlike many, he had a good secondary education. Quite unusually, he served his apprenticeship in a factory owned by his grandfather. Again, he pursued his engineering studies not at the Königliche Gewerbeinstitut in Berlin but at the engineering academies of Hanover and Zurich. Reflecting the movement of the generations, he then found employment not with F. A. Egells but with August Borsig, himself a former Egells employee. Where the budding Gentile entrepreneur, typically, began with a small workshop, Rathenau, in partnership with Julius Valentin, bought a modest factory. Significantly, where the Gentile entrepreneur would supply capital deficiencies through a 'sleeping partner' (whether relative or friend), Rathenau, from the start, drew on banking capital. (This may, however, reflect simply the development of capitalism in the later generation.) Yet even allowing for these differences, Emil Rathenau's career, up to this point, bore many marks of the entrepreneurship of an earlier age. (By contrast, the brothers Loewe, Benno Orenstein, or Arthur Koppel had neither served apprenticeships, served as 'journeymen' nor studied engineering.)

Rathenau's second entrepreneurial career which would make him a leading member of the German corporate élite formally began in 1883 with the setting up of the Deutsche Edison Gesellschaft für angewandte Elektricität AG with a nominal share capital of 5 million marks. Two years earlier, at a Paris exhibition, Rathenau had seen the inventor demonstrate his new electric light bulb. Impressed, he had at once acquired the German patent rights. In 1882, he had characteristically, set up a company mainly to publicize the new invention. The modest risk capital (250,000 marks) had been provided—again characteristically—by Jewish private banks: Jacob Landau and the Nationalbank für Deutschland (in which Landau had an interest), the

Breslauer Diskontobank, and Gebr. Sulzbach in Frankfurt-on-Main. (It is interesting to speculate what would have happened had the Landaus and Sulzbachs not invested modestly in the projects of the suspect failed entrepreneur. Would Rathenau have been able to raise the means himself? Would he have found other sponsors? Or is it possible that there might have been no AEG?)

In 1883, the Deutsche Edison Gesellschaft für angewandte Elektricität AG was founded for the production and sale of electric light bulbs in co-operation with the Edison company in Paris and with Siemens & Halske in Berlin. It was the original consortium of Jewish banks which raised the share capital of nominally 5 million marks on condition that Rathenau not only avoided competition with the firmly established Siemens but, indeed, entered into contractual relationships with him.[81] It was agreed that, while Siemens would build the dynamos, Rathenau would produce the electric bulbs and set up the central generating plant.[82] Moreover a distrustful Jacob Landau had also thoughtfully provided Rathenau with a financial controller in the person of Felix Deutsch.

In 1884, Rathenau concluded an agreement with the city of Berlin under which, in return for permission to lay electric cables under the city streets, he undertook to supply electric current at an agreed price. At the same time, Rathenau established the Städtische Elektricitäts-Werke in Berlin with a nominal share capital of 3 million marks (subscribed in part by Deutsche Edison). The electricity company undertook to buy from Rathenau's firm all machinery, materials, and lamps at preferential prices. Rathenau's company, then proceeded to construct Berlin's first electrical power-station. Demand, however, was slow in coming. During its first four years, the parent company paid the modest dividend of 4 per cent, 4 per cent, 5 per cent, and 4 per cent respectively.[83] Indeed, the first decade of the company would be described by Felix Deutsch, Rathenau's right-hand man, as real years of struggle ('Wirkliche Kriegsjahre').[84] By 1886-7, the company stood on the verge of bankruptcy.[85] Was Rathenau's earlier experience to be repeated once more?

It was the Deutsche Bank under its leading director Georg Siemens

[81] Ernst Schulin, *Walther Rathenau* (Göttingen, 1979), p. 14. [82] Ib.
[83] Pinner, *Deutsche Wirtschaftsführer*, op. cit., n. 14 above, p. 17.
[84] Schulin, op. cit., p. 14.
[85] Ibid., p. 15. Kocka ascribes the financial difficulties of the company to 'drängende Forderungen der Stadtverwaltung und gleichzeitiges Misstrauen der Aktionäre', *Kocka*, loc. cit., n. 78 above, p. 138.

which came to Rathenau's assistance by taking the lead in a major capital reorganization in 1887. The nominal share capital of the company, now renamed the Allgemeine Elektricitäts-Gesellschaft (AEG), was raised from 5 to 12 million marks with Siemens & Halske providing 1 million. The rest of the enlarged capital was subscribed mainly by the Deutsche Bank and by Carl Fürstenberg's Berliner Handels-Gesellschaft (together with some smaller banking houses). Georg Siemens became board chairman of the AEG, a post he would occupy until 1897. Arnold, son of Werner von Siemens, also joined the board. The same consortium assumed responsibility also for the finances of Rathenau's electricity generating company which now became the Berliner Elektricitäts-Werke (BEW).

Following the reorganization, the financial situation of the AEG improved. Credit became more readily available. In 1887, new shares had been issued at 122 per cent. Two years later, with the company paying a dividend of 7 per cent, 4 million marks nominal were raised at 150 per cent. In 1890, with the dividend now 9 per cent, a further 4 million nominal capital was raised, this time at 165 per cent. The additional capital thus acquired was invested in the acquisition of a dynamo factory in Berlin, and in the expansion of both AEG and BEW.[86]

The agreement of 1887 between AEG and Siemens & Halske, while enabling the AEG to expand,[87] gave rise to friction between the two companies. Following a period of severe strain, they parted company in 1894.[88] The AEG was free to develop on its own.

In 1895 the AEG, with the aid of an international consortium, founded a holding company based on American models. The Bank für Electrische Unternehmungen in Zurich, to which it assigned the bulk of its financial participations in various enterprises, became responsible

[86] Pinner, *Deutsche Wirtschaftsführer*, op. cit., p. 21.
[87] '... Das Mass an gewonnener Selbständigkeit genügte der nunmehr auch produzierenden AEG mit ihrer sprunghaft, zunächst durch Bankkapital, später auch durch Selbstfinanzierung anwachsenden Kapitalmacht und unter einer risikobereiten, neuerungsfreudigen Leitung, auf den vom Vertrag mit S & H ausgeklammerten neuen Gebieten der elektrischen Strassenbahnen, der Kraftübertragungen und der Elektrochemie, eine führende Stellung zu erringen.' Kocka, loc. cit., n. 78 above, p. 139.
[88] 'Die AEG zeigte nicht das erwartete Interesse, grosse Zentralen, die abmachungsgemäss der Firma S & H bedeutende Produktionsaufträge eingebracht hätten, zu bauen, da sie dabei an den Konkurrenten gebunden war; andererseits tendierten S & H dazu, die angebotenen Konzessionen nicht an die AEG weiterzugeben, sondern direkt mit den Kommunalbehörden zu einer Einigung zu gelangen. Spannungen, Verfeindungen und Prozesse folgten; viele Aufträge fielen an dritte Konkurrenten, wie Schuckert ...' (ib., n. 85).

for international financing within the organization. The initial capital of this great 'electro-bank' was 30 million Swiss francs.

The AEG, meanwhile, was concentrating its energies on the construction of power-stations and municipal tramlines. To manage the associated electricity generating companies the Elektricitäts-Lieferungs-Gesellschaft was set up in 1897. In the same year, Rathenau helped to found the Deutsch-Überseeische Elektricitäts-Gesellschaft (DUEG) to secure orders overseas and to supervise their execution.

In 1898, the share capital of the AEG was raised to a nominal 60 million marks. Rathenau at the same time, with the advice of Carl Fürstenberg, was building up vast hidden reserves (the balance sheets of the company only showed profits directly attributable to its manufacturing operations, which alone were used for dividend payments; the extensive profits from other activities were transferred to hidden reserves to ensure the financial health of the company in times of financial difficulty).

Thus when, around 1900, over-capacity and financial stringency combined to enforce a rationalization of the over-extended electricity industry, the AEG found itself in a strong position. The 'Union' electricity company, part of the Loewe concern, with valuable American patents (through its association with the General Electric Company of America), especially in relation to steam turbines, finding itself in financial difficulties, in 1902 entered into an association agreement with the AEG. In 1904, it joined the AEG group, bringing with it a valuable connection with the Berlin tramway company (Grosse Berliner Strassenbahn-Gesellschaft) and, through it, also with the Dresdner Bank. Siemens, meanwhile, had acquired the Schuckert works in Nuremberg which, in 1901, had got into financial difficulties and which, after negotiations, the AEG had failed to rescue. To finance the absorption of the Union Elektricitäts Aktien Gesellschaft, the nominal share capital of the AEG has been raised from 60 to 80 million marks.

The next substantial acquisition of the AEG concern was the Elektricitäts-Gesellschaft vorm. Lahmeyer, an electricity company in Frankfurt-on-Main acquired by the Electrobank in Zürich. Following this, Louis Hagen, the industrial 'marriage broker' in Cologne, arranged in 1910 an association between the AEG and Felten-Guilleaume-Lahmeyer AG. The Lahmeyer dynamo works in Frankfurt were absorbed by the AEG, which also became the majority shareholder of the Felten Guilleaume-Carlswerk AG, cable manufacturers in Mülheim near Cologne. (Siemens, in its turn, in 1910 acquired the electrical firm of Bergmann in Berlin.)

In 1907, in terms of nominal share capital, the AEG without its subsidiaries had become the largest single electricity company in Germany:

	Nominal share capital in million marks
AEG	100
Siemens-Schuckert Werke	90
Siemens & Halske	63
Felten & Guilleaume-Lahmeyer	55
Bergmann	14

When Emil Rathenau died in 1915, his place as managing director of the AEG was taken by his chief assistant Felix Deutsch. Under Rathenau, Deutsch had been responsible, more particularly, for the AEG's sales organization. Though Rathenau himself, following American models, had favoured operating through agencies and franchises, he had allowed Deutsch to build up a costly sales organization of 300 commercial-technical offices staffed by sales representatives and engineers, offering technical advice and after-sales services. It was a policy which paid dividends especially when amalgamations had provided a sales volume large enough to justify an extensive rationalized sales organization. Deutsch's career as managing director belongs to the period of the Weimar Republic and will be considered later.[89]

Rathenau's concerns, if not those of the pure engineer, were neither, like those of Deutsch, primarily commercial. His interest, according to his biographer, lay not in the sale of a product or in the techniques of salesmanship. Instead, his prime object was to produce a saleable commodity, to anticipate, and, if possible, to create, demand. Again, Rathenau showed little interest in the manufacture of standardized 'bread and butter' products (however important these might be for the AEG). His peculiar strength, it is claimed, lay in the fact that he was able to anticipate future developments and, hence,

[89] Paul Mamroth, after Emil Rathenau and Felix Deutsch the third prominent member of the AEG management, was responsible more particularly for the financial affairs of the company, for certain of its trading activities, and for the supervision of subsidiaries operating particular enterprises (*Betriebsgesellschaften*).

future opportunities. He was a man of action, not unduly reflective, very unlike his more famous son. In the technical sphere, his training enabled him to appreciate new technical possibilities and innovations for which the time was ripe and, in consequence, to set the right tasks for his engineers. He would furnish them with the means to solve problems and to overcome difficulties. He was quick to see the possibilities of technical inventions.[90] His talents, while industrial-commercial, rested on a firm basis of engineering competence.[91]

However, if Emil Rathenau was the most eminent (together with Albert Ballin) among members of the Jewish managerial élite, he was, in important respects, a far from typical one. That élite, at one extreme, included men who made their way into corporate management from the direction of family connections and private ownership, prominent examples being Carl and Arthur von Weinberg, Franz Oppenheim or Wilhelm Merton. A second group, to which Rathenau also belongs, still a minority in the total number, consists of the creators of large enterprises operating in the main with capital not their own. Besides Emil Rathenau, men like Ludwig and Isidor Loewe, Benno Orenstein, and Arthur Koppel are representative of this group. Lastly, there are the majority of managing directors, 'employees' (if powerful ones) in 'alien' companies—with Albert Ballin and Alfred Berliner as outstanding examples, as are Victor Zuckerkandl or Sally Segall. The first two categories, as already indicated, represent a transitional stage between the pure family owner and the corporate employee, documented by the fact that they tend to dynasty formation (sometimes less than successful as illustrated, among others, by chequered relations between Walther Rathenau and the AEG). Striking examples in the managerial élite of the large banks are Eugen Gutmann and Carl Fürstenberg. Nor do such 'intermediate' managing directors disappear entirely even in the following generation.

More typically, however, the élite of the managing directors, like its counterpart in banking, consists of senior employees making successful careers without capital of their own in the world of developed ('organized', high) capitalism. These are men rewarded (usually on a generous scale) not for the provision of investment capital but for

---

[90] Pinner, *Deutsche Wirtschaftsführer*, op. cit., n. 14 above, p. 27.
[91] '... Emil Rathenaus einzigartige Begabung, sein Genie und das Schöpferische seiner Leistung lagen auf industrie-kaufmännischem und industrie-finanziellem Gebiete ... [aber] ... auf dem, Untergrund einer zuverlässigen technischen Fähigkeit aufgebaut ...' (Felix Pinner, *Emil Rathenau*, op. cit., n. 78 above, p. 365).

placing at the disposal of corporate organizations their talents, commercial, financial, managerial, or, more rarely, technical or scientific.

III

If the Jewish corporate élite can thus be seen in functional terms, distinguishing between directors of joint-stock banks and managing directors of major industrial enterprises (how far the qualities required for success differed in the two occupations would not be easy to determine), it can also be viewed as a positional élite. As such, it is defined through the chairmanship of the boards of major companies (*Vorsitzende des Aufsichtsrats*) and through multiple board membership (*Mitglieder des Aufsichtsrats*). Considered in these terms, the corporate élite consists of a top stratum of key figures in the corporate structure rising above a larger number of men with a more limited scope for action. Here also, some distinctions should be made. The 'pure' managing director employed in an 'alien' company—a Ballin or Berliner come to mind—would, however influential within his own firm, rarely occupy (or wish to) seats on outside boards. Others, of the more 'intermediate' type—Emil Rathenau and, after him, his son Walther are examples—would occupy seats only on boards of companies closely associated with their own. This was the case also with certain directors of joint-stock banks, with Max Steinthal guiding the Mannesmannröhren-Werke on behalf of the Deutsche Bank a prominent example. Selective also, if more numerous, were the board memberships of a man like Carl Fürstenberg, confined in the main to major business associates of his bank. On the other hand, the more typical bank director—Eugen Gutmann of the Dresdner Bank, Louis Hagen, associate of the Oppenheims in Cologne, and Arthur Salomonsohn of the Disconto-Gesellschaft come to mind—would join the boards of dozens of companies, not infrequently chairing those of their closer associates but representing the interests of their institutes on numerous others. Such multiple board memberships could be lucrative;[92] they also provided access to valuable commercial information

---

[92] Already around the year 1905, the Dresdner Bank paid its board members 21,000 marks a year, Felten & Guilleaume 34,000, the Deutsche Bank 32,000. A board member of the Vereinigte Köln-Rottweiler Pulverfabriken would receive 11,500, of Orenstein & Koppel 8,500. Members of the board of the Gelsenkirchener Bergwerks AG earned 8,700, those of the Bayerische Hypothekenbank 13,000. In general, banks

The Corporate Élite

and, on occasion, would enable the director to promote the commercial interests of his own company or its clients.[93] Direct influence on major managerial decisions would be rare as would participation in financial decisions (more likely to be influenced by the directorates of a major financial associate). It is worth noting that multiple board members might be conscientious (like Carl Fürstenberg or Arthur Salomonsohn) in studying and trying to solve the commercial problems of the companies involved or they might be content, like Eugen Gutmann or Louis Hagen, to draw their fees in return for somewhat perfunctory attendance at relatively infrequent board meetings. Many may have occupied an intermediate position both as regards their involvement and the usefulness of their services. Arthur Salomonsohn, himself a conscientious multiple chairman and member, once distinguished between 'Wald-und-Wiesen-Aufsichtsräte'[94] (presumably, on the one

paid more than industrial firms, the large joint-stock banks more than smaller ones. For details see the invaluable study of Dr Franz Eulenburg, 'Die Aufsichtsräte der deutschen Aktiengesellschaften' in *Jahrbücher für Nationalökonomie und Statistik*, series 3, vol. 32 (Jena, 1906). It is worth quoting Eulenburg's general assessment:

'... Loeb überschlug für 1900 die Gesamtsumme der Tantièmen auf etwa 60 Mill. Mark. Inzwischen ist diese Summe jedenfalls wieder erheblich gestiegen und mag jetzt wohl schon gegen 70 Mill. Mark erreicht haben, wenn wir bedenken, dass im Durchschnitt jede Aktiengesellschaft 6/10 Proz. ihres Nominalkapitales als Tantième verteilt und dass mithin *durchschnittlich* jedes Aufsichtsratsmitglied 1/10 Proz. erhält. Bei grossen Gesellschaften ist dieser Betrag natürlich absolut grösser, bei kleinen geringer. Wenn wir aber nur jenen niedrigen Satz annehmen, so entfielen doch schon durchschnittlich mindestens 2100 Mark auf jede Aufsichtsratsstelle. Jene 154 Aufsichtsräte, die die Spitze der Kumulation bilden würden demnach nach der ungünstigsten Schätzung jeder mindestens 30,000 Mark für seine Tätigkeit einheimsen (zusammen 4½ Mill.). In Wirklichkeit ist deren Einnahme oft ganz erheblich grösser, da sie vor allem an den leistungsfähigsten und kapitalkräftigsten Gesellschaften beteiligt sind, besonders oft auch den Vorsitz im Aufsichtsrat führen, der weit besser honoriert wird. Wir haben wenigstens einige Stichproben ausgeführt, um die tatsächlichen Gewinne aus den Tantièmen bemessen zu können, und gefunden, dass für die grösseren Aktiengesellschaften etwa 6–8.000 M. im Durchschnitt als Tantième gerechnet werden muss. Jene 154 Aufsichtsräte würden demnach *jeder* durchschnittlich etwa 100.000 M. beziehen: einzelne natürlich noch ganz erheblich mehr.—Die Kumulation der Aufsichtsräte bedeutet demnach doch auch eine nicht geringe finanzielle Kumulation, die zu der wirtschaftlichen Machtposition noch hinzukommt' (ib., pp. 107 f.).

[93] As Jakob Riesser observes in his classic *Die deutschen Grossbanken und ihre Konzentration* (Jena, 1912, reprinted Glashütte i. Taunus, 1971):

'Die in den Aufsichtsräten der Industrie-Gesellschaften vertretenen Bankdelegierten haben, was ein besonders wirksames Ergebnis der "beratenden Funktion" des Aufsichtsrats ist, stets in grossem Umfange dafür gesorgt, dass die betreffenden Industrie-Gesellschaften Absatzquellen in denjenigen dazu geeigneten Industrie-unternehmungen fanden, auf welche die betreffenden Banken einen Einfluss auszuüben in der Lage waren' (ib., p. 309) (and vice versa).

[94] Arthur Salomonsohn to Jakob Hasslacher, privately, 2 Oct. 1925, Rheinstahl

hand, representatives of major shareholders, of local interests, or of firms that had been absorbed, on the other those of banking connections concerned mainly with drawing their fees and furthering particular interests) and serious board members who not only exercised supervisory functions but who also helped and advised the management.[95]

When Franz Eulenburg, on the basis of the *Adressbuch der Direktoren und Aufsichtsräte für 1906*, examined the question of multiple board membership, he found that 18 men occupied more than 21 seats each, a total of 488 which meant an average of 27 places apiece. A further 136 occupied 10 or more seats each.[96] It should, however, not be overlooked that a purely quantitative assessment may be somewhat misleading as companies differed widely in importance.

Whilst Eulenburg—discreetly—did not publish the names of multiple board members, the *Berliner Tageblatt* had no such inhibitions. In its issue of 17 March 1912[97] the paper published a list of the 16 leading 'pluralists' in the years 1912 and 1908 as follows:

		1912	1908
1.	Carl Fürstenberg	36	44
2.	KR Louis Hagen	44	42
3.	GKR Eugen Gutmann	33	35
4.	Dr Max Schoeller	15	30
5.	Simon *Frhr.* von Oppenheim	40	21
6.	GKR Dr Strupp	26	29
7.	KR Albert Heimann	34	29
8.	Julius Stern	31	28
9.	Heinrich Schröder	15	28
10.	*Geh. Rat* Waldemar Müller	31	28

Archiv in Essen 2.00.01.7. I wish to record my particular gratitude to the Thyssen Industrie AG in Essen and to their archivist Dr Carl-Friedrich Baumann, for the outstanding liberality of their policy in granting access to their archives.

[95] A good example of such relationships is that between Nicholas Eich of the Mannesmannröhren-Werke in Düsseldorf and Max Steinthal of the Deutsche Bank (see Pogge von Strandmann, *Unternehmenspolitik und Unternehmensführung* (Düsseldorf and Vienna, 1978). A similar relationship between the bankers Carl Fürstenberg and Arthur Salomonsohn and managing director Jakob Hasslacher of the Rheinische Stahlwerke AG is documented in the archives of Thyssen-Rheinstahl in Essen, now incorporated in the Thyssen archives in Duisburg.

[96] Eulenburg, loc. cit., n. 92 above, p. 105. A total of 154 people, therefore, occupied 2,257 seats, a considerable concentration of economic influence (ib., p. 106).

[97] Zentrales Staatsarchiv in Potsdam, 61 RE 1, Reichslandbund Pressearchiv, 137 S.6 76.

		1912	1908
11.	*Just. Rat* Robert Esser	25	26
12.	*Geh. Rat* R. Witting	17	25
13.	Hugo Stinnes	22	25
14.	*Geh. Rat* Emil Rathenau	28	25
15.	*Generalkonsul* Eugen Landau	23	25
16.	*Generalkonsul* Max Baer	17	25

Thus, of the 16 leading 'pluralists', 10 (Fürstenberg, Hagen, Gutmann, Oppenheim, Strupp, Heimann, Stern, Witting, Rathenau, Landau, and Baer) were of Jewish origin. In 1912, in purely arithmetical terms, the leading places were occupied by Hagen (44), Oppenheim (40), Fürstenberg (36), Heimann (34), and Gutmann (33). Only then came the Gentile Waldemar Müller (representing the Dresdner Bank) (31) equal with Julius Stern (also 31).

The distribution of these Jewish board members among major companies shows a distinctive interlocking pattern.[98] Isidor Loewe, in 1907, sat on the boards of 12 such companies. These, in the first place, included firms associated with his own concern. They were, besides the parent company of Ludwig Loewe & Co. (7.5),[99] which he directed, the Deutsche Waffen- und Munitionsfabriken (15), of which he was board chairman, Waffenfabrik Mauser AG (2), where he occupied a similar position, the Deutsche Niles Werkzeugmaschinen-Fabrik (6), also as board chairman, and the Gesellschaft für elektrische Unternehmungen (Gesfürel) (37.5), directed by his son-in-law Dr Oscar Oliven, all in Berlin. The last was the residue of the erstwhile electrical interests of the Loewe group which, owing to the large capital requirements, as the composition of its board revealed, had, to some extent, passed out of Loewe control into that of a consortium of joint-stock banks and the AEG.

However, Isidor Loewe's interests extended beyond the Loewe group. Thus he worked in close association with the AEG, to which he had transferred the bulk of his electrical interests in 1904. He occupied seats on the boards of two of Emil Rathenau's companies: the AEG itself (100), and the Deutsch-Überseeische Elektricitäts-Gesellschaft (DUEG) (36), which combined the interests of the AEG with those of a consortium of joint-stock banks. Both of these also

---

[98] Details on the composition of boards are taken from *Handbuch der Deutschen Aktien-Gesellschaften*, 1906–7 edn. vol. 2 (Berlin and Leipzig, 1907).
[99] Figures in brackets: nominal share capital in million marks in 1907.

numbered Oscar Oliven as joint deputy Chairman among their board members. Further, Isidor Loewe sat on two boards chaired by his close friend Eduard Arnhold: those of the Grosse Berliner Strassenbahn (100) and the Berlin-Anhaltische Maschinenbau-Actien Gesellschaft (Bamag) (9) of whose board Loewe was the deputy chairman.

In addition Loewe sat, somewhat more fortuitously, on the boards of Vereinigte Königs- und Laurahütte (27), part of the Bleichröder interest, the Bismarckhütte (10), in which the Born group was prominent, and the Stettiner Chamottefabrik-Actien-Gesellschaft vorm. Didier (12.5).

Furthermore, to some extent outside this structured pattern of companies, Loewe occupied seats also on the boards of the Norddeutscher Lloyd (125) and of the Deutsch-Atlantische Telegraphen-Gesellschaft in Cologne (24), a Felten & Guilleaume associate in which the Oppenheims and Louis Hagen were prominent (98).[100] Documenting his own major banking connection, Loewe had a seat on the board of the Disconto-Gesellschaft. Finally, through Oscar Oliven, Loewe would presently become associated with the Orenstein and Koppel firms Aktiengesellschaft für Feld- und Kleinbahn-Bedarf (11) and Arthur Koppel Aktien-Gesellschaft (10).

Overlapping with the interests of Isidor Loewe are those of his close friend Eduard Arnhold. Arnhold was board chairman of the Grosse Berliner Strassenbahn (100) and Bamag (9), and a member of the boards of the AEG (100), of Ludwig Loewe & Co. (7.5), and Deutsche Waffen- und Munitionsfabriken (15). He was also a board member—later deputy chairman—of the Actien-Gesellschaft für Anilin-Fabrikation (Agfa) (9). His major banking connection is reflected in his membership of the board of the Dresdner Bank (180).

Again overlapping with those of both Isidor Loewe and Eduard Arnhold are the mammoth interests of the AEG represented by the board memberships of Emil and Walther Rathenau. Both, naturally sat on the boards of the AEG (where they were joined by Felix Deutsch) and DUEG, and also on that of their major banking associate the BHG (100). Emil Rathenau as chairman and Walther as his deputy (with Paul Mamroth as one of the directors) also sat on the board of the Elektricitäts-Lieferungs-Gesellschaft in Berlin (8). Walther Rathenau

---

[100] A number of other companies where Loewe was a board member do not figure among the hundred largest enterprises in 1907 and are of lesser importance. They include firms like the Daimler Motoren-Gesellschaft and the Dynamit AG vorm. Alfred Nobel.

was a board member of a subsidiary company, Gebr. Körting Aktien-Gesellschaft in Linden, of which Felix Deutsch was deputy chairman. In addition, he represented the AEG on boards of the Loewe companies Ludwig Loewe & Co. and Gesfürel. Similarly, he sat on the boards of two companies of the Friedländer group, Rybniker Bergbau Aktien-Gesellschaft (6.5), of which he was chairman, and Hohenlohe-Werke Aktien-Gesellschaft (40). Emil Rathenau, on the other hand, represented the AEG on the boards of two Merton companies, the Metallgesellschaft (15) and the Berg- und Metallbank (40), of which Walther Rathenau also was a board member. Finally, Emil Rathenau sat on the board of the Stettiner Maschinenbau Aktien Gesellschaft 'Vulcan' (10).

Fritz von Friedländer-Fuld, whose interests overlapped with those of the Rathenaus, sat on the boards of companies in which he had a major interest as chairman of Oberschlesische Kokswerke & Chemische Fabriken (18.5), of the Russische Montanindustrie-Aktien Gesellschaft (2), and as deputy-chairman of Hohenlohe-Werke and of Rybniker Bergbau. He also occupied seats on the boards of the AEG and of the BHG, his major banking connection (he would later, after a disagreement with Carl Fürstenberg, transfer his custom to the Deutsche Bank, of which he, thereupon, became a board member). The Mertons, notwithstanding some links with the Rathenaus and later association with the BHG, confined themselves to chairmanships and directorships of their own companies, with regional banking connections in Frankfurt-on-Main. Their associations with Berlin interests remained peripheral.

The network of industrial interests which has been described was intertwined with another consisting of board memberships reflecting financial associations. In this, a key position was occupied by Carl Fürstenberg of the BHG. Fürstenberg's interests were far flung, covering a significant segment of German industrial activity. They may somewhat arbitrarily, for the purpose of the present study (though this is not the pattern in which Fürstenberg himself would have ranged his activities[101]), divided into three sections: those associated with the industrial grouping just discussed, those linked to another in which men of Jewish origin were prominent, and lastly his ties with heavy industry, notably in the Ruhr.

In the first group, Carl Fürstenberg, as the principal banker of the

[101] For Fürstenberg's own later evaluation of his business associations see Fürstenberg, op. cit., especially pp. 169 ff., 349 ff.

AEG, was joint deputy chairman of its board, together with Isidor Loewe. As the main banking associate of Fritz Friedländer, on the other hand, he chaired the board of Hohenlohe-Werke and was deputy chairman of Oberschlesische Kokswerke. He also sat on the boards of the Bismarckhütte and of the 'Vulcan' shipyard in Stettin.

The second group of Fürstenberg's board seats consisted of Berliner Elektricitätswerke (31.5), of which he was deputy chairman, of the Oberschlesische Eisenindustrie (25.2), chief representative of the Caro interest, of which he was again deputy chairman, and the Bergwerksgesellschaft Hibernia in Herne (60), associated with the Bleichröder bank and where his partner *Geh. Justizrat* Max Winterfeldt also held a seat.

In the third group, the most conspicuous enterprise with which Fürstenberg was closely associated and on whose board he occupied a seat was the Harpener Bergbau AG (72.2), followed by the Rombacher Hüttenwerke (33) and the Rheinische Stahlwerke (30). Fürstenberg also sat on the board of A. Riebecksche Montan AG in Halle (12) with his partner Winterfeldt as chairman, and, as chairman on that of the Aktiengesellschaft für Verkehrswesen in Berlin (formerly Lenz & Co.) (10). In the latter, Fürstenberg's son-in-law Dr jur. Alfons Jaffé was one of the directors. Finally, Winterfeldt was deputy chairman of the Deutsche Continental-Gas Gesellschaft (21) in Dessau, and another Fürstenberg partner, *Generalkonsul* Hermann Rosenberg, deputy chairman of the Bochumer Verein für Bergbau und Gusstahlfabrikation (25.2).

Unlike the more widely distributed board seats of Carl Fürstenberg and his partners, those of Eugen Gutmann of the Dresdner Bank almost coincided with what, with due caution, might be described as the 'Jewish sector'. Besides his directorship of the Dresdner, Gutmann sat on the board of the associated Schaaffhausensche Bankverein (145). He was deputy chairman of the board of Ludwig Loewe & Co., board member of Deutsche Waffen, deputy chairman of Gesfürel, and had a seat on the board of the Bismarckhütte. He sat on the boards of Grosse Berliner Strassenbahn, of the AEG, and of the Königs- und Laurahütte. He also belonged to the boards of two enterprises outside the 'sector', Gelsenkirchener Bergwerks AG (130) and then Saar und Mosel Bergwerksgesellschaft (21)—closely associated with the Dresdner Bank and which also provided a seat for Gutmann's son-in-law Johann Schuster.

Julius Stern, director of the Nationalbank für Deutschland (80) was a member of the directorate also of the Dresdner Bank. His board memberships, again, were located largely within 'the sector'. Thus Stern sat on the boards of the Loewe associates: Ludwig Loewe & Co., Deutsche Niles and Gesfürel, of Grosse Berliner Strassenbahn, Bismarckhütte, and Oberschlesische Eisenindustrie. In addition, he was deputy chairman of the board of a large property company, Neue Boden-Aktiengesellschaft in Berlin (26).

Bernhard Dernburg, director of the Bank für Handel und Industrie (154), sat on the boards of Ludwig Loewe, Deutsche Niles, Gesfürel, and Neue Boden, also on those of Oberschlesische Eisenbahn-Bedarfs-Actien Gesellschaft (45) and Deutsche Petroleum AG, Berlin (20).

Lastly, S. Bleichröder, the leading private bank of Jewish origin involved in industrial financing, was represented on a number of boards by either Paul von Schwabach or the non-Jewish Alfred Blaschke. Both occupied seats on the board of the Königs und Laurahütte, the old Bleichröder 'heirloom', Schwabach as chairman, while Schwabach and Hans von Bleichröder sat on the board of Hibernia. The 'Loewe seats' were shared, with Schwabach on the board of Deutsche Waffen, Blaschke on those of Ludwig Loewe and Gesfürel. Blaschke also sat on the boards of the AEG and the Grosse Berliner Strassenbahn, while Schwabach was a board member of AG für Verkehrswesen and, as deputy chairman, of the Allgemeine Petroleum-Aktien-Gesellschaft in Berlin (15). Finally, both men were involved with another Bleichröder 'heirloom', the Preussische Central-Bodenkredit-Aktiengesellschaft (39.6).

What emerges from these data is a pattern of interlocking board memberships linking, through a handful of members of the Jewish corporate élite, on the one hand the major Jewish industrial interests among themselves, on the other these industrial interests with several 'Jewish' banks, whether joint-stock or private. Finally, the board seats occupied by these men also indicate links between some banking interests in which Jews were prominent and certain industrial enterprises in which they were not. In the following chapter, these data will be examined in perspective in relation not only to the total board memberships of the companies involved but also to German industry as a whole. The facts, as presented here, are of course, selective.

Below the top stratum of multiple board members, there are others, among them Maximilian Kempner, Siegfried Samuel, director of Schaaffhausen, Richard Witting, and Eugen Landau, connected with the Nationalbank, whose cumulations are only slightly inferior to those which have been considered. An analysis of their board seats reinforces the pattern already described.

Interestingly, a number of Gentiles also fit in the distribution of their board seats into the same corporate pattern, notably: *Geh. Ober-Finanzrat Bank Direktor* Hugo Hartung, *Ministerialdirektor a. D.* (Schaaffhausen), *Wirkl. Geh. Ober-Regierungsrat* Joseph Hoeter, *Ministerialdirektor a. D.* and *Geh. Baurat* Alfred Lent (both Disconto-Gesellschaft), and *Geh. Ober-Finanzrat* Waldemar Mueller (Dresdner). It is clear that retired high officials, with their contacts in official circles and the prestige some of them could confer, were welcome on the boards of 'Jewish' companies (as, indeed on a number of 'Gentile' boards).

IV

Some aspects of the Jewish corporate élite deserve attention. Among them is its prominence in the directorates of all the large joint-stock banks. Contrary to a widely held belief, the Jewish role in banking by no means ended with the decline and absorption by large universal banks of many private Jewish banking houses during the financial crisis of 1903–4. Another aspect is the fact that Jewish involvement in industry in the age of full industrialization is larger than has sometimes been suggested. Men of Jewish origin managed a number of major industrial enterprises that flourished during the upturn of the business-cycle from the mid-nineties onwards. Equally, an examination of the élite illustrates the close links at this time, so characteristic of German economic development, between banking capital and industry, documented by the allocation to bankers of board seats and chairmanships. Moreover, an examination of corporate structures as documented in interlocking board seats, reveals the existence of something akin to a 'Jewish sector' within the German corporate economy. This is, however a matter to be considered further in the next chapters. Finally, the high proportion of people of Jewish origin among the great 'pluralists' of the corporate structure might be held to indicate the general importance of Jews in the capitalist organization of, more particularly, Wilhelmine Germany. In general, it is clear that the Jewish role in the German economy did not diminish with the decline of the notables. As some old families and firms disappeared, others adapted successfully to the new structures. A number of 'self-made' men emerged from the wider Jewish commercial and professional classes to join the ranks of the Jewish corporate élite. There is, in fact, no justification for the view that Jews in Germany lost this economic significance with the emergence of large corporate units in finance and industry and the growth of large private bureaucracies. Jews, as was indeed to be expected, proved eminently capable of adapting themselves to the conditions of the new corporate age.

7
Corporate Structures

BEFORE attempting to evaluate the role of the Jewish 'positional élite' in the corporate structures of the age of full industrialization, it is necessary to consider the composition of the board (*Aufsichtsrat*) of a large German joint-stock company. Such a board (it normally consisted of some ten to fifteen people, though some were larger and all showed a tendency to grow in size) would be a composite body including several different kinds of members. Prominent among these were representatives of the major banking associate (or associates), especially important in the case of expanding companies in capital-intensive industries. Indeed, with the greatest consumers of capital—the major electrical firms are a case in point—banking consortia became the rule. The principal concern of such banking members would be, besides a general supervision of the financial gestation of the enterprise, the proffering of financial (and, occasionally, commercial) advice and assistance to the managing director and the promotion of particular commercial interests (whether those of their own institutions or of other commercial clients).

A second category of board members consisted of representatives of the principal commercial associates, whether customers or suppliers. Their function was both to 'symbolize' and to promote especially close commercial ties. A subspecies of this type of board member might be either a large shareholder or major client (particularly in the case of large joint-stock banks). Less important were representatives of lesser financial interests (smaller banks, which had provided original 'risk capital', or firms which had been absorbed). There were to be found on the boards of some companies (mainly outside the major centres) belated 'notables' representing local commercial or financial interests. On the boards of major companies, it was not unusual also to find one or two retired high officials who not only lent 'tone' to enterprises in the eyes of the authorities and shareholders but who, through bureaucratic contacts, could obtain useful information or help in securing contracts or legitimate commercial favours. Lastly, there would be some 'technicians', the chief legal adviser or syndic or the trained engineer or scientist (usually towards the end of a career in management).[1]

Men of Jewish origin, perhaps predictably, would most often appear on company boards as the representatives of banking interests. They would figure, however, also among the 'technicians' and, particularly in enterprises based in Silesia, also as representatives of local commercial or financial interests.

The role and influence of an individual board member would depend, besides his personality, on the weight of the interest he represented. Plenary board meetings were infrequent; on larger boards, less important members were swamped. The influence of a 'rank and file' member (what Arthur Salomonsohn described unkindly but not unfairly as 'die Wald- und Wiesen-Aufsichtsräte'[2]) on managerial or financial decisions was negligible. The activity of such a member might well be confined to more or less discreet lobbying on behalf of his own institution or its clients.

Somewhat different was the position of the *Vorsitzender des Aufsichtsrats* (board chairman) or of his deputy on boards where the chairman's functions were of a mainly decorative kind. Chairmen, in the majority of cases, would represent either the leading financial associate or, on occasion, usually in the person of a former managing director, a quasi-managerial (even partly proprietary) interest. Where the financial transactions of a large company involved more than one major bank (though rarely more than two), representatives of each would share in overall financial management of the enterprise. The leading banker or bankers would be involved in regular consultation

[1] For a systematic analysis of the boards of more than 100 joint-stock companies in the year 1906 see Franz Eulenburg, 'Die Aufsichtsräte der deutschen Aktiengesellschaften' in *Jahrbücher für Nationalökonomie un Statistik*, 3, 32 (Jena, 1906), pp. 93 ff. Analysing the occupants of 6,783 board seats by profession, Eulenburg arrives at the following distribution: bankers: 29.4 per cent; merchants: 13.4 per cent; officials: 11.8 per cent; manufacturers: 19.9 per cent; living on their income: 10.9 per cent; liberal professions: 11.6 per cent (ib., p. 95). Eulenburg notes that private bankers (406 occupying 1,180 board seats) outnumber joint-stock bankers (286 with 816 seats). He adds that, though a few private banks still controlled capital resources comparable to those of the large joint-stock banks, most now operated on a more restricted scale (ib., p. 97). Such private banks were represented disproportionately on the boards of smaller and local companies (ib.).

[2] '... Ich möchte daher anregen, auch die Mitteilungen an die Wald- und Wiesen-Aufsichtsräte etwas ausführlicher zu halten ...' Arthur Salomonsohn to Jakob Hasslacher, privately, 2 Oct. 1925. Rheinstahl Archiv der Thyssen Industrie AG (RA), Essen 2.00.01.7, fo. 30.

with management (usually in the person of the managing director), more particularly on matters like the desirability and financing of acquisitions (in an age of rapid expansion with a degree of both vertical and horizontal integration), fluctuations in output, pricing, or the formation and renewals of cartels and syndicates. In matters such as these, board chairmen would engage on behalf of companies in extensive 'business diplomacy' involving a variety of negotiations with outside commercial interests. They would not, normally, interfere in any way with the day-to-day activities of management, but would, almost invariably, defer to the advice more particularly of managing directors on both technical and commercial matters. Communications between board chairman and managing director could, in consequence, be a vigorous two-way traffic on which the health of a company might depend.

Much ink has been spilt in attempts to assess the relative weight in decision-making of board chairman and managing director, the relative influence of management and its bankers. Clearly relations would vary from case to case, depending on individuals. They would vary with circumstances (the degree of the need for new capital, among others). They would vary from time to time, depending on the age and experience of individual partners. Clearly the banker was unable to influence effectively—let alone control—management decisions. On the other hand, management, in important respects, would be dependent on sound financial advice and the efficient conduct of corporate financial affairs. Perhaps the most persuasive description of the relationship is that offered by the 'insider' Otto Jeidels:

... nirgends ist aber das Verhältnis der Banken zur Industrie so vollständig auf persönliches Wirken gestellt wie bei dem Institut des Aufsichtsrats. Werden in den Aufsichtsrat eines Industrieunternehmens die geeigneten Männer geschickt, so kann durch Anregungen, Ratschläge, Warnungen, tatsächliche Hilfeleistungen aller Art der Einfluss eines Bankdirektors und damit der hinter ihm stehenden Bank ganz ausschlaggebend werden.[3]

[3] Dr Otto Jeidels, *Das Verhältnis der deutschen Grossbanken zur Industrie* (Munich and Leipzig, 1913), p. 160. For details of Jeidels's analysis see ib., pp. 143 ff. This view is to be preferred to that of Georg Bernhard when he claimed: 'In den allermeisten Fällen ist die Direktion ins Hintertreffen geraten. Sie ist lediglich noch Werkzeug in der Hand ihrer Aufsichtsräte ... Bei den meisten Gesellschaften ist heute das Bankinteresse dominierend ... Die einzelnen Industriedirektoren sind mehr und mehr auf die Stufe von Ressortchefs herabgedrückt worden.' Georg Bernhard, *Berliner Banken* (Berlin and Leipzig, n.d. (probably 1903). See also the same, *Meister und Dilettanten am Kapitalismus* (Amsterdam, 1936), pp. 113 f. While the influence of bankers in some industrial enterprises had been considerable in the nineties, it declined significantly thereafter.

The role of, more specifically, the Jewish bank director as board chairman of a major industrial enterprise, while it cannot be described here in detail, may perhaps be illustrated in a number of cases. The general function of an experienced and weighty board chairman in his relations with the younger managing director is described in a letter addressed by the management of the Rheinische Stahlwerke in Duisburg-Meiderich to its board chairman Arthur Salomonsohn of the Direction der Disconto-Gesellschaft (the fact that this is a *laudatio* on the occasion of a jubilee detracts only marginally from its value as a generalized description of a chairman's functions):

Die Würdigung Ihrer Verdienste um Ihre Gesellschaft wird Ihnen von berufener Seite zuteil werden, wir unsererseits dürfen uns erlauben, Ihnen bei der heutigen Gelegenheit unsern wärmsten Dank dafür auszusprechen, dass Sie von dem Augenblick an, indem Sie als Vertreter Ihrer Bank in unsern Aufsichtsrat eintraten, stets unsere Interessen mit Ihrem klugen Rat and Ihrer tatkräftigen Unterstützung aufs wirksamste haben fördern helfen. Wir geben uns der Hoffnung hin, dass Sie auch weiterhin noch auf eine recht lange Reihe von Jahren hinaus Ihre uns überaus wertvolle freundschaftliche Anteilnahme und werktätige Mitarbeit unserm Unternehmen erhalten und die durch Sie vermittelten nahen Beziehungen Ihres Hauses zu unserer Gesellschaft sich immer enger gestalten möchten.[4]

[4] Board of the Rheinischen Stahlwerke to Arthur Salomonsohn, Duisburg-Meiderich, 1 Apr. 1913, copy RA 2.00.01.30. In a similar spirit, many years later, Jakob Hasslacher, by then a very senior managing director—he had been appointed in 1910 on the proposal of Carl Fürstenberg at the age of only 41—wrote to Fürstenberg, a long-time member of the *Aufsichtsrat* of Rheinstahl, on the occasion of his seventieth birthday:
'... Wenn auch die Vollendung des 7. Lebens-Dezenniums an sich weder ein Verdienst noch ein Freudenfest ist, so gibt sie doch denjenigen, die mit Ihnen zusammen ein Stück Wegs gehen und arbeiten durften, Veranlassung, Rückschau zu nehmen und sich bewusst zu werden des Erfolgs und der Art Ihrer Arbeit hier in unserm Kreise. Für beides schulden wir Ihnen herzlichste Dankbarkeit: mit Ihrem klugen Rat in ernster Sachlichkeit haben Sie unser Unternehmen in oft schwieriger Lage hindurchgeführt und dabei stets rein menschliche Liebenswürdigkeit und persönliches Wohlwollen den in unmittelbarem Betrieb der Verwaltung tätigen Herren, insbesondere meinen Kollegen und mir, erwiesen. Neben dem Gefühl der ausserordentlichen Hochschätzung für die überragende Begabung des geschäftlichen Führers bewegt uns daher auch eine tiefe Verehrung des warmherzigen Menschen...'
Hasslacher to Fürstenberg, 3 Sept. 1920, RA 2.00.01.2.8.
When Arthur Salomonsohn, shortly before his death, retired from the board of Rheinstahl, he wrote to Hasslacher:
'... Ich kann Ihnen versichern, dass das Schicksal von Rheinstahl mir immer besonders am Herzen gelegen hat und dass ich mit grosser Freude wahrgenommen habe, wie berechtigt meine Empfehlung war, Sie an die Spitze der Gesellschaft zu rufen. Ich hoffe, dass wir auch in derselben freundschaftlichen Weise in der Zukunft bei unseren Bestrebungen, die Rheinstahlwerke zu fördern, Hand in Hand gehen werden.

From the extensive correspondence between director-general Jakob Hasslacher of Rheinstahl and the two influential bankers on his board, its chairman Arthur Salomonsohn and Carl Fürstenberg, it is possible to select a few specific episodes illustrating the relationship. Bankers would be closely involved in all matters concerning acquisitions whether arising on the initiative of management[5] or at their own suggestion,[6] whether as scouts, intelligence gatherers,[7] business

So weit ich dazu beitragen kann, wird es gern geschehen.' Salomonsohn to Hasslacher, Berlin, 22 May 1930, RA 2.00.01.7.
On 1 July 1930, a few weeks later, the Rheinstahl board paid tribute to its recently deceased chairman:
'... Dem Nachruf des Herrn Vorsitzenden schloss sich Dr. Hasslacher für den Vorstand und im eigenen Namen noch ganz besonders an, indem er hervorhob, dass seine Berufung in die Leitung der Rheinischen Stahlwerke vor 20 Jahren durch Herrn Dr. Salomonsohn herbeigeführt worden sei, und dass Herr Dr. Salomonsohn in der ganzen seitdem verflossenen Zeit, wie auch früher, vor allem aber in den schweren Jahren des Ausbaus der Rheinischen Stahlwerke zu einem grossen gemischten Unternehmen der Schwerindustrie stets mit seinem wertvollen Rat die Gesellschaft unterstützt und ihr allezeit sein lebhaftestes Interesse zugewandt habe.' (Record of the board meeting, 1 July 1930, in RA 2.00.01.30.)

[5] 'Es ist uns Gelegenheit geboten, eine ausschlaggebende Beteiligung bei der Gusstahlfabrik F. Bischoff in Duisburg zu erwerben ... Wir empfehlen hiernach den Erwerb der Beteiligung als für uns ausserordentlich wertvoll & preiswert ... Wir bitten daher um ihre telegraphische Einverständniserklärung.' Hasslacher to Krawehl and Stein (directors), Carl Fürstenberg, and A. Salomonsohn, 21 Apr. 1921, RA 1.64.05.1a. All gave their consent.

[6] 'Meinem gestrigen Schreiben möchte ich noch nachtragen, dass nach einer Nachricht die der Disconto-Ges. von Düsseldorfer Geschäftsfreunden zugekommen ist, auch die A.G. Balcke, Tellering & Cie [another firm was also under discussion] an eine Fusion mit einem grösseren Hüttenwerk denkt. Sollten Sie geneigt sein, dieser Anregung eine Folge zu geben, so bitte ich Sie, mich zunächst zu verständigen, damit ich mich über den zweckmässigsten Weg des weiteren Vorgehens mit unseren Düsseldorfer Freunden benehmen kann.' Salomonsohn to Hasslacher in strict confidence, 22 Apr. 1910, RA 1.66.03.

[7] Thus Salomonsohn reported to Hasslacher on 3 enterprises in which Rheinstahl might be interested, 'auf Grund unseres Archiv-Materials'. He had no data on a fourth,'
... ich möchte an meinen Mittelsmann wegen näherer Angaben nicht gerne herantreten, bevor nicht im Prinzip entschieden ist, dass die Angelegenheit für Sie Interesse hat ... Ich habe inzwischen aber unser Auskunftsbüro angewiesen, allgemeine Auskünfte über sie einzuholen'. The same to the same, in confidence, 27 Apr. 1910, ib.
The management declared a lack of interest in two of the possible acquisitions. However Düsseldorfer Röhren- und Eisen-Walzwerke (vorm. Poensgen) were declared to be desirable. 'Ich stelle daher ergebenst anheim, ob u. in welcher Weise Sie es für zweckmässig halten, dass wir eine nähere Prüfung der technischen Verhältnisse bei Pönsgen vornehmen können ...' Hasslacher to Salomonsohn, in confidence, 30 Apr. 1910, copy ib.
Salomonsohn's reaction was tepid. '... Leider stehen mir zu Poensgen Beziehungen nicht zur Verfügung; ich kann Ihnen nur anheimgeben, sich konvenierendenfalls direkt oder durch einen geeigneten Vertrauensmann an die bei diesem Werk massgebenden

diplomats, or financial agents.[8] This, while it might involve only comparatively minor acquisitions (however desirable for expansion), could, on the other hand, be concerned equally with major fusions like the creation, in 1925, of the giant Vereinigte Stahlwerke.[9] Carl Fürstenberg might act as an intermediary between Rheinstahl and the AEG, being a prominent member of both boards.[10] Banking

Persönlichkeiten zu wenden. Die Nachrichten, die mir über diese Firma zugingen, sind nicht derart, dass ich daraufhin eine Verbindung suchen könnte.' Salomonsohn to Hasslacher, in confidence, 2 May 1910, ib., 1.64.2.

[8] '... Ich werde den Markt von Harkort überwachen lassen, vorkommendes Material geräuschlos und ohne Steigerung aufnehmen und es bei irgendwelcher nennenswerten Ausdehnung der Aufnahme zu unseren Erwerbspreisen Ihrer verehrten Gesellschaft überlassen.' Fürstenberg to Hasslacher, Berlin, 26 Dec. 1910, RA 2.00.01.2.8.

[9] 'Nach dem ergebnislossen Verlauf der letzten Verhandlungen vom 5 d.M. ... haben gelegentliche Besprechungen mit dem Rechts-Unterzeichneten [Albert Vögler, director of the Gelsenkirchener Bergwerks AG (GBAG) of which Arthur Salomonsohn was also the board chairman] und Herrn Dr. Salomonsohn stattgefunden auf Grund deren wir folgendes als den Willen der drei genannten Werke entsprechend glauben feststellen zu können ... Wir sind—trotz schwerster Bedenken—bereit, auf der vorstehenden Grundlage in weitere Verhandlungen einzutreten ...

Vor Wiederaufnahme der Verhandlungen erlauben wir uns nochmals darauf hinzuweisen, dass Voraussetzung unseres Beitritts die befriedigende Regelung folgender Fragen ist: ... 'Emil Kirdorf and Alfred Vögler for the Rheinelbe-Union and Gelsenkirchener Bergwerks-Aktien-Ges. to Gruben vorstand of the Gewerkschaft Aug.-Thyssen-Hütte, Hamborn-Bruchhausen, the board of Phoenix Aktien-Gesellschaft für Bergbau and Hüttenbetrieb Düsseldorf, and the board of the Rheinische Stahlwerke Aktien-Gesellschaft Duisburg-Meiderich, Essen, 30 Dec. 1925, in confidence RA 170.00.1.

Clearly at what was, perhaps, the critical juncture in the negotiations, Arthur Salomonsohn, board chairman of both GBAG and Rheinstahl, thus helped to make possible the creation of the Vereinigte Stahlwerke.

[10] 'Ich trete heute mit einer Bitte an Sie heran, die bezweckt, den Absatz unserer Erzeugnisse, namentlich auch unserer Verfeinerungs-Erzeugnisse aus dem angegliederten Hohenlimburger Werk, als da sind, Wellen, Qualitätsstabeisen, Kabelbandeisen, Isolierrohre etc. bei der AEG zu fördern, und die ich, soweit Ihre Person in Frage kommt, dahin zusammenfasse, dass Sie die Freundlichkeit haben möchten, Herrn Wilhelm König ... zu empfangen und ihm Ihren weitreichenden Einfluss bei Herrn Geheimrat Rathenau evtl auch den anderen Herren der AEG und ihren Tochtergesellschaften gütigst angedeihen zu lassen.

'... und bin fest davon überzeugt dass Sie damit sowie mit der Weiterempfehlung des Herrn König unseren Interessen eine grosse Förderung zuteil werden lassen für die ich Ihnen schon im Voraus unsern besten Dank sage.' Hasslacher to Fürstenberg, 17 July 1912, copy RA 2.00.01.8, fos. 78f.

It was a two-way traffic:

'Ich habe in der Allgemeinen Electricitäts-Gesellschaft die Vorschläge gesehen, welche Ihrem verehrten Herrn Direktor Esser für die durchlaufende Trio-Feinstrasse und das Reversier Universalwalzwerk gemacht worden sind. Da die Herren des Vorstandes und ganz besonders Sie, verehrter Herr Dr. Hasslacher, zu meiner Freude bei jedem gegebenen Anlass über die geschäftlichen Dinge der Gesellschaft mit mir

representatives, not unnaturally, would look after the interests of their own institutions, whether crudely[11] or in more sophisticated ways.[12]

verkehren, so bringt mich dies in den Ruf, bei Ihnen etwas zu gelten und hierauf pochen naturgemäss, wenn sich eine Gelegenheit bietet, die Gesellschaften, denen ich anzugehören die Ehre habe. Herr Dr. Salomonsohn ist übrigens in derselben Lage; er ist gleich mir Mitglied des Aufsichtsrats der A.E.G., nur ein viel jüngeres Mitglied, dem schon aus diesem Anlass doppelt daran gelegen sein wird, sich nützlich erweisen zu können.

In bessere Hände als in die der A.E.G. kann der Auftrag schliesslich nicht gegeben werden, denn hierbei handelt es sich um eine ganz besonders Stärke der Gesellschaft, und so hoffe ich, aus unserem Zusammentreffen am 30. Juni die Gewissheit mitnehmen zu können, dass die A.E.G. Berücksichtigung findet.' Fürstenberg to Hasslacher, Berlin, 24 June 1911, ib.

Hasslacher in reply explained why, for technical reasons, the bulk of the order would have to go to Siemens-Schuckert, though there would be a 'consolation prize' also for the AEG (Hasslacher to Fürstenberg, 26 June 1911m copy ib.). Fürstenberg, caught in a conflict of interests, was driven to awkward contortions:

'Ich bin Ihnen zu sehr grossem Dank verpflichtet, dass Sie sich wegen meiner ergebenen Bitte, die ich als Fürsprecher der A.E.G. vortrug, bemüht haben, und ich bin überzeugt, dass nach Lage der Verhältnisse ein weiterer Erfolg nicht möglich gewesen ist. Wenngleich ich den Interessen Ihrer verehrten Gesellschaft jederzeit mit ganzer Lebhaftigkeit angehöre, ist es doch für mich eine grosse Freude gewesen, durch die gleichzeitigen Beziehungen nach zwei Fronten mich bewähren zu können.' Fürstenberg to Hasslacher, Berlin, 27 June 1911, ib.

'Ich habe dann noch eine Bitte an Sie, nämlich die, von anliegendem Bericht meines Herrn Kollegen Esser Kenntnis zu nehmen, der sehr betrübt ist über die langsame Lieferungsweise der A.E.G. Wir hoffen beide, dass es Ihnen vielleicht möglich ist Ihren grossen Einfluss bei dieser Gesellschaft für uns mit Erwirkung der Beschleunigung der Lieferungen an uns geltend zu machen.' Hasslacher to Fürstenberg, 21 Dec. 1911, ib.

[11] 'Der Direktor unserer Filiale Essen, Herr Beigeordneter Brandi, hat die Absicht, Ihnen in den nächsten Tagen einen Besuch zu machen. Ich bin sicher, dass Sie ihm eine freundliche Aufnahme bereiten, und hoffe, dass Sie ihm auch angenehme geschäftliche Perspektiven, die sich für unsere junge Filiale aus der Geschäftsverbindung mit Ihnen und dem Ihrer Gesellschaft nahestehenden Konzern ergeben, eröffnen können.' Salomonsohn to Hasslacher, 8 Nov. 1911, RA 2.00.01.30.

Since the desired result, however, was not achieved, there followed a peremptory admonition:

'Sodann wollte ich nochmals die Belegung der flüssigen Gelder von Rheinstahl mit Ihnen besprechen und nochmals, und zwar zugleich im Namen von Herrn Fürstenberg die dringende Bitte an Sie richten, diese Geldgeschäfte bei der Disconto-Gesellschaft und der Berliner Handels Gesellschaft, und zwar bei uns bei unserer Zentrale zu konzentrieren. Wie ich sehe, haben Sie ja mit unserer Filiale in Essen ein neues Geschäft, leider zu für uns sehr ungünstigen Bedingungen, abgeschlossen, und ich höre von unserer Filiale aus diesem Anlass, dass sie sich zu dem hohen Gebot mit Rücksicht auf die Konkurrenz veranlasst gesehen hat. Dies gibt mir Veranlassung, erneut darauf hinzuweisen, dass sowohl Herr Fürstenberg wie ich doch Wert darauf legen, dass wir in der Konzentrierung dieser Geschäfte bei uns ein kleines Aequivalent für die Dienste finden, die wir über den Rahmen unserer Pflichten als Aufsichtsräte hinaus dem Rheinstahl geleistet haben und auch in Zukunft zu leisten gern bereit sind. Beide Institute haben die Rheinischen Stahlwerke stets mit grösster Kulanz behandelt, und Sie dürfen versichert sein, dass Sie auch die Interessen Ihres Instituts am besten

The picture which emerges from the correspondence of Salomonsohn, Fürstenberg, and Hasslacher is one of a sustained, close, and, on the whole, mutually advantageous relationship which, while not free from minor tensions, is based on mutual respect and, indeed, a degree of admiration. On the whole, the managing director emerges as the dominant partner, even in matters of financial policy. On the other hand, he is dependent on the banker (particularly the board chairman) as a watchdog and friend in the intricate game of corporate competition, either to preserve the independence of the enterprise (in the face of share purchases by competitors) or, through business diplomacy, to negotiate the most congenial (or least uncongenial) associations and partnerships. Companies without a dominant family interest, in particular (Harpen, Hibernia, Phoenix, GBAG, Mannesmann, Rheinstahl), might, at different times, require protection of this kind.

A picture similar to that of the relationship between Salomonsohn and Hasslacher emerges from the correspondence between Nicholas Eich, for many years managing director of Mannesmann, and the long-standing chairman of his board, Max Steinthal of the Deutsche Bank.[13] A position comparable to that of Fürstenberg on the board of Rheinstahl was occupied at Mannesmann by Walter Rathenau (who had joined the board as representative of the Berliner Handels-Gesellschaft in 1903). Max Steinthal had become deputy chairman of Mannesmann in 1892 (chairman in 1900), at a time when the firm found itself in financial straits. 'Mir [ist] die Mannesmann

---

wahrnehmen, wenn Sie auf die kleinen Verdienste, die Sie durch Gelegenheitsgeschäfte mit der einen oder anderen Bank hier und da machen, verzichten und statt dessen sich unser warmes Interesse auch fernerhin erhalten ...' Salomonsohn to Hasslacher, Berlin, 15 June 1912, RA 2.00.01.30.

[12] 'Wie ich höre, beabsichtigt auch Rheinstahl eine Amerika-Anleihe aufzunehmen. Sie wissen ja, dass wir über die ersten Beziehungen in New York verfügen und daher auch die Rheinelbe-Anleihe tatkräftig fördern konnten. Ich möchte Ihnen daher unsere Dienste für die Rheinstahl-Anleihe gern zu Verfügung stellen und wäre Ihnen, in der Annahme, dass Ihnen unsere Vermittlung willkommen ist, dankbar, wenn Sie mich baldigst näheres wissen liessen, namentlich wie gross die Anleihe sein soll, welche Werte für erststellige hypothekarische Sicherstellung verfügbar sind, wie gross deren Wert ist usw. Es kommt mir darauf an, mir zunächst einmal einen Überblick zu verschaffen, um die Verhandlungen in Gang bringen zu können. Auf Einzelheiten würde dann natürlich später noch zurückgekommen werden müssen ...' The same to the same, Berlin, 25 Jan. 1926, RA 2.00.01.7.

[13] For the following see Pogge vom Strandmann, *Unternehmenspolitik und Unternehmensführung: der Dialog zwischen Aufsichtsrat und Vorstand bei Mannesmann 1900 bis 1919* (Düsseldorf and Vienna, 1978).

Gesellschaft', he confided in 1898, 'im Jahr 1890 gleich einem Mühlstein auf die Schultern gelegt worden ... unter dessen Last ich lange nicht hatte aufrecht gehen können'.[14] Technically, he considered, the firm had by 1898 found its feet.[15] During the period of reconstruction, the position of Steinthal (who, besides those of the Deutsche Bank represented also the interests of the Siemens family) had been in the driver's seat.[16] Such was the position when, in 1900, following the sudden death of the then managing director, the youthful and relatively inexperienced Nikolaus Eich was appointed his successor. During the early months, while Steinthal felt the need to reinforce his control,[17] Eich (young enough to be Steinthal's son) adopted a deferential attitude.[18] For some time to come, Steinthal would find himself in his relations with Eich in a somewhat 'parental' situation.[19] Gradually, however, with growing self-confidence, Eich began to emancipate himself from board control. In close co-operation with Steinthal he began, instead, to use the board to reinforce his own managerial decisions.[20]

Eich tried in the customary manner to use the influence of board members, and that of Steinthal in particular, to advance the interests of his company. In some instances, Steinthal in reply referred Eich

[14] Steinthal to the directors, 22 Dec. 1898, M(annesmann Archiv), 11/073 quoted Pogge, p. 21.
[15] 'Industriell haben wir unseren Weg gefunden und werden ihn weiter machen.'
[16] 'Bei Mannesmann war jedoch die Macht der Kontrolleure entscheidend, um die Gesellschaft aus der Verlustzone zu bringen.' Pogge, op. cit., p. 21. For details of the firm's massive indebtedness see ib., pp. 18 f. These debts would not be finally liquidated until 1906.
[17] 'Nach Eichs Amtsübernahme glaubte Steinthal, die Kontrolle über Mannesmann verstärken zu müssen. Daraus ergab sich ein Briefwechsel, der zeitweilig so rege war, dass zwei oder sogar drei Briefe an einem Tag geschrieben wurden... Die ursprünglich als Kontrollfunktion gedachte Korrespondenz entwickelte sich zu einer Art Tagebuch, das zwei regelmässige Leser hatte' (ib., p. 24).
[18] 'Eichs Briefe sind dagegen von dem Respekt des Jüngeren gekennzeichnet, während Steinthal sich väterlich-freundlich verhielt. Erst langsam gestaltet sich das Verhältnis zwischen beiden enger' (ib.).
[19] 'Eich schien daran gelegen, sein bewährtes Echo für seine Gedanken und Pläne voll auszunutzen, während Steinthal sich in einer Art Lehrer- und Vaterfunktion befand, von der er ein hohes Mass an Befriedigung durch die weitere Entfaltung der Mannesmann Gesellschaft empfing' (ib., p. 49).
[20] 'Eich sah im Aufsichtsrat weniger eine Kontrollinstanz als vielmehr eine Art Beirat ... Er benutzte die Aufsichtsratssitzungen zur Selbstdarstellung und liess sich für seine Entscheidungen den Rücken stärken. Durch vorherige Absprachen mit Steinthal und anderen Aufsichtsratsmitgliedern stellte er einen Konsensus her, der ihm wachsende Unabhängigkeit verlieh ... Entscheidend blieb für ihn das Verhältnis zur Deutschen Bank und insbesondere zu Steinthal' (ib. p. 26).

directly to relevant members of the Mannesmann board, in others, he tried discreetly to advance the Mannesmann interest. On occasion, he felt unable to help. Thus, when Eich applied to Steinthal for support in dealings with a Romanian oil company in which the Deutsche Bank had an interest, Steinthal refused to intervene (Thyssen had been able to offer the required pipes 10 per cent more cheaply than Mannesmann). He explained to the disappointed Eich:

> Wenn nun auch in diesem einzelnen Fall sich Ihre Wünsche nicht erfüllen liessen, so glaube ich doch sagen zu können, dass die Deutsche Bank durch ihre vielfachen Beziehungen zu industriellen und Bau-Unternehmungen für Ihren Absatz mehr leistet, als irgend einer der Konkurrenten Ihnen leisten kann, ja ich glaube, mehre als alle zusammen.
> Dabei sehe ich von der historischen Anteilnahme der Deutschen Bank an der Mannesmann Gesellschaft ganz ab.[21]

Eich not only expressed keen disappointment at the treatment received at the hands of the Deutsche Bank but demanded compensatory services with some of its other associates.

Pogge von Strandmann sums up the relationship of Steinthal and Eich, bank and industrial enterprise. While, in the early stages, he concludes, the bank may have enjoyed the dominant position, this changed with the self-assertion of the mature Eich. While, occasionally, suggestions for a new departure may have come from Steinthal (or indeed some other member of the board), policy, generally was determined by Eich. Neither the bank nor Steinthal personally had a concept for the overall development of the firm. Except for keeping an eye on the balance sheets, the bank could do little to influence day-to-day decisions. A few isolated episodes apart, no conflicts of interest arose. The bank occasionally voiced reservations with regard to some of Eich's suggestions or considered their timing inappropriate. In general, after making its own comments, it accepted the decisions of the management. While the correspondence between Steinthal and Eich provided the bank with a subtle means of supervision, it (and Steinthal) lacked the technical knowledge, and that of the market for tubes, to be able to intervene effectively. Proposals for increases of capital, the issue of obligations, or the granting of credit did not orginate with the bank (it was the same at Rheinstahl) even though Steinthal in conversation may, on occasion, have offered suggestions. And Pogge sums up:

[21] Steinthal to Eich 18 Apr. 1908, M.11/078, quoted Pogge, op. cit., n. 13 above, p. 26.

Der Rückhalt bei der Deutschen Bank war wichtiger als ihr tatsächlicher oder auch möglicher Einfluss ... Die briefliche und gesprächsweise erreichte Übereinstimmung zwischen Eich und Steinthal wurde der Verteilung zwischen handelndem Vorstand und beaufsichtigendem und beratendem Aufsichtsrat gerecht. Von einer Herrschaft durch die Bank kann jedoch keinesfalls die Rede sein.[22]

The examples of Rheinstahl and Mannesmann thus confirm Jeidels's view of the highly personal nature of the relations between board chairman and managing director. They also point to the institutional preponderance, actual or potential, of the latter, notably after the end of the century. At the same time, there is a good deal of evidence from other sources concerning the prominent role of bankers (Louis Hagen, Arthur Salomonsohn, Walther Rathenau, Carl Fürstenberg, Jakob Goldschmidt) in negotiating the major mergers which are a characteristic feature of what is sometimes described as 'organized capitalism'.

Nor were the examples of Rheinstahl and Mannesmann considered here the only ones of their kind. The characteristic relationships of banker-chairman of the board and managing director are replicated among others at the Harpener Bergbau AG in the persons of Carl Fürstenberg and Robert Müser. Indeed, Carl Fürstenberg, in his memoirs, lists the enterprises in which he and his bank played a major role and with which he cultivated a 'special relationship'.[23] Other banks, Bleichröder and Oppenheim among their number, maintained comparable relations with industrial firms, as did the part-banker part-industrialist Walther Rathenau. The firms in which such relations between prominent bankers on the boards and management developed were, almost without exception, either enterprises with a preponderant interest in coal-mining or manufacturers of finished or at least semi-finished products. They could not emerge in the old family firms of, among others, the steel industry.

---

[22] Ib., pp. 27 ff.
[23] 'Durch die Freundschaften mit Rheinstahl, Bochum und Hibernia, mit Rombach und Harpen ... wurde die Tätigkeit der Berliner Handels-Gesellschaft eine Zeitlang ganz überwiegend nach dieser Seite hin orientiert.' Carl Fürstenberg, *Die Lebensgeschichte* p. 369. For an abortive attempt by Fürstenberg to associate Harpen, Rombach, and Rheinstahl see Fürstenberg to Hasslacher, 6 Feb. 1911 and 23 Apr. 1911, RA 2.00.01.2.8.

II

In considering the place of men of Jewish origin in the German corporate structure, it is useful to make a fourfold distinction. In the first place, there are companies which could be described as 'Jewish' (I). These are enterprises usually founded by men of Jewish extraction, with Jews prominent in management and substantially represented on the board. Leading examples of companies of this type are, on the one hand, the AEG, on the other, the Dresdner Bank. Next, there are companies with men of Jewish extraction prominent on the board, typically as chairmen or deputy chairmen, with others among ordinary board members (II). The third category (III) consists of companies with isolated men of Jewish origin in prominent positions: Ballin at the Hapag or Berliner at Siemens-Schuckert are typical. Ethnically mixed directorates like those of the Deutsche Bank or the Disconto-Gesellschaft fall somewhat between the two latter categories, but may be closer to (II). Lastly, there are companies in which Jews play little or no part (IV).

Compilations, as already indicated, exist of the hundred largest German industrial enterprises in terms of nominal share capital for the years 1887 and 1907 (also for 1927, to be considered separately), and others indicating the composition of their boards. There is also an unpublished schedule of the hundred largest enterprises of all kinds, in the same terms, for the year 1907. These sources yield information about the position in the German corporate structure of men of Jewish origin.

In 1887, with the share capital of companies still relatively modest and the corporate élite in its infancy, the Jewish component also was a modest one. In fact, many of the firms listed for 1887 are obscure and ephemeral. Of the hundred recorded, only twenty would still figure in lists for 1907 and 1927.[24] Moreover, details of board membership are not readily available in all cases.[25] Of those for which information can be found, fourteen had board chairmen of Jewish extraction. These companies (share capital in million marks in brackets) are the following:

Vereinigte Königs- und Laurahütte (27)
Phoenix AG für Bergbau und Hüttenbetrieb, Laar (16.2)

---

[24] Hannes Siegrist, 'Deutsche Grossunternehmen rom späten 19 Jahrhundert bis zur Weimarer Republik', *Geschichte und Gesellschaft*, 6 (1980).
[25] In Saling's *Börsen-Papiere Zweiter (finanzieller) Teil* (Berlin, 1886).

Bochumer Verein für Bergbau und Gusstahlfabrikation (15)
Oberschlesische Eisenbahnbedarfs AG (9)
Harzer Werke, Blankenburg (7.2)
Rheinisch-Nassauische Bergwerks und Hütten AG (6.6)
Königin Marienhütte AG Kainsdorf b. Zwickau (6)
Westfälische Union AG für Bergbau. Hamm (5.5)
Lothringer Eisenwerke, Ars (3.75)
Nähmaschinenfabrik vorm. Frister & Rossman AG (3.9)
AEG (5)
Consolidierte Alkali-Werke, Westeregeln (7)
Harkortsche Bergwerke u. Chemische Fabriken, Gotha (6)
AG für Schlesische Leinenindustrie (9)
Vereinigte Breslauer Oelfabriken (3.99)

Some features stand out. One is the involvement of Jews in early mining and iron and steel-making enterprises. This is, in the main, a reflection of industrial financing involving bankers and entrepreneurs of Jewish origin, notably the Oppenheims, Borns, Landaus, Bleichrödens, Bethel Henry Strousberg, and, more modestly, the Eltzbachers of Cologne. The Bleichröder interest was the largest, including as it did also the Hibernia in Herne (16.8), details of whose board are lacking—exceeding in importance that of the Oppenheim's, concentrated mainly on Phoenix. The chairmanship in companies unconnected with coal, iron, or steel might be held by bankers (Carl Ladenburg and Hugo Landau) or merchants and entrepreneurs (Isidor Friedenthal and Julius Schottländer). Most of the companies involved would fall into (II), with a few on the borderline to (III).

Among banks, a number had men of Jewish origin in prominent positions, in some cases both in management and as board chairmen:

Deutsche Bank (60) (with Hermann Wallich and Max Steinthal in a directorate of 5)
Dresdner Bank (36)
BHG (30)
Deutsche Vereinsbank (24)
Nationalbank für Deutschland (21)
Schlesischer Bankverein (18)
Deutsche Effekten & Wechselbank (12)
Breslauer Disconto Bank (10.5)

Of these banks, the Dresdner, BHG, Nationalbank among the joint stock banks, the Deutsche Vereinsbank (in Frankfurt), and, probably, also the Deutsche Effekten & Wechselbank (also in Frankfurt) were unambiguously (I), the remainder 'mixed' (II).

The data for 1907–8, in the full flowering of industrial capitalism, are fuller and provide a comprehensive picture of the Jewish presence in the corporate sector of the German economy. Among the 100 largest enterprises[26] of all kinds (ranging in share capital from 21 to 200 million marks), the distribution of the four categories is, roughly, as follows:[27]

	number		number
I	17 (18.8%)	II–III	5 (5.9%)
I–II	2 (2.2%)	III	25 (27.7%)
II	14 (15.5%)	III–IV	1 (1.1%)
		IV	26 (28.8%)
	33 (36.5%)		57 (63.5%)

Thus, just under one fifth of the largest companies show a substantial Jewish involvement, a further one sixth or so a significant one. On the other hand, well over a quarter reveal only limited Jewish participation (this includes a company like Ballin's Hapag, which had no Jews on its board), a further quarter no Jewish involvement of note (though this includes some companies with board seats occupied by local worthies of Jewish origin or a firm like Friedrich Krupp which, in fact, had one board member of Jewish origin and business connections with more than one Jewish private banker, notably the Hirschland and Warburg, eventually also the Dresdner Bank). Altogether then, people of Jewish origin may be said to have occupied positions of some degree of prominence in about one third of the largest companies. It is a curious fact that really significant Jewish involvement (I) thus approximates roughly the 'standard' Jewish percentage of the German economic élite.

The figures are however modified if only the very largest companies (with a nominal share capital of 100 million marks or over) are examined. The following picture then emerges:

---

[26] In fact, only 90 can be considered here as the remainder, mainly so-called *Gewerkschaften* and some enterprises that remained essentially family firms, do not conform to the normal joint-stock pattern.

[27] An element of subjectivity unavoidably enters the assignment to categories.

	number		number
I	3 (23%)	III	2 (15.4%)
I–II	1 (7.7%)	III–IV	1 (7.7%)
II	5 (38.5%)	IV	(7.7%)
	9 (69.2%)		4 (30.8%)

What is significant in these figures is the higher level of Jewish involvement, notably in the large 'mixed' enterprises (II). Over two-thirds of the firms have a significant Jewish component, whilst a mere 7.7 per cent are without some degree of Jewish participation.

A different distribution is revealed in companies with a nominal share capital between 50 and 100 million marks:

	number		number
I	4 (19%)	III	7 (33.3%)
I–II	1 (4.8%)	IV	8 (38%)
II	1 (4.8%)		
	6 (28%)		15 (71.3%)

Worthy of note, besides the comparatively low level of Jewish participation in general, is the almost complete absence, in this range, of the 'mixed' company (II). The percentage of firms with a substantial Jewish involvement still exceeds the average for the total sample. Another feature is the percentage increase at this level of capitalization of firms without significant Jewish participation. At the next lowest level, that of companies with a nominal share capital of between 30 and 50 million marks, the Jewish involvement again increases.

Thus Jewish participation in the corporate élite is greater in the 13 companies with a capital of 100 million marks or over than in the 21 with a capital ranging from 50 to 100 million marks. The major reason for the difference is Jewish prominence, in both (I) and (II), in the large, heavily capitalized joint-stock banks. As against this, there is a substantial number of large provincial banks (mainly on the Rhine and Ruhr) in category (IV) with share capital between 50 and 100 million. this can be illustrated in part by a comparison of the 10 largest companies respectively in (I) and (IV):

(I)		(IV)	
1. Dresdner Bank	(180)	Friedrich Krupp AG	(180)
2. BHG	(100)	Rheinisch-Westfälische Disconto-Ges. AG in Aachen	(80)

(I)		(IV)	
3. AEG	(100)	Rheinische Credit-Bank in Mannheim	(75)
4. Nationalbank f. Deutschland	(80)	Bergisch-Märkische Bank, Elberfeld	(75)
5. DUEG	(72)	Essener Creditanstalt	(60)
6. BEW	(64.1)	Barmer Bankverein Hinsberg, Fischer & Co.	(59.83)
7. Preuss. Hypotheken Aktien Bk	(50.59)	Bayerische Hypotheken- u. Wechselbank	(54.29)
8. Oberschl. Eisenbahnbedarfs AG	(48)	Pfälzische Eisenbahnen	(50.27)
9. Gesfürel	(37.5)	Pfälzische Bank (Ludwigshafen)	(50)
10. Süddeutsche Disconto Ges. AG in Mannheim	(35)	Bayerische Vereinsbank	(45)[28]

A number of features stand out. The first is the predictable overall preponderance of banks but more surprisingly, while there are only 5 in group (I) (50 per cent), 8 (80 per cent) figure in group (IV). In terms of capital strength, the two groups are roughly comparable, with a slight weighting in favour of group (I) in the first five places, of group (IV) in the remainder.

Where the two groups differ widely is, of course, in the matter of geographical distribution. Whereas in group (I) 8 (80 per cent) are situated in Berlin (Oberschlesische Eisenbahnbedarfs and Süddeutsche Disconto would, however, have been joined in place 11 by the Berg u. Metallbank in Frankfurt-on-Main), not a single company in group (IV) had its base in the capital. Instead, the first 6 (60 per cent) were located in Rhine–Ruhr, the remaining 4 (40 per cent) in Bavaria and the Palatinate. It could, in fact, be argued that the two groups were so different as to represent virtually two separate economies. Some reasons for the specific locations of industries with strong Jewish participation will be considered presently.

A further difference between the two groups is that whereas (I), taken as a whole, shows a high degree of integration, linking banks and enterprises in the electricity industry through multiple business dealings and the exchange of board seats, group (IV) appears to consist essentially (so far as the evidence permits conclusions) of distinctive

---

[28] For some details on the largest provincial banks which figure so prominently in this column however at a later date, when their joint-stock capital was larger see Karl Erich Born, *International Banking in the 19th and 20th Centuries* (Engl. edn., Leamington Spa, 1983), p. 171.

regional units.[29] Thus Friedrich Krupp & Co., characteristically, eschewed all permanent associations with major banks except when in dire straits; their actual banking links, after early unhappy experiences with the Oppenheim in Cologne, were with the Cologne banking house of Deichmann, to a lesser extent with the Jewish house of Hirschland in Essen; their banking connection in Berlin, maintained through one Carl Meyer, whose ethnic origins cannot be determined, was primarily with the Jewish banker Meyer Cohn whose interests, presently, would be absorbed in the 'Privat' element of what, in 1920, would become the Commerz & Privat-Bank. Another Krupp connection was the Gentile banking house of Delbrück, Leo & Co. (later Delbrück Schickler & Co.). Eventually, Krupp also worked with the Dresdner Bank. Possibly the respective attitudes towards bank capital, indeed the very structure, of the leading industrial enterprises respectively in groups (IV), Friedrich Krupp, and (I), AEG, are symbolic. While the Krupp family owned their simply structured enterprise, the far less wealthy Rathenaus had only a relatively small stake in their highly complex concern. Whereas the Krupps continued under dynastic control, extending to a son-in-law, Gustav Krupp von Bohlen und Halbach, nothing comparable occurred, or indeed was likely to have occurred, in the case of the Rathenaus. The AEG was not, and for good reason, called 'Emil Rathenau AG'. What is true of the Krupps applies, *mutatis mutandis*, also to the Siemenses, not included in IV owing to the presence of Alfred Berliner, leading director of the Siemens-Schuckert Werke AG. Where the Krupps, with the weakest of financial structures, lived a hand-to-mouth existence, the AEG flourished under the skilful financial management of Emil Rathenau and Carl Fürstenberg.

Of the hundred largest *industrial* enterprises in 1907, the seventy-seven organized on the strict joint-stock principle of the AG[30] can be divided as follows:

---

[29] However, three of the banks, the Rheinische Credit Bank, the Bergisch-Märkische Bank, and the Essener Creditanstalt, were in fact associates of the Deutsche Bank, the Barmer Bankverein of the Disconto-Gesellschaft (as, indeed, was the Süddeutsche Disconto-Gesellschaft).

[30] Of the hundred companies listed by Kocka and Siegrist twenty-three are omitted as their organization does not conform to the joint-stock pattern. These are mainly mining companies organized either as *Gewerkschaften* or as the proprietary companies of Silesian magnates (Pless, Schaffgotsch, Ballestrem, also Stinnes in Essen).

	number		number
I	13 (15.9%)	II–III	8 (10.4%)
I–II	2 (2.6%)	III	14 (18.2%)
II	13 (16.9%)	III–IV	3 (3.9%)
		IV	24 (31%)
	28 (36.4%)		49 (63.6%)

The distribution of the categories among industrial firms, thus, somewhat surprisingly, differs hardly if at all from that among all commercial enterprises.

If only the small number of industrial companies with a nominal share capital in excess of 50 million marks is considered (2 engaged in mining, 3 in iron and steel manufacture, and 4 in the electricity industry), a somewhat different picture, not unexpectedly, emerges.

	number		number		number
I	1 (11.1%)	II–III	4 (44.4%)	III	2 (22.2%)
II	1 (11.1%)			IV	1 (11.1%)
	2 (22.2%)				3 (33.3%)

The commonest type (mainly II–III) is that of the mining or steel firm with extensive capital requirements reflected in a degree of Jewish board membership.

Again, the 10 leading industrial companies respectively in (I) and (IV) may be juxtaposed:

(I)		(IV)	
1. AEG	(100)	Friedrich Krupp AG	(180)
2. Ob. Eisenbahnbedarfs	(48)	Kattowitzer AG	(30)
3. Hohenlohe-Werke	(40)	Gutehoffnungshütte	(24)
4. Ob. Eisenindustrie	(28)	Schles AG f. Bergbau, Lipine	(23.5)
5. Ver. Königs- und Laura	(27)	Nordd. Wollkämmerei, Bremen	(22.5)
6. Leop. Cassella	(20)	Saar u. Mosel Bergwerksges	(21)
7. Ob. Koks & Chemie	(18.5)	Farbenfabriken Bayer	21
8. Gebr. Körting	(16)	Reis u. Handels AG, Bremen	(20)
9. Deutsche Waffen	(15)	Essener Steinkohlenbergw.	(19)
10. Deutsch-Oesterr. Bergwerksges., Dresden	(15)	Gasmotoren-Fabrik Deutz	(17.47)

So far as the value of the nominal share capital is concerned, there is little difference between the two groups. Nor, significantly, are the differences in the branches of industrial activity represented more than marginal. Half the enterprises in (I) are found in 'heavy industry'.

There is again, however, some difference in location, five of the enterprises in group (IV) being located in the Rhine–Ruhr, as against not one in group (I). On the other hand five firms in group (I) as against only two in group (IV) are Silesia based.[31] Two of the firms in group (IV) are located in Bremen, a city where men of Jewish origin played no role in commercial life. Except for one enterprise, and that only partially (Deutsche Waffen), Germany south of the Main is unrepresented in either group, probably reflecting general industrial 'underdevelopment' rather than the prevalence of enterprises in the intermediate groups.

III

Each major joint-stock bank maintained a 'special relationship' with a number of industrial clients,[32] a fact, almost invariably, reflected in the composition of *Aufsichtsräte* through multiple representation, chairmanship, or both.[33] These were recognized, stable relationships.

[31] In spite of a fairly extensive literature on the subject, most recently Kurt Schwerin, 'Die Juden in Schlesien', *Bulletin des Leo Baeck Instituts*, 19, nos. 56–7 (Tel Aviv, 1980) and Konrad Fuchs, 'Zur Rolle des schlesischen Judentums bei der wirtschaftlichen Entwicklung Oberschlesiens' in *Zeitschrift für Ostforschung*, 28 (1979), no. 2, pp. 270 ff., no attempt has ever been made to account for the relative prominence of Jews in (early) ownership, finance, and management of Silesian 'heavy industry' (or, for that matter, the Silesian textile industry) from the mid-nineteenth century onwards. To explain why Jews found more openings (and less Gentile competition) in Silesia than in the Rhineland and Westphalia (or in Saxony), it would be necessary to examine in some detail the social structure and evolution of these very different regions. One major difference was undoubtedly the extensive role of Franco-Belgian (and, to a lesser extent, Anglo-Saxon and Dutch) entrepreneurship and capital in the early industrialization of western provinces which had no equivalent further east. Another factor may have been the development of a strong Jewish commercial and banking community in Breslau (based partly on trade with Poland and Russia) which was ready to take advantage of industrial opportunities and to provide 'risk capital' (not always with the desired success) for investment. The corresponding Jewish groups in Cologne, Düsseldorf, or Dresden were almost certainly weaker.

[32] 'Eine solche Emission schlingt dann die Fäden zwischen den Banken einerseits als den Hauptvertretern der kapitalistischen Wirtschaftsordnung, und der industriellen Produktion andererseits so eng, dass sie alsdann beide "auf Gedeih und Verderb" dauernd miteinander verbunden sind. Diese Verbindung pflegt früher oder später auch einen weiterern Ausdruck zu finden in der Delegation von Mitgliedern des Vorstandes der Banken in den Aufsichtsrat der industriellen Unternehmungen und mitunter auch durch Entsendung von "Kapitänen" der Industrie in die Aufsichtsräte der Banken.' Jacob Riesser, *Die deutschen Grossbanken und ihre Konzentration* (Jena, 1912), p. 303.

[33] 'Diese Form "freundschaftlicher" Beziehungen durch Besetzung von Aufsichtsratsposten ist allerdings mitunter, so bei der Erkämpfung zweier Aufsichtsratsstellen bei der Laurahütte durch die Dresdner Bank, erst nach recht unerfreulichen Auseinandersetzungen zustande gekommen' (ib., p. 304).

Corporate Structures

The industrial alliances of the leading banks were recorded by Jacob Riesser, formerly of the BHI (Darmstädter Bank), in 1912.[34]

Of the large joint-stock banks, while Dresdner and BHG belonged to group (I), the BHI might be placed in (I–II) and the Deutsche Bank and Disconto-Gesellschaft in (II). Schaaffhausen, which until 1904, would have figured in group (IV) and thus formed a natural contrast to the rest, had, through the intermediary of Louis Hagen, entered into a close—if temporary—liaison with the Dresdner Bank, a fact reflected in its leading personnel. However, enough remained of its original character to distinguish it from its contemporaries in groups (I) and (II). It is interesting to consider, in the light of this classification, the principal industrial affiliations.

The following among the hundred largest enterprises are listed by Riesser in 1912 as maintaining a 'special relationship' with the Deutsche Bank:

Siemens & Halske (63) (III)
Norddeutscher Lloyd (125) (III–IV)
Deutsche Petroleum AG (20) (II–III)
Deutsch-Überseeische Elektr, Ges. (72) (I)
Ges. f. elektr. Hoch- und Untergrundbahnen (40) (III)
since 1911: Oberschl. Kokswerke u. Chem. Fabriken (18.5) (I)

A feature of these 'special relationships of the Deutsche Bank is the *relative* prominence of partners in group (III).

For the Disconto-Gesellschaft, Riesser lists the following associates:

Gelsenkirchener Bergwerks AG (130) (III)
Dortmunder Union (42) (III)
Kaliwerke Aschersleben (12) (III)
Hapag (125) (III)
Gebr. Stumm, Neunkirchen (21.6) (IV)
Bochumer Verein (25.2) (III)
Rheinische Stahlwerke (30) (II)
Kattowitzer AG f. Bergbau (30) (IV)

Among the associates of the Disconto-Gesellschaft, therefore, the preponderance of enterprises in group (III) is even more pronounced than among of those of the Deutsche Bank.

The Dresdner Bank, in Riesser's compilation, has few industrial partners:

[34] Ib., pp. 308 f. and pp. 651 ff.

Felten & Guilleaume-Lahmeyer 55 (II–III)
Ver. Königs- u. Laurahütte (27) (I)
Saar u. Mosel Bergwerks-Ges. (21) (IV)
Deutsch-Oesterreichische Bergwerks-Ges. (15) (I)

Here the industrial partners are too few to permit conclusions.

The following associations are listed by Riesser for the BHG:

AEG (100) (I)
Harpener Bergbau AG (72.2) (II–III)
Hibernia (60) (II)
Oberschles. Eisenindustrie (28) (I)

Fürstenberg himself, in his memoirs, adds further 'friendships' of his bank which, however, were not exclusive ones:

Rombacher Hüttenwerke (33) (II)
Rheinische Stahlwerke (30) (II)[35]
Bochumer Verein (25.2) (III)

Firms in group (II) predominate.

The A. Schaaffhausensche Bankverein had been, since 1904, somewhat ironically, associated with the Dresdner Bank. Its main industrial partnerships are listed as follows:

Harpener Bergbau AG (72.2) (II–III)
Eisen u. Stahlwerk Hoesch. Dortmund (15) (IV)
Bochumer Verein (25.2) (III)
Phoenix, Hörde (100) (II–III)
Rombacher Hüttenwerke (33) (II)

It is worth noting that, except for Hoesch, these were shared associations, Schaaffhausen almost certainly lacking the capital to sustain major industrial enterprises single-handed.

Lastly, Riesser's own BHI had few substantial industrial clients:

Deutsch-Luxemburgische Bergwerks u. Hütten AG (24) (II–III)
Chemische Fabrik Griesheim-Elektron (14) (IV)
A. Riebeck'sche Montanwerke AG Halle (12) (II)

In an appendix to his work, Riesser adds a fuller list of industrial

---

[35] Financial 'bigamy' and even 'polygamy' was not unusual. Most large enterprises came to deal with consortia, though one particular financial institution usually predominated. But two ties of equal importance were by no means unheard of.

associates great and small of the major joint-stock banks.[36] Here the affiliations of board chairmen as well as multiple board representation indicate further associations.

To the previously mentioned associates of the Deutsche Bank, the following are now added:

Mannesmannröhren-Werke (II)
Hohenlohe-Werke AG (I)
Bergmann Elektrizitätswerke (IV)

There were additions also to the clients of the Disconto Gesellschaft:

Deutsch-Lux, Bergwerks u. Hütten AG (II–III)
Kaliwerke Aschersleben (III)
Phoenix, Hörde (II–III)
AEG (I)
Gesfürel (I)
Allg. Petroleum Industrie AG (II)
Grosse Berliner Strassenbahn (I)
Grosse Venezuela Eisenbahn Ges (IV)

Though several of these relationships were not exclusive, the additions to the Disconto interest were considerable. They mark some increase in the proportion of industrial clients in groups (I) and (II).

The single addition to the Dresdner list is Orenstein & Koppel Arthur Koppel AG für Kleinbahnen (I). Schaaffhausen, meanwhile, not yet aligned with Disconto, had added to its industrial clientele:

Lothringer Hüttenverein (III)
Maschinen-Anstalt Humboldt, Kalk (III–IV)
Deutsche-Mineralöl-Industrie, Cologne (III)
Deutsch-Atlantische Telegraphen-Ges. (II)
Neue Boden-AG (I)

Fürstenberg's BHG has gained two further industrial clients:

Rütgers-Werke (II)
AG für Verkehrswesen (I)

The additions strengthen the links of the bank with enterprises in groups (I) and (II).

Lastly, the somnolent BHI had failed to win a single new associate.

[36] Riesser, op. cit., pp. 651 ff.

Overall, Riesser's data suggest a degree of correlation between the category of a bank and that of its major industrial associates. The correlation is fairly striking in the case of the BHG, and some correspondence is evident also in that of the Dresdner Bank (whose close industrial associations, however, are too few to permit firm conclusions).[37]

In the case of Schaaffhausen, on the other hand, there are notable affinities with enterprises in group (III). The Disconto-Gesellschaft, which would eventually absorb it, during the period covered by Riesser's data shows a slight shift in its associations from group (III) to groups (I) and (II). The industrial clients of the Deutsche Bank, on the other hand, cover the entire spectrum. There is here, as with the Disconto, a slight shift from associates in group (III) to those in (I) and (II).

One notable feature is the relative paucity, 7 (16.3 per cent) of a total of 43 in the sample, among the banks' major industrial clients, of companies in group (IV). These, essentially, are firms which, like Friedrich Krupp AG, sought to avoid permanent banking entanglements, preferring instead to deal *ad hoc* with various banks with the occasional use of large overdrafts, usually secured on their assets. It may be that this pattern, perhaps reflecting a weakening of the position of individual banks in relation to industrial clients, became more frequent with time. The question whether and with what degree of frequency, 'special relations' between banks and particular clients were terminated (or, more often, diluted by the admission of competitors to banking consortia) deserves a separate investigation. Not infrequently, these would be proprietary firms thinly disguised as joint-stock companies. Such enterprises, in ethnic terms, almost invariably lacked significant Jewish participation.

More generally, it is, perhaps, the 'discrepancy' in ethnic terms between the large joint-stock banks and their industrial clients that is worth noting. Whereas all the banks except Schaaffhausen (with 10 'industrial clients') can be categorized as I/II, 24 (55.8 per cent) of the total of 43 clients belong to the categories II–III to IV. The conclusion to be drawn from these figures must be that the joint-stock banks, notably those in (II), frequently delegated to Gentile directors seats on the boards of their 'protégés'. This would apply, more particularly, to

[37] The salient feature regarding the Dresdner Bank is that, though Eugen Gutmann was indeed a multiple board member, few of his board seats represented a really close 'special relationship' of his institute.

the Deutsche Bank (but also, if to a lesser degree, to the Disconto-Gesellschaft). The evidence, in fact, might seem to suggest that these banks, with their ethnically 'mixed' directorates, also strove to maintain some ethnic balance in the allocation of (often lucrative) board seats. Whether, in any way, this was a matter of policy, it is impossible to determine.

Overall, while there is thus some evidence of loose and partial 'ethnic' correlations between banks and their 'special clients', that evidence would seem, perhaps, insufficient to justify the drawing of firm conclusions.

IV

Links among major companies in group (I) are documented in the composition of their *Aufsichtsräte* in 1908. The most significant board, in this respect, is that of the AEG:

Chairman: Admiral F. von Hollman   *Staatssekratär* a.D. (friend of Kaiser Wilhelm II and also confidant of the house of Krupp)
Deputy chairmen: Carl Fürstenberg
Generaldirektor Isidor Loewe
Members:
Generaldirektor Albert Ballin
KR Hugo Landau (BHI)
Geh. Justizrat Maximilian Kempner
Banker Ludwig Born (Nationalbank)
Direktor Oscar Oliven
GKR Fritz von Friedländer-Fuld
KR Eugen Gutmann

Banker Dr Walther Rathenau (BHG)
Bank-Direktor Geh. Regierungsrat Richard Witting (Nationalbank)

Geh. Ober-Finanzrat a.D. Max v. Klitzing (BHI)
Ludwig Delbrück
Geh. Ober-Finanzrat Bank-Dir.
Hugo Hartung *Ministerial-Dir.* a.D. (Schaaffhausen)
Wirkl. Geh. Ober-Regierungsrat Joseph Hoeter, *Ministerial-Dir.* a.D. (Disconto)
Geh. Baurat Alfred Lent (Disconto)
Banker Albert Blaschke (Bleichröder)
Direktor Franz Vortmann (Berlin)
Generaldirektor Dr Heinrich Wiegand (Bremen)
KR Wilhelm Oswald, (Koblenz)
Generaldirektor Ernst Thurnauer (Paris)
Engineer Walter Boveri (Baden, Schweiz)

This was a relatively large board of twenty-four members, a board moreover which, given the dominating role of Emil Rathenau as managing director and Carl Fürstenberg as his financial adviser, was likely to be limited in its influence. Several features are worth noting. The major relationships documented in the composition of the AEG board are those with the BHG (Fürstenberg and Walther Rathenau) and with the Loewe concern (Isidor Loewe and Oscar Oliven). Of the two vice-presidents one represents the AEG's major banking the other its major industrial partner. A further significant feature is the double representation of both Nationalbank and Disconto, represented, characteristically, respectively by Born and Witting on the one hand, Hoeter and Lent on the other. The BHI, also with double representation, sent Hugo Landau (the Landaus, whose bank had been absorbed by the BHI, had, as already indicated, been the original backers of Emil Rathenau and his Deutsche Edison), and the retired official Max v. Klitzing. The Deutsche Bank, at one time closely associated with the AEG and still involved in dealings with its associates is, not by accident, unrepresented. Among the lesser banking connections, Gutmann balances Hartung, while among prominent customers, Ballin matches Wiegand of the Lloyd, Friedländer, Wilhelm Oswald of the Rombacher Hüttenwerke. Maximilian Kempner was, perhaps, Germany's leading corporation lawyer. The board of the AEG thus, even if somewhat lacking in influence, yet reflects the company's major commercial ties, at the same time documenting the relative prominence of men of Jewish extraction within its ambit. The key names linking the AEG board with important 'Jewish' interests are, besides Carl Fürstenberg and Isidor Loewe, Albert Ballin, Fritz Friedländer, Maximilian Kempner, Eugen Gutmann, and Richard Witting. Significant in particular is the close association with the Loewe group.

In the Loewe group itself, Ludwig Loewe & Co. AG., the parent company, had a board constituted as follows:

Chairman: *Wirkl. Geh. Ober-Regierungsrat Ministerial-Direktor* a.D. Joseph Hoeter (Disc.)
Deputy Chairman: KR *Konsul* Eugen Gutmann (Dresdner)
Bank-Direktor Bernhard Dernburg (BHI)
GKR Eduard Arnhold[38]
Regierungsrat a. D. Karl v. Kühlwein
Geh. Baurat Alfred Lent (Disc.)
Banker Albert Blaschke (Bleichröder)

[38] Eduard Arnhold, while closely associated with the Dresdner Bank, was also chairman of the board of Grosse Berliner Strassenbahn as well as a personal friend of

Bank-Direktor Julius Stern (Nat.)	*Ober-Regierungsrat* a. D. H. Schröder (Cologne)
Dr phil. W. Rathenau (BHG)	GKR Gustav Hartmann (Dresden)
	Generaldirektor H. Wiegand (Bremen)
	Hugo von Noot (Wien)

What stands out are the links with Disconto (Hoeter and Lent). Equally significant is the representation of major customers, retired officials in connection with government contracts, Wiegand (Nordd. Lloyd) and Hartmann (Saxon machine builder also associated with Krupp). It is interesting to speculate how far the almost precise ethnic balance (the background of Hugo von Noot, who figures on several boards, is not known) in a small board of thirteen, may have been the result of more than chance.

The most important component of the Loewe group was however the Gesellschaft für elektrische Unternehmungen in Berlin with a board constituted as follows:

Chairman: *Min.-Dir.* a.D. Joseph Hoeter (Disc.)
Deputy Chairman: KR *Konsul* Eugen Gutmann (Dresdner)

Bank-Dir. Julius Stern	*Geh. Baurat* Alfred Lent (Disc.)
Direktor Bernhard Dernburg	Banker H. Blaschke
GKR Isidor Loewe	Hermann Bachstein
Dr Walther Rathenau	Direktor John Hamspohn
	Geh. Ober-Finanzrat Bank-Direktor
	Hugo Hartung (Schaaffh.)
	Regierungsrat a.D. G. Köhler

Again, the special relationship with the Disconto-Gesellschaft is evident. Again there are the retired high officials. Leading customers represented are the AEG (John Hamspohn had passed from Loewe to the AEG with the Union Elektricitätsgesellschaft) and Hermann Bachstein, a prominent Gentile railway entrepreneur.[39] Again there is approximation to 'ethnic parity'. The significant names, in terms of the Jewish corporate structure, are those of Walther Rathenau (linking BHG, AEG, and Loewe group), the Gentile John Hamspohn (linking

Isidor Loewe. It is impossible to say in which of these capacities he occupied his seat on the board of Ludwig Loewe & Co.

[39] For the operations of Hermann Bachstein, the Süddeutsche Eisenbahngesellschaft, and the BHI, see Jeidels, op. cit., n. 3 above, pp. 225 ff.

Loewe and AEG), and Eugen Gutmann as deputy chairman of Ludwig Loewe & Co. and Gesfürel.

It is interesting to compare the Gesfürel board with that of the comparable Deutsch-Ueberseeische-Elektricitäts-Ges. (DUEG) sponsored by the Deutsche Bank:

Chairman: Bank-Direktor Arthur Gwinner (DB)
Deputy Chairman: Dr Arthur Salomonsohn (Disc.)

Geh. Regierungsrat Bank-Dir.	Banker Ludwig Delbrück
Richard Witting (Nat.)	*Geh. Ober-Finanzrat* Waldemar
KR Hugo Landau (BHI)	Müller (Dresdner)
Banker Dr Walther Rathenau	*Direktor* John Hamspohn
(BHG)	*Direktor* S. Kochenthaler
Geh. Baurat Dr Emil Rathenau	Bank-*Direktor* L. Roland-Lücke
GKR Isidor Loewe	(DB)
Dr Oscar Oliven	Senator V. Fris (Brüssel)
	H. Wiener (Paris)
	Ludwig Breitmeyer (London)

This board, in fact, represents in the first place an association of the Deutsche Bank (Gwinner and Roland-Lücke) with the Loewe group (Isidor Loewe, Oscar Oliven, S. Kochenthaler, director of Gesfürel) and the AEG (Emil Rathenau and John Hamspohn). The 'special relationship' of both the Loewe group and AEG with the Disconto-Gesellschaft is reflected in Arthur Salomonsohn's deputy chairmanship. As this is a commercial rather than a manufacturing company, no major customers are represented. Again, whether by accident or design, a rough ethnic parity prevails. It would be interesting to know why Arthur Salomonsohn rather than Hoeter or Lent occupied the deputy chair allocated to the Disconto-Gesellschaft. Within the Jewish corporate sector, the significant names in this instance are those of Emil Rathenau, Isidor Loewe, once again Walther Rathenau, and the Gentile John Hamspohn.

If one looks at the *Aufsichtsrat* of Oberschlesische Kokswerke und Chemische Fabriken, the major company in the Friedländer group, the following picture emerges:

Chairman: GKR Fritz von Friedländer-Fuld
Deputy-Chairman: Bank-Direktor C. Fürstenberg
KR Dr jur. Georg v. Caro   *Bergassesor* Dr Alfred Martin (Berlin)

Generalkonsul Rosenberg (BHG)	KR Rudolf Hegenscheidt (Berlin)
GKR Oscar Caro	*Oberbürgermeister* Kreidel (Charlottenburg)
	Bank-Direktor Berve (Breslau)
	Generaldirektor Dr Stephan (Beuthen)
	Bank-Direktor a.D. Johannes Klewitz (Berlin)
	Central-Direktor Wilhelm Kestranek (Vienna)

The composition of the board reflects in the main Friedländer's major associations, on the one hand with Fürstenberg and the BHG, on the other with the Caro interest (including Rudolf Hegenscheidt). Significant also is the relative importance of local connections (even if some of the people involved had moved their residence to Berlin). As before, once more something like an ethnic balance is evident in a small board of twelve. As regards the Jewish corporate structure, the significant names are those of the Caro brothers as Silesian industrialists, linked to the core group in Berlin through Friedländer and Fürstenberg, the leading figures in Oberkoks.

Another enterprise in which Friedländer had a major interest was the recently founded Hohenlohe-Werke AG in Hohenlohehütte, a partnership of magnate, industrialist, and banker:

Chairman: Banker Carl Fürstenberg
Deputy Chairman: GKR Fritz von Friedländer-Fuld

Banker Dr Walther Rathenau	*Generaldirektor* Paul Link (Slawentitz)
Banker Dr Georg Heimann (Breslau)	*Justizrat* Ferd. Lobe (Berlin)
	Generaldirektor Karl Behrens (Herne)
	Wirkl. Geh. Rat Dr von Kurnowski
	Domänenrat Alfred Pickart (Slawentitz)

The major association reflected in the composition of the board is that of prince Hohenlohe (Link and Pickart) and the BHG (Fürstenberg and Rathenau). In a 'mini-board' of nine persons, there is again an ethnic balance.

With the Hohenlohe board may be compared that of the Bismarckhütte in Bismarckhütte, a smaller Silesian enterprise owing its origin principally to local Jewish bankers (admirers of Bismarck).

Chairman: Banker Ludwig Born
Deputy Chairman: E. Sachs
GKR Isidor Loewe
Banker Adolf Philipsthal
KR *Konsul* Eugen Gutmann
Banker Carl Fürstenberg
Bank-Direktor Julius Stern

Direktor Oskar Vogt
(Schwientochlowitz)
Hugo von Noot (Vienna)

In this gathering of Jewish bankers, director Oskar Vogt, the 'odd man out', may have felt a little 'lonely'. The composition of the board is unique, with the bankers Born, Sachs, and Philipsthal representing the original founders (the enterprise had been started in 1872 by an association of the Born group in Berlin with local Jewish bankers). The significant Jewish names are Isidor Loewe and Carl Fürstenberg.

The industrial interests of the Caro and Kern families, as already indicated, had been merged with others into the Oberschlesische Eisenindustrie in Gleiwitz, a larger enterprise than the Bismarckhütte. Its board was composed as follows:

Chairman: GKR Oscar Caro (Hirschberg i. S.)
Deputy Chairman: Banker Carl Fürstenberg
Banker Lorenz Zuckerkandl   *Bank-Direktor* Emil Berve
Bank-Direktor Julius Stern
Direktor Alois Kern, Breslau
GKR Dr jur. Georg von Caro

This, in essence, reveals a former family business, associated financially with the BHG and, to a lesser extent, the Nationalbank, as well as with some local Silesian banking interests. Emil Berve, again, must have felt somewhat solitary in this board of seven. The significant link is that of the Caro brothers, the most important Jewish industrialists of Upper Silesia (besides Fritz v. Friedländer-Fuld and Eduard Arnhold) with Carl Fürstenberg.

It is interesting to compare the Obereisen board with that of the larger Oberschlesische Eisenbahn bedarfs AG in Friedenshütte, repository, among others, of the former Huldschinsky interest:

Chairman: *Generalkonsul* Eugen Landau (Nat.)
First Deputy: *Regierungsrat* a. D. Dr Ernst Magnus (Nat.)

Second Deputy: *Bank-Direktor* H. Haenisch
Bank-Direktor C. Chrambach
KR R. Landsberg
KR A. Moser
Bank-Direktor B. Dernburg
Geh. Regierungsrat
a. D. R. Witting (Nat.)
Rechtsanwalt Dr jur. Wittkowsky
Direktor S. Nathan (Sosnowice)
Justizrat Berger
Bergrat Gothein MdR
Rittergutsbesitzer Dr Immerwahr
Bank-Direktor E. Berve (Breslau)
Generaldirektor E. Holz
Generaldirektor P. Liebert
Reinhard Steffens
KR Rudolf Hegenscheidt (Berlin)
Generaldirektor Pieler (Ruda)
General-Berg-Direktor Schulte (Waldenburg)

The large board of twenty documents, above all, a close association with the Nationalbank für Deutschland (Landau, Magnus, Witting) as well as strong local connections, both financial and managerial. Apart from Bernhard Dernburg, Rudolf Hegenscheidt, and the ubiquitous Emil Berve, the board shows little affinity to the characteristic corporate groupings of either Berlin or Upper Silesia. Again there is virtual 'ethnic parity'.

The Vereinigte Königs- und Laurahütte, a Bleichröder heirloom, on the other hand, approaches the 'normal' corporate pattern:

Chairman: *Generalkonsul* Dr Paul Schwabach
Deputy-Chairman: *Ober-Bergrat* a. D. Dr Paul Wachler
Generalkonsul Eduard Behrens (Hamburg)
Konsul KR Eugen Gutmann
GKR Isidor Loewe
KR Banker Dr jur. Georg Heimann (Breslau)
Geh. Bergrat O. Junghann (Berlin)
Bank-Direktor M. Schinckel
GKR Schlutow (Stettin)
Banker Albert Blaschke
Rittergutsbesitzer Johs. Klewitz (Klein-Lubars)

The unusual feature, here, is perhaps the 'Hanseatic connection', represented by Eduard Behrens, Schlutow, and Max Schinckel (Norddeutsche Bank). The 'ethnic balance' here extends also to the two leading positions in a board with a large banking component.

Lastly, a company in the Merton group may be considered, the Berg- und Metallbank in Frankfurt:

Chairman: *Privatier* Dr Wilhelm Merton
Deputy Chairman: *Justizrat* Dr Henry Oswald
KR Eduard Beit
KR Jean Andreae

KR Otto Braumfels
Kaufmann Leo Ellinger
Direktor Zachary Hochschildt
Banker August Ladenburg
Kaufmann Alfred Merton
Banker Dr Walther Rathenau
Geh. Baurat Dr.-Ing. Emil Rathenau

Privatier Walther vom Rath
Bank-Direktor Otto Ulrich (Frankfurt)
KR Theodor von Guilleaume
Direktor Louis Fade

This board represents a combination of an extended family group (Wilhelm Merton, Alfred Merton, Leo Ellinger, Zachary Hochschildt) with leading Frankfurt bankers (Beit, Braunfels, Ladenburg, Andreae) and with Emil Rathenau and Theodor von Guilleaume as important business associates. The rationale of the presence of Walther vom Rath (Farbwerke Höchst) is perhaps less apparent. Walther Rathenau represents the BHG, a co-founder of the company, but, curiously no others are represented. Wilhelm Merton, a Frankfurt patriot, was clearly concerned with minimizing the representation of Berlin joint-stock banks. With the exception of the two Rathenaus, no other board members hailed from Berlin.

The board of Fürstenberg's BHG—its influence on the conduct of operations almost certainly negligible—contained, like the boards of other joint-stock banks, in the main representatives of leading industrial clients:

Chairman: *Geh. Regierungsrat a. D.* W. Simon
Deputy Chairman: KR E. Behrens (Internationale Bank, absorbed into BHG)[40]
Second Deputy: *Geh. Baurat* E. Rathenau

Geh. Ober-Regierungsrat Georg Magnus
GKR Fritz v. Friedländer-Fuld
Direktor Felix Klemperer
H. Rosenberg (BHG)
GKR Oscar Caro
Robert Borchardt (Breest & Gelpcke, absorbed 1901)
Banker M. Feilchenfeld (Niederösterr. Escompte Ges.)

Geh. Justizrat Fr. Ernst (prominent corporation lawyer)
Geh. Justizrat Max Winterfeldt (BHG)
Staatsminister K. v. Hofmann Exc.
GKR Fr. Lenz
Banker Dr jur. F. Clemm
KR Robert Müser (Harpen)
Generaldirektor Bergrat C. Behrens (Hibernia)

[40] For the history of this unsuccessful venture of Ludwig Max Goldberger and the Born group see ibid., pp. 275 ff.

Rentier Carl Menshausen
Generaldirektor
W. v. Oechelhäuser
Bergrat O. Müller
KR W. Oswald (Rombach)
KR Dr.-Ing. h. c. H. J. Stahl
(Vulcan)
Generaldirektor Fritz Lob
(Hohenlohehütte)
Central Direktor W. Kestranek
(Prager Eisen-Industrie Ges.)

Fürstenberg's board thus, was in its essence a representation of the BHG's largest industrial clients, a 'back-up' for sustained commercial associations.

Somewhat different in its composition was the board of the Nationalbank für Deutschland.

Chairman: *Wirkl. Geh. Rat* O. Hellwig Exc.
Deputy Chairman: *Regierungsrat* a. D. Dr Ernst Magnus
KR G. Fromberg
Stadtrat Dr M. Weigert
Banker Carl Hagen (brother of Louis Hagen)
Ludwig Born
Adolf Philipsthal
Dr Georg Hahn (Hahnsche Werke)
KR *Generaldirektor* E. Marx (Bismarckhütte)
Hofrat S. von Hahn (Vienna)
Banker F. Andreae
KR Rudolf Hegenscheidt (Berlin)
Geh. *Regierungsrat* Dr Hermann Paasche
Factory owner A. Klönne (Dortmund)
Bergrat H. Kost (Essen)
Dr jur. Paul von Mallinckrodt
KR C. Scheibler

This is an *Aufsichtsrat*—somewhat outside the 'main stream'—combining originally Silesian bankers (Fromberg, Philipsthal) and industrialists (Marx, Hegenscheidt) with similar interests (though somewhat of the 'second order') on the Rhine and Ruhr (Klönne, Kost, Mallinckrodt). This, clearly, was a bank not associated at this time with any major industrial enterprises and thus rightly excluded by Jacob Riesser from his list of major joint-stock banks.

In general, then, the composition of *Aufsichtsräte* of companies in group (I) reveals a central core of enterprises in which a limited number of prominent Jewish bankers and industrialists (who must have known each other extremely well) occupied board seats in an interlocking pattern. This is particularly evident in the relevant sector of the electricity industry with its far-flung associates, due partly to that industry's great need for capital, but spills over into 'heavy industry', more particularly in Silesia, into machine building, and metallurgy (tubes, cables, wire, brass fittings, and so on). The representation on the *Aufsichtsräte* seems to reflect the existence of a large, more or less integrated manufacturing, commercial, and financial complex in which a limited number of men of Jewish origin held key positions. The board seats occupied by some of these in a number of companies will illustrate the pattern:

AEG
Deputy chairmen: Carl Fürstenberg, Isidor Loewe
Members: Hugo Landau, Fritz von Friedländer-Fuld, Albert Ballin, Eugen Gutmann, Ludwig Born, Richard Witting, Walther Rathenau, Maximilian Kempner, Oscar Oliven
Grosse Berliner Strassenbahn
  Chairman: Eduard Arnhold
  Members: Isidor Loewe, Eugen Gutmann
Berliner Elektricitätswerke
  Chairman: Hugo Landau
  Deputy Chairman: Carl Fürstenberg
  Members: Maximilian Kempner
Gesellschaft für Elektrische Unternehmungen
  Deputy Chairman: Eugen Gutmann
  Members: Isidor Loewe, Walther Rathenau
Deutsch-Überseeische Electrititäts-Gesellschaft
  Deputy Chairman: Arthur Salomonsohn
  Members: Hugo Landau, Richard Witting, Emil Rathenau, Walther Rathenau, Isidor Loewe, Oscar Oliven
Berlin-Anhaltische-Maschinenbau AG
  Chairman: Eduard Arnhold
  Deputy Chairman: Isidor Loewe
  Members: Maximilian Kempner

Deutsche Niles-Werkzeugmaschinen-Fabrik
  Chairman: Isidor Loewe
  Members: Walther Rathenau
Ludwig Loewe & Co. AG
  Deputy Chairman: Eugen Gutmann
  Members: Eduard Arnhold, Walther Rathenau
Deutsche Waffen- und Munitionsfabriken
  Chairman: Isidor Loewe
  Members: Eduard Arnhold, Ludwig Born, Eugen Gutmann, Paul Schwabach
Oberschlesische Eisen-Industrie
  Chairman: Oscar Caro
  Deputy Chairman: Carl Fürstenberg
  Members: Georg v. Caro
Oberschlesische Kokswerke
  Chairman: Fritz v. Friedländer-Fuld
  Deputy Chairman: Carl Fürstenberg
  Members: Georg v. Caro, Oscar Caro
Hohenlohe Werke AG
  Chairman: Carl Fürstenberg
  Deputy Chairman: Fritz v. Friedländer-Fuld
  Members: Walther Rathenau
Bismarckhütte
  Chairman: Ludwig Born
  Members: Isidor Loewe, Eugen Gutmann, Carl Fürstenberg
Rybriker Bergbau AG
  Chairman: Walther Rathenau
  Deputy Chairman: Fritz v. FriedländerFuld
  Members: Oscar Caro
Ver. Königs- und Laurahütte
  Chairman: Paul Schwabach
  Members: Eugen Gutmann, Isidor Loewe
Braunkohlen u. Brikett-Industrie AG
  Chairman: Fritz v. Friedländer-Fuld
  Deputy Chairman: Walther Rathenau
  Members: Paul Schwabach

However, if there existed in these companies a handful of men of Jewish origin occupying key positions, it is also worth noting that the composition of most of their boards shows approximate 'ethnic parity'. The phenomenon is too widespread to be the result of pure chance. In fact, it seems highly likely that, in appointments to such boards, the ethnicity of candidates played some part. If this was indeed the case, two conclusions would seem to follow. In the first place, prominent Jewish members of the corporate élite, in advising on (or, indeed, actually making) board appointments, were probably conscious of the 'ethnic' aspect. Moreover, it would then seem likely that they sought to avoid creating an image of their companies (joint-stock, in some cases—with Gentile managing directors) as 'Jewish'. In an odd way, if probably for different reasons, such 'ethnic' policies are the mirror image of those pursued by the directorates of the large and essentially 'Gentile' joint-stock banks, the Disconto-Gesellschaft and the Deutsche Bank, with their 'Jewish' alternate dynasty of the Salomonsohn-Solmssen or the 'dynasty by adoption' from Hermann Wallich to Oscar Wassermann. It is difficult to believe that members of the corporate élite, whether Jewish or Gentile, were, in making certain corporate decisions, unaware of (or wholly uninfluenced by) the 'ethnic' dimension.

Gentiles on boards of companies with strong Jewish associations belong to several different categories. In the first place, there are former high officials with largely decorative functions. These could, however, also be of practical use in branches of industrial and commercial activity concerned with public utilities and dependent on orders from municipalities, postal services, the state railways, and a variety of public authorities. Companies of the Loewe group, the Silesian steel-plate industry, and the Vulcan shipyard in Stettin also had dealings with the military and naval authorities. Some retired financial officials had come also to represent private banking interests, notably those of the Disconto-Gesellschaft and Schaaffhausen. Finally, such officials might help, in the eyes of some, as already indicated, to confer 'respectability' on 'Jewish' companies.

A second Gentile group was that of the 'technocrats', trained engineers with managerial responsibilities: Samuel Kocherthaler, John Hamspohn, H. J. Stahl, Fritz Lob, O. Junghann, and a whole 'gaggle' of *Bergräte*. A third group represented Gentile business associates, prominent among them Rudolf Hegenscheidt, Paul Mauser, Friedrich Lenz, and the Guilleaumes. A few were appointed to document 'special relationships', banking or commercial, with entirely 'Gentile' enterprises. Thus Gentile banking interests are represented by private bankers, among them Ludwig Delbrück or the ubiquitous Emil Berve. Gentile representatives of joint-stock banks (other than retired high officials) are rare.

In this manner, companies in group (I) were embedded, through multiple relationships, in the wider corporate structure. Yet their Gentile board members tended to be somewhat heterogeneous and, to an extent, fragmented. Some names do, indeed, recur but many figure only once and their presence may be somewhat fortuitous. By contrast, the Jewish group involved in these companies appears considerably more compact, with the same names recurring repeatedly and with some leading figures occupying positions in a number of companies. It is difficult to avoid the conclusion that the roles of men of Jewish origin and those of Gentiles in this segment of the German corporate structure were not identical. That reverse conditions may have obtained in clusters of predominantly 'Gentile' companies is, of course, a different matter.

The question may be raised as to the reasons for a degree of ethnic 'clustering' within the wider corporate structure. It may be surmised—but would require detailed study to confirm—that such 'clustering' was, to a great extent, the product of the 'growth strategies' of original 'parent' companies and their closest banking associates. The initiative, as a rule, would seem to have come from the 'leading men' of the parent company: Emil Rathenau, Isidor Loewe, Fritz Friedländer, Wilhelm Merton, Ludwig Katzenellenbogen, Paul Silverberg. On occasion, bankers like Carl Fürstenberg, Louis Hagen, Walther Rathenau, Arthur Salomonsohn, Maximilian Kempner, or Jakob Goldschmidt also would take a hand in promoting the association of companies but this more often was 'cross-ethnic' and, not infrequently, proved temporary, or involved only 'Gentile' enterprises (like the creation of the Vereinigte Stahlwerke in 1926, in which Jewish bankers played a part).

V

In fact, some data concerning fusions of substantial enterprises may have also an ethnic aspect. Some prima-facie evidence suggests that firms of comparable 'ethnic' composition may have tended to amalgamate more readily and more smoothly than those of widely differing 'make-up'. By no means all the evidence points in one direction but at least it would seem that amalgamations, under the aspect considered here, were not wholly random events.

One illustration is the well known process of concentration in the electrical industry. The story begins with a co-operation agreement in 1887 between Siemens & Halske (IV) and the Deutsche Edison-Gesellschaft, later the AEG. The liaison, amidst mounting tensions, survived for seven years, ending in a none too friendly separation in 1894.

Then, early in the twentieth century, due to over-capacity compounded by general financial crisis, rationalization among the seven substantial electrical enterprises imposed itself. The first to seek a partner were the Schuckert works (IV) in Nuremberg. They looked in the first place, to the AEG. The negotiations, much to the chagrin of Walther Rathenau, ended in failure with the AEG board rejecting the merger terms proposed. Within a short space of time, the Schuckert works had become Siemens & Schuckert (III).

About this time, Isidor Loewe felt that, given the growing capital requirements, the time had come for his concern to divest itself of its electrical interests. Smoothly, his 'Union' Elektricitätsgesellschaft became first an associate and presently part of the AEG concern. The two Rathenaus, Isidor Loewe, and his son-in-law Oscar Oliven joined with a banking consortium in forming the DUEG to finance and organize the costly electrification projects overseas. Both the Siemens and Schuckert association and that between the Rathenaus and Loewes proved lasting.

The 'next round' in the rationalization process occurred in 1910. While the Siemens group and the AEG became jointly associated with the Bergmann AC (IV) in Berlin, the AEG, through the intermediary of Louis Hagen, acquired a majority holding in Felten & Guilleaume-Lahmeyer (III) in Mülheim. This proved an uneasy 'marriage' and one destined, after the death of Emil Rathenau in 1915, for progressive dissolution.

For some time, the possibility had been canvassed of forming a giant electrical trust combining the competing interests of Siemens and the AEG and their respective banking consortia. In 1912, the time appeared ripe for a step in this direction. In that year was formed the Elektro-Treuhand AG, with an issue of 4 per cent debentures of nominally 15 million marks.[41] This was a joint venture, in equal parts,

[41] For documentation on the Elektro-Treuhand AG see ZSAP, 80 Ha.1 BHG, no. 14131.

of the Siemens companies and the AEG backed by their financial consortia led respectively by the Deutsche Bank and BHG. The object of the venture was to take over the running and extension of the Hamburg electric railways (Hamburger Hochbahn), for which purpose Elektro-Treuhand (a holding company) took over as a security shares of the Hamburger Hochbahn AG to a nominal value of 15 million marks (25 per cent paid but to be paid up in full). Each party undertook half the financing operation. The new company would have two directors, Alfred Berliner of Siemens and Felix Deutsch of the AEG. Walther Rathenau was to chair a board consisting of Albert Ballin, Carl Fürstenberg (representing the BHG), and Carl Klönne (representing the Deutsche Bank), together with a former Lord Mayor (it is not clear whether of Hamburg or Berlin) and a bank director from the consortium of the Deutsche Bank. The Elektro-Treuhand AG undertook to add to 7 km. of line just put into operation a further 21 km. Its concession for operating the network was to last for forty years.

However, the Elektro-Treuhand AG, which might have become the proto-type of a large electrical combine, did not produce this result. Instead, following the war, the two groups again went their separate ways. Siemens in 1920 entered an illogical association with Hugo Stinnes and Emil Kirdorf. The common council of the new Interessengemeinschaft—to last for eighty years—was to be chaired jointly by Emil Kirdorf, Hugo Stinnes, and C. F. von Siemens. In fact, at least so far as Siemens was concerned, the Interessengemeinschaft was to prove stillborn, with the Ruhr industrialists eventually joining instead in founding the Vereinigte Stahlwerke. It was a failure due to incompatibilities of both interests and personalities.

Meanwhile, the AEG in its turn under the direction of Felix Deutsch had entered into an association (*Interessengemeinschaft*) with the Linke-Hoffmann-Werke AG in Breslau, a wagon-building firm in which men of Jewish origin were prominent.[42] With a nominal sharecapital of 40 million marks in 1927,[43] Linke-Hoffman then figured among Germany's hundred largest industrial companies. Jointly, AEG and Linke-Hoffmann acquired a share in a Saxon

---

[42] Among the co-founders of the original Linke-Waggonwerke had been the Breslau banker Sigmund Sachs. Chairman of the board had been Robert Caro, a son of Oscar Caro. The later joint-stock company had as its board chairman the Jewish banker Carl Chrambach (1853–1929) (Schwerin, loc. cit., n. 31 above, pp. 38 and 49).

[43] Siegrist, loc. cit., n. 24 above, p. 95.

steelworks (Lauchhammer) and joined in the construction of a steel rolling-mill to supply their own needs. This proved to be a more satisfactory association than Friedrich Carl v. Siemens's with Emil Kirdorf and Stinnes.[44] The AEG entered a further partnership when, jointly with the Mertons' Metallbank, it acquired a majority shareholding in the Mansfeldsche Kupferschieferbauende Gewerkschaft which, with a nominal share capital of 37.875 million marks, again ranked among the hundred largest industrial enterprises.[45]

Yet another association of the AEG with a (somewhat smaller) company in group (I) arose more fortuitously. Hirsch Kupfer und Messingwerke AG had, largely as the result of war contracts, been able to modernize its plant and to increase its production. When military orders ceased, Siegmund Hirsch, the managing director, approached both Siemens and the AEG, long-standing customers of the Hirsch trading and manufacturing companies, with an offer to become their exclusive supplier of brass and copper products.[46] As the Hirsches' banking associations were with the Deutsche Bank, their 'natural' partner would, perhaps, have been the Siemens group (of course, the offers to supply the two concerns were not, totally, mutually exclusive). Carl Friedrich von Siemens, together with Köttgen, the managing director of Siemens-Schuckert, paid a visit to the Hirsch lines at Neuwerk. It turned out that, though both admired the modern production facilities, three factors militated against acceptance of Hirsch's offer. In the first place, Siemens were not prepared to forego their independence with regard to the procurement of semi-finished metal products. Moreover, their requirements in this field were in any case less than Hirsch had assumed. Finally, due to the nature of their production, they required a large variety of items each containing small quantities of brass, which, however, must be available at all times in different sizes and qualities.[47] Hirsch and Siemens parted on friendly

[44] For details see Felix Pinner, *Deutsche Wirtschaftsführer* (Charlottenburg, 1925), pp. 262 ff.
[45] Siegrist, loc. cit., n. 24 above, p. 94.
[46] For the following see the chapter 'Siemens und Allgemeine Elektricitätsgesellschaft (AEG)' Siegmund Hirsch, *Revolution im Messing 1908–1929* (Lammersdorf, 1967), pp. 178 ff.
[47] '... Aber ihre totale Unabhängigkeit in der Versorgung mit Metallhalbfabrikaten aufgeben, dazu konnten sie sich nicht entschliessen. Ihren Jahresbedarf hatte ich überschätzt. Er betrug höchstens 4.000 Tonnen. Dafür sei er aber, vom Standpunkt einer Massenfabrikation gesehen, ein sehr unbequemer. Das verursachte speziell der Bedarf von Siemens & Halske. Vom Telegrafenbau angefangenen wurden in den riesigen feinmechanischen Werkstätten Hunderte von Apparaten besonders auch

terms, with Siemens agreeing to buy from Hirsch such semi-finished brass products as they could not conveniently produce for themselves. Friendly business relations continued—without Hirsch's overall object having been attained.

Next, August Elfes, the technical director of the AEG, paid a visit to Hirsch in Neuwerk. Siegmund Hirsch describes in detail the ensuing businesslike duscussions which resulted within a fortnight in an accord making Hirsch the AEG's sole supplier of semi-finished brass products. Hirsch rejoiced at the outcome.[48] His experience led him to reflect on the differences between the two concerns. And though the reasons for the different outcomes of the two negotiations were primarily technical, Hirsch also commented on the different ethos of the two firms, which he ascribed mainly to the surviving family influence at Siemens.[49] What Hirsch did not notice was that the position of the Rathenau family in the AEG, managers but not owners, had never resembled that of the 'possessing' Siemens. Even less was he likely to note that (perhaps with the exception of his own, slightly anachronistic group) owner-dynasties of the Siemens type were not to be found among major Jewish industrial entrepreneurs. Hirsch's comments also prompt speculation as to how Alfred Berliner, who, for whatever reason, could not, in the long run, coexist with the Siemens, would have fared within the ambit of the AEG.

In fact, the expansion of the Deutsch era overstrained the resources of the AEG and the onset of the Depression, following Deutsch's death in 1928, found it in financial difficulties. A salvage operation became necessary. Perhaps the 'natural' solution to the AEG's predicament would once again have been a combination, in one form or another, of its interests with those of Siemens (just as the shipping crisis was met by a close association between the old rivals Hapag and

---

kleinsten Kalibers hergestellt, von denen fast jeder etwas und ganz wenig Messing benötigte, aber dieser musste in unzähligen Dimensionen und Qualitäten vorhanden sein und stets. Dieser Bedarf hatte Siemens vor allem zur Selbstversorgung gebracht' (ib., pp. 179 f.).

[48] 'Das war es: das "elektrische Zeitalter" wurde nun doch noch direkt unser Kunde. Wieder ein Traum erfüllt!' ib., p. 183.

[49] 'Sachlich, klar, klug, kalt, zuverlässig. Das war der Zug in der ganzen AEG. Hier herrschte nicht wie bei Siemens eine Familie. Hier gab es einen ingeniösen Gründer Rathenau und einen Sohn, der früh unverheiratet starb und einen, der als Junggeselle ermordet wurde. Aber das Werk des Schöpfers überdauert bis heute. Bei Siemens überdauert beides: Familie und Werk. Schicksal!' ib., p. 182.

Lloyd or the difficulties of the joint-stock banks by the amalgamation of the Deutsche Bank and the Disconto-Gesellschaft).[50]

Instead, the salvage operation was effected by an international consortium in which, besides the General Electric Company of America, a major AEG shareholder as well as a long-standing associate of the Loewe group, the latter, with some further partners,[51] played the leading role. In 1929 Ludwig Loewe AG, the parent company, still concerned with the manufacture of precision tools, had been amalgamated with the Gesellschaft für elektrische Unternehmungen, involved in the construction and management of public utilities, under the title of Gesfürel-Loewe AG. The management of the new company included Oscar Oliven, Erich Loewe, Eric Sommerfeld, and Richard Wolfes. Chairman and deputy chairman, reflecting the new company's financial affiliations, were, respectively, Arthur Salomonsohn (Disconto) and Herbert Gutmann (the son of Eugen) (Dresdner). The latter link, moreover, was underlined by the fact that Oscar Oliven was, at the same time, deputy chairman of the Dresdner Bank. Gesfürel-Loewe AG formed in turn the core of the group which now came to the rescue of the AEG.

Associated with Gesfürel-Loewe in the enterprise was a long-standing Loewe partner, the Société financière d'électricité (Sofina) of Brussels. This was a company similar to Gesfürel set up by Belgian and other continental banks to finance the construction and operation of electrical power-stations, trams, and railways. Its leading director Dannie Heinemann (not to be confused with Elkan Heinemann of the Deutsche Bank), born in the USA, had completed his engineerng studies at the *Technische Hochschule* in Hanover. He had then joined the 'Union' Elektrititäts-Gesellschaft (Loewe group), from which he had gone on to Sofina. Under Heinemann, Sofina before the war had

[50] The failure of negotiations for an association between AEG and Siemens interests are described in Heidrun Homburg, 'Die Neuordnung des Marktes nach der Inflation. Probleme und Widerstände am Beispiel der Zusammenschlussprojekte von AEG und Siemens 1924–1933 oder "Wer hat den längeren Atem?"' in Gerald D. Feldman (ed.), *Die Nachwirkungen der Inflation in Deutschland 1924–1933* (Munich, 1985).

[51] As v. Winterfeld, a Siemens director, had written in November 1931 in connection with abortive negotiations for a complete or partial merger between Siemens and AEG: 'Wenn der AEG das Messer an der Kehle sitzt, wissen wir nicht, wie weit sie die Amerikaner oder Franzosen in Deutschland engagiert und auf diese Weise von Fremden gestützt, uns tatsächlich erledigen kann.' V. Winterfeld, 'Entwurf, Aktennotiz, Einzelne Gedanken über die wünschenswerten Rückwirkungen der Wirtschaftskrisis auf das Verhältnis Siemens/A.E.G.', 7 Nov. 1931, Siemens Archiv Akte (SAA), 4/Lf 529, fo. 2. I wish to thank Dr Heidrun Homburg for placing at my disposal copies of a number of relevant documents.

participated in some of Gesfürel's major international ventures. Moreover, it had come to the rescue of its German partner by taking over, with the help of an international syndicate, a number of companies liable to confiscation under the provisions of the treaty of Versailles. In the case of the Deutsch-Überseeische Elektricitäts-Gesellschaft moreover, in which the Deutsche Bank had a major interest (administered through Elkan Heinemann), conversations between Dannie Heinemann and Arthur von Gwinner had led to the formation of Chade (already mentioned), registered in Spain and operating from Buenos Aires. Dannie Heinemann had become deputy chairman of the board of Chade. Oscar Oliven in turn, in the mid-twenties, had joined or rejoined the boards of both Chade and Sofina. The latter, after the war one of the leading international holding companies for public utilities, given these past associations, naturally joined in the rescue operation for the AEG.[52]

These then were the major partners in the international consortium which, if it did not quite 'take over' the AEG, made it at any rate part of a larger international grouping. Oscar Oliven, Isidor Loewe's son-in-law, already deputy chairman of the Dresdner Bank, assumed the same function for the AEG. Negotiations were set on foot to associate also the Hirsch Kupfer und Messingwerke AG, placed in jeopardy by the financial crisis of its parent (trading) company in Halberstadt.

A not dissimilar pattern to these electrical relationships can be discerned in amalgamations of the large joint-stock banks. The first here to seek an association was the weakest, the Schaaffhausensche Bankverein (IV). In terms of rational business criteria, its 'natural' partner was the Dresdner Bank.[53] Whereas the industrial interests of the other joint-stock banks were widely spread in both geographical and industrial terms, those of Schaaffhausen and Dresdner were unbalanced in opposite directions, making them and their industrial interests complementary.[54] In 1904, the two banks did in fact conclude

[52] For the following details see Gerald Oliven, 'The Ludwig Loewe Group, its Personalities and Interconnections' unpublished MS, Leo Baeck Institute, New York.
[53] For the following see Jeidels, op. cit., n. 3 above, p. 176.
[54] 'Am deutlichsten tritt diese Eigenart aber bei der Dresdner Bank und dem Schaaffhausenschen Bankverein hervor; wenn man bedenkt, dass der Tabelle die Verhältnisse *vor* Abschluss der Interessengemeinschaft zugrunde liegen, kann man aus der Verteilung der Industriebeziehungen dieser Banken insbesondere in Westdeutschland (13 und 163) und Sachsen (77 und 2) aber auch in Norddeutschland (79 und 29) fast die logische Notwendigkeit einer solchen Kombination ableiten. Dasselbe Bild der beiden Banken gibt Tabelle IV für die Verteilung der Industriebeziehungen nach Gewerben; es sei nun einerseits auf den Steinkohlenbergbau (6 und 55), die Berg-

a long-term partnership agreement which Otto Jeidels considered eminently rational,[55] and which created (by a considerable margin) the largest banking group in Germany. Within five years, the partnership was dissolved.[56] In 1914 Schaaffhausen, still in need of an associate, entered into a successful partnership (prelude to eventual absorption) with the Disconto-Gesellschaft, whose distribution of interests approximated perhaps most closely to its own.

A new phase of concentration followed the restructuring of industry, commerce, and banking following the war, the loss of German overseas assets, of German territory, and the inflation.[57] It was then that it began to be felt, notably in the directorate of the Deutsche Bank, that the great combines in industry (notably IG Farben and Vereinigte Stahlwerke) had to be matched by a parallel concentration among the large joint-stock banks to enable them to deal effectively with the new giants of industry.[58] The ubiquitous Louis Hagen, aware of these sentiments, thereupon established contacts between the *DB* and Jakob Goldschmidt, the 'boss' of the recently founded Danat Bank (I). Serious negotiations about the possibility of an amalgamation ensued.[59] Opinion among directors of the Deutsche Bank was divided. While

---

und Hüttenwerke (12 und 38), andererseits auf die Transportunternehmungen (47 und 19), auf die Textilindustrie (25 und 12) und die Nahrungsmittelgewerbe—insbesondere die Zuckerindustrie Mitteldeutschlands und Sachsens'—(39 und 19) hingewiesen. Bei den anderen Grossbanken ist auch in der gewerblichen Gliederung eine solche Spezializierung weniger vorhanden.' Jeidels, op. cit., n. 3 above, p. 176.

[55] It is interesting that Jeidels, when stressing the inner logic of the association, was unaware of its outcome.

[56] It would be instructive to know the reasons for the breakdown of the arrangement but evidence is lacking.

[57] For the following see Seidenzahl, *Hundert Jahre Deutsche Bank* (Frankfurt, 1970), pp. 312 ff.

[58] This is how Georg Solmssen, then a director of the Disconto-Gesellschaft, summarized the thinking of the Deutsche Bank directorate (in a note dated 16 Sept. 1926): 'Die Zusammenballung der Kapitalien in der Industrie habe solche Dimensionen angenommen und werde sich noch weiter derart fortsetzen, dass die Tätigkeit der Banken immer mehr zurückgedrängt werden müsse und es ihnen unmöglich gemacht würde, sich dieser Unterdrückung zu widersetzen. Um der Industrie das Paroli bieten zu können, sei es erforderlich, einen Banken-Block von solcher Grösse zu schaffen, dass seine Placierungs-Kraft den Inlands-Markt beherrsche und über das Mass des Vernünftigen hinausgehende Unterbietungen von Gegengruppen zwecklos wären' (ib., p. 313).

[59] Georg Solmssen records: 'Es haben, und zwar, wie es scheint, auf Veranlassung von Herrn Geheimrat Hagen, sehr ernsthafte Verhandlungen zwischen dem Vorstand der Deutschen Bank und Herrn Jacob Goldschmidt wegen einer Fusion Deutsche Bank-Danatbank stattgefunden' (ib., p. 312).

Oscar Wassermann was not averse to agreement,[60] the majority raised objections 'on personal grounds'.[61] There is no evidence to indicate whether these were objections to the upstart Jakob Golschmidt (with his possibly over-aggressive business methods), the arrogant parvenu (in terms of personality), the Jew, or, as seems most likely, to a combination of all three. Different members of the majority may have been inspired in varying degrees by different motives. At all events, to the relief of the majority, the negotiations soon faltered on account of Goldschmidt's excessive demands.[62]

The greater number of directors of the Deutsche Bank preferred, instead, fusion with its old rival, the Disconto-Gesellschaft. The Disconto, pursuing a conservative policy of high liquidity, had been losing ground in relation to other, more 'go-ahead', joint-stock banks. By the end of 1925, it had been overtaken in some positions by the Dresdner, by the end of 1926 also by the Danat. A little later, even the Commerzbank was threatening to do the same. Nevertheless, the directorate of the Disconto ignored advances from the Deutsche Bank. On the one hand, it considered its own institute as something traditional and 'special' while, on the other, there was a more specific reluctance to combine with the long-standing rival.[63] Not until the summer of 1929 were the Disconto directors ready to enter serious negotiations. On behalf of the Deutsche Bank, these were conducted by Schlitter who, as early as 1926, had considered Disconto the 'natural' partner.[64] The Disconto in its turn had empowered Georg

---

[60] 'Oscar Wassermann scheint nicht abgeneigt gewesen zu sein . . .' (ib., p. 314).

[61] Solmssen records that Oscar Schlitter (non-Jewish director of the Deutsche Bank and seemingly his main source of information) 'liess durchblicken, dass eine Zusammenarbeit mit Herrn Goldschmidt von vornherein aus persönlichen Gründen auf Bedenken gestossen sei' (Seidenzahl, op. cit., n. 57 above, pp. 312 f.), '. . . aber mindestens die Mehrheit des Vorstandes hatte Einwände' (ib., p. 314).

[62] ' "Die Angelegenheit sei durch die masslosen Forderungen Jacob Goldschmidts bald nach Beginn der Verhandlungen überhaupt zum Stillstand gekommen", notierte Solmssen. In der Deutschen Bank sei man "eigentlich nicht traurig darüber gewesen" ' (ib.).

[63] 'Aber das war für das Chefcabinett Unter den Linden 35 kein Grund, die geprägte Form der Disconto abzustreifen und sich mit einem Institut zu vereinen, mit dem alte Meinungsverschiedenheiten sachlicher wie persönlicher Art bestanden . . .' (ib.).

[64] In the words of Solmssen: 'Deutsche Bank und Disconto-Gesellschaft eignen sich nach Herrn Schlitters Ansicht besonders für eine derartige Blockbildung, weil beide innerlich gesund und im Wesentlichen nach gleichen Prinzipien geleitet würden [clearly in contrast with the other large banks]. Die Deutsche Bank sei in der Kreditgewährung bewusst etwas larger als die Disconto-Gesellschaft, es sei aber in der Kreditpolitik und der Behandlung der Filialen kein so wesentlicher Unterschied vorhanden, dass man Schwierigkeiten begegnen würde, die beiderseitigen Geschäftsmethoden zu vereinen' (ib., p. 313).

Solmssen to negotiate on its behalf but, on account of his mother's death, the task fell instead to Eduard Mosler (who was part-Jewish on his mother's side). Following the preliminaries, crucial conversations between Mosler and Wassermann led to rapid agreement.[65] The Deutsche Bank became the senior partner in the new Deutsche Bank und Disconto Gesellschaft (DeDi Bank or DD Bank),[66] with a nominal share capital of 285 million marks (still far from matching IG Farben or Vereinigte Stahlwerke) and open reserves of 160 million marks, enough to survive the approaching financial crisis, even if with heavy losses.[67]

Not so Jakob Goldschmidt's Danat Bank which on 9 July 1931 had to declare itself insolvent.[68] The only joint-stock bank willing and able to step in despite Danat's valuable industrial connections and real estate, was the Dresdner Bank, of which, with state participation, Danat became a part.

Whether these data do, in fact, show patterns of association in the electricity industry and banking in which the ethnic aspect, besides others, may have played some part, must remain an open question. What is incontrovertible is the fact that there are few amalgamations of the first order and on more or less equal terms across ethnic lines. Perhaps the nearest (relatively minor fusions like those of the Caro, Kern, and Hegenscheidt interests apart) is the successful association of Leopold Cassella with Farbwerke Höchst and, after the war, its absorption into IG Farben. But then, neither of these represented transaction between equal, or near equal, partners. The evidence thus, at any rate, does not controvert the view that the two 'ethnic' sectors of the economy stood, at least to some extent, apart. Of course this says nothing whatever about successful dealings between companies, about co-operation in a variety of cartels or trade associations, or about many recorded cases of cordial personal and, indeed, social relations (those

---

[65] Seidenzahl ascribes the success of the negotiations in part to the fact that both men were free of old prejudices. 'Beide gehörten nicht zu den massgebenden Männern der Vorkriegszeit und mögen daher mit Ressentiments weniger belastet gewesen sein' (ib., p. 317).

[66] In 1937 it would again become the Deutsche Bank.

[67] For the refusal of Dedi and its reasons see Seidenzahl, op. cit., n. 57 above, p. 332 and 339. For those of the Commerzbank and the Reichskredit-Gesellschaft see ib., p. 340.

[68] During the crisis, to support the value on the stock exchange of their falling shares, the Danat Bank had had to buy up 58.3 per cent, the Dresdner Bank 55.9 per cent, the Commerzbank und Privatbank 49.6 per cent but the DediBank only 36.8 per cent of their nominal share capital (ib., p. 342).

between the Salomonsohns and Kirdorfs being among the more surprising) but these are matters to be considered in a different context. There is, in any case, no doubt that the Jewish component of the corporate élite of the age of high industrization formed a fairly distinctive economic and social group.

VI

Objections—perhaps predictably—have been raised to the 'formalist' methodology of the foregoing sections. It is, of course, perfectly true that the mere presence of a Jew on the board (even as chairman) of a company by itself says nothing about his influence, if any, within the enterprise. It may be great or negligible or may even have varied at different times. In theory at least, this is a valid point. In practice, it would be interesting to find the historian capable of assessing in detail (the evidence, in any case, for the great majority of enterprises does not exist) the actual role, on a continuing basis, of even the better-known individual members of a large number of boards or managements. Theoretically a counsel of perfection, the suggestion is entirely impracticable. 'Cliometric methods', unfortunately, cannot detect quality. All that can be established, except in a few individual instances, is the simple presence or absence of men of Jewish origin in management and board, the interests they represented (in the case of the latter), and their relative weight, documented effectively either in the position of managing director or, more often, of board chairman. It is to be assumed that they did not occupy their positions 'by chance'. Beyond this, it is possible to identify (tentatively), through the location of Jews in the corporate system, certain patterns of financial and commercial relationships. Again, the 'formalist' method adopted makes it possible to present a rough picture showing the distribution of Jews within the German corporate élite and, through this, to gain some impression of their distinctive economic role (or function) within the overall corporate system. It then becomes possible to attempt, on the basis of these facts, some historical (or economic) explanation of certain peculiarities.

Objections can be raised also to confining analysis to the hundred largest companies—not necessarily identical with the hundred most important—within the German economy. The criticism may have some validity, but by what practicable criterion, other than share capital, is 'economic importance' to be measured? Reputable economic historians, who compiled the lists, must have found this 'yardstick', however, arbitrary, a meaningful, or at any rate the most feasible one. What other even remotely quantifiable criterion could have been devised? It has also been suggested that the sample examined should have been extended beyond the economic élite (however defined) to incorporate as well medium-sized Jewish enterprises. While this may be a valid proposition in theory it is, of course, impracticable. It is difficult enough to secure the necessary data (also about the ethnic origins of individuals) to identify a group of the size and kind examined here for the purpose of a prosopographical study. To attempt more (if indeed feasible) would require a computerized study by a substantial team—assuming, always, that the necessary information could be obtained and that ethnicity could be established with any degree of certainty.

Similarly objection has been raised to the 'static' approach unavoidably involved in analysing the positions occupied by members of the élite in the corporate system only for the years 1887 and 1907 (1927, if the following chapter is included). This, it is said, ignores dynamic elements of change, expressed in matters like the changing degrees of influence exercised by banks in industrial affairs, the comparative dynamism of enterprises with strong, and those with little or no Jewish involvement, the broader processes underlying changes in the Jewish role. Studies of this kind (that is of economic dynamics) could profitably be attempted—with great difficulty due to scarcity of documentation—for some individual enterprises: in the present context by comparing pairs of comparable firms in different ethnic categories. Such pairs can indeed be found. A number of studies of this kind, though they could, at best, cover only a limited area, *might* permit some conclusions about possible specifically 'Jewish' financial or commercial strategies, risk-taking propensities (and, with them, the greater risk of disaster in times of economic crisis), growth, dynamism, and structure of enterprises. Such comparative investigations, however (potentially fruitful as they may be), lie largely outside the scope of the present study.

A further objection to the method here adopted is that it ignores the question of ownership. While this is, in fact, true, the suggestion to include it is, of course, once more impracticable. For this, there are several reasons. In the first place, the composition of the body of shareholders was, necessarily, fluid. Moreover, as is well known, great numbers of individual shareholders were represented at the Annual

General Meetings of companies by large joint-stock banks (usually representing besides any shares in their own portfolios also those of their clients and, often, others obtained through 'swap' arrangements with sister banks). In any case, it is not immediately apparent how the distribution of share ownership could be of particular relevance to the role of members of the Jewish economic élite. They did, of course, by the very fact of their presence on company boards directly or indirectly document the ownership (or at least representation) of share capital.

VII

The question has also been raised concerning the legitimacy of isolating a separate 'Jewish' component within the wider corporate élite. In fact, as has been shown, men of Jewish origin were prominent in some branches of economic activity, under-represented in others. Equally, their geographical distribution differed from that of the élite as a whole. It seems therefore only logical to seek explanations and to examine some distinctive aspects.

The specific 'Jewish' situation within the German corporate structure owed not a little to the relative Jewish prominence in banking, notably in the large joint-stock banks. The major reasons for such prominence have already been discussed and need not be recapitulated here. The implications of this prominence for the role of Jews in the corporate economy of the age of full industrialization (or fully fledged capitalism) were, necessarily, far-reaching. They were, moreover, accentuated by a distinctive feature of the German economy. As is well known, banks (both private and joint-stock) played a considerably larger part in Germany than in many industrializing or industrialized countries in industrial financing, from providing the risk capital for early entrepreneurs to meeting the financial needs of large expanding or 'modernizing' industrial companies. Especially in the last quarter of the nineteenth century, major industrial companies required amounts of capital for exceeding their abilities at 'self-financing'. Many fell into debt and had to be rescued and nursed back to financial solvency (helped by boom conditions in the years before the war) with the help of major banks (able to draw on vast capital resources provided by depositors and savers). Strong and lasting associations developed between particular enterprises and their bankers, documented by the places occupied by bankers on the boards of major companies. The association, naturally, was closest in the case of expanding companies with the highest and most sustained need for investment capital (after the lost war this would be largely foreign capital: American, Dutch, and French). Foreign capital, though it could also be raised through industrial associates, could often be obtained on terms less potentially dangerous to commercial independence through the international banking system.

The close links between banking and industry characteristic of German economic development led to the emergence of a breed of banking specialists for industrial financing. In every major joint-stock bank from the days of the earliest, the Disconto-Gesellschaft and the Bank für Handel und Industrie, one or two senior directors assumed responsibility for industrial financing and made themselves specialists in the field. Individually, such men occupied important positions within the directorates of their banks, while collectively they constituted a small group of specialists co-operating on an almost daily basis (not without significant rivalries), knowing and watching each other and engaging in the delicate (and not always successful) transactions and operations of financial and industrial diplomacy. In particular, they came to involve themselves in the promotion of a variety of industrial and commercial associations and fusions as, notably, in the liquidation after the war of the Stinnes empire, the state of 'Stinnesia'. The role of industrial bankers in the German economy is in fact considered unique.

So, in consequence, was the role of men of Jewish origin. The reasons were manifold. In the first place, given the importance of Jews in the banking system generally (for reasons which have been explained), it was only to be expected that they would be prominently involved also in industrial financing. There were, however, additional reasons why some Jews were selected for key responsibilities in this field. Not least was their unusual diplomatic skill (it is possible but perhaps unprofitable to speculate whether and to what extent this was a product of the Jewish situation). Some developed special skills as mediators between 'capital' and industry, and between different industrial enterprises. Here the Salomonsohns, Louis Hagen, Carl Fürstenberg, Jakob Riesser, and others distinguished themselves. A further asset often found among Jewish bankers would be a close familiarity with the operations of the stock exchange. Again, with the growing internationalization of the capital market, the expansion of world trade, the widespread urge to export, and the growing importation of foreign raw materials, Jewish bankers, through the international connections of at any rate some of their number, were well qualified to guide the relations between banks and industrial enterprises. And, a significant fact, sometimes overlooked: the role of Jewish bankers in industrial financing was facilitated also by the relative freedom of many industrial managers, well documented in a number of cases, from strong anti-Jewish prejudice. Without such freedom, the position of Jewish bankers, particularly as board chairmen of industrial companies, might have been untenable. Nor would the directorates of large joint-stock banks have entrusted important 'industrial relations' to their Jewish members. Though there were, of course, Gentile counterparts—in particular the name of Carl Klönne, originally of the Schaaffhausensche Bankverein, later of the Deutsche Bank, comes to mind—these were not numerous. The Jewish banker as board chairman or multiple board member (to which might be added leading *syndici*—Adolf Salomonsohn had started in this way, later Maximilian Kempner and Julius Flechtheim were prominent), for whatever reasons, fulfilled an important role within the German corporate élite. His function as mediator between 'capital' and industry, the banks and industrial enterprises was a distinctive one, indispensable to the smooth development of industry in the age of full industrialization. This is a field which, though of course not specifically 'Jewish', was yet one in which the Jewish role (as has been seen for a variety of historical reasons reaching far into the past) was both specific and prominent. There is a direct line leading from the Jewish money-lender, pawnbroker, money-changer, or coinage manager (*Münzjude*), but also from the court financier and military contractor of the age of absolutism, to the Salomonsohn, Hagen, Fürstenberg.

One feature worth considering in this context is the involvement of Jewish financiers in the development of 'heavy industry', particularly in Silesia and in the Ruhr. This, which has occasionally been overlooked, was primarily a result of the heavy capital requirements of growing industrial enterprises, more particularly during the lean period of the Great Depression (which, whatever historians may claim after the event, existed at least in the perception of contemporaries). Indeed the ground for the investment of bank capital in industry had been prepared by the capital requirements of railway construction (which, in turn, had led to some investment in 'heavy industry'—as in the cases of Bethel Henry Strousberg or Gerson Bleichröder) culminating in the *Gründerjahre* (which some of the newly founded enterprises survived). For reasons to be considered presently, while the Jewish role in the industries of Upper Silesia extended also to management, this was not the case in the Rhine and Ruhr. In general, the role of Jewish bankers was a modest one in firms controlled by strong dynastic families (usually owning the bulk of the share capital even where the joint-stock principle had nominally been adopted). It was on the other hand important in a number of pure joint-stock companies Jews had helped to found or where original family influence had disappeared (or, on occasion, waned). There existed in the 'proprietary' enterprises, as exemplified notably in the case of Alfred Krupp, a strong hostility to (and fear of) bank capital, more particularly as represented by the large joint-stock banks. Curiously however such 'proprietary' enterprises, in the age of the large joint-stock banks would, not infrequently, turn to the larger private banks—again often Jewish—to meet their financial needs. In fact, through their place in banking, the role of Jews in 'heavy industry' is considerably more significant than has sometimes been supposed. In their capacity as industrial financiers, men like the Salomonsohns, Max Steinthal, Carl Fürstenberg, Louis Hagen, Jakob Goldschmidt, and others occupied a unique place and made a distinctive contribution.

Equally distinctive was the evolution of traditional Jewish trading activities in the age of full industrialization. Here, a combination of inherited aptitudes and new opportunities (largely through the rise of a 'mass-market'—in the first place mainly among members of the middle classes) led to far-reaching commercial developments. On the one hand, there was demand creation on an unprecedented scale with its by-product, advertising, on the other the satisfaction of consumer demand through developments in retail trade culminating in the establishment of great department stores. Another feature was a hitherto unseen expansion of world-wide international trade, in which Germany participated to the full. A symbolic expression was the role of Albert Ballin and the Hapag. Indeed, Jews were in the van of most of the great commercial innovations of the age. In the sphere of commerce as in that of banking, the Jewish élite of the age of full industrialization played a distinctive part. Its role, to no small degree, differed from that of its Gentile peers. Interestingly, the great majority of the leading Jewish commercial undertakings remained family firms; their owners, strictly speaking, did not become members of the corporate élite. In the cases, however, where wholesale trading activities shaded (or diversified) into production (as was the case with the Mertons' Metallgesellschaft), there would, exceptionally, be a degree of integration into the corporate structure. Such cases, however, were exceptional: commerce, essentially, remained the field of the independent. This, it may be, was part of its appeal more particularly for Jewish members of the élite.

VIII

Some elements of specificity in the Jewish industrial corporate élite of the age of full industrialization emerge from a comparison with its Westphalian Gentile counterpart. Hansjoachim Henning has analysed social origins, internal structure, marriage strategies, and sociability of Westphalian industrialists between 1860 and 1914.[69] Of particular interest in the present context is a group of men who were granted the titles of *Kommerzienrat* and *Geh. Kommerzienrat* between 1895 and 1910,[70] designated by Henning under the description of 'Grossunternehmer'. While it cannot, of course, be determined how far the Westphalian sample is representative of Gentile entrepreneurship as a whole (no men of Jewish origin appear to be included), and while the two 'subgroups' may, in some respects, lack strict comparability, divergences in their profiles are, nevertheless, suggestive.

One characteristic feature of Henning's sample is the high proportion of owner-managers[71] (27 out of 40 appointed in the period 1860–89, 12 of 40 in 1890–1909). Even in the period 1890–1909, employee managers[72] numbered only 24 out of 40—with a further 4 owners in process of transition to management.[73] From these data, Henning draws the conclusion that the heroic age of the 'inventor-artisan' was over, that what was now required for successful owner-entrepreneurship was primarily the possession of capital (essentially the product of economic achievement of an earlier generation) and the ability to employ it. These were moreover the natural preconditions for internal recruitment from within the entrepreneurial group.[74]

[69] H. Henning, 'Soziale Verflechtungen der Unternehmer in Westfalen 1860–1914' in *Zeitschrift für Unternehmensgeschichte*, 23, no. 1 (1978), p. 1 ff.
[70] 'Nach einer beim Oberpräsidium in Münster geführten Liste lebten in der Provinz Westfalen unter Berücksichtigung aller Zu- und Abgänge 1885 27 Kommerzienräte, davon 3 Geheime Kommerzienräte. Im Jahre 1900 lauten die entsprechenden Zahlen 51 und 5 und für 1910 81 und 11. Für 106 Angehörige der Teilgruppe konnten die Daten zum Verflechtungsverhalten erhoben werden' (ib., p. 4).
[71] *Eigentümer-Unternehmer*. [72] *Angehörige des hohen Managements*.
[73] *Eigentümer-Unternehmer im Wechsel in das hohe Management*.
[74] 'Währenddessen war für Westfalen jedoch ... die Zeit der Erfinderunternehmer mit ihrem schnellen Aufstieg aus anderen sozialen Gruppen schon vorüber. Zum Eigentümer-Unternehmer als Grossunternehmer gehörten nicht mehr in erster Linie technisches Wissen und technisch-handwerkliche Fähigkeiten, sondern er musste über Kapital verfügen können, das ihm im Unternehmen den beherrschenden Einfluss

Little of this applied to Jewish industrial entrepreneurs. In the first place, the enterprising 'inventor-artisan', considered by Henning the 'founding father' of Westphalian industry, hardly existed, and for obvious reasons, among Jewish entrepreneurs. In the second place, Jewish industrialists who inherited substantial paternal capital (or, somewhat more frequently, acquired it by marriage) were also comparatively rare. Far more typical than either the virtually non-existent artisan-inventor or the comparatively rare heir to a substantial fortune had been, among Jewish entrepreneurs of the age of early industrialization, the successful war contractor or purveyor of credit of the Napoleonic period. Such a man would invest in manufacturing with ownership not infrequently divorced from technical competence and, sometimes, even from management. In a later age also, the capital needed to start or develop industrial enterprises was only occasionally inherited. Instead, early risk capital was, more often, provided by private Jewish banking houses, later, with expansion of the enterprise, replaced by joint-stock banks or consortia, eventually by the capital market. Prominent members of the Jewish corporate élite, the Loewes, Arnholds, Ballins, Orensteins, Koppels, Huldschinskys, Hahns were, in economic terms, 'self-made men', as was, to an extent, Emil Rathenau (who was unable to 'pass on' his enterprise to his son Walther). A smaller number, among them the Caro brothers and Fritz Friedländer, were indeed the inheritors of relatively modest commercial firms which, however, could not provide the capital basis for the subsequent expansion of their entrepreneurial activities. This again, besides some commercial profits, would have to come from the banks and, eventually, the stock exchange. In consequence, the Jewish industrial élite, particularly as regards the 'great achievers', who perhaps should alone be considered, could hardly be described as 'self-recruiting'. The requirement for success here was less the possession of capital than commercial flair and the ability to inspire confidence. It was this which, for the fortunate few, would open the way to riches and influence, if rarely ownership. Jewish entrepreneurs, by and large, worked with capital provided by others rather than their own (which indeed they rarely commanded, particularly in the early stages of their entrepreneurial careers).

sicherte ... Dieses Kapital und die Fähigkeit, es einzusetzen, waren in aller Regel ererbt, waren also in erster Linie Ergebnis der Leistung der Vätergeneration. Damit waren die objektiven Voraussetzungen für einen hohen Rekrutierungsgrad aus der eigenen Teilgruppe gegeben' (Henning, loc. cit., p. 6).

A second respect in which the economic élite of Westphalia as depicted by Henning may be compared with the Jewish one concerns the social extraction (*Herkunft*) of its members. What is striking in Henning's sample is the high proportion of his 'Grossunternehmer' drawn either from large-scale industry (*Grossindustrie*) or wholesale trade (*Grosshandel*). These two branches account for 24 out of 40 in the period 1860–89 (the 'age of the owner-manager') and still for 18 out of 40 in the period 1890–1909 (with due caution the 'age of management'). Jewish 'Grossunternehmer' by contrast did not originate from Jewish wholesale industry (which, indeed, hardly existed) and only to a limited extent from wholesale trade. More commonly, the fathers would have engaged in 'middle-range' commercial pursuits, frequently in provincial towns. In more than one biography also it is recorded that fathers had at one time owned substantial commercial fortunes but had subsequently lost them. In general, Jewish 'Grossunternehmer' came, more often than their Westphalian counterparts, from Henning's category of 'Gewerbe' (a somewhat ill-defined portmanteau term to describe medium-scale economic activities). Again, a relatively high proportion of Jewish 'Grossunternehmer' were drawn from a background seemingly outside Henning's major categories. These were the sons of members of the professions of doctors and Jewish communal officials (teachers, cantors, and so on) without direct Gentile equivalent. On the other hand, a number of Gentile entrepreneurs were the sons of academically trained officials which, this time, had no Jewish counterpart. Overall, Westphalian entrepreneurs, being the older, were recruited to a much greater extent than Jewish from established bourgeois and, indeed, often *haut bourgeois* families. The background of the Jewish corporate élite on the other hand tended more often to be 'middle-class' or even petty bourgeois. Jewish entrepreneurs, unlike those of Westphalia, were, in their majority, 'self-made' men.

There is, in Henning's examination of the social origins of Westphalian entrepreneurs, one feature that contrasts markedly with the position in the Jewish élite. In his subdivision for 'top management' for the period 1890–1909, of the 24 managers given titles no fewer than 14 are drawn from 'Gewerbe', another 8 from large-scale industry. The majority of 'top-management' is described as possessing little capital but (extensive) previous commercial experience.[75] This

[75] 'Der ins hohe Management aufsteigende kleinere Teil dieses Personenkreises ... setzte sich vorwiegend aus Männern mit kleinem Besitz, aber schon relativ

description of an employee at the highest level, while it might fit men like Albert Ballin or Alfred Berliner, is by no means appropriate for others like Emil Rathenau, Isidor Loewe, or Oscar Caro. By and large, Jewish 'managers' were, if anything, more likely to come from more substantial commercial backgrounds (including banking): they tended to be founders of their companies (unlike their Gentile counterparts), even if they did not own them. Even though salaried, it may be doubted whether the term 'employee' truly describes their status or position. Their managerial functions often are broadly commercial rather than 'managerial' in the narrower sense. There is not in the 'Jewish sector' the same rigid division as in the Gentile between proprietary and managerial enterprises. The Jewish managing director, while less than the member of an owning dynasty, is often a good deal more than a senior employee—the business may or may not bear his name. Their minority interest in the firm they did not own might be—or at least could become—substantial. In short, numbers of Jewish 'managers' occupied a position intermediate in some respects between those of owner and manager. Henning's categories, while appropriate to Westphalian entrepreneurs, are largely inapplicable to Jewish industrialists. It is a fact which points to a fairly fundamental difference between the two groups (though, of course, if exceptionally, extreme proprietary positions like those of the Hirsches of Halberstadt or managerial ones like those of Albert Ballin are to be found among Jewish men of affairs also, but they are not typical).

The evidence, then suggests that the Jewish segment of the German corporate élite possessed some characteristics of its own, stemming from its distinctive origins and, to some extent, evolution. For mainly historical reasons, the Jewish corporate élite, while sharing some features of the Gentile one, can yet be distinguished from it. Some prima-facie differences have been discussed. Further and more detailed study would be needed to establish more accurately the degree of Jewish specificity within the corporate economic élite.

IX

A related question regarding the Jewish corporate élite concerns the extent to which the business strategies of its members may have differed from those of their Gentile counterparts. This is, of course, an

grossen geschäftlichen Erfahrungen auf dem Hintergrund einer kaufmännischen oder kaufmännisch-technischen Vorbildung zusammen' (ib., p. 7).

area of speculation rather than proof, but the matter is on occasion referred to in the literature. Historians, for instance, have more than once alluded to an underlying ethnic component in the notorious rivalry of the AEG and Siemens. About the fundamental differences in the respective managerial styles and ethics of the two firms there can be little doubt. Thus, in a memorandum (November 1931) relating to a possible amalgamation of the two companies, Winterfeld, a member of the Siemens directorate, expressed himself as follows: 'Dazu kommt, dass AEG und Siemens in ihrer Individualität überaus verschieden sind, man spricht verschiedene Sprachen, was sehr schnell wieder zur Verstimmung führt . . .'. And again, in a more detailed development of the argument:

Gegen die Fusion spricht eigentlich nur, dass es sich ausgerechnet um die AEG handelt. Die AEG stellt mit Ihren [sic] vielen Interessen: vom Stahlwerk zur Lokomotive, bei der Verschwelung mit ihren Bankverbindungen, von der Handelsgesellschaft bis zu ihren Aktienbeteiligungen in Amerika einen Partner dar, dessen innerer Wert schwer zu übersehen ist, und der als ganzer Bissen unverdaulich ist . . .[76]

To which the modern historian of the negotiations, on the basis of further evidence from the Siemens archives adds: '. . . Schliesslich wurde der Gegensatz zwischen dem "Siemens" und dem "AEG-Geist" hervorgehoben. Die unterschiedlichen Personalführungsstile und geschäftspolitischen Leitlinien der beiden Gesellschaften ständen einer erspriesslichen Zusammenarbeit auch auf der Managementebene entgegen.'[77]

A concrete example of the contrasting commercial philosophies of the two firms is provided by a characteristic incident described in the memoirs of Felix Deutsch. In the late eighties, when the price of electric light bulbs stood at 3.50 M apiece, an attempt was made to negotiate a 'price-fixing' agreement between three major producers, AEG, Siemens, and Edison Swan Co. in England. Deutsch recalls:

Von unserer Seite wurde der Vorschlag gemacht, den Preis auf 1.50 zu ermässigen, um dadurch die Konkurrenz von vornherein auszuschalten. Es

---

[76] Ib., p. 4.
[77] Homburg, loc. cit., n. 50 above, pp. 35 f. The statement is supported by the following references: Record of the Discussion between Franke, Köttgen, Winterfeld, Haller Gorz on 4 and 7 Oct. 1925, OCT. 1925, SAA 4/Lf 529; SSW Meeting of the board of directors, 20 Oct. 1925; SSW Board meeting, 10 Nov. 1931, SAA 4/Lf 529; Carl Friedrich v. Siemens to Frank, New York, 30 Aug. 1932, SAA 4/Lf 796. Homburg, loc. cit., p. 56 n. 115.

war klar, dass bei diesem Preis zunächst jedenfalls kein Nutzen zu erzielen war, vielleicht sogar Verluste entstehen würden, aber wir waren sicher, keine erhebliche Konkurrenz zu erhalten und nach und nach in den Preis hineinzuwachsen. Werner von Siemens war in hohem Masse indigniert. Solche Vorschläge, meinte er, könnten nur Menschen machen, die vom Geschäft nichts verstünden, und wenn wir die AEG so weiter leiteten, müsste sie zu Grunde gehen. Alles Reden half nichts, er liess sich nicht überzeugen, und wir gingen resultatlos auseinander. Die Folge war, dass nach einigen Jahren ca. vierzig Glühlampenfabriken existierten und schliesslich der Preis bis auf zwanzig Pfennige herunterging.'[78]

The existence in this instance of irreconcilable differences of attitude concerning a major issue on business strategy is clear. Deutsch and Rathenau were willing to take commercial risks to eliminate (or forestall) competition, Siemens was not. Did the differences have an ethnic (as well as a commercial) base? And, if so, how far were they 'typical'? No conclusive answer to these questions can be given.

Repeatedly, Emil Rathenau has been seen (or represented) as possessing characteristic attributable to his 'Jewishness' also in regard to his wider business philosophy. Thus Felix Pinner,[79] numbered by Carl Fürstenberg among the leading experts on German economic affairs,[80] professed to find 'Jewish' characteristics in Rathenau's personality.[81] These, he considered, were reflected in the nature of his economic achievement: 'Emil Rathenaus einzigartige Begabung, sein Genie und das Schöpferische seiner Leistung lagen auf industrie-kaufmännischem und industrie-finanziellem Gebiete ... auf dem Untergrund einer zuverlässigen technischen Fähigkeit aufgebaut'.[82]

His distinctive contribution was 'der fruchtbare Gedanke, den Konsum nicht zu erwarten, sondern den Konsum zu schaffen ... es war die überaus schöpferische Verbindung und wechselseitige Befruchtung von Industrie und Finanzierung, die das System

---

[78] Felix Deutsch, 'Lebenserinnerungen', typewritten MS copy in the archives of the Leo Baeck Institute in New York, pp. 64 f.
[79] Felix Pinner, *Emil Rathenau und das elektrische Zeitalter* (Leipzig, 1918).
[80] See p. 20 n. 18.
[81] 'Auch sonst ist der jüdische Einfluss in Rathenaus Charakter deutlich zu spüren. Der rechnerische Sinn im Schwärmen, der Realismus in der Phantasie, die Kühle im Enthusiasmus, die Selbstkritik im Optimismus und schliesslich die Schärfe und Helle des Intellekts, die trotzdem nicht nur Gedankenblässe wird ... alles das sind Zeichen des einmal bodenständig gewesenen, aber dann entwurzelten, und nun wieder nach Verankerung strebenden, darum in seinen Empfindungen häufig umschlagenden jüdischen Geistes.' Pinner, op. cit., n. 79 above, p. 362.
[82] Ib., p. 365.

Rathenau prinzipiell von dem System des frühern Siemens & Halske unterschied'.[83] Whether the differences in the 'styles' or 'systems' of Werner Siemens and Emil Rathenau justify Pinner's dialectical contrast[84] and the extent to which they rested on an ethnic base must again remain a matter of opinion. All that can be said here is that the rivalry of AEG and Siemens,[85] suggestive in itself, is by no means free from ethnic overtones.[86]

Moreover, an aura of Jewish specificity hangs about another of the 'Jewish big three' in the corporate sphere,[87] Eugen Gutmann's Dresdner Bank. Of the founder and guiding spirit for many years, Carl Fürstenberg speaks in the following significant terms:

... Es ist für mich immer sehr interessant gewesen, festzustellen, wie die führende Persönlichkeit, die eine grosse Bank geschaffen hat, deren ganzem Betrieb einen unverwischbaren persönlichen Stempel aufdrückt. Die Dresdner Bank Eugen Gutmanns unterschied sich in grundlegender Hinsicht von der Deutschen Bank Georg von Siemens' und von der Disconto-Gesellschaft Hansemanns. Auf der einen Seite sollte es Gutmann gelingen, systematische Mitarbeiter zu finden, die in ruhiger Arbeit das Filialwesen gerade dieser Bank zu besonderer Stärke entwickelt haben. Auf der anderen Seite war Gutmann nicht ein Mann des Details, sondern besass einen bemerkenswerten Blick für grosse Gewinnmöglichkeiten und einen ausgesprochenen Börsenverstand. Seinen Einfluss auf Aktiengesellschaften pflegte er sich auf Grund von Aktienkäufen an der Börse zu sichern, wobei er eine ihm persönlich eigentümliche Taktik entwickelte.[88]

[83] Felix Pinner, op. cit., n. 44 above, pp. 25 f.
[84] 'In diesem bewusst Kaufmännischen der Absatzwerbung und der Kalkulation lag der hauptsächliche Gegensatz der von Rathenau geführten AEG gegenüber den Siemensbetrieben ... Siemens & Halske blieben auch bei der praktischen Verwertung der genialen Siemensschen Transportelektrifizierung ihren Geschäftsmaximen treu, das Beste, was sie leisten konnten, zu zeigen, der Leistung eine möglichst grosse Publizität zu geben und dann wie der gute mittelalterliche Handwerker, dessen Tradition Siemens in die moderne Zeit hinein verlängerte, auf die Bestellung zu warten. Diese Bestellungen blieben auch nicht aus.' Georg Bernhard, op. cit., n. 3 above, p. 152. 'Als die Siemensunternehmen sahen, dass mit ihren moderneren Methoden die schnell gross gewordene Konkurrentin ihnen auf ihrem eigensten Spezialgebiet immer grössere Objekte abjagte, blieb ihnen nichts anderes übrig, als das System der Finanzierungsgesellschaften nachzunahmen' (ib., p. 157).
[85] Thus Georg v. Siemens ends a memorandum about the possibility of fusion with the AEG with the words: 'Ceterum censeo Carthaginem esse delendam'. Georg Siemens, On the question of the union of Siemens-AEG, Berlin, 7 Nov. 1931, SAA 4/Lf 793.
[86] See for instance Deutsch, op. cit., n. 78 above, p. 57.
[87] The third being Ballin's Hapag.
[88] Fürstenberg, op. cit., n. 23 above, p. 213 f. The same quotation occurs on p. 226 n. 30 above in a different context.

After describing Gutmann's stock-exchange manœuvres, Fürstenberg continues: 'Diese Methoden, die damals noch als amerikanisch galten, sind erst in späteren Jahren auch in Deutschland üblich geworden. Wenn ich hier andeute, dass Eugen Gutmann wirtschaftliche Vorgänge unter dem Gesichtspunkt der Hausse oder der Baisse anzusehen pflegte, so will ich den Verdiensten dieses grossen deutschen Bankiers damit nicht etwa Abbruch tun. Das vortreffliche Werk, das er hinterlassen hat, zeugt für das hohe Mass seiner Tüchtigkeit.'[89]

In certain respects comparable to Eugen Gutmann, creator of the Dresdner Bank, was Jakob Goldschmidt, who was able to raise his Danat (Darmstädter- und National) Bank into an institute of comparable rank. Hans Fürstenberg, in his memoirs, describes his father's attitude towards Goldschmidt as a banker in terms indicating the similarity of the latter's rise and methods of those of Eugen Gutmann:

Der junge Goldschmidt [from humble beginnings] hatte sich ja nur dadurch mit verblüffender Schnelligkeit in die Höhe arbeiten können, dass er in frühen Jahren den Zutritt zu einer anfänglich bescheidenen Börsenfirma fand, wo er, dank eines geradezu sensationellen Instinkts für Kursgewinne und einer unentwegt den Pulsschlag der deutschen Inflation abtastenden Hand, rasche und grosse Erfolge erzielte und ein sehr reicher Mann wurde.[90]

Carl Fürstenberg, though himself a highly successful 'self-made man', did not wholly approve of Goldschmidt's strategies:

Es ist nach meiner früheren Schilderung klar [wrote his son] dass Jakob Goldschmidt nicht gerade ein Bankier nach dem Herzen Carl Fürstenbergs war. Er fand ihn zu spekulativ, zu ehrgeizig, zu schnell durch Börsenmanöver bereichert. Andererseits entgingen ihm aber gewisse geniale Züge seines Wesens nicht. Auch dass Goldschmidt einen ausgesprochenen 'Börsenverstand' besass, gefiel einem alten Routinier wie Carl Fürstenberg in einer Zeit, wo sich zu seinem Ärger volkswirtschaftliche Theorien mehr und mehr ausbreiteten.[91]

It is not without significance that both Gutmann and Goldschmidt, as 'fathers' respectively of the Dresdner and Danat banks, probably the two most successful corporate Jewish bankers (with Carl Fürstenberg

---

[89] Ib., p. 214. Pinner describes Gutmann, somewhat colourfully, as 'eine Vollblutnatur, ein Draufgänger, eine Persönlichkeit voll Konstruktion und Ideen', who, however, was sometimes carried away by his enthusiasms. Pinner, op. cit., n. 44 above, p. 225.
[90] Hans Fürstenberg, *Erinnerungen* (Düsseldorf and Vienna, 1968), p. 162.
[91] Ib., p. 190.

a good third), thus built their banking careers on early operations carried out in similar style. Both acquired much of the initial capital for themselves, their institutions, and, no doubt, occasionally also their clients, on the stock exchange—and both were commended by Carl Fürstenberg for their uncanny 'stock-exchange instinct' ('ausgesprochener Börsenverstand'). Carl Fürstenberg himself possessed similar gifts though he may have considered the activities of Gutmann and Goldschmidt too speculative for his taste. Another successful stock-exchange 'operator' had been the Cologne banker Louis Hagen whose early career, like those of Gutmann and Golschmidt, had been dominated by operations on the Berlin stock exchange. While not every Jewish banker possessed this 'stock-exchange sense' or chose to exercise it (among the notable exceptions are 'conservatives' like Hermann Wallich, Max Warburg, or the Mendelssohns), it yet appears in a number of cases to have been highly developed. At the same time, it was comparatively rare among Gentile bankers. More widely, men of Jewish extraction played a leading part on the Berlin stock exchange. It was no accident that perhaps its outstanding figure was the Jewish banker Wilhelm Kopetzky.

On the reasons for the widely recognized and often negatively assessed special Jewish aptitude for successful stock-exchange operations, it is possible only to speculate. Was the correct anticipation of price movements (or wider economic trends) the result of 'flair', luck, skilful manipulation, good intelligence, pleasure in gambling, 'self-fulfilling prophecy' (once a 'king of the stock-exchange' had gained a reputation as a pundit, lesser lights would blindly follow his lead whether to a bear or a bull market), or was it, as is indeed most likely, a mixture of several of these? In any case, whatever the qualities required for the successful anticipation of market movements, there is no doubt that a number of prominent Jewish bankers possessed them to an eminent degree. The 'ausgesprochener Börsenverstand' admired by Carl Fürstenberg, on the evidence, was part of a banking 'style' most prominently represented by men of Jewish origin (no counterparts among prominent Gentile bankers—whether directors of joint-stock or of private banks—come to mind). Of course not all members of the Jewish banking élite adopted the style of operations of Eugen Gutmann or Jakob Goldschmidt: some, including even Carl Fürstenberg, while admiring their 'Börsenverstand', disapproved. What may have existed however, and for whatever reason is a predisposition of a number of Jewish bankers towards stock-exchange operations combined with a special aptitude. These clearly were men prepared to take risks at which others might have balked.[92] The Dresdner Bank ran into serious difficulties in the economic and financial crisis in 1901. And was it wholly accidental that, in the great banking crisis thirty years later, Danat and Dresdner, to a greater extent than the Deutsche Bank and/or Disconto-Gesellschaft, found themselves over-extended,[93] and had to pay the price in the form of wholesale state aid and nationalization? More or less close association with the stock exchange (and thus some speculative activities) had long been characteristic of prominent Jewish bankers, probably more than of the bulk of their Gentile counterparts. Not every successful Jewish banker (as Carl Fürstenberg and Hermann Wallich demonstrated in their respective spheres) was also an avid 'speculator', but some of the most prominent (as well as some lesser lights) were. A penchant for stock-exchange transactions combined with a special flair for anticipating price movements may thus have been a feature related to Jewish ethnicity (no doubt less for 'genetic' reasons than through the ambition of the disadvanted leading to a greater readiness to take risks, indeed to gamble, combined, in some cases—the most outstanding—with a 'sixth sense' for price movements and trends). The Hansemanns or Georg Siemens, on the other hand, as Carl Fürstenburg noted, built up their large enterprises with the aid of strategies significantly different from those employed by a Gutmann or a Goldschmidt.

[92] The kind of 'risk' the Dresdner Bank was prepared to take in industrial financing are illustrated in a letter which, in 1901, August Thyssen wrote to Carl Klönne of the Deutsche Bank (his principal financial associate), in connection with a prospective loan operation of which Klönne was claiming the lion's share for his institute: 'Wie Sie wissen, haben mir Dresdner Bank und Schaaffhausen zu allen Zeiten das grösste Vertrauen entgegengebracht. Niemals haben diese Banken unseren Kredit bemängelt und Deckungen verlangt, obgleich wir, d.h. Thyssen & Co., in der schwierigsten Zeit [in the nineties] bis drei Millionen Mark und mehr schuldeten. Es ist meine Pflicht, diesen Banken bei dieser Gelegenheit meine Dankbarkeit zu zeigen, falls überhaupt eine Anleihe ausgegeben wird'. Quoted in Gertrud Milkereit, 'Einige Uberlegungen zum Verhältnis zwischen Industrie und Banken' Jürgen Schneider (ed.), *Wirtschaftskräfte und Wirtschaftswege*, 3 (Nuremberg, 1978), p. 527.

[93] Thus in 1929 the Danat Bank, although 'only the fourth biggest bank in terms of its equity capital ... had the second largest balance sheet ... thanks to its expansionist business policies'. (Born, op. cit., n. 28 above, p. 244.) Two years later, what 'triggered off' the acute phase of the German banking crisis in June 1931 was the insolvency of Nordwolle—a firm involved in speculative transactions, to which both Danat and Dresdner Bank had extended large credit facilities (ib., p. 260). On the other hand, however, the Berliner Handels-Gesellschaft was the only major bank 'to emerge from the crisis without capital reconstruction and Reich aid ... Its directors, Carl Fürstenberg and Otto Jeidels, had on principle not taken up any foreign credit of less than six months. They had also been very cautious in their lending policy.' (Ib., p. 262.) As Fürstenberg's and Jeidels's strategies show, there were also cautious bankers of Jewish origin.

Already, speaking of his banking experiences in Paris at an earlier period, Hermann Wallich had noted what appeared to him the commercial implications of ethnic diversity:

> Es ist für Frankreich beschämend, zu konstatieren, dass bis zur Begründung der jetzt bestehenden grossen Aktienbanken die Träger des eigentlichen französischen Bankgeschäfts deutsche Juden und kalvinistische Schweizer waren. So wie die Nationalitäten, sondern sich auch die geschäftlichen Eigenschaften der beiden Gruppen. Während die erste, leichter beweglich, sich mehr auf das immer mehr in Mode gekommene Effektengeschäft warf und sich zum Herrn der Börse machte, blieb die andere Grupp ihren strengen Grundsätzen treu, betrieb das Bankfach nach gegebenen Formen und legte mehr Wert auf dauernden und festgeregelten Gewinn. Das legitime Bankgeschäft, in dessen Organisation sie den andern überlegen waren, bevorzugten sie einmaligem Nutzen eines mehr oder weniger spekulativen Börsenverkehrs.[94]

As suggested by the careers of, among others, Gutmann and Goldschmidt (as against those of Gentile founders of large joint-stock banks) or by the readiness of the Landaus or Borns to provide risk capital for hopeful entrepreneurs, the distinction may well be of wider validity than the contrast suggested to Wallich by his Paris experiences.

Irrespective of the question whether Jewish economic activity, more particularly at the level of the élite, possessed features differentiating it from Gentile, there is evidence to suggest a fairly widespread awareness of the 'ethnicity' of industrial enterprises. At the time of Louis Hagen's reception into the Catholic Church for instance, a significant little anecdote was making the rounds of the Rhineland:

> Die üblichen Scherze kursierten damals im Rheinland. Der katholische Pfarrer habe ihn beim Vorbereitungsunterricht gefragt, ob er einige gute Werke kenne, worauf der damals noch Louis Levy genannte die Namen 'Harpen, Gelsenkirchen, Phönix'[95] herausschmetterte. Als der verlegene Pfarrer ihm darauf sagte, er meine gute christliche Werke, sei die Antwort 'Siemens' gekommen.[96]

[94] *Zwei Generationen im deutschen Bankwesen 1833–1914* (Frankfurt-on-Main, 1978), pp. 52 f.
[95] Sal. Oppenheim Jun. & Co., financial patron of Phoenix from its beginning, had saved its protégé during the economic crisis of the late eighteen-fifties and had since retained a leading position. See Lutz Hatzfeld, 'Das Phoenix-Rheinrohr-Archiv als Problem industrieller Verwaltung' in *Duisburger Forschungen*, 8 (1965), 136.
[96] Louise, *Freifrau* von Reibnitz-Maltzan, in *Der Mittag* (Düsseldorf, 9 October 1932). Quoted in W. E. Mosse, 'Zwei Präsidenten der Kölner Industrie- und Handelskammer: Louis Hagen und Paul Silverberg' in *Köln und das rheinische Judentum* (Cologne, 1984), p. 331.

What is significant in the anecdote is the fact that both those who 'perpetrated' and those who retailed it must have considered the three first-named companies as 'Jewish' (on account of their Jewish banking connections and board chairmen) and Siemens, for whatever reason, as quintessentially Christian.

In conclusion, a study of the place of Jews in the German corporate élite confutes the view that, with the gradual transition from private firm to joint-stock company, their role underwent a significant diminution. It equally shows that, though they occupied important positions, their influence in the German economy was far from dominant. It confirms also that they were unevenly distributed over the German economy, due largely to the parameters of previous Jewish economic activity. Lastly, some tentative suggestions can be advanced concerning the relationship of ethnicity and economic activity. Here, clearly, nothing can be either quantified or 'proved'. All that can be shown is that some indications suggest the existence of elements of Jewish specificity and possibly of a distinctive Jewish economic 'style' (a view shared, more or less, by some Jews, most anti-Semites, and a number of people who were neither). Economic 'rationality', as illustrated by Deutsch's account of the abortive cartel for electric light bulbs, was not an unambiguous one-way street. It is in fact, more than doubtful whether considerations of 'economic rationality' do indeed provide 'ideal type' single, 'correct' solutions. And, where equally (or nearly) economically rational variants, alternatives, or options exist (or are perceived to be available), it may well be that cultural or ethnic factors also influence the ultimate choice (or economic decision). Ethnic origin, while not perhaps in itself the principal determinant of business strategy, may yet have affected certain economic decisions and preferences (among Gentiles as much as among Jews). Ethnicity thus may have been a relevant, even if secondary, factor in the German corporate economy.

8
Weimar: Decline and Fall?

THE classical age of German entrepreneurial capitalism of the 'second industrial revolution' may be said to have ended with the outbreak of war in 1914. The introduction by stages of a war economy had involved a high degree of state control over matters like imports, the allocation of raw materials, and hence also production, which had had to be geared largely to military needs. When, after 1918, state controls were gradually relaxed, industry and commerce had to adjust to new and unfavourable economic conditions. Firms had lost a large part of their foreign assets, their overseas markets, their international goodwill. Important coal and iron-ore deposits had been lost in both east and west. Nor did years of political instability culminating in the inflation of 1923 favour peaceful economic reconstruction. The burden of reparations, whatever orders it might produce for individual enterprises, of necessity depressed the German economy as a whole. Again, the limitations imposed on the German armed forces (and which could be evaded only imperfectly) could not but affect adversely (compared with the palmy days of Wilhelm II) the market for the products of German 'heavy industry'.

As is well known, currency stabilization after 1923 combined with a flood of foreign investment (much of it, however, on a short-term basis) provided the basis for a short-lived period of reconstruction and expansion. Then, under the impact of the Depression, the Brüning government (and its successors) began to intervene increasingly in economic affairs. During the financial crisis of the summer of 1931, a substantial part of the German banking system passed under state control. Increased financial burdens were imposed on industry to meet the state's need to provide the means of subsistence for, in the end, some six million unemployed. Harsh deflationary policies were adopted (over the opposition of some 'Keynesians'). At the end, a partial economic recovery (fuelled by rearmament and public works) was accompanied by a measure of insecurity attending political revolution and by the earliest stage of partial 'Aryanization'. These, by and large, were conditions hardly conducive to economic expansion or entrepreneurial initiative.

In any case, moreover, the phase of rapid industrialization based on the growth of the electrical industry, on massive armaments, and on rapidly expanding exports was over. The 'electrical revolution' had been completed. The demand for battleships had shrunk to a trickle. Lost export markets could be regained only slowly and were threatened, in any case, by a growing wave of protectionism. Motor car, diesel engine, and aeroplane were insufficient to take up the slack. Even without the other adverse conditions, economic growth had become patchy at best.

It was against this background of relative economic decline that significant structural changes occurred in the German economy. Among these was a marked reduction of the role of banks in industrial financing. This had begun during the war when some industrial firms, out of swollen profits, had been able to repay bank loans. Then, during the period of inflation great conglomerates had been formed (notably by Hugo Stinnes and Otto Wolff) without significant banking participation. Again, while banks might play some part in the creation of giant concerns like IG Farben (1925) and Vereinigte Stahlwerke (1926), the resulting units were too large to form close associations with particular banks. In general, the 'special relationship' between an industrial firm and its banking connection, which had been so conspicuous in the imperial era, had all but disappeared. Capital needs of some of the largest firms exceeded the resources of even the largest joint-stock bank. Industrial managements, at the same time, preferred to deal, where necessary, either with several different banks or with large banking consortia (or, possibly, to take in foreign capital largely through the major private banks). Moreover, the expansion of many enterprises (as distinct from amalgamations and rationalization) and with it the need for new capital (except occasionally for modernization of plants) had slowed down. There was some growth also of state credit institutions designed to assist industry. Taken together, these developments would alter the relationships that had previously existed between industrial firms and 'their' bankers. 'Special relationships', even where they persisted, had lost much of their earlier importance. As a result, the influence of board chairmen in dealings with managing directors (and their managerial organizations) would decline.

As against this, however, the banking system in relation to industry and commerce after war and inflation would acquire a new and important function, to assist the capital reconstruction of companies. Banks, through their international connections, were able to attract into Germany foreign investment capital (largely through Amsterdam) for the benefit alike of private industry, of public utilities, and of municipal corporations. With this, there occurred a limited renaissance of private banking firms, especially larger ones with international reputations and access to international capital markets. A number of Jewish private banks, among them the Mendelssohns, Warburg and Hirschland, Hardy and Dreyfus, benefited from these conditions, as did Jakob Goldschmidt's Danatbank.

A special feature of the unprecedented interaction between economics and international politics was the new concern with currency questions, with reparations, and with a variety of international financial negotiations. Here successive German governments needed not only expert advice but also the services of skilled negotiators acceptable to the international economic community. Among such experts, two men of Jewish extraction stood out, Carl Melchior, partner in the house of Warburg, and Rudolf Loeb, the last effective director of the Mendelssohn bank. Another major figure was Dr Fritz Mannheimer, an associate of the Mendelssohns, domiciled in Amsterdam. Yet another was Otto Jeidels, Carl Fürstenberg's 'right-hand man' at the Berliner Handels-Gesellschaft. In fact, in the changed circumstances after 1918, a number of Jews played an active role in reintegrating the German into the international economy, from which it had been largely excluded.[1]

Within these overall parameters, there operated factors of both continuity and change. On the one hand, there was a high degree of

---

[1] The part played by Jewish private bankers after 1918 in reviving and 'mediating' financial and industrial relations with neutral and 'ex-enemy' centres, in the peace negotiations particularly with regard to reparations, in the negotiation of the Dawes and Young loans, and in the general reintegration of the German economy into world markets merits a special study of its own. One aspect is described in a memorandum of 1931 by Hans Schäffer (state secretary in the ministry of finance) 'Bei den verschiedenen Kreditverhandlungen haben uns immer die Häuser Mendelssohn und Warburg unterstützt. Beide Häuser haben sich um das Reich sehr verdient gemacht. Warburgs haben insbesondere durch Melchior, die schwierigsten und undankbarsten Verhandlungen für das Reich bei aussenpolitischen Behandlungen geführt. Mendelssohns sind bei verschiedenen Gelegenheiten in Kassenfragen zu Hilfe gekommen. Das Reich führt zwar seine Verhandlungen durch die Reichsbank, aber diese beiden Häuser betätigen sich dann nach draussen, wie die Dinge heute liegen, meist als Vermittler.' Hans Schäffer, Memorandum on the discussion with Dreyse, [vice-president of the Reichsbank], Berlin, 6 Jan. 1931, Schäffer Nachlass, Institut für Zeitgeschichte, Munich, ED 93, vol. 30, fo. 2.

continuity of ownership and management in industry. In this respect at any rate, the year 1918 marked no revolutionary turning-point. Equally, territorial losses and the loss of overseas assets, while they hit some particular interests hard, did not produce widespread changes. Neither was the impact of the inflation, though productive of some changes of ownership and of some ephemeral speculative conglomerates, a revolutionary one. On the other hand, within this overall (if financially weakened) continuity, important biological changes were at work in the German economic élite. The 'Wilhelmine' generation of entrepreneurs was rapidly disappearing, to be replaced by another of lesser calibre (as well as diminished opportunities). The age of the 'great captains' was passing, with mediocre heirs reinforcing a tendency inherent in the system towards depersonalization, bureaucratization, and relative anonymity. An exception were the few flamboyant buccaneers emerging from the chaotic fluidity of war and inflation who, by a variety of share transactions, were able to achieve a usually ephemeral prominence in economic life. Of the few who survived the currency stabilization, several came to grief during the Great Depression. The most prominent Jewish newcomers—Ludwig Katzenellenbogen, Jakob Goldschmidt, Paul Silverberg—had fallen victim to economic circumstances (and over-extension of resources) before the advent of Hitler.

It is within these wider developments that the position of the Jewish economic élite in the Weimar Republic must be considered. Several features, sometimes contradictory in their effects, are significant. In the first place, there was a particularly marked generational turnover among Jews prominent in economic life. The following are the years of death of some of the more important figures:

1910	Isidor Loewe	1920	Rudolf Mosse
1913	M. L. Goldberger		Hugo Landau
	Georg v. Caro	1922	Walther Rathenau
1914	Wilhelm Herz	1923	Richard Witting
1915	Emil Rathenau		Oscar Tietz
	Julius Stern	1924	Paul Mankiewitz
1916	Wilhelm Merton		Alfred v. Kaulla
1917	Fritz v. Friedländer	1925	Eduard Arnhold
1918	Albert Ballin		Eugen Gutmann
1919	Adolf Salomonsohn		Sally Segall

At the time of their deaths, most of these men were well past their prime, with their major economic achievements lying well in the past. This is true also of 'survivors' like Carl Fürstenberg, Louis Hagen, James Simon, Benno Orenstein, Maximilian Kempner, Max Steinthal, Oscar Caro, Leopold Koppel, and Arthur Salomonsohn. These were now in the main in their late seventies, 'belated' relics of the 'great pre-war generation'. Their progressive eclipse contributed not a little to the impression of Jewish economic decline in the Weimar Republic.

Given the relative prominence of Jews in banking, both joint-stock and private, the overall decline in the importance of banking capital may have led to some reduction in their economic role. If, however, this was indeed the case, it was at least masked by some countervailing influences. In the first place, while the classic age of the joint-stock bank in Germany as an instrument of industrial financing lay in the past, the prominence of men of Jewish origin in these banks reached its apogee only under the Weimar Republic. Jews, in the days of Weimar, would, in fact, occupy leading positions in every major joint-stock bank. Moreover, some bankers—with Jakob Goldschmidt outstanding —would play a major role in the rationalization of whole branches of industry through concentration and amalgamation. In addition, with some of the stronger private banks once more coming into their own, this also, in the new age of 'mixed banking', brought Jews into positions of some prominence. Leading Jewish private bankers, as already mentioned, played a significant role in attracting foreign investment capital (much of it short-term) and in reintegrating Germany into the world economy. Also, as already mentioned, their services were in demand both as expert advisers and as international negotiators. On the face of it, it might even appear that the golden age' of Jews in German banking occurred only in the days of Weimar.

In the manufacturing and commercial sectors, meanwhile, with continuing processes of consolidation and concentration and with the growth of some individual firms, some industrial enterprises not numbered among the hundred largest in 1907, had reached that position by 1927.[2] They included, firms with Jewish participation. In the commercial sector also, in fields like retailing or publishing, Jews continued to be strongly represented. Overall, in fact, in the non-banking sectors, factors favourable to Jewish enterprise may, until the onset of the Great Depression, have still outweighed adverse ones.

---

[2] According to Siegrist's data, of the hundred largest industrial companies in 1927, 63 were 'newcomers'. Of course these were not necessarily new companies but often enterprises that had gained in relative importance since 1907.

There was, however, an adverse if imponderable influence that accompanied the recession (and, indeed, was fuelled by it); the growth of extreme nationalism with increasingly anti-Semitic overtones. Equally, there was a strong growth of anti-capitalist sentiment. The impact of such political developments on the position of Jews prominent in German economic life is difficult to assess. To some contemporaries at any rate it appeared as early as the beginning of 1928 (that is, before the onset of the Great Depression) that Jews were being squeezed out of important positions in both state and economy, even in banking. Only a few wealthy Jews were now left.[3] This, representing the contemporary impression of at least two informed observers, however, requires a number of qualifications. In the first place their comments on the paucity of very wealthy Jews lacked perspective. While the observation itself may have been correct, Ernst Feder and Martin Carbe might have asked themselves how many very large pre-war Gentile fortunes had in fact survived war, civil war, the loss of territories, of overseas assets, and, above all, hyper-inflation followed by violent deflation (the last of which also had claimed bubble-fortunes amassed by war profiteers, currency and stock-exchange speculators, and share pushers). Moreover, failure to mention extremely wealthy men like the brothers Franz and Robert von Mendelssohn suggests that Feder and Carbe confined their consideration to unbaptized Jews only. In fact, a number of wealthy Jews were baptized. As for the alleged partial elimination (*Zurückdrängung*) of Jews from positions of importance in the economy, this also requires qualification. True, a number of large Jewish (as almost certainly also of Gentile) private firms or companies in which Jews had been prominent had been hit by recent vicissitudes: thus the wealthy textile wholesalers Gebr. Simon had been all but ruined by the effects of the war; the damage caused to the Hapag had contributed to Albert Ballin's presumed suicide. The coal wholesaler Eduard Arnhold had seen his fortunes severely damaged by the fact that his mining interests (unlike those of the heirs of his erstwhile competitor Fritz Friedländer) were located in the part of Upper Silesia ceded

---

[3] The journalist Ernst Feder of the *Berliner Tageblatt* reports in his diary under the date of 6 Feb. 1928 a conversation with Martin Carbe, nephew of the publisher Rudolf Mosse: 'Mit Carbe Gespräch über die Zurückdrängung der Juden aus allen wichtigen Posten in Staat und Wirtschaft, sogar im Bankwesen. Carbe weist darauf hin, wie wenig sehr reiche Juden es noch gibt. Einer der wenigen ist Lachmann-Mosse ...' (Hans Lachmann-Mosse, grandson of Salomon Lachmann, son-in-law and heir of Rudolf Mosse who died in 1920) (Feder, op. cit., p. 155).

to Poland; the world-wide metal-trading firm of Aron Hirsch in Halberstadt, already hit by the copper crisis of 1907, had been almost fatally damaged by British confiscation of 'enemy property'. Coincidentally, Jewish-owned liberal newspapers would soon be losing readers (and, more seriously, advertising revenue) with the steady erosion of German liberalism. All this had hardly been *Zurückdrängung* of Jews but rather the damage done by the war and its aftermath to world-wide German wholesale trade in which Jews were prominent. Other cases of decline like those of the publishing firms started by Leopold Sonnemann and Rudolf Mosse or of the once great Bleichröder bank were attributable largely to mismanagement by incompetent heirs. As for the alleged *Zurückdrängung* 'even in banking', this, as the evidence will show, must have been largely a subjective impression.

At any rate the list of participants at an extraordinary meeting of the enlarged executive (*erweiterte Ausschusssitzung*) of the central organization of German bankers (Centralverband des Deutschen Bank- und Bankiergewerbes) held in June 1931 (with the economic crisis in 'full swing') hardly suggests a significant diminution of the Jewish role. As to Jewish participation in the corporate sector, the evidence suggests that, thanks largely to the interested protection of Dr Hjalmar Schacht, this, in many cases, was not seriously impaired until 1935. There is also some evidence to suggest that, at least down to this date, many Gentile members of the German ecomonic community showed no particular alacrity to rid themselves of their Jewish colleagues. It was only after 1935 that the expulsion of Jews from German economic life appears to have gathered momentum, culminating in their complete exclusion by 1938.

I

Among directors of joint-stock banks in general, the economic journalist Felix Pinner noted in 1925 at the same time a certain mediocrity (compared to the talented 'founders' of the previous generation) and a high average level of technical competence[4]—possibly

[4] 'Wie sehr es auch im derzeitigen Berliner Bankwesen an überragenden Gestalten fehlt, so muss doch zugestanden werden, dass kaum jemals ein so hoher Grad des Durchschnitts, eine so starke Zahl begabter, tüchtiger und geschulter Persönlichkeiten im Berliner Bankwesen tätig gewesen ist wie grade jetzt ...' (Pinner, *Deutsche Wirtschaftsführer* (Charlottenburg, 1925), p. 222).

features typical of a generation of heirs. While lacking originality, these bankers yet possessed the ability to take advantage of such opportunities as offered themselves.[5] However, such opportunities were now significantly fewer than in the 'golden days' of a Carl Fürstenberg or Eugen Gutmann.

Among these 'Weimar' bankers as already indicated, men of Jewish origin figured prominently. At the Deutsche Bank, Oscar Wassermann, a member of the directorate since 1912, filled, from 1923 until his retirement in 1933, the post of *Sprecher* (speaker), the premier position. In Pinner's view, Wassermann owed this position to a combination of intelligence and dialectical skill, respected by his colleagues in the directorate.[6] Among his major contributions is his part in the fusion in 1929 of the Deutsche Bank with the Disconto-Gesellschaft, creating Germany's largest financial institution with a nominal share capital of 285 million marks.[7] Wassermann's counterpart at the Disconto-Gesellschaft was Arthur Salomonsohn, a partner since 1895 and since 1912 chairman of the directorate, a position he would occupy until the amalgamation of 1929. Salomonsohn is described as a cool, determined banking diplomat.[8] On the fusion of the two banks, he became joint chairman with Max Steinthal of the Deutsche Bank. Salomonsohn's younger cousin Georg Solmssen, meanwhile, held a partnership in the Disconto-Gesellschaft from 1911 until the fusion of 1929. Among his major tasks had been the 'reorganization' of the A. Schaaffhausensche Bankverein in Cologne, in whose directorate he had occupied a prominent place from 1914 until 1923. From 1929 until 1934, Solmssen was a director of the Deutsche Bank and thus, with Wassermann, joint leader of Germany's largest financial institution.[9] He continued to be a board member of the Deutsche Bank from 1935 to 1937. Solmssen is described as in many respects a replica of his

---

[5] '... die Fähigkeit zur erschöpfenden Ausnutzung der gegebenen Verhältnisse' (ib.).

[6] For Pinner's characterization of Wassermanns see p. 224 n. 17 above.

[7] For Wassermann's role in the operation, see Seidenzahl, *Hundert Jahre Deutsche Bank* (Frankfurt, 1970), pp. 321 ff. and Zielenziger, *Juden im der deutschen Wirtschaft* (Berlin, 1930), pp. 253 f.

[8] '... zurückhaltend und konziliant, ein pflichtbewusster, aber kühler Geschäftsmann' (Zielenziger, op. cit., p. 120). 'Eine durchaus moderne Bankierserscheinung, die Schneid, Frische und sehr bewusste Geschäftsbestimmtheit mit bankdiplomatischer Begabung verband' (Pinner, op. cit., p. 224).

[9] 'Mit Oscar Wassermann ist Georg Solmssen heute der Führer des grössten Deutschen Bankinstituts' (Zielenziger, op. cit., p. 224).

cousin Arthur Salomonsohn.[10] This continuing prominence of men of Jewish extraction in leading positions in the Deutsche Bank und Disconto-Gesellschaft is surprising. Jews, traditionally, provided between a quarter and a third of the directorates of the two banks.[11] Anti-Semites in 1933 considered the Disconto-Gesellschaft (wrongly) a 'Jewish' enterprise.[12]

Less surprising is the prominence of Jews in leading positions in the joint-stock banks which traditionally had had strong Jewish associations. Thus, in the Dresdner Bank, Henry Nathan had occupied the position of 'senior' (*Senior der Bank*) since 1920.[13] He would remain a director after reorganization and amalgamation with the Danat Bank until his death in 1932. The generally critical Pinner compares Nathan, whom he saw as the undoubted 'spiritual centre' of the Dresdner Bank in the post-Gutmann era,[14] favourably with the majority of his peers.[15] In the Danat Bank, the Dresdner's eventual partner, Nathan's counterpart, though very different in character, was Jakob Goldschmidt.[16] Goldschmidt, among the Jewish directors of great joint-stock banks, stood out as a 'self-made man'. Emerging from humble beginnings,[17]

---

[10] Pinner, op. cit., p. 225.

[11] For details of the directorates and partners of the Deutsche Bank and the Disconto-Gesellschaft see Ernst Wilhelm Schmidt, *Männer der Deutschen Bank und der Disconto-Gesellschaft* (Düsseldorf, 1957), p. 21.

[12] The Disconto-Gesellschaft is listed among institutes 'in ihrer Leitung jüdisch bezw. verjudet' in a memorandum by the *Verein zur Wahrung der Interessen der Chemischen Industrie Deutschlands e.V.*, Berlin, d. 29 June 1933, copy in Gutehoffnungshütte, Historisches Archiv, HA/GHH no. 400 101 220/14a, p. 10. Listed with the Disconto-Gesellschaft are Commerzbank, Dresdner Bank, Darmstädter Bank, Berl. Handelsgesellschaft, Bleichröder, Mendelssohn, Warburg and so on (ib.). Surprisingly, the Deutsche Bank is missing.

[13] Kurt Hunscha, *Aus der Geschichte der Dresdner Bank 1872–1969* (Frankfurt-on-Main, 1969), p. 39.

[14] Pinner, *op cit.* n. 14 above p. 225.

[15] For Pinner's characterization of Nathan see p. 227 n. 34 above.

[16] For Jakob Goldschmidt see Zielenziger, op. cit., n. 7 above, pp. 264 ff., and Hans Fürstenberg, *Erinnerungen* (Düsseldorf and Vienna, 1968), pp. 161 ff. and *passim*.

[17] Jakob Goldschmidt was born in 1882, the second son of a Jewish shopkeeper in the small Hanoverian town of Eldagsen an der Deister. His intention to study law was frustrated by the fact that his father, with a family of seven children, lacked the means to support him. With an incomplete secondary education he had to enter as an apprentice the banking house of H. Oppenheim in Hanover; which he left when it was taken over by the BHI in 1907 (Zielenziger, op. cit., n. 7 above, p. 265).

his rise to the top had been meteoric. A landmark in Goldschmidt's career had occurred in 1918, when the young partner in the modest firm of Schwarz, Goldschmidt and Co. had been appointed a director of the Nationalbank für Deutschland. His bitter rivalry with Hjalmar Schacht, also of the Nationalbank, had been resolved when Schacht was persuaded to enter the public service. In 1922, Goldschmidt negotiated an association with the BHI (Darmstädter Bank), now in decline. This was followed by a fusion in 1923 leading to the creation of the Danat Bank. With the help of leading foreign banks, Goldschmidt had then organized the Internationale Bank te Amsterdam (with a nominal capital of fl.14 million) to act as a link between German industry and foreign capital markets. By these operations, Goldschmidt had laid the foundations for his role in the reorganization of German industry. This began with a cartel of producers of electric light bulbs and culminated in the reorganization of the Stinnes concern and the creation of the Vereinigte Stahlwerke. The Linke-Hoffmann concern was rationalized into the Mitteldeutsche Stahlwerke, while the bulk of Upper Silesian heavy industry became the Vereinigte Oberschlesische Hüttenwerke. Goldschmidt took an active part also in reorganizating the potash industry. He rationalized commercial navigation by the sale of Stinnes shipping interests to the Austral-Kosmos Linie. He then amalgamated that line with the Hapag. Goldschmidt's major achievement in the sphere of navigation, however, shortly before his downfall, was the partnership arrangement between Hapag and Norddeutscher Lloyd. In the process, Goldschmidt became not only a wealthy man but board member of more than a hunred companies including some of the largest and most prestigious in Germany.[18] It has been pointed out that, though his meteoric rise coincided in time with that of a number of successful speculators, Goldschmidt's role as organizer of industry was a constructive one.[19] It was based on financial flair, combined with hard work and great ambition—as well as a personal humanity which some of his

---

[18] Ibid., p. 267.
[19] '... Der jüngste unter allen deutschen Bankdirektoren ist in kurzer Zeit zu ihrem Star geworden. So phantastisch der Aufstieg Goldschmidts vom kleinen Bankangestellten zum mächtigen Grossbankdirektor erscheint, so gleicht sein Weg nicht dem Emporsteigen der ihm gleichaltrigen Inflations-Könige. Denn mit eiserner Energie arbeitet er sich nach oben ... Wenn er als Bankier auch zum Finanzier wird, dann nicht als Spekulant, sondern als der berufene Vermittler für den Ausgleich der Kapitalien' (ib., p. 265). Zielenziger, of course, drew his portrait of Goldschmidt before the collapse of the Danat bank.

Weimar: Decline and Fall? 333

contemporaries lacked. It appears that Goldschmidt tried to model himself on another 'self-made man', Carl Fürstenberg, whom he admired, and to whom he sought to compare himself.[20]

At the Commerz- und Privat-Bank, finally, which, before the fusions, was gaining ground on its competitors, the leading figure was Curt Sobernheim,[21] a stepson of Eugen Landau. Sobernheim, born in 1871, had joined the directorate of the then Commerz- und Disconto-Bank in 1911 and been responsible above all for developing relations with both domestic and foreign commercial and industrial enterprises. He was described as an able negotiator.[22] The Great Depression produced setbacks which led to his resignation as a director of the bank.

During the whole of the Weimar period, then, men of Jewish extraction occupied leading positions in all the major joint-stock banks. While none enjoyed the prestige and influence of a Carl Fürstenberg or Eugen Gutmann, Fürstenberg himself credits them with guiding their respective institutes through the difficult post-war era of civil war, adjustment, inflation, and reconstruction.[23] Though some failed to survive the crisis of 1931, several would keep their positions into the days of the National-Socialist regime.

The prominent place of Jews in German banking (and, indeed, the wider sphere of commerce) under the Weimar Republic is documented in the list of participants of the *Erweiterte Ausschusssitzung* of the

---

[20] Hans Fürstenberg, op. cit., p. 162 and 164.
[21] For Sobernheim see Daniel Bernstein, 'Wirtschaft' in Kaznelson (ed.), *Juden im deutschen Kulterbereich* (Berlin, 1962), p. 743. While Pinner considered Gustav Pilster the leading man of the bank with Sobernheim in second place (Pinner, op. cit., n. 4 above, p. 226), Carl Fürstenberg in his reminiscences ranks Sobernheim among the most prominent bank directors of this generation. Carl Fürstenberg, *Die Lebensgeschichte eines deutschen Bankiers* (Wiesbaden, 1961), p. 546). Clearly Sobernheim's ranking in the Commerz Bank was a matter of opinion.
[22] An early colleague describes Sobernheim as follows: '... ein begabter aber äusserst sanguinischer, ja leichtsinniger Mann, Stiefsohn des einflussreichen Generalkonsuls Eugen Landau, dessen Bruder Hugo Landau der Aufsichtsratsvorsitzende der Bank war ...'. Siegmund Bodenheimer, 'Mein Leben', MS in archives of Leo Baeck Institute, New York. Pinner describes him as 'eine gewandte Vermittlernatur' (Pinner, op. cit., n. 4 above, p. 226).
[23] 'Gerade während der letzten Jahre vor dem Kriege gelangte im deutschen Bankwesen ein Anzahl von Persönlichkeiten in die vordere Reihe, die noch heute Führerposten einnehmen ... Männer wie Oskar Wassermann, Henry Nathan, Oscar Schlitter [Gentile], Georg Solmssen, Kurt Sobernheim sind durch die schweren Zeiten des Krieges und der Inflation hindurch den von ihnen übernommenen Aufgaben treu geblieben ... Dagegen zählt Jakob Goldschmidt, dessen glänzender Aufstieg mich in manchen seiner Begleitererscheinungen an meine eigenen Jugendjahre erinnerte, bereits zu einer späteren Generation' (Carl Fürstenberg, op. cit., p. 546).

Centralverband des Deutschen Bank- und Bankiergewerbes (EV) (CDBB), held in Berlin in the eve of the banking crisis, on 27 June 1931.[24]

Among representatives of the Vorläufige Reichswirtschaftsrat (composed in the main of the leaders of commercial and industrial associations), several were of Jewish extraction:

Heinrich Grünfeld President of the Hauptgemeinschaft des Deutschen Einzelhandels, Berlin

Dr Louis Hagen, *Geh. Kommerzienrat* of A. Levy and Sal. Oppenheim jun. & Co. President of the Industrie- und Handelskammer, Cologne

Franz von Mendelssohn, President of the Deutsche Industrie- und Handelstagand of the Industrie- und Handelskammer, Berlin

Dr Georg Solmssen, Chairman of the board of the Centralverband des Deutschen Bank- und Bankiergewerbes (EV), Berlin[25]

Again, of seven members of the general council (*Generalrat*) of the CDBB attending the meeting, four were of Jewish extraction. These were, besides **Dr h.c. Louis Hagen** and **Franz von Mendelssohn**, **Dr h.c. Max M. Warburg**, of M. M. Warburg & Co., Member of the general council, Hamburg and **Oscar Wassermann**, Member of the board of the Deutsche Bank und Disconto-Gesellschaft, Member of the general council, Berlin[26]

The *Industrie- und Handelskammer zu Berlin* was represented by thirteen men, headed by its president Franz von Mendelssohn and its three vice-presidents including **Heinrich Grünfeld**

The remainder, besides three legal advisers (*syndici*) with Jewish-sounding names and three—Gentile—permanent officials (*Direktoren*) included:

Georg Haberland, *Kommerzienrat*, Member of the board of the Berlinischen Bodencredit-AG[27]

---

[24] Data from *Verzeichnis der Teilnehmer an der Erweiterten Ausschusssitzung des Centralverbands des Deutschen Bank- und Bankiergewerbs (E.V.) am 27 Juni 1931 im Plenarsaal des ehemaligen Herrenhauses zu Berlin*.

[25] It is, perhaps, worth noting that two further members were:
Max Fürstenberg, Manager of the Deutsche Bankbeamten-Verein EV, Benno Marx, Berlin. Manager of the general association of German bank employees, Berlin.

[26] The three Gentile members were Richard von Flemming, President of the Landwirthschaftskammer für Pommern (Stettin), Hans Remshard, *Geh. Kommerzienrat*, member of the directorate Bayerische Hypotheken- und Wechsel-Bank (Munich), and Franz Urbig, chairman of the board of the Deutsche Bank und Disconto-Gesellschaft (Berlin).

[27] For Georg Haberland (1861–1933), a leading real-estate developer in Berlin, see Bernstein, loc. cit., n. 21 above, pp. 784 f.

Dr.-Ing. e.h. Paul Mamroth, *Kommerzienrat*, member of the board of the Elektricitäts-Lieferungs-Gesellschaft
Alfred Zielenzieger, *Kommerzienrat*, chairman of the Börsenvorstand, Abt. Produktenbörse, chairman of the board of directors of the Getreide-Kredit-Bank AG

More surprising was the presence of seven men of Jewish extraction among the twenty-four representatives of the Reichsverband der Deutschen Industrie:

Dr.-Ing. Herbert von Klemperer, chairman of the board of the Berliner Maschinenbau AG, vorm. L. Schwarzkopff, Berlin
Hans Kraemer, deputy chairman of the RDI
Dr.-Ing. William Meinhardt, chairman of the board of directors of the Osram GmbH, KG, Berlin
Dr Edmund Pietrkowski, *Generaldirektor*, Berlin (since 1926 managing director of the Verein zur Wahrung der Interessen der chemischen Industrie Deutschlands EV in Berlin)
Dr.-Ing. e.h. Philipp Rosenthal, *Geh. Kommerzienrat*, Selb (Bayern)
Dr jur. Dr rer. pol. h.c., **Dr.-Ing. e.h. Paul Silverberg**, chairman of the board of the Rheinische Aktiengesellschaft für Braunkohlenbergbau und Brikettfabrikation, Cologne
Dr jur. Walter Sobernheim, *Kommerzienrat*, chairman of the general board of directors of the Schultheiss-Patzenhofer Brauerei-Aktiengesellschaft, Berlin
The *Reichsverband des Deutschen Gross- und Ueberseehandels EV*, in turn, had among its four representatives its vice-president **Dr h.c. Leo Lustig**, *Kommerzienrat* in Berlin.

So far as the directorate (*Vorstand*) of the CDBB itself was concerned, besides **Georg Solmssen**, its president, and **Max Warburg** as one of its four vice-presidents, it included among its eight remaining members:

Dr Max Fraenkel, member of the board of the Deutsche Centralboden-Centralboden-Kredit-Aktiengesellschaft, Berlin
Generalkonsul **Paul v. Mendelssohn-Bartholdy** of Mendelssohn & Co., Berlin.

The wider council (*Ausschuss*) of fifty-two members included at least twenty-two of indubitably Jewish origin. It is worth listing the more important of these to convey an impression of the range of Jewish banking interests in the final years of the Weimar Republic:

Konsul **Adolf Arnhold**, of Gebr. Arnhold, Dresden
Otto Aschaffenburg, partner of the Lazard Speyer-Ellissen KaA, Berlin
Georg Behrens, of L. Behrens & Söhne, Hamburg
Siegfried Bieber, partner of the Berliner Handels-Gesellschaft, Berlin
Siegmund Bodenheimer, partner of the Darmstädter und National-bank KaA, Berlin[28]
Willy Dreyfus, of J. Dreyfus & Co., Berlin
Prof. Dr jur. et phil. L. Albert Hahn, member of the board of the Deutsche Effecten-und-Wechsel-Bank, Frankfurt (Main)
Dr Georg Hirschland, of Simon Hirschland, Essen
Dr Paul Homburger of Veit L. Homburger, Karlsruhe (Baden)
Generalkonsul **Dr Paul Kempner**, of Mendelssohn & Co., Berlin
KR **Dr Richard Kohn**, of Anton Kohn, Nuremberg
Konsul **Dr Rudolf Maron**, of Bondi & Maron, Dresden
Oscar Franklin Oppenheimer, of Lincoln Menny Oppenheimer, Frankfurt
Dr. phil. Paul v. Schwabach, of Bleichröder, Berlin
Julius Schwarz, of Schwarz, Goldschmidt & Co., Berlin
Oscar Wassermann, member of the board of the Deutsche Bank und Disconto-Gesellschaft, Berlin

To these may be added some among the more prominent additional names listed under group B (Vereinigung von Berliner Banken und Bankiers) which, to some extent, overlaps with the members of the council:

Ludwig Berliner, member of the board of Commerz- und Privat-Bank AG
KR **Dr Theodor Frank**, member of the board of Deutsche Bank und Disconto-Gesellschaft
Hans Fürstenberg, partner in Berliner Handels-Gesellschaft
Dr h.c. Jakob Goldschmidt, partner in Darmstädter und National-bank KaA
Rudolf Loeb, of Mendelssohn & Co.
Dr Ernst Picard, partner in Lazard Speyer-Ellissen KaA

---

[28] For the career of Siegmund Bodenheimer, recalling that of Jakob Goldschmidt (his father had been an impecunious shopkeeper in Heidelberg ('Herrenkonfektionsgeschäft en gros u. en detail'), the son, intending to study medicine or law, had been forced to become a bank employee after an incomplete secondary education), see Bodenheimer, op. cit., n. 22 above.

Dr.-Ing. e.h. **Curt Sobernheim**, member of the directorate of the Commerz- und Privat-Bank AG

Dr **Georg Solmssen**, member of the directorate of the Deutsche Bank und Disconto-Gesellschaft

GKR **Max Steinthal**, chairman of the board of the Deutsche Bank und Disconto-Gesellschaft

This then was broadly the German–Jewish banking 'establishment' as it presented itself in 1931. Some aspects are worth noting. Overall, it is clear that the place of Jews in German banking both in the joint-stock and the private sectors, remained significant.[29] It found its reflection in the positions occupied by men of Jewish origin in the professional association of German bankers. Contrary to the conventional wisdom, private banks in general and Jewish ones in particular, in spite of the disappearance of some since the beginning of the century, remained numerous. In particular, a number of old-established houses, Warburg and Behrens in Hamburg, Oppenheim in Cologne (represented by the indefatigable Louis Hagen), Arnhold in Dresden, Mendelssohn and Hardy and, if perhaps to a lesser extent, Bleichröder, Hirschland in Essen (extending also to Hamburg), together with some old houses of the second order, continued to play a not insignificant role in German economic life. Moreover, the recurrence of certain names and the offices and appointments held suggests the existence of the usual inner circle of individuals enjoying prestige and influence.

Overall, there is little to suggest a decline in the importance of Jews within the banking community compared to the pre-war period though there may be, for reasons already discussed, fewer outstanding individuals. Jakob Goldschmidt alone among bankers of Jewish origin—and, arguably, he was out of season—now represents the type of great initiator of which Ballin, Rathenau, and Fürstenberg had been such outstanding examples. Such men now, even where they attain to the stature and position of a Georg Solmssen or Oscar Wassermann, hide (or are hidden) behind a shroud of administrative anonymity. In

[29] Particularly striking is the place occupied by Jews (already discussed in connection with the career of Wilhelm Kopetzky) on the Berlin exchanges. An NS document of June 1933—to be treated with due reserve but seeming in the main reliable in many of its facts—claims that of 147 members of the stock, produce, and metal exchanges, 116, almost 80 per cent, were of Jewish origin. The figures for Jews and Gentiles in the management committees (*Vorstände*) of the 3 exchanges are given respectively as stock exchange 25 and 11, produce exchange 12 and 4, and metal exchange 10 and 2. Similar figures are provided for various exchange committees. (*Verein zur Wahrung der Interessen der Chemischen Industrie Deutschlands EV*, Circular letter to members d. Berlin, 29 June 1933. Copy in GHH Historisches Archiv, HA/GHH, no. 400 101 220/14a.)

the case of Max Warburg, perhaps a more colourful personality, such reticence was a matter of discretion and policy. It was not desirable to share the fate of Walther Rathenau, indeed to become the target of anti-Semitic hostility as some Jews prominent in economic life had done. As to purely economic influence this, for Warburg, in spite of his valuable American connections, was perhaps circumscribed by relative lack of capital. Also the Warburg bank traditionally largely refrained (as did the Mendelssohns) from involving itself in industrial financing (and hence from representation on all but a few boards). Finally, given the amounts of capital involved, private banks were now to some extent confined to either local or special (international) transactions which, while they could be lucrative, were unlikely to be spectacular.

Jewish bankers (like, indeed, Gentiles), then, however prominent their positions, were acting within certain constraints. The large joint-stock banks, by and large, were run on collegiate principles which precluded the autocratic rule of a Carl Fürstenberg or Eugen Gutmann. Private bankers, on the other hand, were inhibited by the relative insufficiency of their funds. Their strength, to some extent, lay in their ability to recruit able men from outside the proprietary families: Adolf Fischel, Fritz Mannheimer, Rudolf Loeb, Paul Kempner (Mendelssohn); Carl Melchior (Warburg); Louis Hagen (Oppenheim); Walther Rathenau (unsuccessfully), Otto Jeidels (BHG); Fritz Andreae (Hardy). Yet such men, though usually of superior ability and almost invariably promoted to partnerships, were handicapped in their turn in the great majority of cases by lack of capital, by their non-membership of the proprietory family (the occasional son-in-law excepted), and by their general position as 'outsiders' without an adequate economic base. Their scope for creative activity in the economic (as in any other) sphere was circumscribed. Though much sought after by the authorities as 'experts', few would make their way into the public service.[30] The economic élite—especially when of Jewish origin—had to operate within narrowing parameters.

A further feature worth noting is the high proportion of men with academic degrees. While a number of such degrees are honorary, the

[30] They were undoubtedly better remunerated as partners in leading private banking houses. Public appointments, moreover, were often political, which reduced their attractiveness. Also, where a Hjalmar Schacht (or Hans Luther, who, however, was not a banker) was quite acceptable as president of the Reichsbank, public opinion would certainly have rejected a Jew, like Carl Melchior, however capable, in that position. The only Jew with close affinities to these Jewish bankers who rose to high office in the public service was the lawyer Hans Schäffer, head of the reparations department in the ministry of economics (1923–9) and state secretary in the ministry of finance (1929–32).

majority represent a completed university course—where the faculty is stated (in a minority of cases) in law but, occasionally, in philosophy. Those with earned academic degrees, predictably, are normally the offspring of old families and represent the second or third generations active in economic affairs at a substantial level. The evidence would seem to suggest that members of the Jewish economic élite have benefited from more formal education than their predecessors under Wilhelm II. This may well reflect a wider trend in the higher ranges of the German economic community.

At the same time, while there are still *Kommerzienräte* and *Konsule*, titles have now become uncommon. While they still occur with somewhat greater frequency among office holders, they are rare among the rank and file. Prominent men like Max Warburg, Heinrich Grünfeld, Paul Silverberg, or Oscar Wassermann use their names unadorned. The predicate of nobility is, of course, under the Weimar Republic merely a 'hangover' from imperial times.

II

The bankers of Jewish origin formed, of course, part of a wider Jewish corporate structure.[31] The details of this wider network are revealed, as before, through board memberships and, particularly, the chairmanships of major industrial companies.[32]

Pride of place among the great 'pluralists' belongs to Jakob Goldschmidt of the Danat bank, whose board memberships numbering over a hundred, included the following:

chairman
Bamag-Meguin (16)
deputy chairman
Kaliwerke Salzdetfurth AG
Consolidierte Alkaliwerke Westeregeln   (48.574)
Kaliwerke Aschersleben
Schultheiss-Patzenhofer   (39.5)
Ostwerke   (26.5)
Mitteldeutsche Stahlwerke, Berlin   (50)

[31] For the following see Georg Wenzel, *Deutscher Wirtschaftsführer* (Hamburg, 1929) and *Reichshandbuch der deutschen Gesellschaft* (Berlin, 1930).

[32] The hundred largest in terms of share capital in 1927 are listed in Hannes Siegnist, 'Deutsche Grossunternehmen vom späten 19 Jahrhundert bis zur Weimarer Republik', *Geschichte und Gesellschaft*, 6(1980). For details of their boards and managements see Saling, *Kleines Saling's Börsen-Jahrbuch 1926–27*.

Vereinigte Stahlwerke (800)
member
Phœnix AG für Bergbau u. Hüttenbetrieb, Düsseldorf (n/a)
Friedrich Krupp AG (160)
Klöckner Werke AG Berlin (90)
Deutsche Edelstahlwerke AG Bochum (30)
Mansfeld AG f. Bergbau u. Hüttenbetrieb (37.875)
Vereinigte Oberschlesische Hüttenwerke AG Gleiwitz (n/a)
AEG (186.25)
Bergmann Elektrizitäts-Werke, Berlin (12)
Continental Caoutchouc & Guttapercha Co., Hanover (34.1)
Linke-Hoffmann-Busch Werke AG, Berlin (49)

Goldschmidt in addition sat on the boards of the Hapag, which does not figure among industrial enterprises, and of a number of industrial companies not included among the hundred largest. Overall, Jakob Goldschmidt, through his reorganizations, thus had some stake in an important segment of German industry.

Next to Jakob Goldschmidt himself, industrial interests of the Danat bank were represented also by his colleague Georg von Simson:

chairman
Berliner Hypothekenbank AG Berlin
deputy chairman
Riebeck'sche Montanwerke, Halle
board member
Oberschlesische Eisenbahnbedarfs AG (27.792)
Schles. Bergwerks- u. Hütten AG Beuthen (16.667)
Linke-Hoffmann-Busch Werke, Berlin (49)
Gelsenkirchener Bergwerks AG
Rhein. AG f. Braunkohlenbergbau u. Brikettfabrikation, (67.2)
  Cologne
Rheinisch-Westfälische Elektrizitätswerke
Elektrizitäts AG vorm. Lahmeyer & Co.
Vereinigte Oberschlesische
Hüttenwerke AG, Gleiwitz (n/a)
Metallbank u. Metallurg. Gesellschaft (45.06)
Degussa, Frankfurt-on-Main (23)
Gebr. Stollwerck AG (16.456)

A further director, Siegmund Bodenheimer, also represented the Danat bank on a number of industrial boards:

Harpener Bergbau AG Dortmund (100.3)
Rütgerswerke Berlin (80)
Ostwerke AG, Berlin (26.5)
Ludwig Loewe AG Berlin (15)
Gesfürel (n/a)

Finally, Ludwig Born occupied two 'second seats' for Danat on the boards of the AEG and of Schultheiss-Patzenhofer. Altogether, Danat representatives in fact occupied seats on the boards of roughly a quarter of the hundred largest companies. Commercial relations of particular importance are documented in Jakob Goldschmidt's deputy chairmanship of four major industrial groupings, Vereinigte Stahlwerke, Mitteldeutsche Stahlwerke, Schultheiss-Patzenhofer-Ostwerke, and the great potash combine of Aschersleben/Westeregeln/Salzdetfurth. In addition, Goldschmidt was chairman of the board of the less important firm of Bamag-Meguin. Further close relationships found expression in the double representation enjoyed by the Danat on the boards of the AEG, the associated Linke-Hoffmann-Busch Werke, and Schultheiss-Patzenhofer. Georg von Simson, in turn, represented special Danat interests through his chairmanship at the Berliner Hypothekenbank AG and deputy chairmanships at the Riebecksche Montanwerke in Halle.

By the side of Goldschmidt's Danat, the industrial interests of the Dresdner Bank, looked after principally by Henry Nathan, continued to be relatively modest. Besides holding the deputy chairmanship of the Vereinigte Königs- u. Laurahütte in Berlin, Nathan occupied seats on the following boards:

Vereinigte Stahlwerke AG, Düsseldorf
Phoenix AG f. Bergbau u. Hüttenbetrieb, Düsseldorf
Gelsenkirchener Bergwerks AG, Essen
Friedrich Krupp AG, Essen
Mühlheimer Bergwerksverein, Mühlheim
Rheinische Stahlwerke, Essen
Deutsche Edelstahlwerke AG, Bochum
Felten& Guilleaume Carlswerk AG, Cologne
Orenstein & Koppel AG, Berlin (36.48)
AEG
Nationale Automobil-Gesellschaft
Elektrizitätswerke vorm. Lahmeyer & Co., Frankfurt-on-Main
Deutsche Petroleum AG, Berlin
Deutsche Erdöl AG, Berlin (100.4)

The absence of chairmanships or deputy chairmanships as well as of double representation would seem to indicate that the Dresdner Bank had failed to maintain 'special' industrial relationships (Gustav von Klemperer, a director of the Dresdner Bank, was, however, board chairman of the Wanderer-Werke, Schönau b. Chemnitz (15.734)).

A more prominent position within the corporate structure was occupied by Georg Solmssen, with his cousin Arthur Salomonsohn principal representative of the industrial interests of the Disconto-Gesellschaft:

chairman
Deutsche Erdöl AG Berlin (in the founding of which
he had played a major part) (100.4)
Deutsch-Atlantische Telegraphen-Gesellschaft, Berlin
deputy chairman
Gebr. Stollwerck AG
member
Berlin-Karlsruher Industrie-Werke, Berlin (30)
Bergmann Elektrizitätswerke, Berlin
Deutsche Petroleum AG Berlin
Felten & Guilleaume Carlswerk AG
Gesfürel
Kaliwerke Aschersleben
Ludwig Loewe AG
Orenstein & Koppel, Berlin
Phoenix AG f. Bergbau u. Hüttenbetrieb

Solmssen's board memberships, besides links with the Loewe group (Ludwig Loewe, Gesfürel, Berlin-Karlsruher—formerly Deutsche Waffen) and Guilleaume interests (Felten and Deutsch-Atlantische), reflect his special associations with the petroleum industry. There is a link with firms in group (I): the Loewe companies and Orenstein & Koppel.

The board seats of Arthur Salomonsohn, the older of the two cousins, to some extent reflect an overlapping interest:

chairman
Ludwig Loewe & Co. AG
Gesfürel
Kaliwerke Aschersleben
Kaliwerke Salzdetfurth AG

Deputy chairman
Consolid. Alkaliwerke AG Westeregeln
member of executive of board (Mitglied des Präsidiums des AR)
Gelsenkirchener Bergwerks AG, Essen
board member
Vereinigte Stahlwerke AG Düsseldorf
Rheinische Stahlwerke Essen
AEG
Henschel & Sohn AG Kassel (45)
Elektrizitäts AG vorm. Schuckert }
Siemens & Halske AG Berlin } (217.5)
Hapag

The board memberships of the two cousins thus reflect 'special relations' with the Loewe concern (Ludwig Loewe & Co. and Gesfürel), the potash combine (Aschersleben/Westegeln/Salzdetfurth), the giant Deutsche Erdöl AG, the Deutsch-Atlantische-Telegraphen-Gesellschaft, and the chocolate makers Gebr. Stollwerck AG. The long-standing association of Salomonsohns and Kirdorfs is reflected in Arthur Salomonsohn's position on the board of the Gelsenkirchener Bergwerks AG. Finally, Theodor Frank, another Jewish *Geschäftsinhaber* of the Disconto (he had risen through the Süddeutsche Disconto, formerly the Ladenburg bank in Mannheim), was board chairman of the Zellstoffabrik Waldhof in Mannheim (34.675).

Compared to the Disconto, the board representation of the BHG in Carl Fürstenberg's declining years had become a modest one. The BHG's leading representative on industrial boards is now the new partner Otto Jeidels:

Deputy chairman
Bamag-Meguin AG
board member
Ludwig Loewe & Co. AG
Gesfürel
Berliner Maschinenbau AG vorm. (18.445)
    Schwarzkopff
Metallbank u. Metallurg. Gesellschaft
A Riebeck'sche Montan
AG f. Braunkohlenbergbau, Cologne

The aged Carl Fürstenberg himself retained only a small number of prestigious seats:

chairman
AEG
board member
Ver. Oberschl. Hüttenwerke
Vereinigte Stahlwerke

Fürstenberg's son Hans, meanwhile, had been moved into the following positions:

board member
AEG
Ver. Oberschl. Hüttenwerke
Accumulatoren-Fabrik, Berlin (20)

A further BHG partner, Siegfried Bieber, occupied a place on the board of the Rütgers Werke. Special links are thus documented with the AEG, with Oberschl. Hüttenwerke, and with Bamag-Meguin AG.

So far as the Deutsche Bank is concerned, Oscar Wassermann, whose industrial interests were limited, occupied the following positions:

chairman
Kaliwerke Neu Stassfurt
board member
Norddeutscher Lloyd
Stettiner Chamotte AG vorm. Didier (14.615)

The veteran Max Steinthal, meanwhile, continued to serve as board chairman of Mannesmannröhren-Werke AG in Düsseldorf (160.264).

Important industrial interests of a different kind fell within the ambit of the Commerz- und Privat-Bank (C & P). Eugen Landau, its deputy-chairman, was a member of the following boards:

chairman
Schultheiss-Patzenhofer Brauerei AG
Oberschl. Eisenbahnbedarfs AG (27.792)
board member
AEG
Linke-Hoffmann
Rütgerswerke

Eugen Landau was stepfather of Curt Sobernheim, director of C & P and of his brother Walter, managing director of Schultheiss-Patzenhofer. Walter Sobernheim was joint managing director of the Ostwerke & Schultheiss-Patzenhofer GmbH.[33] His co-director, Ludwig Katzenellenbogen, managing director of Ostwerke,[34] sat on the following boards:

chairman
Schles. Portland Cement Industrie, Oppeln (27), Germany's largest cement producer
deputy chairman
Schultheiss-Patzenhofer AG
board member
C & P

Through Katzenellenbogen, the group was linked with the Mitteldeutsche Credit Bank in Frankfurt-on-Main, of which Ludwig's brother *Justizrat* Albert Katzenellenbogen was a prominent director and which would amalgamate with the C & P in 1929. Albert Katzenellenbogen in his turn held the following positions:

chairman
Salzdetfurth/Westeregeln/Aschersleben
board member
Ostwerke
Buderus'sche Eisenwerke, Wetzlar (26.3)
Stahlwerke Röchling, Völklingen (15)

This, then, was a grouping linking the Commerzbank with Schultheiss-Patzenhofer (and, through it, Danat), Ostwerke, and Schles. Portland Cement—as well as the interests of the Mitteldeutsche Creditbank in

---

[33] Walter Sobernheim's financial associations were not with his brother's *C & P* but with Danat of which he was a board member. He had married a daughter of Julius Schottländer.

[34] Ludwig Katzenellenbogen was born in 1877 in Krotoschen, where his father Adolf had been founder-owner of Spiritusraffinerien Krotoschin and alderman. In 1903, on his father's death, he took over the management. He then moved to Berlin where he founded the Spiritus-Zentrale. When this was taken over by the state, he became director and majority shareholder of the Breslauer Spritfabrik AG and the Ostelbische Spritwerke AG. Through a variety of fusions he created the Ostwerke AG. He next took over the Portland Cement Industrie AG (in which the Schottländers had a major interest). After this, he organized the yeast industry. Finally, Katzenellenbogen negotiated the association with Schultheiss-Patzenhofer. In addition to his position as managing director of Ostwerke he took over the post of joint managing director of Schultheiss-Patzenhofer-Ostwerke. The concern would collapse during the Depression.

the potash combine. It was a substantial 'Jewish' banking and industrial grouping.

Among private bankers, the most significant industrial connections were those of the aged Louis Hagen (still member of some 90 boards) and the Oppenheims, in whose bank he was now a partner. A number of Hagen's board seats continued to be in major companies:

chairman
Berliner-Karslruher-Industrie-Werke (formerly Deutsche Waffen)
first deputy chairman
Klöcknerwerke AG, Berlin
board member
Vereinigte Stahlwerke   Orenstein & Koppel
Mitteld. Stahlwerke   AEG
Phoenix AG   Bamag Meguin
Rheinische Stahlwerke   IG Farben (1.100)
Rheinische AG f. Braunkohlenbergbau
Demag, Duisburg (25)
Felten & GuilleaumeCarlswerk

Hagen's board memberships are supplemented by those of Simon, *Freiherr* von Oppenheim:

chairman
Basalt AG Linz a. Rh. (24)
board member
Felten & Guilleaume Carlswerk
Klöckner Werke
Harpener Bergbau AG
Rhein. AG f. Braunkohlenbergbau
AEG
Orenstein & Koppel

Eduard, *Freiherr* von Oppenheim, was a board member of the Gelsenkirchener Bergwerks AG, Waldemar von Oppenheim of the Phoenix. The Hagen–Oppenheim special relations, therefore, besides the Phoenix, included the Klöcknerwerke AG, the Berlin-Karlsruher, Felten & Guilleaume, Orenstein & Koppel, the Basalt AG, and the Rheinische AG für Braunkohlenbergbau. The connections, to some extent, were regional ones. Both Hagen and Eduard von Oppenheim moreover sat on the boards of both Schaaffhausen and the Disconto-Gesellschaft, thus indicating their wider banking ties.

By the side of traditional Cologne interest of Hagen and the Oppenheims, the almost equally old banking firm of Simon Hirschland in Essen was gaining a new lease of life through its involvement in the financing and reconstruction of Ruhr industry. Its role was reflected in the industrial seats of two partners. Of these, Kurt Hirschland was a member of the following boards:

Gelsenkirchener Bergwerks AG
Phoenix
Ver. Stahlwerke
Friedr. Krupp
Klöckner Werke
Rhein. Westf. Elektrizitäts Werke
Theodor Goldschmidt

His broader financial ties were expressed through board membership of the Dresdner Bank. Indeed it is possible that, for the Dresdner Bank, Simon Hirschland had replaced its erstwhile partner Schaaffhausen. Kurt Hirschland's brother Georg occupied fewer seats:

deputy chairman
Kaliwerke Neu Stassfurt (19.5)
board member
Mannesmannröhren
Gewerkschaft Constantin d. Grosse

The surviving industrial interests of the house of S. Bleichröder were represented mainly by Paul von Schwabach, who occupied the following seats:

chairman
Ver. Königs- u. Laura (this no longer ranked among the hundred largest industrial companies)
deputy chairman
Deutsche Erdöl AG
Berliner-Karlsruher Ind. Werke
board member
Norddeutscher Lloyd
Dt. Schiff u. Maschinenbau, Bremen (25)
Felten & Guilleaume Carlswerk
Otavi Minen u. Eisenbahn Ges., Berlin (16)
Dt. Petroleum AG

His partner Ernst Kritzler, meanwhile, represented Bleichröder on the boards of AEG, Ludwig Loewe, Gesfürel, and Ver. Königs- u. Laura.

Lastly, Maximilian Kempner, associated through his son Paul with the Mendelssohns, chaired the boards of Stettiner Chamotte vorm. Didier (14.615) and AG für Chemische Produkte vorm. Scheidemandel in Berlin (25).

Thus—though it should again be emphasized that the 'special relationships' of banks had lost some of their earlier importance—bankers of Jewish origin occupied positions as chairmen or deputy chairman or held double representation for the same financial interests on the boards of almost a quarter of the hundred largest industrial companies.[35] These companies, in random order, are the following:

Ver. Stahlwerke	Salzdetfurth/Westeregeln/Aschersleben
Mitteld. Stahlwerke	Gebr. Stollwerck
Klöckner Werke	Berlin-Karlsruher
Mannesmannröhren	Ludwig Loewe
Oberschl. Eisenbahnbahnbedarfs AG	Orenstein & Koppel
Linke-Hoffmann	Neu-Stassfurt
Deutsche Erdöl	Basalt AG
Schultheiss Patzenhofer	Bamag-Meguin
Ostwerke	AEG
	Zellstoffabrik Waldhof
	Wanderer-Werke
	AG f. Chem. Produkte
	Stettiner Chamotte
	Schles. Portland Cement

An analysis of 'Jewish' banking associations of industrial companies reveals a number of different components. In the first place, there are the traditional 'Jewish' concerns (which had already figured with the same associations in 1907), the AEG with its more recent industrial associate Linke-Hoffmann-Busch; Ludwig Loewe and the Berlin-Karlsruher-Industrie-Werke (formerly Deutsche Waffen- und Munitionsfabriken); Orenstein & Koppel; Oberschles. Eisenbahnbedarfs AG, Zellstoffabrik Waldhof, AG für Chemische Produkte; Stettiner Chamotte. In the second place, there are two large

---

[35] There may be a few companies with a higher share capital than some of those included, missing for one reason or another from Siegrist's list. One or two of these would fall into the category described here.

new groupings based in one case on largely 'Jewish' components: Schultheiss-Patzenhofer, Ostwerke (formerly Breslauer Spritfabrik), and Schlesische Portland Cement; in the other on earlier components associated through banking interests: Salzdetfurth/Westeregeln/ Aschersleben. A new company with a capital in excess of 100 million marks and in which a banker of Jewish origin is prominently involved is the Deutsche Erdöl AG. Further, there is a group of enterprises, both old and new, in 'heavy industry', where banking interests represented by men of Jewish origin have either played a traditional role or in which they have become involved through the liquidation (largely through the instrumentality of Jakob Goldschmidt) of the 'Stinnes-empire': Mannesmannröhren-Werke, Klöckner-Werke, Ver. Stahlwerke,[36] and Mitteldeutsche Stahlwerke. Lastly, there is a number of miscellaneous companies (Gebr. Stollwerck, Bamag-Meguin, Basalt AG, Wanderer-Werke, Neu-Stassfurt) where banking representatives of Jewish origin occupy important positions. In general, the data may suggest a certain dynamism of banking interests expressed in the promotion of larger industrial groupings and in the acquisition of some new clients (which did not figure among the 100 largest industrial firms in 1907). It would appear that, compared to the pre-war period, Jewish representatives of banking interests, until the end of the Great Depression, had maintained their positions on the boards of industrial companies.

Those of the hundred largest companies in which bankers of Jewish origin occupied positions of influence were distributed unevenly among the different branches of industry (total numbers in each category in brackets):

III Mining (9):	Dt. Erdöl AG
IV Stone and earth (5):	Schles. Portland; Basalt AG; Stettiner Chamotte
V/VI Iron & Metal production; metal goods (22):	Ver. Stahlwerke; Mannesmann; Klöckner; Mitteld. Stahlw.; Berlin-Karlsr.; Oberschl. Eisenbahnbed.

---

[36] As an anti-Semitic publication of 1928, which, however, appears to be accurate in its information, noted: 'so sind bei Fr. Krupp AG 3, bei den Klöcknerwerken AG 6 ... bei Mannesmann Röhrenwerken 5 jüdische Aufsichtsräte. Die Vereinigten Stahlwerke ... besitzen deren 7, gleich 28 v.H. der Gesamtzahl'. Otto Bonhard, *Jüdische Weltherrschaft?* (Berlin, 1928) p. 281 n. 277.

VII Machinery, apparatus,   Linke-Hoffmann; Orenstein &
    vehicles (20):   Koppel; Bamag-Meguin, Loewe;
                                       Wanderer-Werke
VIII Electrical (5):   AEG
IX Chemical (13):   Westeregeln-Asch.-Salzd.; Neu
                                       Stassfurt; AG f. Chem. Produkte
X Textile Ind. (10):   none
XI Paper & printing (3):   Zellstoff-Fabrik Waldhof
XII/XVII Leather & lino;   none
    shoes (4):
XIII Caoutchouc (1):   none
XVI Food and drink (8):   Schultheiss-P.; Ostwerke;
                                       Stollwerck

What is worth noting here is the relative prominence of Jewish bankers in firms in categories (IV), (XVI), and (V/VI) (partly a consequence of Jakob Goldschmidt's role in liquidating the Stinnes concern). They are relatively numerous also in (VIII) and (IX). In other categories, there are some further firms with Jewish associations, though not through the banking community. What is noteworthy is the absence of Jewish involvement in the large category (X),[37] a matter in need of further elucidation. Certain branches of industry, of course, needed little investment capital or raised such capital as they needed either from family or local sources, or through self-financing.

III

Hand in hand with the relative decline in the importance of the banker-chairman went an increase in that of the leading executives. This was the case not only in vast new agglomerations like IG Farben

[37] It would be interesting to ascertain how far this reflects a general paucity of regular banking associations in textile enterprises. This might be suggested by, among others, the history of the Blumenstein concern and by Hans Fürstenberg's description of the purely family-controlled textile firm of Christian Dierig in Langenbielau (Hans Fürstenberg, op. cit., n. 16 above, pp. 220 ff.), with its nominal share capital of 30 million marks in 1927 and 7,000 employees, narrowly the third-largest textile firm. The Norddeutsche Wollkammer und Kammgarnspinnerei in Bremen, the second-largest German textile company (in terms of nominal share capital), with 24,500 workers in 1927 (mis)managed by the notorious Lahusen brothers, had relied on large credits from both the Danat and the Dresdner Banks. (Born, op. cit., p. 260). Before its collapse in June 1931 it had 'suffered a loss of 200 million RM in speculative transactions' (ib.). The Danat bank alone lost 50 million RM in the Nordwolle affair (ib., p. 263), which was a major contributory factor in its insolvency.

or Vereinigte Stahlwerke, whose nominal share capital exceeded that of the largest banking institutions, but also of medium-sized and smaller companies. Directors of the larger companies would join the boards of associates. They also, as was traditional, were represented on the boards of banks with which their enterprises were associated.

In this managerial élite also, men of Jewish extraction played a part. Thus in IG Farben, the largest industrial undertaken, Jews found a place mainly through two of its component units. The chemist Dr Franz Oppenheim had, as already described, joined the AG für Anilinfabrikation (Agfa) in the eighties to become, in due course, its managing director. When the IG was formed in 1925, he had found a place in its directorate (*Verwaltungsrat*) as well as a seat on its board. He was a board member also of the Dresdner Bank. His son Kurt in turn had entered the IG directorate as managing director of the Agfa division in Berlin. Ernst von Simson, a former director of the Agfa, had, like Franz Oppenheim, joined the directorate as well as the board of IG. Carl von Weinberg, meanwhile, managing director of Leopold Cassella, had, on the foundation of the IG, become deputy chairman both of its directorate (*Verwaltungsrat*) and its board. He had become deputy chairman also of another constituent company, Kalle & Co. AG. He also occupied a seat on the board of the Disconto-Gesellschaft. Carl von Weinberg's brother Arthur, a former director of Leopold Cassella, had also joined the IG as a director and board member. In fact, Leopold Cassella continued to operate as an autonomous unit within the parent company. Leo Gans, a further Cassella partner, also occupied a seat on the IG board.

Elsewhere, directors of parent companies sat on the boards of associates. Thus the associations of the AEG were reflected in the board seats occupied by Felix Deutsch and Paul Mamroth. Deutsch, who died in 1928, occupied the following positions:

chairman
BHG
second deputy
Mansfeld, Eisleben [figures in brackets denote share capital in million marks] (37.875)
board member
Rütgers
Ludwig Loewe
Accumulatoren

Paul Mamroth in turn represented the AEG on some associated boards:

Rütgers
Linke-Hoffmann
Felten & Guilleaume

These were, in fact, the traditional AEG associations, the one with Rütgers being particularly close.

Comparable Loewe interests were documented by Oscar Oliven, managing director of Gesfürel:

deputy chairman
Dresdner Bank
board member
Berlin-Karlsruher
AEG
Orenstein & Koppel

Again, these represent traditional links.

Meanwhile a new figure had become associated with this group of interests, Max von der Porten, managing director of Vereinigte Aluminiumwerke AG, Lautawerk near Hoyerswerda (Lausitz), occupied seats on the following boards:

Gesfürel
Ludwig Loewe
Bamag-Meguin
Mansfeld AG
Metalgesellschaft
Degussa (23)
Rhein. Westf. Elektr. Werke, Essen (RWE)

Porten's associations span Loewe and Merton interests. Richard Merton, managing director of the Metalgesellschaft in Frankfurt-on-Main, was board chairman of the Schlesische Bergwerks u. Hütten AG in Beuthen (16.667), while his brother Alfred occupied seats on the following boards:

Degussa
IG Farben
Disconto

An important newcomer among managers with a significant role in corporate industry was Paul Silverberg, long-time managing director of the Rheinische AG für Braunkohlenbergbau und Brikettfabrikation (Rheinbraun) (67.2),[38] who occupied the following seats:

chairman
Rheinbraun
Harpener Bergbau, Dortmund (100.3)
board member
Ver. Stahlwerke
Gelsenkirchen
Felten & Guilleaume   Siemens & Schuckert
Demag AG Duisburg   RWE
Metallgesellschaft

Four directors of Jewish extraction managing firms numbered among the hundred largest stood somewhat outside the corporate structure. They were Dr.-Ing. Herbert von Klemperer, son of the Dresden banker Gustav von Klemperer of the Berliner Maschinenbau AG vorm. Schwartzkopff (18.445), Friedrich Schott, former director of Portland Cementwerke Heidelberg-Stuttgart in Heidelberg (25), presently chairman of its board, Hermann Schülein of Aktienbrauerei zum Löwenbräu in Munich (13.045), and Hans Bie of Kokswerke & Chem. Fabriken in Berlin (formerly Fritz Friedländer's Oberkoks) (80.3).

Finally, there were some enterprises that effectively remained family

---

[38] For Paul Silverberg see H. Kellenbenz, *Paul Silverberg* (Münster, 1967). Paul Silverberg was the son of the industrialist Adolf Silverberg of Bedburg an der Erft who, beginning with textile manufacturing, had extended his interests to linoleum and lignite production. In 1898, jointly with others (including *Freiherr* Eduard von Oppenheim), he had acquired the lignite mine Fortuna, subsequently turned into a Gewerkschaft. In 1903, having studied law, Paul Silverberg took over the management of the firm. In 1908 Fortuna became the Rheinische AG für Braunkohlenbergbau und Brikettfabrikation (RAG). When Silverberg gave up the post of managing director in 1926 to become chairman of the board, the firm had become the largest lignite producer in Germany. In 1924, with the object of forming a large coal and electricity combine, Silverberg had begun to buy up shares of the Harpener Bergwerks AG, in the first place a packet from August Thyssen. In 1925 he had become a member of the Harpen board. In 1927, on the death of Robert Müser, he became its chairman. Under Silverberg's leadership Harpen, which had become obsolescent, was extensively modernized with, between 1926 and 1931, a total investment (including some American credits) of 110 million marks. In 1928, the RAG board of 28 under Silverberg's chairmanship contained 8 bankers of Jewish extraction: GKR Hermann Frenkel (Jacquier & Securius), GKR Louis Hagen, Dr Otto Jeidels (BHG), *Freiherr* S. Alfred v. Oppenheim, Georg v. Simson (Danat), Max Warburg, and KR Max v. Wassermann. Silverberg's role in public affairs will be considered elsewhere.

firms with men of Jewish origin prominent in management: the Bing Werke in Nuremberg (13.765), Th. Goldschmidt in Essen (29.3), the Blumenstein-Konzern in Berlin (22.25),[39] Adler & Oppenheimer, Berlin (15.12), and Sigle Kornwestheim (Salamander Schuhe) (14). A less marked connection also existed in the case of Rhenania-Kunheim, Berlin (20.540), which had absorbed the originally Jewish chemical firm.

Members of the Jewish managerial group thus occupied prominent positions in the following companies, listed at random:

IG	Portland Cement
AEG	
Mansfeld	Löwenbräu
Schles. Bergw.	Bing
Rheinbraun	Goldschmidt
Harpen	Adler & Opp.
Berl. Maschinen	Sigle
Kokswerke	Blumenstein-Konzern

The companies with Jews prominent in management also can be divided among the official categories (total numbers in brackets):[40]

III Mining (9):	Harpen, Rheinbraun
IV Stone and earth (5):	Portland Cement
V/VI Iron & Metal prod., metal goods (22):	Schles. Bergw., Mansfeld, Bing
VII Machinery, apparatus, vehicles (20):	Berl. Maschinen
VIII Electrical (5):	AEG
IX Chemical (13):	IG, Th. Goldschmidt, Kokswerke

[39] Before the war, the brothers Joseph and Alfred Blumenstein, jute specialists, had traded in sacking in Mannheim. During the war, they acquired a quasi-monopoly for the supply of sandbags to the Engineer Corps of the German army. The Blumensteins owned several factories in Baden. Their profits, during the war, exceeded 10 million marks (they supplied sandbags to a value of over 100 million). Joseph Blumenstein acquired shares in jute mills, also in mills that were customers for sacks. He also acquired a bank. The capital of his Bank für Textilindustrie is given by Siegrist as 22.25 million marks in 1927. For details on Joseph Blumenstein and his *Konzern* see Monika Richarz, *Jüdisches Leben im Deutschland*, II (Stuttgart, 1979), pp. 57 and 459 ff.

[40] The list of companies with Jews prominent in management is incomplete. Several of the firms with Jewish bankers prominent on their boards also had Jewish managing directors (among them AEG, Ludwig Loewe, Orenstein & Koppel, Bamag-Meguin, and Scheidemandel).

X Textile (10):	Blumenstein-Konzern
XI Paper & printing (3):	none
XII/XVII Leather, lino, shoes (4):	Adler & Opp., Sigle
XIII Caoutchouc (1):	none
XVI Food and drink (8):	Löwenbräu

In a small sample, the strongest relative representation occurs in the chemical industry and in leather and shoes. Once more, the textile industry is weakly represented.

IV

If one considers the industrial sector as a whole, men of Jewish extraction were to be found in prominent positions in some 39 of the 100 largest industrial companies listed by Siegrist.[41] Once more, the distribution by branches may be considered (total number in brackets):

III Mining (9):	Erdöl, Harpen, Rheinbraun 3
IV Stone and earth (5):	Portland Cement, Schles. Portland, Basalt AG, Stettiner Chamotte 4
V Iron & metal production, metal goods (22):	Ver. Stahlwerke, Mannesmannröhren, Klöckner, Mitteld. Stahlwerke, Metallurg. Ges., Mansfeld, Berlin-Karlsruher, Oberschl. Eisenbahnbed., Schles. Bergw., Bing Werke 10
VII Machinery, apparatus, vehicles (20):	Linke-Hoffmann, Orenstein & K., Berl. Maschinen, Bamag-Meguin Wanderer-Werke, Ludwig Loewe 6
VIII Electrical (15):	AEG 1
IX Chemical (13):	IG, Kokswerke, Rütgerswerke, Salzdetfurth etc., Th. Goldschmidt, AG f. Chem. Produkte, (Rhenania-Kunheim), Kaliwerke Neu-Stassfurt 7
X Textile (10):	Blumenstein-Konzern 1
XI Paper & printing (3):	Zellstoff Waldhof 1
XII/XVII Leather & Lino; shoes (4):	Adler & Opp., Sigle 2
XIII Caoutchouc (1):	none

[41] Of course this figure says nothing about the size or importance of the companies concerned.

XVI Food & drink (8):   Schultheiss-P., Ostwerke, Stollwerck, Löwenbräu 4

What stands out, besides the prominence in category IV, are the relatively high proportions in the larger categories V/VI and IX. Enterprises with Jews in prominent positions also figure strongly in the small categories XII/XVII and XVI. They still constitute about one third in categories III and the larger VII. Striking of course, in view of the past history of Jewish entrepreneurial activity, is the almost complete absence of representation in category X.[42] Overall, there appears to be no justification for the widely held view that, in the time of the Weimar Republic, there were few people of Jewish origin involved prominently in industrial activity. On the contrary, at least until the onset of the Great Depression, their position in this field was one of relative prominence.

While some of the companies in which men of Jewish origin were prominent dated from the 'second industrial revolution'—Ludwig Loewe, Orenstein & Koppel, the AEG, and the Metallbank u. Metallurgische Gesellschaft are outstanding examples—others had joined the hundred largest only recently. In this connection, it is interesting to consider the 63 overall newcomers to the list between 1907 and 1927. Of these, 20 had Jewish members of some prominence whilst 43 did not. While 'newcomers' thus constituted 50 per cent of the 'Jewish' total,[43] they formed 70 per cent of the Gentile one (62). While these figures allow no firm conclusions without detailed consideration of individual cases, they may suggest a relatively slower growth among 'Jewish' companies in the overall reservoir of enterprises from which the hundred largest were recruited.

Again, with every reserve, an attempt may be made to distribute the

[42] This is in part explained by location in areas where Jewish involvement in industry (indeed in economic activity as a whole) was relatively small. Firms were located in Elberfeld, Bremen, Barmen, Osnabrück, Leipzig, Hamburg, Hanover-Linden, Neusalz. The only enterprise in the area of traditional Jewish textile entrepreneurship is the Christian Dierig AG in Oberlangenbielau which, moreover, established links with the BHG and retained Hans Fürstenberg as a board member until 1937.

[43] The figures are affected by the fact that Siegrist excludes Vereinigte Stahlwerke, IG Farben, and the Salzdetfurth-Westeregeln-Aschersleben Konzern from the number of new companies because their constituents had previously figured amongst the hundred largest companies. If they are considered as new enterprises, which in fact they were, the figures would be somewhat modified. Thus the share of 'new' companies among those with Jews in prominent positions would rise to 58 per cent.

hundred largest companies in the 'ethnic' categories (I)–(IV) already used. The resulting distribution would be the following:

(I)	(II)	(II–III)	(III)	(III–IV)	(IV)	not classifiable
15	16	10	5	3	50*	1

*of which 9 in the textile industry

There is a striking polarization between categories (I) and (II), 31 firms, on the one hand, and category (IV) with 50 on the other. It would seem from this that participation of men of Jewish origin was either fairly marked or non-existent. The 'intermediate' categories contain only 18 firms.

It is possible to compare the ten largest firms in the two groups at the extremes of the spectrum (I) and (IV) (nominal share capital in brackets):

(I)		(IV)	
1. AEG	(186)	1. Siemens	(217)
2. Rütgers	(80)	2. Burbach Kaliwerke	(125)
3. Rheinbraun	(67)	3. Kali-Industrie (Wintershall)	(120)
4. Linke-Hoffmann	(49)	4. Stinnes (Restkonzern)	(80–100)
5. Salzdetfurth	(48)	5. Bergbau AG Lothringen	(80)
6. Metallbank	(45)	6. Gutehoffnungshütte	(80)
7. Schultheiss-P.	(39)	7. Ilseder Hütte	(64)
8. Orenstein & K.	(36)	8. Ver. Glanzstoff AG	(60)
9. Schles. Portland	(27)	9. Opel	(60)
10. Ostwerke	(26)	10. Köln-Neuessener Bergwerksverein	(55)

The companies in category (IV) are markedly larger than those in (I). On the other hand, while there are no known connections among the enterprises in (IV), there are quite close associations on the one hand between AEG, Rütgers, and Linke-Hoffmann with a joint capital of (315), and between Schultheiss, Ostwerke, and Schles. Portland (92). In fact what is represented is two large concerns, the AEG and the Landau-Sobernheim-Katzenellenbogen group, and three 'independents', Silverberg, Merton, and Orenstein. The Mertons and, to a lesser extent, Orenstein have, however, some historic associations with the AEG group. The Loewe interest is missing only because Gesfürel, its major unit, is not classed by Siegrist as an industrial company. The capital of Ludwig Loewe & Co. (presently to be amalgamated with

Gesfürel) is too small to figure among the ten largest. Thus the leading companies in group (I) are the ones of the pre-war era, with the post-war additions of the Sobernheim–Katzenellenbogen and Silverberg interests and the Goldschmidt-sponsored potash grouping (with Arthur Salomonsohn board chairman of two component units, Albert Katzenellenbogen of the third, Jakob Goldschmidt deputy chairman of all three as well as a joint managing director). It is worth noting that this company is smaller than its competitors Burbach and Wintershall. The Friedländer interest has disappeared with the death of its founder. It would appear that, in comparison with the situation in 1907, the relative weight of companies in group (I) has somewhat diminished. There is a difference also in the distribution among different branches of industry. Whilst 5 of the companies in category (IV) come from groups III and V/VI (coal, iron and steel), in (I) only 2 companies fall into these categories.

Finally, it is worth considering the 10 largest enterprises overall (nominal share capital in brackets):

1.	IG Farben	(1.100)	(II)
2.	Ver. Stahlwerke	(800)	(II–III)
3.	Siemens	(217)	(IV)
4.	AEG	(186)	(I)
5.	Krupp	(160)	(III–IV)
6.	Mannesmannröhren	(160)	(II)
7.	Burbach	(125)	(IV)
8.	Wintershall	(120)	(IV)
9.	Dt. Erdöl	(100)	(II)
10.	Harpen	(100)	(II)

Thus, in half of the largest industrial companies, men of Jewish origin play a part of some importance, while in the other half they do not. Comparing this with the situation twenty years earlier, it would be difficult to see in the industrial sector any decided trend. It is, perhaps, symptomatic of the continued role of Jews in German industry that, of its twenty-four representatives at the meeting of the CDBB in Berlin in June 1931, seven, as previously indicated, were of Jewish origin:

Dr.-Ing. Herbert von Klemperer, chairman of the board of the Berliner Maschinenbau AG vorm. L. Schwartzkopff, Berlin
Hans Kraemer MdRWR, Berlin, deputy chairman of the RDI (paper industry)

Dr.-Ing. William Meinhardt, chairman of the directorate of the Osram GmbH KG, Berlin (electric bulbs)
Dr Edmund Pietrkowski MdRWR, general director, Berlin (chemical industry)
Dr.-Ing. c.h. Philipp Rosenthal, *Geh. Kommerzienrat*, Selb (Bayern) (china)
Dr jur. Dr rer. pol. h.c. Dr.-Ing. c.h. Paul Silverberg, chairman of the board of directors of the Rhein AG für Braunkohlenbergbau u. Brikettfabrikation, Cologne
Dr jur. Walter Sobernheim, *Kommerzienrat*, chairman of the general directorate of the Schultheiss-Patzenhofer Brauerei Aktiengesellschaft, Berlin

V

As regards the commercial sector, there is a lack of systematic data. In retailing, while firms like Hermann Tietz expanded (among others by taking over another Jewish chain, A. Jandorf) and Wertheim maintained its position, the rising Gentile store of Rudolph Karstadt in Hamburg (which numbered Fritz Warburg among its board members) prospered under the guidance of a man of Jewish origin, KR Hermann Schöndorff.[44] Schöndorff's major innovations consisted on the one hand in horizontal expansion through the absorption of lesser stores, on the other in vertical growth through Karstadt-owned factories (notably by the acquisition of textile mills and chocolate factories). Karstadt's financing operations were carried out largely with the

[44] For Hermann Schöndorff see Pinner, op. cit., n. 4 above, pp. 277 ff. Pinner calls Schöndorff the guiding spirit ('führende Kopf') of the firm. Father Schöndorff had been a horse-dealer in Westheim (Kr. Düren). One son, Albert, had turned to timber preparation (*Holzbearbeitung*) and the construction of carriages (*Waggonbau*) in the firm of Gebrüder Schöndorff, Holzbearbeitungsfabrik und Waggonbauanstalt, Düsseldorf. He subsequently became a member of the board of Rudolph Karstadt AG as well as of the Barmer Bankverein in Düsseldorf. Hermann Schöndorff, meanwhile, born in 1869, had in 1890 become partner in and manager of a bedding manufacture and shop Gebr. Schöndorff, Bettenfabrik und Bettendetailgeschäft. This he had turned into a shopfitting establishment (*Ladeneinrichtungsfirma*). In 1920, Hermann Schöndorff had entered Rudolph Karstadt and had largely contributed to the striking expansion of the original Hamburg store. Like his brother, he joined the board of the Barmer Bankverein. His son Robert joined the Karstadt directorate in 1927. This is the account given in the *Reichshandbuch der deutschen Gesellschaft*. Wenzel, in his *Deutscher Wirtschaftsführer*, claims that Schöndorff was first employed in the department store of Theodor Althoff in Münster. When Althoff was absorbed by Rudolph Karstadt, Schöndorff moved to Hamburg to begin his career in the larger firm.

assistance of M. M. Warburg & Co. Oscar Tietz and Heinrich Grünfeld, meanwhile, played leading roles in the professional association of department store owners, the Verband der deutschen Waren- und Kaufhäuser.

Among publishers, while after the death of Rudolf Mosse in 1920 his firm declined under weak management, the more dynamic house of Ullstein was forging ahead. Hermann Ullstein, one of the partners, in speaking of the years 1928–9, would later recall: 'Never was there a time in the history of our firm when things progressed more favourably than now. Expanding in every direction, it refused to be intimidated by vague murmurings of unrest beneath the surface.'[45] Thus, though Leopold Sonnemann's *Frankfurter Zeitung* would presently pass into the hands of industrial interests (notably IG Farben), and in spite of severe competion from the nationalist publishing house of August Scherl, directed by Alfred Hugenberg (and, to a lesser extent, the apolitical Generalanzeiger group), the 'Jewish press' overall maintained its position. Theodor Wolff and Georg Bernhard, editors-in-chief respectively of *Berliner Tageblatt* and *Vossische Zeitung*, the leading Mosse and Ullstein 'quality papers', played a significant if controversial role in the public life of the Republic.

Men of Jewish origin continued to play a role also in the field of public utilities—Oscar Oliven in Gesfürel or Paul Silverberg on the board of Rheinisch-Westfälische Elektrizitätswerke—and in communications, with Georg Solmssen as board chairman of the Deutsch-Atlantische Telegraphen-Gesellschaft. They remained prominent in real-estate development, with Georg Haberland and his son Dr Kurt Haberland in Berlin outstanding.

Jews remained prominent also in the traditional metal trade. Leo Lustig, the former protégé of the Caros, directed the Deutsche Eisenhandel AG in Berlin. The old-establshed firm of Aron Hirsch & Söhne in Halberstadt, though overtaken increasingly by more enterprising competitors, continued its trading activities. Other interconnected Jewish firms were active in the same field: besides the Metallgesellschaft in Frankfurt-on-Main, the firm of Beer, Sondheimer & Co. Grosshandel in Berg- und Hüttenprodukten (later Tellus AG

---

[45] Hermann Ulstein, *The Rise and Fall of the House of Ullstein* (London, n.d.), p. 162. Among other ventures, the Ullsteins, in 1929, started a new paper, the *Grüne Post*, designed to appeal to readers in rural areas. It 'caught on' above all in small provincial towns and, within a year, boasted a readership of over one million. The Nazis, in alarm, started an unsuccessful *Braune Post* in competition (ib., p. 158).

für Bergbau und Hüttenindustrie), started by two former employees of the Metallgesellschaft. Its chairman, Albert Sondheimer, also held a seat on the board of the C & P bank. Closely associated with the Metallgesellschaft (then Metallbank und Metallurgische Gesellschaft) was the originally Upper Silesian metal wholesale firm of Rawack & Grünfeld. A former director of the Metallgesellschaft, Edmund Pietrkowski, on moving to Berlin as general secretary (*Geschäftsführer*) of a trade association, joined the boards of both companies. Deputy chairman of the Rawack board was Arthur Netter, partner in the metal wholesaling firm of Wolf Netter & Jacoby, which also owned tin rolling-mills. Alfred Merton of the Metallgesellschaft sat on the board of the Deutsche Gold- und Silber-Scheideanstalt (Degussa) in Frankfurt-on-Main, managed by the Gentile Rössler family, but associated also with the Mertons.

All these were older companies. In the more recent Otto Wolff AG in Cologne, a man of Jewish origin, Ottmar Strauss, played a prominent role as co-founder.[46] Assisted by Louis Hagen, Wolff (a Gentile) and Strauss secured the dominant influence in the Phoenix-AG für Bergbau und Hüttenbetrieb in Düsseldorf. *Freiherr* Simon Alfred von Oppenheim had to give up the chairmanship of the Phoenix board, hitherto a perquisite of his family. Otto Wolff became a board member. In 1923, Otto Wolff & Co. on becoming associated with the Koninklijke Nederlandsche Maatschappij Hoogovens en Staalfabrieken, ceded to the Dutch company part of its Phoenix holdings. Wolff and Strauss then acquired a major interest in the Rheinische Stahlwerke AG in Duisburg-Meiderich. When, in 1926, Phoenix and the bulk of Rheinstahl entered the Vereinigte Stahlwerke, both Wolff and Strauss joined the board of the new company. In the meantime, Otto Wolff & Co. had acquired a major interest in the Mansfeld AG für Bergbau und Hüttenbetrieb. Strauss had joined the boards of Phoenix, Rheinstahl, Mansfeld, and Demag. In fact, the Wolff concern had established links with machine and machine-tool building firms, with metal manufacturers, shipyards, and shipping lines. It had added zinc to its other interests, with Wolff in 1927 joining the board of the largest producer, AG für Bergbau, Blei- und Zinkfabrikation Stolberg in Aachen. Ottmar Strauss played a part in these activities though it is, of course, significant that the firm was called Otto Wolff & Co., not Wolff & Strauss.

---

[46] For the career of Ottmar Strauss see Zielenziger, op. cit., n. 7 above, pp. 257 ff.

These details are presented somewhat at random, simply to show that, in various aspects of commerce, men of Jewish origin continued to play an active role under the Weimar Republic.

VI

Down to 1931, at least, there is little evidence of any significant overall decline of the role of Jews in German economic life. In the banking sector, though some Jewish-owned private banks had disappeared, mainly through absorption by joint-stock banks, this was a process which went back to the beginning of the century. Since then, as part of banking rationalization, many provincial joint-stock banks (as well as a few more private banks) had been absorbed—incidentally opening up undreamt-of career prospects for some of the abler and more determined employees and apprentices (a few of whom would make their way to the top of the joint-stock banking system). The subsequent phase of amalagmation among the major joint-stock banks themselves had done little to impair the position of men of Jewish origin as documented, among others, by the careers of Jakob Goldschmidt and Georg Solmssen. In the larger Jewish private banks, moreover, several men of outstanding ability had been admitted into partnerships—Carl Melchior in the firm of M. M. Warburg, Otto Jeidels, the true successor of Carl Fürstenberg in the BHG, and Rudolf Loeb,[47] its last effective partner (with son-in-law Paul Kempner), in Mendelssohn & Co. To these might be added Dr Fritz Mannheimer, director of a highly successful associate of the Mendelssohns in Amsterdam. All, in their different ways, became prominent figures on the international financial scene. Indeed, between them, they may be said to have brought about, together with the indefatigable Max Warburg, a renaissance in Jewish private banking. This was, in fact, new talent spotted by perceptive private bankers (Otto Jeidels, actually, was recommended to Carl Fürstenberg, greatly to the latter's advantage, by Wilhelm Merton) and rewarded with partnerships and leading positions for outstanding performance. None came from banking backgrounds or had been associated with any of the large joint-stock banks. No government, down to the end of the Republic, would dispense with their expert services. This was a sector where, by adoption, the German–Jewish economic élite was still

[47] For Rudolf Loeb see Wilhelm Treue, 'Das Bankhaus Mendelssohn' in *Mendelssohn Studien* I (Berlin, 1972), pp. 66 ff.

successfully recruiting and renewing itself. Overall (bearing in mind, however, the declining place of corporate banking within the economy as a whole) the Jewish role in the banking system had, if anything, increased.

In industry, whilst the importance of bankers—including Jewish ones—may have diminished somewhat, though Jakob Goldschmidt, for example, played a leading role in the reorganization and rationalization of entire branches of German industry, including the heavy industry of the Ruhr, that of Jewish managing directors, Sally Segall (Rütgers), Hans Bie (Kokswerke), Herbert von Klemperer (Berl. Masch.), Walter Sobernheim (Schultheiss-Patzenhofer), Felix Deutsch (AEG), Moritz Salomon (Scheidemandel), Herbert Peiser (Bamag-Meguin), William Meinhardt (Osram GmbH KG), Benno Orenstein (Orenstein & Koppel), not to mention Paul Silverberg, had, if anything, increased. A number of new Jewish managers had emerged, including both directors of major companies other than managing directors and managing directors of companies not included among the hundred largest. Overall, it would be difficult to claim that the place of Jews in major industrial enterprises had diminished markedly since Wilhelmine days.

In commerce also, as has been seen, the role of Jews had remained significant. In the wholesale metal trade, for instance, the traditional Jewish involvement had, if anything, increased. The same is true of retailing, where Jewish participation had almost certainly grown. In publishing, due largely to the expansion of the house of Ullstein, Jewish enterprise was maintained. In the construction industry, meanwhile, Jews occupied a conspicuous place, not least through the activities of the Julius Berger Tiefbau AG[48] which had, from modest

[48] For Julius Berger see Zielenziger op. cit., n. 7 above, pp. 221 ff. Born in 1862 the son of a waggoner in Zempelburg (Posen), Julius Berger (one of fifteen children from three marriages) had been apprenticed at 13 to a leather wholesaler in Berlin. Financial pressures forced him to return to Zempelburg to work as a waggoner. From transportation of building materials (for roads and railways), Berger moved to road construction. In 1892, he started a building firm in Bromberg. With the active support of GKR Louis Aronsohn, one of the leading bankers of the province of Posen (and with the participation of Schaaffhausen, then associated with the Dresdner Bank), the business, in 1905, was transformed into the Julius Berger Tiefbau AG, (share capital 1 million marks). Julius Berger became managing director, Louis Aronsohn board chairman. In 1910, the management of the firm had moved to Berlin. It concerned itself with railway, road, and, particularly, canal construction. In 1912, the share capital had been raised to 4 million marks. The firm then turned to tunnelling, more particularly a major project in Switzerland (completed in 1915). In 1914, Berger was made a *Kommerzienrat*. During the war, the firm was involved in railway construction for military purposes and in the

beginnings, developed into a world-wide enterprise employing 300 engineers and technicians and a workforce of some 25,000–30,000. This was a pre-war business dating from the year 1905 which, however, had achieved its major expansion, national and international, during the post-war period. On the other hand, among the victims of war, inflation, and Depression had been the old-established firm of Gebr. Simon which finally went bankrupt in October 1931.

While thus, in general, there is little evidence of decline in Jewish economic activity at least at the level of the economic élite, there are indications pointing to a long-term diminution of the Jewish role. In the first place, the biological factor was continuing to remove progressively remaining survivors of the pre-war generation. The following are among the more important:

1926: Benno Orenstein; Gustav v. Klemperer
1927: Maximilian Kempner
1928: Felix Deutsch
1930: Arthur Salomonsohn
1931: Oscar Caro
1932: Louis Hagen; James Simon; Henry Nathan
1933: Leopold Koppel; Carl Fürstenberg (aged 83)
1934: Oscar Wassermann (at the unusually young age of 65); Carl Melchior.

However, many of these men (typically in their early seventies, some a good deal older) had, in the majority of cases, half withdrawn from active participation in economic life. Equivalent pioneers among Gentiles, Werner von Siemens, Georg Siemens, August Thyssen, Carl Klönne, Arthur v. Gwinner, Adolph Hansemann, Alfred and Friedrich Krupp, and, latterly, Hugo Stinnes, had already left the scene if anything marginally earlier than their Jewish counterparts. In fact, German capitalism as a whole had entered a 'silver age'.

Moreover, at least to some extent, the gaps left by the disappearance of the 'Grand Old Men' were being filled by new, usually 'self-made' men, drawn in the Jewish case from the reservoir of (mainly commercial) lower middle and middle-class families. Goldschmidt,

---

building of fortifications. After the war, it engaged in major rail and tunnel construction work in Romania, Turkey, and Iran, in port construction, work on canals, and on the Berlin underground. Berger's position within the construction industry was recognized by his election to the executive council (*Praesidium*) of his professional association (Reichsverband industrieller Bau- Unternehmungen).

Bodenheimer, Ludwig Katzenellenboge, Melchior, Loeb, Jeidels, Silverberg, Strauss, Schöndorff, and others (employees rather than owners) helped, in some degree, to replenish the Jewish economic élite. Some of the 'old dynasties' persisted, the Mendelssohns, Oppenheims, Warburgs, Ladenburgs, Mertons, Weinbergs, Loewes, Ullsteins, Tietzes, together with a less effectual 'second generation', the *'Nachwuchs'* of the Fürstenbergs, Kempners, Wallichs, Gutmanns, Mosses. Others however, Fritz Friedländer, Eduard Arnhold, Louis Hagen, or Felix Deutsch, had no successors. Overall, if there was some decline in the quality of entrepreneurship, this was a slow and gradual process.

Another feature pointing to a slow decline is the fact that, between 1906 and 1927, a relatively lower proportion of companies with significant Jewish participation entered the ranks of the hundred largest. A higher proportion of 'Jewish' firms than of non-Jewish had already figured among the hundred largest in 1907. The implication of this fact might be that more Jewish firms maintained their ranking by preserving or increasing their capital whereas fewer increased it 'disproportionately' to gain inclusion for the first time. This could be a pointer to a relatively slower growth of capital in industrial firms with Jewish associations—though their relative stagnation may be only by comparison with the comparatively rapid capital expansion of certain branches (such as textiles) in which Jews were not represented at this level to any marked extent. More detailed investigations than are possible here would be needed to determine whether, perhaps, the activities of members of the Jewish economic élite were concentrated in sectors with relatively slower capital growth. Furthermore, at least in theory, there is no reason why the comparative figures for 1907 and 1927 should, of necessity, reflect a continuous process.

What is incontrovertible is that the onset of the Depression struck a serious blow at many enterprises where men of Jewish origin occupied prominent positions. But was that blow a disproportionate one? This is a question impossible to answer. So far as the large joint-stock banks were concerned it was Goldschmidt's Danat which, having suffered the greatest loss of confidence and the largest withdrawals, had to close its shutters on 13 July 1931. The Dresdner Bank followed suit and was saved only by heavy government investment (repaid in 1937) in consideration of its readiness to absorb the Danat bank. Danat was, in fact, the only large bank which disappeared. The Dresdner survived, to regain its independence in 1937 and, in due course, become a major banking institute of the Federal Republic. The C & P also survived the crisis with some assistance from the authorities to operate once more successfully in the Federal Republic as the Commerzbank. The DeDi bank, on the other hand, thanks mainly to more cautious borrowing policies, withstood the crisis with the aid of its own resources, though at the price of a substantial reduction in its share capital.[49] On the face of it, it might appear that the banks with the greatest Jewish involvement fared worst. But then, in the DeDi banks with their more cautious borrowing policies also, Jews (Oscar Wassermann and Georg Solmssen) had played a leading role. Furthermore, among private bankers, Carl Fürstenberg, Otto Jeidels, and Rudolf Loeb appear to have decided in good time, contrary to the then widespread practice, not to accept three-month deposits but only moneys lent for at least six months. This, when the banking crisis broke, provided at any rate a breathing space.[50] However, even such prudence had saved neither M. M. Warburg nor the BHG from serious financial embarrassment. It was the American Warburgs who had come to the rescue by investing extra capital (through the International Acceptance Bank-Bank of Manhattan Company, whose vice-president, James P. Warburg, spent the summer months of 1931 in Hamburg) in the Warburg houses in Hamburg and Amsterdam.[51] When the BHG in its turn found itself in difficulties,[52] it was the combined Warburg interests which mounted a successful rescue operation.[53] A close association between the two banks was formed, with Max M. Warburg entering the board (*Verwaltungsrat*) of the BHG. It was a unique case of a private bank acting as an intermediary (for a major American consortium) in the rescue of what had been considered, at least till the successive fusions of the 'D' banks, one of the large joint-stock banks. The association, however, was amicably dissolved before long, since the two firms were in fact conducting similar operations and competing for the same type of customer.[54]

[49] Details in Seidenzahl, op. cit., n. 7 above, pp. 337 ff. To repeat Seidenzahl's figures taken from a speech by Oscar Wassermann, while Danat, in the attempt to support their value on the stock exchange, had had to buy up 58.3 per cent of its own shares and Dresdner 55.9 per cent, *C & P* had 'got away' with 49.6 per cent and DeDi with a mere 36.8 per cent (ib., p. 342).

[50] See Treue, loc. cit., p. 66.

[51] Rosenbaum, 'Albert Ballin' in *Year Book III of the Leo Baeck Institute* (London, 1958), p. 192.

[52] Details in Hans Fürstenberg, op. cit., n. 16 above, pp. 243 ff.

[53] Details in Rosenbaum, op. cit., pp. 192 ff. and Hans Fürstenberg, op. cit., pp. 245FF.   [54] Rosenbaum, op. cit., p. 193.

In fact, the overall effect of the crisis was, in the banking sector, to bring about a further round of concentration. Typically, it was banks with a strong Jewish involvement which tended to combine. This was the case with the fusion, under the auspices of the German government, of the Dresdner and Danat banks. Though Brüning (against the recommendations of Hans Schäffer, the Jewish State-secretary in the ministry of finance) secured the dismissal of Jakob Goldschmidt and substantial changes of personnel,[55] men of Jewish origin remained. The directorate (*Vorstand*) of seven men included four Jews: Henry Nathan, Wilhelm Kleemann, S. Bodenheimer, and Samuel Ritscher.[56] The last named, director of the official Reichskredit-Gesellschaft, as representative of the government, was perhaps among the most important members.

Amongst prominent Jewish private banks, while Mendelssohn & Co., in no small degree thanks to the skill of Rudolf Loeb,[57] appears to have weathered the crisis unscathed, and M. M. Warburg (as well as the BHG) was being kept afloat by 'the American connection', S. Bleichröder & Co., for many decades under weak management, was among the casualties.[58] While, however, Bleichröder lost its independent existence, it amalgamated with a stronger Jewish partner, Gebr. Arnhold in Dresden,[59] to form a viable new enterprise. Other Jewish

[55] Ekkehard Wandel, *Hans Schäffer 1886–1967* (Stuttgart, 1974), p. 219.

[56] 'Unter ihnen befanden sich vom alten Vorstand der Dresdner Bank der (im November 1932 verstorbens) Senior der Bank seit 1920, Henry Nathan, ferner der 1919 aus dem diplomatischen Dienst übernommene Geh. Leg.-Rat Dr. Walther Frisch, der, zugleich Vizepräsident im Centralverband des deutschen Bank- und Bankiergewerbes, in den kritischen Wochen wiederholt als Sprecher der Bank hervorgetreten war, und als dritter Wilhelm Kleemann, in besonderer Würdigung seiner Verdienste um die damals noch zum Interessenbereich der Bank gehörenden Kreditgenossenschaften. Neu hinzu traten aus dem Kreise der Danatbank der für dieselbe bestellte staatliche Treuhänder Staatssekretär a.D. Karl Bergmann und von den bisherigen Geschäftsinhabern S. Bodenheimer, ferner als weiterer Vertrauensmann der Reichsregiegung das bisherige Vorstandsmitglied der Reichskreditgesellschaft Samuel Ritscher, der schon einmal, 1919 bis 1923, aus der Deutschen Orientbank hervorgegangen, dem Vorstand der Dresdner Bank angehört hatte (Hunscha, op. cit., n. 13 above, pp. 39 f). Wandel's information (Wandel, op. cit., p. 219) is erroneous.

[57] Treue (loc. cit., n. 47 above, pp. 65 f), in uninformative on how Mendelssohn & Co. weathered the storm.

[58] See Hans Fürstenberg, op. cit., n. 16 above, pp. 225 f.

[59] 'Obgleich die Nachbar-Banken sich darum bemühten, dass diese Perle der Berliner "Haute Banque" nicht in Verlegenheit geriet, sollte sich am Ende keine selbständige Lösung finden lassen. Schliesslich ergab sich ein Ausweg in Form der Übernahme durch das alte Bankhaus Gebrüder Arnhold, dass sich in Dresden die erste Stelle erworben hatte und durch den Teilhaber Hans Arnhold teilweise nach Berlin verpflanzt worden war, und zwar mit beachtlichem Erfolg. Aus der Übernahme ergab

private banks like the—possibly over-extended—firm of Simon Hirschland in Essen survived, if with much anxiety. It would be difficult, in sum, to claim that the financial crisis of 1931, however traumatic, seriously reduced the German financial establishment, including its Jewish component. This would, in fact, be ready for a financial and industrial upturn expected with some confidence before long.

Elsewhere, the Great Depression hit Jewish commercial and industrial enterprises as it did others. At the AEG there had already been changes before the Depression struck,[60] which, however, had done little to alter its character. Confronted with financial problems under a new and unproven leadership the AEG was tided over its immediate problems by a loan of 20 million marks from its banking consortium.[61] The loan having proved insufficient to solve the difficulties of the group, Bücher, its (Gentile) managing director, began—Hans Fürstenberg claims behind his back—prolonged negotiations which would end in associating the AEG with the American General Electric Company and the international Loewe consortium.[62]

Another group of enterprises affected by the Depression were Jewish publishing houses.[63] The Frankfurter Societäts Druckerei (FSD), publishers of the Frankfurter Zeitung, with most of the shares in the hands of the heirs of Leopold Sonnemann,[64] had found itself in

sich dann die Firma Arnhold & S. Bleichröder, die seit dem Kriege erfolgreich in New York weitergeführt wird' (ib.).

[60] In 1928 Felix Deutsch, managing director since the death of Emil Rathenau, had died. He had recently selected his successor *Geheimrat* Hermann Bücher, a Gentile, who duly succeeded him. In 1929 Carl Fürstenberg, then approaching the age of 80 and still chairman of the board (a chairmanship he refused to relinquish), had his son Hans elected a board member. As Carl Fürstenberg could no longer direct proceedings, a joint deputy chairmanship was established in 1930 with Fritz Andreae, the part-Jewish son-in-law of Emil Rathenau and partner in Hardy & Co., as the senior, Hans Fürstenberg as the junior member. Hans Fürstenberg claims that he then assumed the *de facto* chairmanship of the board, as his father could no longer exercise his functions and Fritz Andreae was an 'outsider' so far as the banking associations of the AEG were concerned. Hans Fürstenberg became chairman also of the bank's finance consortium (Hans Fürstenberg, op. cit., n. 16 above, p. 207).

[61] 'Meine grösste Leistung in jener Zeit bestand darin, dass es mir gelang, noch einen Konsortial-Kredit von 20 Millionen Reichsmark zustande zu bringen. Dass die Bedingungen unter gegebenen Verhältnissen nicht gerade glänzende waren, versteht sich von selbst' (ib., p. 208). [62] Ib., p. 209.

[63] For the following see mainly Modris Eksteins, *The Limits of Reason. The German Democratic Press and the Collapse of Weimar Democracy* (Oxford, 1975).

[64] Now his grandsons Heinrich and Kurt Simon.

financial difficulties as early as 1927.[65] By October 1928, it had accumulated debts of 1.75 million marks.[66] Following abortive negotiations with other newspaper publishers, the Simon brothers, grandsons of the founder, found a financial backer in Carl Bosch, chairman of the managing board and chief decision-maker of IG Farben.[67] 'The FSD needed two million mark; Carl Bosch appeared prepared to provide them.'[68] In February/March 1929, the Simons sold to an intermediary 35 per cent of FSD shares for a price of 1.4 million marks, twice their nominal value. The FSD was granted, at the same time, a loan of 1.5 million marks at the low interest rate of 5 per cent. A representative of the new shareholders joined the advisory board.[69] Changes in editorial personnel followed. Bernhard Gutmann, the paper's Berlin correspondent, was replaced, as was Arthur Feiler, economic expert in the political section. Both were of Jewish origin and both, coincidentally, were replaced by Gentiles. Subsequent changes in personnel, in editorial policy, and in the tone of the paper were gradual. The injection of almost three million marks, however, failed to improve its profitability. While its circulation figures rose somewhat, advertising revenue fell drastically with the onset of the Depression. Within eighteen months of the deal, the FSD had exhausted its new resources. In 1930, a further 14.5 per cent of the shares, owned this time by friends of the Simon family, passed to the new shareholders, giving the IG 49.5 per cent of the share capital.[70] The *Frankfurter Zeitung* continued to make losses, estimated for 1931 at 1.2 million marks. Faced with this situation, the Simon brothers offered a further 25 per cent of the remaining family holding to Carl Friedrich von Siemens, but, in the uncertain economic climate, the offer was refused.[71] Little was left of the legacy of Leopold Sonnemann.

---

[65] 'By the end of 1927 the publishers of the *Frankfurter Zeitung* had, according to one of the directors, "almost reached the dangerous point where debts devour all yields" because of the interest repayable on borrowed capital. The firm's deficit for the business year 1927 exceeded a quarter of a million marks, the second year in succession that enormous losses had been registered. The total deficit now amounted to over RM 700,000' (ib., p. 160).

[66] Ib., p. 163.

[67] One reason was that IG had invested heavily in research on the production of synthetic petrol and had come under attack for squandering national assets. The firm needed to create a favourable climate of opinion and to secure a tariff on the importation of oil (ib., pp. 166 ff).

[68] Eksteins, op. cit., n. 63 above, p. 168.

[69] Ib., p. 172.

[70] Ib., pp. 175 f.   [71] Ib., pp. 178 f.

Matters stood little better with the publishing house left behind by Rudolf Mosse. Under his son-in-law Hans Lachmann-Mosse, in the course of the twenties, the once flourishing business had gone into a steep decline.[72] Lachmann-Mosse sought to meet its financial problems by reductions in editorial staff combined with the 'depoliticization' of its papers. By the end of 1931, some fifty editors and correspondents had been dismissed.[73] The 'depoliticization', moreover, had meant, effectively, also 'de-Judaization'.[74] When this offered no solution to the firm's financial problems, Lachmann-Mosse was forced to turn elsewhere. It appears that in 1932 the Dresdner Bank, in which the state now had a majority holding, provided some 2.5 million marks to help Mosse liquidate some speculative ventures in real-estate development.[75] By 1933, with the uncovered debts of the firm standing at 8.8 million marks, its financial position was desperate.[76] No more than Leopold Sonnemann's had the legacy of Rudolf Mosse been able to stand the test of difficult times.

Unlike its two competitors, the house of Ullstein had at first found itself in a relatively healthy financial position. Whereas both FSD and Mosse had been in difficulties even during the 'fat years' of the Republic, the Ullsteins ended the business year 1930 with profits which, if reduced, were still substantial. In 1931, cutbacks had to be made, but it was not until 1932 that the firm recorded an overall financial loss.[77] The journal *Tempo* was a loss-maker as was the prestigious *Vossische Zeitung*, which in 1931 lost 500,000 marks. By the beginning of 1933 it was costing 200,000 marks a month. Moreover, the firm was beset by a succession of bitter family feuds among the Ullstein brothers and their descendants. When these proved insoluble, the Ullsteins approached the (Jewish) former state secretary in the ministry of finance, Hans Schäffer, who agreed to join the firm as

[72] 'The injudicious nature of Hans Lachmann-Mosse's speculative activities in the 1920s became fully obvious at the turn of the decade. Enormous sums of money had been swallowed by various unsound projects. At first, existing assets had been mortgaged to furnish new capital; then open debts were contracted. When the depression struck, the owners of the Mosse firm found themselves in a financial quagmire. To cover debts elsewhere Lachmann-Mosse began to play with the finances of his newspapers and other publishing interests. He dug into the pension fund for his employees—according to one report 3.6 million marks were appropriated from this fund by 1933 ... The business practices of the Mosse advertising agency became notorious ...' (ib., p. 224).

[73] Eksteins, op. cit., n. 63 above, p. 229.

[74] 'From the large number of Jews among those sacked some historians have deduced that Lachmann-Mosse was trying intentionally to remove the evidence for the right-wing assertions that the Mosse papers belonged to the *Judenpresse*' (ib., p. 229).

[75] Ib., p. 259.   [76] Ib., p. 224.   [77] Ib., pp. 231 f.

director-general. Already, since the autumn of 1930, four Gentiles, a former Reich minister of finance and three men with industrial connections, had been invited to join the management to provide judgement unaffected by the family feuds.[78] Through Schäffer, unobtrusive pressure on matters of editorial policy could be brought to bear by the government. In December 1931, the editor in chief of a major Ullstein paper was dismissed for an article displeasing to the authorities and replaced by a man previously approved by the ministers of defence and finance, the *Reichspräsident*'s secretary, and the state secretary in the *Reichskanzler*'s office.[79] With that the libertarian traditions of Leopold Ullstein had effectively gone the way of those of Sonnemann and Mosse.

While it is, of course, evident that all (non-Nazi) newspapers and their publishers suffered financially during the Depression from loss both of circulation[80] and advertising revenue, the 'Jewish press' with its liberal political leanings was hit additionally by the decline of liberalism and the widespread prejudice aroused by the ethnic composition of its editorial boards and staffs. It was thus in headlong decline (as well as in process of transformation) well before the arrival of the new rulers.

In a very different sphere, the Depression also helped to terminate Paul Silverberg's industrial career. The story is a complicated one of corporate competition and intrigue, sufficiently interesting to be worth summarizing.[81] Early in 1929 Silverberg's company Rheinbraun had acquired from Fritz Thyssen, in addition to its existing holdings, a further packet of Harpen shares for 12 million marks. In the same year, it took over from the Gelsenkirchener Bergwerks-AG (Gelsenberg) Harpen debentures (*Harpen-Anleihe*) to a nominal value of 22.3 million marks in exchange (fatefully) for its own shares to the (nominal) value of 11.7 million marks. While not all the Harpen shares remained in the Rheinbraun portfolio, Rheinbraun, in 1932, still owned Harpen shares to a nominal value of 36,352 million marks. It had become the largest shareholder ever of one of the leading coal producers of the Ruhr.

[78] Eksteins, op. cit., n. 63 above, pp. 232 f.
[79] Ib., p. 236.
[80] 'That the circulation of the Mosse papers declined after 1930 was due in the main to the economic depression rather than to editorial policy. Almost all papers suffered a decline in sales, regardless of their political orientation, in virtually direct relation to the unemployment figures in the country' (ib., p. 231).
[81] For the following see Kurt Pritzkoleit, *Wem gehört Deutschland?* (Vienna, Munich, Basle, 1957), pp. 310 f.

Before the majority shareholder, Dr Friedrich Flick, in the spring of 1932, sold his Gelsenberg shares to the government, he acquired, with borrowed money, Gelsenberg's holding in Rheinbraun, now of a nominal value of 13 million marks. As his own firm, Charlottenhütte had already taken over a packet of nominally 8 million marks of Rheinbraun shares from the tottering Danat bank, and as Fritz Thyssen had gratuitously sold Flick further Rheinbraun shares from his portfolio, Flick now controlled a nominal 21 million marks of Rheinbraun shares. He had become the company's major shareholder. Being however interested in coal (Harpen), not lignite (Rheinbraun), Flick then proposed to Silverberg an exchange of his Rheinbraun shares against Rheinbraun's Harpen holdings. Silverberg declined the offer, which would have terminated his ambitious industrial dreams (of a concern combining lignite, coal, and electricity).

Flick then offered his Rheinbraun holdings to the Rheinisch-Westfälische Elektricitätswerke, a company eager to acquire Rheinbraun and its subsidiaries, in exchange for Rheinbraun's Harpen shares. RWE, previously a minority shareholder in Rheinbraun, having thus acquired the majority, duly transferred the Harpen shares to Flick. Following this deal, Silverberg's days as an industrialist were numbered. On 31 March 1933, he resigned the chairmanship of the Rheinbraun board. On 3 August, he also left the Harpen chairmanship. On 23 January 1934 Flick, now in control of 45.8 per cent of Harpen's share capital, became its new chairman. RWE, from whose board Silverberg had resigned (he had been one of its three deputy chairmen), was left the owner of Rheinbraun. The astute corporate operation that had defeated Silverberg had been assisted by the financial crisis which had induced the Danat bank to make over its Rheinbraun holding to Flick.

Another victim of the Depression (and of his own imprudence) was Ludwig Katzenellenbogen, whose concern collapsed with Katzenellenbogen himself being found guilty by the courts of infractions of the law.[82] Lesser enterprises also got into financial difficulties, sometimes as a result of misguided speculations, as was the case with Aron Hirsch & Sohn in Halberstadt, taken over by another

---

[82] Bernstein, loc. cit. n. 21 above, p. 782. The financial reconstruction of Schultheiss-Patzenhofer was carried out with the help of the BHG which provided the capital other members of the Schultheiss consortium were unable to raise. A representative of the BHG joined the Schultheiss board and its quota in the consortium was substantially increased. (Rolf E. Lüke, *Die Berliner Handelsgesellschaft in einem Jahrhundert deutscher Wirtschaft 1856–1956* (Berlin, 1957, p. 229.)

Jewish firm. The Depression, by weakening many industrial and commercial enterprises, reduced the role of some members of the German–Jewish economic élite—whether disproportionately is difficult to tell. It may be (but this can only be surmise) that Jewish managements showed a somewhat greater inclination to take commercial risks (or to engage in somewhat risky speculations) than their Gentile competitors, and were thus more vulnerable to the havoc wrought by the Great Depression. 'Jewish' enterprises, like Danat, Dresdner, AEG, Aron Hirsch & Söhne, and possibly others were certainly caught over-extended (as, however, were predominantly 'Gentile' firms ranging from Rudolph Karstadt AG, the insurance company '*Nordstern*', and the notorious Norddeutsche Wollkämmerei in Bremen to the two prestigious shipping lines, the Hapag and the Lloyd). It was perhaps a symbolic gesture when, in December 1931, Franz von Mendelssohn, on doctors' advice, resigned from the presidency of the Deutsche Industrie- und Handelstag, a post he had held since 1914 and which had just made him the first ever German president of the conference of the International Chamber of Commerce.[83]

VII

The economic crisis culminating in the events of July 1931 developed, of course, against the background of increasing anti-Semitic agitation and political instability following the death of Gustav Stresemann in October 1929, and the Reichstag elections of September 1930. Yet the impact, if any, of these developments on the position of Jews in German economic life was both delayed and diffuse and is difficult to document. In general, as future events would show, the attitude alike of the German political establishment exemplified by a man like Brüning, of the economico-political one represented perhaps by Dr Hjalmar Schacht, formerly of the Nationalbank für Deutschland, and of the industrial leadership represented by men like Paul Reusch or Emil Kirdorf towards Jews in German economic life was essentially 'functional'. While such men might feel no special liking for Jews they would, nevertheless recognize their usefulness in certain areas (which, indeed, was in the Bismarckian tradition). They could not, at any rate in their majority, be described as anti-Semites in the sense of the vulgar racialist demagogues. As will be seen presently, it was only

[83] Treue, loc. cit., n. 47 above, p. 66.

relatively late that Jewish origin became a bar to appointment to important economic positions. Men like Paul Silverberg, Franz von Mendelssohn, Carl Melchior, Rudolf Loeb, and others—as well as, of course, state secretary Hans Schäffer, or Samuel Ritscher of the Reichskredit-Gesellschaft—were able to play a part for some time in the formulation of economic policies. Even more (though perhaps with some exceptions) the role of Jews in the corporate economic structure continued to be widely accepted in the commercial and industrial community. One instance among several is that of the octogenarian Max Steinthal, board chairman of Mannesmannröhren-Werke until 1936 and associated with the firm's affairs until 1938.

There is no evidence, other than an instance like the loss of readership and advertising revenue of papers like the *Berliner Tageblatt* (due perhaps to economic as much as to political causes) of a direct impact of political developments in the last years of the Republic on Jewish economic activity. Somewhat surprisingly, even Hitler's advent to power made itself felt only gradually. This, was some justification, has been attributed largely to the influence of Hjalmar Schacht. So long as he remained indispensable to the new rulers—he did not finally lose his position until 1938[84]—he protected to the best of his ability, for purely utilitarian reasons, the 'Jewish sector' of the German economy.[85]

Within this relatively 'permissive' framework, the corporate sector of the German economy shed its Jewish members at a very uneven pace. Among early institutions to dismiss their Jewish directors (though not quite all, and not those of Jewish origin alone) was, perhaps predictably, the DeDi bank. Here, only Georg Solmssen remained a director until 1934, a board member until 1936.[86]

[84] Rosenbaum, op. cit., n. 51 above, p. 207.

[85] 'Solange Dr. Hjalmar Schacht seinen Posten bekleidete, blieb es die offizielle Politik des Reichswirtschaftsministeriums—durch die es, wie es nicht anders sein konnte, häufig in Konflikt mit anderen Ministerien und den Parteiorganen gebracht wurde—die meisten jüdischen Unternehmungen ungehindert ihren Geschäften nachgehen zu lassen; ein Beispiel für seinen verhältnismässig starken Einfluss gegenüber seinen Gegnern bot die Tatsache, dass es am 1. April 1938 noch fast 40.000 Firmen in Deutschland gab, die sich in jüdischem Besitz befanden' (Rosenbaum, op. cit., n. 51 above, p. 207).

[86] Already in 1929–30, in a first purge, affecting also Gentile directors, Selman Fehr had transferred to a Jewish private bank (in which the Deutsche Bank was a partner), Paul Bonn had been sacked, while Arthur Salomonsohn had been transferred to the *Aufsichtsrat*. Three years later came the second purge, 'Mit einem tapferen Wort hatte sich Ende 1933 Oscar Wassermann von der Belegschaft verabschiedet. Gleich ihm war Theodor Frank vom neuen Regime vertrieben worden ... Dr. Georg Solmssen hielt

Weimar: Decline and Fall?

In an institution like the BHG, the change, as might be expected, took place more gradually. While Siegfried Bieber had to resign as *Geschäftsinhaber* already in 1934, Hans Fürstenberg kept his position until 1935 and indeed 'stuck it out' on the board until 1938.[87] When a law of 1937 finally made the continuance of men of Jewish origin on company boards impossible, seven such members left the bank in 1938.[88]

The leading Jewish private banks meanwhile (particularly on account of their international prestige) remained an almost irreplaceable economic asset, a fact appreciated by no one more clearly than by Hjalmar Schacht, once director of the Nationalbank für Deutschland. Schacht spared no pains to keep at least the more prestigious Jewish private banks in the consortium for the provision of state loans (*Reichsanleihekonsortium*), a fact Max Warburg attributed to the financial strength of the Mendelssohns and his own firm.[89] When, early in 1938, Schacht had to bow to NS pressure, the last Jewish private banks were removed from the consortium and forced into liquidation. It bears testimony to the prestige of M. M. Warburg & Co. that, when the firm was 'Aryanized' in 1938, the authorities insisted that it continue to operate under its old name. Not until 1941 was it permitted to change its name to that of Brinckmann, Wirtz & Co.[90]

---

sich unter erschwerten Umständen bis 1934 im Vorstand, um noch bis 1936 im Aufsichtsrat auszuharren' (Seidenzahl, op. cit., n. 7 above, p. 433).

[87] 'Ich muss ins Jahr 1935 zurückkehren, wo wir schliesslich Staatsfinanzrat Hans Weltzien als Geschäftsinhaber gewannen, nachdem ich in diesem Jahr als solcher ausschied, jedoch im Interesse der Überleitung noch immer bis 1937 im Verwaltungsrat ausharrte ... Vorher was Herr Bieber schon 1934 zurückgetreten. Dr. Jeidels schliesslich musste 1938 gehen. Man sieht, dass die Überleitung in einem Rythmus gelang, der dem Ansehen des Hauses entsprach ...' (Hans Fürstenberg, op. cit., n. 16 above, p. 262).

[88] They were Hans Fürstenberg, Max Warburg, Siegfried Bieber, Paul Stahl, Herbert v. Klemperer, Hans Gottstein, and Robert Haas. Walter Merton had left the board already in 1937 (Lüke, op. cit., n. 82 above, p. 254).

[89] In his memoirs, he wrote: 'Die Firma (M. M. Warburg & Co.) war noch immer Mitglied des Reichsanleihe-Konsortiums ... Die Zahl der Mitglieder war ungefähr 50. Ein Drittel waren jüdische Bankhäuser gewesen; sie waren allmählich eliminiert worden. Schliesslich blieben nur noch drei übrig. Die NS Partei forderte immer entschiedener, dass die jüdischen Bankhäuser aus dem Konsortium zu entfernen seien. Dagegen wehrte sich Schacht als Präsident der Reichsbank. Er kannte die Bedeutung der Finanzierungskraft der Firma Mendelssohn und der unsrigen. Aber Argumente konnten die Gegenpartei nicht überzeugen. Er hatte nachzugeben' (quoted in Treue, loc. cit., n. 47 above, p. 68).

[90] 'Das Vermögen der Bank wurde auf diese neue Gruppe übertragen, die das Geschäft weiter unter dem Firmennahmen M. M. Warburg & Co. KG fortsetzte. Die Beibehaltung des alten Namens war von den Behörden besonders verlangt worden, weil

This was a compromise Rudolf Loeb, on behalf of the Mendelssohns, disdained. In 1938, the firm arranged to join the Deutsche Bank.[91] The major phase of Jewish participation in German banking thus ended in a deeply symbolic act.[92]

The forced resignation of Jews from the boards of commercial and industrial enterprises also was a gradual process effected with widely differing degrees of dignity and consideration.[93] Though gestures of solidarity with Jewish colleagues were few, they were not entirely lacking. When Paul Silverberg, perhaps the representative 'Jewish' personality (he had been baptized a Protestant as a child) in the economic élite of German 'heavy industry', was forced to give up the presidency of the Industrie- und Handelskammer in Cologne in the spring of 1933, the veteran Emil Kirdorf wrote in an open letter to the *Rheinisch-Westfälische Zeitung* in Essen:

Als ein Verbrechen erachte ich das unmenschliche Unmass der fortgesetzten antisemitischen Hetze. Eine grosse Anzahl um Deutschland verdienter Menschen, deren Familien seit Jahrhunderten hier eingebürgert sind, hat man in grausamer Weise deklassiert und ihnen den Boden unter den Füssen weggenommen ... Der Dolchstoss, welchen man diesen wertvollen Menschen versetzt hat, hat auch mich getroffen. Jetzt ist meine Hoffnung dahin, mein Vertrauen, ein neues, unbeflecktes, stolzes Deutschland noch zu erleben.[94]

Even the Ruhrlade, the unofficial 'cabinet' of Ruhr industry of which Silverberg had been the only 'Jewish' member, maintain a measure of

man sich ungeachtet der neuen Verhältnisse den internationalen Goodwill der Firma zunutze machen wollte' (Rosenbaum, op. cit., n. 51 above, pp. 210 ff.).

[91] For the details of the negotiations between Rudolf Loeb and Hermann Abs on behalf of the Deutsche Bank see Treue, loc. cit., n. 47 above, pp. 68 ff.

[92] The firm of Sal. Oppenheim jun. & Co. was tolerated by the NS regime with two Oppenheims, Simon and Waldemar von Oppenheim, as partners, though under the name of Pferdmenges & Co. In 1944, in connection with membership of a 'suspect' organization, the Union Club, the *Staatspolizei* in Cologne carried out investigations, leading to an official 'regrading' of the brothers Friedrich Karl Simon and Waldemar von Oppenheim '... bisher als Mischlinge II Grades geführt ... nunmehr als Mischlinge I Grades rassisch eingeordnet...' (Staatspolizeistelle, Cologne, IV ib 1814/44AG to *Reichssicherheitshauptamt Sonderkommando* III, Cologne, 4 Aug. 1944). Microfilm copy in Institut für Zeitgeschichte in Munich, MA 553 2 775218 ff. The report contains some curious data on the brothers Oppenheim, mostly based on surmise.

[93] 'Manchmal bewahrte man immerhin noch gute Formen, wenn Teilhaber von M. M. Warburg & Co. aus irgendwelchen Aufsichtsräten abgewählt wurden, aber in ebenso vielen Fällen wurde eine mit Absicht beleidigende Form der Mitteilung gewählt' Rosenbaum, op. cit., n. 51 above, p. 199.

[94] Quoted in R. Neebe, *Grossindustrie, Staat und NSDAP 1930–1933* (Göttingen, 1981), pp. 194 f.

solidarity. In June 1933 they, demonstratively, moved one of their periodic meetings to Silverberg's estate, the Hoverhof.[95] Their founder and leading personality, Paul Reusch, managing director of the Gute Hoffnungshütte, went further. Reusch, who had maintained cordial relations with both Paul Silverberg and Max Warburg, was uncompromising in his rejection of National Socialism. As Warburg records in his memoirs:

Jemand wie Reusch hatte von Anfang an Hitler, und alles was mit ihm zusammenhing, restlos abgelehnt. Am Tage der Machtergreifung des Nationalsozialismus liess er in seinem Park eine steinerne Bank aufstellen mit einem griechischen Spruche des Inhalts, dass wer immer mit dem Tyrannen paktiere, daran zu Grunde ginge. Die Offenheit seiner Kritik ... machte jeden Kompromiss unmöglich, und so legte er seine sämtlichen Ämter nieder und zog sich auf seinen Katharinenhof zurück.[96]

Warburg's friendship with Reusch would survive the NS period: 'Nach dem Kriege war er einer der ersten, mit dem ich die Verbindung wieder aufnehmen konnte. Er war in allen Zeitläuften der alte Freund geblieben. In seinem ersten Briefe nach dem Kriege schrieb er: "Nur diejenigen ändern die Zeiten, die sich von den Zeiten nicht verändern lassen".'[97] If Kirdorf and Reusch were exceptional among Ruhr industrialists, so, perhaps, was a Hitler supporter like Fritz Thyssen. The bulk, probably, occupied an intermediate position,[98] neither protesting at, nor yet actively promoting, the step-by-step exclusion of Jews from economic life.

Of 108 board seats (many in minor companies) occupied by members of M. M. Warburg & Co. at the beginning of 1933, 18 had to be vacated during the course of the year, apparently including those of the Hapag and the Deutsch-Atlantische Telegraphen-Gesellschaft—companies to whose well-being Warburg had made a substantial contribution.[99] That such early action was unnecessary is shown by the fact that partners in the Warburg firm lost the bulk of their board

---

[95] '... dass die Ruhrlade ... ihre Juni-Sitzung 1933 auf den "Hoverhof" Silverbergs verlegte und damit nachdrücklich demonstrierte, dass von den hier versammelten Industriellen (unter ihnen sowohl Thyssen als auch Vögler) der Hitlersche Antisemitismus nicht vorbehaltlos akzeptiert wurde' (ib.).

[96] M. Warburg, *Aus meinen Aufzeichnungen*, privately printed (New York, 1950), p. 152.

[97] Ib.

[98] Neebe claims that the majority of the Ruhrlade were free from anti-Semitic prejudice. op. cit., n. 94 above, pp. 194 ff.

[99] Ib., pp. 199 f.

seats—80—only between 1936 and 1938.[100] Some firms, indeed, their Jewish board members to the bitter end.[101] On 30 June 1934, the secretariat of Rheinstahl notified Julius Flechtheim that the AGM of the company (by then within the orbit of IG Farben) had re-elected him as a board member with a mandate to run until 1939.[102] Hans Fürstenberg lists the companies, 25 in number, on whose boards he remained until 1936 or 1937. Several were foreign companies, other subsidiaries of the AEG. A few were of minor importance. Among the more significant ones, Fürstenberg remained deputy chairman of the board of the AEG until 1937, board member of the BHG also until 1937. Until 1936 (as representative of Fritz Friedländer's heirs) he continued to sit on the board of the Braunkohlen- und Brikett AG. Among companies which retained his services until 1937 were Felten & Guilleaume, Dessauer Gas (formerly Deutsche Continental-Gas-Gesellschaft, a long-standing Gentile connection of the BHG, until 1936 as deputy chairman), and Rheinische Stahlwerke.[103] The latter company[104] had the distinction of preserving two of its Jewish board members, Hans Fürstenberg and Julius Flechtheim, until 1938. On 21 June 1938, the board chairman, Hermann Schmitz, finally wrote to Flechtheim as follows:

... Es war die Absicht, Sie bis zu der im Aktiengesetz vom 30 Januar 1937 vorgeschriebenen demnächsten Neuwahl des gesamten Aufsichtsrats der Rheinischen Stahlwerke in Ihrem Amte zu belassen. Die dritte Verordnung der Reichsregierung vom 14 Juni 1938 zum Reichsbürgergesetz, wonach solche Aktiengesellschaften als jüdisch gelten, in deren Aufsichtsrat Juden im Sinne des Reichsbürgergesetzes vertreten sind, veranlasst mich, Sie hiermit zu bitten, uns Ihr Aufsichtsmandat im Interesse des Rheinischen Stahlwerks schon jetzt zur Verfügung zu stellen...[105]

The personnel files of Rheinstahl, in consequence, contain the following entry:

---

[100] Ib., p. 208.
[101] The law of 1937 declaring that any company with a Jewish member on its board would henceforth be considered a Jewish business.
[102] Thyssen-Rheinstahl Archiv (RA), 2 00 01 1, Folder 6.
[103] Hans Fürstenberg, op. cit., n. 16 above, p. 270.
[104] Its largest shareholder was IG Farben. '... meinem Vertreter im Vorsitz, Herrn Geheimrat Dr. Schmitz von der IG Farbenindustrie, die bekanntlich der weitaus grösste Aktionär unserer Gesellschaft ist.' *Berg-Assessor* Dr O. Krawehl to board of Dresdner Bank, 16 Dec. 1932. RA 2.00.01.1, Folder 25.
[105] Hermann Schmitz to Prof. Dr Julius Flechtheim, 21 June 1938, RA 2.00.01.1, Folder 6, Julius Flechtheim.

Prof. Dr. Julius Flechtheim   1922–1938 } als nichtarisch
Hans Fürstenberg, Berlin   1931–1938 }   ausgeschieden[106]

It was the epitaph of four generations of Jewish participation in German economic development.

[106] Ib.

9

Conclusion

IF one surveys the German–Jewish economic élite as a whole, a number of questions suggest themselves. To what extent did this élite fulfil a specific function in German economic development? How far did its contribution to the growth of the German economy bear a distinctive character marking it off from that of comparable Gentile groups? It is, of course, readily apparent that from Meyer Amschel Rothschild through Joseph Mendelssohn, Gerson Bleichröder, Arthur Salomonsohn, Max Warburg, Oscar Wassermann, to Jakob Goldschmidt and Georg Solmssen, the part played by Jews in German banking—both private and joint-stock—was an outstanding one. What, it may be asked, accounts for the almost unique prominence of Jews in German banking? Perhaps the most important general cause for the Jewish place in German finance was the fact that, unlike their Christian neighbours (existing in what was, essentially, a natural economy), Jews, for many generations, had been living in a money economy. Jewish commercial activity, at whatever level, had been concerned not with the exchange of goods or services but with cash and credit transactions. Jews, thus, almost since 'times immemorial', had not only known how to operate with money but had been conditioned to think in monetary terms. They had thus formed (and in a sense continued to form) a 'capitalist enclave' in a still largely 'pre-capitalist' economy.

Specialization in banking activities had developed organically out of the general commercial (trading) occupations engaged in by Jews. At first, banking transactions had been simply a by-product of trade with, for example, Meyer Amschel Rothschild trading in rare coins, or the founders of the Kaulla dynasty supplying the Habsburg armies. Court Jews, as often as not, had been suppliers (merchants) as much as financiers. In fact, commerce and banking, in many cases, remained undifferentiated well into the nineteenth century. Trading, the major economic activity engaged in by Jews, involved almost invariably, and at whatever level, an element of banking. In the first place, this arose from the unavoidable (or almost) necessity of selling goods on credit—with its necessary corollary, the taking of interest (usually high like the risk involved). Moreover, since Jews, through their commercial activities, were normally possessors of some mobile wealth (money), it was natural that those in need of money should approach them for loans (which might or might not be repaid). More particularly, it was princes great and small who borrowed money from their court Jews (whether in return for privileges or under threat of loss of favour). Financial partnerships tended to develop between princes and court Jews, containing a substantial banking component and not infrequently issuing in the founding of court or state banks. Princes, eventually, came to look for financiers rather than suppliers. Typical, perhaps, of the evolution from *Hoffaktor* to private banker were the careers, of two leading Bavarian bankers, Aaron Elias Seligmann and Jacob Hirsch:

> The war economy and the financial exigencies of the State made a few bankers and particularly the court-bankers, Aaron Elias von Eichthal and Jacob von Hirsch powerful figures in the State. They had made great profits on war-supplies, became large creditors of the state by deferring payments due to them and by cash loans and subsequently also personally promoted the State's credit standing by advising the government and by the sale of State obligations.[1]

Moreover, banking (in essence 'money-lending', though it later came to embrace also some other activities) had gained among Jews early respectability and status (second only to 'learning'). The conspicuous success of the Rothschilds and Mendelssohns, of Habers, Heines, and Oppenheims, not only made banking generally respectable but, particularly among Jews, conferred upon it a status well above that of 'mere' trade or industrial entrepreneurship. Under the aegis of the Rothschilds (and of their fabulous wealth) there developed something like a mystique of the (mainly Jewish) private banker, a mystique continued through generations of Mendelssohns, through Gerson von Bleichröder, and eventually, perhaps, through Carl Fürstenberg, a legend in his lifetime, and Max Warburg. Jewish bankers, in fact, had become almost (if not quite) the equals of nobles and even of princes. Daughters of the wealthiest and most prominent among them became eligible, from a relatively early period, for marriage into the nobility. Bankers, at the level of greatest success, would themselves become

---

[1] *Die Bayerische Staatsbank von 1780–1955* (1955) p. 96, quoted in Kurt Grunwald, *Türkenhirsch. A Study of Baron Maurice de Hirsch, Entrepreneur and Philanthropist*, (Jerusalem, 1966), p. 3.

barons and *Freiherrn*. Banking, as numerous examples showed, was for aspiring young Jews from modest backgrounds a most promising avenue of upward social mobility. From a humble station it would remain possible, to the end, to become a Hermann Wallich, an Eugen Gutmann, a Jakob Goldschmidt, or, at least, a Siegmund Bodenheimer. Banking, for numbers of young Jews, must therefore have possessed a magnetic attraction.

A further aspect of importance was the existence, from an early period, of a Jewish banking network operating, like other networks, through informal contacts, recommendations, apprenticeships, and, above all, an element of mutual trust. Jewish bankers, as a rule, received their training in Jewish banks or under the auspices of fellow-Jews (of which the Jewish 'elective dynasty' at the Deutsche Bank, Bamberger—Wallich—Steinthal—Mankiewitz—Wassermann, is an illustration). Jewish private bankers chose Jewish partners (Fischel, Mannheimer, Loeb, Melchior Jeidels, Paul Kempner, Bieber, Walther Rathenau at the BHG, Paul Wallich, and so on). The Jewish banking élite, to the end, remained largely self-perpetuating, increasingly through co-option as much as dynasty formation (though that also was not lacking, as shown by the Landaus, Salomonsohns, Gutmanns, Fürstenbergs, and others).

A special feature of the network promoting the Jewish role (and assisting Jewish success) in German banking was, of course, its 'internationalism'. Capital movements on a large scale during the revolutionary and Napoleonic periods, whether concerned with the transmission to the Continent of British subsidies, the private financial operation of princes like the duke of Hessen-Kassel, or the collection and transfer of French reparations payments, transcended the boundaries of states and brought together Europe's major financial centres. Only the network linking the major Jewish banking houses (which, in essence, became that of the Rothschilds and their clients) was capable of carrying out such large-scale international financial transactions. International links, often reinforced by kinship ties, remained to the end an important ingredient in the ascendancy in German banking of men of Jewish origin.

Also of importance to Jewish success in German banking was the existence of an associated 'intelligence network' both national and, above all, international. Extensive and sustained contacts among Jewish bankers yielded valuable (often profitable) intelligence on a variety of financial matters (as indeed did regular encounters at the stock exchange in Berlin or for luncheon (*Frühstück*) at a small number of favoured restaurants). Prominent Jewish bankers, those who 'belonged', in fact, formed something like a 'closed society' with a 'grape-vine' in active operation. Of course, membership of the network (or networks) by no means excluded rivalries and on occasion fierce competition, among Jewish banks and bankers, although, on the whole, a co-operative spirit (based on a philosophy of 'give and take' and 'fair shares for all') prevailed. By and large, an accepted member of the network (in return for certain standards of financial probity) could count on a 'fair deal' from his Jewish fellows. The strength of the Jewish banking élite in fact (to a degree) lay in its solidarity. Such solidarity, of course, more particularly in the large joint-stock banks, might extend, up to a point, across the ethnic divide—the career of Hjalmar Schacht being a case in point.

It is, then, clear for what reasons and how Jews came to play a significant role in German banking. They enjoyed, by virtue of their history, cultural background, minority status, and ethnicity, certain advantages not shared—or at least shared to nothing like the same degree—by their Gentile counterparts.

What then were the major contributions of 'Jewish finance' to the development of the German economy? Clearly, given their prominence in German banking in general, Jews made a major contribution to every aspect of banking activity. Beyond this, however, there were some areas where the role of Jewish bankers were especially in evidence. Among these was the field of public finance, lending to governments and estates, floating and subscribing to government issues, developing public credit. This, of course, was a sphere in which Jews had traditionally been conspicuous and would continue to be at least till the age of Bleichröder and Bismarck.

A second important sphere of Jewish banking operations was the financing of railway construction. One reason for Jewish prominence in this field was perhaps simply the fact that, at the time the major railway lines were being built, private Jewish banks enjoyed a conspicuous position in the capital market through both their own capital and that of their wealthy clients. Beyond this, however, there is some evidence of a special Jewish interest in matters of transportation. Perhaps early experience of having to move sometimes heavy loads over considerable distances had developed in some Jews a special sense of the economic possibilities of transportation; more particularly with the aid of the steam engine. They may, on the other hand, have done little more than follow the general investment trend of the 'railway age' and offered clients what, to many, appeared opportunities of lucrative investment. Lastly, it is possible that there may have been in some Jews elements of the economic visionary. Salomon Oppenheim may have foreseen a 'railway age' just as Emil Rathenau would become the apostle of an 'electrical age' or Albert Ballin of an age of transoceanic steam navigation. (Subsequently, Jewish concern with railways would shift from financing to construction and to the provision of railway materials and accessories. From having been mainly financial, the interest became commercial and industrial.)

A third area in which some Jewish banks made a major contribution was in the realm of foreign flotations on the Berlin market, more particularly Russian and Italian ones. Again, Jewish banking connections in foreign countries played a part. These, moreover, were operations which often had political connotations and which impinged on international relations (more particularly dealings relating to Russian securities). A large part of Russia's native banking establishment consisted of Jews and, notwithstanding its anti-Jewish prejudices and discriminatory policies, the Russian government was happy to operate in Berlin through the intermediary of Jewish banks, more particularly the Mendelssohns.

Perhaps the most important sphere of Jewish banking activity, however, was its association with industrial entrepeneurship. The particular service performed by German banking in this respect (as compared for example to British) has repeatedly been stressed.[2] Carl Fürstenberg, whose main banking activities lay in this field,

---

[2] Among others by Helmut Böhme: 'Nur mit Hilfe des Finanziers war in Deutschland Neues zu schaffen. Während z.B. in England der Unternehmer durch die hohen Profite seiner frühindustriellen Erfolge so gut mit Kapital versorgt war, dass er auch seine langfristigen Investitionen selber durchführen konnte und sich also von den Banken nur mehr oder weniger kurzfristige Umlaufs- Kapitalbedürfnisse decken liess, war eine solche "Insider-Finanzierung" in Deutschland nie möglich gewesen. Das Signum der deutschen Wirtschaftsentwicklung war die chronische, oft katastrophale Kapitalnot. Deutschland—und voran Preussen—war ein "pays de petite fortune". Die deutsche Industrie war und blieb ständig auf ein leistungsfähiges System von Industriebanken angewiesen, die die notwendige Fremdfinanzierung durchführen konnten, und die die Möglichkeit hatten, nicht nur solche Ersparnisse der Industrie zuzuführen, für die sie auf lange Sicht keine andere Verwendung hatten, sondern die auch fähig waren, kurzfristige Mittel des Geldmarktes zur Verwendung in langfristigen Investitionen als industrielles Unternehmenskapital mobilisieren zu können.' Helmut Böhme, 'Bankkonzentration und Schwerindustrie 1873–1896' in H. -U. Wehler (ed.), *Sozialgeschichte Heute* (Göttingen, 1974), pp. 442 f.

was in a position to appreciate its importance.[3] Already members of the families of court Jews had branched out into entrepreneurial activity, Salon Haber,[4] David Seligmann,[5] Joel Jacob Hirsch.[6] Mendelssohns and Oppenheims had been closely associated with the AG für Anilinfabrikation in Treptow, the Oppenheims in Cologne, and Gerson Bleichröder with various industrial ventures. However, the major role of Jewish bankers in the financing of large industrial undertakings is associated with names like Adolf and Arthur

[3] 'Spezifisch das Bankiersgewerbe, meint Fürstenberg, habe zu dem beispiellosen wirtschaftlichen Aufstieg des Wilhelminischen Deutschland einen einzigartigen Beitrag geliefert. Es seien die deutschen Banken, die "durch ein wohlverstandenes Unternehmertum den grandiosen Aufbau der deutschen Industrie in finanzieller Hinsicht" überhaupt ermöglicht hätten. Länder wie Frankreich oder England lieferten Beispiele dafür, wie langsam sich industrielle Betriebe ohne die aktive Unterstützung von Banken weiter bildeten".' (W. E. Mosse, 'Die Juden in Wirtschaft und Gesellschaft' in W. E. Mosse (ed.), *Juden im Wilhelminischen Deutschland 1890–1914* (Tübingen, 1976), pp. 110 f.)
In general, Fürstenberg describes the role of capital in the development of industry as follows:
'Ein Land wird modernen Wirtschaftsformen erschlossen, ein Eisenbahnnetz wird errichtet, eine umwälzende Erfindung der praktischen Verwertung zugeführt, eine Industrie aufgebaut. Wie wenige machen sich wohl klar, dass zu alledem nicht nur technischer Erfindungsgeist, Organisationstalent, menschliche Arbeit und politische Unterstützung gehören, sondern auch ein schaffender und ordnender finanzieller Geist, 'Nervus nerum'—ein abgegriffenes Wort und doch heute die beste Definition für die Rolle des Kapitals in allen Fragen der Wirtschaft.' Carl Fürstenberg, *Die Lebensgeschichte eines deutschen Bankiers* (Wiesbaden, 1961), p. 180.

[4] 'Er wurde Hauptgläubiger von drei grossen badischen Fabriken, der Zuckerfabrik Waghäusel, der Baumwollspinnerei Ettlingen, der Maschinenfabrik von Kessler in Karlsruhe, welche ohne seine Beteiligung nicht ins Leben gerufen werden konnten . . .' Heinrich Schnee, *Die Hochfinanz und der moderne Staat*, 6 vols. (Berlin, 1953–67), p. 76.

[5] 'in Baden wurde 1809 eine staatliche Spinnfabrik in St. Blasien gegründet, die primär der Karlsruher Hofbankier [David] Seligmann finanzierte und verwaltete.' Monika Richarz, *Judisches Leben in Deutschland* (Stuttgart, 1976), i. 36.

[6] '. . . He mechanized farming and improved stockbreeding. He added sugar-refining to beer-brewing on his large sugar-beet plantation in Rottersdorf, which he kept busy in the off-season with imported Indian crude sugar, alcohol being the by-product of this industry. A brandy-still may have been connected with his vineries, the products of his Franconian vineyards. Turf-cutting and lumber were additional industries based on agriculture, as was also wool-spinning, for which in 1826 he imported 3.000 modern English water-drawn spindles to replace the traditional hand-spindles.
He reorganized the Franconian lumber trade, thus breaking a Dutch monopoly . . . and he started to use the Danube–Main Canal for floating lumber to the Rhine. He was active in the establishment of the Donau–Main Dampfschiffahrts Aktiengesellschaft and participated in various railway ventures . . . In 1835, he was one of the prime movers in setting up the Bayerische Hypotheken- und Wechselbank, for which he won the collaboration of the Rothschilds, who subscribed 1.5 million florin to Hirsch's 1 million florin. And he served on the committee which drew up the statute of this bank.' Grunwald, op. cit., n. 1 above, pp. 4 f.

Salomonsohn, Eugen and Hugo Landau, Max Steinthal, Bernhard Dernburg, Carl Fürstenberg, Louis Hagen, Georg Solmssen, and Jakob Goldschmidt, to name only the most important. A substantial part of German industry, and this affected alike east, centre, and west, developed under the auspices or with the assistance of Jewish bankers. Such bankers provided indispensable links with the Berlin capital market and, on occasion, with the great international financial centres. German industrial development, as it took place more particularly from the eighties onwards, is unthinkable without the Jewish bankers who helped to man the *Aufsichtsräte* of so many of the larger industrial companies. Of special significance perhaps, besides the provision of early risk capital for new ventures (by the Landaus or Sulzbachs) or activities as 'company doctors' (Bernhard Dernburg, Max Steinthal, Jakob Goldschmidt as chief liquidators of the bankrupt Stinnes concern), was the role of Jewish bankers in 'organizing capitalism'. This would range from Hagen's 'industrial marriages', through Leo Lustig's organization of the iron trade and that of the potash industry through Maximilian Kempner, Hugo Herzfeld, and Jakob Goldschmidt to the latter's part (in conjunction with Arthur Salomonsohn) in the creation of the Vereinigte Stahlwerke. Indeed the significant part played by Jewish bankers in the growth and rationalization particularly of Ruhr industry awaits detailed investigation.

If the most conspicuous economic contribution of the Jewish élite probably occurred, overall, in the sphere of banking, its members also played a significant role in the area of the Jews' original economic activity, trade. Among the branches of trade in which Jews achieved special prominence, the outstanding one in the early nineteenth century was, undoubtedly, war contracting. It was this activity which may be said to have laid the foundations of the fortunes of the German–Jewish economic élite. This was, unquestionably, the major source of early Jewish capital accumulation. It not only laid the basis for the growth of individual fortunes, but also provided the economic foundations for subsequent diversification into both banking and entrepreneurship. The successful war contractor, who, after the return of the peace in 1815, branched out into other forms of economic activity, is unquestionably the characteristic figure of the German–Jewish economic élite in at any rate the first quarter of the nineteenth century.

Moreover, Jewish war contracting did not end in 1815. In particular it was resumed during the wars of 1866 and 1871, creating, among others, the great fortunes of men like Julius Schottländer, Salomon Lachmann, and Siegmund Aschrott. Nor did the story end with the wars of German unification. It continued in the war of 1914 with Jewish (among other) suppliers of the armed forces—among them notably the Tietzes or, among newcomers, Joseph Blumenstein, the 'sandbag king'. Jews in many instances (frequently attacked as war profiteers) were among those rendering signal if often unappreciated services to the German armies as suppliers of necessities.[7] Nor was it accidental that raw-material supplies and distribution, during a critical period, were organized by a Jew, Walther Rathenau, food distribution by Wilhelm Merton, and essential food imports by Max Warburg and Carl Melchior. Crucial dealings with neutrals—Sweden, Holland, Switzerland—were conducted largely through Jewish intermediaries and their contacts. The provision of war supplies (of which, so long as cavalry had been important, that of horses also had formed a part) thus formed a special sphere of activity (and success)—as well as of unappreciated service to whatever 'national interest' may have been at stake—from the Napoleonic beginnings of the Jewish economic élite almost to its bitter end.

Why, it may be asked, should army contracting have become a major sphere of Jewish economic activity? One part of the answer is beyond a doubt to be found in the traditional prominence of Jews in the agricultural produce trade: transactions in grain, cattle, meat, horses, fodder, wool. This was a sphere of activity in which, in many regions, Jews enjoyed a quasi-monopoly. The reasons for this are not readily apparent. Why was a crucial area of economic activity left almost entirely in the hands of Jews until the tardy advent of co-operative societies and *Raiffeisen*-banks? Why, moreover, did noble (not infrequently anti-Jewish) landowners almost invariably choose to market their produce through Jewish intermediaries? Part of the explanation must be that, historically, particularly in southern Germany, Jews were totally, or almost totally, excluded from guild-dominated cities, but permitted to live in villages or small 'rural' townships and the residences of interested princes. Given the fact of their trade-orientated activities, this necessarily led to trading in local (agricultural) produce. Furthermore, through often exemplary dealings, Jewish dealers (who moreover rarely competed with each other) would build up (sometimes hereditary) positive associations with local landowners

---

[7] It was not entirely their fault that the authorities were willing to pay any price while the state failed, almost to the bitter end, to tax enormous war profits.

—whether knights or peasants—for whom, moreover, they might, at the same time, act also as suppliers and as purveyors of credit. Such rural links (and Jews were engaged also in transportation), possibly through hierarchies or associations of Jewish dealers, would form the essential (indeed, before the railway age the only possible) organization for the mobilization of large (or relatively) quantities of agricultural produce—the essence of war contracting. It may be that, through the carefully developed networks for the trade in local produce, Jews enjoyed what amounted to almost a natural monopoly.

The second relevant factor almost certainly came from the opposite direction, the special relations of some Jews with princes, generals, and, above all, commissariats. These, in the first place, were relations arising from the position of Jews as 'contractors', as factors and, moreover, ones almost invariably willing to supply goods on (fairly long-term) credit. Furthermore, there can be little doubt that some Jewish entrepreneurs made a particular point of cultivating relationships (corruption, in more or less subtle forms, was a not unusual part of business dealings, especially with the authorities) with those responsible for awarding military contracts. It was, of course, clear to Jewish traders that here was a large market (actual or potential) for produce of different kinds which they were uniquely able to supply, where need was urgent, and where few questions were asked about price (moreover, even sentiments of loyalty or patriotism may, at times, have played a part). Jews, in fact, were links in a chain joining the agricultural producer (whether peasant or noble) to commissariat and supply services. There were, furthermore, men and beasts to be fed—on a regular contractual basis not only in war, but even in times of peace. There was thus, in fact, good reason why Jews occupied a special position with regard to war contracting.

Moreover, this time more fortuitously, Jews would become involved in military supplies also from other directions. Jews from early times had been prominent, almost to the point of monopoly, as dealers in scrap-metal. Again, their involvement in the textile industry could assume a military dimension (they also, on occasion, employed prison labour, provided by the authorities).

Finally, at a later stage, Jews became prominent also in the armaments industry, more particularly in the provision of infantry weapons (including bayonets) and parts of munitions. In the best-known instance, that of Ludwig and Isidor Loewe, involvement in arms production had been, in the first place, a by-product of the use of precision machinery (introduced originally to manufacture sewing-machines!)

There may be yet a further, more general reason for Jewish prominence in army contracting. An unfortunate history had bred in many a Jewish trader a rooted attitude of servility towards the powerful who, at any moment, could make or break them (a servility still conspicuous for instance, in the disagreeable (if not untypical) relationship betweent Gerson von Bleichröder and Otto von Bismarck). And Jewish servility, originally in the interest of survival, would express itself, beyond an extreme show of deference, also in costly presents (ranging from jewellery or furs to caviar and Havanas). Christian satraps (Bismarck a typical example) liked to deal with 'their' court Jews, Jewish clients who showed deference, brought gifts, and, what is more, 'delivered the goods'. (Of course cruder forms of corruption were not excluded). The Jew, in the unequal relationship, found protection and profit—even a modicum of mutual human sympathy was not excluded. There is much evidence to suggest that relations of this kind persisted (even Walther Rathenau still sought, on the whole without success and for psychological rather than economic reasons, a position as 'Schutzjude' to some potentate like his 'neighbour' Theobald von Bethmann-Hollweg). Such relationships—to which among others some of the recommendations for the conferment of commercial titles bear witness—must have played some part also in the position of Jews as war contractors.[8]

A second field in which the Jewish contribution to commercial life was unique was that of retail trading. This, in itself, given the preponderant Jewish involvement in trade, was, of course, not surprising. What was less predictable was the specific form of the Jewish contribution, more particularly in the shape of chains of department stores. These were stores distinguished by the fact that they sold under one roof large varieties of goods at fixed, clearly marked, and usually competitive prices made possible by economies of scale, large turnover, and, in some lines, the sale of self- or specifically produced goods. The introduction in Germany of such stores from the eighties onwards (a controversial undertaking) was of great benefit to a mass of,

---

[8] A late, but none the less instructive instance is that of Joseph Blumenstein, in the First World War the large-scale manufacturer of sandbags for trenches. 'Er arbeitete hart, verstand es glänzend, seinen Konzern aufzubauen und wusste die Offiziere des Ingenieurscorps, die für Armeeaufträge zuständig waren, geschickt zu nehmen.' Edward Gans in Richarz, op. cit., ii. 459.

mainly middle-class, consumers, indeed contributed to the early development of a 'mass market'. The department store was, of course, not a German–Jewish invention. It probably originated in Paris and received a certain development in New York (with Jews being involved, if by no means preponderantly, in both cities). The contribution of members of the German–Jewish economic élite consisted primarily in the business acumen and organizational skill with which they transferred retailing techniques pioneered abroad to Germany at the time when a potential middle-class mass market was developing in the major urban centres. A significant feature was the relatively early emergence of chains of stores, spanning large parts of the country, rather than the expansion of one individual store. A further feature, highly resented by competitors, was extensive and systematic advertising (not only by conventional methods but also by the introduction of a variety of 'gimmicks'). The creation of demand, indeed (or, at any rate, its attempted creation), was a feature common to much Jewish commercial enterprise and could be regarded as peculiarly (though by no means exclusively) characteristic of the 'Jewish' style of business. Nor was it wholly accidental that Jews inaugurated systematic and specifically directed advertising by means of specialist advertising agencies.

A different aspect of Jewish retailing was the creation of high-class specialist shops (for leather goods, fashions, textiles, household goods, trousseaux, china, and so on) for the better-off members of the aristocracy and bourgeoisie. Such stores, as often as not, would sell largely their own products, obviating the need to buy through the intermediary of wholesalers. They would acquire and cultivate a reputation for quality. This was a development reflecting social change (the emergence of a well-to-do bourgeoisie), resulting in the growth of a new market. Jewish manufacturers-retailers, it would appear, were quick to see the possibilities.

Finally, the stores managed by Jews were quick to adopt a further element of publicity: the elaborate illustrated catalogue. Only antiquarian research could establish where and by whom the catalogue as a means of salesmanship was first employed. The possibility of doing so would be dependent on the development of printing techniques and the introduction of moderate postal charges. In Germany, it would appear, Jewish-owned stores were in the van of the development. Catalogues were sometimes sent out to special categories of selected potential customers. There was some development also of mail-order business.

Overall, members of the German–Jewish economic élite thus made a major (and not uncontroversial) contribution to the introduction of modern marketing techniques. Goods in Jewish-owned stores—this had not always been the case—acquired a reputation for combining good quality with reasonable price. The new stores altered the shopping habits of large parts of the population. In some cases, moreover, the store-owners were concerned with design as well as utility. Jewish stores thus may well have had some influence also on the development of public taste. There was, almost certainly, a special Jewish flair for innovative (at any rate so far as Germany was concerned) and imaginative retailing. German Jews also (like the British) could, not without some exaggeration, be described as a 'nation of shopkeepers'. This also was an important part of the economic activities of the German–Jewish economic élite.

Another major feature of Jewish commercial activity may be seen in the development of trading links with central, eastern, and southeastern Europe: the Habsburg monarchy and its successor states, Poland, Russia, and the Balkans. Jews in particular were engaged in a variety of trading ventures in all these areas, assisting, in effect, German economic penetration. Indeed, the German–Jewish economic élite could, in this respect, be seen as an agent (though not consciously in political terms) of German economic imperialism. The economically underdeveloped (or relatively) areas in which they traded were alike a source of raw materials, a market for manufactures, and an area for investment and development (notably railway construction and 'heavy industry'). It was, in fact, a 'natural' area for German economic expansion. Jews (partly through contacts with fellow Jews whether in Vienna or Budapest, Łódź or Warsaw, St. Petersburg, Kiev, or Bucharest) were well placed to take advantage of the opportunities. They were, objectively, the 'natural' protagonists of German 'commercial imperialism' in the east.

Yet a further significant commercial contribution—this time in the indeterminate borderland of trade and industry—was Albert Ballin's achievement in turning the Hapag from a somnolent shipping line of the second order into a world leader in its field. It was Ballin who made the Hapag a flag carrier on the world's oceans whose splendid ships contributed immeasurably to Germany's international prestige. The vast increase in the Hapag's tonnage achieved under Ballin's management provided the German economy with a priceless commercial asset (an asset largely lost as a result of the war). Again, by his skilful pool negotiations, Ballin succeeded in integrating Germany's new-found maritime strength, relatively painlessly, into the world shipping community. Thanks primarily to Ballin, Germany was able to enter in an unprecedented manner a new and expanding field of world-wide economic activity: the German economy branched out in a new direction, entered flamboyantly a sphere where German participation had, hitherto, been modest.

Why, it may be asked, should it have been a Jew and, moreover, a Jew of modest origin, who was responsible for this development? Ballin's professional background (an agency for moving East European [mainly Jewish] emigrants to the New World) did, in fact, combine a Jewish element with that of transatlantic transportation. This, however, hardly accounts for the fact of a Jew becoming the successful managing director of the largest and most prestigious shipping line. What, it should therefore be asked, were the qualities that account for Ballin's unique achievement? Here, several considerations, perhaps, are relevant. Among these is Ballin's position as an 'outsider' in Hamburg shipping circles, an outsider, however, endowed at the same time with marked charisma. This Ballin combined with the more mundane qualities of sound judgement, willingness to innovate, as well as (characteristically) useful British (though in this case largely Gentile) contacts.[9] It has also been claimed that the transactions which marked the early stages of Ballin's rise in the shipping world reveal a characteristic 'style', attributable in part to a mixture of Anglo-Saxon and Jewish elements.[10]

[9] 'Mr. Wilding, one of Ballin's earliest, most cherished and life-long friends in British shipping circles, had told him about new developments in English shipbuilding, particularly the introduction of twin-screw engines, on which the opinions of technicians were still divided to such a degree that the Norddeutscher Lloyd continued to stick to one-screw system even for the bigger and faster ships which were put into service in 1890.
Ballin, who had always weighed the evidence himself and who until the end never allowed an engineer on the managing board of his company, was impressed by the first British experience and persuaded the Board of Directors in the autumn of 1887 to agree to the construction of four fast ships with twin-screw engines and to raise the necessary capital by the offer of new shares and debentures.' Eduard Rosenbaum, Albert Ballin', *Yearbook III of the Leo Baeck Institute*, (London, 1958), 265.

[10] '... the typical elements of Ballin's business strategy: First: the breaking of new ground and the acceptance of considerable risk by his agreement with the Carr Line, without discarding the carefully built up relations with his British correspondents. Then the negotiating "from strength" ... with the Hapag, without casting off his moorings to his old firm too quickly.
With this mixture of boldness and caution, with this careful choice of the conditions of attack without neglecting the lines of retreat, he testified to his thorough study of English

A further feature of Ballin's career, revealed more particularly in his negotiations for international shipping 'conferences' (agreements on freight-rates and sharing of traffic) and 'pools' (agreements among shipping-lines involving elements of profit-sharing), is his diplomatic and persuasive skills and talents for the reconciliation of rival interests.[11] It is in this sphere, above all, that he revealed his qualities of charismatic leadership,[12] to the point where eventually 'the British partners refused to attend meetings if Ballin was prevented from presiding'.[13] Ballin's skills, in fact, were above all those of the persuasive and reasonable business diplomat rather than those of the financier or engineer. These were skills shared in some measure with not a few members of the German–Jewish economic élite, with Eduard Arnhold, Carl Fürstenberg, or Louis Hagen. The case of Ballin shows that talents of this kind could be sufficiently broad and general to produce triumphant results even in the (for Jews) perhaps somewhat esoteric field of navigation. (However, Kunstmann and Bernstein, shipowners respectively in Stettin and Hamburg, Hecht, shipowner on the Rhine, and Eduard Arnhold, interested in navigation on the Oder, point to the fact that Ballin's involvement in shipping, if wholly outstanding in its scope, was not unique.)

Thus the contribution of members of the German–Jewish élite in several areas of commerce was outstanding. If, overall, it was somewhat less significant in manufacturing, it was yet not unimportant also in this sphere. Three aspects of Jewish entrepreneurship left, perhaps, the greatest mark. The earliest of these was Jewish participation in the textile industry, particularly in Berlin and Silesia (but also in south-western Germany), marked by names like Meyer, Loewe, Nauen, Goldschmidt, Liebermann, Reichenheim, Kauffmann,

business methods. One may perhaps also recognize the characteristic wariness of a member of the Jewish minority, though in a town like Hamburg . . . too much must not be made of this argument' (ib., pp. 206 f.).

[11] 'It was one of his fundamental tenets that every conflict of interest could be solved among reasonable human beings by discussion, persuasion and compromise' (ib., p. 265).

[12] '. . . any meeting called for a certain purpose was immediately changed in atmosphere by Ballin's presence. There was so much of the essence of real power concentrated in him that everybody felt his magnetic pull and talked and behaved differently from what they would have said and done without his presence. When Ballin was chairman he handled the business with a very quiet voice and with very few, expressive gestures, in the masterly and suggestive manner of a great conductor, or, to use Max Weber's term of a "charismatic leader"' (Rosenbaum, loc. cit., pp. 264 f.).

[13] Ib., p. 264, n. 3. The *London Shipping Gazette*, in an issue of 1911, described Ballin as 'this past-master in the art of negotiation' (ib.).

Grünfeld, Fränkel, Rinkel, Weigert, and Elsas.[14] The prominence of Jews in this sphere has been linked (doubtfully) to their involvement in the second-hand clothing and rag trade, perhaps more persuasively to their special opportunities for operating a 'putting-out' system, more particularly in rural areas. What brought Jews to the textile industry may, however, have been equally well general entrepreneurial drive leading them to the 'growth area' more particularly of cotton printing. Again, widespread British contacts would help to promote the introduction of English power-driven machinery as well as of English technical processes (the shoddy-manufacture introduced by Albert Hahn and Salomon Huldschinsky in a case in point). Had not the first English Rothschild begun a great banking career by buying Lancashire cotton goods for export to Germany? Again, while domestic contacts (not infrequently with fellow-Jews) would ensure supplies of wool, contacts abroad would facilitate the necessary imports of cotton. Last but not least, textile manufactures involved a substantial trading component designed to make them congenial to Jewish entrepreneurs. The textile industry, from the start, supplied extensively foreign and overseas markets. On the other hand, it would lead to the development of the garment industry, *Konfektion*, more particularly in women's fashions and raincoats—to become a major area of Jewish industrial activity. In this field of manufacture, however, Jewish involvement declined in the imperial period when the centre of the German textile industry shifted to the north-west, to Elberfeld and Barmen, Krefeld, Münster, Bielefeld, and Bremen (as well as Saxony), areas where Jewish entrepreneurship was relatively feebly developed.

A second sphere where German–Jewish entrepreneurship made an impact was in the industrial development of Upper Silesia. Marked by names like Friedländer, Caro, Kern, Hahn, Huldschinsky, Pringsheim, Zuckerkandl, Arnhold, Bie, and Lustig, Jewish entrepreneurship was conspicuous in the development of—more particularly—Silesian heavy industry. Significant in relation to this aspect of Jewish activity was the existence in several Silesian towns (notably Breslau, Gleiwitz, and Beuthen) of substantial Jewish communities. Breslau, in particular, early became the home of a number of Jewish bankers and traders ready to invest in industrial undertakings (mining, iron and steel production, metallurgy, cement). Jews in Silesia engaged also in

---

[14] For details of Jews prominent in the textile industry outside Berlin and Silesia see Toury, *Soziale und politische Geschichte der Juden in Deutschland 1847–1871* (Düsseldorf, 1977), p. 90.

industrial management (Huldschinsky, Kern, Caro, Bie, Zuckerkandl). The collective role played by Jewish entrepreneurs in the economic development of what was perhaps Germany's second industrial region (the relative important of Silesia and Saxony with its, on the whole, smaller industrial units can be debated) was a substantial one.

A final feature of Jewish entrepreneurship was the creation of the AEG concern with its associated companies. The AEG, under the guidance of Emil Rathenau, developed into a large industrial grouping which, though based firmly in the electrical industry, came to extend well beyond it. Significant aspects of the AEG's policies were the energetic (indeed aggressive) creation of demand, which included the setting up of Felix Deutsch's three hundred foreign bureaux, the financing of expansion through a steady increase of share capital (rather than, like the major competitor Siemens, through bank loans), and a cautious financial policy (in conjunction with Carl Fürstenberg and the BHG) of building up large hidden reserves. The AEG in fact, through its industrial and commercial activities, was able to contribute conspicuously to the realization of Emil Rathenau's dream (or vision) of a coming 'electrical age'. The AEG did much to construct an electrical 'infra-structure' of power-stations, generators, transformers, cables, and transmission systems, not only in Germany but in many different parts of the world. It helped to spread the use of electricity not only for public utilities (particularly street lighting and tramways) but also as a source of power for domestic purposes. In doing this, it was making a major contribution to the 'second industrial revolution', while at the same time contributing to German exports world-wide and enhancing Germany's place in the world economy.

How did a handful of members of the German–Jewish economic élite (the two Rathenaus, Felix Deutsch, Paul Mamroth, the Landaus, and Carl Fürstenberg) come to make this major contribution to German economic development? There is clearly no necessary or organic connection between traditional forms of Jewish enterprise and the new electrical industry. Nor was there a strong traditional association with metallurgy—the background to Emil Rathenau's entrepreneurship (and the chosen field also of Ludwig and Isidor Loewe, of Benno Orenstein, and of Arthur Koppel). Indeed the proximate cause of Rathenau's involvement, grandfather Liebermann's addition of a machine-building establishment to the family's textile mills, had been a mildly eccentric undertaking. What eventually brought Rathenau to an appreciation of the Edison inventions and through them to what would be his life's achievement, was perhaps little more than chance. What is significant here is that Emil Rathenau, himself in a shaky financial position, saw opportunities the better-placed Werner von Siemens refused to recognize. And Rathenau vigorously applied his managerial skills, technical flair (in the early years he personally refashioned much American and/or Siemens-designed equipment to suit his particular purposes), and 'electrical vision' to the realization of these possibilities. Others too had seen the same 'wave of the future'—to which the large number of electrical enterprises competing at the turn of the century bears witness—but it was Rathenau and his assistants' commercial and managerial talents which made the AEG first one of the two survivors in the race and, finally, the front runner. It was these skills which not only helped to determine the specific contribution made by the AEG but which may contain elements possibly attributable to ethnic factors. There were certain specific combinations of commercial, financial, and technological flair which, in a small group, were perhaps more likely to emerge among members of the Jewish rather than the Gentile component of the German economic élite.

If, then, one takes an overall view of the place of the Jewish élite in German economic life two features, perhaps, would appear to be of particular importance. These may be said to represent the broad effects of Jewish economic activity, not the conscious intentions of the participants. They also helped to make the Jewish role in particular a controversial one in Germany society, exposing the Jewish economic élite to attack from anti-Semites, from German nationalists, and, on occasion, from socialists as well. The first of these features is the marked contribution of German Jews (conspicuously of leading members of the Jewish economic élite) to the development of German capitalism. In the first place, what was important here was the role of Jewish banks in the mobilization (or concentration) of capital resources both through their own accumulated wealth, through that of their clients, and through stock-exchange activities popularizing a variety of bonds and obligations. The development of the Berlin Stock Exchange, in which Jewish brokers played a leading role almost from the beginning,[15] also promoted the process of capital mobilization and to some extent formation. These were developments which, on the one

---

[15] See Hans Goslar, 'Die Zeit der Anfänge der Berliner Börse und der Judenemanzipation' (source not stated) in the Mendelssohn files in the archives of the Leo Baeck Institute in New York.

hand, advanced the techniques of government borrowing (through the issue of loans and obligations) while, on the other, promoting the construction, financed mainly by private bankers and capitalists, of the major railway lines. In both these aspects of capitalist activity, Jewish bankers played a decisive part. Indeed the claim has been put forward that Jews in economic life, in consequence of their distinctive starting-point, for a time anticipated what later became the broader general capitalist development.[16] This is a thesis which, while it contains an element of truth, must not be pressed too far. As Schnee has shown, German princes borrowed from non-Jewish as well as Jewish bankers.[17] Still, the Rothschilds in particular, through the unrivalled scale of their financial operations (and after them the Habers, Heines, Bischoffsheims, Hirsches, and Oppenheims), could indeed be seen as pioneers of German capitalism of the age of early industrialization. In a later generation, Gerson von Bleichröder, with his railway and industrial ventures, his operations on behalf of the Prussian state and also of the arch-capitalist Bismarck, could be (and was) regarded as the leading representative of German capitalism. Again, in the Wilhelmine era, many leading capitalists, Louis Hagen, Carl Fürstenberg, Eugen Gutmann, Arthur Salomonshon, were of Jewish origin. The final generation, that of private capitalism in partial eclipse, was dominated, at any rate on the financial side, by Jakob Goldschmidt and Georg Solmssen (with, perhaps, Max Warburg and Oscar Wassermann). Possibly the most important function of these Jewish 'high priests' of German capitalism was, as has been seen, the financing of private capitalist industry (more particularly of such enterprises as were willing to enter into a permanent or semi-permanent partnership with 'finance capital'). Moreover, prominent capitalists from Louis Hagen to Jakob Goldschmidt contributed significantly to the capitalist concentration or 'rationalization' of industry through a variety of fusions and associations. Moves towards 'organized capitalism' and industrial concentration were in many cases (not in all and less in the post-war period as shown in the operations of a Hugo Stinnes, Otto Wolff, or Friedrich Flick)

---

[16] '... kann der jüdische Trend demach zusammenfassend als eine "vorübergehende Vorwegnahme der allgemeinen kapitalistischen Entwicklung durch diesen in seiner Ausgangsposition dazu besonders geeigneten Bevölkerungsteil" definiert werden.' Toury, op. cit., p. 99, quoting from H. Genschel, *Die Verdrängung der Juden aus der Wirtschaft im Dritten Reich* (Göttingen, 1966), p. 31.

[17] This is documented in detail for Baden where, in the first two decades of the nineteenth century, while Jewish *Hoffaktoren* lent a total of 12,887,471 fl., Christian financiers lent 10,960,000 fl. Schnee, op. cit., n. 4 above, p. 85.

initiated or promoted by Jewish financiers. It could be claimed that, almost to the end, Jews played a not inconsiderable role in the evolution of German capitalism.

This was, as already indicated, a role which exposed members of the Jewish economic élite to attack from opposing directions. German society, in its historic evolution and social values, was, as already suggested, essentially hostile to all forms of capitalist development. Capitalism was attacked consistently and virulently in the name of pre-industrial values (real and imaginary). And, of course, general anti-capitalism could all too easily be directed into anti-Jewish channels, given the prominence of Jews in capitalist development. Particularly was this the case following the severe crisis of German capitalism in the years after 1873. The Rothschilds, Bleichröder, and, finally, Albert Ballin were, in turn, used by anti-Semites as symbols of 'Jewish' capitalism; Walther Rathenau, though the emphasis here was perhaps slightly different, may be added to the list. In 1912 the anti-Semite Diederich Hahn noted, not without at least some measure of justification, that though there were many Gentile capitalists, Jews, especially among large German owners of mobile capital, formed an inner core, around which the rest grouped themselves, 'der innerste und am festesten organisierte konzentrische Kreis, um den die anderen sich gruppieren'.[18] It was, moreover, the prominence of Jews among the leading protagonists of capitalism which reinforced arguments about the 'alien' and 'un-German' nature of capitalism itself. And had not Karl Marx himself—gleefully quoted by Sombart—argued the virtual identity of the terms 'Jew' and 'capitalist'? Marxist socialism, in all its manifestations, necessarily attacked members of the German–Jewish economic élite, whether as 'capitalists' or (more covertly and only occasionally) as Jews.

The second important function of Jewish economic activity at the highest level was one of integration: one aspect of this was the gradual creation of a German national economy. In this process, men like Abraham Oppenheim, Bethel Henry Strousberg, Gerson Bleichröder, Louis Hagen, Eduard Arnhold, Emil Rathenau, and Georg Solmssen, among others, had played a major part. They did this, more particularly, by developing communications between the eastern and western halves of the Prussian monarchy, by linking both commercially and by rail and water transportation, the remote province of Silesia

[18] Hans-Jürgen Puhle, *Agrarische Interessenpolitik und preussischer Konservatismus* (Hanover, 1966), p. 131 n. 110.

with Berlin, and by associating parts of Ruhr industry with the capital market in Berlin. Industrial links were forged between enterprises in the Ruhr and others further east, notably by Louis Hagen's industrial and financial marriages. Again, Jews were prominent in the creation of regional banks (notably those in Darmstadt and Dresden) which, by moving to Berlin, helped to 'nationalize', in the economic sense, their regions of origin. It is significant, however, that such economic integration extended south of the Main only occasionally (as was the case with the Loewe concern and, to a lesser extent, the AEG. The Ladenburgs in Mannheim, under the guise of the Süddeutsche Disconto-Gesellschaft, eventually joined their industrial interests to those of the parent bank in Berlin. Hermann Tietz flourished in Munich before moving to Berlin.) In such links between north and south as did in fact occur, Jewish enterprise thus also played its part.

The major aspect, however, of this Jewish integrative function was the integration of the (relatively parochial) German into the world economy. This, in the first place, was of course a function of capitalism in general—in the development of which, as already discussed, Jewish economic leaders in Germany played a prominent part. No less important, however, was Jewish membership of an internationally dispersed commercially articulated minority—its dispersion, furthermore, constantly accentuated by emigration from Germany. Among the emigrants, moreover, were men like Ernest Cassel, Charles Hallgarten, Alfred Beit, or the brothers James and Edgar Speyer, destined themselves to occupy leading positions in the economic life of their new countries. This gave to the economic activities of many German Jews, however great their German patriotism, something of an international or 'cosmopolitan' dimension. Particularly in the 'Rothschild era', Jewish commercial activities outside Germany were facilitated by a strong sense of Jewish solidarity and mutual trust, often reinforced by kinship ties. Later, with a weakening of the ties of social solidarity based on traditional Jewish observance, Jewish contacts across national frontiers persisted on a basis of common networks of acquaintance, of apprenticeships, of long-standing commercial relations occasionally reinforced by kinship ties. Rothschilds, Speyers, Bischoffsheims, Beits, Erlangers, Sterns, Mertons, Loewes, Warburgs, Bambergers, and Hardys were numbered among families with economically prominent members in more countries than one. However, even members of the corporate élite largely lacking such ties (Albert Ballin, Emil Rathenau, Carl Fürstenberg come to mind) still tended to make a special point of cultivating relations, both personal and economic, across international frontiers.

Jews, whether as bankers, merchants, or industrialists, tended, perhaps more than their Gentile counterparts, to look to the markets of the world. They did so as exporters of German goods and services (the AEG's three hundred sales offices or the Hapag luxury liners' appeal for American tourists are cases in point, as are the Mendelssohns' financial dealings with the Russian government). Mention of extensive exports recurs in the earlier recommendations for Jewish *Kommerzienräte* in the textile industry. Nor was it accidental that a Jew became co-founder and only German member of the London metal exchange.

One significant aspect of the Jewish contribution to German integration into the world economy was, of course, the 'technology transfer' which laid the foundations for a not inconsiderable part of Jewish (and German) commercial success. Imported British machinery and techniques, gradually replaced by German, figure prominently in the story of Jewish textile manufacturers. Albert Hahn brought to Germany first the British manufacture of shoddy, then that of seamless tubes for heating installations. The Loewe brothers and Emil Rathenau built large enterprises on the initial exploitation of American patents. Benno Orenstein and Arthur Koppel, before embarking on their own enterprises, had studied the uses, outside Germany, of narrow-gauge railways for industrial and agricultural purposes; Albert Ballin learnt from his English friend Mr Wilding of the success of British experiments with twin-screw navigation. Oscar and Georg Tietz, finally, brought to Germany lessons learnt in the department stores of Paris and New York. German Jews, in short, as a result of study visits (or, more rarely, their normal commercial associations in advanced western countries), made a major contribution towards raising Germany to the level of world achievement. In this respect, imperial Germany could be seen as the 'Japan' of its day. This was a major aspect of German integration into the world economy.

At the same time, the fruits of German industry were then passed on to 'less developed' areas of Europe and the world: the Iberian Peninsula, Italy, eastern and south-eastern Europe, Latin America—with the AEG's (and to some extent Ludwig Loewe's) construction of power-stations, provision of electric trams, street lighting, and so on a prominent example. Other significant instances were the Metallgesellschaft's exporting, to Australia among other places, of mining and smelting equipment and 'know-how', or the railway constructions, largely overseas, of Orenstein and Koppel or the Fürstenberg-sponsored firm of Lenz & Co. (later AG für Verkehrswesen). Alike through the import and export of advanced technology, Jewish enterprises thus played a conspicuous part in the integration of Germany into the international economy.

This integrating function of the German–Jewish economic élite had an important corollary. The so-called 'export-orientated' industries, in which, as in the 'import-orientated' ones, Jews had a major stake, had a vested interest in international free trade. It was an interest paralleled by that of 'finance capital' in the unimpeded flow of capital across national frontiers. In consequence, members of the Jewish economic élite were, by and large, convinced protagonists of free trade and adherents of the 'Manchester School'. As they would show in the battle with the Prussian government over control of the Hibernia mine in 1904, they rejected state intervention in economic affairs (in which attitude they found themselves ironically in partial agreement with the 'master in our own house' school of (mainly Gentile) industrialists). In addition, however (and here they parted company with the entrepreneurial 'individualists' of heavy industry), they also rejected the protectionism introduced by Bismarck after his abandonment of free trade. Not accidentally, it was Ludwig Max Goldberger, a Jewish banker, who stood at the elbow of Caprivi in his attempt to dismantle protectionism. Again, members of the Jewish economic élite were prominent in the *Handelsvertragsverein* of 1900 (those attending the inaugural gathering including Carl Fürstenberg, Jacob Riesser, Ludwig Max Goldberger, Eduard Arnhold, Franz Oppenheim, Emil Rathenau, Isidor Loewe, and Albert Ballin).[19] The effects of these endeavours, though perhaps less the conscious intentions of the protagonists, were again directed towards a greater integration of the German economy into the world trading system.

However, this attitude, stigmatized by right-wing and protectionist elements (in agriculture, the *Mittelstand*, and heavy industry) as 'cosmopolitan', 'un-national', and, indeed, unpatriotic, tended once more to make the German–Jewish economic élite a target for attack. That their ideology in this sphere coincided largely with their economic interests made it easier for opponents to question their motives. Like their role in developing German capitalism, their parallel

---

[19] Some details in Peter Pulzer, 'Die jüdische Beteiligung an der Politik' in W. E. Mosse (ed.), *Juden im Wilhelminischen Deutschland 1890–1914* (Tübingen, 1976), p. 228.

part in integrating Germany into a capitalist world economy thus earned the Jewish economic élite little thanks and much opprobrium. However, among those who showed a degree of insight into the functions and importance of the élite was none other than the Emperor Wilhelm II. Although not partial to Jews, Wilhelm II saw the need for his 'over-populated' empire of economic development and of exports to pay for food and raw materials. Thus he shuddered at the thought of Germany's future were the Jews to be removed from German economic life.[20]

Two broad questions about the Jewish role in the German economy have formed the subject of (possibly somewhat sterile) discussion. One concerns the 'Jewishness' of the Jewish economic contribution. The nature of the question needs definition in two directions. If it asked whether there were aspects of Jewish economic activity common to all (or the great majority of) Jewish undertakings but not to be found in Gentile ones, the answer must of course be that no such features can be established. There was, in this sense, no absolute correlation between 'Jewishness' and form of economic activity or style. A similar answer must be given to the narrower question of whether the nature of 'Jewish' business decisions differed from 'non-Jewish' ones or whether both were not based on identical criteria of economic rationality (or presumed rationality). Here one might have to examine the twin questions how successful (or functional) decision-making differed inherently from unsuccessful (or dysfunctional). It would then have to be considered whether, in two ethnic samples (whether of the successful or the unsuccessful) comparable in their starting chances, there is a significant quantitative difference in the numbers of 'functional' or 'dysfunctional' economic decisions. The question has only to be put in these terms to show that it is completely unanswerable on the basis of empirical data.

However, the position is entirely different if the issue is approached from a different angle. It is, of course, incontrovertible and supported by much empirical evidence that both cultural ('Jewish') and environmental ('Gentile') factors played a major part in determining the character of Jewish economic activity; as did social factors, resulting

[20] In rejecting (in 1912) anti-Jewish measures proposed by the anti-Semite Heinrich Class, he wrote: 'Sie [the Jews] würden ihre enormen Reichtümer entnehmen, und wir würden unserm Nationalwohlstand und Erwerbsleben einen Schlag versetzen, der uns auf den Zustand vor 100 Jahren zurückwerfen und zugleich aus der Reihe der Kulturnationen ausscheiden würde.' Quoted in Lamar Cecil, 'Wilhelm II und die Juden' in W. E. Mosse, op. cit., p. 343.

from ('Jewish–Gentile') minority status. As a result of all these influences, the Jewish economic situation was, and remained, distinct from that of comparable Gentile groups. Among other things, as the result of both cultural and social factors, there developed something akin to a 'Jewish sector' of the German economy which, though not a 'closed society' was yet a clearly perceptible entity. Jews, at all levels, often did business with other Jews, almost certainly beyond the call of 'purely economic necessity'. Moreover, more particularly at the highest level of economic activity, a number of prominent Jewish bankers and industrialists did form part of an international network (or of international networks) in which fellow Jews were prominent. When Walther Rathenau spoke of the 300 men who, in his opinion, controlled the economic destinies of Europe and of whom each knew every other, he did not, of course, consider the question of ethnicity. However, if his general claim was correct, it would be interesting to speculate (though this will not be done here) how many of the 300 were of Jewish (or part-Jewish) origin. It is introvertible that Jews—markedly at the highest level of economic activity—had through their 'Jewishness' and Jewish contacts a streak of cosmopolitanism which left its mark also on their commercial opportunities. It was a 'cosmopolitanism' which (Albert Ballin is a case in point) was neither reprehensible in itself, nor detrimental to a strong identification with Germany and her fortunes (and which stands honourable comparison with the 'patriotism' of Hugo Stinnes and others of his ilk). Thus, due to a combination of cultural, social, and environmental factors, the role of the Jewish economic élite in German economic development was, as has been seen, a fairly distinctive one, complementary in certain respects to that of its Gentile counterpart. The German economy needed for its development—and in fact had the benefit of—both components of the German economic élite.

Another question which has been discussed concerns the 'originality' or otherwise of the Jewish contribution to German economic life. Were Jews pioneers or 'merely' successful imitators? The question, of course, is asked almost invariably from the prejudiced point of view of the *völkisch* dialectic contrasting alleged German 'inventiveness' (with Werner von Siemens as the symbolic figure) with Jewish 'copying' and exploitation of other people's inventions (with Emil Rathenau as the inferior 'antitype'). With this is associated the further dialectical contrast between the 'honest' and 'productive' Germanic machine builder (with August Borsig as the prototype or perhaps Alfred Krupp) and the Jewish textile or garment manufacturer with his essentially commercial and 'exploitative' activities. The contrast, as widely adumbrated, is prima facie malicious nonsense. Inventions, essentially, are made by engineers (or, as in the chemical field, trained scientists) and not by entrepreneurs. The comparison of Jews and Gentiles respectively as scientists, applied scientists, or inventors does not arise in the present context. In the field of entrepreneurship and industry what matters is less the invention—a fact to which the unfortunate Rudolf Diesel, Heinrich Ehrhardt (who, however, would assert himself in the end), or the brothers Mannesmann among others bear witness—than its practical commercial or industrial application. Had not the great Werner Siemens himself designed a wholly viable system of electrical tranways which, however, was never put into operation? It would appear to matter little whether practical application is the work (rarely successfully) of the inventor himself (even the great Thomas Alva Edison is not known for his entrepreneurial talents), of the inventor or scientist with the aid of bankers and entrepreneurs (as was the case, among others, with A. von Martius, Heinrich Caro, or Arthur von Weinberg), or of a 'mere' entrepreneur who had acquired the inventor's patents. True Jewish entrepreneurs, like the bulk of their Gentile colleagues, were not themselves either inventors or scientists (an exception is the chemist Nikodem Caro). The innovative aspect of Jewish entrepreneurship in Germany lay essentially in the introduction of foreign technology and techniques (from Joseph Liebermann and Albert Hahn to Ludwig Loewe, Emil Rathenau, Albert Ballin, and Oscar Tietz) and, in some cases, their adaptation to specific requirements. Jewish entrepreneurs often were (in the German context) innovators without for that being inventors. In any case, how 'inventive' or 'innovative' were successful Gentile entrepreneurs? Had not the Rothschilds been more 'inventive' and 'innovative' in their techniques than the old-established Bethmanns, Bethel Henry Strousberg and Maurice de Hirsch than Gentile railway entrepreneurs? Was not Albert Ballin more 'innovative' than his somnolent competitors at the Norddeutsche Lloyd, Oscar Tietz than Gentile retailers?

There is a related question which its apparent silliness has never prevented from being asked: that concerning the innovative or progressive quality (or otherwise) of Jewish entrepreneurial activity in Germany. Were Jews economic pioneers? Or did they enter fields where others had done the pioneering but which promised economic success? Or did they merely join in the broad mainstream of economic activity? Apart from being somewhat pointless, the question is almost impossible to answer. Is it not likely that, while some Jews were pioneers in their particular fields (but then what, in any case, does the term 'pioneering' mean in the economic sphere?), others may have followed well-trodden paths and invested in established success? In what ways could the wildly successful and incomparable Rothschilds, the fabulously wealthy Bleichröder, or men like Emil Rathenau or Ludwig Loewe who saw, seized, and by hard entrepreneurial and technological grind exploited large economic opportunities be considered (or not) innovators or pioneers? Vagueness of the terms employed forbids both an answer and any comparison with Gentiles. If the question is discussed in terms of innovative or imitative economic behaviour, of pioneering (hence 'high risk') activity or the march along safe, well-trodden paths, then it is wrongly put. With little enough sense in regard to economic activity in general, it comes close to nonsense when complicated by the introduction of ethnic categories.

What is however incontrovertible is the fact that, as proved by their economic success, members of the German–Jewish economic élite made a major contribution to the satisfaction of wants and, with it, to German economic development in general. Werner Sombart, an unqualified admirer neither of capitalism nor of Jews, pays the classic tribute to their role in the development of the German economy:

... so wird man dennoch zugeben müssen [he writes] dass unser Wirtschaftsleben, wie es sich im neunzehnten Jahrhundert gestaltet hat, ganz undenkbar wäre ohne die Mitwirkung der Juden. Stellt man sich auf den Standpunkt der neuzeitlichen Entwicklung des Wirtschaftslebens, betrachtet man die Entfaltung kapitalistischen Wesens und damit die Freisetzung starker produktiver Kräfte als einen Fortschritt, legt man Wert auf den Rang, den ein Land heute auf dem Weltmarkt einnimmt, so kann man gar nicht umhin, die Existenz jüdischer Wirtschaftssubjekte als einen der grössten Vorzüge anzuerkennen, über die dieses Land in ethnischer Hinsicht verfügt: *si le juif n'existait pas, il faudrait l'inventer.*[21]

---

[21] Sombart, *Die Juden und das Wirtschaftsleben*, p. 112. These words were first written in 1903. Twelve years later, in an essay *Die Zukunft der Juden* published in Leipzig in 1912, Sombart, after expressing himself in favour of Jewish emigration to Palestine, wrote—somewhat naïvely—that not all Jews would find a place there. Germany could never permit that its wealthiest and most enterprising citizens ('seine reichsten und betriebsamsten Bürger') should emigrate, which would be equivalent to a collapse of the German economy ('was einem Zusammenbruch der deutschen Volkswirtschaft gleichkäme')—perhaps an over-statement. Quoted in Wanda Kampmann, *Deutsche und Juden* (Frankfurt-on-Main, 1979), pp. 427 f.

Bibliography

Achinger, H., *Wilhelm Merton in seiner Zeit* (Frankfurt-on-Main, 1965).
Achterberg, Erich, *Berliner Hochfinanz Kaiser, Fürsten, Millionäre um 1900* (Frankfurt-on-Main, 1965).
Arnhold, Johanna, *Eduard Arnhold: ein Gedenkbuch* (Berlin, 1928).
Arnsberg, Paul, *Die jüdischen Gemeinden in Hessen* (Frankfurt-on-Main, 1971).
Bernhard, Georg, *Meister und Dilettanten am Kapitalismus* (Amsterdam, 1936).
Bernstein, Daniel, 'Wirtschaft II: Handel und Industrie' in Siegmund Kaznelson (ed.), *Juden im deutschen Kulturbereich* (Berlin, 1962).
Cecil, Lamar, *Albert Ballin: Business and Politics in Imperial Germany 1888–1918* (Princeton, 1967).
Diamant, Adolf, *Chronik der Juden in Dresden* (Darmstadt, 1973).
Eulenburg, Franz, 'Die Aufsichtsräte der deutschen Aktiengesellschaften' in *Jahrbücher für Nationalökonomie und Statistik*, 3, 32, (Jena, 1906).
Euler, Friedrich-Wilhelm, 'Bankherren und Grossbankleiter nach Herkunft und Heiratskreis' in H. H. Hofman (ed.), *Bankherren und Bankiers* (Limburg and Lahn, 1978).
Friedeberger, Paul (ed.), *Industrielle Vertreter deutscher Arbeit in Wort und Bild* (Berlin, n.d.).
Fuchs, Konrad, 'Zur Rolle des schlesischen Judentums bei der wirtschaftlichen Entwicklung Oberschlesiens', *Zeitschrift für Ostforschung*, 28 (1979), 2.
Fuchs, Max, *Max Steinthal* (Berlin, 1930).
Fürstenberg, Carl, *Die Lebensgeschichte eines deutschen Bankiers*, recorded by his son Hans Fürstenberg (Wiesbaden, 1961).
Fürstenberg, Hans, *Erinnerungen Mein Weg als Bankier und Carl Fürstenbergs Altersjahre (Düsseldorf and Vienna, 1968).*
Grünfeld, Fritz, Das Leinenhaus Grünfeld: Erinnerungen und Dokumente ed. Stefi Jersch-Wenzel (Berlin, 1967).
Grünfeld, Heinrich, *Falk Valentin Grünfeld und sein Werk* (Berlin, 1934).
Grunwald, Kurt, *Türkenhirsch: A Study of Baron Maurice de Hirsch, Entrepreneur and Philanthropist* (Jerusalem, 1966).
Haas, Rudolf, *Die Entwicklung des Bankwesens im deutschen Oberrheingebiet* (Mannheim, 1970).
Hamburger, Ernest, *Juden im öffentlichen Leben Deutschlands* (Tübingen, 1968).
Hirsch, Siegmund, *Revolution im Messing 1908–1929* (Lammersdorf, 1967).
—— 'Die Kupferhirschs in Halberstadt 1780–1930' unpublished MS.
Homburg, Heidrun, 'Die Neuordnung des Marktes hach der Inflation. Probleme und Widerstände am Beispiel der Zusammenschlussprojekte von

AEG und Siemens 1924–1933 oder "Wer hat den längeren Atem?" ' in Gerald D. Feldman (ed.), *Die Nachwirkungen der Inflation in Deutschland 1924–1933* (Munich, 1985).

Hunscha, Kurt, *Aus der Geschichte der Dresdner Bank 1872–1969* (Frankfurt-on-Main, 1969).

Jeidels, Otto, *Das Verhältnis der deutschen Grossbanken zur Industrie*, 2nd edn. (Munich and Leipzig, 1913).

Jersch-Wenzel, Stefi, *Jüdische Bürger und kommunale Selbstverwaltung in preussischen Städten 1808–1848* (Berlin, 1967).

Kaelble, Hartmut, *Berliner Unternehmer während der frühen Industrialisierung* (Berlin, 1972).

Kampmann, Wanda, *Deutsche und Juden* (Frankfurt-on-Main, 1979).

Kellenbenz, Hermann, *Paul Silverberg 1876–1959* (Münster, 1967).

—— *Louis Hagen 1855–1932* (Münster, 1974).

Kocka, Jürgen, *Unternehmensverwaltung und Angestelltenschaft* (Stuttgart, 1969).

—— 'Siemens und der aufhaltsame Aufstieg der AEG' in *Tradition*, 3–4 (1972).

—— and Johannes Siegrist, 'Die hundert grössten deutschen Industrieunternehmen im späten 19. und frühen 20. Jahrhundert' in Norbert Horn and Jürgen Kocka (eds.), *Law and the Formation of the Big Enterprises in the 19th and early 20th Centuries* (Göttingen, 1979).

Koenigsfeld, Ernst, 'Viktor Zuckerkandl—ein oberschlesischer Wirtschaftsführer' in *Gleiwitzer-Beuthener-Tarnowitzer Heimatblatt*, 21 *(1971).*

Krüger, Alfred, *Das Kölner Bankiersgewerbe* (Essen, 1925).

Kuznets, Simon, 'Economic Structure and Life of the Jews' in Louis Finkelstein (ed.), *The Jews: Their History, Culture and Religion* (London, 1961).

Ledermann, Lisbeth, 'Familie David Schottländer', typescript MS in the archives of the Leo Baeck Institute, New York.

Lerner, Franz (ed.), *Das tätige Frankfurt* (Frankfurt-on-Main, 1955).

Lewinsohn, Richard, *Die Umschichtung der europäischen Vermögen* (Berlin, 1926).

Lewy, Max, *Die Nationalbank für Deutschland zu Berlin 1881–1909* (Berlin, 1911).

Luke, Rolf, *Die Berliner Handelsgesellschaft in einem Jahrhundert deutsche Wirtschaft 1856–1956* (Berlin, 1956).

Martin, Bernd, and Ernst Schulin (eds.), *Die Juden als Minderheit in der Geschichte* (Munich, 1981).

Martin, Rudolf, *Jahrbuch des Vermögens und Einkommens der Millionäre in Preussen* (Berlin, 1912, (2nd edn., 2 vols., 1913).

—— *Jahrbuch ... etc. in der Provinz Brandenburg* (Berlin, 1913).

—— *Jahrbuch ... etc. in Bayern* (Berlin, 1914).

—— *Jahrbuch ... etc. in Württemberg* (Berlin, 1914).

—— *Jahrbuch... etc. im Königreich Sachsen* (Berlin, 1912).
—— *Jahrbuch... etc. in den drei Hansastädten* (Berlin, 1912).
Mitteilungsblatt der Industrie- und Handelskammer zu Köln, 'Abraham Freiherr von Oppenheim (1804–1878)', 5, no. 19 1 Oct. 1950).
Mosse, Werner, 'Judaism, Jews and Capitalism. Weber, Sombart and Beyond' in *Year Book XXIV of the Leo Baeck Institute* (London, 1979).
—— 'Zwei Präsidenten der Kölner Industrie- und Handelskammer: Louis Hagen und Paul Silverberg' in *Köln und das rheinische Judentum* (Cologne, 1984).
—— (ed.), *Juden im Wilhelminischen Deutschland 1890–1914* (Tübingen, 1976).
Oliven, Gerald, 'The Ludwig Loewe Group, its Personalities and Interconnections from the early foundations until its forced dismantlement under the Nazis', unpublished MS in the archives of the Leo Baeck Institute in New York.
Perlick, Alfons, *Oberschlesische Berg- und Hüttenleute* (Kitzingen, 1953).
Pinner, Felix, *Emil Rathenau und das elektrische Zeitalter* (Leipzig, 1918).
—— *Deutsche Wirtschaftsführer* (Charlottenburg, 1925).
Pogge v. Strandmann, Hartmut, *Unternehmenspolitik und Unternehmensführung* (Düsseldorf and Vienna, 1978).
Pritzkoleit, Kurt, *Wem gehört Deutschland?* (Vienna, Munich, Basle, 1957).
Rachel, Hugo and Paul Wallich, *Berliner Grosskaufleute und Kapitalisten*, 1939 vol. iii (Berlin, 1939).
Rathenau, Walther, *Zur Kritik der Zeit*, 5th edn. (Berlin, 1912).
Redlich, Fritz, 'Two Nineteenth-century Financiers and Autobiographers' in *Economy and History*, 10 (Lund, 1967).
Reichshandbuch der deutschen Gesellschaft (Berlin, 1930).
Richarz, Monika (ed.), *Jüdisches Leben in Deutschland: Selbstzeugnisse zur Sozialgeschichte 1780–1871* (Stuttgart, 1979), vol. II.
Riesser, Jacob, *Die deutschen Grossbanken und ihre Konzentration* (Jena, 1912).
Rosenbaum, Eduard, 'Albert Ballin: A Note on the Style of his Economic and Political Activities', *Year Book III of the Leo Baeck Institute* (London, 1958).
—— and A. J. Sherman *Das Bankhaus M. M. Warburg & Co. 1798–1938* (Hamburg, 1976).
Rosenthal, Heinz, 'Jews in the Solingen Steel Industry' *Year Book XVII of the Leo Baeck Institute* (London, 1972).
Schiefel, W. *Bernhard Dernburg* (Zurich, n.d.).
Schmidt, Ernst. W., *Männer der Deutschen Bank und der Disconto-Gesellschaft* (Düsseldorf, 1957).
Schnee, Heinrich, *Die Hochfinanz und der moderne Staat, Geschichte und System der Hoffaktoren an deutschen Fürstenhöfen im Zeitalter des Absolutismus*, 6 vols. (Berlin, 1953–67).
Schulin, Ernst, *Walther Rathenau* (Göttingen, 1979).

Schwabach, Paul v., *Aus meinen Akten* (Berlin, 1927).
Schwerin, Kurt, 'Die Juden in Schlesien' in *Bulletin des Leo Baeck Instituts*, 19 nos. 56–7 (Tel Aviv, 1980).
Seidenzahl, Fritz, *Hundert Jahre Deutsche Bank* (Frankfurt-on-Main, 1970).
Siegrist, Hannes, 'Deutsche Grossunternehmen vom späten 19. Jahrhundert bis zur Weimarer Republik' in *Geschichte und Gesellschaft*, 6 (1980).
Solmssen, Georg, *Gedenkblatt für Adolf und Sara Salomonsohn zum 19 März 1931* (Berlin, 1931).
Sombart, Werner, *Die Juden und das Wirtschaftsleben* (Leipzig, 1911).
—— *Die Zukunft der Juden* (Leipzig, 1912).
—— *Die deutsche Volkswirtschaft im neunzehnten Jahrhundert*, 4th edn. (Berlin, 1919).
Stern, Selma, *The Court Jew. A Contribution to the History of the Period of Absolutism in Central Europe* (Philadelphia, 1950).
Tietz, Georg *Hermann Tietz: Geschichte einer Familie und ihrer Warenhäuser* (Stuttgart, 1965).
Tischert, Georg, *Aus der Entwicklung des Loewe-Konzerns* (Berlin, 1911).
Toury, Jacob, *Soziale und politische Geschichte der Juden in Deutschland 1847–1871* (Düsseldorf, 1977).
—— 'Der Eintritt der Juden ins deutsche Bürgertum' in Hans Liebeschütz and Arnold Paucker (eds.), *Das Judentum in der deutschen Umwelt 1800–1850* (Tübingen, 1977).
Treue, Wilhelm, 'Caesar Wollheim und Eduard Arnhold' in *Tradition*, 6 (Apr. and June 1961).
—— 'Das Bankhaus Mendelssohn als Beispiel einer Privatbank im 19. und 20. Jahrhundert' in *Mendelssohn Studien*, 1 (Berlin, 1972).
Ullstein, Hermann, *The Rise and Fall of the House of Ullstein* (London, n.d.).
Wallich, Hermann, Aus meinem Leben (private printing Berlin, 1929).
—— *Aus meinem Leben* in *Zwei Generationen im deutschen Bankwesen 1833–1914* (Frankfurt-on-Main, 1978).
Wallich, Paul, *Lehr- und Wanderjahre eines Bankiers*, in *Zwei Generationen im deutschen Bankwesen 1833–1914* (Frankfurt-on-Main, 1978).
Warburg, Max, *Aus meinen Aufzeichnungen* privately printed (New York, 1950) and published (Glückstadt, 1952).
Weinberg, Carl. v., *Jubiläumsschrift* (Frankfurt-on-Main, 1931).
Wenzel, Georg, *Deutscher Wirtschaftsführer* (Hamburg, 1929).
Zelzer, Maria, *Weg und Schicksal der Stuttgarter Juden* (Stuttgart, 1964).
Zielenziger, Kurt, *Juden in der deutschen Wirtschaft* (Berlin, 1930).

Index

Abel, Rudolf 213
Adelsbürger 30 f., 36
AG f. Anilinfabrikation (Agfa) 241, 241 n. 70, 254
AG f. chemische Produkte vorm. Scheidemandel 234, 239, 350
AG f. Verkehrswesen vorm. A Lenz & Co. 256 f., 281
Allgemeine Elektricitäts-Gesellschaft (AEG) 19, 21, 47, 56, 64, 229, 234; Deutsche Edison Ges. f. angewandte Elektricität AG 244 f.; relations with Siemens & Halske 245 f., 246 n. 88, 254 ff. *passim*, 265, 275, 277, 280 f., 283 f., 296 ff. *passim*; AEG and Siemens compared 299; rescue by international consortium 299 ff.; contrast with Siemens 315 ff., 317 n. 84, 344, 350, 368, 378
Allgemeine Petroleum Industrie AG 281
Andreae, Fritz 338, 368 n. 60
A. Riebecksche Montan AG 256, 280
Arnhold
  Adolf 335
  Dr Adolph 153
  Eduard 22, 53, 130, 154 ff.; commercial activities 155 nn. 133 and 134, 181, 193, 208 f., 236, 254 f., 284, 292 f., 326, 328, 401
  Georg 200
  Max 200
Aron Hirsch & Sohn 55, 372 f.
Aschrott, Sigmund 101, 147 ff., 182, 193, 208
Asser-Kaufmann Richard v. 183, 194
A. Wertheim GmbH 191 n. 32

Badische Anilin- u. Sodafabrik 197
Baer, Max 183, 185; commercial activities 185 f., 194, 253
Ballin, Albert 7 ff., 19, 21, 193, 195, 213 n. 59; career of 237 f., 249, 250, 283, 292, 297, 326, 391 ff., 392 nn. 9 and 10, 393 n. 11 and 12, 401

Bamberger, Ludwig 108, 221, 222 n. 8
Bank f. Electrische Unternehmungen 246 f.
Bank f. Handel u. Industrie (Darmstädter Bank) 230 ff., 280 f., 284, 332
banking and industrial entrepreneurship 384 ff., 384 n. 2, 385 n. 1
Basalt AG 346, 349
Bayerische Vereinsbank 196
Becker, Moritz 91, 156 f., 156 n. 136
Beer
  Jakob Herz 50, 59
  Michael 50
  Wilhelm 50 f., 90
Beer, Sondheimer & Co. 360 f.
Behrend
  Heinrich 106
  Joseph 105
Behrens
  Eduard Ludwig 201, 289
  Georg 201, 336
  Theodor 201
Beit
  Eduard (Beit v. Speyer) 179 n. 15, 181, 189 n. 28, 194, 210 f., 214, 289
  Ferdinand 179 n. 15
Benary
  Ernst 91
  Julie 196 n. 42
Benda, Sigismund 101
Bendemann, August Heinrich 90
Berend
  Bacher Beer 49
  Bernhard Samuel 49 f.
  Levin (Louis) 49, 59, 97; commercial activities 97 f.
  Samuel Bacher 49, 59
Berger, Julius 363, 363 f.
Berg- u. Metallbank 255, 289 f., 298
Bergwerksgesellschaft Hibernia 256 f., 272, 280
Berlin-Anhaltische Maschinenbau AG (Bamag, later Bamag-Meguin) 154, 254, 341, 344, 350
Berliner, Alfred 239 f., 249, 250, 297, 299

Index

Berliner Elektricitäts-Werke (BEW) 246, 256, 275
Berliner Handels-Gesellschaft (BHG) 134, 151, 155, 228 ff., 246, 254 f., 272, 274, 280 f., 290 f., 297, 343 f., 366, 375, 378
Bernhard, Georg 262 n. 1., 360
Bernstein, Daniel 46, 46 n. 31
Berve, Emil 288 f.
Bie, Hans 242, 353
Bieber, Siegfried 230, 336, 344, 375
Bismarck, Otto v. 21, 22, 69 n. 3, 72, 73 n. 12, 75 f.
Bismarckhütte 134, 242, 256 f., 288
Blaschke, Alfred 257, 284, 289
Bleichröder
  Gerson v. 10, 21, 22, 76, 90, 101 f., 106; assistance to Prussian government 106 n. 14, 108, 165
  Hans v. 181, 194, 208
  James v. 181
  Samuel 101
Blumenstein, Joseph 354 n. 39, 389 n. 8
Blumenstein-Konzern 354 f.
Bochumer Verein f. Bergbau u. Gusstahlfabrikation 256, 272, 279 f.
Bodenheimer
  Gumpert 103
  Siegmund 231, 336, 340 f., 367
Borchardt
  Moritz 172
  Robert 290
Born, Ludwig 283 f., 288, 291 ff. *passim*, 341
Braunfels, Otto 184; commercial activities 186 n. 23, 189 n. 28, 194, 290
Bücher, Hermann 368, 368 n. 60

Caro
  Georg v. 131, 133; commercial activities 133 n. 82, 161, 174, 183, 194, 286, 288, 293, 326
  Heinrich 46, 240
  Moritz 130, 134
  Nikodem 404
  Oscar 131 ff.; commercial activities 132 n. 79, 161, 229 n. 37, 242, 287 f., 290, 293, 327, 364
  Robert 130 f., 161, 173
  Robert (2) 133
Caspar, Bernhard 213
Cassella, Leopold 156, 187 n. 25
Centralverband des deutschen Bank- u. Bankiergewerbes 221, 333 ff.
Cohen, Philip Abraham 188 n. 27
Cohn
  Meyer 90, 101, 173, 276
  Moritz 109, 150
  Simon 91, 101, 144, 144 n. 99, 145 n. 101, 174
Commerz- u. Privat-Bank 333, 344 ff., 366
Compania Hispano Americana de Electricidad (Chade) 224, 301
Continental Caoutchouc- u. Gutta-Percha Co. (Conti) 56 f., 213, 241
Coppel
  Alexander 56, 233
  Alexander (2) 56 f.
  Gustav 56, 66
court Jews: descendants as bankers 34 f.; disappearance 37, 37 n. 10; and industrial entrepreneurship 385, 385 nn. 4, 5 and 6
Coutinho., Caro & Co. 133

Dahlheim, Louis 103, 118, 160, 172
Darmstädter u. National Bank (Danat) 11, 232, 303, 304, 320, 320 n. 93, 332, 341, 365, 372
Dernburg, Bernhard 2, 22, 186, 231, 257, 284 f., 289
Deutsch, Felix 21 n. 26, 192, 242, 245, 248, 254 f., 297, 299, 316 f.; board seats 351, 364
Deutsch-Atlantische Telegraphen-Ges. 254, 281, 360, 377
Deutsche Bank 19, 52, 197, 199, 221 ff., 245 f., 272, 279, 281, 297, 302 ff., 330 f., 344
Deutsche Bank u. Disconto Ges. (DeDi) 11, 281, 304, 366, 374
Deutsche Continental-Gas Ges. 256, 378
Deutsche Eisenhandels AG 133 f.
Deutsche Erdöl AG 342 f., 349
Deutsche Niles-Werkzeugmaschinenfabrik 141, 253, 257
Deutsche Petroleum AG 239, 257, 279, 342
Deutsche Waffen- u. Munitionsfabriken 141, 244, 253 f., 256 f., 277; later Berlin-Karlsruher Industrie-Werke 349
Deutsch-Luxemburgische Bergwerks u. Hütten AG 280 f.
Deutsch-Überseeische Elektricitätsges.

(DUEG) 224, 247, 253 f., 275, 279, 296, 301
Direction d. Disconto-Ges. 141, 198 f., 219 ff., 233 f., 254, 279, 281, 284, 303 f., 330 f.
Dortmunder Union 165, 279
Dresdner Bank 19, 141, 155, 199, 225 ff., 232, 234, 247, 254, 272, 274, 276, 279, 281, 300 ff. *passim*, 320, 320 n. 92, 331, 341 f., 365
Dreyfus, Willy 336

Eich, Nikolaus 268 ff.
E. Ladenburg 186, 186 n. 24, 188 n. 27
Elektricitäts-Lieferungs-Ges. 254, 335
Elektro-Treuhand AG 296 f.
Elfes, August 299
Elkan, Philip 106; assistance to government 106 n. 15
Ellinger
　Leo 290
　Philip 188 n. 27
Embden, Max 195
Erlanger & Söhne 185, 228
Eulenburg, Franz 252, 261 n. 1

Fehr, Selmar 225, 374 n. 86
Feilchenfeld, M. 290
Felten Guilleaume-Carlswerk 234, 248
Felten Guilleaume-Lahmeyer AG 247, 280, 296, 378
Fischel, Adolf 338
Flatau
　Joseph 105
　Theodor Jacob 105 f.
Flechtheim, Julius 234 f., 239, 375 f.
Flick, Friedrich 372
F. Mart. Magnus 111 ff., 115
Fraenkel, Max 335
Frank, Theodor 336, 343, 374 n. 86
Fränkel
　Albert 118, 161
　Samuel: career 43 f., 101, 103 f.; commercial activities 104 f., 119
Frankfurter Metallges. 188, 188 n. 26
Frankfurter Societäts Druckerei 368 f.
Frankfurter Zeitung 189
Freud, Siegmund 29, 29 n. 47
Freudenberg, Philipp 127; commercial activities 127 n. 68, 184, 190, 194
Friedenthal, Isidor 91, 108, 272
Friedländer
　Emanuel 105 f., 108, 151, 153, 172

Fritz (v. Friedländer-Fuld) 46, 130, 151 f., 155, 161, 174, 179 n. 14, 181, 193, 208 f., 229 n. 37, 236, 255 f., 283, 286 f., 290, 292 f., 326, 328
　Moritz 102, 172
　Otto 101 f.
Friedmann, Gustav 174
Friedrich II (Emperor) 28 n. 46
Fromberg
　Georg 90, 174 f., 291
　Heinrich 108
Fürstenberg
　Carl 8, 19, 20 n. 18, 22, 132, 183, 186, 194 f., 226, 228 ff., 229 n. 37, 247, 249 ff. *passim*, 255 f., 264 ff., 270, 276, 283 f., 286 ff. *passim*, 292 f., 299, 317 ff. *passim*, 327; board memberships 344, 364, 366, 368 n. 60, 401
　Hans: on economic role of Walther Rathenau 21 n. 27, 230, 336; board memberships 344, 368 n. 60, 375, 378 f.
F. V. Grünfeld: reasons for success 125 f.

Gans
　Adolf 183, 187, 189 n. 28, 211 f.
　Fritz 183, 187, 189 n. 28, 211 f.
　Leo 156, 156 n. 135, 183, 187, 211 f., 351
　Pauline 187 n. 25, 194
Gebr. Arnhold 200, 367
Gebr. Körting 277
Gebr. Mauser KG (later Waffenfabrik Mauser AG) 139, 197, 253
Gebr. Simon 128 f.; commercial activities 128 n. 70
Gebr. Sulzbach 245
Gelsenkirchener Bergwerks AG 256, 279, 343
Gerson
　Benny 101, 103, 127; commercial activities 127 n. 66
　Jacob (Julius) 127; imperial patronage 127 n. 67
　Moritz 103, 127; commercial activities 127 n. 65
Gesellschaft f. elektr. Unternehmungen (Gesfürel) 141 f., 253, 255 ff. *passim*, 275, 281, 285 f., 300, 360
Goldberger, Ludwig Max 76 n. 26, 91, 173 f., 183 f.; commercial activities 184 n. 20, 194, 214, 326, 401

Index

Goldschmidt
 Hans 46
 Hayum Benedikt 179 n. 14
 Jakob 11, 19, 183, 232, 232 n. 52, 302 ff., 318 f., 326; career 331 ff.; board memberships 339 f., 367
 Karl 46
 Maximilian Benedikt 179 n. 14
 Ruben Bendix 45, 97
 Theodor 45 f.
 Theodor (2) 46
Goldschmidt-Rothschild
 Albert Frhr. v. 181, 210 f.
 Erich Frhr. v. 182, 210
 Lucy Freiin v. 181, 210
 Maximilian Frhr. v. 179 n. 14, 180, 194, 210 f.
 Rudof Frhr. v. 181, 210 f.
Graetz, Leo 196
Grosse Berliner Strassenbahn-Ges. 247, 256 f., 281
Grosskopf, Louis 162
Grünfeld
 Falk Valentin 119 ff., 126, 161
 Heinrich 122 ff., 135, 334, 339, 360
 Ludwig 122 f.
Guggenheim, Emil 135, 240
Gumpert, Louis 91
Güterbock
 Baer Levin 58
 Levin Isaak 58 f.
 Moritz 58 f., 90, 101, 106, 108, 172
Gutmann
 Eugen 19, 183, 186, 194, 199 n. 47, 225 ff., 225 nn. 23–6, 226 n. 30, 249 ff. *passim*, 256, 283 ff. *passim*, 288 f., 292 f., 300, 317 f., 326
 Herbert 227
Gwinner, Arthur v. 221, 286, 301

Haber, Fritz 46
Haberland
 Georg 334, 360
 Kurt 360
Hagen
 Carl 291
 Emma 234
 Louis 10 f., 19, 22, 22 n. 31, 184, 187, 194 f., 212, 232 ff., 247, 250 ff. *passim*, 302, 319, 321, 327, 334; board memberships 346, 364
Hahn
 Albert (banker) 336

Albert (industrialist) 46, 91, 118; commercial activities 119 n. 43, 136 f., 160 f., 173
 Georg 291
Halle, Friedrich Gottlieb v. 111
Hallgarten, Charles 189 n. 28
Hamburg-Amerikanische Paketfahrt AG (Hapag) 11, 19, 237 f., 279, 332, 377
Hamspohn, John 285
Hardy, James 183 f.; commercial activities 184 n. 19, 208, 214
Harpener Bergbau AG 230, 256, 280, 371 f.
Hasslacher, Jakob 264 ff.
H. C. Plaut 113, 115
Hegenscheidt, Wilhelm 131, 134
Heimann
 Albert 252
 Ernst 108
 Georg 183, 185, 194, 212, 287, 289
 Heinrich 90, 101
Heine, Salomon 201
Heinemann
 Dannie 300 f.
 Elkan 224, 301
Heinrich Kern & Co. 131
Helfft, Edmund 91, 174 f.
Henning, Hansjoachim 61 n. 51, 311 ff.
Henoch
 Hermann 58, 60
 Moses 57 ff., 97
Hermann Tietz 22 n. 35, 190 n. 31
Herz
 Michael 212
 Salomon 51, 97, 172
 Wilhelm 51 f., 54 nn. 42 and 43, 56, 66, 74, n. 17, 90, 103, 172 f., 184 f., 194, 326
Heymann, Carl 96 f., 99; commercial activities 99 f.
Hirsch
 Aron 54 f.
 Aron (2) 55
 Benjamin 55
 Emil Frhr. v. 196
 Gustav 55
 Joel Jacob 381, 385 n. 6
 Joseph 55, 102 ff.; commercial activities 104 n. 8, 105 f.
 Moritz v. (Baron Maurice de) 10, 37 n. 10, 101, 109, 114, 118, 196
 Siegmund 22 n. 40, 54 n. 44, 55 f., 135, 298 f.

Index 415

Hirsch Kupfer u. Messingwerke AG 298 f., 301
Hirschland
 Georg 336; board memberships 347
 Kurt: board memberships 347
Hochschild, Zacharias (Zachary) 188 n. 27, 290
Hohenlohe-Werke 255 f., 277, 281, 287
Holländer, Benjamin 161
Huldschinsky
 Oscar 137, 181, 193, 208 f.
 Salomon 118; commercial activities 119 n. 43, 136 f., 136 nn. 85–7, 161, 173

IG Farben 11, 235, 241, 351, 369, 369 n. 67
Internationale Bank te Amsterdam 332
Israel, Berthold 183, 189

Jacob Landau 233, 240, 244 f.
Jacob S. H. Stern 186, 188 n. 27
Jacoby, Kiwi David 97 n. 1, 99 f.
Jaffé
 Alfons 256
 Bernhard 90, 108
Jeidels, Otto 230, 262, 270, 325, 338; board memberships 343, 362, 366
Jewish entrepreneurial activity 9 ff.; geographical distribution 11; and early metallurgical industry 64; general characteristics 157 ff.
Jewish entrepreneurs: social characteristics 38 f.; in textile industry 39 ff.; compared with Gentile textile entrepreneurs 47
Jüdell, Felix 228

Kantorowicz, Nazary 161
Kaskel
 Carl Frhr. v. 199 nn. 46 and 47
 Emma Freifrau v. 200, 200 n. 48, 212
 Felix Frhr. v. 37 n. 7, 199 n. 47, 200, 214
 Michael 199 n. 46
Kattowitzer AG f. Eisenhüttenbetrieb 242, 279
Katzenellenbogen
 Albert: board memberships 345
 Ludwig 11, 326; board memberships 345; commercial activities 345 n. 34, 372

Kauffmann
 Hermann 101, 103, 105, 172
 Julius 118, 161
 Meyer 42 f., 48
 Salomon 42 f.
Kaulla
 Alfred v. 37 n. 10, 109, 197 f., 326
 Hermann 197
 Jeanette 197
 Lucie Eva 197
 Rudolf 197 f.
Kempner
 Leopold 101
 Maximilian 11, 234, 283, 292, 327, 348, 364
 Paul 336, 338
Kern
 Alois 130, 288
 Heinrich 130 ff., 161
Kirdorf, Emil 376
Kleemann, Wilhelm 227, 367
Klemperer
 Felix 290
 Gustav v. 226 ff., 364
 Herbert v. 335, 353, 375 n. 88
 Victor v. 227
Klöcknerwerke AG 349
Kommerzienräte: qualifications 70 ff.; wealth qualifications 72 f.; political qualifics 74; quotas 75 f.; decline of title 76 ff.; Jewish applicants 78 ff.; Jewish share 83 ff.; geogr. distribution 86 f.; structure of Jewish KR 87 ff.
Kopetzky, Wilhelm 183 f.; commercial activities 185 n. 21, 194, 214, 319
Koppel
 Arthur 46, 191, 249
 Leopold 182; commercial activities 182 n. 18, 193, 195, 208 f., 214, 327, 364
Kraemer, Hans 335
Kritzler, Ernst 348
Kunheim
 Erich 53
 Hugo 53, 90
 Louis 52 f.
 S. Heinrich 49, 52, 59 f.
Kunstmann, Wilhelm 213
Kuznets, Simon: model of Jewish economic activity 166 ff.

Lachmann, Salomon 101; assistance to government 107 n. 16; commercial

Index

Lachmann (*cont.*)
  activities 144, 144 nn. 98–100, 150, 173 f.
Lachmann-Mosse, Hans 150, 328 n. 3, 370
Ladenburg
  August 184, 186, 186 n. 24, 194, 290
  Carl 198 f., 272
  Emma 188 n. 27
  Ernst 90, 184, 186, 194
  Johanna 179 n. 15
  Mathilde 196
  Seligmann 109
Landau
  Eugen 186, 253, 288; board memberships 344
  Heinrich 103
  Hugo 272, 283 f., 286, 292, 326
  Jacob 90, 138, 165, 173
Landes, David 28
Lazard Speyer–Ellissen 188 n. 27, 336
Lehfeld, Wilhelm 90, 101
Lehmann, D. J. 103
Leonhard Tietz AG 190 n. 31
Leopold Cassella & Co. 156, 161, 187 n. 25, 277, 304
Lessing, Ludwig 172
Lestchinsky, Jakob 30
Levi, Max 197
Levin, David Aron 161
Liebermann
  Adolph 10, 172
  Benjamin 40, 74 n. 16, 90, 101, 103
  Joseph 40 f., 48, 97
  Max 41
  Philip 40, 101 f., 105
Linke-Hoffmann-Werke AG 133, 297, 332, 350
Loeb
  Rudolf 325, 336, 338, 362, 366 f., 376
  Salomon 201 n. 51
Loeser, Hermann 162
Loewe
  Erich 300
  Heinrich Joseph 101 f.
  Isidor 22, 91, 130, 137 ff.; commercial activities 139 ff., 174 f., 183, 194, 236, 249, 253 f., 256, 383 ff. *passim*, 288 f., 292 f., 296, 326, 401
  Ludwig 46, 63 n. 52, 66, 130, 137 ff., 249
  Sigmund 138 n. 91
Lohnstein, Emanuel 173

Ludwig Loewe AG 47, 64; growth of 137 ff., 244, 253 f., 256 f., 284 ff., 350
Lustig, Leo 133 ff., 335, 360

Mamroth, Paul 192, 242 f., 248 n. 89, 254, 335; board memberships 352
Manasse, Georg 213
Manheimer
  Ferdinand 81 f., 82 n. 38, 174 f.
  Gustav 81 f., 82 n. 38, 174
  Valentin 91, 101, 103, 105; commercial activities 105 n. 11, 118, 161, 172
Mankiewitz, Paul 192, 223, 223 n. 14, 326
Mannesmannröhren-Werke AG 222 f., 267 ff., 281, 349
Mannheimer, Fritz 325, 338
Mansfeldsche Kupferschieferbauende Gewerkschaft 298
Martin, Rudolf 5 f., 8, 11, 20, 75 ff.
Marx, Emil 242, 291
M. A. v. Rothschild & Söhne 112 f., 115
Meinhardt, William 335
Melchior, Carl 325, 338, 362, 364
Mendelssohn
  Alexander 74 n. 19, 90, 111, 172 f., 241
  Franz v. 90, 183 f., 193 n. 35, 194, 209
  Franz (2) v. 328, 334, 373
  Joseph and railway financing 110 f., 110 n. 25
  Robert v. 182, 208 f., 328
Mendelssohn-Bartholdy
  Ernst Paul v. 91, 180 n. 16, 181, 335
  Paul 90, 108, 241
Mendelssohn Bartholdy, Otto v. 184, 194
Mendelssohn & Co. 111 ff., 115, 228, 367, 376
Merton
  Alfred 290, 352
  Ralph (Raphael Moses) 188 n. 27, 194
  Richard 352
  Walter 230, 375 n. 88
  Wilhelm 22, 183, 186 n. 24, 188 n. 27, 189 n. 28, 194, 237, 249, 289, 326, 362
Metallgesellschaft 255
Meyer
  Abraham 173
  Carl 276
  Jacob Abraham 39 f., 75 n. 19, 90, 97, 172
  Joel Wolff 40, 90, 97

Index

Julius Wolff 40
Louis Ephraim 90, 101
Philip 40, 90, 97 f.; commercial activities 99 n. 4, 101 f., 105
Meyerbeer, Giacomo 50
M. I. Caro & Sohn 130 ff., 132, 134 f.
Mitteldeutsche Creditbank 345
Mitteldeutsche Stahlwerke 332, 341, 349
M. M. Warburg & Co. 201, 202 n. 52, 360, 366, 375, 377 f.
Montesquieu, Charles Louis de Secondat, Baron de 27
Mosler, Eduard 304
Mosse
  Emil 180, 180 n. 17, 184
  Rudolf 181, 193, 208 f., 326
Münzer, Emanuel 162
Müser, Robert 230, 270

Nathan, Henry 227 f., 227 nn. 33–4, 331; board memberships 341, 364, 367
Nationalbank f. Deutschland 227, 232, 244, 272, 275, 284, 291, 332
Neue Boden AG 257, 281
Norddeutscher Lloyd 11, 19
Nothmann, Adolf 242

Oberschl. Eisenbahnbedarfs AG 137, 272, 275, 277, 288 f., 349
Oberschl. Eisenindustrie AG 131 f., 135, 242, 256 f., 277, 280, 288
Oberschl. Kokswerke u. Chemische Fabriken AG 151 f., 242, 255 f., 277, 279, 286 f.
Oberschl. Portland-Cementfabrik 147
Oliven, Oscar 253 f., 283 f., 286, 292, 300; board memberships 252, 360
Oppenheim
  Abraham 10, 90, 101, 106; railway finance & management 109 f., 118, 230
  Albert Frhr. v. 181
  Eduard Frhr. v. 181, 346
  Emma 199 n. 47
  Franz 46, 240 f., 241 n. 71, 249, 351, 401
  Hugo 174
  Kurt 351
  Moritz 189 n. 28
  Simon 37 n. 7, 73 n. 14, 90, 101
  Simon (2) Frhr. v. 234, 252; board memberships 346, 376 n. 92
  Waldemar Frhr. v. 346, 376 n. 92

Orenstein, Benno 46, 191 f., 237, 240, 249, 327, 359, 364
Orenstein & Koppel AG 64, 192, 238, 240, 254, 281
Otto Wolff AG 361

Paderstein, Emil 212
Pariser, Heymann 160
Peiser, Herbert 363
Pfeiffer, Eduard v. 196 ff.
Pflaum, Alexander 198 n. 43
Philipsthal, Adolf 288, 291
Phoenix AG f. Bergbau u. Hüttenbetrieb 234, 271, 280 f.
Pietrkowski, Edmund 335, 361
Pinkus
  Hans 44
  Joseph 44, 91, 118, 161
  Max 44
Pinner, Felix 20, 20 n. 18, 21 n. 26, 316 f., 329, 331
Plaut, Moritz 90, 101, 106, 106 n. 13
Pogge v. Strandmann, Hartmut 269 f.
Porten, Max von der 352
Portland-Cementwerke Heidelberg–Mannheim 199
Preussische Central-Bodenkredit AG 257
Preussische Hypotheken Aktien Bank 275
Pringsheim
  Alfred 196
  Hugo 91

Rachel, Hugo 20, 38 nn. 12 and 15, 62, 62 n. 53, 66
railway financing & construction 10; Jewish participation 101 ff., 108 ff.; failures 113 ff.
Rathenau
  Emil 7 f., 19, 21, 41, 63 n. 53, 64, 78, 102, 192, 229 n. 37, 230, 242 ff., 250, 253 ff. *passim*, 276, 284, 286, 290, 296, 316 f., 326, 395 f., 401, 403
  Walther 7 f., 7 n. 5, 21, 21 n. 27, 22, 22 n. 28, 230, 249 f., 254 f., 267, 283 ff. *passim*, 290, 292 f., 296 f., 326
Reichenheim
  Leonor 41, 66
  Louis 41, 90, 118, 160, 173
  Moritz 183, 194
Reichshandbuch der deutschen Gesellschaft 20
Reusch, Paul 377

Rheinische AG f. Braunkohlenbergbau 353, 371 f.
Rheinische Stahlwerke 256 263 ff., 279 f., 378 f.
Rheinisch-Westfälische Elektrizitätswerke 360, 372
Richarz, Monika 42 n. 23, 47 n. 33, 48, 62 n. 52
Riesser, Jacob 186, 221, 231, 231 n. 45, 279, 401
Rinkel, Hermann 129; commercial activities 129 n. 73, 161
Ritscher, Samuel 227, 367, 374
Robert Warschauer & Co. 111 ff., 115, 228, 231
Rombacher Hüttenwerke 256, 280
Rosenberg, Hermann 230, 256, 287, 290
Rosenthal, Philipp 335
Rothschild
 Carl Meyer v. 189 n. 28
 Mathilde, Freifrau v. 181, 189 n. 28, 210
 Meyer Amschel 179 n. 15
 Minna 179 n. 14
 Nathan v. 90
 Willy v. 179 n. 14
Rütgers-Werke AG 238 f., 281
Rybniker Bergbau AG 255

Saar u. Mosel Bergwerksges. 256
Sachs, E. 288
Saling, Bonheim 102 f.; commercial activities 103 n. 7, 105
Salomon, M. 239
Salomonsohn
 Adolf 183, 186, 194, 220, 326
 Arthur 220, 250 f., 263 ff., 286, 292, 300, 327, 330 f.; board memberships 342 f., 364, 374 n. 86
 Georg see Solmssen
Sal. Oppenheim jun. & Co. 112 f., 115, 234, 376 n. 92
Salzdetfurth-Westeregeln-Aschersleben 341
Samuel, Siegfried 233
S. Bleichröder & Co. 111 f., 115, 141, 228, 233, 367
Schaaffhausenscher Bankverein 141, 232 ff., 256, 280 f., 301 f.
Schacht, Hjalmar 329, 332, 374 f., 374 n. 85
Schäfer, Hans 43
Schäffer, Hans 367, 370 f., 374

Schiff, Jacob H. 189 n. 28, 201 n. 51
Schles. Portland Cement Industrie 345, 349
Schlesinger, Martin 161 f.
Schlitter, Oscar 303
Schnee, Heinrich 9, 9 n. 8, 20, 34 f.
Schöndorff, Hermann 359, 359 n. 44
Schott
 Friedrich 353
 Paul 199
Schottländer
 Julius 145 ff., 181, 272
 Loebel 101, 145 f.
 Paul 147, 183, 212
Schück, Johanna 120, 122
Schülein, Hermann 353
Schultheiss-Patzenhofer 11; Schultheiss Brauerei AG 51; Schultheiss-Patzenhofer Brauerei AG 51, 240; Aktienbrauerei Gesellschaft Friedrichshöhe vorm. Patzenhofer 165, 240, 341, 345, 350, 372 n. 82
Schuster, Johann Jacob 227 f., 256
Schwabach
 Julius Leopold 90, 101
 Paul v. 183 f., 194, 208, 257, 289, 293; board memberships 347
Segall, Sally 229 n. 37, 238 f., 249, 326
Seligmann
 Aaron Elias Frhr. v. Eichthal 381
 Bernhard 90
 David Frhr. v. Eichthal 54 n. 41, 385 n. 5
 Siegmund 241 f.
Siemens & Halske 19, 239 f., 245 f., 296 ff. *passim*
Siemens & Schuckertwerke 239, 298
Sieskind, Sieskind 212
Silverberg, Paul 11, 22, 22 n. 32, 135, 326, 335, 339; board memberships 353, 353 n. 38, 360, 371 f., 376 f.
Simon
 Eduard 182, 208
 Isaak 128, 173
 James 22, 181, 208, 327, 364
 Lewin 91, 128 f.; commercial activities 128 f., 129 n. 72, 173 ff.
Simson
 Ernst v. 351
 Georg v. 231; board memberships 340
Sobernheim
 Curt 233 n. 55, 336, 345
 Walter 240, 335, 345

Index

Société financière d'Electricité (Sofina) 300 f.
Solmssen, Georg 135, 220 f., 233, 303 f., 303 n. 64, 330 f., 334 f., 337; board memberships 342, 360, 374, 374 n. 86
Sombart, Werner 1; on alleged Jewish racial characteristics 14, 14 nn. 11 and 12, 25, 27 ff.; on alleged Jewish 'idolatry' of money 28 n. 43, 66 n. 56, 398, 405, 405 n. 21
Sondheimer, Albert 361
Sonnemann, Leopold 183, 189, 189 n. 30, 194
Speyer
  Edgar, Sir 179 n. 15
  Franziska 181, 189 n. 28
  Georg 179 n. 15, 189 n. 28, 221
  James 179 n. 15
  Joseph Lazarus 179 n. 15
  Lucie 179 n. 14
Speyer-Ellissen, Gumperz (Eduard Joseph) 179 n. 15
Steiger, Louis v. 228
Steiner, Kilian v. 197, 198 n. 43, 222 n. 9
Steinthal, Max 183, 186, 194, 222 f., 222 nn. 10 and 13, 250, 267 ff., 327, 330, 337, 344, 374
Stern
  Fritz 21
  Julius 227 f., 232, 252, 256 f., 285, 288, 326
  Theodor 189 n. 28
Stettiner Chamotte AG vorm. Didier 234, 349
Stettiner Maschinenbau AG 'Vulcan' 255 f.
Stinnes, Hugo 11, 253, 297
Strauss, Ottmar 361
Strousberg, Bethel Henry 10, 46, 101, 109; commercial activities 114 f., 118, 165
Strupp, Louis 252
Süddeutsche Disconto Ges.-AG 186 n. 24, 199, 275
Sulzbach, Walter 189 n. 28

Teichmann, Moritz 161
Tietz
  Georg 22, 123, 126
  Hermann 190 n. 31, 191
  Leonhard 190 n. 31, 191
  Oscar 19, 22, 126, 135, 190, 190 n. 31, 195 f., 209 f., 326

Toury, Jacob 9, 9 n. 9, 30, 34 n. 1, 41 n. 22, 54 n. 41

Ullmann, Moritz 108
Ullstein
  Hermann 360
  Leopold 191 n. 32
Union Elektricitäts-Ges. 141, 247

Valentin, Julius 244
Veit, Hermann Eduard 90
Vereinigte Köln-Rottweiler Pulverfabriken 139, 234 f., 239
Vereinigte Königs- u. Laura–Hütte 165, 256 f., 271, 277, 280, 289
Vereinigte Maschinenfabrik Augsburg–Nürnberg 240
Vereinigte Oberschl. Hüttenwerke 332, 344
Vereinigte Stahlwerke 11, 332, 341, 349

Wallich
  Hermann 76 n. 27, 78 n. 29, 174, 186, 192, 193 n. 35, 209, 221 f., 222 nn. 8 and 12, 224, 321
  Paul 20, 38 nn. 12 and 15, 62, 62 n. 53, 66, 230
Warburg
  Felix 201 n. 51
  Fritz 359
  Gabriel Georg 197
  James P. 366
  Max M. 22, 202, 334 f., 337 ff. *passim*, 366, 375 nn. 88–9, 377
  Moritz M. 201 n. 51
  Paul 201 n. 51
  Siegmund 197
Warschauer, Robert 90, 101, 180 n. 16
Wassermann
  Amschel Elkan 224
  Emil 224
  Oscar 192, 221, 223 f., 303 f., 330, 334, 339; board memberships 334, 364, 374 n. 86
Weber, Max 1, 14 n. 11, 28 f.
Weigert
  Abraham 42
  Hermann 42
  Max 42
  Salomon 42, 101 f.
Weinberg
  Arthur v. 46, 183, 187, 187 n. 25, 189 n. 28, 194, 210, 249, 351

Weinberg (*cont.*)
   Bernhard 187, 187 n. 25, 194
   Carl v. 46, 183, 187, 187 n. 25, 194, 210, 249, 351
   W. H. Ladenburg & Söhne 111, 115, 198 f.
Wilhelm II: 82, 402, 402 n. 20
Winterfeldt, Max 256
Witting, Richard 232, 253, 283 f., 286, 289, 292, 326
Wolfes, Richard 300
Wolff
   Anton Emil 165
   Heinrich 90, 165, 173
   Moritz 103 ff.; commercial activities 104 n. 9, 108, 118, 172
   Theodor 360
Wollheim, Caesar 22 n. 36, 152 ff.
Württembergische Vereinsbank 197, 199, 222 n. 9

Zellstoff-Fabrik Waldhof 198, 350
Zielenziger
   Alfred 335
   Kurt 19, 19 n. 13, 29, 29 n. 48, 34 n. 2
Zuckerkandl, Victor 131 f., 242, 249